The Complete Guide to Music Technology
Using Cubase 13

By Darren Jones

Darren Jones
1022 Ringwood Road
West Howe
Bournemouth
Dorset
BH11 9LA
UK

email: darren@musictechtuition.com
web site: musictechtuition.com
youtube: youtube.com/c/musictechtuition

First Edition 2023

©2023 Darren Jones

ISBN 9798850592387

Contents

How MIDI Works 55

Effective Sequencing 71

Contents

Contents

Contents

Arrangements 219

Synthesizers 231

MIDI Remote 273

Multi-Track Recording... 455

Contents

Mixing 619

Binary, Hexadecimal and MIDI Communication 673

Glossary 681

Keyboard Shortcuts 691

Index 695

Introduction

This book is intended to give you a solid grounding in a wide range of practical areas that you will need to be a productive and competent Music Technologist - be it a producer of your own work or other people's. It has been written to take you from your first steps using Cubase to making large-scale recordings and producing completed mixdowns of your work. It assumes no prior knowledge of Music Theory or Music Technology, although both will naturally be an advantage. It is the culmination of years of note and handout-making as a teacher of Music Technology as well as an active recording engineer and producer and a Steinberg Certified Trainer. It is aimed to give a good all-round grounding in Music Tech for anyone who would like to become more competent in it. Music Tech is a vast, ever-growing topic, and to fully explore each area of the book would mean each chapter would be the size of the entire book, so in some cases the most expedient (but still correct) route has been taken through the subject matter, and of course in any artistic endeavour there are often as many opinions as there are options. You should never be afraid to experiment and draw your own conclusions from doing so, and you should question everything you are presented with to ensure that it fits with other established facts.

This book is solely the work of the author, written, drawn, edited and published entirely independently. While copyright is something which is of decreasing value as the world moves forward, I would appreciate it you refrained from making copies of this book in any way, shape or form, as it is not the product of a faceless company, but one man's effort to improve the teaching of a subject where there seems to be no all-encompassing textbook to give an all-round grounding in this area. For this reason, the book is only available as printed matter, and not electronically. I hope you will enjoy it and find the information within as useful as I have done over the years.

Conventions used in this book

In an attempt to make the text of the book clearer, some formatting has been used throughout. Whenever there is a button or text on screen which you need to read, alter or click, it has been **presented in this font**.

Whenever there is a keyboard shortcut given, it has been **presented in this font**. All the keyboard shortcuts given are the defaults; while there are many which could be edited to make working within Cubase easier, referring to custom keyboard shortcuts would make matters less clear. Remember that keyboard shortcuts will make working in Cubase much quicker and easier, so some of the most useful ones have been included on page 691. To aid clarity, the editors have been set to be much lighter than standard, under **Preferences > User Interface > Custom Colors > Editor Area Background** and choosing a lighter shade by clicking the grey square.

Cubase is available in a number of different versions - Pro, Artist, Elements, AI and LE - each with fewer features. While highlighting which features are available in every version would make the text of the book difficult to read, where a section covers a version available only in Pro or Artist that has been highlighted using the following graphics.

ARTIST PRO

If you can't find the menu option, tool or icon mentioned, check if your version has the feature in question by consulting the chart at:

https://www.steinberg.net/cubase/compare-editions/

This edition of the book features a mixture of graphics taken from both Windows and Mac versions of Cubase to improve the printed appearance of screenshots as the Mac version has higher resolution text. The function of the program is the same in both versions, and any menus have been edited to remove reference to keyboard shortcuts.

This book was created using Cubase 13.0.0 Build 92. Due to the ongoing nature of software development, there may be variations in appearance and function from this text and the version you are running on your system.

Acknowledgements

I would like to thank my wife Tammie for being so supportive of the creation and completion of every edition of this book and for her proof-reading skills. It has been something which has taken a great deal of time and she's had to hear far too much detail about!

The Complete Guide to Music Technology
Using Cubase 13

by Darren Jones

Sequencing

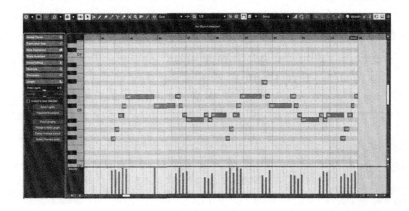

Cubase is music production software - often called a Digital Audio Workstation (DAW) - and one of its features is that it is a sequencer. This means it can record notes that you play on a keyboard, and then play them back through a synthesizer, allowing you to create compositions and hear what they sound like without using other musicians. Very complex pieces of music can be built up doing this as you can create one track at a time and re-record it until you are totally happy with it, all at your own pace. You don't need to be a good keyboard player to get good results, either (although having some keyboard skills is a big help). It's important to remember that it deals with MIDI (which will be covered fully later on), and that really means notes being played, usually on a keyboard, so you can change the sound of what you've recorded afterwards, but there are some limitations to how it will sound.

Getting Started

Firstly you will need to start your computer and any other items in your setup. The order of this will change depending on your specific equipment, but there is a good rule of thumb here:

Tip: The speakers should be the last thing you turn on, and the first thing that you turn off – this is to avoid any 'thumps' damaging them (or your ears) when you turn the equipment on. Usually the computer will be one of the first things to be turned on and the last to turn off. Once this is done, you can start Cubase.

 Once it loads (which can take some time as it's a large program), you will see a screen like the one on the left, it is the **Steinberg Hub** and it is there to allow you to pick from a number of templates, as well as tell Cubase where you want your project to be saved.

Tip: Whenever you use Cubase, it's important to make sure your files are where they should be – in some situations the computer is used by a number of people, and in addition it's really important to save each project in a separate folder – this means you will easily be able to back your work up later on.

To create a new folder for your project, click in the area next to Project Folder at the bottom right of the Steinberg Hub window, and type the name of the folder you want to create, and then in the upper section click **More** and then pick **Empty**. Now click the **Create** button at the bottom and Cubase will make the folder and a new project.

Tip: Remember that USB flash drives and external hard drives are becoming increasingly affordable, and their cost is small compared to the amount of time that you would need to recreate any work if it was lost. Backing up your work is a necessity, as is regularly saving your work. Computers crash, particularly when running complex software such as sequencers, and hard drives fail. If you save regularly and back up often then you will not lose a great deal if the worst happens.

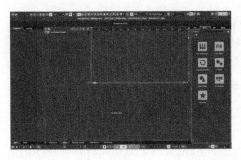

Here we see the main Cubase window, with the Transport Bar at the bottom. The transport bar is like the remote control for a video recorder, although it has more functions, the basic controls are the same, as we'll see later on. The central area is the project window. This is where all your tracks will be created and the majority of your work will be.

The first thing to do is to create a new track. Go to **Project > Add Track > Instrument,** and a new window will appear where you can select an Instrument.

Click where the window says **No VST Instrument** and a list will appear of the instruments your computer has available. Pick **Halion Sonic** from the Synth folder (as it is available on all Cubase systems), and click **Add Track**. You should now see a screen similar to the one shown below.

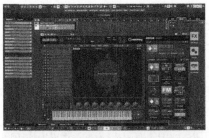

Here is the Cubase window, with Halion Sonic located in the centre of the screen. While you will be editing the controls later on, at the moment we don't need to see Halion Sonic, so close the window to reveal...

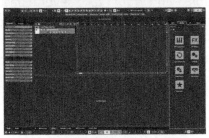

... the project window with Halion Sonic track in it. On the left of the screen is the Inspector, showing details such as track name, inputs and settings. If the inspector isn't present...

... click this button to make it visible. It can also be enabled with **CTRL + ALT + L**.

The Inspector is very important as it allows you to alter the volume and panning of a track (more of this later), and most importantly pick the sounds you wish to use. We will see how this works in a while, but firstly we will look at a few things we need before we get started.

The Transport

The transport (hit **F2** if you can't see it) allows us to control Cubase, making it play, stop, record, rewind and a host of other features. We won't cover them all here, but we will cover the basic controls that you need to get you sequencing.

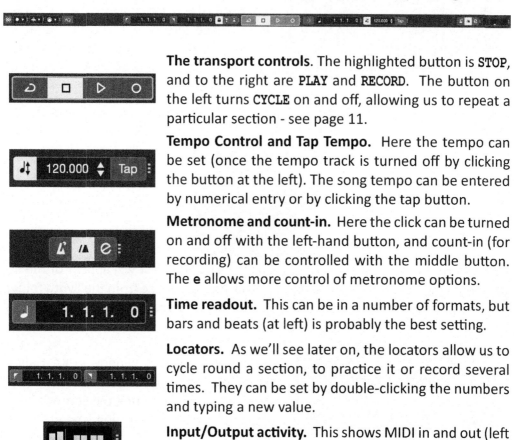

The transport controls. The highlighted button is **STOP**, and to the right are **PLAY** and **RECORD**. The button on the left turns **CYCLE** on and off, allowing us to repeat a particular section - see page 11.

Tempo Control and Tap Tempo. Here the tempo can be set (once the tempo track is turned off by clicking the button at the left). The song tempo can be entered by numerical entry or by clicking the tap button.

Metronome and count-in. Here the click can be turned on and off with the left-hand button, and count-in (for recording) can be controlled with the middle button. The **e** allows more control of metronome options.

Time readout. This can be in a number of formats, but bars and beats (at left) is probably the best setting.

Locators. As we'll see later on, the locators allow us to cycle round a section, to practice it or record several times. They can be set by double-clicking the numbers and typing a new value.

Input/Output activity. This shows MIDI in and out (left two meters) and audio input and outputs (stereo).

The Transport Bar in Cubase is highly configurable - and would take several pages to describe all the available options - but suffice to say that you can turn sections on and off right-clicking on an empty section of the transport bar, and selecting the sections that you want to see from the set up window that appears. You can alter the appearance of each section by clicking the three dot menu to the right of each section.

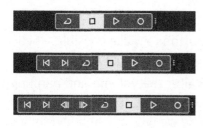

Here we see the effect of this on the transport controls section. The first view is the default with just four controls present. The next mode adds buttons to move between markers, and the third mode adds fast forward and rewind controls.

The Metronome

It is very important that when you play music into Cubase that it is in time with the metronome. Computers may work extremely quickly, but they do not have much intelligence, and as a result they need to be told things that we may take for granted. One of them is the tempo of a piece of music – Cubase can't really work that out, so to make life easy in the long run, you should play in time with the metronome. This is easily achieved, firstly by turning it on using the button above - it will turn white. Pressing **Play** on the transport bar should now mean you hear an indication of the tempo of the piece.

Changing Tempo

If you want to change the speed, make sure that the tempo track is turned off click the button above on the transport bar so that it is dark grey, and then enter the tempo that you want by double-clicking it and typing the speed you want, or tapping the tempo on the **Tap** area to the right of the tempo indication. You may need to experiment to find the right speed, and remember that you can always change the speed of what you've recorded after you've done it. This has an important benefit if you're finding a part difficult - you can record difficult parts slowly to make them easier to play, then return the tempo to normal afterwards.

Picking a sound

Many synthesizers provide a wide range of sounds (referred to as patches) and these should cover most eventualities – there are usually over a hundred on a basic synth, and on some there can be thousands. However, picking them can be a little difficult as there are so many to choose from, but the Inspector makes it easier.

Here is the routing section of the Inspector of the Halion Sonic track. You may need to click on **Routing** to expand it to see this section in full. When a sound is selected it will appear where it currently says **Program Selector**, so click there...

... and the patch list appears. Here you can list all the sounds that the synth has, and there are many (6120, as shown at the top right). If you want to explore, feel free to do so, you can scroll through the list and click once on a sound and you will be able to hear it played using your MIDI keyboard – you may find a sound that inspires you or takes your compositions in new directions.

There are so many sounds that it's hard to find the right one quickly. If you click where it says **Search MediaBay** and enter a word (or part of one) then it will only show you sounds that are relevant to that – both in their names and also their categories/description, so if you enter piano (as seen here) then you should get piano sounds, even if their name doesn't make that obvious. Not all instruments have descriptions in their patches, however.

Naming Tracks

It's important to name each track – at first it's easy to know what's what as you may only have one or two tracks. When your piece develops, you may end up with many tracks, and knowing instantly what each one is will help. To name it, double click where the track says **Halion Sonic 01** and name it appropriately – melody, bass, chords or whatever you want to call it.

The Info Line

If you have the Info Line present (if it isn't, click the icon above right and select it from the menu that appears), then you can name the parts you create as well, avoiding confusion if you have musically different parts. It can also be of benefit to use the colour palette to colour parts, providing an instant visual clue when a part is different from its neighbours.

Toolbar and Transport Setup

There is a great deal of information that can be present on screen in Cubase, and both the toolbar and transport bar area have too many options to fit on most screens. As a result, you will need to be familiar with getting the tools you need on screen. This is done right-clicking in empty space on the area in question, and using the pop-up window to select the appropriate sections. If a tool, icon or menu is mentioned in this book and you can't see it, then right-click the area and turn that section on. You may need to turn other sections off to see the desired section in full - particularly in the case of the transport bar (where some sections can be expanded in size, as seen on page 4).

Making a recording

Cubase will record whatever you play on the keyboard. To do this, select a track (if you only have one it will already be selected, this is shown by it being lighter than the others), and look to see that the red 'record enable' button is lit up on the track itself – it should be as soon as you select the track, but it's possible for it to be turned off. This button doesn't mean that the track is recording straight away, but it means that when you press record it will record on this track. Next, we need to tell Cubase to give us a count-in (normally this is 2 bars). This is done by activating the **Count-in** button, near the metronome button– it looks like this:

If you can't see the count-in button, press the three dots to the right until you can see it. Now make sure Cubase is at the start of the song, and hit **Record**. Cubase will give you a 2 bar count-in, and then start recording. Play something on the keyboard, and you should see it appear as you're recording. Once you're happy, press **Stop**. Go back to the beginning of the piece (pressing , on the keyboard next to M will do this, although a good way to remember it is to think of the < pointing back to the start of the project) and press play to hear what you recorded.

If you're not happy with the recording, then often the best thing to do is to delete it and start again – unless there is some unique part of it that you think you could never reproduce, the best thing to do is to start again, as this will improve your keyboard skills quite quickly if they need to be improved, and mean that in the future you can sequence things with much more speed and accuracy.

Tip: To delete a part, select it (left-click it) and then hit **Backspace** on the computer keyboard.

To record again, just repeat the steps above.

Snap

Snap is extremely important. Without it, it would be very difficult to make parts in the project window which were exactly the right length, whether it's bars or beats we are after. What snap does is makes sure that any movements you make and any edits you do are constrained to a grid, which minimizes the room for errors. Whenever you're making any changes in the project window, make sure that snap is turned on, and initially make sure that it's set to **Bar**. The settings for Snap are found at the top of the project window, and the correct ones are shown below:

The button at the left turns snap on or off. Next to it is an area that shows the current setting (which is set to **Grid**). The size of the grid is set by the next two boxes - the first is currently set to **Bar** (which we want). Ignore the 1/16 section for the time being – this only applies if the middle menu is set to **Use Quantize**, which you will need later on.

Later on, as your sequencing develops, you will find times when you don't want to use snap, or you want it set to different values. But initially it's best to stick with it set to a grid of bars, as this leaves the least room for problems!

Trimming a part to size

When creating a song, it's often made up of smaller 'building blocks' – these could be a verse, chorus or other section of a song that you wish to repeat. When you originally record them, they might end up being too long, for instance if you didn't hit stop right on the end of a bar, you may well end up with a bar of silence. This can be easily trimmed away – just hover your mouse over the part in question, and it will have small 'handles' at the bottom corners – one for the start and one for the end.

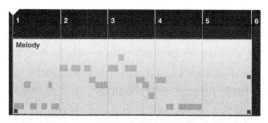

Here we see the part, with a bar of silence at the end. At the bottom corners there are 'handles' which you can click and drag to size the part.

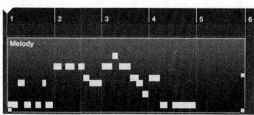

If the part has been selected, it will look like this - dark with the 'handles' being lighter.

In either case, you can click and drag the end one to the left...

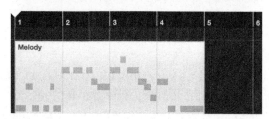

... to produce a part of the correct length. Note that if you do this to an area which has notes in it, they will not be played, but they are not lost – you can extend the part again using this technique and they will re-appear.

Make sure snap is turned on when doing this, or the timing of your part will suffer.

Adding another track

To add another track, you can do so in the way you did before – go to `Project >` `Add Track > Instrument`. It is important to experiment with the different Instruments you have on your system, which can create a wide range of sounds.

Adding Drums

Drums are an important part of many styles of music, so adding them is often needed. To do this, create an instrument track as shown above, but this time you will pick `Groove Agent SE` from the Instrument menu. Now, using the patch selector (as shown on page 5) pick the Dry Standard Kit (remember you can search for it with the keyword 'drum'). This means that instead of playing notes, the keyboard will play drum sounds – on most keyboards/synths you will find that the C note to the left of the keyboard will be a bass drum, with snare above it on D and E, toms above that, while the hi-hats will be on F♯, G♯ and A♯. Learning what sounds are where will take some time (experiment to find which sounds are where), but the basic parts of the drum kit are found on the left-hand end of the keyboard. There is a map of some of the keyboard in the MIDI Chapter on page 62. As before, recording drums is just like recording any other MIDI, although the playing may be more complex if you're trying to play a full kit's worth at once.

Adding more notes to a part

If you have problems playing all of a drum track at once, then there are a number of ways to do it. The first way is to record 'on top' of the first part you have recorded. Simply go back to the beginning of the track, and then record again on the same track – the notes you've already played will be played back to you, and you'll create a new part on top of the original one; Cubase will show the part with diagonal lines on it to show you that there is more than one part in that location, and once you're happy with the second part you have made, you can select the 'glue' from the toolbar at the top and glue the top part to the bottom – you'll now see a part with both sets of notes in (see diagrams below). Once you're finished working with the glue, you can return to the arrow tool, either by using the toolbar, or right-clicking on the white area of the project window and selecting it from the pop-up menu.

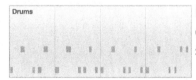

Here we see the initial part that has been record-ed. Cubase is set to record from the start on the same track, and we see below.....

... that the notes get recorded and seem to be in the same part, but the part has a diagonal pattern on it - this shows that there is another part below this one. Both still play, even though they are on top of each other. If we want them to be one part, we select the glue from the toolbar above, and click on the part, leading to...

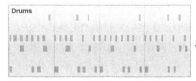

.... a final part which has the notes of both parts.

Picking which tracks play

Cubase has two important buttons which will let you hear the tracks you want, and stop others from playing.

Mute

Mute will stop any track that has it turned on from playing. Click on the button so that it is selected in yellow, and play your track back - the track will not be heard. You can do this for as many tracks as you want. To un-mute them, either click the mute button on the track, or you can clear all mutes with the clear mutes button which is in the toolbar at the top of the window.

If you want to mute a track you have selected (i.e. it is in white in the list) then press **M** on the keyboard.

Solo

Solo will mute all tracks other than the one(s) you have soloed (press **S**). This makes it quick and easy to hear a track you want to hear in isolation. You can solo multiple tracks if you want, and each one is toggled by clicking the solo button on the track in question. **CTRL** clicking a Solo button will mute any other already soloed tracks. As with mute, there is a clear all solo button in the toolbar at the top of the window.

Creating an arrangement

Usually, a song will consist of several parts, some of which will be repeated. This can be done quickly and simply in Cubase. Firstly, create the parts that you want to use for the song – you can do this on several tracks, using different instruments, but for clarity the diagrams below will only show one track.

The first thing to realise is that you can move any part to a new location by clicking and dragging it there. When you do so, make sure you have snap turned on, as then your part will be in time. You can also drag a part to a new track to make it play on a different sound – sometimes this happens accidentally.

However, often copies of the original parts are needed, to make the piece larger – repeating sections of an entire song, or copying a bar from one place to another. There are a few ways to do this, as seen below.

Here we see the original part, 4 bars from bar 1 to bar 5. For each step below, the first part has to be selected.

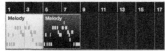 **Edit > Functions > Duplicate**. A single copy is made, directly after the original part.

 **Edit > Functions > Repeat**. A new dialogue box appears, asking for the number of copies – here 3 was entered. Useful for creating many copies.

 Holding down **ALT** while dragging the part to a new location will create a copy – this is useful when a copy doesn't need to be directly after the original.

Using these simple techniques allows a song's structure to be built up quickly and easily.

Practicing a section

When a part is simple to play, then it can often be done with little practice. But sometimes it's necessary to repeat a section so you can practice or work out what you want to play. Here's where the locators come in. Cubase has two main locators, left and right. They can be used to create a cycle which Cubase will repeat until you tell it otherwise. To do this, firstly we need to set the left and right locators. This can be done in a number of ways:

1 – Double-click the area on the transport bar where the current value of the locator is, and enter a new value. For bar 5, just hit **5** and **Enter** on the keyboard.

2 – You can **CTRL-click** on the ruler (showing the bars across the top of the project window's white area) to set the left locator, and **ALT-click** to set the right locator. This needs accurate mouse placement, though.

3 – If you have a part or parts that you want to cycle round, select them and then hit **P** on the keyboard.

All of these will set the locators, and once you have done this, you can activate **Cycle** on the transport bar (the button to the left of stop – it will turn blue when it's on), and Cubase will cycle round the contents between the two locators. You can now practice the section that you wish to record or create until you get it right.

Cycle Recording

While cycling to play a section and practice it is useful, it is also useful sometimes to record while in cycle mode. This gives a number of different options, including recording several different versions of the same part, or to add notes to the part as you go. We will look at three of the available options.

Adding notes to a part

A common need is to add notes to a part. While we have seen this being used when recording without Cycle mode, in cycle mode it is possible too. The first thing is to ensure that the MIDI Record Mode is set to Mix, by clicking the button on the next page.

11

Clicking here will summon the MIDI Record Modes menu:

Now, with the locators set, a part can be played. Each time round the cycle, the notes you play will be added to the previous notes - they will not overwrite them. This is a quick way of building up a drum part, as seen here. The first time round the cycle, the bass and snare drums were played:

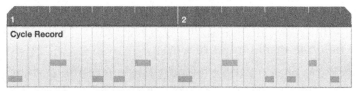

The next time round the hi-hats were added:

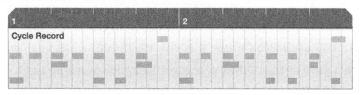

You can cycle round as many times as you like, and whenever you add a note it will become part of the recording.

Keeping only the last version

If you want to keep only the last version you record, this is easily done. Set the MIDI Record Mode to **Keep Last**:

Now proceed as in the previous section; when you stop, only the last version you did will be left. This can be useful when you are trying to get a part right, and will stop as soon as you have done that. Often if you keep starting and stopping to record, it can stop you from getting in the feel of things, so having Cubase cycle round until you get it correct can save time.

Recording different versions

Sometimes, you may want to keep recording while you play different versions of that section, and then decide later which version you want to keep. To do this, set the MIDI Record Mode to **Stacked**, from the right-hand side of the pop-up menu on the Transport Bar.

As you record with cycle turned on, you will see each part recorded, and it may look as if the other versions have been lost (much as in the previous section) - here is the result after four cycles.

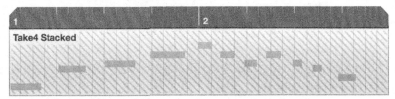

Note that the part says Take 4 - this was on the fourth repeat. If we play the track back, we get the fourth version that was played. However, the others are still present. Clicking the Show Lanes button will reveal the previous 3 Laps.

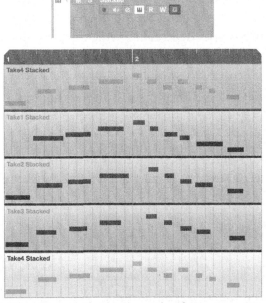

At present, Lap 4 is the version that is heard. If you want to hear another one, you can use the Comp tool - see page 522 - or you can use the Mute tool to mute

13

one of the lanes, and then again to allow another one to play (see page 30 for the Mute tool). The Comp tool is explained on page 522 in the Audio Editing chapter, but works for MIDI as well as audio, so the instructions there will show you how to use it for more than merely choosing which lane to play. Note that with either method, if you change the lane which is active, the note display on the track changes to reflect the part that will be played - here Lap 2 has been chosen, and the track part reflects this both in name and note content.

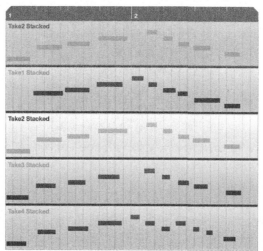

If you want to return the track back to being viewed normally (without lanes), then click the Show Lanes button again.

Retrospective Record

There will be many times when you will play an idea that you think worked well, but you weren't recording it - and sometimes it can be difficult to remember exactly what you did. In the past, this would have been gone forever, but Cubase has a feature called retrospective record which essentially means Cubase is always recording MIDI input. This means all you need to do is press the retrospective record button and the events will be put onto the currently-selected track.

Here's an example - while it is difficult to see something that hasn't happened in a screen shot, you can try this yourself to get a chance to see how useful retrospective record can be.

The setup is simple - a single instrument track in a project. Play was pressed (but **NOT** record!) and a MIDI keyboard was played for a few bars of melody. After hitting stop, this was the result:

No MIDI data has been recorded to the track.

However, pressing the retrospective record button will make Cubase behave as if record had been pressed:

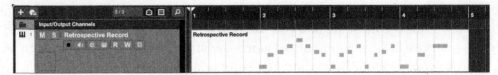

The MIDI data can now be edited as normal - it is now a normal MIDI part. Retrospective record has another trick up its sleeve - you don't even need to have pressed Play - if you have just been playing MIDI while Cubase has been in Stop mode, it will still record. Again, starting from a blank track, but not pressing play, MIDI notes were played on a keyboard. Pressing retrospective record this time once more generated a recording:

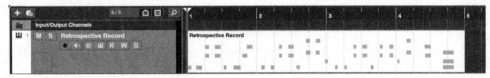

Clearly the timing of this may be off (as there was no metronome to play along with), but it can still be invaluable to capture those inspirational moments that come along every now and then.

Editing

One of the most powerful reasons to use a computer for creating music is that you can alter what you've played after the event – you can change the sound that something is played back on, and you can also alter the notes that you've played. Simple editing will save you hours of work – while it is always a good idea to try to improve your keyboard skills and play something in real time, there will always be times when you will need to edit what you have played. To open the editor, double-click a part you have recorded. This will open the 'key editor', which is like the paper roll from a player piano.

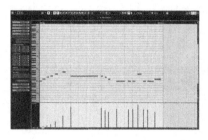

Here we see the key editor, with time running from left to right, and the notes going up the left-hand side of the screen, from low to high. The notes of the part are represented as rectangles, and the colours show how hard the note was hit (called Velocity in MIDI terminology), from blue to red (soft to hard).

The first editing is quite simple. As we've seen in the project window, each note can be moved to a new location, and again it is controlled using snap – this will make the notes 'stick' to a grid, and we can set the size of the grid.

Listen to the part you've created, and work out the grid that it should fit to – if it has only one note per beat (quarter notes/crotchets), then set the snap to ¼. If it has two even notes per beat (eighth notes/quavers) then set it to 1/8, etc. Once you have done this, you can move the notes to the 'correct' location by clicking and dragging them – note that the position that you click on the note is crucial – if you click at the beginning or end you drag the note out. If they are all fairly close and you have set the snap setting correctly, then hit Q on the computer keyboard for 'quantize' – this will move each note to the nearest 'correct' grid position; this may or may not work well depending firstly on if you've chosen the correct snap setting, and secondly if you've played it accurately! It's not unusual to have to correct some notes by hand, but quantizing can save a lot of manual work. There is more information on this on page 84.

If there are any notes that you don't want, you have two choices - either double-click a single note, or select one or more and hit **Delete**.

You can also edit the velocity of the notes that you have played (i.e. how hard you played them – for most synths this translates into the volume of the notes being played). This is done in the "controller lane" at the bottom of the window, as seen on the next page:

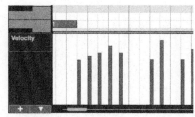

If there is no controller lane, click on the plus at the bottom of the editor area and one will appear.

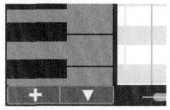

If the controller lane is not displaying velocity, click on the triangle that appears on the current controller name to bring up the pop-up menu, and pick Velocity from it.

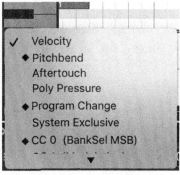

You can pick a variety of parameters to edit with the pop-up menu on the left of the lane, but Velocity is what we're after at the moment. You should see coloured bars which represent the velocities of each note that you have played – by default, they will be short and blue for lightly-played notes, tall and red for notes that were played loudly, and in-between for others. You can see that in this example, they are all the same velocity (100 in this case, from a range of 1-127).

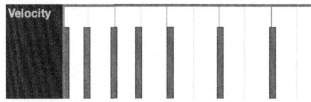

To edit the velocities, you can move the selection tool over the velocity area - note that it turns into a pencil when you move there. You can now click and drag the note velocities to the desired levels, and you should hear the effect of doing so.

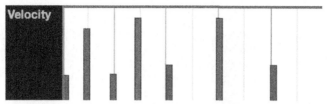

You can also use the line tool in a variety of modes (see page 31), which will allow you to alter the velocities in a number of different ways.

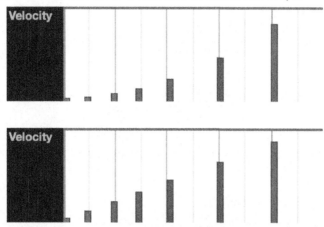

Once you're finished in the editor, hit **Enter** and you'll be back to the project window.

Non-Keyboard player tips

If you are not already a competent keyboard player then you may find sequencing quite frustrating or difficult – particularly if you are trying to sequence something that already exists. There are a number of things you can do to help your situation:

Keyboard Skills – improving these will pay the largest dividends. If you can learn basic keyboard technique it will enable you to translate your ideas into parts a lot more quickly. Knowing where the notes are on the keyboard is important, as is being able to play simple chords. If you can gain some independence between your two hands then this will make matters even better, particularly when you start to program drum parts in real time.

Slowing things down

Often a complex part will be difficult to play at the correct speed, and one way round this is to slow Cubase down, and then play the part at a lower (achievable) speed – see page 5 – and you can then put Cubase back to the original speed.

Recording rhythm then changing the pitch

This is a useful skill when you know what you want to play but can't do it quickly enough (or it's too complex to get). Firstly, pick a note that fits OK with whatever backing you have, and then record the correct rhythm of the piece, but all played at the same pitch – this should be doable for just about everyone.

Here we see the rhythm of our melody has been recorded, all on a single note.

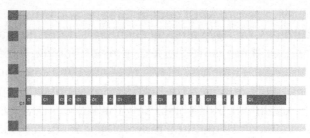

The next step is to correct the pitches of the notes that you've played in. You can do this by editing each one, but it can be laborious. If you know what notes you need to play (which is often the case with a melody which you know or that's written down) then open the part you have just recorded in the key editor. Select the first note of the melody, and then click the MIDI Input button at the top. This enables input from the MIDI keyboard. You will see there are three buttons with notes on to the right of this. Make sure the ones with the arrows are turned off - this will mean only the pitch of the note is being altered as you press keys on your keyboard. The correct setting is shown below.

You can now play the correct pitches in, one at a time, and Cubase will alter the pitch of the current note, and move to the next one. In this way anyone who can't read music quickly can input a rhythmically accurate version and then change the pitches quickly - below is the part with half the notes replaced.

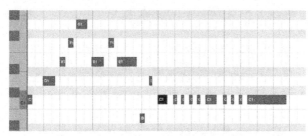

Below is the completed melody. Don't forget to turn MIDI Input off after completing the task, as otherwise you may accidentally alter a part without realising.

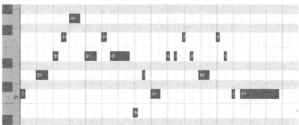

Step Input

There is another way to record MIDI data in Cubase, and instead of being in real-time (like the recordings we have already seen), it is done in what is called 'step time'. This means that there is no clock or timing running, instead Cubase will move forward in time each time you play a note, and you can wait as long as you like between them. This removes the need to play notes in quick succession, which can often be useful for those first using the keyboard, or when sequencing parts which are too difficult to play at a reasonable speed. It also opens up some more creative possibilities as well.

To use Step Input, firstly create a new, empty part. This can be done in a number of ways, either selecting the pencil tool in the project window and clicking and dragging to draw the part:

Or if you have your locators set you can double-click between them on the appropriate track.

Once you have your part, double-click it to open it in the editor. You will now need to turn Step Input on, using the icon located towards the top of the editor. (you may need to enable `Step/MIDI input` by clicking the cog in the top right of the editor window)

Next, set the step size. This is done by altering the quantize value at the top of the editor, seen here set to 1/8.

You may have noticed that as soon as you turned Step Input on, a blue indicator appeared at the play position on screen, as seen below:

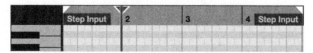

This is where Step Input will be active. If you want to alter where the notes appear, use the left and right cursor keys on your keyboard to move to the correct location. You can also set it by clicking in the main section of the editor window (where the notes appear).

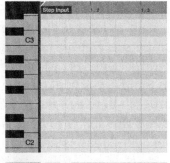

Here is the empty part, with the step input line on the left . You should see the blue triangle and line showing where the input will occur. Cubase is ready to take the next note or chord played, and when you do so and release it...

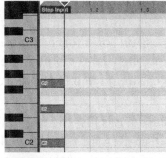

...two things happen: Firstly, the note or chord that you played has been created in perfect time - it starts precisely where the input location was set, and it is exactly the length you set. Secondly, the blue step input line will have moved on to the next grid division, ready...

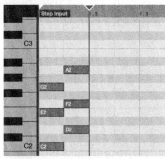

... for the next one. Once it is played and released, the same thing happens again - the 'perfect' chord/ note is created with the right start and end points, and the step input line moves another division forward.

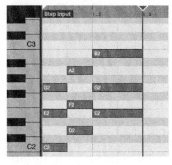

It is possible to alter the duration of the notes created using the cursor left and right keys. Here the right cursor key was pressed twice before releasing the notes, leading to a chord of double the usual duration.

Note that when you are using Step Input, once you press a key on the MIDI keyboard, you can press more keys to make a chord, and it is only when you release them all that the input is actually taken, so you don't have to hit all the notes at the same time. As with MIDI note input above, ensure you turn Step Input off when you have finished, or you can enter notes without realising it!

Pitch Bend

So far, the notes we have seen have all been discrete, and at least a semitone apart, like the notes on a piano keyboard. Many instruments as well as the voice are capable of playing notes which don't fit into this 'grid' of pitches. MIDI has the facility to achieve this by using what is called Pitch Bend - which allows the alteration of the pitch of a note to another pitch - whether in-between the 'grid' of pitches, or sliding from one to another. Pitch Bend has the ability to bend a note up or down in pitch from the original, so the display in Cubase starts with zero in the middle.

Pitch Bend can be created by using the controller lane as already seen (strictly speaking, it's not a controller, but we'll leave that discussion for another time). By selecting `Pitchbend` instead of `Velocity` in the controller lane, it's possible to enter any pitch bend which is already present, or to create pitch bend data as we'll see next.

Here is a single note, which lasts for four bars. When played, it is just the pitch of C3, and it doesn't change. A synthesizer sound has been chosen for this as it will sustain (sound) for the entire length of the note, which is needed - if the sound stops before the pitch bend happens, its effect will be unheard.

With the controller lane set to `Pitchbend`, it is possible to draw in a single point which will alter the pitch at that time - instantly changing pitch, but without playing a new note.

By default, most synthesizers have an up and down pitch bend range of 2 semitones. Here the Pitch Bend is under half of the range available from the default (the centre), so it will be a bit below a C♯ note. The default display of pitch bend uses Cubase's values with a maximum of +100 and a minimum of -100, with 0 in the middle as no pitch bend. This is not how MIDI actually sends the values, so for more information on how MIDI works for pitch bend, see page 56 if you want to go deeper. Here the point has been moved up the maximum (note the 100 readout):

To use a more musical range of semitones for pitch bend, click the cog in the controller lane ...

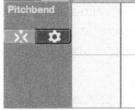

... and in the window that appears, select **Show Semitones Grid**.

Notice that two things have happened - firstly, there is now a scale of +2 to -2 semitones at the left, and secondly, moving any point tells you the pitch in semitones, rather than raw MIDI data (note the **2.00** readout):

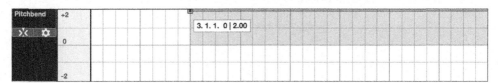

Clicking on the line and dragging to a new location will draw another point, allowing the pitch to alter again when played back:

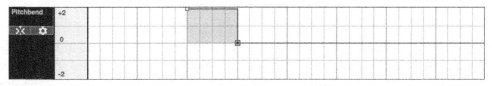

Turning on snap with the button to the left of the cog allows easy creation of accurate pitch bend data.

Altering Pitch Bend Curves

Once you have more than one pitch bend event, hovering the mouse between them will show a circle:

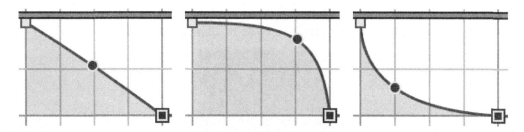

Clicking and dragging this circle will allow the creation of smooth curves between the points, as seen in the examples below (note that the two pitch bend points have not moved, but the transition between them has been edited by dragging the circle).

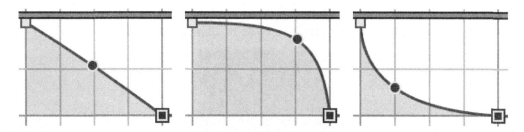

In this way it is possible to build up smooth transitions between pitches with a minimum of effort as Cubase will create the data needed to make the change smooth, and altering the start or end points can be done quickly, while retaining the smoothness of the transition.

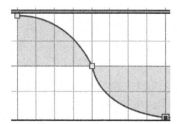

Editing MIDI Controller Data

MIDI controller data can be created and edited in the same way as already seen for pitch bend, although the range of data is typically 0-127 instead of -8192 to +8191. Use the same method of creating points first, and then altering the line between them to achieve the desired transition. This will allow accurate and smooth edits and transitions to be created.

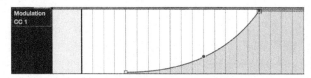

Once you are more familiar with the basics and move on to the techniques shown in the Effective Sequencing chapter on page 71, you will find these skills invaluable.

Saving your work

This is the most important thing you can do! Make sure that you save your work regularly. It is an unfortunate fact of life that computers crash sometimes. Cubase is a very complex piece of software – we've just scratched the surface of it here – and sometimes it crashes. Whenever you've done something that you like, save your work! It's quickly done by pressing `CTRL+S`, and it can save you hours of time if something goes wrong. You can also set Cubase to auto-save by going to `Edit > Preferences > General` and ticking `Auto Save` – it's really easy to forget to save work in the middle of a sequencing session, so this is a good idea. If you need to back your work up, then see page 51 for how to do this.

The Toolbar

At the top of the project window and editors in Cubase you will see the toolbar.

This allows you to select different tools, making the mouse cursor perform different tasks. We will now look at the tools that are available to you, and some of their uses.

The Selection Tool   (Press 1)

This is the default mode - the arrow that you have already been using - where you can click and drag a part to a new location, and use the sizing handles that appear to alter the length of parts. This is the mode you will use more than any other, and it can be accessed by pressing **1** on the main keyboard. If you click and hold on the tool on the toolbar, a pop-up menu appears:

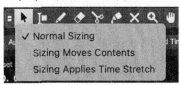

This allows the selection of different modes for the tool, which alter what happens when you re-size an event. Note that pressing **1** repeatedly will cycle through these modes.

Normal Sizing

As we have already seen, it is possible to click and drag a start or end handle, and change the length of a part. This is the default mode.

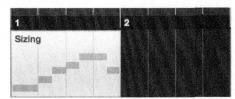

Sizing moves contents

In this mode when you re-size a part, the contents will move when you do so. Here is an example to show that in action.

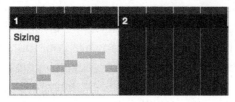 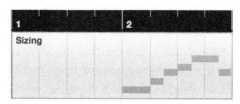

Sizing applies Time Stretch

In this mode, when you re-size a part, the contents will be stretched or squeezed according to the change in length that you apply. Here is an example to show that in action.

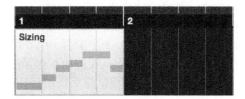 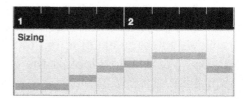

The Range Selection Tool   (Press 2)

The Range Selection Tool lets you click and drag to select an area across a number of tracks, and then move the contents of the area you have outlined to a new location by clicking and dragging. It can be useful for making large changes to a sequence without having to spend a long time separating all the parts that you want by using the scissors (see the next section for the scissor tool). Here we see a sequence which has had an area selected by clicking and dragging.

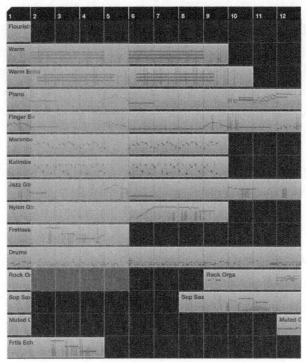

Once the area has been selected, hover the mouse over it - it will turn into a hand and now the area can be moved by clicking and dragging.

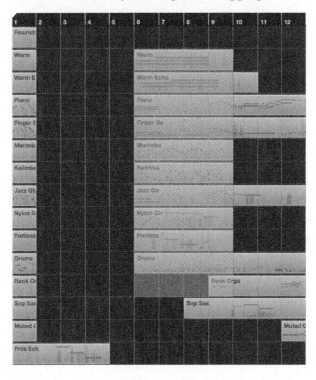

Combine Selection Tools (Press **ALT + SHIFT + 1**)

It is possible to use both the selection and range selection tool by clicking the button to the left of the selection tool. In this mode, range selection works in the top half of a track, and selection in the bottom half. It can save on mouse mileage, and make for a faster, more productive workflow once you have mastered its intricacies.

However, it can be frustrating to use at first as you need to be accurate when working in the project window , and it may well be something that is best left turned off while you master the use of each tool individually.

The Scissors (Press **3**)

The scissors allow you to cut existing parts into smaller ones. Here we will see the scissors in action - here is an existing part:

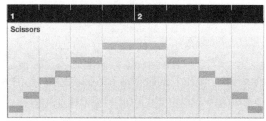

Clicking with the scissors at bar 2 creates 2 parts from the original.

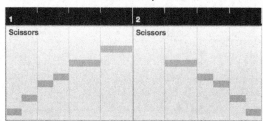

Note that the long note from the end of bar 1 (which extended over the bar 2 line where the cut was made) does not appear in the second part - the notes themselves are not cut. Looking inside the first part shows us that the note is intact, and extends beyond the new part.

This can lead to some confusion when cutting parts with MIDI notes in, so be aware that things like this can happen.

The Glue

(Press **4**)

The Glue tool allows parts to be glued together and become one part. Taking the parts created by cutting above, we can see that the reverse of the cutting process happens:

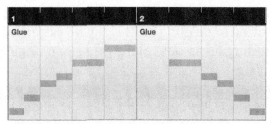

Clicking on the first part glues it to the following one, as seen on the next page:

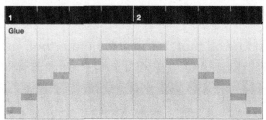

Note that the long note from the first part now has its true length shown. Glue can bridge the gaps between parts, as seen here:

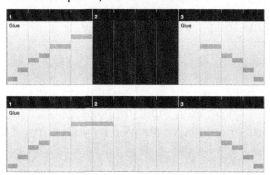

Later on, when working with audio, note that glue will only glue audio events together that originally belonged together; if they didn't then an audio part will be created, which is a container with multiple audio events in it.

The Eraser

(Press **5**)

The eraser allows you to delete parts by clicking on them. It is often quicker to stay on the Selection tool, click on a part and hit Backspace on the keyboard, but you may prefer using the erase tool.

The Zoom Tool

(Press **6**)

As its name suggests, the zoom tool controls zooming in and out. It has two main ways of working. If you click on a track without dragging, it will zoom in. **ALT**+click will zoom out. However, if you want to zoom into a particular area, you can click and drag that area using the zoom tool, and once you release the mouse button, that area will fill the screen.

The Mute Tool   (Press 7)

The Mute Tool can be extremely useful - it allows the muting of a part, stopping it playing without moving or deleting it. This can be extremely useful for creating arrangements and testing ideas out. Here we see an original track, with three parts:

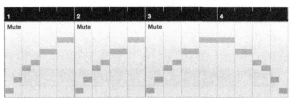

The middle part will now be muted using the mute tool - note that it has gone grey (easier seen on screen than in print!), and it will not be played.

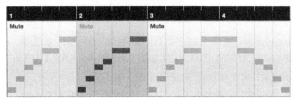

Clicking again will allow the part to play normally.

The Pencil Tool   (Press 8)

The Pencil (or Draw) tool allows the creation of parts and events - this has already been seen on the section on Step Input on page 19. Clicking and dragging with it will create new parts or events, controlled by your current snap settings.

The Play Tool   (Press 9)

The Play Tool allows you to play a part by clicking and holding on it. Note that only the part you click on will be played - if there are other tracks which happen at the same time they will not be played. This is similar to using Solo, as covered on page 10.

The Line Tool

The Line tool has a number of modes, as seen below.

 Line - creates straight lines

 Parabola - creates curves. Pressing **CTRL** flips the curve

 Sine, Triangle and Square - create repeating waveforms, with the wavelength (i.e. how often the cycle repeats) is set by the Snap value. This can be extremely useful for creating repetitive data. **CTRL**, **SHIFT** and **ALT** act as modifiers to change the creation mode.

The Line tool allows the creation of notes in the editor, the editing of velocities and controller data in the controller lane (as seen on page 16), as well as automation data (see page 341). In the line and parabola mode it can be very useful for making smooth edits of velocity and controller data (as seen in the Effective Sequencing chapter on page 71). If you are feeling avant-garde, it can also be useful for creating unusual patterns of notes in the key editor.

In the key editor, another mode - Paint - exists, allowing free creation of note data.

The Time Warp Tool

PRO

The Time Warp Tool allows you to alter Cubase's tempo by dragging bars to a desired location, producing complicated and accurate tempo changes quickly and visually. This is covered in the Audio Editing chapter, starting on page 489.

In addition, it has a third mode where it can be used to apply AudioWarp to audio events directly in the project window. This is covered on page 506.

The Comp Tool

ARTIST PRO

The Comp Tool allows you to piece together a best performance from a number of tracks you have recorded. This is covered on page 522.

Editing Drums

While it is possible to edit drum parts that have been played using the key editor, it is often better to do this editing in the drum editor – this is for two main reasons. Firstly, the length of a drum note is irrelevant – the sound will play for the same duration regardless of how long you hold the key down. Secondly, with a drum part it is often important to be able to edit the velocity and quantization of each drum instrument individually, and this is not easily achieved in the Key editor. To open the drum editor, select a drum part and pick `MIDI > Open Drum Editor`. You will see a window like the one below.

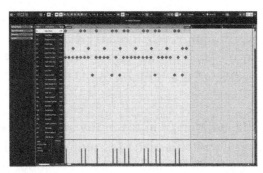

There are many similarities to the Key editor, but the main differences are listed below.

Each note (a drum sound) is represented by a single line, and named for convenience. It is possible to alter the order of the notes by clicking and dragging them by their names) to their new position.

The controller lane will only show the velocity of the currently-selected notes – notice in the above diagram only the bass drum velocities are shown.

Quantize can be applied globally or set individually; with `Use Snap from Drum Map` selected (as seen with the -|+ button below) then each drum instrument can be quantized to the appropriate value quickly and easily. It's also possible to pick `Use Quantize` from here, and set a single value across all drum instruments.

By default, note duration is not shown – each note is simply shown as a diamond, but the button below right can show note lengths if this is required.

The length of any notes created with the drumstick (the pencil tool, essentially) can be set with this menu - linked to the drum map or explicitly set.

Volume and Panning

The last thing we'll cover here is setting volumes of parts – this is important as the balance between instruments is totally under your control – you can do this by setting the volume using the slider in the inspector, as seen on the next page.

 The volume fader – from off (left) to loud (right) – click and drag the slider at the bottom to set it.

 The pan control – this allows the sound source to be placed from left, through centre, to right; again click and drag the slider to set the position.

Both these controls work per track - it's important to remember that the Inspector works on tracks, not on parts.

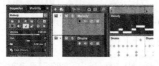 **Incorrect** - a part on the Melody track is selected, but the inspector shows the settings for the track which is selected, in this case the Drums. Changing settings will alter the Drum track, not the Melody one.

Correct - the Melody track has been selected, so the inspector is now showing the settings for that track.

Getting the balance right between instruments can make a big difference to your composition and how it is perceived by the listener, so take some time to get this right. Also note that if they are set to "off" then it means that no value has been sent yet; it's never a good idea to leave them like this as you may inherit odd settings from a previous sequence.

The MixConsole

You can also set the volume and panning using Cubase's mixer, known as the MixConsole. It can be summoned using the **F3** key or via **Studio > MixConsole**. You should see a window similar to the one shown below.

 At the bottom right are the mixer channels. These have faders which allow you to control the level of each channel. The channels are colour coded - by default, red for input or output channels, and cream for instrument channels. Moving the fader up or down will alter the volume of that track. The input seen on the left-most channel is the audio input - we will not be using this yet, but you may see a signal there (as seen in the screenshot) - don't worry about it for the moment. The right-most channel is the Stereo Out, and it controls the overall volume of your project.

It is the same control as seen on the section on the Transport Bar earlier in this chapter. On the left, there is a section covering **Visibility**, **History** and **Snapshots**. This will be covered in the mixer chapter, but you can make a channel disappear from the mixer by clicking the tick to the left of its name. The section at the top right is where more in-depth manipulation of each channel can be performed, adding in a variety of effects and processing. We will not be using this section yet, but it will be covered later on in the mixer chapter and others. Remember - the mixer's appearance will change as you add more tracks, but the basics will remain the same. The MixConsole is covered in detail in its own chapter on page 587.

Instrument Tracks vs Rack Instruments

Cubase has two kinds of tracks with very similar features and function - Instrument Tracks and Rack Instruments. Originally, there were only Rack Instruments, but as Cubase has developed, Instrument Tracks came into being, combining MIDI data and a VST into one entity. When they were first introduced they had some limitations which have now largely gone, and as a result the two track types are now broadly similar. Let's examine both and look at what can be done with them.

Instrument Tracks

These are the type of track we have already used, and they allow us to create and edit MIDI information, but to have that information turned into sound using a VST Instrument (often called VSTi). As with all software synthesizers, they rely on using the computer's processor to create the sound, which can limit the number of sounds you can make (depending on how powerful your computer is, and how complex the synthesizer is). There are two big positives to using them – firstly you can create more than one copy of these to make more sounds – with a physical synthesizer that is not the case. Secondly, all of the information about and editing of the track occurs in one place, on the track itself - the diagram below shows how an instrument track works - it consists of a track with MIDI Data in it (which you will already have edited), but also contains a VST Instrument. The track then sends its output to the mixer.

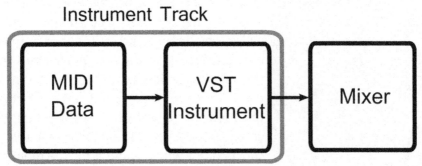

Instrument Track

Don't worry if you find this confusing, you will probably find for most applications that Instrument Tracks will do what you need.

VST Instruments and Separate MIDI Tracks

This way of using VST Instruments involves more steps – firstly you create the VST Instrument, and secondly you create a MIDI track to send data to it.

Firstly, go to **Studio > VST Instruments** and the VST Instruments window will appear. It can be accessed using **F11** as well as the menu, and you can run up to 64 VST Instruments, depending on the version of Cubase that you are running. If you have Instrument tracks, the instruments will appear in the top of the window, but to create a Rack instrument, click on the right, where it says **Rack**...

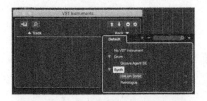

...to see a menu of the available instruments – we will select the Halion Sonic that is included with Cubase. Your list may be different to this, depending on the plug-ins that you have installed.

You will be asked if you want to create a MIDI track for Halion Sonic – you will usually want to, so click **Create**

Next, Halion Sonic will appear on screen. It can be played with the on-screen keyboard, but we will need to route MIDI to it to use it for any sequencing work or playing live with a keyboard. You will also need to select a patch (sound) for Halion Sonic to be generate any sound.

Here we see the routing section of the track. Note that **Halion Sonic** is the output, that **Channel 1** is currently selected, and that there is no program selected (**Program Selector** will be replaced when a program is chosen). A program can be selected by clicking here, or...

... in the right-hand section of Halion Sonic. Search for text in the search area, and then click the All patches category icon to see a list similar to the one seen on the right. Then double-click a program to load it.

The diagram below shows the connection between MIDI tracks and a VST Instrument which is in the rack. As can be seen, multiple MIDI tracks can be sent to the same VST Instrument.

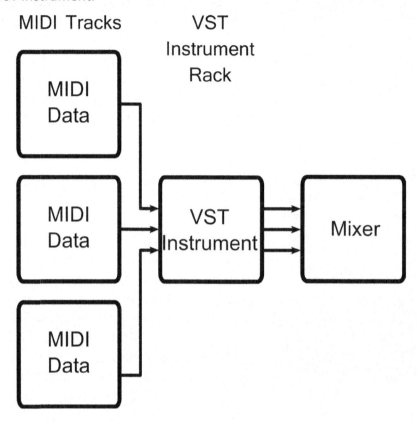

Advantages and Disadvantages

Clearly, using Instrument tracks is much quicker and simpler. In addition you will notice later on when you start using automation that it is much easier to do this using Instrument tracks, because everything is in one place; if you are automating a "rack" VST then you will need to go and find the track for the VST Instrument you are using, and in a large project this can take time. In the past, Instrument Tracks were limited - they only had a single stereo audio output, and could only accept MIDI from the instrument track itself. Now this is no longer the case, your preference is the main deciding factor between using Instrument Tracks and Rack Instruments. If you like having everything integrated into one track, then Instrument Tracks are the way to go. However, if you want to work with purely MIDI tracks and then send them to a single instrument (aping the way MIDI studios worked with physical synthesizers), then Rack Instruments may be the way to go. When working with many instruments at once, you may find that you need to use each synthesizer to produce many timbres at once (Multi-Timbral synths provide up to 16 different sounds), and then it may be simpler to use Rack Instruments. But at the moment, if you're unsure then stick to using Instrument Tracks until it becomes apparent that you need to do something else.

Sending MIDI to an Instrument Track

There are two main reasons to use extra MIDI tracks with an Instrument. Firstly, you may want to have multiple parts played by a multi-timbral synthesizer. Some synths (such as Halion Sonic SE) have the ability to play 16 different sounds, and when using this facility it makes sense to have each part on a different track. Secondly, it may be desirable to have the musical parts that are played by a synth split across multiple tracks to allow construction of layered and complex parts easily. Whatever the reason, doing it will involve a new type of track - the MIDI Track.

MIDI Tracks contain only MIDI data. There is no synthesizer integrated into them, so their output needs to be sent to a synth to turn the MIDI data into audio.

Creating one is done in the same way as other tracks - either right-clicking in the track list area, or going to `Project > Add Track > MIDI`.

There are two important settings to alter. The first is the `MIDI Output` - this picks the destination instrument that the MIDI data will be sent to.

The other setting may or may not be crucial, depending on the synth; the MIDI channel. MIDI data streams can contain up to 16 channels, and the synth may be 'listening' on a specific channel, or it may listen to all of them (this is called OMNI mode). If you are not sure, leave it on `Channel 1`, and see if you get any sound when you play your MIDI keyboard. If not, you can try changing it after creation, either in the inspector's routing section, or in the track itself, as seen here:

Both are the same setting, so use whichever is most convenient.

Using more than one output on a VST Instrument

While in many cases as single audio output for a VST Instrument (VSTi) will be appropriate, there are some occasions when more than one output is useful, for instance having a multi-timbral VSTi (such as Halion Sonic), and wanting to apply Effects (see page 537) or Automation (see page 341) to one of the sounds without it altering any of the others. In such a situation, it is possible to use more than one audio output on a VSTi, and the next section shows how to do this. If you are just starting out in sequencing this may not be needed at this point, but there will come a time when you'll want to do this - so if you're following the book from start to finish, you may want to remember this and return at a later date. There are three main steps to achieving this - two are mandatory, and the last makes working in the project window a lot easier when you have multiple tracks using different outputs on the same instrument.

Setting up the outputs in the rack

The first step is to activate the extra outputs needed in the VST Instruments rack - either in the Right Zone (**CTRL + ALT + R**), or in the VST Instruments Window (**F11**). By default this area is smaller than needed to see the outputs menu directly ...

... so resize the window to show all the options.

To turn an output on or off, summon the menu using the outputs button...

...and a menu will appear showing all the possible outputs from that instrument:

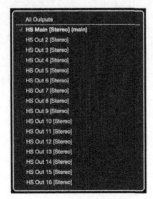

Extra outputs can be turned on here, and you will see a change in the Instrument track in the project window when it changes from 1 output...

... to 2:

This can be repeated for as many outputs as needed. Remember that each output will add a track to the project window and mixer, so you may want to only turn on outputs as they are needed.

Assigning an output from inside the instrument

The next step is to change the audio output that a part inside the instrument is using. This is different for each instrument. Here is Halion Sonic, on the Mix page, and the outputs are currently all set to Main at the right hand side of the window.

Selecting a new output is as simple as clicking on the current output - which is `Main` by default - and picking one from the list.

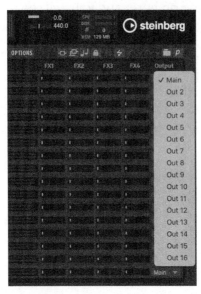

Selecting a different output will now cause the audio for that channel to be output there, allowing processing for that track to be achieved separately. Note that it is possible to select an output inside a VST Instrument which has not been turned on in the rack, and this will lead to that channel being silent. Note that it is possible to select an output inside a VST Instrument which has not been turned on in the rack, and this will lead to that channel being silent.

Separate outputs are not only useful for multi-timbral synths - many percussion synths can benefit from this (with the kit effectively being a timbre per MIDI note, you could consider it a massively multi-timbral synth). The same process can be applied, for instance, to Groove Agent SE5, by selecting a different output per drum pad. The output is selected in the Main area of Groove Agent, as shown below, and the output selected from the same list of 16 possible outputs.

Linking the Inspector to the Output Track

One of the biggest drawbacks of using separate VST Instruments and MIDI tracks is that there are two tracks for the overall part - one for the MIDI data, and another for the audio output of the instrument. This can make editing a little more complex, and using Automation (see page 341) also means splitting attention between two tracks (some parameters will be part of the MIDI track, others will be part of the instrument). To make this a little easier, Cubase can be told which VST Instrument output track is being used by the MIDI track, allowing the Channel Settings window for that track to be opened quickly to view audio settings. By default, it will be set to the main output of the instrument in question, as seen in the routing section of the Inspector. This is viewed by clicking on the Activate Outputs button:

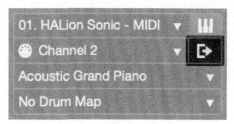

This can be changed to any output available on the VST Instrument in question. If the output is not already enabled, selecting it will also enable it on the VST Instrument, as seen previously.

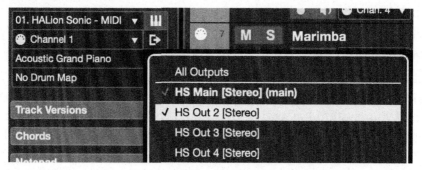

Now any audio-related sections of the inspector will relate to the output which has been selected, and the Channel Zone will also show settings for the appropriate output of the Instrument. This alone can make the separation of multiple audio outputs from the MIDI tracks that they are being driven by much simpler to understand.

Setting up multiple outputs properly can take a little time, but the increase in creative possibilities it opens up compared to using a single stereo output mean that it is worth spending the time on it. The first time you do this it will probably seem complex, but after a few sessions using it you will wonder how people got by without access to individual outputs for each part of a 16-part multi-timbral synth!

Considerations for VST Instruments

Bear in mind that each VSTi uses your computer's processing power to create sound (some more than others), so you may find that you can only run a few on your system before it runs out of processing power. There is a great advantage of software synths though – if you need another one (and have the processing power) then you can just create another one in the rack – no extra expense!

Another issue is called latency – you may find that when you press a key, there is a delay before sound is heard. This is latency, which is the delay between the CPU processing some audio (in this case making a sound) and it being output by the sound card. If there is a significant delay, you may need to alter the latency – see the Audio Setup chapter on page 651 for details on this, or you can record your parts using a "normal" MIDI synth, and then play them back using a VSTi – this is possible because Cubase can take the delay into account when playing back a part from a MIDI recording.

MIDI Devices

When looking at the output list in the Inspector, you may wonder why there are different groups of outputs – there is always **Not Connected** available at the top, but in addition there can be three other groups.

The bottom group is a list of 'actual' outputs – these will be physical MIDI ports which exist on your setup, and often the Microsoft software synth that is part of Windows. These will allow you to play MIDI, but Cubase will not give you any listings of patches that are available with them.

Above this there can be two different groups, which may alter depending on how you have the system set up.

There can be a list of "MIDI Devices" – this is a way of telling Cubase about the synthesizers you have in your studio, and what MIDI connections they use. For instance, if your system has two MIDI outputs with a JV1080 attached to output 1 and an Emu Proteus 2000 attached to output 2, you could use the MIDI Device Manager to set these up. They would then appear in the output list. Although the MIDI information will still pass to the same output (output 1 if you have selected the JV1080), Cubase will now give you a list of the patches that a JV1080 has available, making sound selection a much easier proposition.

There can also be a list of VST Instruments – if you have set any of these up (as shown previously in this chapter) then each VST Instrument will appear here.

The Project Window in Detail

You have already been using the Project Window - it is where the majority of your recording and arranging work will take place. There are a number of features that have not been covered, so we will now look in more detail at the sections of it. It consists of a number of different areas, most of which can be hidden from view, allowing you to give maximum space for the task you are working on.

We will look at the different areas of the project window that are available, and how to alter the set-up; the default view may be a little crowded on some screens, and you will soon get used to altering the setup quickly to suit whatever you are working on at any given time. Good knowledge of what information is available where, and how to control this quickly and efficiently is important to ensure that you are concentrating on the task in hand (creating music) rather than searching for information. Many settings in Cubase are available in multiple locations, so being aware of this is also an important part of learning how to work efficiently.

The Main Area

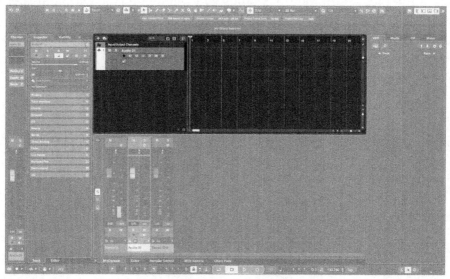

This is where your tracks are shown, and any parts (be they MIDI, Audio or any other type) will be displayed. On the left of this section is the track listing area, and on the right is the main area where your parts will be. Time runs from left to right, and here the time shown in bars. This part of the window is always in view, and is where you will be doing a considerable amount of the work you do in Cubase.

The Left Zone

CTRL + ALT + L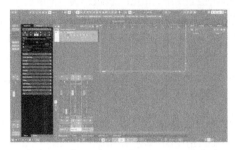

The left zone holds two main tools - the Inspector and the Visibility list. It can be toggled on and off with the keyboard shortcut **CTRL + ALT + L**, or with the button at the top right of the tool bar (where the other zones can be toggled as well):

The Inspector

The Inspector allows a wide range of settings for the selected track to be altered. The information that is available here will depend on the track type. Here is the Inspector view for four example tracks - Audio, Instrument, MIDI and Sampler - which are the most common track types you will be dealing with, but there are others with different functions available here. Many of the changes you will make that apply to a track can be made here, although there are some (such as audio effects) which can also be made in the mixer (see page 599) as well as the channel settings window (see page 547).

| **Audio** | **Instrument** | **MIDI** | **Sampler** |

The Inspector can work in either Track or Editor mode; if an editor is open in the lower zone, then the editor section will become available, and the Inspector's mode will depend on which window has focus.

Visibility

The Visibility section allows tracks to be hidden. Note that hiding a track does not stop it playing back. It is possible to sync the visibility settings between the Project Window and the Mix Console by selecting that option in the menu to the right of Visibility - without this activated, the two are independent.

The Channel Zone   CTRL + ALT + C

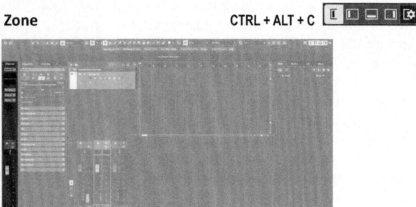

The Channel Zone is a smaller area which allows a dedicated display of a sub-set of the Inspector information for a given channel, allowing the channel fader and meter to be permanently in view, even while other parameters are being altered in the main inspector section.

The Right Zone   CTRL + ALT + R

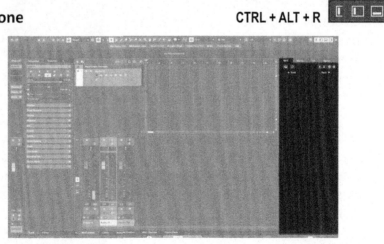

The right zone holds four sections - VST Instruments, Media Bay, Control Room and Meter. As with other zones, it can be toggled on and off with the button at the top right of the tool bar, or with the keyboard shortcut **CTRL + ALT + R**.

VST Instruments

This section (visible by default) shows any VST Instruments that you are using - the software instruments that take your musical information and convert them to audio. The two types of VST Instruments are both present here - the top section shows Instrument track instruments, while the lower section shows any which are being used as separate VST Instruments and MIDI tracks (Rack Instruments) - these are both covered in the section starting on page 34. Most of the controls available here are available in the Inspector, but some - such as activation of extra outputs - are not. Note that under each instrument there are a number of controls available, giving quick access to the most-used settings, avoiding the need to open the instrument editor.

MediaBay

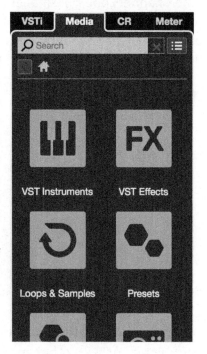

MediaBay gives quick access to a great deal of musical resources in one place, combining search of samples, sounds, MIDI loops and other information into one search engine. Once a search has been completed, the results can be dragged directly to tracks (or to create new tracks if the search result is an instrument/sound combination) to quickly create music from the available resources. Making use of MediaBay's facilities can vastly speed your workflow, allowing quick, seamless access to the considerable amount of content that is included with Cubase. It is covered in more detail on page 117.

Control Room

The Control Room allows complex routing for audio for performers to be achieved from within Cubase. It is outside the scope of this book.

Meter

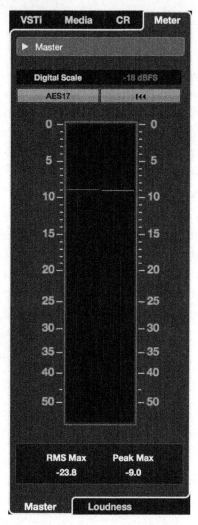

The meter section allows monitoring of the output level of your project in Cubase without having to open the Mix Console. This can be particularly useful if you are working on a laptop or any other computer with limited screen space.

There are a number of options available here, and choice between a Master output meter or a loudness meter. More details on this are available in the Mix Console chapter on page 617.

The Lower Zone

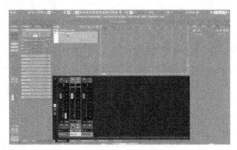

The Lower Zone has five modes - MixConsole, Editor, Sampler Control, Chord Pads and MIDI Remote. The first two offer a particular view of an editor/function which is available elsewhere, but Sampler Control and Chord Pads can only be seen here. The lower zone allows a fuller range of functions (such as editing and mixing) to happen while keeping Cubase in a single-window environment, allowing work on laptops to be achieved without a myriad of overlapping windows. It, too, can be toggled on and off with the button at the top right of the tool bar, or with the keyboard shortcut **CTRL + ALT + E**.

MixConsole

The lower zone MixConsole view allows the viewing of some of the features of the full MixConsole (see page 587 for a full description of the MixConsole). By default, it will show the faders for the channels in the project - usually inputs, the tracks in the project and the Stereo Out - and it gives quick access to levels, panning, mute, solo and automation controls.

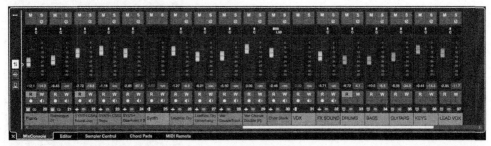

There are two other views - Inserts (selected on the left-hand side of the MixConsole view)...

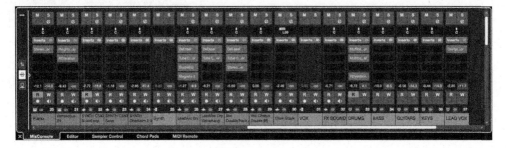

...and Sends (see page 538 for a description of how these work.)

Editor

The editor view provides a version of the Key Editor (covered on page 16), allowing quick access to MIDI information on MIDI and Instrument tracks, or an audio editor when audio events are selected.

Sampler Control

This mode provides all the controls for Sampler Tracks (see page 297), which can also pop out into a floating editor window.

Chord Pads

Chord Pads (see page 209) reside here, and this is the only location they can appear.

MIDI Remote

Cubase's MIDI Remote system is accessed via this tab of the lower zone, and is explained starting on page 273.

Transport

In addition to the Transport Zone (see page 3), there is a floating transport bar (**F2**) which can be placed anywhere. On larger screens it can be useful to place it near your work area, and on smaller screens you can use only minimal controls and hide the Transport Zone to save space. The features it has are identical to the Transport Zone, and learning to configure it to suit your needs at any time is an important skill in smoothing your workflow in Cubase.

The Status Line

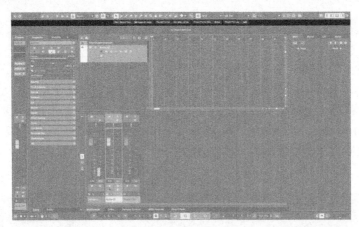

The Status Line gives information about the current project and setup - by default whether audio inputs and outputs are connected, and information about project setup and recording time.

Info Line

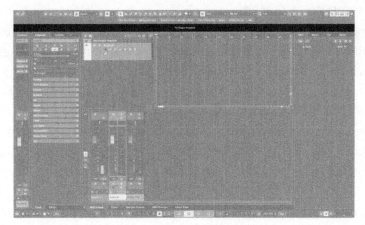

The Info Line provides information about the currently selected object (the actual information displayed will change depending on the type of object selected). From here it is often possible to double-click to alter a value (useful when you want to make a precise setting). If multiple objects are selected, then the information will be in yellow, and it is possible to alter all the objects at once here (useful when you want to apply the same change to multiple objects).

Project Window Layouts

The default setting for the project window is to have all of the areas viewable, and depending on your screen resolution this may be an acceptable setting. On smaller screens (such as laptops), it may be more suitable to have fewer zones viewable, and indeed the near-minimal setting of only the inspector, info line and main area viewable is a more minimal setup for workflow in many situations. The active zones can be set by clicking Setup Window Layout (the triangle to the left of the cog at the top right), and selecting them from the menu that appears:

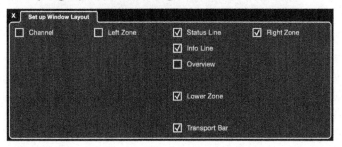

Backing up your work

It's a fact of life – computers crash. Modern computers are massively complex systems, and a single fault can render a computer unusable. A hardware fault in a hard drive can mean a total loss of data, and with it hundreds (or even thousands) of hours or work lost. In addition if you are working on a shared computer there is a chance of accidental data loss, and if your computer is connected to the Internet there is always the chance of a virus or similar program wreaking havoc on your computer and possibly with your data. Many school computers will be restored from an image in the case of problems, and that usually means all the data on the computer is erased.

How can data loss be avoided? Simple – back your work up. Whenever you have made a significant change to a piece, save it, and whenever your session ends, save the work on the computer you're working on and on another storage medium. If you don't, you run the risk of losing everything – if it's in two places it's extremely unlikely that both will suffer a fault at the same time.

The biggest issue here is making sure that all the data for the song is saved. If you merely do **Save As**... then you are only saving Cubase's project file (.CPR) – if you have only MIDI information then this will be adequate, but if you have any audio in the project then you need to save the audio files as well.

To do this go to **File > Back up Project**... You will see a new dialog box where you can pick the location of the new project; this needs to be in an empty folder.

Once you have done this a new dialogue box will appear where you can name the project file, and also choose backup options. If you are aiming to make a complete backup, then leave the boxes ticked as shown below – this will not alter the audio files in any way, but will use the most space.

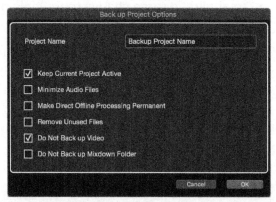

The unticked options are only relevant to audio operations, and will decrease the amount of space needed for the backup, but will decrease the possibilities for further editing. What they will not do is alter the sound of your project, however. Once you hit OK Cubase will save the project file to the new folder, and also create new audio files for it, inside that new folder. The entire folder is self-contained and therefore can be taken to any other Cubase setup.

If you regularly back up your project and audio files, you will never have a significant loss of work. It is a good idea to alternate between two flash drives for backups – after all, they are physically small, and easily lost. Bear in mind that "my data was lost" is not a viable excuse either when at school, college or when working professionally recording clients!

Exercises

Here is a list of tasks that will help you get started with sequencing - each chapter will have some exercises if they are relevant. Whenever you start out with a new topic, getting started is far more important than the material you are working on - the skills and techniques are important; the music itself isn't. Don't attempt to sequence anything complicated at first; simple melodies such as nursery rhymes are a great starting place and will mean you spend more time sequencing than worrying about what to work on.

Sequence a simple melody

Make sure you set Cubase to an appropriate tempo (turn the tempo track off and set the tempo on the transport bar), and sequence the melody accurately. Use a simple sound such as a piano for this part of the task.

Sequence chords

You may already have the keyboard skills to play the correct chords or even harmonise the melody at sight. If not, make use of step input (on page 19) to input the chords. If you can't work out what chords to play, then try to find out what they should be, or harmonise the melody using the information on page 150 if you can.

Sequence a bass part

Your first bass part can just be the root notes of the chords you have played, but if you want to increase the complexity, you can create a more interesting bass part by changing the rhythm, or creating a part which doesn't just use the root note of the chords.

Sequence drums

Adding drums can be a challenge for many beginning sequencing students - both because drummers are usually playing more than one part of the kit at a time and also knowing what to play. You can get round the 'two things at once' issue by either using cycle recording (page 11), step input (page 19) or using the editor to input your part (page 14). If you don't know what to play, this drum part may get you started, so try to input it and then come up with developments of your own.

Change sounds

This will be done by using the inspector for the tracks in question, or changing the VST instruments to give a greater change in sounds.

Apply volume and panning

By using the mixer - as seen on page 33 - you can apply volume and panning to your tracks. Remember that you can make some drastic changes to the way your piece is perceived by altering just the pan and volume of your parts.

Summary

The sequencing techniques you have seen above are basic, but they are the foundation of all MIDI sequencing that you will do. Understanding them and performing them quickly will enable you to capture musical ideas quickly, and being able to quantize quickly and effectively can mean creating accurately sequenced parts quickly. The only way to gain these skills (as with many others) is to practice. Do this by picking a simple song to sequence at first (such as a Folk, Traditional or Christmas Carol tune), and then progress onto longer, more complex songs with more parts and increased complexity within them. It is often a good idea to practice on some music which already exists rather than your own composition as then you will only need to practice one element (sequencing) rather than working on creative elements as well.

How MIDI Works

```
00002E70  1  --   80   17   40   1  B  0 Note Off
00002E90  1  --   90   26   40   1  D  2 Note On
00002E9C  1  --   80   1D   40   1  F  1 Note Off
00002F03  1  --   80   26   40   1  D  2 Note Off
00002F6A  1  --   E0   0E   4F   1  --- Pitch Bend
00002F75  1  --   E0   5A   4E   1  --- Pitch Bend
00002F7E  1  --   E0   25   4E   1  --- Pitch Bend
00002F88  1  --   E0   70   4D   1  --- Pitch Bend
00002F93  1  --   E0   46   4D   1  --- Pitch Bend
00002F9C  1  --   E0   24   4D   1  --- Pitch Bend
00002FEA  1  --   90   19   40   1  C# 1 Note On
0000309C  1  --   80   19   40   1  C# 1 Note Off
000032C2  1  --   B0   16   3F   1  --- CC: 22 (E-MU)
000032CB  1  --   B0   16   3E   1  --- CC: 22 (E-MU)
000032D5  1  --   B0   16   3F   1  --- CC: 22 (E-MU)
000032E0  1  --   B0   16   3F   1  --- CC: 22 (E-MU)
000032E9  1  --   B0   16   3F   1  --- CC: 22 (E-MU)
000032FE  1  --   B0   16   3F   1  --- CC: 22 (E-MU)
00003307  1  --   B0   16   3F   1  --- CC: 22 (E-MU)
0000332F  1  --   B0   16   3F   1  --- CC: 22 (E-MU)
0000333F  1  --   E0   03   4D   1  --- Pitch Bend
00003357  1  --   B0   16   3F   1  --- CC: 22 (E-MU)
0000389C  1  --   90   17   40   1  B  0 Note On
000038BC  1  --   90   1D   40   1  F  1 Note On
00003948  1  --   80   17   40   1  B  0 Note Off
0000395C  1  --   80   1D   40   1  F  1 Note Off
00003AC3  1  --   90   25   40   1  C# 2 Note On
00003B29  1  --   80   25   40   1  C# 2 Note Off
00003B69  1  --   90   17   40   1  B  0 Note On
00003B75  1  --   90   1C   40   1  E  1 Note On
00003BDC  1  --   80   1C   40   1  E  1 Note Off
```

In order to learn sequencing and Music Technology on any platform, it's important to be able to understand the basics on which the sequencing system is built. This falls into two main categories, MIDI and Audio.

MIDI

MIDI stands for Musical Instrument Digital Interface, and is a standard that was created in 1984. Before this it had been difficult or impossible to link polyphonic (many note-playing) synthesizers, even when they were from the same manufacturer. MIDI changed all this, allowing synthesizers to be linked together and played in unison. But what does MIDI do? How does it work? This chapter will tell you all of that. While you may think that the information in the next section is dry and technical, it is important to have an idea of how MIDI works as later on you will be using programming techniques which rely on understanding this. Don't worry if you don't understand it all at first sitting (particularly the communication section), you can re-read it when you've become more familiar with sequencing.

First, the information in this chapter refers to the original MIDI standard, which is now called MIDI 1.0. In 2020, the MIDI Association published MIDI 2.0 as a standard, which is designed to update the original specification (which was nearly 40 years old at this point), providing up-to-date functionality, while still maintaining backwards compatibility with MIDI 1.0. At the time of writing this book, MIDI 2.0 has still not gained much traction, and there are currently no hardware devices available which support it. MIDI 2.0 is a much more complex protocol than MIDI 1.0, and gaining an understanding of it lies outside the scope of this book - it's much more involved than MIDI 1.0. From version 13, Cubase has started to integrate features of MIDI 2.0, and those areas will be discussed at the end of this chapter.

It is the author's belief that a good understanding of MIDI 1.0 will stand the reader in good stead for a long time, as much data will still be sent in a manner that is either MIDI 1.0 or so similar as to make no difference. While MIDI 2.0 will produce some interesting abilities, the vast majority of people will be happy using only MIDI 1.0 features.

Communication

MIDI 1.0 is a serial protocol, meaning that only one piece of information can be sent at a time. It works at a data rate of 31.25kHz, which means that 31250 bits of information can be sent in a second; slow by today's standards, but in the early 80s this was a fast technology. However, the overhead in the data transmission means that in fact around 3000 messages can be sent per second (as each message is made up of 10 bits or so). This sounds fast, but as we'll see later on it means that there can be audible delays between notes. MIDI provides 16 separate channels on each connection, allowing for different instruments to be played at any time, as we'll see later on. But first we'll take a look at what actually gets transmitted by a MIDI connection (for more detail on this, see page 676)

The first thing to understand is that MIDI doesn't transmit sound per se; it only transmits information about what notes are being played and how they are being played. It does this by telling the synthesizer (or sequencer) what notes have been played (with a 'Note On' message) and which have been released (with a 'Note Off' message). It does this using three separate messages, the first a 'Status Byte' (instruction) for 'Note On', followed by two 'Data Bytes' (with a range of 0-127) - the first saying which note has been played (the pitch) and the second saying how hard or loud the note has been played (the velocity). The notes are normally referred to by "friendly" names, with their pitch (A-G) and octave (from -2 to 8) with middle C being C3. If you press middle C on a MIDI keyboard, it sends the following three messages:

Raw Data	145	060	095
Message	Note On Channel 1	Pitch is C3	Velocity is 95
Function	Status Byte	Data Byte 1	Data Byte 2

When you release the key, a similar thing happens:

Raw Data	129	060	044
Message	Note Off Channel 1	Pitch is C3	Velocity is 44
Function	Status Byte	Data Byte 1	Data Byte 2

Notice that a 'Note Off' event has a velocity too; when MIDI was created it was thought important to convey the speed at which a note was released, but most sound modules do not respond to this information, and few keyboards send it, normally sending 0. In a similar manner, playing a three-note C Major chord would produce the following data:

Message 1	Note on Channel 1	Pitch is C3	Velocity is 95
Message 2	Note on Channel 1	Pitch is E3	Velocity is 102
Message 3	Note on Channel 1	Pitch is G3	Velocity is 87
Function	Status Byte	Data Byte 1	Data Byte 2

Releasing the notes would produce a similar set of messages. The problem of 'MIDI Delay' arises because each message above takes about 1mS (1/1000 second) to be transmitted, so the last note is played at least 2mS after the first one, a delay which could become noticeable if several notes were playing on each channel. To try to overcome this, an idea called 'running status' was incorporated into the MIDI standard. What this meant was that instead of sending a 'note on' message repeatedly, the keyboard would instead keep just sending data bytes after the first status byte. This can happen because Status Bytes (such as note on) look different to Data Bytes, so the receiving device can tell them apart. Using running status can mean that there is a saving of 1/3 on all subsequent notes. Another saving is also made by not sending 'Note Off' messages, but instead sending them as 'Note On' messages with velocity of zero; nearly all modern modules will work in that way, but some synths (of early 80s vintage) don't recognise those messages and think of them as more Note Ons instead, and will just play more and more notes....

Another important thing to remember with MIDI is that the note's duration is not transmitted (or known) by the MIDI device; it just plays the note until it is told otherwise. This is why hanging notes sometimes happen, as if a note off message isn't received then it will just keep playing; when working with a sequencer, it's easy to think of the notes seen on screen as being entities in themselves, but they are in fact two messages – the start of the note and the end.

So, that covers notes, but what other things can MIDI send? One of the most obvious is 'Pitch bend'. Most MIDI keyboard controllers have a pitch-bend wheel by the side, and this is transmitted as a different form of data – a pitch bend status byte, followed by two data bytes, The first number is multiplied by 128 and then added to the second. This gives a range of 16384 different pitch bend positions (commonly interpreted as –8192 to +8191), which gives the effect of a seamless change in pitch. Again, the sending device only transmits the pitch bend value itself; it doesn't 'know' how much (in semitones) the pitch-bend will be. This is normally plus or minus two semitones, but can be adjusted to a wider range (an octave is normally available, and often more).

Controllers

MIDI has a range of 'continuous controllers' – CCs for short. These are extremely common, and allow MIDI to transmit a wide range of non-note information about a musical performance – volume, Pan, Expression, Foot pedal positions and a wide range of other information. They are transmitted as three bytes, as shown next:

Raw Data	177	007	107
Message	CC on Channel 1	Value 1 is 7	Value 2 is 107
Function	Status Byte	Controller Type	Controller Value

As with all data bytes, their range is 0-127, so there are a total of 128 controllers available with a range of 0-127 each. Initially these controllers were left up to the manufacturers to use for whatever purposes they saw fit, but this led to a lack of compatibility, and a later addition to the MIDI specification saw a large number of messages standardised; the most common ones are shown in the table on the next page.

Common MIDI Controller Messages

No.	Name	Description	Range	Result
1	Modulation	Control over vibrato depth	0 – 127	none – max
5	Portamento Time	Time taken to slide between notes	0 – 127	short - long
7	Channel Volume	Volume level (absolute)	0 – 127	min - max
10	Pan	Position in stereo field	0 - 63 - 127	L - C - R
11	Expression	Relative volume	0 – 127	min - max
64	Sustain Pedal	Simulates a piano's sustain pedal	0, 127	OFF , ON
65	Portamento Pedal	Turns pitch sliding on or off	0, 127	OFF, ON
91	Reverb Depth	Amount of Reverb applied to channel	0 – 127	off - max
93	Chorus Depth	Amount of Chorus applied to channel	0 – 127	off - max
120	All sound off	Turns all sound off on the channel	N/A	N/A
121	Reset All control- lers	Resets all controllers to their default values	N/A	N/A
123	All notes off	Turns all notes off on the channel	N/A	N/A

The full MIDI specification defines more controllers, but these are the most common ones. As we'll see in a practical situation, all of these controls give quick access to a wide range of sound-altering controls, from simple volume controls to being able to dramatically alter the timbre of a sound. Next, there is the ability to change the basic timbre being played on a channel. This is referred to as a "Program Change", and again the MIDI specification started without any definition of what each program change meant; PC #1 on one module could be a synth sound on one unit and a violin on another. The later "General MIDI" specification (which a great many devices conform to) also defined a wide range of program change values, which meant some compatibility between any synths with a General MIDI mode; PC 1 is always a Grand Piano sound, and so on. Full details of the program changes are given on the next page; note that the instruments are grouped together as similar sections, and give a wide range of sounds to the user. Note that program changes are transmitted as 0-127, not 1-128. Most programs use the more 'human' range of 1-128, but some sequencers are an exception to this, and this fact can cause some confusion, either when using software which uses an unfamiliar scheme, or in particular editor windows (for instance in Cubase when looking at the program changes in a MIDI file using one of the editors they are shown in 0-127 format, while the Inspector uses the 1-128 format).

Another area of confusion is the naming of these controllers, and that there are some pedal controllers which act as switches. All of these controllers are continuous controllers, but some parties insist on referring to pedals as "Switch Controllers" – while this may be their function, they are still referred to officially as "Continuous Controllers", a source of some confusion.

General MIDI Program Changes

The following table shows all 128 General MIDI program changes. While you may not remember all of them, it is useful to have an idea of the order of the groups, to make searching for the sound you want on a GM module easier. Bear in mind as well that some of the group descriptions are not entirely accurate - Timpani, for instance is not a string instrument, but is grouped in with the orchestral string instruments.

PIANO	1	Acoustic Piano	**ENSEMBLE**	49	Strings Ens 1	**SYNTH EFFECTS**	97	Rain
	2	Bright Piano		50	String Ens 2		98	Soundtrack
	3	Electric Grand		51	Synth String 1		99	Crystal
	4	Honky Tonk		52	Synth String 2		100	Atmosphere
	5	Electric Piano		53	Choir Aahs		101	Brightness
	6	Electric Piano 2		54	Voice Oohs		102	Goblins
	7	Harpsichord		55	Synth Voice		103	Echoes
	8	Clavinet		56	Orchestra Hit		104	Sci-Fi
TUNED PERCUSSION	9	Celesta	**BRASS**	57	Trumpet	**ETHNIC**	105	Sitar
	10	Glockenspiel		58	Trombone		106	Banjo
	11	Music Box		59	Tuba		107	Shamisen
	12	Vibraphone		60	Muted Trumpet		108	Koto
	13	Marimba		61	French Horn		109	Kalimba
	14	Xylophone		62	Brass Section		110	Bagpipe
	15	Tubular Bells		63	Synth Brass 1		111	Fiddle
	16	Dulcimer		64	Synth Brass 2		112	Shanai
ORGAN	17	Drawbar Organ	**REED**	65	Soprano Sax	**PERCUSSIVE**	113	Tinkle Bell
	18	Perc Organ		66	Alto Sax		114	Agogo
	19	Rock Organ		67	Tenor Sax		115	Steel Drums
	20	Church Organ		68	Baritone Sax		116	Woodblock
	21	Reed Organ		69	Oboe		117	Taiko Drum
	22	Accordion		70	English Horn		118	Melodic Tom
	23	Harmonica		71	Bassoon		119	Synth Drum
	24	Tango Accord'n		72	Clarinet		120	Rev. Cymbal
GUITAR	25	Nylon Guitar	**PIPE**	73	Piccolo	**SOUND EFFECTS**	121	Gtr Fret Noise
	26	Steel Guitar		74	Flute		122	Breath Noise
	27	Electric Guitar		75	Recorder		123	Seashore
	28	Electric Guitar		76	Pan Flute		124	Bird Tweet
	29	Muted Guitar		77	Blown Bottle		125	Telephone
	30	Overdrive Gtr		78	Shakuhachi		126	Helicopter
	31	Distortion Gtr		79	Whistle		127	Applause
	32	Harmonics		80	Ocarina		128	Gunshot

		BASS			SYNTH LEAD
33	Acoustic Bass		81	Square Lead	
34	Finger Bass		82	Saw Lead	
35	Electric Bass		83	Calliope	
36	Fretless Bass		84	Chiff Lead	
37	Slap Bass 1		85	Charang Lead	
38	Slap Bass 2		86	Voice Lead	
39	Synth Bass 1		87	Fifths	
40	Synth Bass 2		88	Bass & Lead	
41	Violin		89	New Age	
42	Viola		90	Warm Pad	
43	Cello		91	Polysynth Pad	
44	Contrabass		92	Choir Pad	
45	Tremolo Strings		93	Bowed Pad	
46	Pizzicato Strings		94	Metallic	
47	Harp		95	Halo	
48	Timpani		96	Sweep	

As can be seen from the table, there are a wide range of sounds available, which will cover many eventualities, and creative use of the GM soundset can allow the creation of an extremely broad palette of sounds

Drums

You may also be wondering about drums; the GM specification places these on channel 10 by default; there is a standard 'map' of drum notes which all units will play, as shown in the table to the right – the bottom note is C1, usually at the left hand side of the keyboard, but this can depend on the keyboard and transposition you have on it when you play.

In addition to this there are a range of 'standard' drumkits, which can be changed by program changes – at startup the unit will default to program change 1, but the others are as follows:

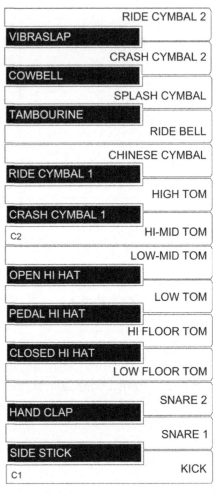

PC	Name
1	Standard
9	Room
17	Power
25	Electronic
26	TR-808
33	Jazz
41	Brush
49	Orchestral
57	Sound FX Kit

Note that the Orchestral kit replaces the toms with Timpani.

As ever with MIDI, the actual sounds of these kits is controlled by the module, so one Brush kit could sound markedly different from another one, but each should provide broadly similar sounds.

In addition, many modules offer extra sounds above and below these ranges and also other kits; the manuals of each device will give details of what is provided by them. When programming sequences that may be played back on other equipment, though, be sure to stick to the standard map or your sequence may sound quite odd when played back by others.

Less Common Messages

There are other less common messages, such as Channel Pressure (which transmits a measure of how hard keys are being held down), Aftertouch (which is similar, but transmitted on a note-by-note basis), and also System events, which allow control of the entire system and the transmission of data, such as programming details and other information. See page 676 for more on this.

Interpretation

Again, throughout this it's important to remember that the sonic outcome of all this data is down to the synthesizer that receives the data and plays it, NOT of the keyboard that generates the data. The quality of sound is down to the synth; there is no guarantee of accuracy or quality defined in the MIDI specification, and in addition there is also a wide range of interpretation between synths, so it's quite possible for an identical piece of MIDI data to sound quite different between one synth and another.

General MIDI Standards

As mentioned above, after the initial "ad hoc" phase of MIDI, General MIDI was introduced as a way of standardising features across a range of synthesizers. These features are summed up as below:

16-part Multitimbral (one for each MIDI channel), with drums assigned to Channel 10

Minimum of 24-note Polyphony overall (most exceed this greatly)

Must respond to note velocity

Program Changes to General MIDI standard (see page 60)

Drum Map to GM standard (see page 62)

Must respond to controllers 1,7,10,11,64,91,93,120,123 (see page 59)

On-board Reverb and Chorus effect processor

This meant that it was now possible to exchange MIDI data between setups and know that your piece would at least sound similar to the way you intended it to; as said above there is no guarantee of quality of the sounds, and clearly there will be variation between each synthesizer's sound, but this compatibility was a huge step forwards, and remains the bedrock of the MIDI specification's enduring popularity as GM-enabled devices are common even in mobile phones (many 'polyphonic ringtones' are played back on GM synths as part of a phone, for instance).

Later, General MIDI 2 was created, which extended the capabilities, including the varying drum kits as shown above, support for more control changes (as outlined in the table previously), and bank changes (sending a controller change after a program change to access a 'variation' of the original sound). Due to clever design, all of this was backwards-compatible with a GM1 synth, and there are a number of synths which provide many of the GM2 facilities while only advertising themselves as being GM1 (such as providing varying drum kits). In practice you will need to experiment to see what your synth responds to and work to its abilities or limitations. With the advent of software synths, however, the use of GM standards seems to be in decline; while some seem to be GM-compatible they may not provide all of the features above but still stick to the same GM sound set, and in addition some software synthesizers provide a huge range of sounds, but still stick to many other GM ideals such as MIDI Controller numbers and drum maps.

MIDI Connections

MIDI is connected using 5-pin DIN plugs, as seen below:

The cables need to be MIDI cables as similar-looking audio cables don't always have the right connections internally. Devices can have MIDI In, Out and Through. A MIDI Out connection will go to a MIDI In, while a MIDI Through (or Thru) pro-vided on some synthesizers allows the signal that is present at the MIDI In to be passed on to another synth, unaltered. This allows daisy-chaining of synthesizers, either to provide thicker textures (with multiple sounds being used), or in situa-tions where only one MIDI output is provided, and each synthesizer responds on a different channel or group of channels. On many modern computer-based set-ups a MIDI keyboard will have a USB connection – the data transmitted is exactly what is described above, but it's passed over USB instead of MIDI – many modern music setups don't have any 'true' MIDI in them as a result of this and the rise of computer-based virtual synthesizers.

In an example setup, a keyboard's OUT would be connected to a computer's IN, and then the computer's OUT would connect to a synthesizer's IN (see page 66). This would provide a chain of control from the keyboard via the computer to the synth; either the computer or the keyboard can issue commands to the synthesizer. This is how many sequencing systems work, as we'll see later on.

MIDI Files

There is often confusion between MIDI itself (the method of communication be-tween synthesizers) and MIDI Files (more correctly called Standard MIDI Files, or SMF).

A MIDI file is a way of storing a collection of MIDI instructions, which are usually mostly notes but can be any MIDI data. It also stores the time of each event, meaning that it is possible to play it back, and it be a piece of music. MIDI files have advantages and disadvantages:

Advantages – MIDI files are universal – they are compatible with a wide range of software products (all sequencers can import MIDI files, plus most media players can play them, and a wide range of hardware devices – keyboards, even most mobile phones).

MIDI files are small – they store data in an efficient way, and because they only store the important information for the song, they are often smaller than the same information when saved in a sequencer's file format

Disadvantages – MIDI files do not store the "structure" of a piece in the way a sequencer does. As you will see, in most sequencers it is possible to separate groups of notes into smaller parts, even if they are closely spaced. A MIDI file wouldn't store this information, which can mean the structure of parts or sections can be less apparent

MIDI files can use more than 16 channels, but this ability is rarely used, whereas most sequencers have a much larger number readily available. This wasn't that important when MIDI was first created (16 channels was thought to be enough), but as time has passed, the number of instruments available has increased, making this more of a limitation.

Often MIDI files are maligned as being of poor quality. This generally is down to two factors – firstly, the programming may be poor – many MIDI files that are downloaded from the Internet have been programmed in a very basic way, with little musicality or respect of the original performances. Secondly the playback system may not be good – it's important to remember with MIDI that the sound that is heard is only guaranteed to be the right type of sound – the quality of it can vary greatly. A synth from 10 years ago may sound nowhere near as good as one of today, playing identical MIDI data.

MIDI File Types

There are two common types of MIDI file – Type 0 and Type 1. A Type 0 file has no internal "structure" – all the MIDI data is in one part, which can contain more than one MIDI channel in it. A type 1 file has separate tracks, each of which only contain information from one MIDI channel. Most MIDI files are type 1, but you may come across a Type 0 file now and again. Most sequencers allow you to "explode" these into separate tracks, which can then be edited as normal.

Typical MIDI setups

MIDI setups have changed dramatically since MIDI was introduced – for many users the original function was merely to connect two keyboards together to generate thicker textures with doubling and detuning. However, as technology became more capable and affordable MIDI setups increased in complexity greatly. Many modern studios now have far simpler MIDI setups as much of the sound generation is done using a computer – all the "MIDI Instruments" are really pieces of software running inside the computer. A selection of different MIDI setups follows, but there are so many permutations it's impossible to show all of them.

Note that the computers shown below are pictured as a laptop but could of course be a desktop computer, and could be a PC running Windows or Linux/Unix or a Macintosh – they are all interchangeable and all are capable of performing MIDI sequencing tasks. Windows and Macintosh are copyright of their respective copyright holders, and all such copyrights are respected.

A 'dumb' controller keyboard connected to a synthesizer

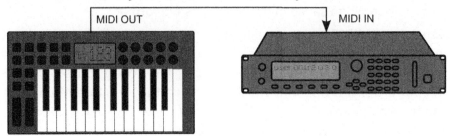

A dumb controller is one which has no sound generating ability - it can only send out MIDI data. Anything played on the keyboard is sent to the synthesizer, which turns it into sound. There is little complication and little to go wrong with this setup, and this was the way that many musicians worked when MIDI first arrived – it gave the ability to play one or more sounds using the same keyboard, which had previously been difficult to achieve.

A controller keyboard, a computer and a synthesizer

This setup allows whatever is played on the keyboard to be recorded and edited on the sequencing PC, and then played back by the synthesizer. It's also possible for the PC to pass the MIDI messages straight on to the synth, allowing real-time playing of the sounds. Problems with playing sounds can be either the cabling, or a fault with the PC or its software. Note that normally some kind of music software will need to be running to allow the data from the MIDI IN of the PC to be passed to the OUT. With many of today's sequencing packages, it is possible to run "software synths", which can take the role of the Synthesizer but instead of being an external, physical unit they are internal, software-based devices that run 'inside' your sequencer package (or sometimes as a separate program).

A controller keyboard and computer

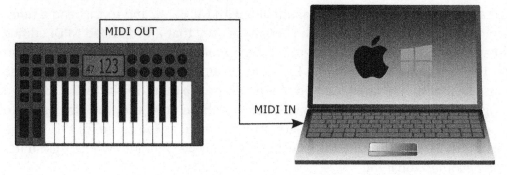

Here a MIDI keyboard is used to input data to the sequencer, as in the previous setup. The big difference is that instead of using an external sound source, the PC has software synthesizers which generate sound from the MIDI data, often allowing a much wider range of synthesis types to be available, and often increasing the number of sounds available (if you run out of MIDI channels, you can just 'create' another synthesizer), providing the PC has enough processing power to do this. This setup is becoming increasingly common, and offers a number of benefits, including the ability to make mixdowns faster than real time. This is becoming the most common setup in many studios today, particularly for "home" setups.

Keyboard with built-in sounds and a computer

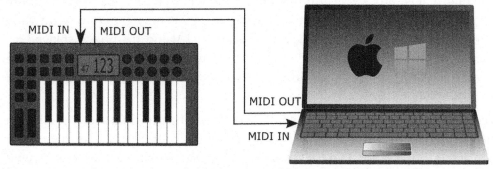

This setup involves a keyboard that has sounds in it, and a PC for sequencing. The MIDI out of the keyboard connects to the IN of the PC, and vice versa. This means that the PC can record what is played on the keyboard, and play back the sounds on the unit too. However, there is one problem; if the PC is set to pass the sounds through to the keyboard, it will end up playing two notes of the same pitch at the same time – one because playing a note on the keyboard generates the sound, and the other (a few milliseconds later) because the PC has told it too as well. This can lead to some undesirable effects, so in this case there is a control on the MIDI keyboard called "Local Off"; this disconnects the unit's keyboard from the sound generating section, so that it only plays sounds that it receives from its MIDI IN. This makes the system work in the same way as example two above.

Changes made to Cubase to accomodate MIDI 2.0

Cubase 13 introduced some compatibility with MIDI 2.0, and to this end a number of changes were made which change the way that any detailed MIDI editing takes place. For many users, there will be no difference, but if you use the Logical Editor (see page 357) or the List Editor (see page 373) then you will notice these changes. The detail-focused reader will notice that the MIDI 1.0 Pitch Bend range values are not visible in any editor in Cubase now; they are translated to user-editable values in the range -100 to 100, with 0 as the centre of this. While this will make sense for the casual user, there may be situations where this limitation becomes apparent.

It is now possible in some editors to edit 'high resolution' MIDI data, which is presented with the familiar range of 0-127, but adds decimal values. Under this regime it is possible to have a velocity of 96.256 or a Pitchbend value of -64.253. Display of these higher-resolution values can be enabled in the preferences (under **Editing > MIDI**), and this will allow situations where the limitations of reduced resolution to be overcome. When enabling these changes, making edits in the controller area in particular will show the changes, but the columns in the List Editor will also show the level of data now being transmitted.

The other changes made when compared to previous versions of Cubase are the renaming of data in the List and Logical editors. What was previously Value 1 (in MIDI 1.0 terminology) is now referred to as Subtype, which can make sense for a Controller Value, but is less intuitive for a note, where a C3 is a different Subtype to a D3. What was previously referred to as Value 2 is now generally Main Value, although Program Changes break with this as their Value 1 is now displayed as a Main Value. All of this has been designed to create a layer of abstraction between the editors in Cubase and any underlying data type. It is for the reader to decide the desirability of this.

There are some underlying changes in the MIDI engine of Cubase to allow the translation of data between MIDI 2.0 and MIDI 1.0. For the most part, they should be invisible, but it is possible that there will be some difficulties, particularly when working with older MIDI 1.0 equipment.

Summary

Although much of the information in this chapter may be seen to be dry and academic, it is extremely important to understand what MIDI is, and what it is capable of (and also what it is not). If you're not aware of all of the tools at your disposal you may find it difficult to create a piece of music or particular technique that you wish to, and being able to use MIDI to its fullest will enable you to make the most musical sequences that you can do.

Effective
Sequencing

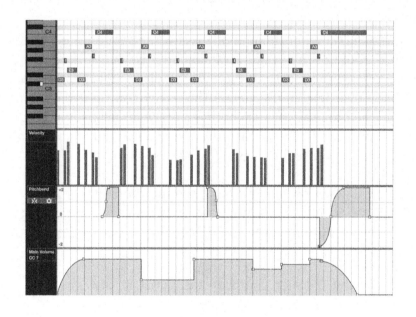

For your sequencing to be successful, it needs to be more detailed. The reason for this is simple – most of the music we listen to has been played by people, and whenever they do something they put in slight variations (whether intentional or unintentional) in what they do, both in terms of their timing, and also of the loudness of each note they play – their performances may well be consistent, but when compared to the rigid metronomic precision of a computer, they are often quite varied.

In addition to this, to effectively sequence an instrument realistically, we need to understand how the instrument makes its sound, and how it is played.

The Guitar

The guitar can be a difficult instrument to sequence effectively, especially for the non-guitarist, but use of some knowledge of the guitar and playing techniques will allow you to produce sequenced guitar performances that are convincing to most, if not all listeners.

Firstly, chord playing – the most common error when sequencing a guitar sound is to use simple, root position triads for guitar chords. While these are possible on the guitar, it is not the most common way to play chords, and certainly isn't something that is evocative of the guitar. The reason for this is the tuning of the instrument and the physical way the chords are played. Take, for instance, a simple C major chord played on the guitar – this would be played as an "open" chord, meaning that open (unfretted) strings are used.

Here we see the C major on the keyboard, root position. It consists of C, E and G. It is called root position because the root note (C) is at the bottom of the chord; the notes appear in ascending order of root, third and fifth.

However, playing the C major chord on the guitar in the shape that most guitarists would use gives us these notes – like two triads on top of each other, but with the top note missing. It consists of C, E, G, C, E. This will sound somewhat different to the root position triad that a keyboard player would probably initially play.

There are several common open chords, are shown below with the keyboard versions first, followed by the 'guitar' versions.

Note that some of these chords can only be played as 'open' chords – you can't necessarily take a shape or pattern of intervals as shown and move it to another root note to make another chord, although in some cases you can do so. Unless you are producing a piece for playing by a 'real' guitarist then this may be irrelevant – if you produce a sequence which is mostly correct in this respect it will sound convincing to most listeners.

However, it is important to note that most chords can be played in a number of positions, as we will see now. The next type of chords is a "barre" chord, which involves using the first finger of the fretting hand fretting all the strings at a given fret, and then forming a shape above that fret. The most common of these are the "E shape" and "A shape" barres, which take their names from the open chords whose shapes they use. They are not E or A chords, but can be any note, depending on the root note of the chord (which is played by the first finger, as we will see), but are often referred to as E or A shape as it tells the guitarist what chord shape to use. An example should show this more clearly.

To construct this type of chord, take two root position triads and put them on top of each other – in this case F,A,C and F,A,C, although this is a "moveable" chord form, so it could be based on any root note, and could also be a minor chord as well. The lowest pitch playable on the guitar is the E chord a semitone below this one.

Then remove the 3rd note of the bottom triad (in this case A). This is because it is not physically possible to play the two triads on the guitar because of the tuning of the instrument

Finally, add another note on top (F), giving us F, C, F, A, C, F. This same pattern (Root, Fifth, Root, Third, Fifth, Root) would be repeated on any note if this shape of chord was played on the guitar.

For an A-shape chord, the situation is similar, but they are only played across 5 strings, not 6. Take two root position triads, and place them on top of each other. As with the 'E-shape' chords, they can be major or minor, but with an A-shape chord, it should not be lower in pitch than the first A below middle C.

Remove the 3rd note from the bottom triad (in this case E). Because the chord is played across 5 strings, there is no note to add on top. The pattern of notes in this case is Root, Fifth, Root, Third, Fifth.

In addition to these major and minor chords, it's common to have to play Dominant 7th (7) chords and minor 7th chords. For a dominant 7th chord, construct the chord as you would normally – in this case we see the completed F Major chord (E shape), as seen above.

Next, the root note of the upper triad (F) is moved down by a tone, to E♭. This is the dominant 7th (♭7) note, giving us a Dominant Seventh chord.

Note that if this procedure was carried out on an F Minor chord, you would obtain an F Minor 7 chord.

For the A shape chord, the procedure is the same – here's the finished C major (A shape) chord. Again, a minor chord could be used as the starting point to generate a Minor 7th chord.

The root note of the upper triad (C) is moved down a tone, to B♭. Again, this is the dominant 7th (♭7) note.

To sum up, on the guitar it is possible to play one chord in a number of positions – these may not affect the pitch of the root note, but can alter the number and pattern of the notes inside the chord, although they will all belong to the chord – see this example for three different ways to play a C major chord:

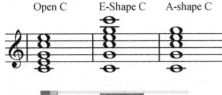

Open C   E-Shape C   A-shape C

Here are the three versions on a treble staff – the Open-chord version, and the E- and A-shape Barre chords. All three are C, but each will have a different sound.

Here are the same three chords, but in Cubase's Key Editor window, showing the pitches of each. Despite them looking different here, it's important to remember that each chord is still C Major, but a different inversion of it, and some players could use all three within a song.

In addition to this, when guitars are played as rhythm instruments (i.e. with a chord being played), then it is extremely uncommon for the notes to all be played simultaneously – most of the time they will be played with a slight delay between first and last as they are strummed, and sometimes the player will accentuate this natural tendency by making the strum last over a noticeable period. See the example below for details on this.

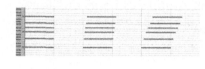

Here is a chord played three different ways – all the notes being played at the same time and then two 'strummed' patterns, where there is a lag between the first and last notes.

These strums can be generated using the trim tool (seen to the left) by clicking and dragging across existing quantized chords (holding **ALT** to allow the front of the notes to be removed) to create the progressively staggered starts.

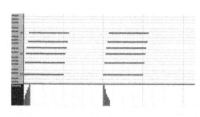

Next is velocity – in the real world, notes aren't played totally consistently and in addition it's common for them to be played with varying loudness depending on the musical situation. For many guitarists, the strum will start with a high velocity and die down, but sometimes the reverse is true – here are two examples, the second of which is more common, but both have their places.

Rhythmic emphasis/feel is also an important part of sequencing – the same notes can sound dramatically different because of their placing in relation to the beat.

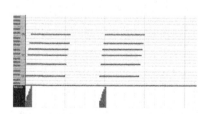

The example to the left shows two identical chords that have been placed differently – the first one starts the strum on the beat, the second one ends on the beat, giving a markedly different feel as a result – the first one is 'behind' the beat, while the second 'pushes' the beat forward.

Each has its own merits, and only experimentation and a keen ear can decide which option is suitable at any given point.

Solo playing

In addition to the eccentricities of chord playing on the guitar, there is another area to tackle with sequencing, that of the melodic or solo guitar part. Because of the nature of the guitar, it is possible to add effects after a note has been struck that are simply not possible with instruments such as the piano – this is one of the things that has made the guitar so popular as an instrument of self-expression, but also makes it difficult to sequence as much of what you hear is not the notes themselves, but other non-note information and phrasing/playing techniques.

Vibrato

Vibrato is a fairly easy thing to simulate – many guitarists add vibrato (some un-consciously), and this adds a lyrical quality to a section. This can be done in one of two ways – either using the modulation controller (which adds a vibrato at a fixed speed with most synth modules), or using pitch bend.

Typically using modulation will work, and often only a small amount is needed to give the desired effect; adding in too much will sound rigid and unnatural. However, for some situations this will not suffice and careful use of the pitch bend wheel (or programming) will help – see the example below for two ways of achieving this end:

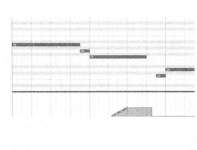

Firstly, modulation. Here we can see that is has been progressively applied (although not to the full amount), so the long note in bar 12 will have some vibrato applied, as will the following ones. It's important to note with this technique that the vibrato that you obtain will be totally down to the sound module you are using, both in terms of speed and intensity. Sometimes this can sound artificial if over-used.

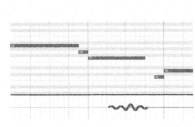

Here, the same passage has been programmed using pitch bend, to give total control over the vibrato. This, however, is a more involved technique and can mean there is a great deal of MIDI data generated, which some synth modules can have problems with. With good programming, this can be a very convincing technique, however.

Bending Notes

Another extremely common technique on the guitar is that of bending strings – this allows the player to move outside the confines of the fretted notes (fixed at semitones) and smoothly move between pitches, and possibly use microtonal (smaller than a semitone) intonation, using notes between the frets on the guitar. In either case, pitch bend is the way to simulate this, although in most cases the range will only be 2 semitones, which is less than most guitarists can bend a note (see the next paragraph on how to get round this). There are two common ways to add bending to a performance – either hold the pitch bend wheel down before playing the destination note and then releasing it, or to hit one note, use the pitch bend wheel to get to the new note, then release it and play the new note; the two (seen below) give quite different results.

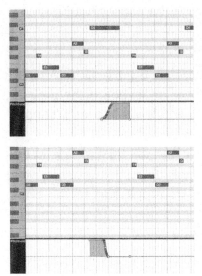

Here we see a passage where one of the notes has a simulated string bend – the note is played, and then bent up a tone using pitch bend. The original note is a C, but it is bent up to a D. Note that the bend is released while there is nothing playing.

Here we see a note which is 'pre-bent' – the pitch bend is applied before the note is played, and then released after the note is played. In this example, while the original MIDI note is a B♭, it would be heard as a C, then released to a B♭.

If the range of the bend is more than 2 semitones (3 is not uncommon, and 4 is possible), then you will need to plan ahead, and apply negative bend before the note is played, and then keep a positive bend amount on while the final note plays.

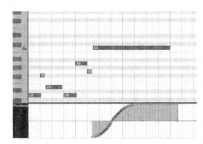

Here is an example of this technique – there is a tone's worth of downward bend applied before the note is played, so the played C will be heard as a B♭. The pitch bend will then bend the note up to be a D, smoothly as if a guitarist had applied a 4-fret string bend.

Multiple note bending

There is another technique that is performed on the guitar that is not possible using a single MIDI channel – that is bending notes against a pedal (or static) note. To do this, you will need to use two MIDI channels, both playing the same sound; one will be used for the pedal note, one for the bent note which can be programmed as above. It is not uncommon for a guitarist to play a pedal note and bend a note a semitone below up to 'meet' it – for instance, play an E and then bend the D up. In addition it is also possible to bend two strings at once, but moving them the same amount physically on the guitar doesn't yield the same amount of pitch bend – for instance doing this on the G and B strings will give a bend of 3 semitones for the G string and 2 for the B string, so you would need to place these on two different MIDI tracks and bend accordingly to simulate this.

This programming technique can be taken to the extreme of using a single MIDI channel per string – this will give complete control of the sound and simulate a guitarist effectively, but can take some time. Some guitar synthesizers provide a mode which does this, allocating a MIDI channel per string and generating a huge amount of data, albeit with a convincing performance. For most situations, however, this is overkill and two channels will suffice.

Strumming sounds

One of the most limiting aspects of trying to sequence a guitar is to emulate strumming – when doing this with a MIDI sequencer or keyboard the problem is that the sound of the previous chord gets cut off and leads to a very 'choppy' sounding sequence.

This can be overcome using a technique similar to the one above – using two MIDI tracks (which must be sent to different channels on an instrument or two separate instruments), where the notes alternate from one part to the other, thereby allowing them to decay more naturally. It's not perfect, but often gives far more convincing results than a single track/channel will do.

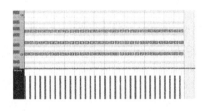

Here we see the original part, which features a strummed eighth-note pattern. However, when played it sounds unnatural as the notes cut off too sharply.

To stop this, we will play every other note on a different MIDI channel (using the same sound/instrument so that they sound the same).

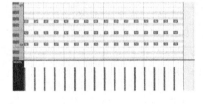

To do this, duplicate the original track (right-click on the track and select **Duplicate Tracks..**, and once you have done that delete every other one on each track, as shown to the left (one will play the 'odd' notes, one the 'even' ones). Here is the above part having had this technique applied to it.

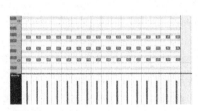

Often just doing this on its own will suffice, but you can also increase the lengths of the notes a small amount to make them overlap more to give more convincing effect.

Tuning

Sometimes a guitar may be slightly out of tune – normally this would be taken care of in the recording, but it is not uncommon for a guitar to be slightly out of tune, and also this can intentionally add to the sequence by thickening the texture (in much the same way as a 12 string guitar can do). To do this, simply add a small amount of pitch bend to the track in places – a small amount positively or negatively can bring a part to 'life', making it sound far more like the real thing. Also if you have two guitars playing similar (or identical) parts then making one of them slightly out of tune will add depth to the sequence. Remember that if you are going to use a GM synth then you can use Controller 93 to add chorus to the part, or you can add chorus as an insert effect on a VST Instrument (see page 540)

Slides

The last technique on the guitar we will cover is sliding – a common thing to do on the instrument. This can be simulated by using a number of notes (not necessarily rhythmically placed, so turn quantize/snap off for this) which chromatically approach the destination note.

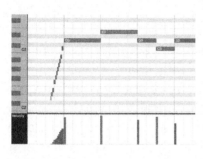

Here is a slide, programmed as a number of notes which are extremely short and a semitone apart, leading to the desired note that happens at bar 5. They are all short, and mostly of low velocity, leading to the note that is heard at the end. Care is needed whenever using this technique to get timing and velocities right to make this sound natural rather than machine-gun like!

The Bass Guitar

Many of the techniques outlined above apply to the bass guitar, although usually less so; while it is possible to play chords (albeit with only 4 or 5 notes on most basses), it is uncommon. Bending notes isn't too common (although again, some do it), but slides and vibrato are common. If you are simulating a fretless bass, using the 'bending' technique will do this (as the notes are not fretted, it is simple to slide the finger up the fret board in a smooth manner), and also you may use some small elements of pitch bend to simulate poor intonation on a fretless sound (don't go too far with this, but some 'colour' can certainly be introduced), as with the guitar "tuning" technique.

However, there is another area which is common with the bass guitar, and that's 'slapping' – often, more accurately, the 'popping' of notes as they are pulled by the fingers of the picking hand, usually to snap back against the frets. To simulate this, it is often best to duplicate the bass part into two tracks, and play one on a "normal" bass sound (to play the notes that are played with the thumb) and one to play a "slap" sound (for the 'popped' notes). Decide on the notes that are to be slapped, and delete them from the 'normal' part, and then delete all the non-slapped notes from the slap part. Now some careful blending of the two sounds should give a convincing facsimile of a slap bass player.

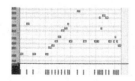

Above left is the original bass part - some of the notes we want to be played as 'popped', so the track is duplicated and then the appropriate notes deleted from each part.

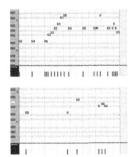

The next two diagrams are the two MIDI tracks, generated from the original bass part. This one is the "fingered" sound...

...while this is the "popped" sound. Because the two don't occur together and have been mixed well, they sound like a single player playing slapped and popped notes.

The Drums

The drums can be sequenced without knowing much about drumming technique, but learning something about the instrument will greatly improve your sequencing. Firstly, for the most part, drummers have only one pair of arms and one pair of legs, so there shouldn't be more than 4 things happening at any one time, and much of the time one of their legs will be controlling the hi-hat, so this should be remembered along with the other leg mostly playing the kick (bass) drum – most drummers don't move from these two items at all, leaving their hands to provide the most variation, therefore allowing only 2 other sounds to be triggered at any one time.

The next thing to remember is timing – there are very few drummers who are totally metronomic and 'accurate' – there are two areas to look at here. Firstly the position of the first beat in the bar – some drummers will play slightly ahead with some part of the kit, some behind; this gives "feel" or "groove", as shown below:

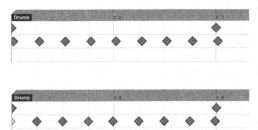

This first example shows the hi-hats behind the beat, although only minimally. This will be enough to give a 'laid back' feel.

Here the hi-hats are ahead of the bass drum, giving a 'pushed' feel and making the drums sound a little faster than they actually are.

Note that if everything is ahead or behind the beat, the effect will be lost – there needs to be something that the feel is being created against.

Secondly, the way the beat is divided up within the bar can alter too – although the bar should be 4 equal divisions, it is not uncommon for a drummer to get to beat 2 or 3 early or late; this is usually most noticeable when trying to place samples of two different drummers together – many grooves will not fit together as a result of this.

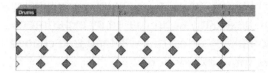

Here are three different hi-hat feels superimposed over one bass drum – one is 'accurate', one is 'late' the other is 'early'.

All 3 in isolation will work, but when played with each other they will usually not sit well together.

Simulating these two playing techniques can give considerable life and feel to your sequenced tracks; in some cases you can use groove quantize to move your original playing nearer to the beat without totally removing your original feel, but sometimes you might need to edit notes manually to achieve this – it depends on the original method of input and the desired end product.

Another often-overlooked area of drum programming is use of velocity. Listen to any good drummer and you will hear a huge amount of variation in dynamics of the whole kit, and most often in the hi-hats – listen to Stewart Copeland's playing on Regatta De Blanc to hear a good example. Many drummers will accent certain beats within bars, and also build dynamically throughout sections, and if your sequenced drum track is missing these details it won't sound as good as it could do.

The next area to look at is cymbal use – the best way to learn this is to listen to drummers in the style of music that you are sequencing. Cymbals are often used to demarcate different sections of songs, either highlighting the end of one section or the beginning of a new one. However, it is not uncommon for a good drummer to use them in a less obvious way, and listening to a great drummer making use of his entire kit to help build an arrangement is something that you can learn a great deal from – here it's more a case of knowing what to play rather than how to actually sequence it, but again listening to real players will teach you a great deal in this area.

String Instruments

Accurately sequencing string instruments can be one of the most challenging tasks to complete effectively. The reason for this is fairly simple – an instrument such as a piano or organ has little other than the notes themselves and how hard they are played, making them easy to sequence correctly and convincingly. However, instruments such as the Violin offer a huge number of techniques for generating the sound from the instrument, and as a result can make an equally wide range of sounds. In addition to this, MIDI was never really designed to communicate such a wide range of playing information – at the time of its conception, just being able to play notes on another synthesizer was an achievement in itself!

There are, however, a number of ways of sequencing string instruments more effectively. Firstly, using some of the techniques above for the guitar will help – often the intonation can be simulated using small amounts of pitch bend. Secondly, using up-to-date software synthesizers or sampled sounds will often give a much better performance even using exactly the same MIDI information – this area of music technology has improved greatly in recent years, allowing a convincing simulation of solo string players. This can be greatly accentuated by experimenting with the velocity of the notes that you play – often this will lead to a change in the timbre that will allow you to create more expression.

Another area to be aware of is the different playing techniques used by string players – at the most basic level this is to be aware of the use of pizzicato (plucked) playing, which is quite a common technique, and usually a separate MIDI channel is needed for this along with a different sound. If you wish to be more accurate, there are a number of ways of bowing the strings and different levels of 'attack' which produce quite different tones – short and long notes tend to be articulated quite differently, so again splitting these onto different MIDI tracks and channels using different sounds (but ones which sound similar enough to be the same instrument) will make the performance sound far more convincing.

Choosing between "solo" sounds and "section" sounds can also make or break a sequence – usually when sequencing a smaller string section (such as a quartet) it is far preferable to sequence each line individually using a solo sound, but in some cases judicious use of a 'section' patch may thicken the sound up. Conversely there are sometimes situations where you have a section which needs a solo instrument in addition to clearly define the way the part is being played.

Another often-overlooked detail when sequencing string sections (usually with ensemble-type samples or synthesizer string 'pad' sounds) is arrangement of the notes that are used. It is quite typical to put too many notes in while attempting to thicken the texture and ending up with a mess instead.

The general rule is this – the lower the note, the larger the interval to the next note. In the left hand (Double Basses) the sound is often clearer and more powerful if only octaves are present, often of the root of the chord.

As the chord moves upwards, the intervals can become smaller, so that 5ths can appear, and in the right hand/treble clef, all of the notes can be present without the sound becoming too dense – to the left we see such an arrangement, with an A minor chord as an example, with an octave interval at the bottom, then fifths, then two triads.

The Voice

The human voice is one of the hardest instruments to imitate – it is capable of a huge range of expression, both in terms of the sounds it produces and the message that is conveyed with words. The sequencing that you are going to do will clearly not imitate a human voice in terms of the words, etc – the technology to do this does exist, but it is at best embryonic. However, it is possible to simulate a melody being sung by a human with another instrument (such as an oboe or clarinet) and add programming techniques to this to closely emulate the melodic performance – here again attention to detail will pay off in the long run, although to do so can be quite time consuming and involve analysis of each note of the original performance.

Firstly, many singers take liberties with the material they are performing – their timing may be quite a way from the rigid, metronomic performance you might expect from another instrument. This is extremely important as it is often the thing that people listen to first, and also incorporates much of the 'feel' of the piece. Simply listening to the timing of your sequence against the original (if you are copying one) should help here (once you have mastered the Tempo Mapping technique on page 90 this will be easy as the MIDI and audio will align perfectly, allowing you to use Cubase's grid accurately), listening through for the phrasing of each line/note.

Secondly, the voice is not a fixed pitch instrument such as the piano – it is quite possible to move smoothly between pitches with the voice, and a great many singers do this in their recorded performances; some will actively slide between notes (something that is less common), but a great many will 'scoop' into notes, and this is something that can be achieved with careful pitch-bend programming.

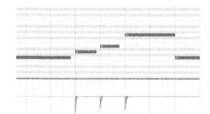

Here we see that technique sequenced – small amounts of negative pitch bend have been applied to make the played note momentarily a small amount flat, and this is quickly released to the 'correct' pitch.

Using this technique gives a bit more life to the attack of the notes, although it shouldn't be used too often or too strongly – the range of the pitch bend needs to be quite narrow for this to work in the desired manner (i.e. subtly), although sometimes this can be used over a wider range where a note can be 'slid' from a semitone or tone below.

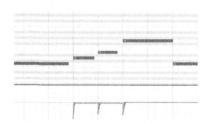

Thirdly, many singers are not totally accurate with pitch – quite often they will be slightly out of tune, and sometimes they will be considerably so. This can be achieved with a small amount of pitch bend being added on the appropriate notes, as seen to the left.

It takes very little to make a sequenced vocal melody sound more authentic – often just a few notes within the scale need to be made a little sharp or flat to add some 'life' to a performance. However, some singers can be quite a way out of tune, although this is often a part of their appeal; simulating their performances will take more effort.

Vibrato is another area which is often overlooked – most singers will add vibrato to longer notes, and simulation of this can be done in two ways, as for the guitar; either use the modulation controller to add some vibrato courtesy of the synthesizer's onboard LFO, or use programmed pitch bend to achieve this, remembering as ever that this technique will give you total control but may generate enough MIDI data to confuse or slow the receiving synth. See the section on guitar sequencing on page 72 for details of this, and remember that listening to the original is the best way to sequence this accurately.

General Techniques

There are a number of programming techniques that can be applied to a wide range of situations, each of them will allow the production of a more realistic sequence, regardless of the instrument/sound in question.

Velocity

The velocity of notes is one of the areas where many programmers fall down. As mentioned above, each performance by a human will contain small differences between notes in terms of volume.

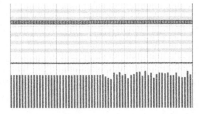

When dealing with MIDI data that has been recorded, these velocity changes will be present, but if the data has been input using an editor then all the notes will be at the same velocity - this can be fixed manually or using the Logical Editor (see page 364)

This example shows the difference, and the second section sounds far more natural, having only had this small change applied.

Quantization

Often the most basic form of quantization (moving notes directly to the nearest point on the grid) is adequate when starting sequencing – it is useful to overcome sizeable errors in playing when recording in real-time and for some players the only way to get a usable performance. However, as we develop as listeners and players, we realise that the totally metronomic performance (with each note being played at precisely the right time) can be somewhat lacking in 'feel' – this is the human element in a performance where notes may be played before or after the 'actual' beat, imparting a different rhythmic feel to the part and indeed the whole piece.

There are a number of ways that this sort of performance can be sequenced. Firstly, it can be done when recording a performer whose playing is accurate enough to have this feel already – many good players will be able to play either 'in front of' or 'behind' the beat, giving the required result.

Soft Quantize

It is possible to have a player who may be too sloppy (with 'too much feel') –

manually fixing these issues would be long-winded and tedious, but fortunately there is a way of applying quantize to a performance to make it closer to being in time without removing all traces of the feel that is desirable, and it is called Soft Quantize.

Here we see the original performance – the notes are often in front of the beat, but too much so in some cases. Over-quantizing would destroy the feel of the part, so...

... Soft quantize is used instead. This has moved the notes 50% of the way towards the grid positions they should be at, removing some of the sloppiness. Doing this again...

... will remove more of that, but eventually the notes move close enough for them to be ignored. Each setting (Soft Strength and Safe Range) can be adjusted in the Quantize Setup box, which is in the key editor's Inspector (to the left of the editing area).

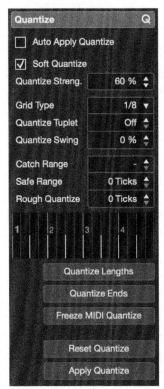

Here we see the quantize settings, as seen in the editor inspector in the left zone. To activate Soft Quantize tick the box (here seen as active), and you can adjust the strength (here set to 60%). You can also adjust the **Safe Range** here, which is the range where notes will no longer be quantized; this is useful for retaining some of the feel, and often a setting in the low teens will be adequate. You can now apply Soft Quantize by hitting **Q** or clicking the **Apply Quantize** button which is at the bottom of the section in the inspector. You can reset the quantization you've applied with the **Reset Quantize** button - note that these buttons work for all forms of quantize, not just soft.

Swing

By default, Over Quantize uses a straight grid – i.e. the grid is divided up equally, with every beat or sub-beat having the same length. But this is often not how people play - when most people play an eighth-note part, they tend to add "swing" – this is the tendency for the first note to be a bit longer than the second. When performed to a greater degree, it will often end up being notated as such (hence the familiar sign seen to the right).

It is possible to alter Cubase's grid to reflect this, making such swung parts quick and easy to create. Adding swing is done in the quantize section of the Inspector, and can be from 0 to 100% and then adjust the swing slider to suit.

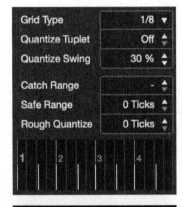

Here is the relevant part of the inspector, with 30% swing set - note how the graph at the bottom displays how the swing will alter the grid positions, and you may note that the grid in the key editor also does so.

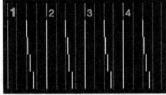

The diagram to the left shows the difference that swing makes, from 0% through 20%, 50% and finally with 100% at the bottom.

Many parts that do not have an overt swing feel can benefit from small percentages being added here, while some styles (such as swing Jazz) may need up to 50% to give the right feel - experimentation is the key, particularly when you are first using swing. Hit **Apply Quantize** or **Q** to hear the difference, and remember that this technique can be combined with Soft quantize as well.

Randomness

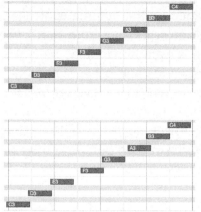

If a part has been created using the editor with snap turned on and is therefore completely rigid, it can sometimes be difficult to add any random human feel to it. However, the quantize setup box has another setting we can make use of – Random Quantize.

This adds in a random timing element to each over quantize operation, meaning that each note will be in a random position centred on the quantize grid, with a distance defined by the number of ticks set in the Quantize Setup box, up to a maximum of 48 - as seen to the left.

NOTE that if you leave a random quantize value in there, you may forget and then get odd results later on!

Controllers

MIDI controllers are extremely important when it comes to detailed MIDI programming. As we have seen in some of the specific examples above, controllers such as Modulation can be used to simulate real-world performance techniques such as vibrato, but using other controllers can improve a sequence and also make programming easier to do.

Using Volume / Expression / Velocity

When reading through the MIDI specification it would be possible to see some redundancy – there seem to be three ways of controlling how loud a given note is – Velocity, Volume and Expression. But it is important to realise that they each have a specific task, and correct use of them will improve your sequences and also make them easier to edit.

Volume – Controller 7

Originally called Main Volume (and now correctly called Channel Volume), this sets how loud sounds are on the specified MIDI channel. It is an absolute measure of how loud a sound is, from 0 (off) to 127 (maximum). Nearly all MIDI synthesizers respond to it. While it is possible to send different Volume messages throughout a song, it is not good practice to do so – it is best to just send one Volume message at the beginning of the song (to control the overall level of the channel within the piece) and then use Expression and Velocity to control the rest, as seen below. The reason for this is simple – Expression and Velocity will take care of the dynamics within the piece (i.e. relative changes in volume), so the Volume message should just be sent once to control the overall volume, allowing a change in the mix (i.e. bringing an instrument up or down in volume overall) to be done with just one message, Volume, at the beginning.

Expression – Controller 11

Expression is best defined as a relative change in volume, from 0 (off) to 127 (maximum). It only works within the range provided by the Volume controller, so if Volume is set very low (say 40) then expression will range from that level at maximum down to nothing at zero. Expression is used for creating dynamics within a performance, such as crescendos, diminuendos and other such directions. As explained above this is to allow the programming of relative settings for dynamics, leaving a single volume message to control the overall level in the mix. It is unfortunate, however, that many current synthesizer plugins do not respond to expression, making changes much harder to perform than before. Conveniently, Cubase has a remedy for this, as we will see next

Editing controller data in a relative manner

The lack of response of some synthesizers to Expression could mean a real problem, as needing to use Channel Volume leads to the problem above of making it difficult to then set the overall volume and retain the dynamic changes you have programmed in. There are two ways to approach this - editing the data itself, or altering the audio output fader.

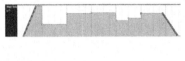

Editing the data is straightforward in Cubase. Make sure the controller lane is set to CC7 (Main Volume).

Click in the controller area and then hit **CTRL + A** on the keyboard. All of the controller data will be selected, and it should be highlighted.

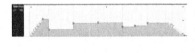

You should also see a square "handle" in the middle at the top of the data - ▪ When you hover your mouse over this, it will turn into a downwards-pointing V; clicking and dragging scales the data.

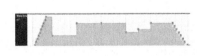

There is something important to remember here though - if you reduce the levels greatly and then increase them again, resolution will be lost as some of the points will have been rounded up or down.

The last example shows how the originally smooth fades in and out have now become visibly (and audibly) stepped. As long as you are careful to avoid this, this method works well.

An alternative method is to use Volume for dynamics, and then using the channel fader (of a VST Instrument / Instrument track) to control the overall level. If you are creating a MIDI file, however, this may lead to overall level issues with your final output file as the channel fader level will not be exported.

Velocity

Velocity is not a controller, it is information that is sent with each and every MIDI note. It is used to provide the note-to-note changes which make a piece sound well performed and dynamic, and in the case of some sounds to change timbre as well; most sounds respond to velocity with a change in level but some also change tone. Using this in combination with Expression and Volume allows a complete range of dynamic control to be achieved.

Viewing Multiple Controllers

If you need to read controller information and make sense of it you may need to view multiple controllers at once - for instance, to see the effects of modulation and pitch bend on a part. You will already be familiar with the Key Editor, and the default controller lane (which you have used to view various data), but you can make use of Cubase's ability to show more than one controller lane at a time.

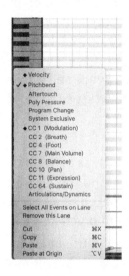

To add another controller lane, **SHIFT-right-click** in the note area and select `Create Controller Lane`, and another will appear. The default is to show note velocities, but the lane can show any controller (plus non-controller data such as pitch bend and velocity). To see the menu of the most common options, click the small black triangle, and the menu shown will appear. Note the most commonly used options are present, but also importantly some of the options have a diamond by them. This shows that this information is present in the current part – here aside from Velocity there is also Pitch Bend and CC1 Modulation. Either of these could be selected individually, but if you want to see the overall picture, you can create another controller lane, and then set one to `Pitch Bend` and one to `Modulation`. This will allow you to see exactly what's going on, as shown below.

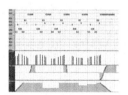

Here we can see that the volume is being altered with the Main Volume (bottom track) controller, while some of the notes have pitchbend applied, and we can still see an overview of the note velocities as well for the complete picture.

Without viewing the controller lanes in this way, it can be difficult to keep track of what is happening, particularly if you have two controllers which overlap in terms of their effect on the sound (such as Expression and Main Volume, or pitch bend and modulation).

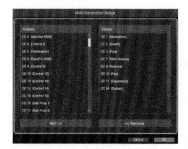

The most commonly-used controllers are normally available in the pop-up menu for the controller lane, but if you need to add a specific one, then it can be done by picking `Setup Available Controllers...` from the menu where you select the controllers. This will create a new window where you can pick any of the missing controllers.

Note that the descriptions given for them are from the General MIDI standard (see page 60), so may not always be interpreted in the same way by any given synth, if at all. Viewing the instrument's MIDI implementation or experimentation is a good way to find out, and remember that many allow you to program their response to controllers.

Tempo Mapping

While many sequenced pieces will follow a fixed tempo, live performances seldom do – humans will change tempo subtly throughout a piece, and in some cases quite dramatically; sometimes this is intentional, sometimes not. To successfully sequence a piece such as this requires mapping the tempo of Cubase to the tempo of the audio. Although this process can take some time, it will make work easier in the long run as it will mean that learning/practicing the parts can be done as a straight comparison (playing along with the piece), that the bar numbers of the original and your sequenced versions will tally, and it will be possible as a result of this to use quantization, etc, on the sequence, while still listening to the original audio for comparison. The half hour or so that you use to work to map the tempo out will pay great dividends.

Importing the Original Audio File

This can be done from an audio file that is already on the PC, such as an MP3 or WMA file. To do this, go to `File > Import > Audio File` and find the file you wish to import. Make sure that `Copy to Working Directory` is ticked as we want to work on a copy of the file, not the original – this is always good practice.

If the song is on a CD, then go to `Pool > Import Audio CD` and in the new dialogue box tick the track you wish to import and then click hit `Copy`. Once it has ripped the file to your hard drive, click `OK`.

You should then have the audio file placed on a track in the project, as seen below. Note that in this case there is some silence before the song starts. Also note there is a very definite start to the piece. Listen to your song now, and get an idea for where the song starts, and also what beat it starts on – this may be immediately apparent, or it might take several listens to get right. When first doing this, it's best to start with a song which starts very definitely and does so at the beginning of a bar – any other case makes things more complex which isn't ideal for your first attempt.

Trimming the Audio

The first thing to do is to trim any silence (or any unwanted noise before the song starts) from the audio file. This is done by clicking on the audio part with the arrow tool, and then using the white 'handle' at the bottom left of the part to drag the beginning of the audio part to the correct position. See the example below:

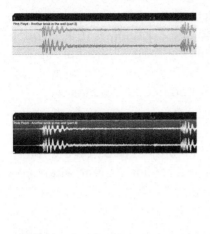

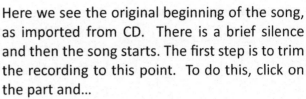

Here we see the original beginning of the song, as imported from CD. There is a brief silence and then the song starts. The first step is to trim the recording to this point. To do this, click on the part and...

... 'handles' will appear - what we're interested in is the little square at the bottom left - this allows the start point to be moved. Make sure that Snap is Off (Hit **J** to toggle it), and then click and drag the handle to the right, and.....

... to the appropriate point. Now you should have an audio part which starts at the right place, precisely on the beat (we are talking in terms of listening at the moment, not the beat as far as Cubase is concerned). Now turn snap on, and move the part to start at Bar 1, Beat 1. This means that Cubase and the song both agree at this point in time....

... and it should look like this. In this process we have aligned only one point of the song – Bar 1, Beat 1.

Next, turn the metronome on (**C**), and listen to the audio and metronome play together. You should hear that the first click (for bar 1 beat 1) happens at the right time, but after that things will probably go a bit awry (unless the song is at, or close to Cubase's default tempo of 120bpm). Turn the click off (**C**), and listen carefully and note where bar 2 starts (in the audio, not Cubase's bar 2). You can usually do this by hitting **SPACE** in time with the music (remember you need to do this where bar 2 will start, not where the last beat of the first bar is; this can take some practice). Now what's needed is to alter the tempo to make Cubase's bar 2 coincide with the song's bar 2. This used to be a case of trial and error, but now there's a much quicker way to do it: The Time Warp Tool.

The Time Warp Tool

As its name suggests, the time warp tool warps time in Cubase. Well, more precisely, it allows Cubase's tempo to be changed to fit with anything visually. This is done by selecting the time warp tool and then clicking on a bar in the project window's main area (not the ruler) and dragging the bar to the desired location. Once this has been done, Cubase will work out the tempo that is necessary to make that happen, and alter the previous event on the tempo track accordingly. This sounds complex, but in practice it's reasonably simple.

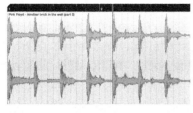

Here we see the original audio from the example above. The vertical play position pointer shows where in the audio Bar 2 actually is (this is found by listening and hitting Stop at the appropriate point). Cubase's bar 2 doesn't align with it correctly - Cubase's tempo needs to be faster.

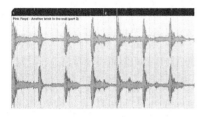

Once the time warp tool is selected, the ruler turns red. To correct Cubase's tempo, move the tool over Bar 2 on the project (**NOT** on the ruler), and you will see a vertical line appear where you are. You can now **SHIFT + click** and drag Bar 2 to the 'correct' position (i.e. where bar 2 happens in the actual audio).

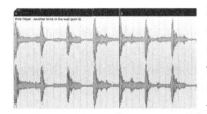

Here we see the effect of doing that – Bar 2 is now is the correct place, and Cubase's tempo has been altered to make this happen. We have found the tempo of the first bar - turn the click back on and play this back and you should hear that the click is in time.

Now, if our players were super-human, they might stick to precisely the same tempo all the way through the piece. But this is almost unheard-of; the tempo will usually alter throughout the piece – one tempo won't fit everything. So what we have to do is insert new tempo points in the tempo track before things go out of time, and then perform the same time warp action as shown above.

Here we are continuing with the track - Pink Floyd's Another Brick in the Wall, Part 2 - which is clearly being played by musicians of the highest calibre, but also allows us to see where beats are visually, to aid in explanation. From our previous example, the first bar is correct – when bar 2 starts, it's perfectly in time. In our ideal world the song might continue at precisely this tempo for some time without needing alteration.

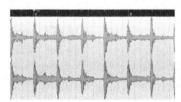

By the time we reach bar 3, things are wrong, as seen to the left. In fact, all of bar 2 is at the wrong tempo - Cubase is running slower than the audio is. The tempo of Bar 1 is correct, but Bar 2 needs a different tempo to work correctly.

What we need to do is to add a new tempo at Bar 2, which is done using the Time Warp Tool. When you click on the project window without using **SHIFT**, a new tempo will be inserted at the point that you click.

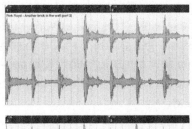

Without moving anything, Bar 2 has been clicked below the ruler using the Time Warp Tool. This means we can now repeat the process we did before, but this time we will be making sure that the beginning of Bar 3 is correct.

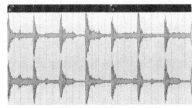

Using the procedure on the page before, Bar 3 has been moved to the correct location, and now all of Bar 2 sounds in time.

Repeating this over a number of bars will look like the next diagram, and indeed the entire song can be mapped in this manner.

With this technique, it is a case of listening for a section which is drifting out of time, then going back to check where Cubase was perfectly aligned with the audio, and once you have found that point, inserting a tempo change at that point and then using the time warp tool to re-align the following bars. It can take some time to do this for a song if the performers have changed tempo a lot during the performance, although often you will find that several bars (if not entire sections) maintain a constant tempo. Although these changes can be minimal, mapping them has two effects – firstly, it means you can use Cubase's quantizing features while still listening to the original track in audio form – this means it is far easier to transcribe an original track as you can listen to your version and the original head-to-head. Secondly mapping these tempo changes mimics the original performance perfectly, and often these changes are put in by the performers as a reaction to the material they are performing – some sections are faster, some slower.

Here are the tempo changes for the first few bars of the song - note that the tempo changes a little on almost every bar. They are viewed in the Tempo Editor (**CTRL + T**), which allows you to alter or insert tempo changes as you wish.

You may notice that there is a pattern, with specific sections slowing down or speeding up; there may also be a general progression, such as the tempo speeding up throughout the piece (as happens in Pulp's "Common People"). Such changes in tempo, when applied to your sequenced version, will make for a far more realistic-sounding sequence. In addition, using a tempo map like this is a seldom-used technique for improving your own compositions – for instance, it is possible to record a performance which has been done without reference to a click track (whether the tempo changes are subtle and unintentional, or are pronounced), and then use a similar technique to that above to map out the tempo of the MIDI information that has been recorded. It is important when doing this to ensure that the MIDI track is set to Linear Timebase - - this will ensure that the original MIDI performance is unchanged by the changes that are made to the Tempo Track when using the Time Warp tool. With a few minutes' work it is possible to work out the tempo of the piece when played, and this can either be kept wholesale, or a new one programmed, as shown next.

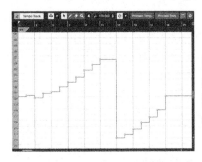

Here we see the original tempo map, which has been created by using the above techniques but on a MIDI part. It is accurate, but there are steps in each bar – usually acceptable, but you may want to smooth things out...

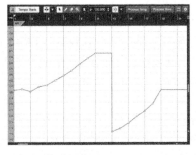

... using ramps instead of steps (changing the **Insert Curve** setting at the top of the editor). This will make for a smoother change, and also facilitate further alterations (changing one point will alter the whole ramp, whereas a group of steps would need to be altered above).

The Tempo Track

The tempo track has already been seen on page 91 - the Time Warp tool allows generation of tempo changes by dragging Cubase's grid. It is, however, capable of more, and we will examine some of these possibilities next.

Changing Tempo

As already seen previously on page 91 it is possible to create tempo changes using the Time Warp tool, usually to allow Cubase's tempo to match the tempo of a recording. It is possible to enter changes directly into the Tempo track, however. The Tempo editor is opened with **CTRL + T**, and looks like this:

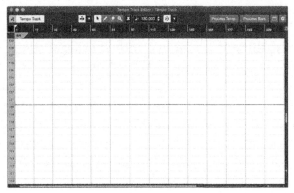

As with other Cubase windows, time runs from left to right. The tempo is represented by a line which shows the current tempo at a given time. Each tempo change is shown as a square. There are two kinds of tempo event - jump and ramp. A jump event will lead to an instantaneous change to the tempo, which will remain at that speed until a new event occurs.

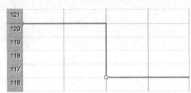

A ramp event will progressively alter tempo from one event to the next, allowing a smooth transition between tempi.

To create a tempo event, pick the type of event you want to insert (Jump or Ramp), and you can insert it in one of two ways - either click and drag on the tempo line, or use the Pencil tool and click wherever you want to insert the tempo. Setting the insert type to automatic will let Cubase insert the same type of events as those already around the location you are putting a new tempo into.

When creating a composition, it is often useful to be able to alter the tempo of sections of a piece, or to introduce gradual changes in tempo, and the tempo track will allow you to do this quickly and easily.

Deleting a Tempo event

To delete a tempo event, you can either select it and hit **Delete** on the keyboard, or use the Eraser tool.

Using Tap Tempo

As seen on page 4, it is possible to enter a tempo using the **Tap** button located on the transport bar. Clicking several times on the Tap button will lead to Cubase inserting a new tempo into the tempo track. If there is nothing selected, then the tempo will be inserted at the current play position. Otherwise the insertion will happen at the start of any selection. The tempo inserted will be a Jump type, regardless of the selection in the Tempo Track Editor.

Changing Time Signature

At the top of the tempo track, there is a section where the time signature of the piece can be altered. By default Cubase starts with a single event, a 4 4 at the beginning of the piece.

If you want to change the existing time signature, you can do it by double-clicking on the event, and entering the signature you wish to use.

If you want to change signature during the course of a piece, you will need to use the pencil tool to insert it at the appropriate bar of the piece. Once you have created it, you can enter the signature (which by default will be 4 4).

Deleting a Time Signature

Changes you have made can be deleted either by selecting and pressing **Delete** on the keyboard, or using the Eraser tool. It is not possible to delete the time signature that appears at bar 1.

Transpose

Often, you will want to change the pitch of the notes of a part, and often multiple parts or even an entire track. While you can do this manually by opening the editor and moving the notes up or down, it is often quicker to use Cubase's transpose function. This is accessed via `MIDI > Transpose Setup...` once you have selected the parts you wish to transpose, and you will see the following dialogue box.

It has a number of features, the most important of which is the Semitones box at the top. This is where you set the number of semitones up (positive) or down (negative) you want to transpose the part by. There are 12 semitones in an octave, so applying large transpositions is easily done.

We will look at some examples - firstly, semitone-based transposition. Here Cubase will move the notes by the set amount, with no changes in the relationships between notes being changed. In this example, 2 semitones have been set, so the original melody (which was in C major) will now be in D major. In this mode,

Cubase has no idea what key a part is in, and just moves the notes up or down by the set amount.

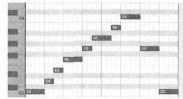
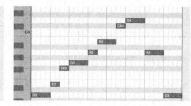

Transpose set to 2 semitones | The original melody, in C major | The transposed melody, now in D major

Next, scale-based transposition. By activating the Scale Correction box, it is possible to tell Cubase what key the original part was in, and the desired destination key. With the same 2 semitone transposition applied, we see the different effect of this when trying to keep the new part in the original key (C Major) - notes which previously were ending up being sharp have now been moved to a natural note, but this changes the relationship between some of the notes, and changes its sound.

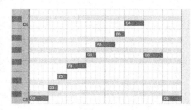
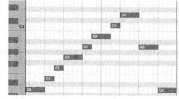

Scale correction enabled | The original melody, in C major | The transposed melody, also in C Major

This technique can be extended to use the transpose dialogue box to alter the tonality of a piece. By applying a 0 semitone transposition (so the notes will not change because of a transposition) and then picking a desired key, it is possible to alter the scale that a melody (or chords) are based on. Here the melody has been set to change from Major to harmonic minor.

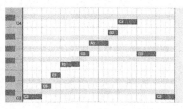
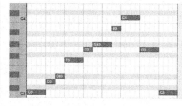

C Harmonic Minor selected as New Scale | The original melody, in C major | The altered melody, now in C Harmonic Minor

It's important to remember that this setting is applied to the notes in the part in the same way as if you had edited them yourself - the transpose setting is not 're-membered' for each part. If you apply a 2 semitone transposition to a part, and then come back to it and apply a 3 semitone transposition, it will be 5 semitones away from the original pitch, not 3.

Marker Tracks

Cubase has Marker tracks - these allow you to place markers at any point in your project, and they can be extremely useful. Firstly we will see how they work, and secondly look at some applications of them.

Creating the Marker Track

Marker tracks are created in the same way other tracks are - right-clicking in the track list area, or going to **Project > Add Track > Marker**. The end result will look like this:

The first type of marker allows us to locate a section and mark it. They are created at the current play position by pressing the **Add Marker** button, as seen here.

You will see the marker appear.

It can be named in the **Description** section of the info line.

You can also colour them as you would any part in the project window.

Markers can be dragged to any location using the selection (arrow) tool.

Active Marker Track

Cubase can have multiple marker tracks, but only one can be active at any time. When more than one marker track is present in a project, a tick button appears on each track, and the active one has this button turned on.

Cycle Markers

Cycle markers allow quick setting of the left and right locators to allow quick setup of cycling. First, set the locators at the range you want to set the cycle locators at.

Next, click the `Add Cycle Marker` button

You will see the cycle marker appear:

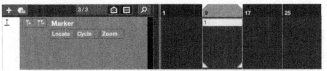

It can be named by editing the Description in the info line.

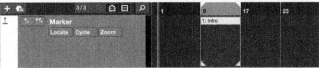

You can select Cycle markers to use from the Cycle menu which appears on the marker track:

Note that this only sets the locators, you will have to turn cycle on manually. You can edit a cycle marker after it has been created. Here we see the original.

The start and end points can be edited by clicking and dragging the triangles...

... while the entire marker can be moved by dragging the bar at the top to a new location.

Applications

Markers can be extremely useful when creating a piece of music - if you are given a brief for a composition, and you have timings you need to stick to, then creating them can be really useful. If you are given timings such as these, ensure that you have set the marker track to Linear (i.e. based on time) rather than Musical (based on bars and beats) - the reason for this is that if you change tempo, a Musical-based marker will move. You can use markers to show where you want specific things to happen in your composition, making it much easier to plan, and also to mark issues you may notice when you are working on a piece that you want to make note of but rectify later on.

Cycle markers make the process of setting your locators much quicker. They also have another use - you can select a cycle marker range from the Zoom menu, and Cubase will zoom in to that range. If you find yourself working on a few different ranges within a piece, this can make that process much easier and quicker.

The Arranger Track

The Arranger Track allows you to make quick changes to the structure of your project. In addition it will allow you to create different versions of a project and compare them quickly before deciding on a final structure. It works as follows. Firstly, create the Arranger track in the usual way - right-clicking in the track list area, or **Project > Add Track > Arranger**. The Arranger track will appear, and it looks like this:

It is inactive, and in addition, no events have been defined, so firstly we will define some events to arrange. Events are created in the track itself, using the pencil tool. Here we see our original arrangement, with the blank arranger track.

Next, using the pencil tool, events are drawn onto the arranger track.

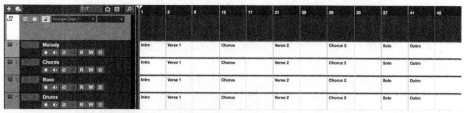

Here each section of the song has had an event created for it, and each event can then be named by selecting it and altering the Description in the info line. To make more sense, the arranger track events have been named as per the song's original sections.

Note that in the inspector the Arranger track now contains all these events.

Now the Arranger chain needs to be filled - this will control the order in which the events are played. To alter the structure of the piece, we will start out with a Chorus, then Verse 1, Verse 2, Chorus 2, Solo, Chorus 2 and Outro. This is done by dragging the events from the **Events List** into the **Current Arranger Chain** box above it, building up as seen below.

Once you have created your arranger chain, it is turned on with the Arranger Mode button, found on the Arranger track.

Note that the play position may change depending on how you have created your chain. When you press play, the sections will play in the order of the events in the arranger chain, rather than the linear order you originally had. This allows you to make large structural changes to your piece without lots of copy and pasting. In addition, you can create more than one arranger chain to allow you to quickly compare different versions of an arrangement - this is very useful when trying out experimental changes to a piece, and there is no danger of losing your original arrangement as you can simply turn the arranger track off to go back to it.

To create a new chain, click on the drop-down menu where the current arranger chain is listed, and pick **Create New Chain** from the menu.

You can edit that chain as you wish, and switch between them by picking from the menu. Note that you can rename the chains from this menu as well.

Each event can be played up to 999 times - to repeat one within a chain, just change the number from the default value of 1 to whatever you want.

One point to note is that the same bars can be part of more than one arranger event. If you wanted at some point to play just the second half of a verse, you can create an extra event which covers just this, as seen below.

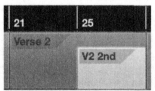

Once you have decided on a chain that you want to keep permanently, then you can pick **Flatten Chain** from the pop-up menu - this will rearrange the parts in the way you have selected, and delete the arranger chain. Here we see the effect of the arranger chain seen above.

Melody	Chorus	≡ Chorus	≡ Verse 1	Verse 2	Chorus 2	≡ Solo	Chorus 2	≡ Outro
Chords	Chorus	≡ Chorus	≡ Verse 1	Verse 2	Chorus 2	≡ Solo	Chorus 2	≡ Outro
Bass	Chorus	≡ Chorus	≡ Verse 1	Verse 2	Chorus 2	≡ Solo	Chorus 2	≡ Outro
Drums	Chorus	≡ Chorus	≡ Verse 1	Verse 2	Chorus 2	≡ Solo	Chorus 2	≡ Outro

You can undo this while the project is still open, but bear in mind you will not be able to undo those changes after you have closed the project, so be sure you want to keep them.

Good and Bad programming

Many MIDI files which are available on the Internet are not well programmed. Some suffer from rudimentary errors such as incorrect notes and rhythms, but many have the notes correct but are not good to listen to, and as a result MIDI is often thought to be at fault. However, close examination of a typical MIDI file will show why the performance is not convincing, and point to where things can be improved; while these points have already been covered, it is a good time to recap some of these techniques and show how a badly-programmed part can be improved dramatically by editing the relevant parameters.

Velocity

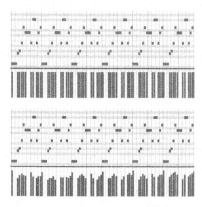

Here we see a guitar part which has been sequenced badly. Straight away you can see that no velocity shaping is present – every note has a velocity of 64. This will mean the part has no dynamics at all.

Here is the same guitar part which has been sequenced with the appropriate velocity values – it sounds much more convincing as a result , accenting some notes in each phrase as per the original.

Note that there are repetitions of the same phrases, but the parts are varied enough to make them sound as if they have been played. Velocity is probably one of the simplest and easiest ways to achieve a convincing performance – often just using the pencil tool in the controller lane can yield good results – there is no excuse for leaving a part with all the same velocity when it should be varying.

Quantization

This part is totally quantized throughout (as indeed was the entire song this was taken from). When starting out in sequencing (particularly when lacking in real-time performance skills) it's common to use quantization to improve the timing of an errant performance, or to use step-time or the key editor to enter parts. This accuracy simply isn't present in live performances.

Here the same part has notes which are not exactly on the grid (either by playing or detailed editing), and the end result is far more pleasing – the 'groove' imparted by this is subtle but worthwhile achieving, and the other parts in the sequence reflected this giving the whole arrangement much more life.

Controllers

A lack of controller data will mean that typically a piece has not been well programmed – it's a part of the GM standard that these messages are acted upon (so nearly all playback devices will benefit from them), and they provide fundamental elements of a performance. While most sequencers will export 'basic' controller data when creating a MIDI file (with blocks at the beginning of each track to set Volume, Pan, Expression and effects depths), this may not be enough, and using Expression, Modulation and other creative effects throughout will improve the end result.

Pitch Bend

Pitch Bend is really a prerequisite for any vocal performance to be accurately sequenced – vocalists almost unknowingly bend into notes and slide smoothly between them, as well as suffer from minor intonation issues that make them sound more 'human' – the same often can be said for guitars and unfretted string instruments.

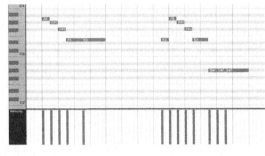

When a vocal sequence looks like this one, it's probably not going to be convincing. When it's supposed to be Eddie Vedder, it definitely won't be! Note also the uniform velocity of 127 throughout the piece.

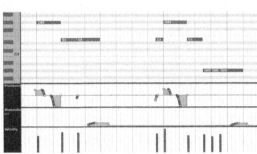

Seen to the left is a good example – so much so that three controller lanes are needed – pitch bend has been used for notes which smoothly change, but in addition modulation has also been used (see controller section above) to add vibrato to the voice, and the velocities are well programmed to replicate the original.

Sound Selection

Many MIDI files are ruined by poor sound selection; this can often depend on the original choice of sounds and how the programmed version is to be played or assessed – if the end result needs to be a MIDI file using the GM soundset then clearly you are limited to the 128 sounds that are provided, but it is still possible to sequence many pieces reasonably well with some creative use of programming skills and effects. If you are to produce an audio recording using any softsynths you have access to, then you should be able to reproduce almost any sound convincingly - using synths such as Halion Sonic SE and other free instruments.

Exercises

Sequencing Guitar Parts

There are a number of different challenges when sequencing guitar parts - the main areas are outlined below.

Chords

Sequence a part, firstly using 'keyboard' type root position chords. Now, using the information on page 72 alter these to be guitar-like, and listen to the different sound of the different chord 'shapes' shown on the relevant pages.

Strumming

With the chords you have now sequenced, experiment with making them appear strummed, altering the relative timing of the notes within the chord. Remember that chords can be up- and down-strummed, and experiment with these techniques as well as the length and timing of the strums.

Bending

Sequence a solo guitar melody, and then use pitch bend to transition between some of the notes in the melody, as a guitarist would, as seen on page 76. Note that the curve that you use for the pitch bend is important - most guitarists will start out bending quickly, and then slow as they reach the destination, so a simple straight line will sound quite artificial.

Bending more than 2 semitones

By applying pitch bend before a note is heard, the commonly-used 3-semitone bend can be sequenced, and doing this in practice takes a bit of thought as the note which is played is not sounded at that pitch. Try to alter the melody from the previous example to incorporate at least one 3- or 4-semitone bend.

Unison Bends

Use multiple tracks to achieve this, by having the static note on one track (which must be routed to a separate MIDI channel if you are using a VST instrument), and the bent note on another. The previous notes about bending and having practiced them will be important here to achieve a believable result.

Slides

Using the techniques on page 79, add a slide to the melody. Note that careful programming of the note velocities and choice of sound is important to get a realistic result with this technique.

Drums

Sequencing drums can be difficult - particularly if you are not a drummer - so practicing it is important. Doing the following will increase your ability to program drums and understand what works for a drummer.

Sequence a simple drum part

Create a part with bass drum on beats 1 and 3, snare on beats 2 and 4, and with the hi hat playing 8th notes. Do this using the cycle record mode (see page 11), playing in each instrument on a separate cycle, building them up as you go. Do this at around 100bpm.

More complex playing

Sequence the same part, but playing the bass and snare in on the same cycle. This will allow you to practice some independence between your hands, and to create the part that much quicker.

Change the hi-hat

Sequence the same part, but add in an open hi-hat on the last 8th of the bar. This increases the complexity of what you are playing a little more.

Repeat with 16ths

Repeat the above three exercises, but with a 16th note hi hat pattern instead of 8ths.

Use written music

Sequence some drum parts from drum music - this is a useful skill to have, and using drum music can help improve your overall reading skill.

String Instruments

While it is possible to merely move a keyboard part to a string sound, it will generally sound better if the observations on page 81 are followed, and the intervals at the lower register are larger than those at the top. To this end, copy a chord part (such as you sequenced in the Sequencing chapter's exercises on page 53), copying it and transposing it over several octaves - instead of a single chord (seen here), you should end up with the same chord across a number of octaves. It will sound too thick like this, so experiment by removing some of the notes on the lower register to improve the sound.

Voice

Sequencing of the voice needs a number of techniques to be mastered for it to work convincingly, and practicing them is important.

Large range pitch bend

It's common for singers to 'slide' between notes which are of a wider range than the standard +-2 semitones that most MIDI synths default to, so practicing the technique shown on page 76 (the same as for guitars) is important as it will be needed in many situations.

Vibrato

As mentioned on page 76 there are two main ways to create vibrato, so both should be practiced. Firstly, by using the modulation (CC1) controller, remembering that this is dependent on the settings on the synth (which you may or may not be able to alter). Secondly, by subtle use of pitchbend to create vibrato from scratch (as seen on page 76)

"Scooping" into notes

An extremely common technique (which many singers are not aware they do), with pitch bend needed before many notes, just allowing the pitch to raise into the note in question (and sometimes down to it, depending on the note before). Practicing inputting this for each note, without snap turned on and using the line tool set to Parabola will allow you to work quickly.

Tuning

Some singers are out of tune, mostly in a subtle and pleasing manner. Adding a fixed amount of pitchbend to a phrase is a common technique to use, and needs to be practiced to allow you to do so quickly.

Volume / Expression

Many current VST Instruments do not provide much information about what MIDI controllers they respond to. In addition, many do not respond to Expression (CC11), only Main Volume (CC7). It is important that you know whether an instrument does, and to do this, create a MIDI part with notes in it, and then use the line tool to add Expression data in an increasing ramp. If the volume does not change, then the synth doesn't respond to CC11. Delete that data and replace it with a ramp of Main Volume (CC7) data, and see if the synth responds to this. Some synths ignore both pieces of data, many only respond to CC7. Knowing which do and don't can save you a lot of time in programming.

Tempo Mapping

Tempo Mapping can be important for a wide range of situations, so practicing it is important. To do so, follow the instructions on page 90, but make sure you do it with a track which has a clearly-defined beat, which has been played without the aid of a click track, and that doesn't have an anacrusis at the beginning - i.e. the first beat you hear is bar 1, beat 1. Once you have tempo-mapped something straightforward, it is worth trying again with something a little more complex, such as a track which features an anacrusis, or that has marked tempo changes. To really test your skills, try a track where there are time signature changes as well, using the information on page 94 to insert time signatures where appropriate.

Summary

MIDI is often derided as being an inferior way of creating a piece of music, but when used well with the techniques outlined above, it is quite possible to achieve a good facsimile of an original musical performance. The difficulty in doing this doesn't come from capturing the original note information (although this is a skill in itself), but in replicating the nuances of each player's performance to achieve a far more realistic sequence. The key to doing this is to listen to what is being played, and then attempt to replicate it using the facilities that MIDI gives you – the techniques outlined above demonstrate some of the more common ways of replicating a 'real' performance, but you should always be prepared to work out how to approximate a new technique should you not be able to do so with the ones outlined. While it may not be perfect, it is possible to take an otherwise stale-sounding sequence and make it extremely convincing given attention to detail, skill and time. Many of the MIDI files that you can obtain (from the Internet, etc.) are programmed only at the most basic level, having captured the notes and very little else about the performance – mostly they will have fixed velocities for each note, and be rigidly quantized. This has led to MIDI being maligned, when often it is in fact the skills (or lack thereof) of the programmers that are at fault.

Having a good grasp of these techniques is important for anyone intending to produce their own music using MIDI - you can create a huge range of expression, and detailed MIDI programming and attention to detail is often the difference between a mundane-sounding piece of music and one which really involves and absorbs the listener.

Sequencing an Entire Song

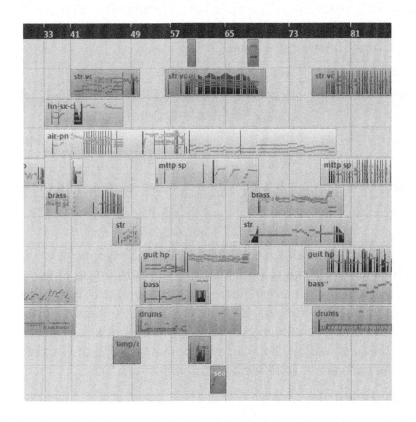

To make a sequenced version of an entire song, there are a number of elements to complete, and it often makes sense to approach it in the following order:

Listen and Analyse

Before starting out on a task like this, it's a good idea to listen to the entire song several times – this will allow you to produce a 'map' of the song, showing times, sections, numbers of bars, instrumentation, texture changes, effects and anything else that you want to note down. Having this kind of plan can make your sequencing much easier and often more accurate – it's possible to forget small details later on when you are directing all your attention towards sequencing rather than the overall pattern and shape of the song. Your analysis can take any form you like, but something like the table below (with part of a song filled in) can make things much easier – much in the same way you would need to do when making a multi-track recording of a song.

Time	Section	Bars	Instruments	Comment
0:00	Intro	1 – 8	Drums Guitar	Guitar Riff is repeated, distorted sound. Drum fill at end
0:17	Verse 1	9 – 40	+ Bass +Vocals	Bass follows intro guitar riff, guitar plays chords
1:25	Chorus	41 – 56	+ B. Vox	Backing Vocals repeated throughout
1:59	Verse 2	57 – 89	- B. Vox - Guitar	Just Vocals, Drums and Bass Delay on Vocal

Another way to map out a song is to do so after Tempo mapping it (shown in the next section). Once you have the original song in your Cubase project, you can create an instrument track for each instrument or sound you hear, and then use the pencil tool to draw in empty parts whenever the instrument is playing. In this way you will have a ready-made map of the song and a quick comparison of your progress and the final version. You can add comments using the marker track or by changing the part names to reflect any comments you have.

Tempo-map the entire song

This will make working in Cubase much simpler as you will always be able to refer back to the original version straight away, knowing you are listening to the correct bar at any given time. Comparisons are then easy and instant to make – this alone will dramatically improve the end result, and the time invested in this will lead to a more natural and convincing-sounding sequence just by virtue of your version following the tempo of the original precisely. See the section on Tempo Mapping on page 90.

Create Markers

Using the marker track, set out the sections of the song that you've noted before. This will make your navigation through the track much quicker (the transport buttons take you quickly to the previous/next marker), and avoid confusion when copying or editing sections common to different parts of the song.

Create parts

There are several stages to creating the parts for your sequence - tackling this in a logical order can make the task easier and

Create empty parts

In conjunction with your analysis of the song from above, you can now create tracks for all the instruments that you can hear, and use the pencil tool to draw in parts where the instruments are playing. This will provide you with a broad outline of the entire piece, and show you where you will need to work out what is being played.

Work out the parts in a basic form

Next, sequence the entire song in a basic form – make sure that all the instruments that you listed are included, and if you have a score available then ensure that these parts are correct (sometimes they have errors, particularly when taken from the Internet) – remember that the recorded version of a song is always the definitive version to be adhered to. If you don't have a score of the song, then you will have two options – either work things out by ear (which can be difficult when you first start doing it, but will dramatically improve your aural and keyboard skills if work is needed in these areas), or sometimes printing out the score from a MIDI file version can help – this is no different than using a score, but remember the accuracy of things you download will always need close scrutiny. Sometimes, though, they can help you with passages you are finding awkward – even if they just provide a clue to the correct notes.

Tuning

Sometimes the entire original song will be out of tune. In this case, use a correct sequenced note as a reference, and process the audio (select the audio event, right-click and pick **Processes > Pitch Shift**) and try various values of the Cents slider to get the song in tune with Cubase). Remember that if you need more than 100 cents your sequenced note was probably wrong! See page 579 for more on audio processes.

Repetition

Many songs feature a great deal of repetition – bass, drum and guitar patterns are often repeated, entire sections (such as choruses or verses) can be repeated in a wholesale manner or repeated with development. At this point do not try to work out everything in complete detail – it's a much better idea to have a rough version of the entire song than to have one section in incredible detail and the rest missing completely. At this time don't add in complex programming such as pitch bend and expression – just get the notes in without any errors or omissions – the details will come later. Sequence the vocal part/s and/or instrumental solos last as they will usually need the most work and often are the most complicated and involved to do.

Another technique that is very useful and easy is to name parts with their contents. You should already be in the habit of naming your tracks (meaning that any parts you record will be named to suit), but adding in the name of the section or the chords which are inside will make copying and comparing things much quicker and easier. An extension to this technique is to use colour to differentiate different versions of a part; often a part will be repeated but with variation, and marking these variations with some colour will make finding them a lot quicker.

Modify and improve the parts

The next step is for more detailed MIDI programming to take place – here you should be working on adding in pitch bend, detailed timing (using groove quantize and some small randomisation of note on events, for instance), velocity programming (both on small and large scales of the song). The kind of programming which is shown in the Effective Sequencing chapter (see page 71) should take place now. The amount of detail that is needed will depend on the track, but don't under-estimate the amount of time needed to complete this step – in the case of vocals in particular the amount of liberties taken with both timing and tuning can lead to a lot of fine, detailed work being needed to achieve a good performance. For many guitar parts (particularly strummed acoustic guitar) the work needed is also considerable as timing and note duration are both critical to achieving a lifelike sound.

Subtle variations

In addition if the part has been performed by a person, it will have subtle variations throughout – sometimes these are small and unplanned, but often they will be part of the arrangement – the way that a part is performed may increase in intensity throughout a song, meaning that straight repetition isn't an option, and each iteration of a section will need to be treated individually. Even parts which sound identical should have some tiny variations added to them in most cases, and this can usually be done quickly by suitable use of the Logical Editor (See page 357).

Here you may find that programming of sounds may already come into play – in many cases a vocal performance may need a pitch bend range greater than that given by default (±2 semitones), and while this should be programmable for GM synths via a controller message using RPNs, many software and soundcard-based GM synths do not obey this, so it could be time to use a VST Instrument which allows this programming done via its front panel straight away.

Listen with the original

Once you think you have sequenced an entire instrument throughout the piece, solo the original track and listen to it twice – once with the original track slightly dominant (so you can hear if you've missed any notes out) and once with your version slightly louder (so you can hear anything in your version that may be wrong or not present in the original). Often parts which are mostly repetitive (such as drum or bass tracks) will actually feature small detailed differences throughout a piece which all add up to develop the arrangement as it progresses – missing these out will mean your sequence will not sound as musical and accurate as it should do.

Programming of sounds

Initially you will have been using preset sounds, but modification of these tones is an important part of making any sequence sound convincing – knowledge of how synthesizers produce their sound is an important part of this, as is placing the recording in context – the technology available to the original artist will govern the sounds and can give you a clue as to what equipment to use. Tailoring sounds to any situation is an important skill to have, but in this case the tailoring should mimic precisely the original sounds (or as much as possible).

In the case of subtractive (analogue) synthesizer sounds, make sure you're familiar with how they work (see page 235 for more on this), try to break down the sounds you are hearing into individual components – firstly the waveform itself; if you are familiar with how the different waveforms (sine, triangle, sawtooth, square) sound, then you should be able to pick a suitable one quickly. Listen for common techniques such as detuned oscillators (adding a thick sound by detuning one of them a small amount) or harmony (by detuning one oscillator by a number of semitones, typically 5, 7 or 12). Vibrato is added by using the LFO to alter the oscillator's pitch, and if the sound is a square wave the use of PWM (Pulse Width Modulation) is common to provide a changing, evolving sound (when the LFO is at a low frequency) or a detuned sound (when the LFO is at a faster rate).

Dynamic changes

Analyse the way the sound attacks and releases – the start and end fade in/out of the notes is critical to simulating a sound, so programming the amplifier's A and R parameters is the most critical part here.

Filtering

The filter is probably the most-used part of a sound, and also the most complex to get right. The basic filter settings (Cutoff and Resonance) are a good starting point (but bear in mind many synths have different filter types – high, low and band pass – and also different filter settings – 12db or 24db / octave are common settings), but also listen to how the filter sound develops over time – if it does alter with the time of each note use the ADSR controls to mimic this, and bear in mind that if the filter can either open or close based on the ADSR setting – usually this is achieved with a positive or negative setting for the filter envelope – sometimes this is a simple switch (often with a drawing of the way the envelope will work), other times it is a knob that allows polarity and amount to be selected.

For drum parts, the same filtering can often be used (in the case of samplers or units such as the SR-202), and with the addition of basic tuning of the sample it is often possible to create a wide range of timbres to mimic original sounds – taking samples a long way from their original pitch range is a useful technique to be aware of.

Sampled sounds are often more complex – having access to the original sample makes things a lot easier (if, for instance a song makes use of a specific sample which has then been manipulated or used as the basis for a piece), but if you don't, then you will need to either find a similar sample, or create one (by recording it yourself or possibly by sequencing something and bouncing that down). The manipulation offered by most samplers follows a subtractive synth closely (see the Samplers chapter on page 293 for more on this), offering Amplitude and Filter control with ADSR and modulation from an LFO in many cases.

EQ

It is rare that a sound you program will sound identical to the original - it's often the case that it will sound thinner or fatter than the sound you are trying to mimic, and it's important to keep in mind that you have access to a very powerful tool for this kind of work in the form of the channel EQ - whether you are using an instrument track or a VST Instrument in the rack, it will have an audio channel for its output and the EQ can provide huge tonal shaping capability. If you need to, refer to the section on EQ in the Effects chapter (page 545) and the Mixing chapter (page 626).

Performance characteristics

Another area to pay close attention to is the playing/performance characteristics of the synth – careful selection of things such as CC1 - Modulation routing (sending modulation to the LFO and making it control pitch and/or filtering), pitch bend range (providing a wide enough range for things such as octave-wide slides) and monophonic slide times (simulating sliding between notes by making them overlap in a "mono" mode rather than having to program every single slide) can make the sequence better to listen and quicker to program.

Fine-tuning a synth sound can take some time, and in addition to continually comparing your sound to the original, it is often best to make edits and then come back to a sound later; it is very easy to lose objectivity when programming sounds!

Mixing and Effects

Effects are an important part of most contemporary recordings, and adding them to your sequence can really transform the sound of it. Careful listening to the original recording and analysis of the production of it and then applying this same production to your sequence can really make it sound more authentic. As you will mostly be using VST Instruments, remember that their output channels have the same facilities as any audio channel, so adding any kind of VST Effect is possible. You can use nearly all of the techniques used with a multitrack recording mix (as indeed the original recording would have) – see the Mixing chapter on page 619 for more on this.

If you are making use of VST Instruments, you will probably have to be more aware than usual of the limitations of the computer you are using – each instrument will use up some CPU power (more than just an empty audio track would do), and sharing any effects where possible (using FX Sends rather than Insert effects) will greatly improve the situation.

This order is, of course, a recommendation, and you will probably find that as you progress through the process you need to do more work on previous steps as you become more discerning about your sequencing.

Summary

Sequencing an entire song from scratch can be a daunting task for anyone; there are many parts which need to be worked out and programmed, sounds which need to be replicated and then the entire piece needs to be mixed. Breaking it down into small chunks is the best way to approach it, and by doing this the overall task will become more manageable. In most cases, it is the attention to detail that will make the difference between a sequence sounding artificial and synthetic and being convincing to many listeners, and your awareness of the techniques available to program performances forms a huge part of this, combined with the ability to analyse sounds and program suitable substitutes. Bringing all these techniques together is challenging, but can produce surprisingly convincing results.

MediaBay

MediaBay is a way to present all of the sounds, settings and samples that have been referenced by Cubase. While not all sounds will appear in it (third party plugins may not work with it without some extra work), the default content installed by Cubase does, and has a huge variety of sounds, settings and samples available to work with. There are two views for MediaBay - one is the main view (accessed by pressing **F5**), and the other is the Right Zone view, which gives quick access to Media Bay, but doesn't present all the options available in the full view.

The Full view

The "Full" view of the MediaBay is in its own window, and is summoned using **F5**. It is seen below.

On the left are the locations where MediaBay searches for media. At the top are filters, below that is the list of current media files, and at the bottom a preview area. There are several ways to quickly select media, so that will be what we look at first.

Attribute Filter

The first is to use the Filter section to quickly filter out unwanted options. Many of the entries (particularly the Steinberg content) is categorised, so these filters can quickly allow selection of a sound, sample or setting.

Here we see a selection being made - firstly drums (**Drum&Perc**)...

... then **Beats**...

... then **Electronica/Dance**...

... then **Classic House**...

... then **Electric**.

Note that each time a selection is made, the numbers update to show the Media matching the selected criteria. Also note that the final **Character** column can have multiple selections made - here **Dark** has been selected as well, leading to 20 possibilities rather than the original 100.

The search can be cleared progressively (by deselecting a selected filter), or by clicking the reset button.

Text Search

Media can also be searched for by entering text - this can be in addition to the filters seen already, or on its own. To search using text, simply enter the text you want to search for and MediaBay will search straight away, presenting the results list as soon as it has found a match.

This search can be cleared using the reset button found in the results area.

In addition, the results can be shuffled into a random order to promote a less uniform approach to any often-used search results:

Auditioning

Media can be auditioned without having to create a track or insert the media into your project. Clicking once on one of the presets temporarily loads it to be auditioned.

MIDI

If the media is MIDI it will be played using the built-in player.

Patches

If the media is a playable sound (such as a patch for a VST Instrument) then playing your MIDI keyboard (or the on-screen keyboard) will audition the sounds.

Audio

If the media is an audio file, the waveform will be displayed at the bottom of the MediaBay, and it can be played with the player that is present here.

There are two useful buttons at the right-hand side of the audio audition area:

 Align Beats to project - this will automatically adjust the tempo of the audio to the project, giving an idea of how the sample will fit in with the project.

 Wait for Project Play - this hands control over to the main transport in Cubase; particularly useful if you want to audition in context, and setting up a loop to cycle with the locators will allow the auditioning of audio samples in succession in context.

To import the selected media (regardless of the type), double-click it, and an appropriate track will be made in the project, with the content selected. Alternatively, Audio and MIDI files can be dragged to appropriate existing tracks in a project.

Filtering Media Types in MediaBay

Often there will be too many results in MediaBay, or a specific Media is required. In this case, the results can be filtered by media type. Here, from MediaBay's home, the text 'piano' has been searched for, leading to 916 results.

There are many types of media matching the search term, but it is possible to narrow this down by selecting one or more types by clicking the Media Types menu, shown to the left of the screen here, and picking the type of media you are interested from the menu - you can select more than one.

The list of results will now be updated to reflect your selection, and the sigma symbol will now reflect your selection (if you have chosen multiples, it will be a three-shape symbol). Here, by selecting only Plug-in Presets, the original 916 options have now been reduced to 400.

Resetting the types of media can be quickly achieved by pressing the reset button, but this also resets a text search term. To avoid this, open the media type selection menu, and select `All Media Types`.

Search using Logical Filters

The default method of using the filter section is via Attributes; they are selected to narrow down the results, and this allows quick selection of suitable media. While this is useful, there is another mode which offers a much more versatile (but less immediate) method of filtering - Logical filters. These work in a similar manner to the filter section of the Logical Editor (see page 358), and while the learning curve may be steeper than the Attribute mode, Logical mode can be more powerful.

Using Logical Mode

To start using Logical Mode, click the **Logical** button in the filter section; the attributes section disappears, and is replaced by a single line:

Entering any text here performs a similar search to entering the same text in the search results area as already seen on page 119.

The initial filter is set to **Any Attribute - Matches**, but clicking on **Any Attribute** allows selection of any attribute that is referenced by MediaBay - and there are a lot:

Extra lines can be added to the logical filter to make it more specific by clicking on the + button at the right hand end of a line:

Unwanted lines can be deleted by clicking the **x** in the same area (note that delete is not active until there are multiple lines present):

The power of logical filter mode lies in the ability to add extra lines of filtering, and the ability to search a wide range of attributes. The following examples will make the power of logical filter mode clear.

Filtering by type and tempo

Often a search is more vague than a simple search for text can provide. Consider the following search:

These two lines will search for any media containing the word drum whose tempo is equal to or greater than 130bpm, yielding 529 possibilities in the default media, a combination of MIDI loops, audio files and instrument presets. Filtering by type is easy using the results section, and if tempo is key concern (perhaps looking for a loop which is nearer 130) then clicking on the Tempo column in the search results list will sort the results in ascending tempo order.

If searching for a range of tempos, then it is possible to add an extra line, setting the maximum tempo. Here a third line adds an upper limit of 140, using the <= operator.

As with many areas in Cubase, there is more than one way to achieve the same end - it is possible to select **in range** for tempo, and set the upper and lower limits on the same line. Often this would be how you would search if the range had been the idea straight away:

Filtering by Key

The following single line allows selection of attributes via key:

Adding another line searches solely for minor tonality:

As MediaBay indexes a large number of possible attributes, there are many options to experiment with here, but even making use of the examples above can quickly speed searches in MediaBay beyond the simple options possible in Attribute search mode.

Media Bay in the Right Zone

Once active on the Right Zone of the Project Window, MediaBay gives the choice of four categories - Instruments, Loops and Samples, Presets and User Presets.

Instruments

Clicking **VST Instruments** gives a visual menu of the instruments present, and then any installed libraries present.

Here **Groove Agent SE** was chosen ...

... followed by **Production Grooves** ...

... leading to a list of results.

From here it is possible to further filter the results, by clicking on the **Sub Style** and **Character** to narrow down the number of available options.

Here **Rap/Hip Hop** and **Processed** were chosen, leading to 11 options.

As with the main MediaBay, it is possible to audition any found Media files and settings using a MIDI keyboard or the built-in audio player, seen at the bottom area of the Right Zone.

Using MediaBay to scan your own samples

In addition to scanning the content included with Cubase, MediaBay can scan sample files that you have stored on your computer. This can make the use of third-party sample libraries much easier, particularly with the ability to audition them in the context of a project.

Firstly, open MediaBay (**F5**), and expand the File System tree on the top left, and keep expanding until the folder/drive where the samples are stored is visible.

Next, tick the tickbox next to the folder where the samples are stored; in this case the Samples folder was ticked so that all the folders inside will be indexed.

The indexing process takes place - the folders will change colour while they are being indexed, and once the process is complete they will all go white.

Clicking on a folder in the left-hand pane now shows all the samples in that folder in MediaBay's results area, and they can be auditioned in the same way as any other content. Note that while the filter section will not yet work for these samples (as their attributes will not have been set), a search by text for any part of the filename will work.

Editing Attributes

As seen earlier, MediaBay's default method of searching is via attributes, but this leads to a problem when using media that you have imported yourself - the attributes will not be set. To rectify this, MediaBay contains an attribute editor, which resides on the right zone of the MediaBay window, which can be turned on with the right zone button at the top right of the MediaBay window.

Viewing the Attribute Inspector will allow editing to take place - often resizing of the window is needed as otherwise MediaBay can be pretty large when all the sections are present.

Here it is possible to edit the attributes for any media, and this is particularly useful with samples. There is a wealth of sample loops available on the Internet, often well arranged and ready to use, but depending on the sample in question, Cubase may mis-recognise the tempo of the sample, leading to some unexpected results. To this end, we will look at the process of adding Tempo and other information to a set of loops which have been downloaded. While this process can take a little time, it is a one-off effort, and usually pays dividends in saved time later on.

Editing Tempo Information

Here is the contents of a typical folder, containing a number of drum loops, all of which have tempo indications in the file name, but whose tempo does not appear in the tempo column:

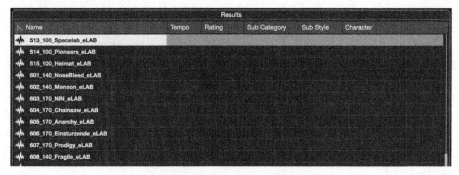

They are an assortment of different tempos. Clicking on any one will allow its attributes to be viewed in the right-hand pane - aside from the file name, it currently has no information present.

Double-clicking the **Tempo** field allows information to be entered:

Once it has been entered, Cubase works out the number of bars present, and fills that information in as well:

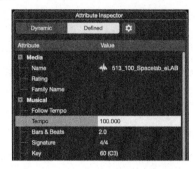

This process could be completed for each individual file, but this would be long-winded. To minimise the amount of time doing this, searching beforehand can help greatly. A search for the text _100 leads to 15 results (from the file names, as each one has the tempo noted with an underscore before it):

It's now possible to select all of the files in the results area (click on the first one, **SHIFT** click on the last one to select all of them), and note that the information in the Attribute inspector is displayed in yellow (as there are multiple files selected). Double-clicking and entering the tempo (94) will now update the tempo for all the samples.

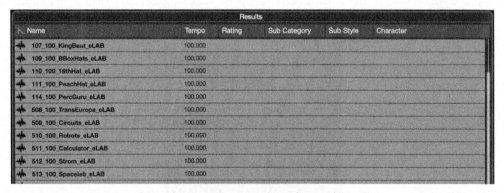

Note that sometimes if you have a tempo already in place for one of the files, you will need to change the value to something else, and then change it back to the correct one so all the files are updated.

Editing Categories

The editing doesn't have to be confined to tempo - categories can be added (allowing searching via the attributes filter) and if the sample library is well organised, this can be a much quicker process.

Here the entire folder of drum breaks is selected:

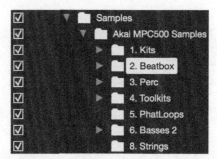

And once more the entire set of samples is selected by clicking on a sample and pressing **CTRL + A**:

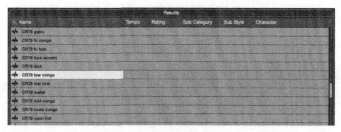

Selecting 200 samples in one go. They can now all be set to the category `Drum&Perc`:

And the sub-category (`Beats`)

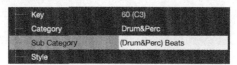

In addition, depending on the sample library structure selecting a folder at a time can allow the setting of sub-style, character and genre to allow third-party samples to be fully referenced using the filter section. Character selection involves a window with choices being either one of two options (left or right in each column), or unset:

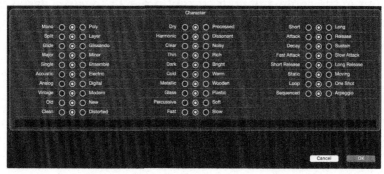

Selecting a few options relevant for all the samples in a folder allows the filtering to be more accurate:

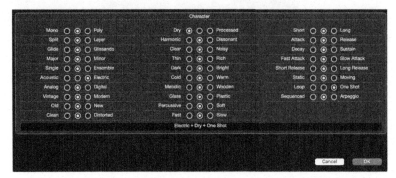

Here the attributes applied to the samples edited in the previous section have been selected (across the entire library, not just the folder edited previously), and they are the only ones in the media library that fit those criteria.

Summary

MediaBay offers a powerful way to index the vast majority of sound content that is available in Cubase - Audio and MIDI parts as well as instrument, effect and track settings. Making use of it can facilitate a faster workflow, and the ability to audition loops in the context of your current project can vastly ease selection of appropriate material without the hit-and-miss of importing audio without hearing it alongside existing parts. Spending some time getting used to the workflow and filtering options available can increase your productivity hugely.

Music Theory

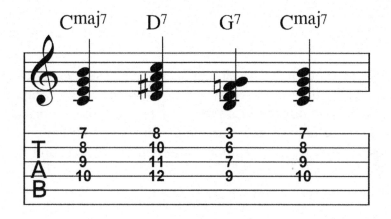

There is one thing above all others that seems to stop Music Tech students from getting the most from their equipment and natural abilities, and that is music theory. Or rather, the total lack of it!

It is a common misconception that learning music theory will "stifle my creativity" and other nonsense. It won't. Yes, there are people who are taught in a way where they become unable to think for themselves musically, and do not develop creativity or musical memory as a result. But that is not because of music theory. What it will do is give you the tools to create more interesting compositions and also understand what others have done. Imagine you couldn't read English. All of the information you have learnt from reading this book and all the others you have read wouldn't have been easily available to you. If you were at Town A and needed to get to Town B, you wouldn't be able to just get in a car and drive there, following the road signs or a map, you'd have to ask people on the way, and it would take much longer. If you didn't speak the language, then all of the information would be lost to you. Music theory is simply a way of organising information to make it easier to understand – rather than saying a chord is "That one, you know, the one where it sounds like this and you put your fingers here", you say "C Major" – already you know some theory if you can name a chord you can play – imagine if you couldn't do that.

The other problem is that some who already know music theory guard it secretly to protect it and boost their egos – they can make things sound complex when they are quite simple (although this isn't to say that some music theory isn't complex – it can be). Unfortunately, there are people like this in all walks of life. Remember, if music theory was that complex, then musicians wouldn't be able to understand it!

With that in mind, let's look at some basic concepts.

Musical Notation

Musical notation uses a system of lines and dots to represent notes. There are a number of different clefs which mean that the pitch of the notes for a given line or space is different, but the most common are the treble and bass clefs.

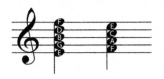 The Treble clef. The spaces between the lines represent the notes F, A, C and E, while the lines are E, G, B, D and F, often remembered with the acronym **E**very **G**ood **B**oy **D**eserves **F**ootball.

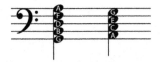 The Bass clef. The spaces here represent A, C, E and G, while the lines are G, B, D, F and A, which has been memorably known as **G**iant **B**ears **D**ance **F**or **A**lan.

There are notes which are between these two clefs (and also above and below their extremes), and they are placed on extra lines which are drawn in, called leger lines. There is only one line between these two clefs in terms of pitch, and that represents middle C (the middle note on a piano keyboard) – it's the first line down from the treble clef, and first line up from the bass clef. Reading note pitches quickly and accurately takes practice, and there are a number of software applications that will help you do this by showing them on screen for you and asking you to name them. The only way to improve is to practice, and after a while you will wonder what all the fuss was about.

Rhythm

Rhythms are written using notes of different lengths, and their corresponding spaces. For the time being, we will look at the most common time signature, 4/4 which has four quarter notes to a bar. Here are the notes, with their equivalent rests and names in both systems.

Note	Rest	Per bar	English name	US Name
		1	Semibreve	Whole note
		2	Minim	Half note
		4	Crotchet	Quarter note
		8	Quaver	Eighth note
		16	Semi-quaver	Sixteenth note
		32	Demi-semi-quaver	Thirty-second note

The US naming system bases the note names on a bar being divided up equally, with each note being half of the previous note duration – the English names are more esoteric, and few sequencing packages make reference to them, using the numerical system instead.

A 4/4 bar can be made up of any of the following:

	1	Whole Semibreve
	2	Half Minim
	4	Quarter Crotchet
	8	Eighth Quaver
	16	Sixteenth Semiquaver
	32	Thirty-Second Demisemiquaver

When notes are written, they can be tied to another note to extend the duration – for instance, if you wanted a note to last one and a half beats, then it would look like this .

A note with a dot after it is 50% longer than the original value – in this case the dotted quarter note would sound the same as the example above – both are one and a half beats.

While learning to read rhythms is outside the scope of this book, it is an important skill which will allow you to understand music a great deal better; rhythm is an underestimated component of music and far more important than many give it credit for. Again, there are a number of software programs which will test you from the very lowest level up to the highest, and in addition there are a lot of books on the subject of rhythm reading. Being able to read is a very useful tool for any musician, regardless of their area of expertise, and if you want to make it as a session musician then it's a pre-requisite.

The Major Scale

The Major scale is the fundamental scale on which all other concepts we will look at are based. For reasons that are not too clear, C major is the 'original' key, where there are no 'sharp' (♯) or 'flat' (♭) notes. Traditional notation (we will only use the treble clef for the time being to avoid confusion) places a note's head either on a line or in a space, with each representing a specific pitch. Middle C (the middle note on a piano keyboard) is shown first, with others following.

This is the scale of C major, from C to C. When played or sung, it is the familiar "do re mi fa so la ti do" which anyone who has seen 'The Sound of Music' will know.

However, looking at a piano keyboard or guitar fretboard will show that the 'gaps' between the notes are not always the same – there is a smaller gap between E and F and also B and C – all the other notes have a 'black' note between (making the gap 2 semitones), while these jump directly to the next note (with only a one semitone gap). This means the pattern between the notes goes as follows:

Note	C		D		E		F		G		A		B		C
Gap		2		2		1		2		2		2		1	

Or Tone-Tone-Semitone-Tone-Tone-Tone-Semitone – this is the pattern for a major scale, so to play one, once you have the first note, you just need to jump up the correct amount of semitones for each note to get a scale which sounds the same.

Sharp Keys

While this is reasonably easy to follow, it does mean that in any key other than C there are some black notes involved. For instance, if we start on the note of G, and move upwards from there playing white notes only, we get a scale which sounds right until the last note:

Note	G		A		B		C		D		E		F		G
Gap		2		2		1		2		2		1		2	

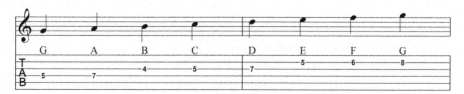

For the most part, the pattern is correct, but the last note (F) is too low. We need to move it up a semitone (to F♯) to regain the same sound. This is why the key of G has a single sharp note in it, F sharp. For each key it is tradition that each note should be represented once – you would not have a G and a G flat in this key.

Note	G		A		B		C		D		E		F♯		G
Gap		2		2		1		2		2		2		1	

The way we create each "sharp" key (i.e. the keys which have notes sharpened) is to start on the fifth note of the key before (in this case we started on the 5th note of C, which was G), to inherit any sharps that are already present, and then sharpen the last note (in the case of G, there were no sharps to inherit, and we sharpened the last note, F, to F♯). We will now do that again. The fifth note of the key of G is D, so we will start from there, and inherit the sharp, in this case just an F♯.

Note	D		E		F♯		G		A		B		C♯		D
Gap		2		2		1		2		2		2		1	

The same can be done for the next key (A)

Note	A		B		C♯		D		E		F♯		G♯		A
Gap		2		2		1		2		2		2		1	

.... and so on for the following keys (E, B, F♯, C♯).

The order that the sharps appears in is always the same – F C G D A E B – and is often represented with an acronym such as **F**ather **C**harles **G**oes **D**own **A**nd **E**nds **B**attle. It doesn't matter what acronym you use, as long as it allows you to remember the order in which the sharps appear.

The Sharp Keys in order

Here is a table showing the progression of sharps as they are introduced.

Key	1	2	3	4	5	6	7	8
C	C	D	E	F	G	A	·B	C
G	G	A	B	C	D	E	F♯	G
D	D	E	F♯	G	A	B	C♯	D
A	A	B	C♯	D	E	F♯	G♯	A
E	E	F♯	G♯	A	B	C♯	D♯	E
B	B	C♯	D♯	E	F♯	G♯	A♯	B
F♯	F♯	G♯	A♯	B	C♯	D♯	E♯	F♯
C♯	C♯	D♯	E♯	F♯	G♯	A♯	B♯	C♯

This table shows the sharps being introduced with the seventh note and then being carried into each following key (starting on the fifth degree of the previous one). You may have noticed something on the last two rows – we have notes which are unusual introduced – E♯ and B♯ - all the other sharp notes we have seen have been black, but in the case of E♯ we would play an F on the keyboard, and for a B♯ we would play a C. While there are some instruments where there would be a small difference between these two notes (any instrument where the pitch can be controlled precisely, such as a violin or other unfretted string instrument), for our purposes we will treat them as one and the same.

Flat Keys

You may have noticed that we have not covered the key of F. This is because it needs a different method applied, and is a "flat" key – i.e. the original notes are flattened to make the same sound of the Major scale. If we play the white notes of the piano from F upwards, we get the following scale, which sounds like the Major scale for the most part, but the fourth note is wrong....

Note	F		G		A		B		C		D		E		F
Gap		2		2		2		1		2		2		1	

.... the fourth note is too high, and needs to move down one semitone to sound correct. This leads us to the following scale:

Note	F		G		A		Bb		C		D		E		F
Gap		2		2		1		2		2		2		1	

This is the key of F Major, and it is the first 'flat' key. The rule for creating a flat key is to take the previous key (in this case C major), and then start from the fourth note (inheriting any flats already present), and flatten the fourth note of the new key to make it sound correct. This means the next key will be Bb, and it will have two flats, Bb and Eb.

Note	Bb		C		D		Eb		F		G		A		Bb
Gap		2		2		1		2		2		2		1	

The next key is E♭, which has 3 flats:

Note	E♭		F		G		A♭		B♭		C		D		E♭
Gap		2		2		1		2		2		2		1	

Next is A♭, then D♭, then G♭ and finally C♭.

The order in which the flats appears never changes either – B E A D G C F – and is the reverse of the order of sharps, so you can reverse the acronym for sharps to get **B**attle **E**nds **A**nd **D**own **G**oes **C**harles' **F**ather. The next table shows the progression of flat keys.

The flat keys in order

Here is a table of the flat keys as they are introduced

Key	1	2	3	4	5	6	7	8
C	C	D	E	F	G	A	B	C
F	F	G	A	B♭	C	D	E	F
B♭	B♭	C	D	E♭	F	G	A	B♭
E♭	E♭	F	G	A♭	B♭	C	D	E♭
A♭	A♭	B♭	C	D♭	E♭	F	G	A♭
D♭	D♭	E♭	F	G♭	A♭	B♭	C	D♭
G♭	G♭	A♭	B♭	C♭	D♭	E♭	F	G♭
C♭	C♭	D♭	E♭	F♭	G♭	A♭	B♭	C♭

As with the sharp keys, the last two involve notes which may be unfamiliar – in this case the C♭ is played as a B and the F♭ is played as an E.

It is also extremely important to remember that being able to read music (in any key other than C) needs an understanding of which notes are sharp or flat – the key signature will tell you this, but unless you remember the notes (best done by being familiar with that key) you will find it hard to play, and the way to do this is to start out by reading music that is in C, and then learning keys which have one or two sharps or flats, and getting used to remembering those notes – walk before you try to run and play in 6 flats!

Here we have seen the notes that make up the keys, but writing them out each time would be long-winded and make the piece look messy (and indeed more difficult to read and understand), so instead they are written at the beginning of a piece of music, and then remembered each time that note is played.

For instance, if you are in the key of G major, you have one sharp, F♯. The key signature would look as shown on the left. The sharp appears on the F line, meaning that all the Fs should be played as F sharps.

The key signature for E♭ Major has three flats (B♭, E♭, A♭) and looks as shown to the right. The sharps or flats should always be in the correct order, and that is the order in which they occur above.

Reading Key Signatures

We have just seen how the keys are created, but reading a key signature is another skill. After some time and practice you will be able to remember many of the keys, but before this happens, there are simple rules you can use to work out what key a piece is in. If it is a sharp key, then the key is a semitone up from the last sharp (remember to read them in the order they appear, left to right) – if the last sharp is an F♯ then you are in the key of G. If the last one is a G♯ then you are in A. If you read a flat key, then the last but one flat is the key you are in. B♭ has two flats – B♭ and E♭ in the key signature, in that order. If you see B♭ E♭ and A♭ then you are in the key of E♭. The only key that this rule doesn't work for is F, which only has one flat. Alas, you will have to remember that one!

The Circle of Fifths

The relationship between the keys we have looked at in the previous sections is often shown as the circle (or cycle) of fifths. This shows all the key signatures in a circle, usually showing sharp keys as clockwise from the key of C and flat keys as anticlockwise. Some keys overlap (with enharmonic notes - see page 142), as you can imagine as we have seen more than 12 keys in total. Here is a representation of the circle of fifths . The major keys are shown around the outside, with minor keys shown in lower case around the inside. The number of sharps or flats is shown within the circle itself, and around the outside are the key signatures themselves.

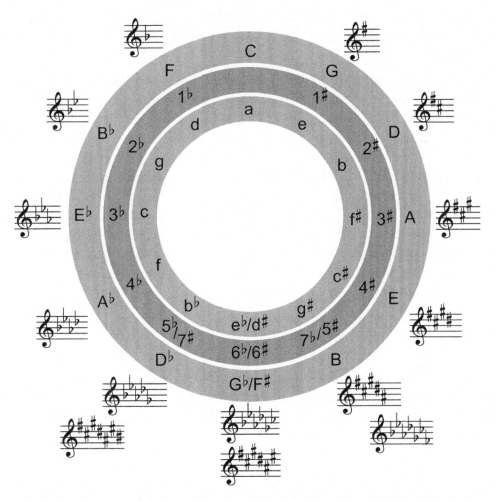

The further round the circle you go from any given key, the less they have in common. Being familiar with the keys here and the number of sharps or flats in them is useful knowledge to acquire, and often it being presented in this form helps it to be committed to memory.

More complexity

Musical notation is intended to be logical, and to cover most eventualities. However, the nature of it can mean that sometimes it can be daunting to the beginner, and some of the following information may help.

Enharmonic Notes

These are notes which are written differently, but sound the same. For instance, all the sharp notes have a corresponding flat – F♯ is the same as G♭, but it is important to avoid using the incorrect term. The key of G contains an F♯ not a G♭, and (as mentioned above) each key should contain one of each note. Enharmonic notes can become important when describing intervals too. You should also know that there is a small difference between these two notes when played on an instrument where the player has control over intonation (such as the violin), but for our purposes we can treat them as one and the same.

Dynamics

Dynamics are an important part of any performance – the difference between quiet and loud and the application of those two extremes (and everywhere in between) can make or break a piece. As with many musical notation terms, the words originated in Italian. *p* is short for Piano, which means quiet. *f* is short for Forte, which means loud. To encompass a wider range, multiple letters are used, so *pp* means very quiet, while *fff* means very, very loud. In between these they can be combined with *m* (meaning mezzo, 'moderately'), making *mf* and *mp*. These terms describe basic dynamic levels, but in addition, there are graphic symbols which show a progressive change between levels, the crescendo and decrescendo (or diminuendo). They are shown below, and are straightforward – the lines moving further apart mean an increase in volume while closer together mean getting quieter.

There are many more esoteric pieces of musical syntax that you may encounter, but for the most part if you know basic rhythms, are able to read the bass and treble clefs and have learned how dynamics work, you should be able to get by in many situations.

Intervals

An interval consists of two notes. They can be played together (a harmonic interval) or separately (a melodic interval) – in either case, the interval is the same. They describe the distance between two notes, and these descriptions are based around the major scale.

Bottom Note	Top Note	Semitones	Interval Name	Abbreviation
C	Db	1	Minor 2nd	m2 / b9
C	D	2	Major 2nd	2 / 9
C	Eb	3	Minor 3rd	m3
C	E	4	Major 3rd	3
C	F	5	Perfect 4th	4 / 11
C	Gb	6	Diminished 5th	b5
C	G	7	Perfect 5th	5
C	Ab	8	Minor 6th	m6 / b13
C	A	9	Major 6th	6 / 13
C	Bb	10	Minor 7th	m7
C	B	11	Major 7th	7
C	C	12	Perfect Octave	

If a **major** interval is **decreased** by one semitone, it becomes **minor**

If a **minor** interval is **increased** by one semitone, it become **major**

If a **perfect** interval is **decreased** by one semitone, it becomes **diminished**

If a **perfect** interval is **increased** by one semitone, it becomes **augmented**

Some intervals (2,4,6) are usually referred to as flat 9,11,13 as they are usually played an octave above the root.

In theory, intervals can be more complex than this (for instance, although Gb and F# are the same note to the listener, the interval from C to Gb is a diminished 5th, while the interval from C to F# is an augmented 4th), but for the most part these descriptions will stand. It is good practice to be able to identify intervals by ear, and a range of ear-training software is available for this task – as with many other elements covered here, practice makes perfect, and with just a few minutes spent on it each day you can become very good at recognising these intervals. If you play the guitar, it is a good idea to know the shapes that intervals form on your instrument (bearing in mind they may change depending on the combination of strings you are playing them on). Without understanding intervals, it is difficult to see how chords are constructed.

Chords

Chords are groups of notes – three or more. They can be constructed from a variety of different notes, but the simplest are three-note chords which are constructed by taking the first note of a scale, and then adding two notes above, one a third above (missing out the next scale step), and one a fifth above the original (which is a third above the third itself). In the case of a chord built on a C using the notes of C Major, the notes C – E – G are used, and this makes a major triad. It has two intervals inside it, a major third (from the C to the E) and a perfect fifth (from the C to the G).

If the notes of the C major scale have chords built upon them using the same method (skipping notes), then the following chords are made:

Note	1	2	3	4	5	6	7
Root	C	D	E	F	G	A	B
3rd	E	F	G	A	B	C	D
5th	G	A	B	C	D	E	F
Chord	Major	Minor	Minor	Major	Major	Minor	Dim.
Degree	I	ii	iii	IV	V	vi	vii
Notes							

The chords built on the 1st, 4th and 5th notes are Major – they are the "Primary" chords of the key, and often used in many songs, as we will see.

The chords built on the 2nd, 3rd and 6th notes are Minor – the distance from the root note to the fifth is a perfect 5th (seven semitones), but the distance from the root to the third is a minor third (3 semitones), hence the chord being a minor.

Chord	Third	Fifth	Symbol
Major	Major	Perfect	maj or M
Minor	Minor	Perfect	min or m or -
Diminished	Minor	Diminished	dim

The last chord (built on the seventh note) is different to all the other chords, in that it has a minor third, but also the distance from the root note to the fifth is smaller than the other chords, being 6 semitones – a diminished fifth.

The 'degree' row shows how chords are often referred to in theoretical analysis. The reason for this is simple – the analysis itself doesn't depend on what key the chord progression is, so it's simpler to talk in terms of "Chord 5" rather than G, as G could belong to a number of keys. The use of roman numerals makes it easier to distinguish between chords (as we'll see later), and using small letters for minor and capitals for major makes analysis simpler too.

The order of chords that are created when harmonising a major scale never alters – it is worth doing it in full several times so that you get used to the order of notes when building chords (skipping every other note), but you should memorise the order of chords, Major, Minor, Minor, Major, Major, Minor, Diminished. It is also important to remember that these are triads, and to refer to them as such – as we will see later on there are other chords which have four (or more) notes in them, which need to be referred to correctly to avoid confusion.

Inversions

Chords are not always presented in the manner we have seen. What we have seen so far is called root position – i.e. the root note of the chord is at the bottom. They can, however, have any note within the chord as the lowest note, and this is called inversion. Take the chord of C major seen above – it can be played with either the C, E or G as the bottom note of the chord.

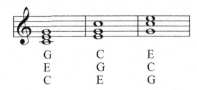

G	C	E
E	G	C
C	E	G

All three are C major, but they sound different as the pattern of intervals inside the chord is different. Whenever you look at a chord, you should look to see if it isn't actually a simpler one that has been inverted. Inversions are named according to the bottom note only – if the bottom note is the third of the chord, then it is a first inversion chord. If the bottom note is the fifth, then it's a second inversion and so on. The order that the other notes appear above it doesn't change the inversion's name. We will see shortly that inversions can be used to create variation without actually changing chord.

It is also important when looking at music which is not played on the keyboard to realise that sometimes the root position versions of a chord may be difficult or impossible to play on other instruments, such as the guitar, and also may simply be uncommon anyway, due to the 'standard' chord voicings on an instrument.

For instance, if you were to harmonise the scale of C major, you would get the following:

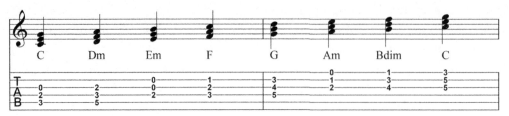

This shows the chords in musical notation, and how they could be played on the guitar, in TAB. However, if you were to ask a guitarist to play them, you would be far more likely to get something like this:

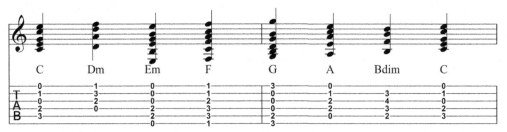

Which contains all the right notes, with the correct note at the bottom, but looks a lot more involved at a first glance. This may also explain why many guitarists find reading notation intimidating – something that they learnt to play at a very early stage looks quite daunting when written on manuscript. If you look in the Effective Sequencing chapter on page 72 you will also see a guide on how to sequence convincing-sounding guitar parts, using these kind of chords.

Chords with more notes

So far, we have only been dealing with chords that contain 3 notes. However, it is possible to use more when writing a piece of music, so we will now look at the next step, chords with 4 notes in them. They are constructed in the same way, by 'skipping' notes, and they actually just add another note on top of the original triad we have already seen.

Note	1	2	3	4	5	6	7
Root	C	D	E	F	G	A	B
3rd	E	F	G	A	B	C	D
5th	G	A	B	C	D	E	F
7th	B	C	D	E	F	G	A
Type	Maj7th	Min7th	Min7th	Maj 7th	Dom. 7th	Min 7th	Min 7th b5
Degree	I	ii	iii	IV	V	vi	vii
Notes							

Here we have new chords – two variations that are Major (Major 7th and Dominant 7th) and two Minor (Minor 7th and Minor 7th(b5)). They are shown in the table below, with the intervals present, and also common symbols for writing them.

Chord	Third	Fifth	Seventh	Symbol
Major 7th	Major	Perfect	Major	maj 7 or Δ7
Dominant 7th	Major	Perfect	Minor	dom or 7
Minor 7th	Minor	Perfect	Minor	min7 or m7 or -7
Minor 7th(b5)	Minor	Diminished	Minor	m7(b5) or Ø

Here are the chords, and their TAB versions for guitar:

These are uncommon shapes on the guitar as they are difficult or impossible to play for many – the following voicings are far more common:

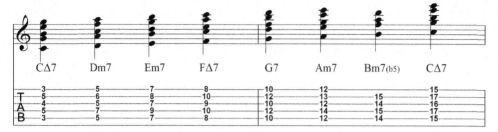

Reading Chords

It is an important skill to be able to read chords when written down, and analyse what is happening – not only is this a useful musical skill, it will almost certainly be a part of your A level course. To this end, you should learn how to read chords. There are a few pointers to take into account –

Remember the Key

When a piece of music doesn't have any accidentals in it (sharps or flats which are not a part of the key signature) then any chords present will be those found by harmonising the major scale. As you have seen on there is a fixed pattern of chords in each key – when triads, chords I, IV and V are always Major, chords ii, iii and vi are always Minor, and chord vii is Diminished. If you know these chords well, and see a chord in root position which is based on one, you will know if it's major, minor or diminished straight away. If it's a four-note chord, then the pattern of chords shown on page 147 will be the ones to know – if it's Chord V (for instance) then it will be a Dominant 7th chord. This can make analysis and playing much easier and quicker, and the more you do it the more natural it will become.

Make sure you take the bass note into account – this is one of the most common errors made when reading parts. If you see the notes of a chord played on an upper-register instrument (such as the guitar or right-hand of a keyboard part), make sure you take the bass note into account (often played by the left-hand of the keyboard part or a bass instrument). Without doing this you will often read the chord incorrectly.

Here is an example – the right-hand of the piano part plays the same triad twice (C major), but the bass note changes – in bar 1 it is a C (so the chord is still C), while in bar 2 it is playing an A (making an A minor 7 chord). This can often happen in real-world situations as many keyboard and guitar players will play a triad which gives the required chord only when added to the appropriate bass note.

Once you have analysed a chord, check to see if it fits in the key you are in – if it hasn't got any accidental notes, then it should fit with the same pattern of chords seen above; if it doesn't then you may have misread it. Also it is often a good idea to make sure that the chords fit in context – there are situations where some chords will fit because of what precedes and follows them.

Get the notes in the right order

A common problem to have is to get notes in the wrong order, and thereby over-complicate matters. This can be overcome by firstly making sure you are starting on the right note, and secondly by re-ordering the other notes that appear into one that makes musical sense. To find the root note of the chord, it is often best to look in the bass part – either a separate bass instrument, or the left-hand part of a keyboard instrument. There are exceptions to this (sometimes the bass will be inverted, playing a third or fifth of a chord), but in many cases this will help.

Next, order the notes correctly – this is done by looking at all the notes which are present in the chord, and then ordering them in thirds, ascending from your bass note. Take the following example:

Here we have a chord which is inverted. It is played over an F bass note, and in the right hand we have the notes C,E,F and A.

Starting with the bass note, we will put these notes into ascending order, climbing in thirds.

To remember this order, if you memorise the following – ACEGBDFACEGBDF (which repeats indefinitely) you will be able to re-order the notes quickly. Starting at the F, we find we have A, C and finally E. This means we have an F Major 7 chord, which was in 2nd inversion (as it had the fifth, C, as the lowest note in the main chord). The following diagram shows the original inverted chord, and how the notes move to the correct order to find the original.

More examples

Here is a first inversion chord, so only the B♭ has been moved an octave above its original position. Re-ordering the notes gives us B♭, D, E♭ and A♭, which is a B♭ dominant 7th chord (B♭7).

This is a second-inversion chord, with the original order being C♯, E, F♯, A. Placing these in the correct order gives us F♯, A, C♯ and E, which make F♯ Minor 7.

This is a third inversion chord; the notes of the right-hand part are G, with A, C and E above it. Re-ordering it gives us A, C, E and G, which is an A minor 7 chord (Am7).

This is also a third inversion chord, but features five notes instead of the four of the previous examples. Initially the notes are G,B,D,C and E, and re-ordering them gives us C,E,G,B and D, making a C Major 9 chord, sometimes written as CΔ9

In all the examples above, the bass note has been given in the left-hand part of the piano (or would be read from the bass instrument), but sometimes the bass note that's being played isn't the right one for the chord; sometimes this will make itself apparent when you analyse the chord and it seems overly complex (in an otherwise simple piece), and sometimes you will need to look for other clues as to the 'real' bass note (such as examining the motion of chords that is occurring at a given time). If you see the section on 'Using the Bass Note' (on page 155) then you will see more on this – often experience and a good ear will help you through this, so try to analyse simple pieces at first! Reading music is a skill which only improves with practice – the more you do, the better and quicker you become at it. Being able to read and analyse chords with reasonable speed is an important skill and one which will be helpful throughout your musical career.

Harmonising a Melody

There are a number of ways to use these chords, but one of the simplest (and often most effective) when trying to create an arrangement is to look at the notes of a melody and then try playing chords that have the melody note in. Take the following melody:

It is in the key of C Major. Because we are using 3-note chords, we have three options for each – the melody note could be the root, third or fifth of each chord, as shown to the right.

The melody note here is a C, so we can use either C (C-E-G), Am (A-C-E) or F (F-A-C), each of which will work with the melody note. You can play this on the keyboard, or on the guitar – if you want to do so on the guitar, just play a normal chord shape, but ensure that the melody note is the highest pitch that you play (usually this will just mean missing out one or two notes at the top of the chord).

Using this technique, for the first bar it would be possible to use three different chords for each beat, giving us up to 81 possibilities, without any variations being introduced. However, you will not normally want to listen to this many versions, and would often not wish to change chord each beat, possibly only using one chord per bar. Here is one version of the melody, with chords shown below.

Or, for the guitar:

Here bar 1 has been harmonised with a C Major (I) (from the C first note in the melody), bar 2 with an E Minor (iii) (from the E in the melody), and the rest with C Major (I). While this is functional, it's somewhat boring, as what has happened is the first note of each bar has been harmonised, and lasts for the rest of the bar.

Even with this simple accompaniment there are 81 different options we could take (3 for each bar), so you could make many different versions – try them out with your own melody.

There are many different tools available to the arranger, and to cover them all would take several books. One of the most important to remember is that some chords 'want' to resolve to another chord - the tension that has been created will be released, and the chord progression will sound finished. The most common example of this is that the V chord (in this case G Major) resolves to the I chord (C Major).

This is extremely common, and will introduce some tension (with the V chord) that is then released when the I chord is played. This is a technique we will see more of later on, but the creation and then release of tension is a powerful tool in composition and arrangement. Once added to our melody above, we get something like this:

Or for the guitar, this:

This is already more pleasing than the original, with the simple addition of the G (V) chord in bar 3. This creates some tension which is resolved by the C (I) chord in bar 4. We will see a further use of this technique later on.

Movement

There is another aspect to harmony that should never be forgotten – context. Taken in isolation, many harmonies may not make too much sense, but when they are viewed as being a part of a whole, and movement is taken into account, then they can work well.

It's possible to make chords move in the direction they are eventually headed, to 'fill in the gaps' as it were. This is shown in the example below, which bridges the gap between the C (I) and Em(iii) chords with a Dm (ii) chord.

Or for the guitar:

The Dm (ii) chord with an E above in bar 1 sounds a little odd when played on its own, but in context it makes sense as the chords are climbing up to their destination, Em (iii), and again in bar 2 the otherwise discordant Dm with a G works because there is movement that resolves this and makes sense of it.

This is also commonly seen where lines descend – whether it is a bass note or a melody note, sometimes they may sound odd in isolation. Take the following example:

Or for the guitar:

Or, rearranged for the guitar (the melody line has been moved up an octave):

This sounds fine when played in time, but if we take the what's happening at bar 1, beat 4 and play it in isolation, we get the bar shown to the right – while it may not be the most offensive chord ever, it's certainly a little tense, and needs to resolve.

When in context, however, due to the movement that is happening, it barely raises an eyebrow. Movements such as these should not be ignored when writing or analysing the works of others – it is possible to 'over-analyse' by looking at each chord in isolation, and to come up with some extremely complex harmonies, when in fact what is happening is actually far simpler.

Voice Leading

While it is not possible to cover all the aspects of harmony here, another important thing to remember is often referred to as 'voice leading' – that is the process of making harmonic changes as smooth as possible, while retaining the same notes. While there are many rules which need to be applied to this technique (see "Harmony" by Walter Piston for this subject at some length), at a simple level this mostly occurs by using inversions of chords. Taking our example from earlier on, it is possible to make Bar 3 sound more smooth simply by inverting the chord and moving the root to the top of the chord.

And taking the example from the previous page, we get a much smoother version:

The chords themselves have not changed, but the changes sound a lot smoother as a result of the inversions of the chords. Note that the limitations of some instruments (such as the guitar) can make this a more difficult technique to perform on them. However, when arranging for a number of single-note instruments (such as individual voices or a small ensemble) this technique can lead to much simpler parts which sound far more pleasing to the ear not only in isolation but when played together as well. Creating contrast is often desirable, so a mixture of using smoother parts and those with larger jumps in can also be valid.

Using the bass note

Another area to explore is the use of the bass note for a chord. It is extremely important not to forget about the bass note when analyzing a piece of music (especially from the score), and also when writing music. The three-note chords that were first seen can also be viewed as the top three notes of a four note chord, with the bass providing the last note.

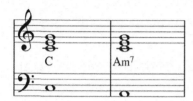

The example on the left shows this – the triad in the left-hand of the piano part doesn't change, but the chord does – firstly (with the C bass), it is a C Major triad. With the A bass, it becomes an A minor 7 chord.

This is an extremely common thing to do – many players of piano and guitar will play a triad that will only form the complete chord when the bass is taken into account, and this is a common thing to see on scores. In addition it can also give rise to some creative possibilities, where you are effectively using voice leading over a whole chord, only altering the bass note and nothing else.

A common use of this is "slash chords", which are commonly seen in jazz and guitar parts. They are written in the form "C/B", which means "play C over a B bass". Sometimes this will actually be a note which is part of the chord (such as the common "D/F♯" which is really just an inversion of D major with the F♯ (the third) in the bass), but other times they will not, and again here it is important to analyse the progression in terms of time – it might well be that the bassline is moving in a certain direction, and forgetting this will make things look far more complex than they actually are. Take the classic chord progression:

While it sounds simple, if you don't take into account the descending bassline, it's easy to 'over-analyse' the chords present and come up with something far more complex than what's really happening as seen on the next page.

This is clearly far more complex than what we hear when listening to it, so whenever you analyse something and it seems to be really complex, try to see if this is being caused by movement which is apparent over time.

Using different chords

So far, we have just seen chords which are 'diatonic' – i.e. they are made up solely of notes within the key we are in. But that isn't something that is used all the time – there are chords which are commonly used which use other notes, and this is often done by 'borrowing' from another parallel key, and these chords are called 'borrowed' chords.

There are quite a wide range of borrowed chords which are used, many of them for certain styles of music – pop, rock and grunge often use this technique. Popularly-used borrowed chords in popular music are shown below:

Scale Degree and chord	Written	Notes and chord in C Major	Notation
Major triad on the flattened third	bIII	Eb, G, Bb Eb Major	
Minor triad on the fourth	iv	F, Ab, C F Minor	
Major triad on the flattened sixth	bVI	Ab, C, Eb Ab Major	
Major triad on the flattened seventh	b VII	Bb, D, F Bb Major	

Modes

So far we have looked at the Major scale, and seen the chords built upon it. Some of the chord progressions we have already seen start and end on the root note of the major scale (C in the key of C), but it is possible to create a chord progression which uses the chords from the key of C but whose arrangement means it will sound at rest on a different chord. Look at the following four chord progressions:

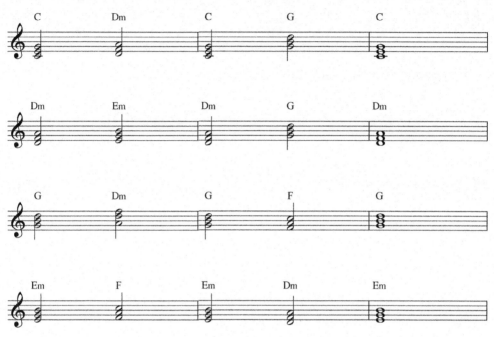

They all use chords from the key of C, but their emphasis is different - each sounds finished, but they 'settle' at different chords - C, Dm, G and Em. If we want to play a melody over them, the notes of C major will fit, but they sound best if the scale starts and ends on the root note of the 'home' chord. Here we see an example which starts and ends on C, so the scale works best when it does the same.

Next, an example starting and ending on Dm with the scale starting and ending on D.

The next example follows suit, starting and ending on G

Finally, another example, starting and ending on an Em chord, with the note of E being played.

What is happening here is that we are using 'modes' - these scales take the notes of a major scale, but use them in a different context by changing the 'home' note; their emphasis (and therefore their sound) is different. The C major scale that we have already seen looks like this:

However, we can start on the second note, to produce a different scale, D Dorian:

When you start a major scale on the second note, the mode is called Dorian.
We can start on each note, and create a different scale each time.

E Phrygian - starting on the third note of a major scale gives a Phrygian mode:

F Lydian

G Mixoydian

A Aeolian

B Locrian

However, creating them like this slightly masks their sound; it can be difficult to hear their true effect because they all use the notes from the key of C, and we tend to remember that when listening to them. The way to hear their true effect is to transpose each one so that they all start on the correct note (easily done by recording the examples before in Cubase and then transposing them down the correct number of semitones so the first note is always C). Then we get the following scales:

C Major

C Dorian

C Phrygian

C Lydian

C Mixolydian

C Aeolian

C Locrian

Now it's much clearer to hear that each scale has its own personality - this is because each one has at least one note which is altered from the major scale. It can be a good idea to listen to each of the scales along with a sustained C bass note - this will provide some context for the scale.

Alterations from the Major Scale

As seen on the staves above, each mode features some alterations from the major scale. The following table shows those alterations, and is presented in order of the number of changes from the major scale, with the least altered scales first and the most altered ones at the end; note that this is not the order that they appear in when created as above.

Major	1	2	3	4	5	6	7
Lydian	1	2	3	♯4	5	6	7
Mixolydian	1	2	3	4	5	6	♭7
Dorian	1	2	♭3	4	5	6	♭7
Aeolian	1	2	♭3	4	5	♭6	♭7
Phrygian	1	♭2	♭3	4	5	♭6	♭7
Locrian	1	♭2	♭3	4	♭5	♭6	♭7

In the above table the 'characteristic note' has been marked with a grey background - this is the note that sets it apart from the other modes. In the case of the dorian, the natural sixth combined with the minor third is its characteristic as it's the only mode to feature this combination, hence both being marked. Note that while the Lydian is the only mode to feature a ♯4 note, the others all feature flats, and those flats accumulate - all the modes after the Mixolydian in the table have the ♭7 note, and all the modes after the Dorian have the ♭3, etc.

Tonal Quality

Arranging the modes in order of 'brightness' is a good task to do; some listeners disagree on the exact order, but in general the preferences go like this:

Brighter	**Lydian**	has more brightness from the ♯4 note
	Major	the reference point
	Mixolydian	a darker version of the major scale with the ♭7
	Dorian	a minor scale, but still bright in tone from the ♮6
Darker	**Aeolian**	a straightforward minor sound
	Phrygian	has a middle-eastern feel from the ♭2 note
	Locrian	a dark-sounding scale with a ♭5 giving an uneasy tonality

Careful use of these modes can help to create specific moods in a piece of music - this can be useful when composing or arranging as it's possible to apply the alterations shown in the table above to alter the nature of a melody and the chords that accompany it.

Scale Assistant

The scale assistant is a tab in the Key Editor inspector. It allows the editing grid to display notes which fit into a selected scale. It can follow the project chord track (see page 186 for details), or work in a manually-set standalone mode. This can be useful for checking if your knowledge of a scale is correct in any key, or for discovery of new scales.

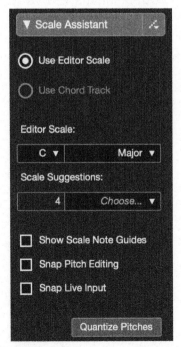

The scale assistant is shown to the left. To activate it, select any of the three options at the bottom - **Show Scale Note Guides**, **Snap Pitch Editing** or **Snap Live Input**. The scale to be used can be chosen by picking the root note and scale type from the two drop-down menus (showing **C Major** by default).

Initially, activating the assistant may be missed - as what it alters is the 'white / black note' colouring in the key editor grid. If you select C Major, then there will be no difference in appearance as this is what the editor defaults to, following the black and white notes of the piano keyboard.

Here is a C Major scale, and the assistant is set to C major, so everything looks as normal. The black notes correspond to the sharp / flat keys of the piano keyboard.

Here, the scale is still C Major, but the assistant has been set to C Aeolian (Natural Minor). Note how three note are now on 'black' lines - E, A and B, because they don't fit in the C Aeolian Scale.

Snap Pitch Editing

Enabling **Snap Pitch Editing** means it is only possible to move notes to a new pitch belonging in the selected scale. An example will show this in action when using the cursor keys.

Here is the original note, an E, which doesn't belong in the scale.

Pressing up moves the note up to F, as normal...

... pressing up again moves it to G - as the F♯ doesn't belong in the scale, and is ignored.

Snap Live Input

As the name suggests, when this is active, any MIDI input will be altered by the scale assistant to follow the selected scale - much like the live transform of scales shown on page 197.

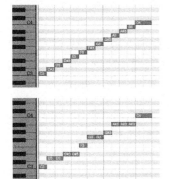

Here is a chromatic scale, played on a keyboard - note that every note is present.

Here, the same scale was played with Snap Live Input active, and any notes not belonging to the scale were altered to fit in.

Note that this will only work if the editor is open and in focus (with a white border) with Record in Editor active - this is indicated at the top left of the window with the red recording indicator. If it is grey or white, then snap live input will not work.

Using Modes to alter a melody and chords

Here we see a familiar melody, 'Twinkle Twinkle Little Star', which has been harmonised using simple chords in the key of C Major.

By applying the alterations in the table on the previous page, it's possible to change the melody and chords to suit new modes.

Lydian: The first alteration will be to use the #4 note, which is F in this case. It changes the melody to a somewhat awkward sound, but the chordal change to F# diminished is quite pleasing:

Mixolydian. This has no effect on the melody in this case as there is no B present, but the change to Gm alters the harmony considerably.

Dorian. This creates a minor sound due to the ♭3(with the Cm joining the G minor), but the natural sixth allows it to retain a bright tonality.

Aeolian. This mode removes this brightness, and the melody sounds considerably 'sadder' than before - the ♭6 note in the melody really does change it greatly, and adds an F minor chord to replace the previous F major, and the chords in the descending section are also altered as a result of the change from A to A♭

Phrygian. This adds the ♭2. This makes for some more interesting harmony, particularly with the G diminished chord which is now present. The melody is affected by the change as well, sounding even sadder than the Aeolian.

Locrian. This is quite a difficult listen, and indeed so much so that the descending chord section in bars 3-4 sounds as if it's from another key. This version suffers from the ♭5 meaning that it's far less easy to discern the home note - our start and end chord is a diminished one.

It is worth experimenting with modes to see what alterations they can provide to a pre-existing idea; they will often throw up harmony or melody ideas which would be unlikely without knowledge of them, and can lead to new and interesting ideas as a result of them. It is not always the case that they can be applied without some further modification (as often some notes will need adjustment particularly in melodies to make them work well), but they can considerably expand your palette as a composer or arranger.

Chords from Modes

The previous sections have concentrated mostly on the alterations away from the major scale for melodies, and altered the chords in an 'incidental' manner. But as we saw on page 143, the order of chords created by when harmonising a major scale is always the same - Major, Minor, Minor, Major, Major, Minor, Diminished. And this is true for the modes - they all create their own order, but plotting them out in a table shows how those chords change between modes:

	1	2	3	4	5	6	7
Lydian	Maj	Maj	min	dim	Maj	min	min
Major	Maj	min	min	Maj	Maj	min	dim
Mixolydian	Maj	min	dim	Maj	min	min	♭Maj
Dorian	min	min	♭Maj	Maj	min	dim	♭Maj
Aeolian	min	dim	♭Maj	min	min	♭Maj	♭Maj
Phrygian	min	♭Maj	♭Maj	min	dim	♭Maj	♭min
Locrian	dim	♭Maj	♭min	min	♭Maj	♭Maj	♭min

Note that the ♭ before any chord shows that it is a chord built on the flattened degree of the scale (such as E♭ Major for the third chord in the Dorian mode). By following a column vertically, it is possible to see the alteration in the chords as the modes proceed. Note how chord 1 starts out as Major (for Lydian, Major and Mixolydian), becomes minor (for Dorian, Aeolian and Phrygian), and then becomes diminished for Locrian. This table makes it possible to see where the chords shown on page 156 come from, and also highlights which modes are appropriate for them; for instance, the major triad on the flattened 7th of the scale (♭Maj) is common to Mixolydian, Dorian and Aeolian, and depending on the situation, any of those modes may fit at that point. It is also possible to see how any of these chords can provide a "gateway" to another mode if that chord (or more than one) is common between two modes.

Development of a Melody or Rhythm

The techniques already seen will allow you to develop a chord progression and alter chords and a melody to a different mode, but there are other techniques that can be used to develop a melody (or a rhythmic pattern for most of these techniques); for most listeners the most memorable part of a song is the melody, so being able to alter it in a musical and memorable manner is important. Here is our original melodic idea, which will be developed using the following techniques.

As can be seen, it starts and ends on C, and features a number of different note lengths.

Repetition

Repeating a melody without any changes is a valid technique, but it is important not to over-use it; while it is extremely common in some styles such as Blues, it needs to be used sparingly, although in some styles use of repetition can help give a listener some structure to hold onto.

Transposition

Transposition means moving a melodic idea to a new starting note. There are two main ways of achieving this.

Tonal

This is when the starting note of the idea is moved to another note within the scale. The movement between notes is preserved, but only in scale steps, not in terms of semitones. This means the intervals between notes will change, and it will sound different as a result of this, but it will stay within the key it is in, and therefore usually fit with the current accompaniment. The example shows the original melody from the previous page transposed with two different starting notes, firstly with an E:

Here it is starting with an F.

Note that no accidentals occur - both melodies are diatonic and 'fit' within the key that the original piece was in.

Exact

This method of transposition is where the exact intervals between notes are pre-served - it is moved into another key. Compare these two versions with those in the section above. Each starts on the same note, but the end result is different as clearly seen in the notation - first the example starting on an E:

Here it is starting with an F:

Note how each example includes accidentals, and in this case (as the original started on a C and was in the key of C) these are from the key of the starting note. Depending on the accompaniment, there may be some changes needed to allow this to work.

Sequences

A logical progression when transposing is to repeat the a melody or phrase at a number of pitches, as seen below.

Inversion

An inversion is where a melodic idea is turned upside-down. As with transposition, there are two ways to approach this, Tonal and Exact.

Tonal

Here the steps within the scale are inverted - they are moved in terms of scale steps, not in terms of semitones.

Exact

Here the inversion is performed in terms of semitones, so it is an exact semitone-based mirror image of the original, but due to this it will often involve notes that were not present in the original key, generating a more colourful phrase which is less like the original.

Retrograde

There are several ways of creating a retrograde, which means to reverse the phrase. The first is the most common, but the other two methods have their uses.

Strict

Here the entire idea is reversed - the notes appear in the reverse order of the original.

Pitch

Here the original rhythm is retained, but the note pitches are played in the reverse of their original order.

Rhythm

Here the rhythm is reversed, but the note pitches are retained in their original order

Adding Notes

Any long notes within an idea can be subdivided into shorter ones. It can be particularly useful to do this in a manner where there is a new rhythm which is carried within these long notes (if not for the entire phrase)

Removing Notes

This is the removal of notes, typically those which are off-beat and possibly ones that fall on beats 2 and 4 (depending on the style of music you are writing).

Augmentation

The increase in note (and rest) duration in an idea. This is easily performed in Cubase by setting the Selection tool to `Sizing Applies Timestretch` and doubling the length of the part.

Diminution

This is the counterpart of augmentation, where note and rest lengths are divided by a given amount. Again, in Cubase this is achieved easiest by using `Sizing Applies Timestretch` and halving the length of the part.

Rhythmic Offset

By changing the timing of the first note of a phrase, it can be altered significantly with respect to the backing. This technique is extremely easy to achieve in Cubase, by setting **Snap** to a small figure such as a **Beat**, 1/8 or 1/16 and moving the part in question in relation to its backing. Here the original idea has been offset by 1/8.

While this may look only slightly different when written down, when heard with an accompaniment it can transform the function of a melody; many composers have made significant use of this technique as it offers so many possibilities.

Common tricks

In addition to what we've seen above, there are a number of common techniques which can be applied to a chord sequence to create more interest; in any given situation some will work and some will not, but only experimentation will tell.

Relatives

The first technique to try is to replace a major chord with its relative minor (or a minor with a major). The relative minor of a major chord is found a minor third (3 semitones) below the original. For instance, C major has a relative minor of A minor, and E major has a relative minor of C♯ minor.

The relative major is the complement of that – it is 3 semitones above a minor chord, so the relative major of F minor is Ab Major, and the relative major of B minor is D.

Take the following chord progression –

The relative minor of C is Am, F is Dm (already present), and of G is Em. Any combination of these can be inserted, as seen below (where the first and last have been replaced with relative minors)

However, as the original chord progression wasn't particularly exciting, while this gives some more interest, it is not a dramatic departure from the original. We can alter it by using the original chords for the first two beats of each bar, and the substitutes for the third and fourth beats.

This provides far more interest, with very little effort. However, if the original is a non-diatonic chord progression - using chords which are not made using only the notes which are in the original major key - the results can be far more interesting.

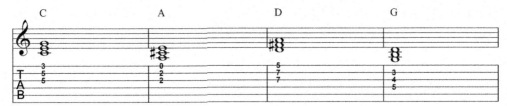

Here we have a chord progression which isn't in the key of C as it features an A major (with a C♯) and D major (with an F♯). The relative minors of these chords are Am, F♯m, Bm and Em respectively, and using them as the second half of each bar gives us the following result:

This is far more interesting than the original, with a lot of movement. You needn't replace every chord, or use the 'alternating' method here, but relative chords offer a lot of scope to obtain more mileage from original material.

Two Before Five

This is a commonly-used technique in Jazz, but can be applied to many other styles. It involves putting the ii chord before a V chord. Take the following chord progression:

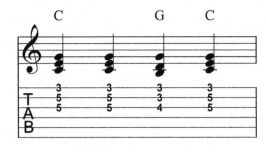

It is extremely simple, with just the I (C) and V (G) chords being played in it. It can be made more interesting by placing the ii (Dm) chord before the V chord, as seen below....

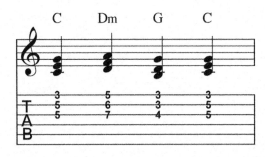

.... the addition of which creates another sensation of "dropping down a fifth" as the Dm is a fifth above the G, but stays completely in key.

This is extremely common, and the resulting "Two Five One" (ii V I) chord progression (in this case, Dm-G-C) is a staple of many jazz and pop compositions alike.

Five of Five

Another similar technique is called "Five of Five", in which the V chord is treated as being the I chord of a new key, and then preceded by that key's V chord.

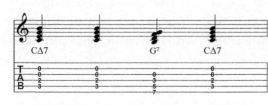

Again, we start with the original chord progression involving just CΔ7(I) and G7(V) chords, nothing else. However, the V chord can be treated as the I chord of a new key (G major), the V of which would be D7.

… which leads us to this – it is similar to the ii-V-I we saw previously, but as it has a 7 chord, the 'pull' to the next chord is stronger, and the introduction of a non-diatonic note (in this case an F#) which creates colour and interest. This idea can be extended further….

… to precede the D7 with its V chord, being A7, which creates even more colour, but still logically descends down to our original target chord, CΔ7.

Note that you can mix these two techniques up, as seen here:

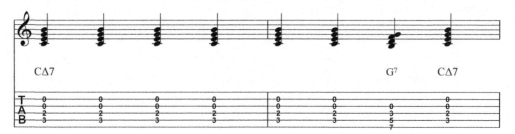

Here is our original chord progression, all CΔ7 with a G7 on the last but 1 beat.

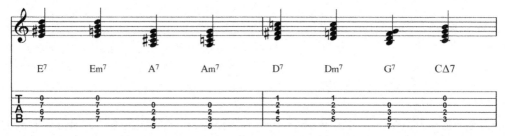

Here is the 'final' version – each 7 chord is the V of a chord that follows it (for instance the E7 at the beginning is the V chord of the following A7 chord), while the m7 chords are created using the "ii before V" technique – the Em7 is the ii chord to the A7 (V) following. When this is played at a brisk tempo, there is too much information occurring at one time, but given enough time for each chord to be taken on board (perhaps a bar or so), then this works well, and even using the technique once can take you in new directions. There are many examples of songwriters using V chords to create some colour within an otherwise mundane chord progression.

Flat Five Substitution

Another common trick makes use of the symmetry which is contained in a dominant 7th chord (V7). The interval between the 3rd and 7th is a flattened 5th, which is 6 semitones. The octave is made up of 12 semitones which means the interval will be the same whether the 3rd is below or above the 7th. This means it is possible for the 3rd and 7th to be swapped over, and be the 7th and 3rd respectively of another dominant 7th chord; the chord in question will be a flattened fifth away from the original root note. Here is an example:

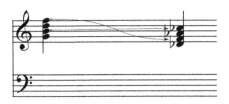

The first chord is a G7, whose 7th is the 3rd of the second chord, a Db7. The 3rd of the G7 is a B, and this is the 7th of the Db7, although it is written as a Cb - the notes are enharmonic and the same pitch in practice.

This means that it is possible to substitute a seventh chord for one that is a flattened fifth away from it - when the original is followed by chord 1 (i.e. a C in the key of C) then it will create interest and colour with a chromatic movement (such as from Db7 to C).

Here is the original progression, IV V I with the G7 chord (V) resolving to C (I). While it is functional, it is quote boring.

Here the flat 5 substitution has been used, to replace the second G7 (V) chord with one a flat fifth away, in this case a Db7 chord, which is a semitone above the destination of C.

Again, this substitution can work in other areas, but it needs to be applied with care if it is to work well.

Modulation

Modulation is another word for changing key. Many songs do this – sometimes this is used to get more mileage out of otherwise identical musical material, sometimes it is used to make a change of section more pronounced. However, there are several ways to change key, some of them simple, some of them less so.

Direct Modulation

This is where the piece simply modulates (normally up) by a certain amount, often a semitone or tone, with no new musical section to bridge the gap between the two keys, and no 'hinting' that the key is about to change – almost as if a switch has been thrown, suddenly the piece is in a new key. It is often disparagingly referred to as the "Truckdriver's Gearchange" as it mimics the sound of a truck's engine when going uphill and a lower gear is selected, although while it has become cliché, as is often the case that has happened because it is a technique which works and has been repeated often. Here is an example of this.

Here, the song simply shifts up a semitone into the new key (from C to D♭, repeating the original material with no changes. This serves to create more excitement/ interest with very little cost (other than credibility). This is the simplest method of changing key, and is somewhat limited in its scope, although it has been used a great many times (and indeed more than once in a song, if you take the example of "My Generation" by The Who, for instance). It can also be used with a larger interval (such as a fourth or fifth), although this is less common, often due to the large vocal range needed to encompass such a piece.

Reinforcing the Key Change

There is a simple technique you can use to allow you to change successfully into any other key, and that is using the Perfect Cadence (from chord V to chord I, such as G to C in the key of C). This resolution is so strong that it will make the listener feel that they are in the new key straight away. Here is an chord progression, with a direct modulation to the new key.

It works, but in a sort of "Boy Band" way – the key change is felt after a short time in the new key, but it's not a great way to change from one key to the other.

We need to use the V chord of the new key, in this case it is A Major. The key of C contains an A Minor, so as soon as the A Major is played the addition of the C# will create interest (making the listener feel that a change has occurred), and also by next playing a D, the modulation will be complete. With no other preparation, we have a more solid and definite key change – the A chord is replacing the last two beats of the G chord, creating harmonic interest for a couple of beats, and leading us to our destination.

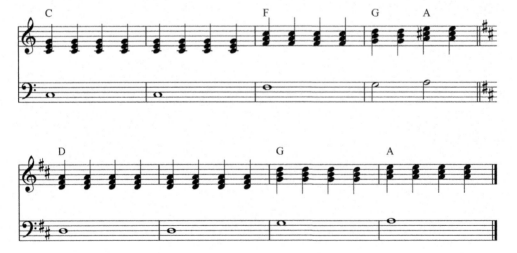

This works far better than the previous example, and yet it is the most rudimentary way of introducing the V chord of the new key. With a more suitable chord progression and more time spent getting to the V chord, the change can be made more interesting and work more smoothly.

Here is where your creativity will come into play – the way of introducing the new key (and firstly the V chord of the new key) will depend on three factors:

The original chord progression – this may well control how easily the new chord slips into the progression; some make it a straightforward replacement, while others will need more invention. Remember that it's the destination that's important – often you can introduce completely new chords which eventually lead to the desired chord and it will make sense (a bit like being led through a maze, and coming out the other end and it suddenly making sense).

The change between the two keys – this again can control how easy it is to introduce the new key's V chord. For instance, if you are in the key of C, and want to change to F, then the V chord of the new key is C as well, so to emphasize the change the chord can be played as C major 7 (the I chord of C Major), and then C 7 (the V chord of F major). Other changes are not as convenient.

The musical style you are writing in and your interpretation of it. Some styles allow for complex changes to be introduced – jazz, for example, can take just about anything as long as the destination is reached and indeed a level of complexity is almost required. In a pop music tune, such complex changes may be less welcome.

In addition your inventiveness will control the outcome – you should look for several ways to bridge the gap between the two keys, looking for similarities in chords or notes of them to create an interesting and competent key change.

Hinting at the new key

Another method is to use accidental notes to hint at the key change that is coming – for instance, if the song is currently in C, but we wish to go to G Major, the only difference (apart from the emphasis on given chords) is that there is an F♯ present – all the other notes are unaltered. It is possible to 'hint' that the keychange is coming by using this accidental, as seen below, while not actually changing key – this will happen particularly if the V-I change used above to reinforce a key change is avoided, or is used in the original key. Once the modulation does occur (using one of the other methods shown here), it will have been anticipated by the listener and will be welcomed.

Using a pivot chord

Sometimes a more dramatic change of key is desired, and this can be achieved by using chords which are common to both keys (called a "pivot" chord). There are many keys that share chords, and the more closely related they are, the larger the number of shared chords. Take the following two keys, C and G, one step from each other on the cycle of fifths. The chords are as follows (written starting from C for both keys to make comparison easier)

C	**C Major**	D Minor	**E Minor**	F Major	**G Major**	**A Minor**	B Dim
G	**C Major**	D Major	**E Minor**	F♯ Dim	**G Major**	**A Minor**	B Minor

Here we can see that there are four chords which are common to the two keys – G Major, A Minor, C Major and E Minor. Any of these chords can be used as a pivot chord between the two keys, as we will now see.

Here is an example which demonstrates the change that using the V of the new key can make (even though it is only one note that changes). If you play the following chord progression, the G at the end feels unresolved, as we still feel that we are in the key of C and we have ended on an unresolved V chord.

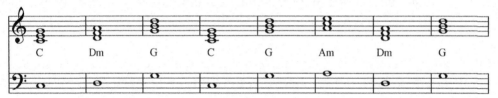

However, if you alter the F to an F♯ then the G now feels like the I chord of the new key, and is resolved.

When analysing such a progression, it is possible to analyse the pivot chord/s as belonging to either key, but once the modulation has actually occurred (i.e. a chord from the new key has been played) then the key has actually changed, and it now belongs to the new key. On the next page we see an analysis of the chords above:

C	Dm	G	C	G	Am	D	G
I	ii	V	I	V	vi	D	I
				I	ii	V	

The G and the Am can be analysed as being in either the key of C or G. Once the D has occurred, the key has changed to G, and this is reinforced by the following G (the I chord of the new key, not the V chord of the previous key), forming a V – I progression.

If you move to a key which is one step round the cycle of fifths away then it will share four chords. If you move two steps then only two chords will be common, limiting your choice of shared chord. Chords iii and V of the original key are common as chords ii and IV of the new key (as seen in the table).

C	C Major	D Minor	**E Minor**	F Major	**G Major**	A Minor	B Dim
D	C♯ Dim	D Major	**E Minor**	F♯ Minor	**G Major**	A Major	B Minor

However, this 'limitation' opens up other creative possibilities – there are a number of chords now which change type while remaining on the original root note (in this case the D Minor in the key of C becomes a D Major in the key of D, while the A Minor of C becomes an A Major in D) – this change of chord from major to minor (or vice versa) can be used to add harmonic interest to the piece. If you are using four-note chords, then even the common Major chord features a change as it will be a Dominant 7th chord in the original key, but become a Major 7th in the new key, also offering similar possibilities. This is part of a concept called 'Pitch Axis Theory' where a succession of chords uses the same root note, but will change chord due to what is effectively a change of key/mode. Some artists have made extensive use of this, creating chord progressions where the root note stays the same, but the chord changes as the key (or rather the mode) changes, leading to different harmony.

Bear in mind that this example was taken going from C to D – if the movement was in the opposite direction (D to C) the chords would still be common, but the changes of chord type would work in the opposite direction as well.

Common Tone Modulation

As we have already seen, there are common chords between different keys, although only a few. There are far more common tones – indeed there are far more notes in common between neighbouring keys (6) than chords (4), and if you jump two steps then you only have two chords, but still have 5 notes. Common tone modulation works by using a sustained note to 'bridge' between two keys, where the note is common between both keys.

Ear Training

One of the most important things you can do to improve your ability as a musician, composer and arranger is to practice ear training – i.e. to learn to recognise musical elements by ear, without reference to an instrument to work things out on. Once you can do this to a good level you will find that all aspects of your musical life will be enhanced – your musical memory will improve, you'll be able to understand more complex ideas, and you'll be able to work out what other people have done quickly and easily.

There are some people who are fortunate enough to have 'perfect pitch' – they can hear a note and know what pitch it is, in the same way most of us see something that is red and know that it is red without having to work it out. For those of us who don't have this ability, it's possible to make great improvements in your listening skills by using software to play different musical concepts and fragments to you, and you can learn from these and then be tested by the program. Clearly you could do this with another person, but their patience could be limited, whereas a computer will repeat exercises until you get them right (or give up). One very good FREE program to do this is GNU Solfege (www.solfege.org) which provides a wide range of drills in rhythm, chords and scales. Even practicing this for 10 minutes a day will see huge improvements in your abilities, and becoming good at recognising rhythms, intervals and chords when you hear them will improve all aspects of your understanding of music.

Exercises

Harmonise a melody

Adding harmony to a melody can take two forms - creating chords for the melody, and also adding a harmony part. Take a simple melody (such as the one you first sequenced on page 53), and then create chords for it, using the information on page 150. You should also try creating a harmony part for the original melody, with the melody being transposed up or down by an interval such as a 3rd. Note that you can try to do this using Cubase's transpose feature, as seen on page 96.

Add extensions

Take the chord part you have just created, and add extensions to the chords, to make them in to 7th, 9th, 11th or 13th chords. Listen to the difference that the extensions make by comparing the two chord parts back-to-back.

Voice lead

The chord parts you have created may not be very 'smooth' - they may jump up and down a considerable amount. By moving some of the notes up or down an octave (changing the inversion of the chords as a result), it is possible to create a smooth part, such as that shown on page 154.

Develop Melody

The techniques on page 168 onwards are extremely important - not only for A level tasks, but to create interesting music in its own right. Being able to take an original idea and expand upon it is important, and can be even more useful when you are feeling short on inspiration. Take the melody you have used previously, and develop it using the techniques outlined.

Develop Rhythm

Some of the techniques given on page 168 onwards also apply to rhythm, so practice applying them rhythmic elements of a piece you have sequenced, such as the drums or altering the rhythm only of a melodic instrument part, such as the bass.

Summary

Music Theory is a much-maligned subject, often by those who do not understand it fully. Many songwriters are using quite advanced techniques without being aware of what they are doing, but being aware of the possibilities in any given situation is always a benefit – when you are short on inspiration you can use these techniques to allow you to create music, and often they will point you in directions you may not have thought of independently. Being able to read and write music opens up a whole new world in terms of quick acquisition of information and knowledge and will make you a more complete and able player, regardless of your instrument or level of ability.

Cubase and Chords

Introduction

Cubase has a number of tools which will help you learn, understand and apply music theory to create and extend your compositions. In this chapter, we will see some of the ways those tools can be used. Some build on ideas we have already seen in the chapter on Music Theory (page 131), others supplement your keyboard skills - allowing much quicker creation and entry of new musical ideas - and others will augment your existing ideas with new material. Broadly speaking, these tools are in three categories - Chord Tracks, Chord Editing tools (page 201) and Chord Pads (page 208).

Chord Tracks

Chord Tracks allow you to define the chord content of your song without it being tied to a specific instrument. This is a great advantage as often a chord or idea will need to be spread amongst a number of tracks, and defining the chord in the chord track will make it quick and easy to apply this chord to Instrument or MIDI tracks. There is more to be gained by using them than just expediency - Cubase provides tools which apply music theory to your existing chords, and allow generation of new chords, either as an extension of an idea, or to bridge between two existing chords.

Creating a Chord Track

Chord Tracks are created in the same way other tracks are - either by right-clicking in the track list area, or by going to **Project > Add Track > Chord**. The Chord Track looks like this:

At first it is blank, so let's look at how chords can be created. The quickest way is to use the pencil tool, which creates an empty chord event (signified by an X).

Editing a Chord Part

Once created, it can be edited by double clicking on it with the selection tool. The chord editor will appear, allowing selection of root, chord type, extensions and bass note, as shown on the next page.

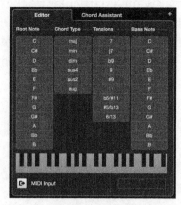

Note that once you've started making a selection in the editor, unsuitable selections are greyed out and can't be picked (for instance, it's not possible to have a ♯9 note in a minor chord, as ♯9 and minor 3rd are the same note pitch).

The arrows at the top right of the chord editor window allow quick navigation between chord events. Creation of a chord progression is quick and simple using this method.

However, if there are no MIDI or instrument tracks in the project, the chords will not be audible at the moment. Creating an Instrument track will allow them to be heard when you play the song back, despite there apparently being no MIDI information on the track in question.

In effect, the chord track creates a MIDI source which will be played back by any Instrument/MIDI track which has record enable or monitor turned on by default. On occasions that you don't want this to happen, go to the Chord track, and deactivate the **Acoustic Feedback** button - this will stop the chord track generating MIDI.

Sometimes, however, you may want a particular track to play the chords, and that can also be done - if you click on **Use Monitored Tracks** and select the track in question, it will play the chords and other tracks will not. This happens regardless of their Record or Monitor status (this is worth checking if the chords are always playing and you're not sure why!).

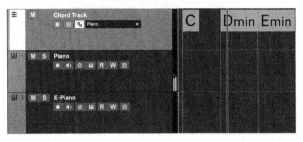

Voicings and Instruments

So far, we've seen how to make chords using the track, but more control is available. You may have noticed in the Chord Editor that the chords (by default) are not simple triads in root position:

This can be selected in the voicings menu. Piano, Basic and Guitar are available, each following rules to create chords that are generally suitable for the instrument in question. Basic will produce simpler voicings (usually starting out in root position), and the three are shown below:

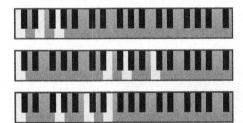

Basic - the chord is in root position, C-E-G

Piano - the root (C) has E-G-C above

Guitar - the root (C) has G-C-E above

Each of these voicings is intended to represent the way a typical player might play the generated chord on the instrument in questions, and in addition, for Guitar and Piano, it's possible to select sub-types of chord, again producing different voicings:

Guitar Voicings

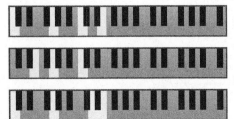

Triads and 4-note chords - the same voicing as seen above.

Three String Triads - a common voicing used by guitarists.

Modern Jazz - adds in the 9th (D), with a widely-spaced voicing.

Some of the rules at work aren't apparent with a triad (they will produce identical results), so for the Piano options, using a C Major 7 chord (C-E-G-B) the differences become clearer:

Piano Voicings

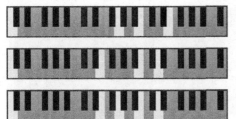 **Rock / Easy Jazz** (Pop 1 & Pop 2 did the same) - plays G B and E over the C root.

Altered Jazz - omits the 5th (G), adding the 9th (D), producing a jazzy sound.

Jazz (Five Sounds) - plays the complete chord over the root, including the 5th.

As with most of the tools in this chapter, the output is heavily dependent on the input - chords and sometimes context - so it's important to keep experimenting to understand what each option can do.

Creating New Chords

While what we've seen so far is useful, Chord Tracks are much more powerful than simply a way to enter chords to play on other instruments - they have the ability to apply theory to generate new chords. Creating a new part and opening the editor allows us to view the Chord Assistant, which is where it's possible to create new chords:

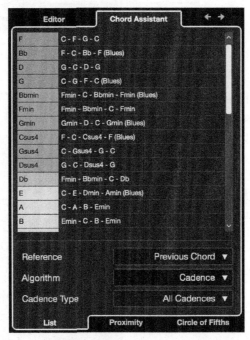

There is a list of chord possibilities in the centre of the Assistant, and the bottom section selects the different ways of generating chords - it's currently set to use the **Previous Chord** in **Cadence** mode with **All Cadences** available. The list will depend on the settings that you pick, so let's look at some of the features and how they work.

Chord Assistant Modes

Near the bottom is the **Mode**, and there are two to select from - Cadence and Common Notes.

Cadence Mode

Cadence uses knowledge of chord pro-gressions to create the chord (you can select the type of cadence from the drop-down menu below). For instance, if you have a C chord as the previous one, you will be shown where this C could be within a progression, and the suggestion for the next chord would be either an **F** (C-F-G-C) or a **D** (G-C-D-G) from the top of the list (where the ca-dences are less complex) or an **Amin** (C-Amin-Bmin-Emin) or any of the other choices from lower down.

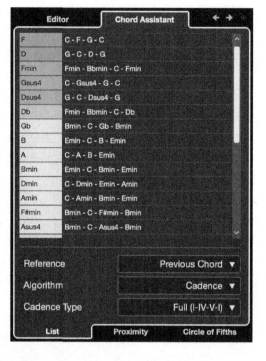

Common Notes

Common Notes generates chords based on having shared notes with the existing chord. At the top of the list we can see three simple chords which share notes with the preceding C chord (C-E-G) - **C minor** (sharing C and G) and **E minor** (sharing E & G), A minor (sharing A & C). Lower down the list are chords which share fewer notes, or where the shared notes lead to a less common choice or change of chord.

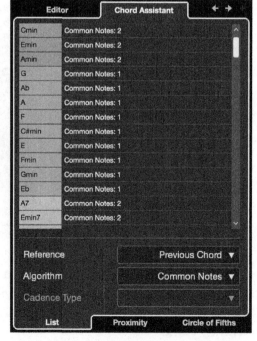

Previous and Next Chord

In the previous examples, the Chord Assistant has been working using the previous chord to provide suggestions. It has another mode - Previous and Next Chord - where it will look at the chord before and after to provide suggestions, allowing the bridging between chords to be performed.

For this first example, there are three chord events - a C, an undefined chord and a G, as shown below:

Opening the X in the Chord Assistant, Gap mode is activated with the button on the right:

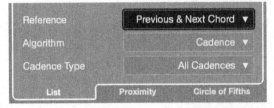

The chord suggestions will now depend on the Algorithm selected. In Common Notes mode, the top suggestions are Cmin and Emin, whereas in Cadence mode, F, Bb and D are at the top of the list.

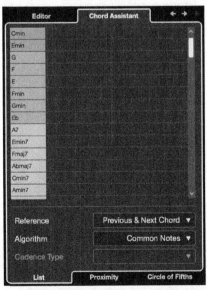
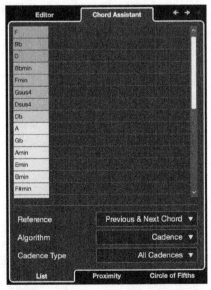

Moving down the list, the complexity increases, as does the number of options. It's important to audition the simpler solutions first as they may well be what you are looking for. Given the large number of options that are available as chords to either complete or bridge between, it's clear that there are a myriad of possibilities here waiting to be explored.

Chords From Audio

It is possible for Cubase to analyse an audio track and create chord events from it. The audio file must contain three or four-note chords, tuned to 12 pitches per octave, and must the the same sample rate as the project. If your audio meets these criteria, then you can attempt to create a chord track from it using the following method.

Below you can see an example project which contains two tracks - a Chord Track (which is currently empty) and an audio track with suitable audio present.

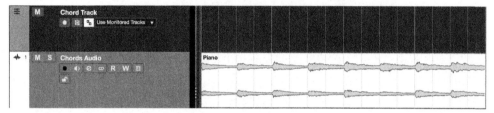

To create the chord events from the audio file, click and drag the audio event to the chord track:

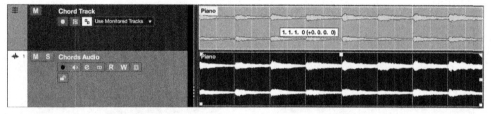

Cubase will then analyse the audio ...

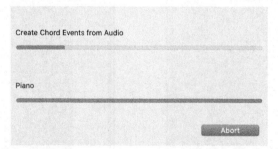

... and create chord events for any chords that it detects:

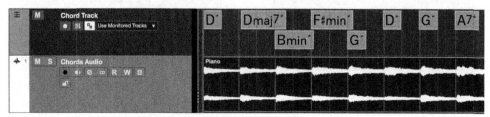

It is also possible to perform this action by selecting an audio event and going to `Project > Chord Track > Create Chord Events`.

Note the audio waveform next to each generated chord event:

When editing an audio-generated chord event, there is a list of probable chords, shown in decreasing likelihood (note the **Detected** tab at the bottom of the window):

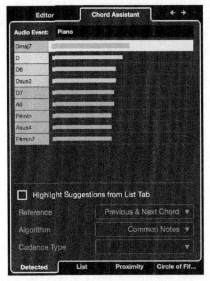

If you decide that one of the other options is preferable, clicking on it will instantly reflect this change in the chord track, as seen below:

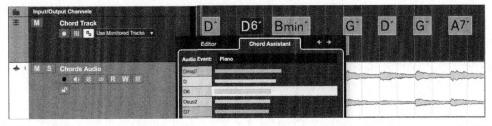

Note that it is also possible to manually edit the chord event as normal. The event will retain the list of detected probable chords, and you can return to them in the Detected tab if you want to.

Converting Chord Track to MIDI

Up to this point, we have relied on the ability of the chord track to generate MIDI to be played 'live' by a track which is monitoring it, but there usually comes a time when the chords need to be turned into MIDI data, allowing the fine-tuning that's needed in nearly any performance.

A Single Part

Converting a single chord part to MIDI is as easy as dragging and dropping from the chord track to the MIDI/Instrument track of your choice. A part gets generated with the current notes present in it, and it's named after the chord track part.

Here we see the original chord part, and an empty MIDI track below.

Select the part, and drag it to the track below ...

... and the MIDI part is created with the right notes and name. Note that it is not necessary to press **ALT** when dragging from a Chord Track to a MIDI/Instrument one - the Chord is left in place, to be used again where needed.

All Chord Parts

While it is possible to repeat this for each chord part, there are times when you will want to convert all of the parts in one go, and fortunately it is easy to do. Select the MIDI/Instrument track that you want the part generated on, and then go to `Project > Chord Track > Chords to MIDI` and a part will be generated for the entire length of chord parts you have present.

Shown below is a chord track with 8 chords present, and the destination track selected.

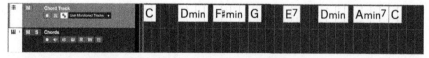

Going to `Project > Chord Track > Chords to MIDI`...

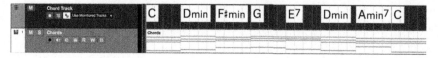

194

... creates a part with all the chords present. Note, however, a minor drawback - the chords are all in one part, and therefore each chord is not named. If chord recognition is not a strong point, you may want to convert each chord individually instead.

Live Input

While being able to do all this with MIDI data is useful, there is still more to come from Chord Tracks. It's possible to use the information in them to modify a live performance that you play on a MIDI device, to ensure that you never play a wrong note. Cubase takes the notes that you've played and if they don't fit with the chord track, the notes get moved to ones that do fit. To some, this may sound like cheating, but if you're lacking in keyboard skills you may find this a useful way of improvising - Cubase will merely apply instant correction to any errant notes that you play, and you can create music in a more accessible and organic way than solely editing it.

Setup

To use Live Input, you will firstly need to create and program a Chord Track, as seen below.

Next, create a MIDI/Instrument track to use with Live Transform - in this example, a Piano was used.

Following Chords

The crucial setting is in the Chords section of the In-spector - here **Live Input** has been set to **Chords**, so the function will be following the notes present in the chords track.

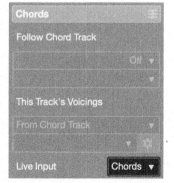

Next, to stop the MIDI track from playing the chords at each change in the Chord Track, the Chord Track needs to be muted.

Recording using a MIDI keyboard on the Piano track will now produce an interesting result - the notes played will be altered to suit the chords on the Chord Track. The track seen below was recorded by playing a C major chord on the keyboard throughout - it's clear to see that the same chord is not recorded ...

... and looking in the key editor confirms that the notes now follow the chord progression.

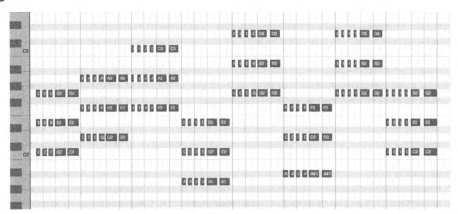

Clearly there are a huge number of possibilities available using this technique - if your keyboard skills are not up to being able to play a basic chord progression, you can use this technique to allow you to still create a piece of music using live recording and improvisation. If your skills are good enough to play that, you can use this to play a progression which you find impossible at present.

Following Scales

Live Transform is not limited to following only chords - it can also follow scales, allowing the same idea to be applied to melodic improvisation. By default the scales that Cubase will use are hidden, so you will need to show them using the button on the chord track:

The chord track now shows the scales that have been automatically selected by Cubase.

Note that for the B♭ chord, a B diminished scale has been chosen which then carries on for the G chord, but that for the C Major chord at the end, the scale returns to C Major. Next, the track we are to record on needs to be set to use the scale from the Chord Track instead of the chords - again, this is done in the Chord Track section of the Inspector.

Recording on the MIDI track will now adjust the played notes to fit with the scales chosen by Cubase, allowing in-key improvisation to occur, regardless of any wrong pitches played.

From the Project window it's not as clear to see the impact of this, but looking in the key editor on the next page...

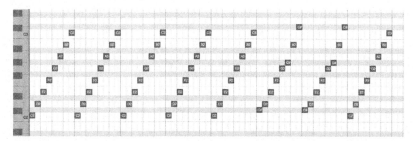

... it's clear to see that the input (which was a C major scale played throughout) has been altered to fit the prevailing scale at any time. However, in this particular

197

case, the choice of scale is not optimal - the section based on B diminished is not completely successful. In addition, it can be useful to try out new scales and possibilities, and being able to do so by letting Cubase control the scales being played allows quicker experimentation and also learning of new ideas without errors creeping in. To do this, the scales will need to be selected manually, and the first step to doing this is to alter the Chord Track to turn off automatic scales. This is done in the Inspector, by deselecting automatic scales, as seen below:

Once this is done, a selected chord event will have an area below it ...

... and clicking on this area will display a menu of scales which Cubase deems suitable to use at that given time, as seen on the right. The list is considerable, and will probably include options that you may have overlooked! Generally, the most common/obvious choices will be at the top, less so at the bottom. Here, F Major was selected, and now the scales section of the Chord Track reflects this.

A# Major
F Major
D# Major
D# Harmonic Minor
D Harmonic Minor
F Melodic Minor
D# Melodic Minor
C Blues 1
G# Blues 1
G Blues 1
A# Pentatonic
A# Myxolydic9/11
E Myxolydic9/11
C# Myxolydic9/11
B Lydic diminished
G# Lydic diminished
D# Lydic diminished
A# Blues 2
G Blues 2
A# Major Augmented
F# Major Augmented
D Major Augmented
C Arabian
D Balinese
B Hungarian
D# Hungarian
D Hungarian
A Oriental
E Oriental
G RagaTodi

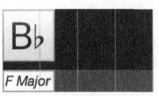

Deleting the originally recorded MIDI part and recording again (with the same input - C major scale) leads to a new result:

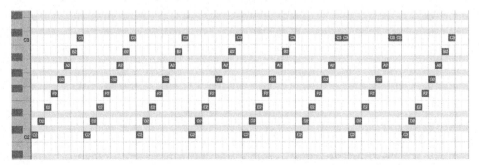

However, this result is not without some unexpected results. As seen below, the B that was played became a C, rather than what might have been expected, a B♭.

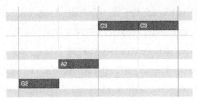

While this may be not entirely as expected, every note played fits in the destination scale, F major.

It is, of course, possible to extend this use of scales by creating more scale events on the Chord Track - remembering that in each musical situation there is often more than one possible choice. Here is the same chord progression, with a scale choice made for each chord:

Once again, recording on the MIDI track, and playing a C major scale produces the following result:

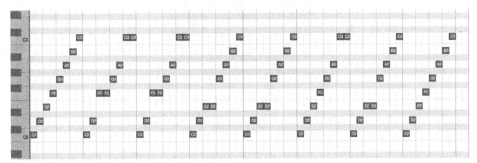

The possibilities - both for creating new music and also learning the many possible scales that are applicable in a given musical situation - are nearly endless.

Chord Tracks and Audio

The power of Chord Tracks is not limited solely to MIDI data - they can also be used to influence audio tracks as well. While this doesn't happen live, the processes can be applied to recorded audio (any audio which is monophonic and can be analysed using VariAudio, as seen on page 510), with a similar result to those seen in the previous section. Here, an audio track has been added to the project, and on it a recording made - in this case, of a guitar playing a C Major scale in each bar.

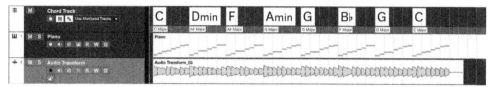

To activate the Chord Track, `Follow Chord Track` needs to be selected in the inspector.

A pop-up menu appears with several options, and in this case, **Scales** was chosen.

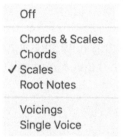

On doing this, the audio will be analysed - Cubase has two options here, as seen in the dialogue box:

The second option is used when the Chord Track is not already populated, but in this case we will use the first option, `Follow Directly`, and click OK. The audio is then analysed, and the desired pitches that VariAudio uses are altered to suit the scales on the Chord Track, much like the MIDI example we saw with Live Transform on page 199.

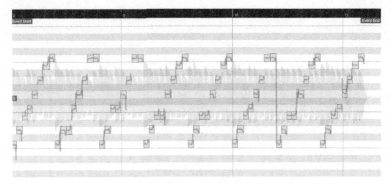

As with MIDI, the scope of this is huge - fitting audio that's already been recorded to new chord progressions can be done semi-automatically, adding another layer where this function can alter workflow and provide new creative possibilities.

Chord Editing Tools

The Key Editor contains a section where it's possible to alter chords using tools which analyse the notes that you have selected, and allow quick manipulation of those chords - providing both a quicker workflow and a better understanding of the editing being made, and also offering a fast route to new possibilities. The chords used in the examples were created using the Chord Track, as seen on page 186, and seen below:

A MIDI part containing these chords was then created using **Project > Chord Track > Chords to MIDI**, as seen below:

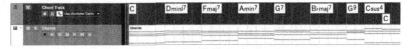

It's important to ensure when using Chord Tracks that **Follow Chord Track** is turned off in the Inspector, or any edits you make will be fixed to suit the Chord Track - usually stopping the changes you make from working!

Opening the part in the Key Editor shows the MIDI notes generated from the chord track.

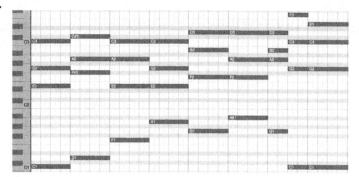

The Chord Editing section is located at the left of the Key Editor, and contains the tools we will be working with.

Highlighting a chord in the Key Editor will allow the Chord Editing section to display its analysis of the notes that are selected - here a C Major chord has been selected, and this is reflected in the display.

Note that if you select the notes of a chord and the bass note is not the root of the chord, the chord display will reflect this:

For chords which have four different notes in, then the lower section will become active - in this case indicating that the chord is a D minor 7:

So far, we have seen that Cubase can analyse chords that we have created, but the tool is much more powerful, as it can also alter notes in a chord.

Here, the Dmin7 chord has been selected, and correctly analysed by Cubase.

It can be altered to Dmaj7 by clicking in the appropriate location on the Chord Editing section.

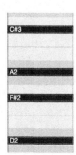 

Doing so changes the chord appropriately, in this case altering the F to an F♯ and C to a C♯, and this change is reflected in the Chord Editor.

It's possible to change between a 4-note chord and a triad (depending on the umber of notes present originally) - here a close-voiced Dmaj7 is turned into a triad using the `Maj` button - it can be turned back by pressing the `Maj7` button.

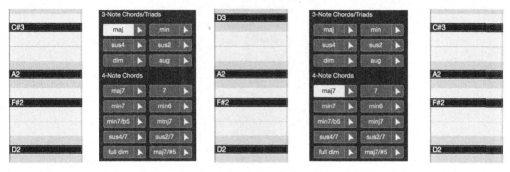

Inversions

The Inversion buttons are useful tools, taking the top or bottom note of a chord and moving it down or up an octave.

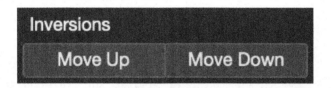

Here is the initial chord - pressing the down inversion button ...

... moves the top note down by an octave. Doing it again ...

... moves the top note (now E) down an octave.

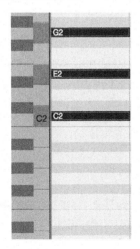
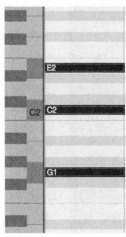
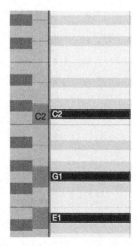

Inserting Chords

The Chord Editing section also provides a quick way to insert chords - click on the arrow icon to the right of the chord variety that you want to insert - it will be highlighted, as seen here:

In the key editor area, the cursor will turn into a pencil, and clicking will create a chord based on the note that you select, with the chord inserted based on it.

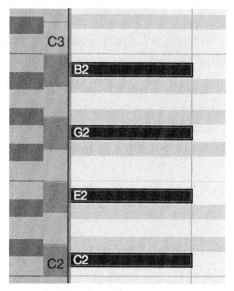

As you would expect, the tool will obey the current settings for Snap and Length, and remember that if you hold **CTRL** down you can temporarily defeat snap and insert the chord at the exact time position you want.

Drop 2, 3 and 2/4

A common way to voice chords is for notes to be spread out over the more than one octave - these are voicings often used by jazz players, and can provide a more interesting alternative to more simple voicings. The Chord Editing section gives tools to quickly perform these changes:

This example will use a root position DMaj7 chord - D-F♯-A-C♯.

Once selected, the drop voicings are easily created by pressing the relevant button, as seen below - each of these starts from the original chord shown above.

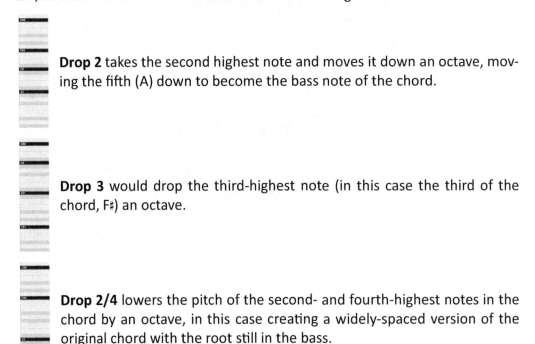

Drop 2 takes the second highest note and moves it down an octave, moving the fifth (A) down to become the bass note of the chord.

Drop 3 would drop the third-highest note (in this case the third of the chord, F♯) an octave.

Drop 2/4 lowers the pitch of the second- and fourth-highest notes in the chord by an octave, in this case creating a widely-spaced version of the original chord with the root still in the bass.

Add to Chord Track

After you have edited your chords in a part, you may want to alter the Chord Track. While it is possible to edit the Chord Track directly (as seen on page 186), there is another way to do this, using the data on a MIDI track. Here is the original Chord Track, with Dmin7 present:

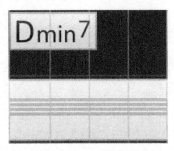

The part has been opened up in the chord editor, and altered to Dmaj7.

Choose **Add to Chord Track** to propagate this change to the Chord Track:

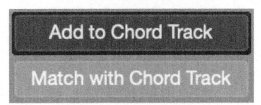

The new chord is now reflected in the Chord Track, as seen here:

Note that this can be used not only to edit existing Chord Track parts, but also to create new Chord Track parts; it's a quick way to take MIDI data that you have already recorded and then transfer this data to the Chord Track to allow the other techniques we have already seen in this chapter to be used.

Match with Chord Track

It's possible to use the Chord Track information to alter MIDI data that's on a track - whether this is to apply new chord information to a part or to quickly alter changes you have made - and this is achieved using the Match with Chord Track button.

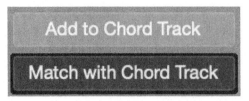

Highlighting MIDI data in a track and then pressing the button will alter the selected data to match the appropriate chord or scale.

In this case the initial chord was G♭/D♭ (displayed as F♯/C♯) - none of the notes are chord tones of the prevailing Chord Track chord at this point, a Dmin7 (D-F-A-C).

Pressing the button altered the chord to Dmin/C, which fits with the Chord Track's Dmin7.

However, it should be noted that depending on the original chord, not all of the notes of the Chord Track's chords may be present after the process - in this case despite the Chord Track being Dmin7 (D-F-A-C), the chord that is created ends up missing the D, being F/C (C-F-A-C). This clearly isn't incorrect, but it may not be the expected result, so check that any tensions you want in the chord are present after performing this action.

Chord Pads

Chord Pads allow quick, easy and accurate entry of chords by pressing a single button. While this may appear merely a simple function at first, it can provide a huge amount of creative power, and due to the Chord Pads' programmable and adaptive nature they can produce individual and musical results quickly.

Activating

To activate Chord Pads, go to `Project > Chord Pads`, or hit **CTRL+SHIFT+C**. You will see something like this in the lower zone of the project window:

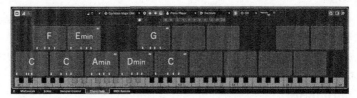

If you have a MIDI/Instrument track Record-enabled or in Monitor mode, clicking on any of the pads will play the chord on the pad in question. It's quick to create a new chord progression in this manner, and recording is done in the same way any other MIDI information would be recorded.

The default choice of chords is reasonably useful, but there is a lot more to explore. Firstly, loading presets - clicking on the Presets section of the toolbar...

...will summon the preset loading window where you can choose from the presets included with Cubase. The Content Summary column includes useful descriptions, but as with many situations, experimentation will be the best way to get to grips with the chords that are included.

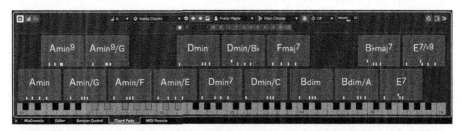

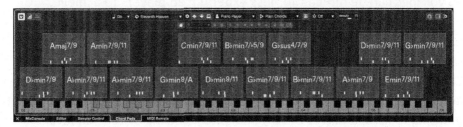

Editing

Most chord pad editing duties are performed using the toolbar, seen below.

However, if you just want to alter the chord on any pad directly, double-click the chord pad. The Chord Editor (seen earlier in this chapter) will appear, allowing quick editing of the chord pad. Note that you can enter text at the bottom right if you prefer. The editor can also be summoned by clicking on the chord display area in the toolbar.

Chord pads can be dragged to any new location (dragging to an occupied one will perform a swap).

Assign from MIDI Input

Once this is selected, any chord played on a MIDI device will be analysed and assigned to the selected pad.

Transpose

These buttons allow quick transposition of selected chord pads

Tensions

These buttons allow the tension in the chord to be increased or decreased. This is particularly useful if your understanding of music theory lags behind your musical ambitions, and can lead to interesting results.

Voicings

These buttons cycle through the available voicings of the chords, allowing the same harmonic information to be spaced more appropriately depending on the situation. This can be extremely useful if your keyboard skills are less advanced, as the voicings can be difficult for less experienced players to achieve.

Lock

A locked pad will not be altered by any other editing procedure. This can be particularly useful when selecting multiple pads for change (such as transposition) but wanting to keep a pad at the original pitch, voicing or tension level.

Adaptive Voicing

Any pad with this active will alter its voicing to match the currently-played pad as closely as possible. Consider the pad seen below, which has Adaptive Voicing turned on, and has changed voicing as different chords have been played. This mimics the behaviour of an advanced player who alters the voicing to the current musical context.

 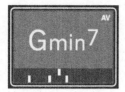  

Adaptive Voicing Reference

When this option is active, any pads with adaptive voicing set will stay at the voicing that matches this pad. This can be useful where a particular pad is leading to an undesirable voicing, by fixing the voicing to another pad.

Players

The second element to voicings are Players. In a similar way to that seen on the Chord Track (page 188), it's possible to pick Players to suit specific instruments for Chord Pads. Players are chosen from the toolbar:

The most obvious change when selecting a Player will be the voicing of the chord - here is the same C pad, but on Piano Player and Guitar Player (Note the pad needs to be triggered before the voicing will alter):

Piano Player

Guitar Player

There is more to this than meets the eye. It is also possible to further refine the player's performance from the menu, choosing a chord voicing style from the menu, or customising it from the custom voicing menu.

Player Mode

It's possible to alter the player so that it not only plays particular voicings, but also can play the chords in a rhythmic manner. To do this, change from the default of Plain Chords on the toolbar...

... to Pattern on the window that appears.

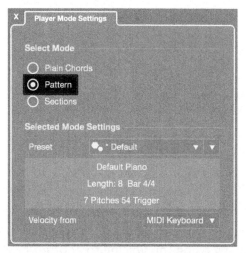

Playing any chord pad should now lead to the chord being played in a pattern, rather than just as plain chords. It is possible to select a preset from the window

...

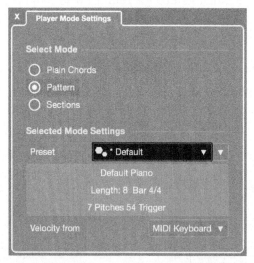

... or even to drag a MIDI event to this part of the toolbar ...

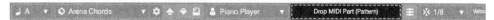

... which will lead to chords being played with the rhythm and notes from the MIDI part, adapted to the prevailing chord. In this way it is possible to develop original ideas even with limited keyboard skills. Once a MIDI part is recorded, it can be adapted to almost any chord imaginable with this method.

Below, the same chord pad has been played. On the left, **Plain Chords** was selected. On the right, **Pattern** was selected with the **Default** pattern.

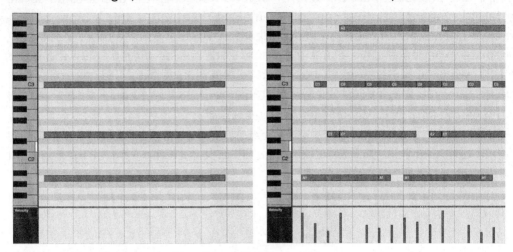

Copying Chord Pads to the Chord Track

It can sometimes be useful to transfer chords from chord pads to the chord track. This can be achieved in two different ways.

Dragging

As the heading suggests, clicking and dragging a chord pad to the chord track will create the chord event at the point that the chord is released. This gives complete control (as snap is available at any resolution), but can involve a significant drag distance depending on your screen resolution and project arrangement.

Step Input

It is possible to use a form of step input to create chord events using chord pads. Activate Step input with the button on the top left of the lower zone:

Once this is active, the step input indicator will appear in blue, and can be moved with the cursor keys. Activating a chord pad (on screen or via MIDI) will create the chord event at the selected position, and move the step input cursor to the next location. The main limitation of Step Input mode is that the resolution is one event per bar.

Move Insert Mode

Activating Move Insert Mode ...

... will move any chord events that are later than the insert point, allowing the insertion of chord events in an existing chord progression.

Remote Control

While it is possible to control Chord Pads via a mouse, it is useful to do so via a MIDI keyboard (or other controller), making them into a much more performance-orientated function, and allowing improvisation to be a more tactile, immediate experience. By default the Chord Pads can be played using the notes C1-B1, which are often the left-hand octave of a four-octave MIDI controller keyboard (but you may need to set your transpose function to play in this octave) - this allows playing of the pads as seen on screen.

However, the remote has some extra features which are usually initially turned off. To turn them on, click the Chord Pads Remote Settings icon, at the top right of the Lower Zone.

This will open the Chord Pads Remote Settings window, seen on the next page.

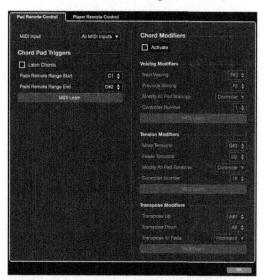

Clicking **Activate** on the right will enable the second level of control, which assigns the notes shown to remotely control:

Voicings (either by F2 & F♯2 and CC1 - Modulation)

Tensions (G2 & G♯2 and CC16 - General Purpose 1)

Transpose (A2 & A♯2 and Pitch Bend)

Enabling these and spending some time experimenting with them in live performance will allow much more control over the Chord Pads - it's possible to quickly introduce tensions, and also transpose a pad a semitone at a time, allowing a huge amount of control to be had, all playing live.

The Chord Assistant

The Chord Assistant provides a useful representation of the cycle of fifths (as seen on page 141), or chords of a given proximity (with a shared number of notes) and does so on-screen, altering the display to suit the chord you select. The Chord Assistant has two visual modes - Circle of Fifths, and Proximity. Both are available in the pop-up mode (when editing a chord on the chord track), but only Circle of Fifths is available when editing chord pads. To use the Assistant with Chord Pads, enable the right zone of the chord pads area:

You will then be able to see the Chord Editor, List Assistant and Circle of Fifths modes, selectable at the top of the section.

Circle of Fifths

In Circle of Fifths mode, the entire circle is represented, with the currently selected root key at the 12 o'clock position.

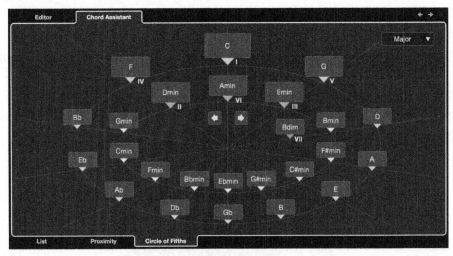

The diatonic chords of the key are indicated with Roman Numerals, and the other chords in the cycle are visible, with Major on the outside, and Minor on the inside. When working with chord events, clicking any chord in the assistant will alter the event to match. When working with Chord Pads, it is possible to not only see, but also audition chords, played in the currently selected Player style (including rhythms if applicable) by clicking on a chord symbol. It's possible to transfer any chord back to any unused pad by double-clicking or by right-clicking and picking **Assign to First Unassigned Pad**.

Proximity

In Proximity mode, the Chord Assistant shows chords which are closely related as near to the original chord (which appears at the bottom centre).

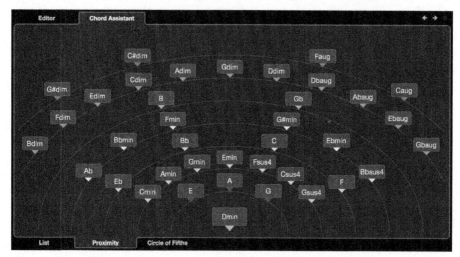

As with the Circle of Fifths mode, clicking any chord will audition it, and also alter the chord event to match.

The List Assistant

The area to the right of the chord pads can also host the List Assistant, which shows the relationship between the currently-selected chord pad and any others. This provides similar functionality to the Chord Assistant as seen on page 215, and enabling the list assistant view will provide an insight into the calculations it performs whenever a new chord pad is played.

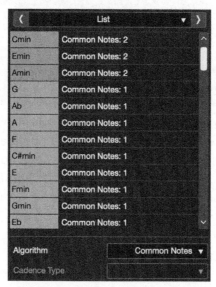

It may also provide some guidance as to which chords are suitable to play next, providing a visual representation of the available options when creating a new chord progression.

Exercises

Chord Tracks, Editing and Pads is an enormous topic - not only because of the features that Cubase provides, but because there is a near-infinite number of possibilities to explore. A few example exercises to follow are given here to get you started.

Simple Chord Parts

A first, basic use of the Chord Track is to create simple chord parts (typically a bar long), and then convert them to MIDI, providing quick, straightforward error-free entry. Creation of unfamiliar chords, or those that sound complex (such as F#m7♭5) is easy and accurate using this method.

Using Cadence mode to suggest new chords

Create a chord progression using the Chord Track, and once you are happy with it, add an undefined chord, and use the Chord Assistant in Cadence Mode to offer suggestions for the chord. You can then extend the chord progression further using this method, remembering that the further down the list you go, the more adventurous the chord choices will be.

Using Previous and Next Chord mode to bridge between chords

While Cadence mode adds a chord at the end of a progression, Previous and Next Chord mode fills in between chords. Create a progression with four chords that you are happy with, and then insert undefined chords between them, using Previous and Next Chord mode to complete the progression.

Use the Arpeggiator

While the Player modes can provide a great deal of interest for Chord Pad parts, it's possible to insert an arpeggiator such as Arpache SX into the MIDI/Instrument track that you are using for playback of your Chord Pads, and combine the power of Chord Pads with the interest that can be generated by an Arpeggiator. With the appropriate settings for each, many a song idea can be created quickly and easily.

Arrangements

Making an arrangement is the act of taking the musical information from a piece and then organising that information for a new group of instruments, often not those of the original piece. It involves musical knowledge as well as inspiration, and in many cases an arrangement of a piece can drastically transform it – it is possible to introduce new musical information as well as arrange the piece for new instruments or have them play in a different style. Usually a combination of these techniques would be used to arrange a piece in a given style. Here we will look at some techniques that you can use to create your own arrangements of pieces.

Listen

The first thing to do is to listen to arrangements that others have come up with – often this can inspire (in terms of the concept of the arrangement), and also when suitable analysis has been performed, then musical and arranging concepts can be gleaned from this. It is important to remember that you can always learn what others have done if you take the time to listen to it and analyse it. While some of the techniques that are used by arrangers may be too complex to grasp at first, there are many techniques that can be used straight away to make an arrangement work in a new style.

Musical Elements in an Arrangement

There are several elements you can manipulate to create an arrangement – they are outlined below along with some ideas and their effects.

Form

The form and structure of a piece has a great effect on the way it is perceived by the listener. Form is the overall concept (such as "a 3 minute pop song") whereas structure is how it is constructed – if you use the analogy of a house (the form is a 3-bed semi, the structure is brick-built) then you should remember which is which.

Many songs follow a straightforward structure (Intro – Verse – Chorus – Verse – Chorus – Bridge – Chorus – End), but some deviate from this with varying amounts of complexity; some songs alter sections each time they repeat, some use 'odd' lengths or numbers of bars, and some eschew a standard structure for something quite different.

It is important when making an arrangement to realise that you can use sections of the original song in a different manner; the original introduction doesn't have to function as the introduction in your version. If you listen to Mark Ronson's version of Radiohead's "Just", the original guitar solo now forms the introduction, and this sort of use is common. In addition it is perfectly acceptable to use parts in different functions, such as using the melody as part of the bass line. Being imaginative with the original material you have been given is the key to an interesting new arrangement (as opposed to a simple 'cover version').

Instrumentation

This is another area where it is possible to make a huge difference to an arrangement, even without altering any parts musically. By simply playing the same parts on different instruments, it is possible to alter the style of the piece of music, and by adapting them subtly to the instrument in question, this effect can become even more effective – take the following examples:

Rhythm

Rhythm is one of the most important parts of any style of music – something that is often forgotten. Indeed the rhythm can define a style more than any other element. Take the simple motif shown below:

It is simple, plain and uninteresting. However, simply changing the rhythm (using triplets to give a 'swung' feel) will impart a far more 'swing jazz' feel to it, with nothing else changing:

While changing the rhythm to this offbeat pattern will (given suitable accompaniment to give a clear indication to the listener where the beat is) give a reggae feel.

In addition to this, it is common to develop the rhythm of a piece, often by taking a single note and dividing it into several smaller ones – this can easily be accomplished in Cubase using the scissors tool – or in other cases to either shorten the rhythm of a phrase or lengthen it.

Time Signature

While many styles of music are in 4 4 time, there are some which use different time signatures, and as a result an arrangement can easily take on that style if such a time signature is used. Progressive Rock, for instance, often used odd-meter times (such as 7 8 or 15 4), a song such as Dave Brubeck's "Take Five" used 5 4 while a waltz will be in a signature based on threes such as 3 4 or 3 8.

Arranging your source material into such a time will quickly make it sound more interesting and reminiscent of that style, and altering the piece to a new time signature can drastically alter its feel. Here is an example - the original (the theme from "Mission Impossible" by Lalo Schifrin) is in 5 4.

For the 1996 film version, the theme was reworked by Larry Mullen Jr. and Adam Clayton of U2, and was changed to be in 4 4 to suit the dance music style chosen:

The two dotted notes at the beginning of the original phrase have been repeated, adding an extra 3 beats to the overall phrase to make it fit in the new time signature (with an originally 5 beat long phrase now extended to 8 beats). Changing time signature needs to be done in a musical way for it to be effective, but when it is done well, it can be almost invisible to the casual listener.

Melody

Avoidance of straight repetition is important when arranging a piece of music. To create something new from the original there are a number of techniques that can be applied to the melody. These (and more) are covered on the Music Theory chapter on page 131, but we will look at examples of their applications here.

The original melody is shown above – there are a number of ways to develop this, firstly an inversion:

This takes the original contour of the melody and substitutes "up" for "down", creating a mirror image of the original melody. When compared with the original, it sounds related, but different – because the rhythm is the same we hear them as closely related. Depending on the note you start on, you may find some of the notes will need alteration to sound 'correct', but this is something you will have to judge for yourself.

The next technique is to reverse the original melody (called a "retrograde")

And finally, you can apply both techniques to get a retrograde inversion:

You can also use a "sequence" – this is taking an original melodic idea, and taking that pattern and moving it up within the scale. Here we see the first bar of the phrase used above. It originally starts on C and is then repeated on D, E and F.

While this can sound somewhat twee when used in a straightforward manner, careful and clever use of this technique in a more subtle way can get a lot more mileage from a simple idea without great effort. Combining them in intelligent ways can create a new but related melody that will interest the listener for a much longer period. Remember with these techniques that they can be used piecemeal, just using them here and there to alter a part, or to inspire you in new directions – you are not simply showing that you can do textbook inversions or retrogrades.

Harmony

Harmony is an extremely important part of an arrangement and indeed any musical style, and in addition it is important that this harmony develops throughout an arrangement – if it is just the same throughout, then the piece will not be as interesting as it could be if it becomes more complex later on. The style that an arrangement is in can define the complexity of the harmony that is used – chords that are appropriate in a jazz context (with altered notes and extensions) would probably not be as suitable in a rock or pop context. Harmony itself is an enormous subject, with a wide range of techniques and styles applicable - an area which could be studied for many years, but some simple examples here will demonstrate how a change of harmony can alter the perception of a piece.

Here is a well known melody (Good King Wenceslas), with commonly-used chords.

They can, however, be substituted for others which work in a less obvious manner.

The choices can be even less obvious, leading to a far more unusual sound:

Clearly there is a great deal that can be done with chords, and learning how to use them and what can be done is a very long endeavour; some arrangers make much use of this, particularly when arranging for a large ensemble or in a jazz style, but even simple changes such as those shown above can radically alter the context in which a melody is perceived.

Example Arrangements

There are a great many cover versions of songs, some of which make little or no attempt to re-arrange the original or play the song in a new style. The examples below show some of the techniques that can be used to effectively make a song change from the original, and while some of the changes are to do with the production and recording, there are also changes made in terms of the techniques outlined above in this chapter.

The Ace Of Spades – Motorhead / Hayseed Dixie

This is a great example of much of the music of Hayseed Dixie – they take classic rock pieces and play them in their bluegrass style, having produced several albums of this. They are clearly very accomplished musicians, and can therefore achieve this with great accuracy. Here are some of the points of interest:

Structure

The structure of the two songs is identical. They are in different keys (Motorhead – E♭, while Hayseed Dixie is in E), but this could simply down to detuning of the guitars in the Motorhead recording.

Instrumentation

The instrumentation is completely different - Motorhead's version features drums, bass, guitars and vocal, while the Hayseed Dixie version features acoustic bass guitar, acoustic guitar, banjo, mandolin, fiddle and vocals. The initial riff is played on the Acoustic guitar (instead of electric), and then on the fiddle, and the original's guitar solo is shared by banjo (8 bars) and fiddle (4 bars)

Musical changes

Musically the songs are extremely similar – the melody has very little embellishment or alteration made either melodically or rhythmically – the change of the accompaniment makes most of the stylistic difference.

The outro features a 16th-note acoustic guitar phrase, whereas the original features a simple unison bend.

Most of Hayseed Dixie's work is worth analysis, being a textbook example of how to take a piece of rock music and play it in another style with a live band.

Don't Stand So Close To Me – The Police (1979 and 1986)

This is a rarity, the same musicians re-working a song into a dramatically different arrangement. The original version was recorded while they were a 'functional' band, during their most creative phase. The second version was recorded as a contractual obligation, some time after they had ceased to be a band, and indeed the relationship between Sting and Stewart Copeland had deteriorated to the point where they allegedly never met during the recording of this version. Some points of note:

Structure

The structure of the song has changed slightly , as seen below.

Original	Bars	'86	Bars
Synth Intro	-	Intro	11
Intro	8		
Verse 1	16	Pre-Verse	4
		Verse 1	16
Chorus	9	Pre-Chorus	8
		Chorus	9
Verse 2	16	Verse 2	16
Chorus	9	Chorus	9
Verse 3	16	Instrumental	16
Chorus	11	Chorus	9
Instrumental	16	Verse 3	16
Chorus	8	Chorus	8
Chorus	8	Chorus	8
Chorus (fade out)	8	Chorus (a capella)	8
		Chorus (fade out)	8

In the '86 version, Verse 3 and the Instrumental have swapped positions. In addition the '86 version has some extra sections before the first verse and the first chorus. The '86 version's verse is three chords as opposed to the original's two.

Instrumentation

While on the face of it the band hadn't changed lineup, the instrumentation is quite different – the original features drums, bass, guitar and vocals with the addition of a synthesizer as well; the vocal and guitar have multiple takes recorded (adding harmony parts to both), but largely it is in an "as played" state. The second version is quite different with far more tracks, use of samples and more synthesized parts, and a far more complex vocal arrangement – the 'a capella' section towards the end allows these parts to be clearly heard.

Production

The second version is far more 'polished', with not only the drums, but the guitar and vocal parts also being far less dynamic; the bass part is far more prominent in the second version too. In addition, Stewart Copeland had a broken shoulder at this time, so the drums were all recorded/sequenced using his Fairlight Sampler, using sounds which at the time were quite fashionable whereas today they sound somewhat hackneyed and are totally lacking the dynamics and detailed rhythmic accenting which he became famous for (and indeed that the first version demonstrates).

The version you prefer is obviously down to personal choice, but they are certainly dramatically different versions of the same song.

Sex Type Thing / Swing Type Version- Stone Temple Pilots

This is an example of a band taking their own music and making it into pastiche. The original version has an extremely heavy guitar riff, played with lots of distortion.

The alternative version takes this same descending musical line and plays it instead on a vibraphone, with the notes 'swung' to mimic the swing jazz era.

The guitar part in the swing version follows a similar descending pattern, but with the E pedal note above instead of below the descending note:

The contrast between the two versions is massive, and yet musically they are extremely similar. The vocal part is altered in a similar manner to the riff, being a swung version of the original. The structure of the two versions is very similar - the swing version features a longer introduction, and the penultimate 8 bar section is different (featuring a single chord as opposed to the original's repeated riff section), but other than that they have the same sections of the same length and in the same order.

Black Hole Sun – Soundgarden / The Moog Cookbook

The original piece is one of the cornerstones of the early 'grunge' style, and features some interesting arpeggiated figures (played on a heavily-effected guitar sound), a dark-sounding vocal melody, and a bridge that is in 9/8 – it was one of the original grunge songs, and helped popularise the style. The Moog version is so dramatically altered as to be almost unrecognisable at first. Some of the changes that have been made are:

Instrumentation

The instrumentation used has been chosen to mimic early 1970s cover versions, using analogue synthesizer patches (such as the eponymous Moog), and layering the melody parts across a number of sounds. The drum part mimics the sounds of a home keyboard of the time, with extremely synthetic-sounding drums and a mock bossa nova feel.

Rhythm

The melody's rhythm has been altered to make it more swung, in keeping with the style.

The end of the verse has a melodic riff added (doubled in the bass), and then an obvious V7 – I progression

Introduction

The introduction starts in a totally different manner to the original – the original features arpeggiated chords, (A♭, B, G♭, F, E, E♭) whereas the Moog version takes most of this progression (transposed), and makes use of some clichéd synth-cover riffery to make it sound like a different song altogether. Both it and the original feature a semitone resolution to the last chord, often seen as a 'flat 5' substitution.

Structure

The form of the song features some interesting twists – while the overall pattern is similar, there are a number of places where there are extra bars inserted (mostly to insert a V7 chord which will then resolve back for the next section), the 9/8 section is played in 4/4 instead, and there are several changes made during repeats (often missing out the inserted V7 chords mentioned before)

The rest of the Moog Cookbook "Modern" album follows this formula very effectively, including a similarly obtuse cover version of "Basket Case" by Green Day, featuring a similar arranging techniques, including a great demonstration of a flat 5 substitution at the end, where the B♭ (which would resolve to an E♭) is replaced with an E, which resolves down to the E♭. There is also a great example of taking a small melodic phrase and making it last for some time (the cover of Weezer's "Buddy Holly" has an introduction lasting nearly two minutes based on a four-bar phrase taken to extremes).

It's Raining Men – The Weather Girls/ Geri Halliwell

On the face of it, it would be easy to think that the original version of the song is straightforward in terms of structure and section lengths, and that the cover version is much the same. This would, however, be wrong. While the instrumentation of the two versions is largely the same (and the cover is clearly intended to sound similar in this respect), the two songs have rather different structures:

Structure

The Weather Girls version has the bridge section played twice as opposed to the cover's once, and in addition features a third verse which is much longer than any others (with an extra 8 bars on chord I before the usual verse progression starts and an extra two bars at the end), a feature that is entirely absent from the cover version.

Introduction

These are different - the Halliwell version is four bars shorter, and misses the voice introduction of the original.

Choruses

Both versions feature unusual-length choruses (7 bars long in places), but the original has a double 8 bar first chorus (each time linked with a single bar's rest with the line 'It's Raining Men' sung over it), while the later version is only 7 bars long; this odd length chorus happens later in the original.

Summary

The topic of arrangement could (and indeed does) fill an entire book, or a number of them. It is a wide-ranged subject which you could spend a great many years studying as it has so many different areas in which it can be explored. This chapter has just scratched the surface but will hopefully give you an idea of what is expected of you when you are asked to take an original piece of material and create an arrangement in a given style. Careful analysis of the desired style should allow you to pick out traits which will - when applied to the original material - give the sound of that style. Most music sounds the way it does because of a combination of factors, both in terms of musical elements and also sonic ones such as instrumentation and production. When all these elements are combined with a piece of music which has been developed from the original in an interesting and musical way, the end result can be a new piece of music which stands up in its own right, but still shows a clear heritage of the original.

Synthesizers

Synthesizers come in many shapes and sizes, but a great many of them share similar concepts. Understanding these will allow you to program them more intuitively and get improved results. Here we will look at Subtractive synthesizers, a method of synthesis which is used in most analogue synthesizers and as a result has become synonymous with "synth". Many of these concepts are used in Samplers as well (as you will see in the Sampling chapter on page 293).

History

While there were some experiments made in the late 1800s and first half of the 1900s, the first programmable synthesizer was the RCA Mark II Sound Synthesizer, made in 1958 at the Columbia-Princeton Electronic Music Center in the USA, gaining some credibility with a number of composers creating music for it specifically. The first commercially available synthesizer was sold by Moog in 1964, although the real breakthrough was the 900 Series, a range of modules which could be connected together to create diverse and complex sounds which became the bedrock on which the future sound of electronic music would be built. While there were many detractors, some musicians saw the potential of these new instruments - not to imitate other instruments, but as a new instrument in its own right. Wendy Carlos' seminal "Switched On Bach" demonstrated this to the wider public, with Bach's complex music seemingly a natural choice for such innovative sounds. Inevitably, other companies entered the growing market, and Moog's high-end expensive and complex devices were undercut by simpler synthesizers leading Moog to produce the classic Minimoog, a synth which was not modular but gained a huge reputation for its sound which still carries on today, despite it being monophonic, meaning it could only play one note at once - a synth which can play more than one note is polyphonic, although the number of notes will depend on the synth in question. Japanese companies such as Yamaha, Korg and Roland released models which through the 1970s and 1980s redefined the sound of many forms of popular music, and the sounds of the synthesizer were transformed from being the unusual and experimental to becoming mainstream and popular. During the 1980s alternative forms of synthesis came to prominence, augmenting the subtractive synthesis model with additive, Frequency Modulation and other forms, and eventually in many cases incorporating an element of sampling by using waveforms from real instruments. By the late 1980s the original wave of analogue synthesizers were unfashionable and unwanted in many corners, but they became popular once more with the advent of House music, leading some previously unloved devices such as Roland's TB-303 (which was originally a tool to provide bass accompaniment to solo musicians) to become hugely popular and extremely valuable. The increasing power of computer technology led to the possibility of simulating the behaviour of a synthesizer in real-time during the 1990s, and this led to the decrease in value of many physical synths as many felt the sound of the simulated versions of them was adequate and convenient enough to warrant their use over the originals - certainly there are far fewer who could afford an original Moog Modular compared to the £200 or so for the software emulation which is smaller and more reliable aside from any other factors. While there is clearly still a place for hardware-based keyboards it seems that software is where the main developments will be; after all many hardware synthesizers now are running software internally, and there are very few 'real' hardware synthesizers left.

Hardware

The RCA Mark II filled an entire room with rack-mounted components, all of which made up the synthesizer. They could be connected in many different ways and connecting ('patching') everything together was a complex and long-winded job, but necessary before any sound could be generated. The Moog Modular that followed nearly 10 years later was still a formidable piece of equipment; while it was considerably smaller than the RCA unit (due to its use of solid-state circuitry instead of valves), it still required patching between the various modules to allow a sound to be heard (and indeed programmed), and changes between sounds normally meant a considerable amount of re-patching. As many owners often made use of the same combinations of oscillators, amplifiers, filters and envelope generators, synthesizers were released which had them connected in a fixed manner, with the sounds being altered solely by changes to the parameters of each component using knobs (as the original modular synths had featured). This made them much more immediate to use and led to a rise in popularity as a non-technical user could quickly experiment and get a sound from them. This led to the rise of many now-popular models from manufacturers such as Moog (the miniMoog, seen right), Roland (the Jupiter and Juno series), Korg (Polysix, below left) and Yamaha (CS-80). Up to this point all of the hardware had been analogue - in general the devices were all simple ones, initially being made from individual transistors, resistors, capacitors and inductors, but later on the popularity of the synth market led to some manufacturers such as Curtis making some elements of synthesizers (such as filters) available as a chip instead of a larger number

233

of individual components. While this was expedient at the time, they are now discontinued and extremely rare, so repairs of some synths that use them can be expensive if not impossible! During the 1980s, digital technology began to be used; at first it was solely for controlling the analogue parts of the synthesizer (that still made the sounds), but increasingly the technology became available to create the sounds digitally - instead of using components to make the audio, it was calculated using mathematics and computer programming, and then converted into analogue audio for the listener. This led to synthesizers which were more stable in terms of tuning and behaviour, but generally made them far less user-friendly; to keep costs down the number of physical controls was reduced in many cases, and in some there were no knobs or sliders, just an LCD readout and a number of buttons to press to change settings, making programming a far cry from the original tactile experience that it was, and leading to many giving up on programming sounds and using presets instead; this combined with the complexity of some forms of synthesis (such as FM - the Yamaha DX7 seen right being the most famous of them all) led to many 1980s recordings making use of the same sounds. One of the advantages of such digital synthesis and control was that many synthesizers became multi-timbral. This is when a synth is capable of producing more than one different sound (timbre) at once. We take this for granted now with many synthesizers and the advent of General MIDI, but it was a groundbreaking feature when first introduced in the 1980s.

The advent of House music led to a resurgence in popularity of many analogue synths, as the ability to alter sounds readily in real-time meant they were ideal for making music where the music was largely static, but the sound changed; the altering of filter settings is something which is still popular in many electronic forms of music 20 years later. This time was the peak of the 'physical' synthesizer, however; advances in computer technology meant that a general purpose computer (such as a PC or Mac) had enough processing power to be able to simulate the sound generated by an entire synthesizer, calculating what would happen at any given moment with enough accuracy to replicate the sound to all but the most discerning of ears, and the fashion for simulating 'real' instruments inside a computer progressed hugely during the 1990s, with previously desirable analogue equipment becoming unwanted once more. This trend has continued throughout the start of the 2000s, with the ever-increasing power of computers meaning it's not only possible to simulate one of a given synthesizer, but many at once; one often overlooked advantage of this approach is that you are not just buying one synth when you purchase a software synth, you are buying as many as you can get your computer to run at once.

234

Structure

There are several different types of synthesis in use today, but the most common one is called subtractive synthesis – this is where an initial waveform is generated that is harmonically complex (see page 411 for details of this concept), and then this is filtered to reduce the amount of harmonics present, and the volume of the output is also controlled. Many of the classic analogue synthesizers revered today used exactly this method to produce their sounds, and in addition a great many software-based synthesizers (such as VST Instruments) use such a method.

Their structure is shown in the diagram below. The signal flows from left to right – the MIDI input goes to the oscillator, and this generates the appropriate sound which is then passed through a filter and an amplifier. These use ADSR envelopes (a way to alter a parameter over time) to control their outputs. In addition there is also an extra oscillator (the LFO) which generates low-frequency waveforms which can be applied to any of the three main sections of the synthesizer to control their output. When the LFO is applied to the oscillator, it produces vibrato because the output frequency is changing. When applied to the Amplifier, it will produce a tremolo effect (a rapid variation in volume), while applying it to the filter will produce a cyclic change of the filtering of the sound, altering the brightness.

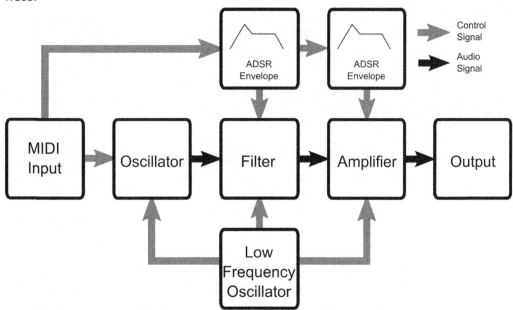

Some synthesizers feature two (or more) oscillators to allow each note played to produce more than one tone – it's possible to offset these in pitch (producing a doubling effect), detune them (producing a chorus or out-of-tune effect), and often to change the waveform of each as well, producing different effects.

Editing a synthesizer

To demonstrate the principles of editing such a synth, we will use the freeware

PG-8X VST Instrument (see page 662 for details of downloading and installing a synth) – create one now (`Project > Add Track > Instrument`) and it should appear as follows.

Here we see the PG-8X with its default `Init` setting, which gives a basic sawtooth wave sound (see page 410). Looking around, you should see that the sections present in the schematic seen earlier are present (don't worry if you don't understand the controls listed, they will be explained later):

Oscillators

There are two oscillators here: `DCO-1` and `DCO-2`. Both have basic tuning and waveform selection, and `DCO-2` adds some extra controls such as fine-tuning. `DCO` is a reference to Digitally Controlled Oscillator, aping the naming used in the Roland JX-8P which the PG-8X is based on.

Filter

The filter features cutoff frequency and resonance, as well as a number of controls to allow dynamic manipulation of the settings. `VCF` stands for Voltage Controlled Filter - a term from the true analogue era of synthesis.

Amplifier

The Amplifier section is simple, but has the choice of using an envelope or gate to control its level, allowing quick changes between the envelope sound and an on/off setting. `VCA` stands for Voltage Controlled Amplifier.

Envelopes

There are two envelope sections, which can be used to control the oscillator, filter, amplifier and mixer. An envelope generates a signal that changes over time, allowing the sound of the synth to develop whenever a note is played.

LFO

The **LFO** - Low Frequency Oscillator - has three waveforms, as well as controls to alter the speed and time before the LFO starts working.

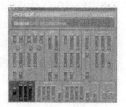

We will be working from this **INIT** sound, so if you want to return to it, you can use the red **NEXT** button to select another **INIT** patch if you want to put the synth back into its starting setup.

The simplicity of this synthesizer and its sections belie the amount of sonic editing potential that is present. To illustrate that, we will first alter the Oscillator to produce a waveform that is rich in harmonics, and then use the amplifier and also the filter to illustrate some of the possibilities that this setup allows. First, change the waveform to **Square** using the switch in DCO-1. A square wave has a sharp sound which will make hearing the filter's effect (later on) much easier.

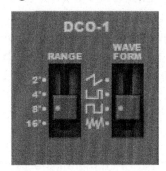

Playing this via MIDI will give a bright, clear tone which is reminiscent of early TV video games. The shape of this waveform makes it very rich in harmonics – as well as the fundamental frequency there is a wide range of harmonics present as multiples of the original frequency. This gives us lots of potential to use the filter to alter the sound, but firstly we will look at the amplifier section.

The Amplifier Section (VCA)

In a subtractive synthesizer the amplifier plays an important role - it changes the level of the signal from the oscillator. This may not sound hugely important, but it is useful because the amplifier can be linked to an envelope generator, allowing the signal level to be altered over time automatically by the synthesizer. It is this that allows the dynamics of the signal to transform over time, and is the first step in creating interesting sounds.

Controlling the Amplifier

When the Amplifier is controlled by the envelope generator, the volume of the synthesizer's output will change over time, allowing the creation of sounds which can emulate real instruments, or new, synthetic timbres. The most common type of envelope generator is called an ADSR because it has four controls - **A**ttack, **D**ecay, **S**ustain and **R**elease. Three of these parameters (Attack, Decay and Release) are time-based, while Sustain is a level, as shown next, where the parts of the envelope are described. The PG-8X has two ADSR Envelope generators, and they can work entirely independently of each other, controlling different areas of the synth.

The Envelope Generator

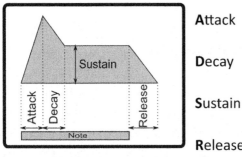

Attack	The time between hitting the key and the level reaching maximum
Decay	The time taken from the maximum to reach the Sustain Level
Sustain	The level which is maintained while the key is held down
Release	The amount of time for the envelope to reach zero once the key is released

To hear this in action, we will need some MIDI data to be sequenced and then played back by the PG-8X, to allow concentration on the changes the controls make. For this example, sequence a series of 16th notes at around 120bpm – this will mean you will hear the effect of the Amplifier. The notes themselves are not important, just that they are present, something like the sequence shown below.

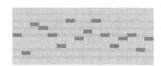

Next, we will examine the effect of changing the **ENVELOPE 2** settings; by default it is Envelope 2 that controls the amplifier in the PG-8X, so altering these controls will allow quick experimentation and discovery.

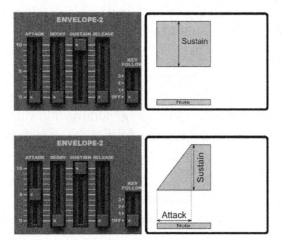

With the controls set as shown, the Amplifier is effectively either ON or OFF – as soon as the key is pressed the A and D times expire, leading directly to the sustain level, which is set to maximum. Releasing the key leads to an instant stop to the sound.

Moving the A control upwards will make each note 'fade in'. As long as the A time is less than the note length, it will reach maximum and then stay there, as shown.

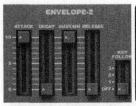
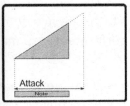

However, if the A control is made too long for the notes that are being played, the maximum level will never be reached (shown with the dotted line in the right-hand diagram).

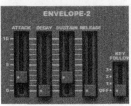
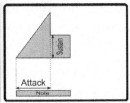

Next, set the S control to around 25%. This will mean as soon as the attack is over, the amplifier will instantly drop to the sustain level, as seen to the left.

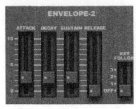
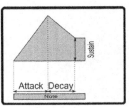

Now set the D control to around a quarter of the way up. It will now take some time for the amplifier to reach the sustain level after the maximum has been reached - this is useful for simulating the decay of real instruments.

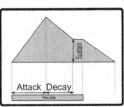

Now add in the R control - this will lead the sound to fade out slowly after the key has been released - this is often used to add more realism to sounds (very few 'real' sounds stop instantly), or to create more pad-like sounds which keep sounding after the note has been released.

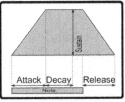

If the S control is set to maximum, it makes the D setting redundant - it doesn't matter how long it takes to change between the end of the attack (100%) and the sustain level (100%), and the end result looks like the diagram on the left.

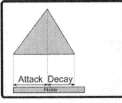

Conversely, if the sustain level is set to 0, then (providing the note is long enough) the release control will do nothing as the sound will already have stopped; only the A and D controls will make any difference.

The last settings will make a sound which is of a fixed length. Using this technique it's possible to create sounds which are percussive - with a short attack and a medium decay they will fade like a 'real' percussion instrument.

With these simple controls it is possible to create a wide range of envelopes for controlling volume and to simulate the performances of many 'real' instruments.

The Dynamics Switch

The **DYNAMICS** switch makes for a more realistic performance by allowing MIDI Velocity to control the overall level of the amplifier. When switched **OFF**, MIDI velocity is ignored, and all the notes are the same volume. The other settings progressively increase the effect of velocity on the audio level.

The Filter Section (VCF)

Before experimenting with the filter, ensure that either **ENVELOPE 2** is put back to the settings shown below, or set the **MODE** switch in the **VCA** section to **GATE** - this will disable the Envelope, and switch the amp fully on whenever a key is pressed.

This is to ensure that only the effect of the filter is heard, rather than the amplifier and envelope being responsible. Below we see the filter in its default state – it is not filtering anything out, because the cutoff frequency is set to maximum (99).

To hear the filter work, it is best to sequence and repeat a short (2 or 4 bars) section of short notes (such as the one shown for the Amplifier examples), and then alter the **Cutoff Freq** control while this plays back. You should hear the sound alter quite dramatically as you reduce the cutoff frequency.

Tip: Be careful with your monitoring level when using the filter, particularly with resonance in the next section as it is possible to get extremely loud sounds, which could damage your hearing if you are not careful!

Here is a frequency analysis of the original sound. We can see the fundamental tone on the left, and then all the harmonics, which extend into the high frequency range, giving this a sharp sound.

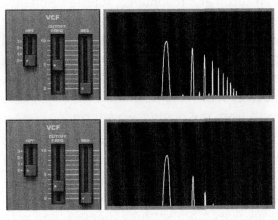

The cutoff frequency has been set to around the half way mark, and the result is this - there are far fewer harmonics present, and the sound is much duller, approximating the tone of a triangle wave.

The cutoff frequency has been reduced even further, and leads to a very dull, near sine-wave sound which has none of the rich, bright tone of the original sound.

The effect of the filter will vary depending on the original waveform you are filtering; as seen in the audio chapter on page 411 a sine wave has no harmonics, so it would not change tone (The PG-8X doesn't feature sine waves, but many other synthesizers do). Square and Sawtooth waves have lots of harmonics, and so will be considerably altered by the low pass filter removing them progressively.

Resonance

The PG-8X's filter is like many others, in that it has control of the resonance of the filter - this means it can boost the frequencies present at the cutoff point. This can make the sound of the filter a great deal more dramatic, and as seen later on in this section it is possible to create some interesting and varied sounds, but first we will take a look at the effect of resonance.

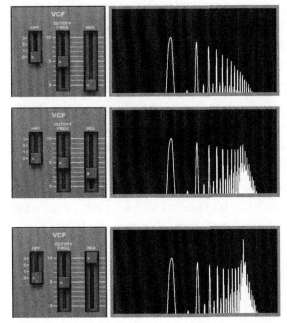

Here we see the original frequency analysis of the sound. The cutoff frequency is below that of the original example above, and some harmonics are being filtered out.

The resonance control has been turned up slightly, and the effect can be seen and heard - the sound is brighter, as the highest harmonics are being boosted.

Here the control has been set to maximum, and there is a clear peak where one harmonic is being boosted more than all the others, but in addition the entire high frequency area is louder (compare this with the first diagram).

To demonstrate the interaction between cutoff and resonance, set the resonance control to around the 50% mark and move the cutoff frequency control, starting at 100% and moving all the way down to 0. This resonant low-pass filter sound is one that is extremely common and has been used widely both on synthesized sounds and also on samples (see the Samplers chapter – page 293 – for details of this) Note that with the correct values of cutoff and resonance it's possible to produce sounds which are quite different from the original waveform.

However, to get the traditional analogue "squelchy" sound, an extra element is needed – the filter needs to alter over time. To achieve this, the filter's cutoff frequency will be changed using an envelope so it opens/closes automatically. This is a more complex piece of modulation (the controlling of one part of a synth using a signal from elsewhere), and it involves more settings changes than with the amplifier, as we need to set how much effect the envelope will have on the filter. This is done with the **ENV** control in the filter section:

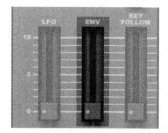

As a starting point, set the **ENV** slider to about 80, **CUTOFF FREQ** to around 40, and **RES** to around 70. This should allow for audible results (and ones that are visible in Cubase's EQ section spectrum analyser as well). Setting the **ATTACK** control of **ENVELOPE** 1 and playing a note should demonstrate the effect well; the filter will take a few seconds to reach its peak value, and the sound will 'open up' as it does so.

Once you have this working, it's possible to alter the controls to observe the effects - the envelope controls will work in a similar manner to those on the amplifier, but remember that the amplifier is currently set to turn off as soon as you release a key, so to hear the release control's effect you will need to alter the amplifier's envelope **RELEASE** control to allow that.

With the initial settings, the envelope is working in a 'positive' mode - it will increase the cutoff frequency, and allow more harmonics to be heard. It is, however, possible to invert the envelope's signal, and make it 'close' the filter. This is done with the **MODE** switch at the bottom of the filter section.

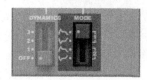

It has four settings - positive and inverted for each envelope - it's possible for the filter to follow either envelope 1 or envelope 2. Changing the polarity of the filter usually means that you need to alter the **CUTOFF FREQ** setting, as often it will mean the filter will be going too far in one direction or the other. As with all things, experimentation is the key to success here.

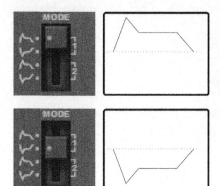

Envelope 1, Positive – the filter will follow the ADSR envelope, starting from the static cutoff frequency (shown as a dotted line), giving a sound which will brighten over time and then hold at the sustain level.

Envelope 1, Inverted – the filter will follow the envelope, but 'upside-down', starting off open and then closing with time, making a sound which will become more muffled.

The dynamics switch works in a similar way to the one in the Amplifier section, and can make for a more 'playable' sound by allowing MIDI velocity to have some effect on the filter envelope. In essence, it controls the setting of the **ENV** slider - a lower velocity means the envelope will have less effect than a high velocity, imitating real-world instruments which not only get louder when played harder, but whose tone changes to become sharper and brighter.

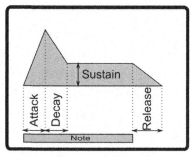

Here the note that is played is a low-velocity one, and as a result although the filter follows its usual ADSR envelope, all levels are reduced as result of the velocity. This leads to a note that is duller in tone as the filter doesn't open as far as it does when....

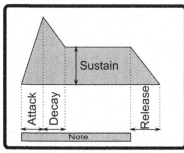

... the note is high velocity. This causes the envelope to act more strongly on the filter, and open it up further, giving a brighter, clearer sound. Routing note velocity to the filter envelope is an important technique when trying to emulate real instruments as well as making synthesized tones more expressive.

Finally, it's also possible to control the filter with the Low Frequency Oscillator.

Low Frequency Oscillator (LFO)

The LFO is an oscillator which runs constantly, and as the name says, at low frequency – typically it will be from around 0.01Hz (one cycle every 100 seconds) to 20Hz (20 cycles per second), although each synthesizer varies. The LFO doesn't generate audio itself (it is at too low a frequency), but is usually used to control other areas of the synth. If it is applied to the oscillator section's frequency, then the result is vibrato as the LFO will change the output of the oscillator over time. If it is applied to the amplifier, then the result is tremolo. If it is applied to the filter, the result can vary greatly from a subtle change in brightness to bizarre, special-FX type sounds.

LFOs usually feature a number of waveforms. In the case of the PG-8X there are three: Sine, Square and Random.

The PG-8X LFO has two main controls - **RATE** which controls the speed of the LFO, and **DELAY TIME** which is how long after a note has been played that the LFO starts to work. This can be useful to simulate performance characteristics of real instruments and voices.

The routing possibilities and functions of an LFO vary greatly between synthesizers – some (like the PG-8X) offer basic facilities, while others have a wide array of options, and sometimes several LFOs, which can be synched to MIDI or the sequencer's tempo to give more musical applications.

The Oscillators (DCOs)

The next area to consider is the initial sound that is generated – i.e. the Oscillator section. The PG-8X oscillator section is fairly typical of its era (it is based on a 1980s design). Some synths only have one oscillator, while some have several, and their functions can vary, but the PG-8X covers most of the basic, common functions.

RANGE: This is the basic (octave) tuning of each oscillator, and takes its values from the pipe length in organs - hence being marked in feet. A smaller number means a higher pitch. Note that the noise waveform does not respond to pitch or tuning.

WAVE FORM: The PG-8X has four waveforms available - Sawtooth, Square, Pulse and Noise. Each generates its own balance of harmonics, giving it a different tone. The noise waveform is useful for adding a percussive element to a sound, or for creation of ambient, evolving tones without any tonal element.

TUNE: This allows for detuning of the oscillator from the played pitch, over a range of +-1 octave.

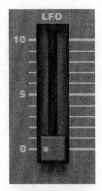

LFO: Provides pitch control from the LFO, allowing creation of vibrato effects. When used in conjunction with a square-wave LFO it is possible to create musical effects, particularly when using two oscillators at once.

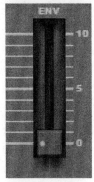

ENV: Allows overall control of the envelope's influence on pitch, opening up interesting creative possibilities. A fast-attacking envelope applied to pitch can create a much more apparent attack to the sound, while a slower, strong drop in pitch can make for interesting textural effects.

DYNAMICS: Controls the routing of MIDI Velocity to the **ENV** slider. When it is turned off, the **ENV** slider will work normally, but turning to **1–3** will control the setting dynamically, requiring a high velocity for the full **ENV** value to be heard.

MODE: In conjunction with the **ENV** control, picks the envelope and polarity of control of the sound's pitch.

FINE TUNE: This allows fine-tuning of OSC2's pitch, allowing subtle detuning to give a thicker sound.

CROSS MOD: This allows OSC2 to be linked to OSC1 in a number of different ways, with 3 (XMOD) offering some interesting possibilities when altering the tuning of OSC2 relative to OSC1

Two Oscillators at once

As mentioned above, using more than one oscillator has creative possibilities – it is possible to create a number of effects, using the settings outlined below, once **OSC2**'s Volume control has been set to make it audible too (set both to 99 to start out with)

Slight detune on OSC2 (around 6 cents) gives a thicker sound, mimicking a chorus effect, multiple players or an out-of-tune analogue synth.

The 'classic' fifths harmony sound, which plays the fundamental with OSC1 while playing a harmony seven semitones higher with OSC2.

By setting OSC2 to an octave below OSC1, an octave-doubled sound is achieved, thickening the texture greatly. This can be combined with the detuning shown above for a larger sound again.

With this example, the two oscillators are set similarly, but OSC2's CROSS MOD is set to XMOD (3) (as well as being set to be an octave below OSC1), creating a sound which has more power and attack than the two oscillators working independently.

There is a myriad of possibilities when using two oscillators, and their combinations are almost endless, especially when waveform types are taken into account. Experiment with the controls to see what you can create and discover.

MIDI Learn

Many synthesizers offer 'MIDI Learn' - a quick way to link an on-screen control to a real-world MIDI control, allowing much more expressive performance to be achieved. While each VSTi differs in its implementation, a quick look at how it works on the PG-8X is worthwhile, as many follow a similar scheme.

Controlling Cutoff Frequency

Let's control the CUTOFF FREQ using the Modulation controller on a MIDI keyboard (you can use any physical control you want to that outputs MIDI data - if you have a control keyboard with multiple such controls you can alter many settings at once in live performance). To do this, right-click on the control in question, and you will notice that the top-right area of the PG-8X alters to MIDI Learn mode:

The selected control is shown in the display, along with the current MIDI control for it - None.

Now alter the MIDI control on your keyboard, and it will be assigned to CUTOFF FREQ - this is reflected in the display.

In this example, the modulation wheel (CC1) was used, hence the display. Moving that control now alters the CUTOFF FREQ slider in real-time, allowing dynamic, musical performances to be created and captured by recording the MIDI data. It can, of course, be edited as with any other MIDI data - see page 87 for details of how to do this.

If the range of your controller is too great for the control on screen, then this can be altered using the MIN VALUE and MAX VALUE sliders. In this case, the filter was moving over too large a range, so this was restricted using the sliders, and giving more detailed control in the desired range.

It's possible to reverse the direction of a controller's influence by making **MIN VALUE** larger than **MAX VALUE**:

Adding more MIDI controllers to the synth is simply a case of repeating the process. It's possible to use the same MIDI controller to alter multiple parameters at once, and being able to limit or reverse the direction of the controller's influence can make for some impressively complex sonic changes with just a single control.

While this is the specific method that the PG-8X uses, many other VST Instruments offer MIDI Learn, allowing performance control to be quickly assigned and then recorded.

Storing A Sound

One of the great advantages of using virtual instruments in Cubase is that the setting of every control is saved with your project. In a physical studio with an analogue synth with no storage, you would have to reset every control to its previous setting to recreate a sound; a long-winded and often inaccurate task. While most synths now come with memories (sometimes referred to as 'Patch', 'Preset', 'Voice' or 'Timbre' storage), it can still be difficult to manage these when dealing with physical equipment.

However, sometimes you will want to mimic this procedure; imagine that you program a fantastic sound on the PG-8X that you want to use in other projects. To do this, we will look at how you can create and load Preset sounds in Cubase, making the recall of any sound quick and easy. This will work for nearly every VST Instrument, but a tiny minority don't provide the information to Cubase to allow this to work. The same process works for most effects as well, allowing you to use any sound you have created across multiple projects.

Firstly, ensure your sound is one you want to keep. Here is a sound programmed on the PG-8X:

To save it, click in the triangle at the top of the window ...

... and select **Save Preset**:

A new window will appear, showing the current presets for this synth - none in this case.

Type a name for your preset at the bottom, and hit **ENTER**.

The preset is now saved, and you will be able to load it whenever you have loaded a PG-8X.

Loading a Preset

There are two ways to load a preset - you can either navigate through the list using the arrows to the left of the triangle:

Or you can click on the current name or in the black area to the left of the cube, or in the small cube at the top of the window and select Load Preset:

The load preset window features filters by default - you can ignore these if you haven't set any, but they can be useful for filtering out results; see page 251 for how this works. Clicking on a preset loads it straight away, so be sure you only do this after you've saved your current sound if it isn't already saved.

Choosing a Preset by using Attributes

It's possible to choose a preset by an attribute - this could be its name, or how it has been described. This is done by choosing Using Track Preset... from the right-click menu in the project window track list.

The Choose Track Preset window will appear.

To pick sounds solely from synthesiser presets, select **VstPreset** in the left-hand column.

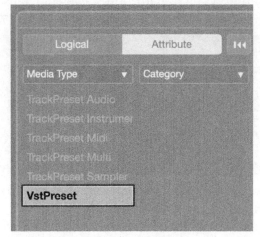

It will now be possible to search the presets using the following methods.

Searching by name

Often, searching by name is the quickest way to find a specific patch. Click in the **Search** box and start typing - as soon as you do, the list of patches is reduced to match. As seen below, just typing **bub** (for bubbles) gives the 11 possible sounds very quickly:

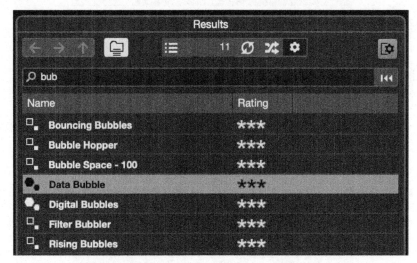

It's possible to audition the sound by clicking on it once, waiting for the synth to load (this happens in the background, so you won't see a synth appear), and then playing on your MIDI keyboard.

Once you find the sound you are after, click **Add Track** or hit **ENTER**, and the track (with the synth and preset loaded) will appear in the project, with the track named after the selected sound.

Filtering Results

Here, the filter section shows all the attributes available, plus the instruments on which they are played. The initial starting point here shows 7384 sounds.

Clicking on any character lists only the sounds that match that description. **Distorted** yields 704 results ...

... adding **Analog** to the filter reduces this to 244 ...

... and **Dark** reduces the number to a much more manageable 40 sounds to audition.

Bear in mind this system is not perfect - it's down to the programmers of the sounds to have attached appropriate attributes to the sounds, but it can allow navigation of the sizeable standard content that comes with Cubase, as well as any sounds that you have added attributes to.

Adding Attributes to Sounds

If you want to use the attribute system, then adding some attributes whenever you save a sound will allow you to reference your own sounds using this method. To do this, you will need to re-save the preset you are working on - if it has already been saved, you will see the preset name with .vstpreset at the end, as seen below:

Now in the attribute inspector (click the button at the top right if it is not visible), you can pick the appropriate attributes by clicking the value column.

Clicking in the **Character** section will open this window ...

... where you can choose the appropriate terms for your sound.

Once this is done, click **OK**, set any other values you wish, and click **OK** to save. You'll be asked if you want to over-write the preset (you do), and then you will be able to search for that sound via its attributes like all the others.

Converting to VST Presets

If clicking on the name of the current sound leads to a list of presets, this is because these sounds are stored in the previous format that Cubase used. This will often be the case with older freeware synths. Converting these sounds to VST Presets has some advantages in that they can become searchable when creating a new synth; if you remember the name of a preset, then Cubase will load the appropriate synth. Converting is easy to do, and only needs to be done once for each synth. Click on the cube, and select `Convert Program List to VST Presets`...

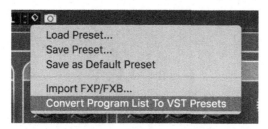

... and you will see a progress bar as Cubase converts the programs to presets.

Sometimes it will find duplicates - usually (if this is the first time you have done this), you can tick `Please, don't ask again`, and then `Overwrite`.

Once this is done, the presets will be added to Cubase's database, allowing a synth to be loaded by searching for the patch name. If you want to add attributes - not a small task for every preset, but possibly worthwhile for your most-commonly-used sounds - then you can follow the process earlier in this section.

Halion Sonic

Halion Sonic (HS) is a synthesizer, but it works in a different way than the subtractive synths we have seen earlier in this chapter. It combines tdifferent 'engines' to produce sound, and as a result has become an interesting and useful synthesizer in its own right. We will take a quick tour of its features - both as a General MIDI workhorse which will provide basic everyday sounds for simple sequencing tasks, but also the programming features that it provides when working in its other modes - 'Trip' and 'Flux'.

The Main Window

Here we see the initial window of HS, where you can select sounds for each of the 16 parts that run down the left-hand side of the window. The right-hand side of the window is the Load Panel, an implementation of MediaBay (see page 117) which allows search, filtering and loading of sounds.

This follows the same principle of search which is used across Cubase, and which is outlined in the section on choosing sounds on page 250 of this chapter. Double-clicking a sound causes it to be loaded in the currently-selected slot. It's also possible to open the load Panel area by clicking on the folder icon at the right-hand end of a selected slot:

This is useful when you are in another area of the synth, or have closed the Load Panel to save space, with the icon on the toolbar, located at the top right of the main synth window:

The Edit Page

HS generates many of its sounds from samples - wavetables - and for these it doesn't offer the same level of editing as a subtractive synthesizer might do, but there are still creative possibilities to explore here. In addition to basic tuning controls and flexible pitch-bend range controls (with independent settings for up and down pitch bend), there are filter and amplifier sections, with similar controls to those of a subtractive synth; these alone can take a mundane sound such as a simple piano and make it much more interesting by altering the attack, release and filter from those expected, as seen in the screenshot below.

The MIDI Page

Here it's possible to alter MIDI-based characteristics - notably the note range that each part will respond on, as well as transposition and polyphony.

This can be useful as a substitute for altering the MIDI data that you are working with.

The Mix Page

The Mix page gives access to level, pan and effects send controls, as well as selection of outputs when using multiple outputs to allow audio effects and processing to be applied outside of HS. There are also level meters which show the audio level from each track as it plays.

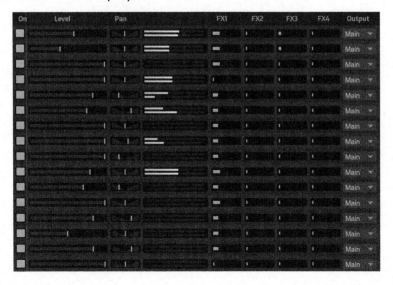

The Effects Page

HS has four effects sends built in. When loading a MIDI file, FX1 will typically contain a reverb and FX3 a chorus as this is part of the General MIDI specification, but each slot can contain up to four effects from a large selection as seen here.

An effect's settings can be changed by clicking the **e** and editing them in the panel below.

The Options Page

Here a large number of settings are available, most of which may not be needed for most users, but allow complete control of settings to improve performance.

Trip

Trip is a virtual analogue (subtractive) synthesizer. To access it, load a Trip sound by going to the Load page, and picking 'TRIP' from the menu that appears. You can then select a sound, and the Edit page will look similar to the one shown below.

If you have spent some time with the PG-8X, then this should look familiar to you - there are many of the controls you've already learned here. At the bottom there is a filter (with selectable filter types), and an ADSR for the filter and amplifier, plus an overall amplifier level and velocity control.

There are four edit pages, the first of which is the Oscillator.

Oscillator (OSC)

Trip has three oscillators, whose features are common to many such synths - waveform selection, tuning and level can all be edited, and there are three to blend together.

Sub (SUB)

The sub page contains a sub-oscillator with several waveforms to choose from, plus a ring modulator, which produces the sum and difference between the selected oscillators - this is often used to add a metallic tone to a sound. There is also a noise oscillator with four noise waveforms to choose from, as well as some standard configuration options such as number notes and overall tuning.

Modulation (MOD)

The modulation page contains a standard LFO which can be routed to a number of different areas of the synth - which have been usefully colour-coded. The bottom section controls how much effect the modulation wheel MW will have on the selected areas of the synth, as well as a frequency control for this.

Arpeggio (ARP)

The arpeggio section of the synth offers some control - but not a full range - of the effect of the arpeggio section, which is present in the presets and can't be turned off - this should be taken in the context that HS is a reduced version of the full Halion Sonic synth, and as a result not every feature you may want is available. If the arpeggio pattern is suited (or inspirational) to what you are doing, then it will be positive, but it limits the programming and musical potential of Trip if it is not aligned with your musical vision.

Flux

Flux is a wavetable synthesizer; while HS is generally based on this sound synthesis method, Flux gives access to a number of controls and facilities to make it a useful sound-generating synth in its own right. Getting access to it is achieved by loading a Flux sound - easily done by going to the Load page, and then picking Flux from the graphic menu that appears. Picking a sound is then done in the usual manner; as a starting point for editing shown, 'Be Free' was chosen. Once loaded, the Edit page is transformed, providing the controls to edit the synthesizer in much more detail than the standard edit page. While the features of the Flux engine would take many pages to cover in full detail, it is worth taking a look at what it is capable of, as it can be extremely creative and capable of a real variety of sounds. Each section of the synth can be turned off using the buttons at the top:

In addition, Flux presets in HS usually feature a number of effects which can only be accessed via the performance controls section at the bottom of the screen. While these can be useful, they do not aid learning what's happening at a deep level in the synth, so turn them off while experimenting with the different sections of the synth so that you can hear what's happening without it being altered by several audio effects.

The full version of HS allows control over these effects, but you may want to select a preset to work from on the basis of the effects which are included with it - some auditioning of the presets will allow this - for instance, 'Be Free' includes a Ring Modulator, a Resonator and a Reverb, while 'Alarm Device' features a Multi Delay. The controls present for these effects depends on the preset, and are not editable, so you may well end up bypassing them entirely, and then using separate outs into Cubase's mixer to allow full control of the audio and effects applied. See page 38 for details on how to do this with HS.

The Bottom Section

The bottom section is visible in all pages aside from Arpeggio, and gives access to controls which have been seen previously on a subtractive synth; on the left there is the filter (with many filter types and options available)

The filter has its own ADSR envelope (if you're unsure of filtering or use of the ADSR here, go to page 240).

The right-hand part of the bottom section has three tabs - The first has controls for the two ADSR envelopes (one for the filter, one for the amplifier) - if you're unsure of how this can alter the sound, read the section starting on page 237.

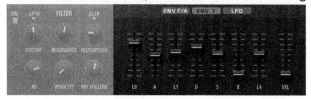

The second tab has access to a third envelope generator, which has more features than the ADSR seen previously; there are level controls for the start (**L0**), attack (**L1**) and end (**L4**), allowing signals that a standard ADSR cannot produce. It is not pre-configured for any particular part of the synth, so its use will become apparent in the Modulation page.

The third tab has controls for the two LFOs - again, these will become of importance after seeing the Modulation page, as it is there where the section(s) controlled by the LFO is set.

OSC Page

The OSC page allows control of the two wavetable-based oscillators. To allow better understanding of the OSC section, turn everything off aside from **OSC1**:

Each oscillator has a range of waveforms available by clicking in the top section (**Saw x Sine RM Sweep** in the screenshots following), and even just changing waveform here can drastically alter the sound produced. Standard controls for octave, course and fine tune allow for control of the sound's pitch, while the position control alters the wavetable sound considerably - to hear this, turn Formant off, and disable the filter (with the 'On' button at to the left of the filter section), and sweep the control while listening to the change in tone.

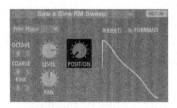 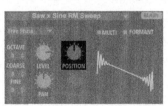 

The **FORMANT** control alters the harmonic content - again, achieving drastic changes in the case of some waveforms. Turn it on and sweep the control through its extremes; at the 12 o'clock position the harmonics are unaltered; turning to the left decreases the harmonic content and to the right increases it, creating a much harsher sound.

 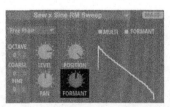 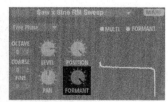

Activating **Multi** allows up to 8 oscillators to be triggered when each sound is played, with detuning thickening the sound considerably.

SUB Page

The Sub page has a fairly standard **Sub Oscillator**, with choice of waveforms, level and pan.

The phase controls allow some control over the relationship between the sub oscillator and the others. There is a lot more interest in the **Noise** section:

This is another wavetable oscillator with an varied selection of wavetables available.

Some are glitchy electronic sounds, while there are also drum attacks which can add a real punch to a sound when used appropriately; this can save a lot of effort doubling a sound up with a sampled drum, as it's all present in the synth itself.

MOD Page

The Modulation page is where some of the most powerful creative possibilities lie within Flux. Here it is possible to use one or more signals to control an aspect of the sound generation engine, allowing complex, evolving tones to be generated using the wide selection of sources and destinations for modulation. The possibilities are almost endless, but a brief overview of the facilities is in order. We will start from a blank slate, so turn every row off aside from the first one...

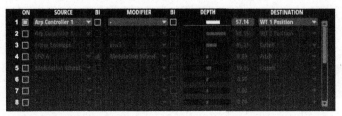

... and then reset the settings on the first slot to be completely clear:

A simple task would be to send an LFO to an oscillator, which will lead to vibrato. This is assigned by picking the source **LFO A**, and the destination **Pitch**, and picking an amount by altering the depth - 2 semitones in this case.

Note that you may need to go to the LFO tab of the bottom section and alter the rate - the default speed from the preset is very fast.

Simple enough, but that will affect notes all the time - not something that's always wanted. To rectify this, using the **Modifier** section will allow control of whether the source gets to the destination. Changing this to **Modulation Wheel** will mean that the MIDI keyboard Modulation Wheel will control how much (if any) of the LFO signal gets through to control Pitch.

Using the modulation section, it is possible to control almost any aspect of the sound with almost any part of the synth that is capable of sending a suitable signal - this includes **Env3** that we saw earlier on. There is a huge amount of control available in this section, and experimentation (and examination of the modulation used in some of the preset sounds) will really pay off here.

Voice Page

The Voice page has typical controls - polyphony (number of simultaneous notes playable), plus setting up Mono mode (often useful for lead sounds with performance controlled by overlapping notes in MIDI data), Glide, and pitch bend settings, etc.

ARP Page

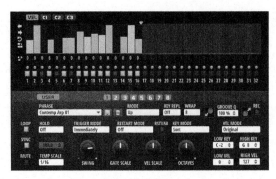

The Arpeggio generator is powerful and has many features - another section which would require many pages to cover it in full. In short, it has up to 32 steps, and can not only output notes, but also other data (C1, C2, C3) which can be used on the MOD page to control the synth's sound rhythmically, and has a wide range of presets to learn from and develop.

Using the Arpeggiator

We will take a quick look at use of the Arpeggiator through a few examples. It's possible to alter the arpeggiator pattern length by dragging the triangle at the top of the pattern section to the appropriate location. In the default pattern for the preset we have been using, it is 16 steps long.

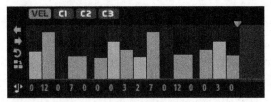

Dragging it to 4 makes it a beat (4 16ths) long.

It's now quick and easy to create a simple 'octaves bass' pattern - Turning step 2 off and step 3 on, using the buttons below them ...

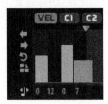

... reducing the velocities of steps 3 and 4 ...

... and changing the transpose of steps 3 and 4 to 12 ...

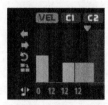

... gives a classic house bass sound from a single note. Note that step 2, while still set to 12, is ignored as it is turned off. Playing a single note applies the programmed rhythm to that single note. The effect of the swing control can now be heard - play a note on a keyboard to hear the pattern while altering the control.

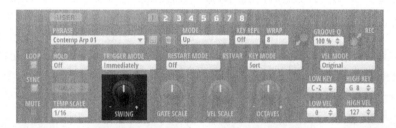

A setting of zero sounds fixed and robotic - reminiscent of the 1980s. Around 30 sounds swung and more human ... ... 100 changes the feel of the rhythm considerably ... ... while -100 accents the beat differently.

Setting the steps as follows ...

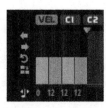

... and playing a 3 note chord creates a pattern with an alternating bass note played at the beginning of each cycle. Many of the classic arpeggiator-based pieces of music (such as that of Tangerine Dream) is based on there being a different number of steps to the musical information present - whether that is the number of notes played, or the number of steps in a bar (so that the pattern shifts position in the bar each time it repeats). Even with just these features, there is a lot of experimentation and creativity to be had.

The Lower Section

The lower section of the arpeggiator has many options (including loading presets) - again, far too many to cover in full in this brief tour - so spend some time playing with each; some of the highlights are the **Mode** option (which allows playing of a complete chord on each step in **Chord** mode, as well as some more varied patterns than the initial **Up** one), **Trigger Mode** (which can help with performance and alter the way you approach the arpeggios), the **Octave** control (for creating bigger arpeggios), and the **Gate Scale** control which (depending on the sound you are using) can produce some vintage-style arpeggio sound sweeps.

Using the Arpeggio Controllers

We have seen how to use the arpeggiator to control notes, but it can also be used as a step sequencer for controlling any modulation destination. An example will help with the understanding of this. Take the previous phrase and use the duplicate phrase button to copy it across the entire 32 steps quickly and easily:

Pressing the button a few times will save time, and produce a pattern with a note on every step, as seen next:

Now switch to the C1 lane:

... draw in a pattern ...

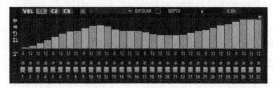

... and play. Note that there will be no change because of the C1 controller at the moment - this is because the MOD page is not set to control any part of the synth with it. Switch to the MOD page, and note the setup from earlier - using the Modwheel to control vibrato:

Now use the second modulation row to set C1 to alter the filter cutoff frequency:

Arp Controller 1 is being sent to Cutoff, with a value of around 60. Playing a pattern now alters the filter cutoff (you may need to alter the number you have put and the pattern you have created for C1, and also ensure the filter is turned on - the default settings from the preset shown below give audible results).

There are 3 controllers and many destinations in the modulation section, so there is a lot of control available with this feature. While this has covered some of the specifics of HS Flux's arpeggiator section, the ideas are common to other synths, effects and standalone step sequencer plugins (such as B-Step Sequencer), opening your creative possibilities many times over.

Other Synths

An important part of learning to program synthesizers is to use multiple different instruments. There are a number of reasons for this:

Different Controls

There are hundreds of VST Instrument subtractive synthesizers available, from freeware models such as the PG-8X and TAL's excellent range of synths, through powerful commercial synthesizers such as Sylenth 1 and Massive, right up to complex modular synths aping real models from Moog and beyond. Many of these will offer different (and in some cases unique) methods of controlling the synth's settings and modulating the sound creation process. Getting as much experience as possible of these is important, providing it doesn't leave you feeling overwhelmed. The controls of a Moog Modular are daunting at first, but a significant portion of such a synth is made up of building blocks you already have experience with - Oscillators, Amplifiers, Filters, Envelope Generators and LFOs. There will, of course, be new elements to learn, understand and harness, but they will probably work in a way you can understand once you have the basics down.

TAL Elec7ro

Here is the Tal Elec7ro. It has a total of four oscillators (two fully functional, a third SUB oscillator, and a noise oscillator). The filter is generally easy to follow, but here the Envelope Depth control seen on the PG-8X is replaced by a CON-TOUR control. The envelope section has a standard ADSR (which controls the level of Oscillators 1 & 2), and another simpler AD envelope, which can be sent to a number of destinations (here it is set to OSC1). There are two LFOs with multiple destinations. Nearly every feature of the synth has already been seen in the PG-8X, but they are arranged in a different manner, and it takes a little practice to understand the differences in controls and modulation options.

Sylenth 1

This is Sylenth 1. While it is a top-of-the-range synth - and a full explanation of all its functions would run to many pages - a quick look around shows features that you have already seen in the PG-8X. Along the top there are two oscillators, with an Amp ADSR that controls both of them. There are actually four oscillators in the synth, but the others (in part B) are the same as the ones seen here. There is a filter with cutoff and resonance controls, and on the right there is a mixer for mixing parts A and B. There are two more envelopes along the bottom, each of which can have two destinations (see that here Modulation Envelope 2 is set to alter cutoff and resonance of the filter). There are two LFOs (again with selectable destinations), and finally some other modulation areas where it's possible to select simple sources (such as modulation wheel or velocity as seen here) and send them to destinations on the synth. In the LCD section there are a number of extra features such as an arpeggiator and a number of audio effects, but there's nothing fundamentally new here, just high-quality synthesizer elements linked together with excellent modulation options.

Different Sounds

It's easy to think that if you set two synths to the same settings, they will sound the same. That may be true in theory, but in reality most synths sound different to each other, and that is because they don't do the same job in the same way. Here are square waves on three different synths - none have been filtered, and all are playing the same pitch.

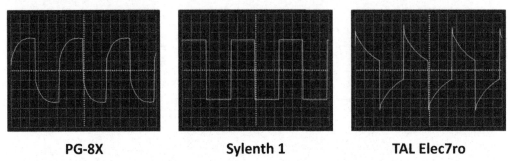

| PG-8X | Sylenth 1 | TAL Elec7ro |

Clearly these three are all different - all sound like square waves, but have their own character. These differences spread to just about every part of a synth, particularly the filters, an area which many analogue subtractive synth buffs say is where the real sound of the instrument comes from. It may simply not be possible to get a sound that one synth makes using another synth - it will be close, but not identical. Experience and experimentation will help you know which synth will be right in any given situation.

Different Features

While many of the elements that make a synth up will be similar (details notwithstanding), some synths offer features which are not available elsewhere. Native Instruments' Massive offers modulation possibilities that most other synths can't match, while Arturia's Modular V offers the equivalent of a Moog Modular that would cost you the price of a house to own. But it's not solely expensive synths that have unusual or unique features; Greenoak's Crystal (while not solely a subtractive synth) offers unusual sound synthesis and preset generation tools. The Tyrell N6 offers complex modulation and a ring modulator for some unusual sound-creation options. While there are many free VST Instruments which are simple and not particularly interesting, there are some which are professional-sounding and worthy of auditioning and use. The more of them you use, the better you will understand all of them.

Exercises

Listen to waveforms

Being able to identify different basic waveforms by ear is an important skill - hopefully at first the sine wave will sound quite different to the others, but hearing the difference between the others outlined on page 410 can take some practice. While there are a near-infinite number of waveforms, being able to recognise the basic ones will help you in being able to analyse sounds that you hear in other people's music, and program synthesizers to mimic them.

Use the amplifier's ADSR

The ADSR is the cornerstone of making synthesized sounds dynamic; without one the sound would be static with respect to time. Spend some time practicing using the ADSR to create sounds and mimic the dynamic changes of real instruments, and mastering the controls. Many people find the A and R components are easy to understand, but remembering that the signal level always reaches maximum at the end of the A phase, and that S is a level, not a time is something to keep in mind, as well as the D control becoming irrelevant if the S control is at 100% (as there is no change in level, the time taken is meaningless).

Use the filter

Filtering is the next important concept in subtractive synthesis (and indeed many forms of modern music production). Being able to recognise different kinds of filter is important; while a great many filtered sounds that are heard will be low pass filters (often with resonance), being able to recognise high-pass filtering and band-pass filtering is important, and with practice should be second nature. Remember that not all synths give a choice of filter type; while the PG-8X (see page 240) offers a low pass as the main filter, many others (such as the TAL Elec7ro-II) offer a selection, and learning which filters to use when is important.

Use the filter's ADSR

While a static filtered sound is more interesting that an unfiltered one, the change of filter cutoff over time is important to create truly interesting and dynamic sounds. The ADSR is the same as featured in the amplifier section, but controlling the tonal balance gives a completely different result. While experimenting it's important to ensure that the amplifier ADSR settings are not stopping you from hearing the effects of the filter ADSR; if the amplifier ADSR has already gone to 0% you won't hear what's happening with the filter as there is no signal.

Use multiple oscillators

A single-oscillator synth gives a wide range of sounds, but adding extra oscillators gives many more options - it's possible to detune the two oscillators relative to each other, both fine-tune and interval-based tuning will create interesting effects. There is also the option of using different waveforms for the two oscillators, giving a much wider range of tonal options. Listening to the effects of this as you experiment is important, as it will allow you to recognise where others have used similar techniques.

Summary

Subtractive Synthesis (as outlined in this chapter) gives a huge range of timbres, and there are many, many virtual synthesizers available today, some of which are new designs, some of which mimic hardware devices of yesteryear. In addition, 'real' synthesizers still exist, and knowing the basics of how to program any one of these devices will give you the ability to create unique sounds, mimic sounds that you have heard and also provides a basis for many activities that are done with conventional samplers. Familiarity with the controls and facilities of each synthesizer is a pre-requisite for being able to program them successfully, and this takes time and experimentation to fully master. However, even casual familiarity with features such as filters will allow quick programming of many effects that have become trademarks of modern music production. It is important to remember that even the most complex subtractive synthesizers which offer a huge range of modulation possibilities (such as Native Instruments' Massive) and modular synthesizers such as the Moog Modular (whether the real thing or Arturia's software equivalent) are based on the principles shown in this chapter, and only when mastering programming of a synth with simple architecture (such as the PG-8X and its real-world equivalent the Roland JX-8P) can the programming of a more complex instrument be possible.

MIDI
Remote

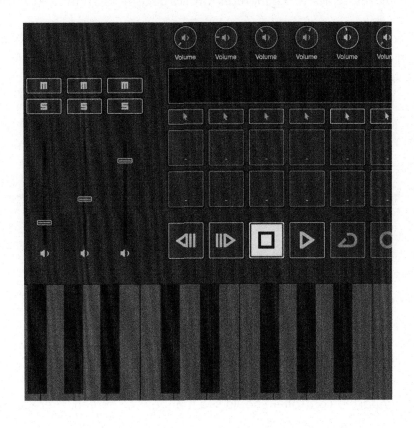

Cubase 12 introduced a new way for Cubase to interface with physical controllers that send MIDI data - MIDI Remote. The system has two modes of operation:

Script API Mode - this mode allows Steinberg and device manufacturers to create dedicated scripts with complex functionality. The list of supported devices will grow over time, and they are included when Cubase is installed. Plugging in a supported controller should lead to it being recognised by Cubase and the script activated automatically.

MIDI Controller Surface Mode - this mode allows creation of a user-defined set of controls, allowing any device that generates MIDI to be used as a remote controller.

Both modes are accessed in the lower zone, so enable it either using the zone control button at the top right, or using the keyboard (**CTRL/⌘ + ALT + E**). Click the **MIDI Remote** tab, and an empty MIDI Remote area should look as seen below:

Script API Mode

While it is possible for a user who is proficient in JavaScript programming to create their own script, for most users, this mode will be 'plug-and-play'. If you plug in a supported controller, it should be recognised by Cubase and appear as a MIDI Remote straight away.

Connecting a supported controller should see it appear on screen. Here an Akai MPK Mini Mk3 has been connected:

Movement of the controls on the device should be reflected on screen. In the case of the MPK Mini, the pads need to be set to CC mode for the buttons to operate - details like these will be specific to each device. Clicking the *i* at the top right (if present) will open an included PDF with help for the device and any settings changes needed.

Once the device is connected and working, you can add to its functionality by adding additional mapping pages as seen on page 286. Due to their complexity, creating scripts using JavaScript falls outside the scope of this book.

MIDI Controller Surface Mode

This mode allows use of any device that generates MIDI as a remote control. While it doesn't offer some of the complexity of script API mode, it will work with any device that generates MIDI, and doesn't require any knowledge of coding to use. This section will cover the basics of getting up and running with a MIDI controller, and use a simple example to demonstrate the process. Most MIDI controllers provide a large number of buttons, faders or knobs, but once you are familiar with the creation workflow, adding extra controls is merely a case of repeating the same actions.

Adding a MIDI Controller Surface

The first step to adding a MIDI Controller Surface is to connect it to your computer. With many controllers, this will be done by connecting a USB cable, but some older units will be connected via MIDI cables and a MIDI interface. In this case, if you want the device to show visual feedback of control status, then you will need to make sure there is a MIDI Output connection back to the controller.

With the device connected, open the lower zone, and click the large **+**, and you should be taken to the **Add MIDI Controller Surface** screen:

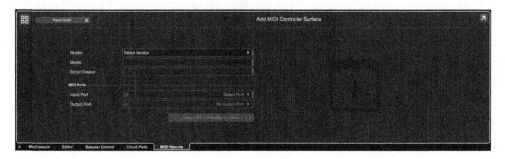

Add the required information for Vendor, Model, Script Creator and also select the MIDI Input and Output for the device. In this case, an Akai **MIDIMix** was added:

Once the settings are correct, click the **Create MIDI Controller Surface** below the settings to go to the surface editor:

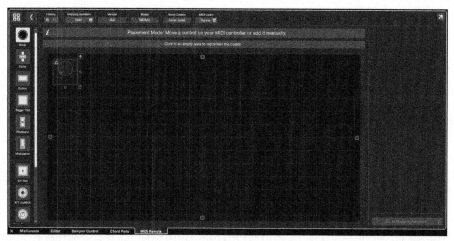

This is the page where controls are added to the surface. Note that there are multiple types of control available on the left-hand-side - **Knob**, **Fader** and **Button** are the three controls we will be making use of (as the MIDIMix features these), but the others on the left work in the same way as seen here. In the case of the MIDIMix, each 'channel' consists of three knobs, two buttons and a fader. To keep this example simple, only one of the 8 channels will be created here.

While it is unlikely that you will have a MIDIMix available, most MIDI controllers have a combination of knobs, buttons and faders, and once you have created a MIDI Remote using these, you'll have the skills needed to add any of the other controller types available in the editor.

The surface editor will create a new control of the selected type as soon as it gets a new MIDI message. In the current mode, it is 'waiting' for a new MIDI message, and the control that will be created is on screen in red. Moving a control on the MIDIMix will do two things:

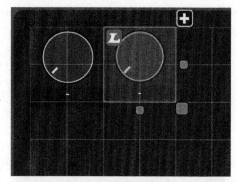

A knob has been created, linked to the MIDI message that the control sent. In addition, a new knob is present, waiting for MIDI data to be sent.

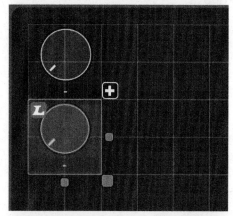

Before this is created, it will be moved to match the physical layout of the controls on the MIDIMix by clicking on the grid in the desired location:

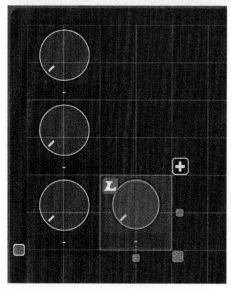

Moving the second knob on the MIDIMix attaches this message to the control. Another knob is ready to be created, which once again is moved before sending the MIDI message by turning the third knob:

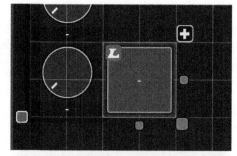

The next two controls on the MIDIMix are buttons. Select **Button** on the left-hand side, and the waiting control will change in appearance:

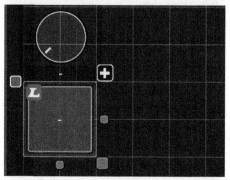

Move the button to below the bottom knob ...

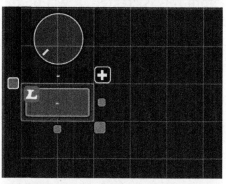

... and then click and drag the square handle at the bottom right of the square to resize the button:

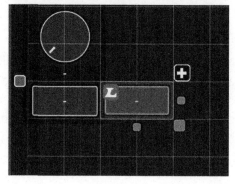

With the button set correctly, pressing the button on the MIDIMix attaches the MIDI message and creates a new button ready to be used:

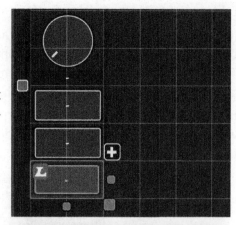

Moving the second button to the correct location and pressing the button on the MIDIMix completes the needed buttons.

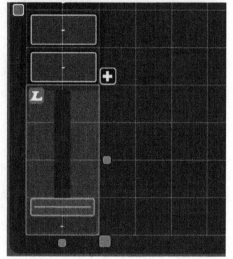

Finally a fader is needed, so press **Fader** on the left-hand side of the screen. The waiting fader will need to be moved and resized ...

... and sending the MIDI message by moving the fader completes the channel's controls. Once controls are added, they can either be edited (as seen next), or allocated functions in the Mapping Assistant, as seen on page 280.

Below, the complete MIDIMix Remote is shown, with all controls created.

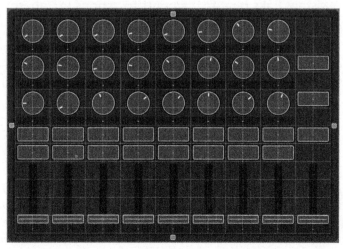

Editing A MIDI Controller Surface

It is possible to edit a controller surface once it has been created by clicking the pencil in the `MIDI Controller` section at the top of the MIDI Remote lower zone. This will return to the learn stage seen above. Adding new controls here is simply a case of following the instructions there.

Editing any existing control is performed by clicking on the relevant control. It will turn blue, and the right-hand side of the lower zone will show the assigned properties for the item.

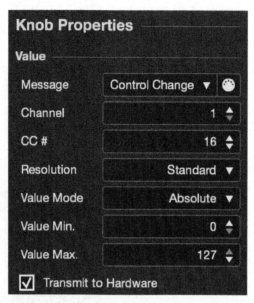

Here it is possible to edit the resolution and value mode of the learned control, and also indicate whether the incoming signal should be repeated back to the controller, allowing disconnection of a button and the indicating LED, for instance.

The Mapping Assistant

The Mapping Assistant links remote elements to actions in Cubase, and it is here where most of the setup of a MIDI Remote is completed. It can be reached by clicking the > at the bottom right of the lower zone from the surface learn / edit mode. You can also open the mapping assistant using the button in the MIDI Remote section of the lower zone, or at the right of the toolbar in the project window:

Here is the mapping assistant after creating the controls seen previously:

The top section of the window is where controls (on the left) are linked to functions (on the right). There are two ways to select a control - either on the surface which is shown in the middle of the window, or by moving a control on the control surface. In this case, the fader on the MIDIMix was moved, leading the fader to be selected, as seen on the left of the top section:

Next, a Cubase function needs to be linked to the control. There are two ways to do this, either by clicking it in Cubase, or by the functions browser.

Using The Functions Browser

The browser makes it easy to locate a given function, so that is the route that will be initially taken here. Open the browser by clicking the button in the top right of the mapping assistant window:

While it is possible to expand the functions in the right-hand side of the window, it's often more productive to make use of the search bar at the top. In this case, the fader on the MIDIMix is to be linked to the channel fader, which is called **Volume**. Typing **volume** in the search area will reveal a suitable list of candidates, and here we will choose `Selected Track > Volume`. Clicking this shows an appropriate icon in the Cubase Function section of the Mapping Assistant:

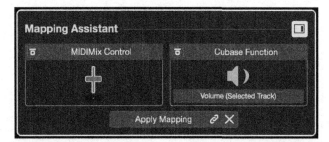

The final step to apply this mapping is to click `Apply Mapping` at the bottom of the top section of the mapping assistant. The bottom section of the mapping assistant now shows that the mapping is in place:

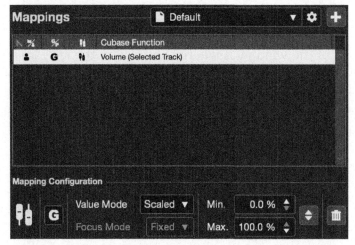

Note that it is possible to apply a mapping directly from the Functions Browser by double-clicking the function.

If you need to edit or delete the mapping, see the section on page 284.

Clicking A Function In Cubase

The other route to create a mapping is to select a function directly in Cubase, although this can lead to an incorrect function being selected. For this example the **Mute** control will be linked to a button on the MIDIMix. Firstly, the button is pressed on the MIDIMix:

Next, the desired control is right-clicked in Cubase - here the selected track's **Mute** button was right-clicked:

Selecting **Pick For MIDI Remote Mapping:Mute** will alter the settings in the mapping assistant:

This illustrates the issue that can occur when using this method to map functions. While this will operate the mute button, it has actually selected the mute for the first channel in a 'Mixer Bank Zone', rather than for the 'Selected Channel'. This may work in some situations, but in others it will mute a different channel than the one expected, so always be sure that the correct function is being mapped. In this particular case, the button was re-mapped using the functions browser to **Selected Channel > Mute** as this was more suitable for a single set of controls.

Potential Pitfalls

Cubase is a complex piece of software, and this is highlighted by the difference shown above between the 'Selected Channel' mute and 'Mixer Bank Zone Channel 1' mute. Programming a MIDI Remote will mean you may encounter some of these issues and need to alter your mapping, but this is easily done using the tools seen in the following sections.

Note that the remote will not function until you close the Mapping Assistant window, so you will need to test the newly-created remote first, and re-open the mapping assistant afterwards.

Altering Mappings

Once you have created a mapping, it is possible to alter the details of it in the lower section of the mapping assistant window. Here is the full set of mappings created for the MIDIMix:

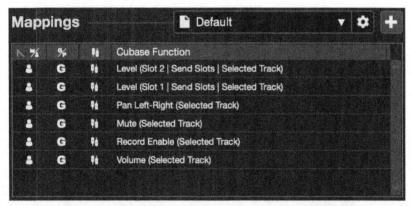

Selecting any mapping enables editing in the bottom section of the window:

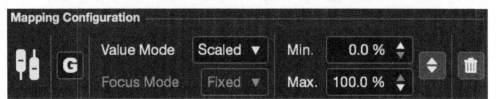

There are a number of settings here, from left to right:

Mapping Scope

Here it is possible to set a mapping to be **G**lobal (so it will be present whenever the controller is connected, regardless of the project), or **P**roject, where it will only appear in a given project. It is often useful to add a mapping which is specific to a given project, and this makes this simple to achieve without altering mappings in other projects.

Takeover

This has three modes - Jump, Pickup and Scaled:

Jump: As soon as the controller sends a message, Cubase follows it. This is generally what you would want for buttons, but can also be useful for knobs and sliders. The issue is that a physical control will not be where Cubase is set to initially, so this can lead to big jumps when the control is first touched.

Pickup: In pickup mode, Cubase's control stays where it is until the remote control reaches that point, and then it takes full control. This is a useful way to avoid sudden changes which jump mode creates, but it disconnects the physical control from Cubase until they agree, which can be confusing - it's possible to move a control and get no changes on screen from this.

Scaled: Scaled attempts to fix the 'dead spot' issue of pickup mode, without the sudden changes of jump mode. It does this by scaling the difference between the physical control and Cubase's current setting, allowing control to still work until the two agree. Once they do, the control directly alters the setting. This is the default for Volume mappings.

Toggle

Toggle is useful for controls which have two states (typically on and off). When you press a button on a MIDI controller it sends an 'on' message, and when you release it, it will send an 'off' message. Take the example of a Mute button; if toggle mode is disabled, then the Mute will follow the controller button press exactly - as soon as you release the button, it will no longer be muted. While this can be desirable in some situations (such as creating stutter effects, etc.), for most switched controls, a 'Press once to activate, press again to deactivate' is the desired function, and toggle achieves this.

Minimum and Maximum Values

These alter how much control the MIDI Remote has over the mapped control. For instance, setting the maximum to 50% for a volume control will mean that even when the remote fader is all the way up, Cubase's fader will only reach 50% (which equates to around -8dB). Swapping these two values with the **Invert Minimum and Maximum** button can be useful when a control does the opposite of the desired effect.

Deleting A Mapping

To delete a mapping, simply select it in the list, and press the 'Remove Selected Mapping' button at the right-hand end of the **Mapping Configuration** section:

Mapping Pages

Initially, surface mode maps come with a single Default mapping page. Script API mode maps may come with other pages, but in both cases it is possible to add more mapping pages, allowing more flexibility. Adding a mapping page is quick, and once added, it is possible to add mappings as seen earlier in this chapter.

Adding A Mapping Page

There are two options for adding mapping pages - either starting from scratch, or duplicating an existing mapping page. If you have a mapping page with multiple controls and want to keep several of them (such as a bank of channel faders), then duplication followed by altering/deletion of the controls to change is a good route to take.

To duplicate an existing mapping page, press the cog to the right of the current map...

... and select Duplicate from the menu that appears. Once duplicated, you can use the menu to rename the page (if appropriate), and then edit it as seen on page 280.

Alternatively, you can create a new page from scratch by clicking the + button to the right of the existing mapping page...

... naming the mapping page and then mapping the desired controls as seen on page 280. This will be the route that you need to take if you want to add a new page to a factory script, as the factory functions cannot be deleted from a page.

Selecting A Mapping Page

It is possible to select a mapping page from the drop-down menu at the top of the MIDI Remote section in the lower zone.

It is also possible to assign this function to buttons on a MIDI Remote, which will allow quick selection of pages from dedicated hardware controls, meaning that it is possible to change mapping pages without having the editor open or using the mouse. If your MIDI Remote has enough buttons available to do this, it's worth planning ahead when creating an initial page which can then be duplicated as a template for other pages to add to.

MIDI Remote Manager

The MIDI Remote Manager allows a number of useful features, some of which will be covered here. It is summoned from the top of the MIDI Remote lower zone:

MIDI Controllers Tab

The MIDI Controllers tab shows the details of any MIDI Controllers present on the system - including ones which are not currently connected:

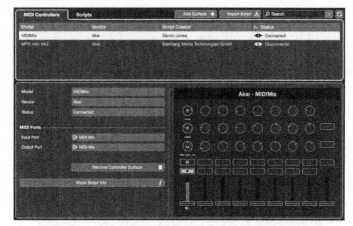

It is possible to remove a script API-based controller surface from this window. This will not delete the script file, just make it invisible in Cubase until the controller is reattached.

Scripts Tab

The scripts tab shows all the scripts that Cubase can currently access - both factory scripts and user-created ones.

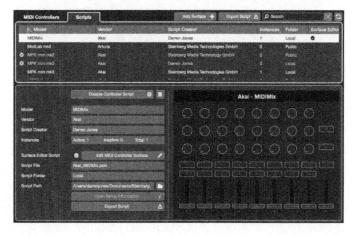

Here you can disable any script you choose in the list, which can be useful when creating multiple scripts for the same MIDI controller (you will need to give each-script a unique name). The window here shows two MIDIMix scripts, one of which is disabled.

It is also possible to delete any user-generated scripts here, so if you have experimented and want to try again, this is the quickest place to remove the previous surface script you have created and start again.

It is also possible to export and import as .midiremote files here, allowing you to share your scripts between different systems and users.

Quick Controls

Quick Controls allow MIDI Remote to control VST Instruments and effects without the remote needing to be specifically programmed for each one. Many factory scripts implement quick controls for knobs/encoders that are present, such as these on the factory MPK Mini Mk3 script:

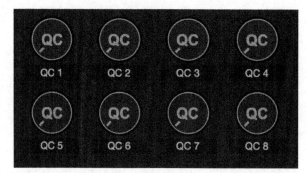

When a track is selected which has Quick Controls set up, the values assigned are reflected in the MIDI Remote:

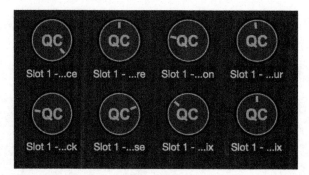

In the case of most Steinberg instruments (such as Halion Sonic SE, Groove Agent, Retrologue), these will be assigned for each patch, giving access to the most relevant controls for editing the sound quickly. Many of the included effects will also have suitable quick controls set up, and focusing on the effect will show these reflected in the names of the quick controls on screen. For any other synths and effects, it is possible to set the quick controls up to allow this, as will be seen in the next section.

Quick Control Learn Mode

In this example a PG-8X Instrument Track was used, but the procedure should be similar for any instrument or effect. First, open the inspector for the relevant track and expand the `Quick Controls` section. Click the learn button.

Next, open the instrument / effect in question, and move the desired control. It will be reflected in the first quick controls slot:

This process can be repeated for any other desired controls by clicking in the desired quick controls slot in the inspector and then moving the appropriate control:

These will now be present in the MIDI Remote if Quick Controls are in operation:

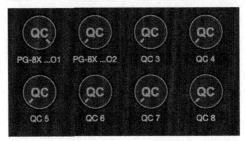

Remember to deactivate learn mode once you have finished mapping new quick controls. Note that the pre-programmed quick controls on Steinberg effects and instruments will not show up in the track's quick controls, but it is possible to override these selections and create your own using the learn method shown above.

Quick Control Focus

Pressing the cog to the right of the quick control focus section allows selection of one of the three modes.

The default follows track and plug-in windows, but the other two modes allow following of only track or plug-in window, allowing further flexibility of Quick Control use.

Locking Quick Controls Focus

Normally, Quick Controls on the MIDI Remote will follow the current focus - whether this is a track, instrument or effect. The current quick control focus is shown at the top right of the relevant window:

The indicator on the right shows that the current window is in focus. When it isn't, the indicator will be dark:

It is possible to lock a given window to hold the focus even when it is out of view - either by clicking the padlock at the top right of the window...

... or by clicking it at the top of the MIDI Remote section of the lower zone:

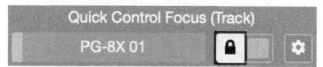

The focus will remain on the selected window until one of the padlocks is clicked to return to unlocked mode.

Summary

MIDI Remote offers a great deal of potential to bridge the gap between the physical world of knobs, buttons and faders and the instruments and effects that can run inside a modern DAW. Spending some time experimenting with the ability to control parameters via physical controls is worthwhile, and with the advent of user-created MIDI Surfaces, it is possible for a non-technical user to control the DAW in the way they want to. Even a cheap MIDI controller can become and indispensable tool when used appropriately in Cubase.

Sampling

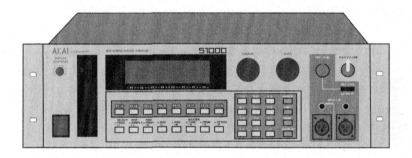

In short, sampling is using clips of audio for a different purpose. This can vary from being used for a single 'effect' in a MIDI composition or live recording to a piece which entirely made up of samples of other instruments, music and found sounds all used in a new context.

The History of Sampling

While the technique of using a piece of music in a new context had been around for several decades including the experiments of Musique Concrete (with the phonogene, an early tape-based sampler seen to the left) and other niche styles, the record considered by many to be the original record to use sampling – 'Rapper's Delight' by the Sugarhill Gang – didn't actually do so! It is commonly believed that it used a sample of Good Times by Chic, but in fact this record featured a re-recording of the music which was then rapped over. However, the concept of sampling certainly dates to this era - the DJ technique of taking two identical instrumental versions of a song and mixing them together to produce a never-ending backing was certainly the original use of another piece of music as the basis of a new one, and before long technology caught up and became affordable to use in this way. This involved the digitisation and storage of short pieces of sound, and then them being replayed on command. Initially this was just taking very short samples (under a second in some cases), and playing them back - the classic use of this is to take a dog barking and then play something like "how much us that doggie in the window", for instance, or the repeated use of a short vocal phrase, with the initial syllable repeated, such as N-n-n-n-n-n-Nineteen, although this use became quite hackneyed and fell from popularity quickly. However, the use of sampling did not suffer the same fate, and went from strength to strength. Many rap artists used the whole sections from other songs looped repeatedly to create a new backing which could then be rapped over (mimicking the Sugarhill Gang's original concept, but with digital technology), while others took a more creative route, and used smaller elements from other pieces in combination with each other, often in totally new and unexpected contexts (for good examples of this, listen to Endtroducing by DJ Shadow, an album which consists entirely of samples used in this manner, from small, short sounds to entire sections of other songs, each used in a new context - all produced on an Akai MPC3000, as seen to the right).

In addition to this, the use of found sounds and spoken words from other sources became commonplace - the use of speech from documentaries and obscure sources became something which is still in use today (Little Fluffy Clouds by The Orb samples an interview with Rikki Lee Jones, 2 Million Ways by C-Mos samples an interview with legendary (and odd) musician Sun Ra, while the record which still embodies sampling for many, Nineteen by Paul Hardcastle, used samples from a documentary about US soldiers in the Vietnam war).

Sampling Hardware

Originally, samplers were hardware-only devices, some adapted from general-purpose computers. The first commercially available one was developed in the 1970s, but was extremely expensive and found limited success. Probably the first commercially successful system was the Fairlight CMI (seen left) which was a computer-based system (costing £20,000+) which allowed sampling of an existing sound or creation of a new waveform by drawing it on the screen. Other systems that followed were the Synclavier, which again was a bespoke system which offered huge capacity for the time, but came with a price tag to match – sampling was really the reserve of the extremely rich. The American Emulator (with three versions of their keyboard-based sampler) improved matters with their product, but it was still around £10,000 for a system which by today's standards would do very little. All of this changed in 1984 when Akai released their first sampler, the S612 (seen at the right). Although it only offered a tiny amount of memory (it was capable of 1 second of sample at its highest speed, 32kHz), its price (around £1000)

was a fraction of that of the previous systems, and it opened up the possibility of sampling to many more, changing the musical landscape completely. While other manufacturers produced samplers, Akai became the most common manufacturer, following the original S612 up with the S900 and the ground-breaking S1000

(seen to the left) which offered editing of samples including reversing and other effects.

Throughout the 80s and 90s the sampler became a more powerful and complex beast, involving onboard effects, hard drive and CD-ROMs. Memory sizes increased, and the increasing popularity of computers meant prices dropped significantly.

In the late 90s, the development of sequencing software (incorporating audio as well as MIDI facilities) meant it was now finally possible to make a software-based sampler, using a standard computer instead of dedicated hardware. The original one was Gigasampler, which gave access to the complete hard drive of your PC as a sampler, meaning suddenly a far larger library of samples could be kept and used, and the ability to import standard formats such as Akai meant it instantly gained ground, and the seeds had been sewn. Within a few years, most sequencer manufacturers would offer their own software sampler, and the sales of hardware devices dropped as a result. Software samplers were generally cheaper, offered more sample memory (often effectively unlimited due to clever software techniques), and possibly most importantly offered complete integration into the sequencer package – on re-loading a song every parameter would be saved exactly as it was before; at minimum a hardware sampler would need to have programs reloaded, but sometimes would need much more work. The programs on a computer based sampler can be enormous and cover many different folders of storage, whereas a hardware sampler using samples from 3 different CD-ROMs would mean each would need to be loaded manually or saved together to a new storage medium.

The line between sampling and synthesizers has blurred greatly in the last few years - many sound sources now use samples as their base, this being in part due to the massive rise in availability of digital storage - hard disc sizes have increased greatly recently, and the prevalence of DVD-ROM drives means that a sample library of 10GB for one instrument is now not unusual, whereas the first Akai samplers may only have had 128kB, 80,000 times smaller. In addition, many devices present themselves as being a synthesizer when in fact they are really far more sampler - they may use a small waveform as the basis for their sound and then apply filtering to this sound to shape it, in much the same way as a sampler does. The main difference is that these synths do not give the facility to record and use your own samples.

Most samplers do not simply play back the audio that they have stored, they manipulate it while doing so and the most common thing for them to do is to use a 'filter', which more specifically is usually a low-pass filter with resonance. This means that it will allow frequencies that are below the set frequency to pass, but those above are blocked. This produces the typically heard "muffled" sound which has become extremely common in much of today's sample-based music. In addition, the filter has a "resonance" control which boosts the signal at the cut-off point, highlighting those frequencies. If this doesn't appear clear, don't worry – once you've heard the sound of a low-pass filter a few times, you will know and identify it easily.

How a Sampler Works

If you have read the Synthesizer chapter (page 231) then this should be very familiar. A sampler takes MIDI input information, and then plays back sampled (recorded) sounds as a result of this. This sampled signal is then passed through a filter (which allows the tonal content of the original sample to be altered), then through an amplifier (which allows control of the signal level as we will see later), then this signal is sent to the outputs of the sampler. While the actual content and facilities offered by each section of the sampler may differ, most follow this same layout. There is little difference between this sampler and the synthesizer shown previously – in fact, the only difference here is the original source of the sound; in a synth it is an oscillator (or oscillators) and in a sampler it is a replayed sample.

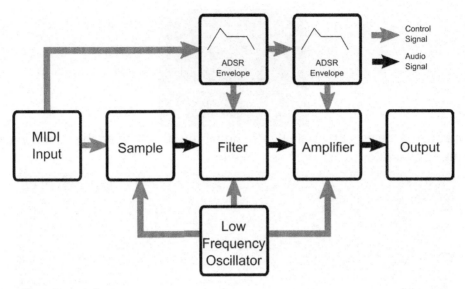

Sampling in action

Because of the wide range of software and hardware samplers available today, it is not possible to cover every possible setup. We will cover two sampling methods - using Cubase's Sampler Tracks, and a freeware sampler called Shortcircuit (before installing it, please see page 487 for an issue which may affect use in some situations), but many software and hardware samplers use much the same paradigm, dealing in key and velocity zones for sample playback and with similar filtering capabilities. If you are using different hardware or software you should find that the concepts apply to your setup. Familiarity with the sampler is a prerequisite, although this can be read in conjunction with your sampler manual to explore new territory.

Sampler Tracks

Sampler Tracks in Cubase provide a quick and easy way to do a number of sampling tasks. While they don't have the ultimate power and flexibility of a full-featured sampler such as shortcircuit (see page 318), they do make many jobs simple and quick, integrate completely with Cubase, and have a couple of tricks up their sleeve that make for quick and easy sampling.

Creating

Creating a new sampler track is done in the same way as any other track type - either **Project > Add Track > Sampler...** or right-clicking in the track listing area and selecting **Add Sampler Track...** The Add Sampler Track dialogue box will appear, where you can name your sample track:

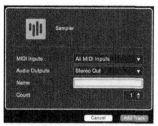

If the Lower Zone wasn't visible before doing this, it will be enabled, and you will see the Sampler Control section selected in it:

A sample needs to be loaded before anything can happen; there are two ways to do this. Either drop a sample onto the sample area (this can be from a current audio event on a track , MIDI data from an instrument track (which will be rendered to audio for you and then loaded), from the Audio Pool, or any file from your computer dragged from Explorer/Finder) or click the folder icon to the left of the **File Name** area at the top of the sampler, and browse to select a file from there:

You will notice that there are now a number of changes that have happened. First, the sample is now visible, with the waveform displayed in the upper part of the sampler control section:

Second, Cubase will attempt to detect the sample's tempo (seen in the bar at the top of the sampler control section):

Third, the Pitch and Amp controls will now be available:

Finally, the range that the sample will play on will be visible at the bottom of the sampler control section, with the root key (the key that will play the sample at the original pitch and tempo) highlighted in blue.

Playing any of the keys in this range (by default, C0-C6) will play the sample - this works for any MIDI keyboards connected to Cubase, or for the keyboard on screen.

Pitch Section

You can alter the pitch of the sample using the pitch controls - course tune alters by a semitone per step, while fine tune does by cents (100ths of a semitone).

The glide control alters how long a newly-played note takes to get to pitch (from the previously played pitch), allowing sliding between notes. This often works best in conjunction with Monophonic mode (see page 317).

Amp Section

You can alter the **Volume** and **Pan** position with the controls in the Amp section. For basic playback of a sample, these controls are all that is needed, but there is more to come.

Trimming the sample

Sampler tracks offer quick and easy trimming and fading in/out of samples. The sample start and end points are defined using the trim markers which appear by default at the beginning and end of the sample.

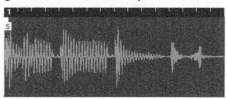

To alter the start or end, click and drag the S on the appropriate marker...

...and drag it to the left or right to alter the start point of the sample.

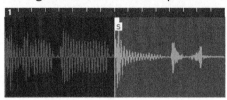

The same procedure works for the end point.

Fading the sample

It's also possible to quickly create a fade in or out for a sample, using the fade handles which appear above the sample start/end point markers. Click on the fade in handle...

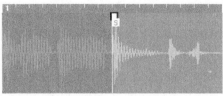

... and drag to the right ...

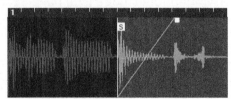

... to make a fade in. As with trimming, the same procedure works to create a fade out at the end of the sample.

The Filter

Sampler tracks have a filter, which can be used to alter the tonality of a sample. To turn the filter section on, click the power button at the top left of the section.

The filter will now alter the audio as it is played back. With the default settings, the effect of the filter will not be audible as the Cutoff frequency is set to 22kHz.

Playing the sample back while altering this will make the effect of the default filter (a low pass - LP - filter) audible. Turning up the **Reso** control increases the resonance of the filter, adding a narrow bandwidth boost at the filter's cutoff frequency. This makes the filter 'ring' at the frequency in question, leading to a clearly discernible pitch if the resonance is high enough, and changing the effect from a general dulling of frequencies to a very specific highlighting of a given tone. Finally the drive control increases the input level into the filter, which can lead to the tone becoming distorted as the filter is overdriven.

There are many filter settings to pick from the types and shapes available; The types control the internal function of the filter, and generally the drive control will allow you to fully explore the extremes of the characteristics of the filter. The **Bit Red**(uction), **Rate** and **Rate KF** modes all produce some particularly extreme effects when driven hard. The shapes control the frequencies that are being controlled by the filter; High Pass (HP), Low Pass (LP), Band Reject (BR) and All Pass (AP) are all available, and their effects are shown in the table below:

Low Pass   **LP**

Audio below the set frequency is passed unchanged. Audio above is attenuated, with various slopes available (6, 12, 18 and 24dB/octave). Resonance accentuates the level at the set frequency, accenting the pitch at this frequency.

Without Resonance   With Resonance

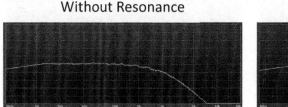 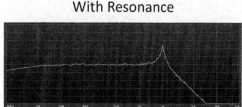

High Pass   **HP**

Audio above the set frequency is passed unchanged. Audio below is attenuated, with various slopes available (6, 12, 18 and 24dB/octave). Resonance accentuates the level at the set frequency, accenting the pitch at this frequency.

Without Resonance   With Resonance

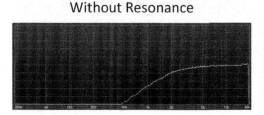 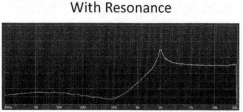

Band Pass   BP

Audio at the set frequency is passed unchanged. Audio above and below is at-tenuated, with two slopes available (12 and 24dB/octave). Resonance accentu-ates the level at the set frequency, accenting the pitch at this frequency.

Without Resonance   With Resonance

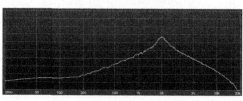

All Pass   AP

While audio at all frequencies is passed unchanged in terms of level, the phase of the signal at the set frequency is altered, which can produce the frequency response shown, depending on the input signal.

Without Resonance   With Resonance

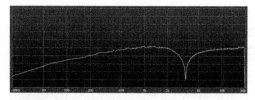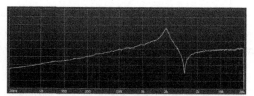

Band Reject   BR

Audio at the set frequency is attenuated. Audio at other frequencies is unchanged, with two slopes available (12 and 24dB/octave). Resonance accentuates the level at the set frequency, making the filter narrower, with less attenuation.

Without Resonance   With Resonance

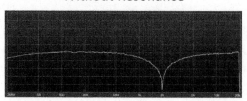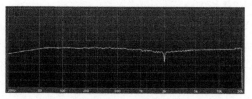

In addition, there are various combinations of filters available, which combine the basic types together to allow multiple changes to the frequency response to be made in one step.

Modulation

While being able to control pitch, amplitude and filter settings is useful, being able to change these dynamically will allow a much more dynamic and evolving sound to be created, and this is where modulation comes in. Each of the three sections has its own modulation controls, and they can be accessed by clicking on the **mod** button at the top left of each section:

Here you can see the modulation page, which is divided into two sections - Envelope on the left and LFO on the right.

These work in a similar way to the sections described in the Synthesizers chapter on page 238 and page 243 respectively, so if you're unsure about what each section does, take a look there. Here we will focus on the practical application inside the Sampler track.

Envelope

Here you can see the default envelope, for the amplifier section. It starts out with an instant attack, and a decay time of 0.25 seconds - although the sustain is set to 100% so it doesn't have any effect - and a release time of 0.2 seconds.

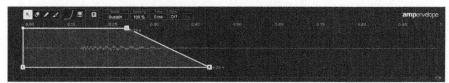

Playing the note shows a diamond-shaped cursor passing through the envelope; note that it stays at the sustain point while the key is held down, and then passes down the release section when the key is released. The times can be altered by dragging the relevant square handle to an appropriate point; here the attack time has been set to 0.2 seconds by dragging the square shown at the top left in the previous image.

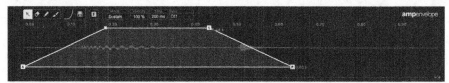

The decay time is set by dragging the **S** handle to the left or right; however, as we saw on the synthesizers chapter on page 240, this will not have any audible effect until we alter the sustain level. The reason for this is that the attack is currently reaching 100%, and the sustain is set to 100%.

The decay time is irrelevant as the level is not changing (it goes from 100% to 100%).

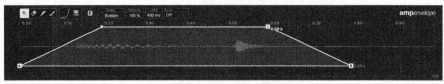

It is only when the sustain level is changed by dragging it down that the decay has an audible effect:

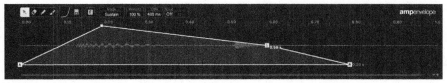

While this replicates the controls that are typically found on most envelopes (ADSR), there is more to come. Firstly clicking and dragging on a line between two points (in this case the release) makes it into a curve, either up:

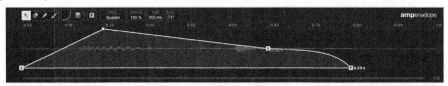

Or down:

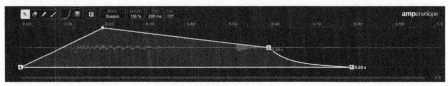

In addition, it is possible to create a new point on the envelope (taking it beyond the standard ADSR) by simply double-clicking on the line at any point:

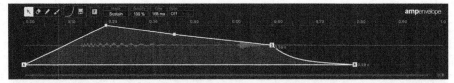

... and then dragging it to an appropriate time and level - here a silent moment was created before the sample goes into the sustain phase:

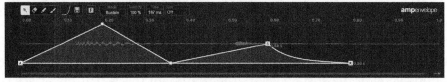

The point can be moved around flexibly as with any other point, allowing the construction of more complex envelopes than the standard ADSR model. You can delete a point by simply clicking on it and hitting **Delete** on your keyboard.

Draw Mode

In addition to freehand, it is possible to use Draw mode to create predefined shapes into the envelope editor. Select Draw Mode from the toolbar:

Then click the shape to the right of the toolbar, and a window showing the predefined shapes should appear:

Select a shape, and the window should close. Now click in the envelope editor, and the shape should appear...

...creating points which can be edited in the normal way. Clicking and dragging while creating will allow the size to be controlled before creation.

Paint Mode

Paint mode works in a similar manner to draw mode ...

... but allows creation of multiple shapes when clicking and dragging:

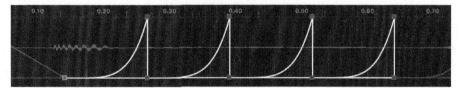

Editing Nodes

Once you have finished creating with the draw or paint modes, the created nodes will remain selected. It is possible to edit these nodes in a similar manner to automation editing, using the handles which appear around the selection:

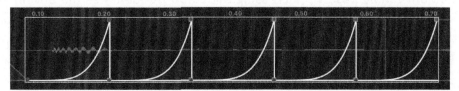

It is possible to scale...

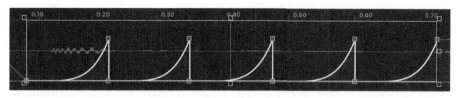

... re-time

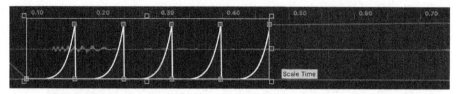

... and tilt the created data...

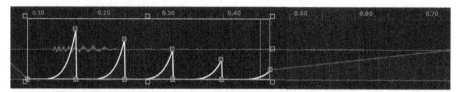

using the handles in a similar manner to those seen on page 345.

Synchronising the Envelope to Cubase's Tempo

The editing of any envelope can be set to time-based or tempo-based, allowing musical synchronization of any edits performed. To do this, turn Sync On in the top section of the envelope editor.

The grid can then be altered, and edits easily set to musical time divisions.

Filter Envelope

Pitch, Filter and Amp each have their own envelopes. The Filter Envelope controls the cutoff frequency; much as seen with a subtractive synth on page 243, the filter setting at any moment in time is dependent on three main factors - the cutoff setting, the envelope value at that time, and also the 'Amount', a slider which is to the left of the envelope, as seen below.

The amount can be positive (increasing the cutoff frequency as the envelope increases), or negative (decreasing the cutoff frequency as the envelope increases) - both have quite different effects with any filter type, and in combination with the many filter types available, the tonal possibilities are manifold.

Pitch Envelope

The pitch envelope has an amount slider (as seen above for the filter envelope) giving the ability for the envelope to apply a positive change (the pitch of the sample will go up) or a negative one (the pitch of the sample will go down).

In addition it the envelope itself also has the ability to apply a negative value - it can go below zero - so that a single envelope can change the pitch of a sound in both a positive and a negative direction at some point, as seen below:

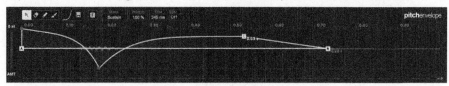

With these settings, it is possible to create new, complex and evolving sounds using samples - there are a huge number of possibilities with these three sections manipulating the sound of the sample.

Advanced Envelope Modes

So far, we have just looked at the envelopes working in their default mode - Sustain. Sampler Tracks have some powerful alternative modes for envelopes which can lead to some interesting creative possibilities, and providing functionality similar to the LFOs seen in other samplers such as Shortcircuit (see page 331)

Sustain

In sustain mode (the default), the envelope runs until the sustain point is reached, and stays at this level until the key is released. This is the way that many envelopes on many synthesizers and samplers work (with the default 4 points, this is an ADSR envelope), and for many purposes this is completely adequate.

Loop

Once loop mode is selected, a pair of loop markers appears on the envelope (at the attack and sustain points by default). When the sample is triggered, the envelope will loop continuously through the section between the loop markers, until the note is released. This can offer a number of interesting creative possibilities, allowing for cyclic modification of pitch (giving a vibrato effect), volume (tremolo) and filter settings.

One Shot

In this mode, the envelope plays from start to finish, without stopping on the sustain point. Combined with the complex envelope shapes that are available, it is possible to create more complex filtering, pitch and amplifier changes than traditionally available.

Sample Loop

In this mode, the envelope holds at the top of the attack until the loop begins. Once it does, the envelope proceeds through the decay as normal, until it reaches the sustain point.

Shaper

In this mode, the envelope becomes like an editable LFO - it will cycle round, and the first and last nodes are connected to ensure a smooth transition round each cycle.

LFO

Sampler Tracks have two LFOs, which are across all elements of each Sampler Track, and you can select which LFO you are using for a given parameter by using the buttons above the control.

The LFO section of the modulation page allows cyclic alteration of the functions available - in the case of the amplifier, this is the level (**Volume**) and **Pan** controls. Both have a basic setting control, and next to them the LFO control:

Here the volume is being controlled by LFO 1 at a level of 100%, and the pan is being controlled by LFO 2 at a level of -50%

The LFO

The LFO section works in a traditional manner - producing a signal which is generally below the audio frequency range - and it has some nice extra features.

Waveform

The LFO waveform can be selected and viewed in the graphic section at the bottom left, and each waveform can be altered using the shape control, as seen in the table on the next page.

Waveform	0%	50%	100%
Sine			
Triangle			
Saw			
Pulse			
Ramp			
Log			
S&H 1			
S&H 2			

Being aware of the variations available can open up creative possibilities or save time - it's probably quicker to set **Triangle** and **Shape** **100%** than set **Pulse** and **Shape** **50%** quickly, for instance.

The **Sync** and **Freq** controls interact. If Sync is off, then the frequency control sets the speed of the LFO with no restraint. The next two sync modes are tempo-based, so the frequency control will then be set to note divisions (which is often desirable). In **Tempo + Retrig** mode, the LFO is tempo-synched, but not locked to Cubase's grid - i.e. it's possible to start the LFO at any point in a bar. In **Tempo + Beat** mode, the LFO is tempo-synched, and locked to the bar, so it will always align with the beats in the project. To get an understanding of the effect of these modes on the LFO, it is useful to set a slow LFO speed (so that the indicator above is clearly visible during the cycle), and then seeing the effect of MIDI notes played on a keyboard on the indicator (and therefore the LFO).

Retrigger

In the first two sync modes, retrigger is available, and has three possibilities:

Off - The LFO is free-running, and not triggered by a note playing. This can be useful when you want each note played to be different in terms of the LFO behaviour.

First Note - The LFO is triggered when the first note is played, but not again. 'First Note' refers to the first of a number of overlapping notes (such as a broken chord) - if you release all the notes and play again, the LFO will be retriggered again.

Each Note - In this mode, the LFO is retriggered when a note is on its own or part of a group of held-down notes. This leads to a different performance dynamic to the First Note Option.

Phase

The phase control allows control of the relationship between the LFO being triggered and the waveform itself, allowing control of the placement of the initial effect of the LFO. In the amplifier, the first setting (0 degrees) will mean the waveform will start out at 50% level, but setting the phase to 270 degrees leads to a minimum level from the LFO, and the possibility of a silent start to the note. The effect of the phase control on a sine wave is shown below. Note that 360° is the same as 0°.

0°	90°	180°	270°	360°

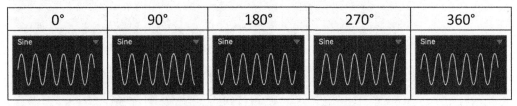

AudioWarp

One of the most useful and time-saving elements of modern music production software such as Cubase is the ability to fix a piece of audio to fit with the tempo of the current song. This is achieved in sampler tracks by activating AudioWarp on the left of the `Pitch` section. Turning it on enables the controls in this section:

Playing the sample at different pitches now should show that the pitch is changing but the tempo is fixed. Because of this, it is possible to play the sample at different pitches while keeping in time with the project, expanding greatly the usability of any given loop. This is not only useful for pitched loops; even percussion only samples can benefit from this approach, allowing them to be played at different pitches in different parts of a song, or to layer multiple simultaneous or offset samples (by playing trigger notes later on in a loop) to create new and interesting rhythmic combinations. With **Sync** turned off, the **Speed** control allows percentage-based alteration of the sample playback speed, while keeping the pitch approximately constant. With **Sync** turned on, the control changes to `Orig BPM` and allows editing in a different manner, setting the putative original BPM of the sample. In either mode, **CTRL + Clicking** the control will return to the default value. Experimentation with the different modes available will lead to different audio and musical results as other controls are available.

Changing the Pitch

There are two main elements to defining the notes that a Sampler Track plays - the Root Key and the range.

Root Key

The Root Key sets the MIDI note that will play the sample at its original pitch. It can be set either at the top of the Sampler Control window:

Or at the bottom by clicking and dragging the white triangle.

Note that this does -not- mean that the sample's audio is actually at the pitch specified, only that it will be at the original pitch when this note is played. While many of the included Sampler Track presets are set correctly (i.e. a C3 will be heard as a C3), this will often not be the case when importing your own sample, so ensure that the tuning is correct if this is what you are after. Often sample libraries will include the pitch in the file name which may help with tuning, or you can use the same technique as outlined for Shortcircuit on page 330.

Range

The range of notes a sampler track will play is shown at the bottom of the sampler track. The entire MIDI note range is shown across the bottom, and the upper and lower limits are set by clicking and dragging the two markers (here shown set to C1 and C4).

Here the sample's range has been set to C3 - C4, but note that the root key is outside this range:

Initially this may appear nonsensical, but it simply means the sample will not be heard at its original pitch, only above it.

Slice

A common technique used in music production is to take a sample (such as a drum loop) and break it up into 'slices', each of which is a part of the loop. In the case of a drum loop this will typically be each drum hit that happens. Next, each sample 'slice' is assigned to a different key on the keyboard, allowing the loop to be played as it was (by playing the notes in the original order), or to create an alternative 'cut and paste' version of the loop by playing the parts at different times, or by playing different parts at the original timings.

Sampler Tracks allow this process to be automated using the slice mode, located on the left-hand side of the sampler track:

Select **Slice** and then press the power button next to it to activate slice mode. Once active, if slices are detected, they will be indicated with markers in the sample window:

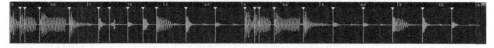

Altering the **Thresh** control will set the level at which slices are detected. By increasing the threshold, the number of slices will be decreased ...

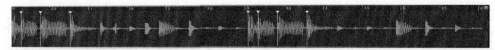

... and by decreasing it, the number of slices will be increased - note that even the smallest transients are now included (in the middle of the sample seen here):

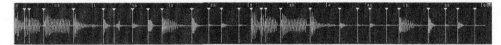

The number of notes that the sampler track responds to will alter to match the number of slices.

Here is the map with a high threshold (smaller number of slices) ...

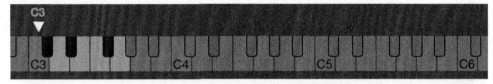

... and here it is with a low threshold (leading to more slices):

MIDI input will now trigger the appropriate slice, and you will see the played slice highlighted:

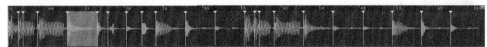

It is, of course, possible to record MIDI to play the slices, but an option to reconstruct the original sample (and to act as a jumping-off point for experimentation) is to click and drag the MIDI icon ...

... to the sampler track in question:

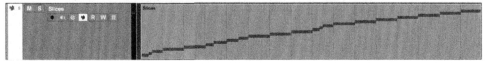

Pressing play will now perform the original sample before the slicing, but it's possible to mix this up quickly. By changing the pitch of the notes, you will mostly preserve the rhythmic intent of the sample, but alter the sounds (reminiscent of cut & paste breakbeat drums, which typically used this technique), or alter the positions to change the timing and feel of the part.

313

Looping

So far, we have only seen samples being played in their entirety, from start to finish. However, it is often the case that we want a sample to repeat a section or the entire sample once the end has been reached. This is called looping, and there are a total of 6 modes that the sampler track supports. The loop mode is selected using the menu at the top of the sampler area, as shown below

The modes are as follows , illustrated with the sample at the top, a key being pressed shown below, and time running from left to right.

No Loop

The sample is played from start to finish, and once the end is reached playback stops. If the key is released before the sample finishes, then playback stops.

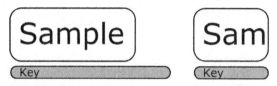

Continuous

The sample is played from the start until the loop end marker is reached, and then playback continues from the loop start marker. This loop is repeated until the key is released.

Alternate

This operates in a similar way to Continuous, but when the loop end marker is reached, playback is then backwards, until the loop start marker is reached, when playback then becomes forwards again.

Once

This is similar to Continuous, but the loop is only played once; then playback continues until the end of the sample.

Until Release

This is similar to both Continuous and Once; the looping will be continuous until the key is released, then the sample will play until the end. Note that this mode will only be useful if you have a long release time in the Amp section (otherwise the audio will stop before hearing the effect of this mode).

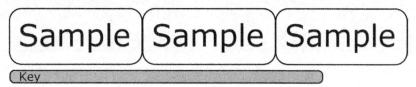

Alt Until Release

This is similar to Until Release and Alternate; the looping with be continuous and alternate until the key is released; once a forward direction is reached after this the sample will play until the release time is completed. As with Until Release, the release time in the Amp envelope needs to be long enough to allow this to be heard.

Other Features

There are a number of buttons along the top of the Sampler Control window which offer important facilities and control:

Fixed Pitch

As the name suggests, this fixes the pitch of the sample at the set pitch. This can be useful for allowing the triggering of multiple simultaneous copies of a sample - not something which is possible without this mode.

One Shot

In One Shot mode, the entire sample will play back after a key is pressed, regardless of the length of the key press. This is often useful for percussion sounds and any other samples which need to be heard in their entirety every time they are triggered.

Normalisation and Gain

In this section it is possible to quickly alter the gain of the sample. The first button will normalise the sample, taking the peak level to the selected normalisation level (which can be set in the first text box):

By default, this is 0dB, allowing the sample's peak to be as high as possible. Once this button has been pressed, the sample waveform will reflect this change:

Before   After

Note that the gain section will now show the gain that has been applied:

This can be edited manually to achieve the desired sample level, or to remove the effects of normalisation.

Sample Trim

This allows the sampler track to remove any unwanted parts of a sample - this can be particularly useful when working with long samples (such as entire songs), allowing the zoom controls to work more appropriately for the wanted section of the sample. Once a desired section of the sample has been selected in the waveform display...

... clicking the trim button will remove any other areas of the sample, and re-set the start and end points to suit the new sample:

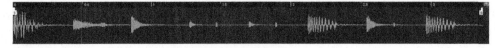

This can be undone with the undo button.

Reverse

This plays the sample in reverse. Note that the sample display reflects the reverse audio direction, to make editing easier.

Monophonic Mode

As the same suggests, this allows only one sample to be played at a time on the Sampler Track. This can be useful for playing lead/solo parts, particularly when used in conjunction with the Pitch section's Glide control.

Monophonic Legato Mode

Once Monophonic mode is enabled, this allows the sample to continue playing when a new pitch is played in legato (i.e. with notes overlapping), instead of re-starting from the beginning when a new note is played (which is the default). This allows for more expressive playing, and also creative possibilities when using longer samples and loops.

MIDI Reset

This stops playback and resets any MIDI controller values to their defaults. It's useful when playing back long samples in One Shot mode.

Transfer to New Instrument

This button will produce a pop-up menu showing which Steinberg instruments are available to transfer your current Sampler Track settings to. Selecting one (such as Groove Agent SE) will create a new instrument track with the chosen instrument in it, and a sample assigned to the root key, allowing further and more in-depth programming to be performed as appropriate with the chosen instrument. The original Sampler Track will be left unchanged.

Sample Backup

It should be noted that the samples that you have imported (regardless of their original location on the computer) appear in the audio pool, in a "Sampler Track" folder. This means that if you use backup project (as seen on page 51) to make a backup/archive of your project, the samples will also be backed up to the new location - not something that third party plugin solutions such as Shortcircuit can do - making for a convenient way of ensuring that your project will play on another computer system, or be fully backed up.

Summary

As seen in this section, sampler tracks offer a convenient, built-in method to perform a wide range of sampling duties whilst in Cubase. Other software samplers such as Halion, Kontakt and Shortcircuit offer more facilities and a much wider range of manipulation, but there are many features in sampler tracks which make for a creative workflow which is native to Cubase, and allows the sharing of projects between users without any additional software being needed.

For more advanced and creative sampling duties, however, a sampler plugin is typically needed, and the facilities available in samplers will be demonstrated in the following pages using a plugin called Shortcircuit.

Shortcircuit

Shortcircuit is a software sampler, which is only available as a 32-bit VST plugin for Windows systems (so if you want to use it, you will need to use a VST Bridge such as jBridge which is explained on page 658). Shortcircuit offers a huge range of options and sampling power, and while it is a little more complex to use than Cubase's built-in sampler tracks, it can perform sampling duties that are much more advanced than Sampler Tracks can do.

The Shortcircuit Window

This shows the main window of shortcircuit – the main area above the keyboard is where you can see what samples have been mapped to MIDI notes, and at the top there are a few buttons, including the one we will need first, load... which is located at the top left.

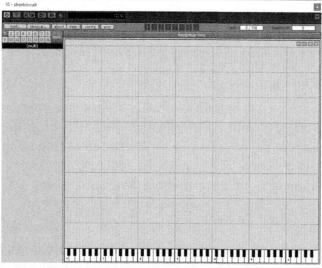

Sampling for a percussion instrument or single note

The first, most basic use of a sampler is to provide a piece of percussion or a sample which is to be played back at a single pitch when a given key is pressed - this is a simple playing back of a specific sound at the right time. For this, you will need a sample of a drum or other percussive sound, and it can be in a number of different formats, but we will use a simple wave (.WAV) file; such files are easily available from sample libraries, many music technology magazine cover DVDs or the Internet.

Loading the sample is straightforward – click the **Load. . .** button at the top left of the Shortcircuit window, and you will need to locate the sample and click **Open**. Shortcircuit will load the sample, and present you with the zone edit window, showing all the settings for the sample you have just loaded.

Here we see a kick drum sample has been loaded, and by default Shortcircuit will allocate it to key C1 (or the next available key when you load another sample). If you can play that key on a MIDI keyboard you should hear the sample being played back.

Tip: If you don't hear anything, common issues can include your MIDI keyboard being in the wrong pitch range, or the keyboard being set to the wrong MIDI channel.

You may wish to change the key that triggers the sample, and this can be done in the "zone range" area, which is on the left-hand side of the screen, just below the waveform display.

zone range		
808 Kick_long.WAV		
low key	C 1 L	127	max vel
root key	C 1 L	0	min vel
high key	C 1 L	1	MIDI ch
	Learn all	0	coarse tune
vel. sens.	-30.0dB	0.00	fine tune
keytrack	100.0%	2	PB range

Here we can see the zone range in more detail – it shows the sample in question (in this case 808 Kick_long.WAV), as well as the MIDI allocation, and a number of other settings which we will cover later on. To assign the sample to a new key, the easiest way to do so is to click the Learn all button on the left, Learn all and then play a key on your MIDI keyboard - the sample should then be triggered by that key.

While this technique is often used for percussion sounds, you can also use this for samples that you simply wish to replay, such as vocal or spoken samples and found sounds – they are simply required to be replayed on command, without their pitch being changed by playing different notes.

If you want to change the pitch of the sample, you can do this using the coarse tune and fine tune boxes – they will alter the playback pitch of the sample, allowing you to tune percussion to your needs, or to create extreme effects.

319

Melodic Sampling

This is the 'next level' when using samples – originally the sound was just being played back at a single pitch – we will now load a pitched sample and play it back at different pitches using the facilities of shortcircuit.

To do this, firstly, remove the original percussion sample you have set up; this is done by clicking the **remove...** button at the top left. Shortcircuit will ask if you are sure, so click **Yes**.

Now you will need to load up a new sample; we will need one which has a clearly-defined pitch, such as a piano or vocal note (in the examples we will load up a piano sound) – you may need to record such a sample if you don't have access to one, but the loading process is identical to the previous example for percussion.

Now we need to make the sound play on a wider range of notes. This is still done in the 'zone range' section – once again, use the **Learn all** button to assign the note to a key on your keyboard (it is a good idea to use a note in the middle of your keyboard) and check that the sample plays back on this key. Now we will change the low key and high key to expand the range. Click the **L** to the right of the low key readout, and press the bottom key on your keyboard. You should see the MIDI note change on the readout. Now click the **L** to the right of the high key readout, and press the top key on your keyboard.

You should now be able to play the sample at any position on the keyboard. If you want to see how the sample is stretched across the keyboard, click on **(multi)** above the sample list on the left-hand side - it should look something like the screenshot seen below.

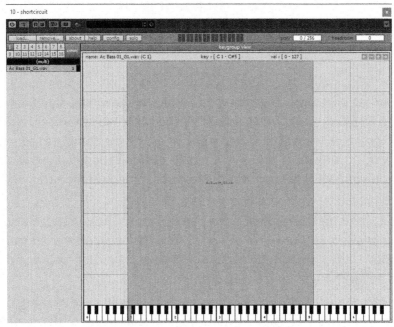

To return to the sample edit screen, click on the sample name on the left-hand-side.

Shortcircuit is speeding the sample up or slowing it down to play different pitches, so extremes of pitch may sound odd. Note that the slower pitches last longer, and the higher pitches last less time, again a function of the sampler playing the sound quicker or slower to achieve the desired pitch, referred to as "munchkinisation". To stop this happening and to obtain a more realistic sample playback, it's important to record the original sound at a number of pitches - generally every two or three semitones, but sometimes every semitone if real accuracy is required. The example shown to the left uses an octave scale sung with 'white' notes, which have then been stretched to the note above (if needed).

Multiple keyzones are needed for this, and programming a large range can be quite time-consuming, but often the end results are well worth it.

Sampling with velocity zones

In addition to the step described above, it is sometimes useful to be able to alter the tone produced depending on the velocity of any played notes - typically a sampler will play low-velocity notes quietly while high-velocity ones are played at higher volumes, instantly producing a playable version of the original. However, many sounds change timbre as well as volume when played at higher volumes, so it is also often desirable to record each pitch at a number of volumes, and then map the velocities of each note to these different recordings, giving a far more natural progression providing the programming is well done. To the left is an example (in this case a drum kit), where again each sample is only used on one semitone, but in this case some of the notes feature several velocity zones for a very convincing performance. There are a total of three keyzones, in this case all assigned to the same note, C1. Each keyzone has a different range of velocities that it handles, however.

40	max vel
0	min vel

82	max vel
41	min vel

127	max vel
83	min vel

Here is the first keyzone, which handles velocities 0-40

Next, the middle keyzone, handling from 41-82; in this case it has a 'harsher' sound.

Finally, the top velocity zone, from 83 upwards. It has a much harsher and 'harder' sounding sample.

By building up a sample using these techniques it is possible to create extremely convincing sample kits and instruments; some professional sample libraries use 8 or more velocity-switched samples per note for ultimate realism.

Altering the sample's volume over time

While what we have seen is useful for simple playback of a sample, there are times when we want to change the volume of the sample over time – for instance, we might want to make a note "fade in" over a short (or long) period of time, or perhaps when we release the key, for it to die off gradually rather than be like turning a switch off.

To do this, we use an Envelope generator, as seen in the Synthesizers chapter on page 238. This is a method of controlling something over time, and usually it has four parameters – Attack, Decay, Sustain and Release – which sometimes lead to it being known as an ADSR Envelope, or even just an ADSR. Three of these parameters (A, D and R) are time-based, while Sustain is a level, as is shown on the next page, with the parts of the envelope described next to it.

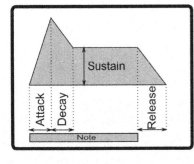

Attack — The time between hitting the key and the level reaching maximum

Decay — The time taken from the maximum to reach the Sustain Level

Sustain — The level which is maintained while the key is held down

Release — The amount of time for the envelope to reach zero once the key is released

Setting these parameters can drastically alter the way your sample sounds when played back. It is important to remember that if you set your times too long, the sample may run out before the envelope has completed its changes, so you will need a sample long enough to encompass what you are intending to do. Next we see some examples of an envelope being used to shape the playback of an otherwise unchanging sound.

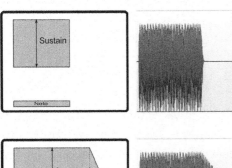

Instant attack and release – when the key is pressed the sound starts playing, and when released it stops. The level in between is not controlled by the envelope, and is at maximum (this is much like a switch, on and off)

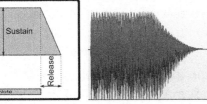

Release time is added, so when the key is released (at the same time as the example above), the sound fades out rather than turning off instantly, giving a more natural end to the sound.

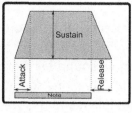
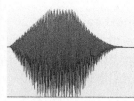

Attack time is added too, so the sound fades in when the key is pressed rather than reaching maximum instantly. As above, when the key is released, the sound fades out.

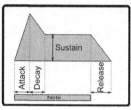
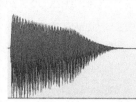

Here the sustain level and time has been added, so once the maximum is reached, the sound then drops to the sustain level (in this case less than the maximum) while the key is pressed.

The examples shown above use the 'classic' ADSR envelope, but Shortcircuit extends this with a Hold control - this allows the peak level to be maintained for a time before the Decay comes into effect.

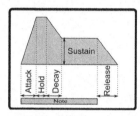

Here we see the AHDSR envelope, with the level held at maximum by the H control after the Attack phase. This allows more control over the development of the signal, and can be particularly useful when using an envelope to control a filter, to allow the sound to remain at a given tone before the D phase begins.

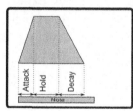

Here we see the same envelope, but with the S level set to 0. This effectively turns it into an AHD envelope which will fade in, hold and then decay down to 0 as long as the key is held (if the key is released then the R phase will still occur, so then the R setting will be important).

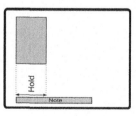

Here the H control becomes really useful; it is possible to create an envelope which opens and closes regardless of the note length (as long as the note is longer than the H time), making it possible to play back percussive sounds, etc., which need to be triggered in their entirety (or to play a given section of a sample). The A D S and R controls are all set to 0.

There are many variations on this theme, but they are usually an extension of the concept shown above. Note that with this simple tool it is possible to shape the dynamics of the most basic of samples – the top diagram shows the original sample (a hummed note), which has no dynamic changes throughout, while the last one (still using the same sample) has dynamic interest throughout, and sounds far more musical in practice.

Using filters

The filter in a sampler is probably the most commonly-used effects, and also one of the most recognizable. Making use of it can drastically alter the interest of your sample if it is being repeated, and also can make a sample sound far more effective when trying to imitate an acoustic instrument – after all, many sounds do not only change volume when hit softly, they also become duller, and this was the original reasoning behind the inclusion of filters on samplers.

Shortcircuit offers a wide range of filters, but we will start with the classic "low pass" filter, which is the most widely-heard sound used in sampling. In the **filter 1** section, click on **none** and select **LP2**:

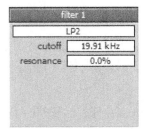

The first thing to do is to experiment with the filter in a "static" mode – i.e. just hearing the effect of altering the cutoff and resonance controls. Bear in mind that if the cutoff is too high you will hear no effect, and also that if you put too much resonance in it's possible to create distortion and even damage equipment or your ears with the high levels that can be generated, so be careful when experimenting. To hear the effect of the filter, play back a sample that has lots of high-frequency content (such as a drum loop with cymbals or the human voice) and then slowly reduce the cutoff frequency – the sound of this should be quite familiar. Now set the resonance control to around the half-way point and try the cutoff sweep again – the effect should be more pronounced, and this is because the resonance is highlighting the frequency at which the cutoff control is working.

In addition to being left in a static setting, the filter can be controlled by other things (such as an ADSR as seen in the Synthesizers chapter on page 240) to make it change with time or vary with the performance. However, to do this we need to learn about one of shortcircuit's most powerful facilities - the modulation routing section.

Modulation

In a musical context, Modulation means changing key. In the context of shortcircuit, it means something different, controlling one signal or setting with another signal. This is an extremely powerful tool, as it allows us to control the settings of the sampler to alter over time or using controls on the MIDI keyboard, or automatically. However, it can be extremely complex, so we will start with a simple example and move on from there.

Altering the filter over time

We have already looked at how the Envelope Generator (**EG**) can alter volume over time. We will now use another EG (**EG2**) to alter the filter's settings in a similar way.

Firstly, make sure you have your sample playing correctly, and add an LP2 filter as seen in the previous section. Make the cutoff frequency low enough that the filter makes the sound dull. Now what we will do is use EG2 to control the filter over time to 'open' it – it will do this by increasing the cutoff frequency.

Firstly go to the **EG2** section, and set the attack time to around 500ms. This should give long enough for the effect to be heard.

The next stage is the most important – we need to take EG2's signal and use it to alter the cutoff frequency of our LP2 filter which we have placed in filter 1. To do this, we go to the modulation routing section.

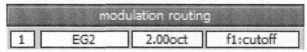

On line 1, in the first column, click **none** and change it to **EG2** (this is the source of the signal). Next, in the third column, click the none and change it to **f1:cutoff**. This has now sent the signal from EG2 to control cutoff, but there is one more setting to make – we need to tell it how much of a change to make. This is done in the second column – you can click on it and drag to the right to change it to **2.00oct** to make a 2 octave difference when the EG2 signal is at its maximum. Note that you can double-click the figure and enter it using the keyboard.

Now when you play the note on the MIDI keyboard, you should hear the sound, starting off dull and then becoming clearer after half a second. Clearly the effect you hear will vary depending on the original sample and the filter settings, so you may want to experiment with them to really hear what's happening. You can increase the resonance to make the effect more pronounced. You can also make the amount negative – this will cause the filter to be open normally, and close as the EG progresses; this can lead to some interesting sounds.

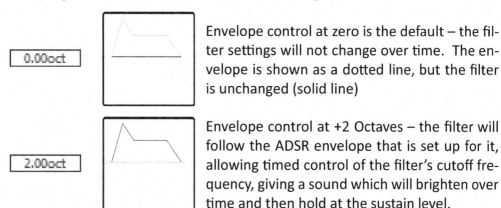

Envelope control at zero is the default – the filter settings will not change over time. The envelope is shown as a dotted line, but the filter is unchanged (solid line)

Envelope control at +2 Octaves – the filter will follow the ADSR envelope that is set up for it, allowing timed control of the filter's cutoff frequency, giving a sound which will brighten over time and then hold at the sustain level.

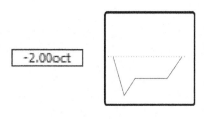

Envelope control at -2 Octaves – the filter will follow the envelope, but 'upside-down', starting off open and then closing with time, making a sound which will become more muffled. The envelope's original output is shown as a dotted line.

Velocity control of the filter

Velocity control of the filter can be achieved in a similar way – instead of using EG2 to control the filter cutoff, then velocity can be selected in the first column.

modulation routing			
1	velocity	2.00oct	f1:cutoff

Now you should find that the harder a key is pressed, the more the filter opens, leading to a sharper, clearer sound. Again, alteration of the amount may be needed to get the right effect.

Velocity and envelope control of the filter

The great strength of shortcircuit's modulation is that it's possible to use several things at once to control a parameter. By setting line 1 to EG2 and line 2 to velocity (both set to control the filter cutoff) then both can alter the cutoff frequency at the same time.

modulation routing			
1	velocity	1.00oct	f1:cutoff
2	EG2	1.00oct	f1:cutoff

Bear in mind, however, that the more sources that there are controlling a given signal, the more care will need to be taken with the amount (column 2), as it is possible for the multiple sources to 'overwhelm' the destination; in this case this would lead to the filter being permanently open, so the amount has been reduced for each line to allow them to interact better. How you choose to set these will often be down to experimentation.

Looping a sample

While some samples will be the length that is needed, it is common for them to be too short - particularly in the case of melodic instruments, where the original sample may well be only a few seconds long, and a longer version needed if sustained notes are to be played. In this case it is necessary to 'loop' a part of the sample - this is to play it repeatedly without gaps. This can extend the length of a sound and make it playable in many more musical situations, but there are techniques needed and skill required if this is to be achieved to a good standard.

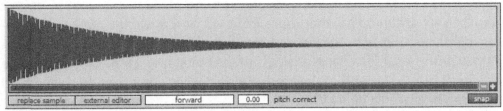

Here we see the original sample - it is a bass sound, but is quite short and does not sustain; what is required is a note which will play infinitely. To do this, we will need to pick a playback mode which will loop the sound from the menu that appears when you click on forward under the sample:

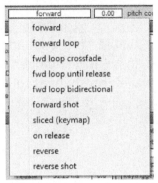

Pick forward loop, and you will notice that the sample changes to a blue colour. This shows the area that is being looped. You may also notice two blue "handles" which allow you to move the section which is being looped.

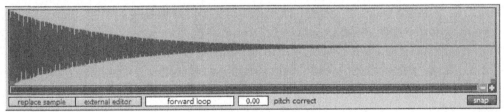

Initially the entire sample is being looped, so press and hold the key and listen to the effect. While it may play indefinitely, it is not a smooth musical effect at the moment - the loop points need to be moved closer to each other.

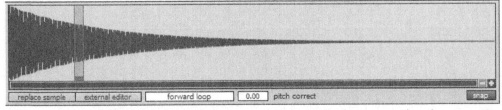

Now we have a sample which will loop more musically, but even the short section we have selected has some changes in it - the volume changes quickly during the loop, so we don't get a smooth, musical and natural-sounding loop, but a noticeable and rhythmic one; this technique has been used a great deal in modern music production, so it's worth noting how it is done, but we are after a smooth loop. In the case of this sample, we need to zoom in enough to see the individual wave

327

cycles, and to set the loop markers around just one of them; note that by default (because snap is turned on) that shortcircuit will only move the markers to zero-crossing points; this is to minimise the chance of there being a click, although the waveforms may still change enough to generate one. In the case below, the waveforms are so similar that the loop is perfect, giving us a triangle-wave sound which can be played indefinitely.

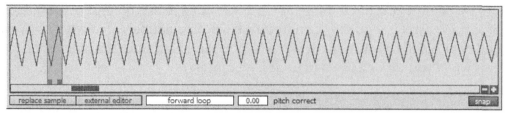

However, it is not always that simple - most sounds are not simple mathematical constructs which repeat in an identical manner, they contain lots of different harmonics meaning that the waveform changes subtly with time

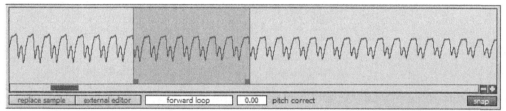

Looping a single wave of this type will lead to a "stuck CD player" kind of sound (something we will be making use of later on), so an alternative is needed, and this is the 'crossfade loop'; rather than changing completely from the end sound to the beginning, the sampler will fade from one to the other (quickly) to smooth the transition between the two. In shortcircuit, this is selected in the same place as the original forward loop mode, picking forward loop crossfade.

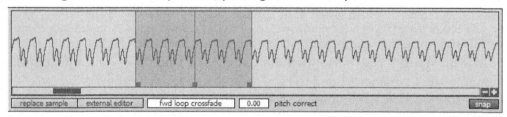

A third handle appears (to the right of the loop end marker) and this allows us to move the crossfade to the left, to allow part of the sample to be crossfaded; with experimentation you can usually get far smoother results using this technique than you would when doing so without crossfading, and many commercial sample libraries make use of this technique to achieve sustained notes.

Making use of short cycle waveforms

When making looped samples as above, it is possible to generate some extreme and unusual sounds; if you have experimented with short sample loops you will probably have made the sampler's output squeak and change pitch dramatically. This is a technique which can be put to good musical use by taking advantage of the unusual sounds which are generated by it. Generally speaking this technique works best with samples where there are a wide range of frequencies and harmonics present, and this usually means entire mixes of music; if you have any songs in WAV format then they will be ideal for these purposes; if not then you will need to convert some audio to WAV format to allow you to do this - see page 636 for how to create audio mixdowns, which you can do having imported the file you wish to convert to WAV.

Firstly, import the sample into shortcircuit as normal. Here we see an entire song has been imported.

Next, pick a part of the waveform which is of high amplitude (i.e. loud), and looks to have a lot of activity there, such as the section in the song below. Note that the start point has been moved to the beginning of this large peak.

Zooming in on this shows this waveform, which has a lot of high frequency activity as well as lower frequencies as well - the low frequencies are the bigger waves, while the HF content is visible superimposed on the bigger wave.

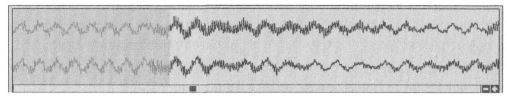

It is now a case of setting your loop to a short number of cycles to repeat, and importantly setting the sample start point to be the beginning of the loop - the idea isn't to have a section of music play and then 'stick', but just to play the extremely short repeated section; it will be completely unrecognisable as music.

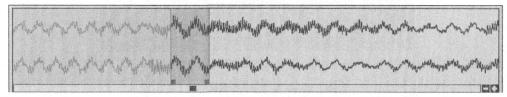

Next, experiment with the loop end point; notice that a small change in position will often lead to a change of pitch as the effective wavelength has changed, and usually not in a musical manner.

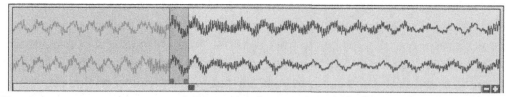

You can now use this as a starting point for your sound; the application of filtering is extremely important in this example as it is currently a very harmonic-rich sound which will overpower most others, so careful application of filtering (and indeed an envelope to the filter to make a dynamically-altering sound) will lead to musical results; it is possible to generate some sounds which would be difficult if not impossible to generate with a traditional subtractive synthesizer as their initial waveforms would not be rich enough in harmonics.

If you pick a less extreme sound to loop, it is possible to generate a wide range of more 'traditional' sounds which will again be completely unrecognisable from the original sample they are taken from, but still will provide an interesting sound which can be further modified using shortcircuit's huge modulation options.

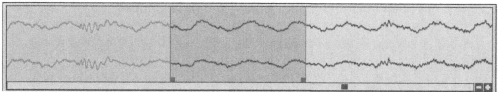

Tuning a sample

In many cases, once you have imported or created a sample and particularly if you have used short cycle looping, you will need to tune the sample - it is very unlikely that it will be in tune - not only in terms of fine-tuning but it will be semitones out more often than not, and the easiest way to deal with this is to tune the sample to concert pitch and then you will not have to think about it again.

There is an easy way to do this in Cubase, and that is to make use of the built-in Tuner, which can be found under **Tools > Tuner** - create it as an Insert effect on the channel in question (see page 540 for how to do this if you are not sure), and then play a C on your MIDI keyboard.

The tuner should give a readout of the note that is being played, and you can now use the course tune and fine tune controls on shortcircuit to get the sample in tune - here we see a note which is 18 Cents flat, so it needs to be tuned up by 18 cents to make it in tune (see below for shortcircuit being set to this).

127	max vel
0	min vel
1	MIDI ch
0	coarse tune
0.18	fine tune
2	PB range

Bear in mind that it is not always possible for the tuner to track your note accurately, and sometimes the pitch of a sample will change as it is being played. In this case, a method to check is to create another instrument track with a simple synthesizer in it (PG-8X or Halion Sonic SE Piano), and to enable monitoring on that channel as well; by doing this both instruments will play at the same time when you press a key on the keyboard, and you should be able to hear if they are in tune and rectify any problems that are happening.

Using the LFOs

An LFO is an oscillator which produces a low frequency signal which is used to control other parameters of the sampler, such as the sample pitch to create vibrato or the amplifier level to create tremolo. Shortcircuit has 3 LFOs and they have more features than a plain LFO. They are all located at the bottom right of the main window, and are all identical. Note that they are called stepLFO, this is because the waveform they produce is actually a series of steps (which can be smoothed), but more importantly this allows you to create your own waveforms easily.

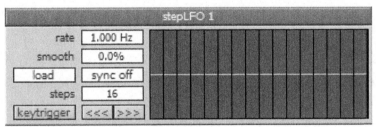

Creating a waveform for the LFO

The easiest way to create a waveform is to use the load... button - clicking it produces a menu of the waveforms available, with a series of commonly-used ones stored here. Picking one from the menu will see it loaded in the display on the right. You can alter the waveform by clicking and dragging each column to the desired height, and the waveform can be rotated using the <<< and >>> buttons. The speed is controlled using the rate control, and finally there is the keytrigger button - this will re-start the LFO when a key is pressed, which can be useful for certain effects as we will see later on.

Assigning the LFO

The LFO signal is currently doing nothing - it isn't routed to any part of the sampler, so it will not change anything. As with the filter setting shown on page 324, the signal needs to be sent somewhere using the modulation matrix. Here the LFO is routed to amplitude, so it is controlling the volume of the sample when played, leading to a tremolo effect.

modulation routing			
1	stepLFO1	+20.0dB	amplitude

When doing this it's usually a good idea to reduce the output level by the same amount so the peak level is the same, otherwise it's easy to end up with a distorted output.

output	
p.f. gain	0.0dB
amplitude	-20.0dB
balance	0.0%
	out 1-2
aux level	0.0dB
	aux:off

Spend some time experimenting with the LFO settings - here you should be able to see the power of being able to draw the waveform as you can easily customise it to get the effect you want, with a square wave providing a far harsher tremolo sound, while being able to round the corners of the waveform slightly will soften it while it is still an effective sound. The LFOs can be routed to any parameter that you like, so spend some time experimenting with different destinations. The Keytrigger option can be useful, particularly if you have created an effect which you want to repeat each time a key is pressed (such as the LFO altering the pitch of a note).

Advanced Modulation

While earlier we have used modulation in a basic way to alter a parameter over time, one of shortcircuit's most powerful features is the ability to use the modulation matrix to use one parameter to control another which is in turn controlling another; This allows some complex sounds and effects to be built up, and while the possibilities may be near-endless, some examples will show the potential which is available.

Using a MIDI controller to alter LFO speed

Here we will first use an LFO to alter the volume and filter cutoff applied to a sound, and then we will assign a MIDI controller to allow us to alter the speed of the LFO in real time; this is a commonly-used technique in dubstep wobble bass sounds amongst others. Firstly, import a synth bass sound (create one as a sample if you don't have one) and map to the keyboard as shown on page 320, and then set up a sine wave LFO with a frequency of around 2.5Hz. Apply the LFO to the amplitude (as seen on page 331) and also add a low-pass filter (LP2) as seen on page 323, and set the cutoff frequency to 400Hz or so, with the resonance set to 50-60%. Now the LFO needs to be assigned to the filter as well; this can be done in the second line in the modulation matrix, with an amount of around 3 octaves.

modulation routing			
1	stepLFO1	+20.0dB	amplitude
2	stepLFO1	3.00oct	f1:cutoff

When you play the note now, you should hear two things - the sound should change in volume and also tone; you should hear the filter altering in time with a 'squelchy' sound as the filter opens and closes. This is a start, but the problem is that it is static; what is needed is a sound where the speed of the LFO can be altered in real time, so the next stage is to do this using a MIDI controller. For our purposes here we will route the data entry control of a MIDI keyboard (CC#6) to control the speed of the LFO - to use the modulation controller (found on most keyboards), it can be selected directly in SC's modulation matrix. For more on MIDI controllers, see page 59. The first thing we need to do is to tell shortcircuit which MIDI controller we will be using, and this is done in the configuration page, which is accessed by clicking the config button at the top of the shortcircuit window.

Here we see the configuration window, and it's the bottom part we are interested in - here we can map shortcircuit to use specific controllers. In the first line we will set the type to MIDI (by clicking it) and set the number to 6 as seen below.

id	type	number
c1	CC	6

Shortcircuit's c1 controller is now mapped to MIDI CC 6, Data Entry. If your MIDI keyboard generates different controller data when using a control then you will need to insert it here. Click **OK** to go back to the main shortcircuit window.

Now we need to get the controller to alter the speed of the LFO. This is achieved in a line of the modulation matrix - c1 is the source and stepLFO1 rate is the destination while the amount was set to 3.00 octaves as seen below (all three lines are included, but the first two are ones you have already set).

modulation routing			
1	stepLFO1	+20.0dB	amplitude
2	stepLFO1	3.00oct	f1:cutoff
3	c1:	3.00oct	stepLFO1 rate

You should now find that playing the note and then altering the modulation control on your keyboard will alter the speed of the LFO. You can alter the depth of the speed change by altering the 3.00 octave setting.

Using automation to control LFO speed

The initial sound and LFO are set as above, but automation will be used instead of the MIDI control. Automation controllers do not need to be set up as such, they can just be accessed directly in the modulation routing window. There are 32 of them, referred to as **auto00** - **auto31**, and they can be selected in Cubase's automation lanes (for more on automation see page 341) - you will need to select **More...** from the automation lane and then from there you can select the automation controller that you want to use. You can then draw in the values you want and they will control the parameter. It is possible to use up to 32; remember that while there are only 12 modulation slots per sample zone, you could have many sample zones on the same shortcircuit.

modulation routing			
1	stepLFO1	+20.0dB	amplitude
2	stepLFO1	3.00oct	f1:cutoff
3	auto00	3.00oct	stepLFO1 rate

Using one LFO to control another

While using a single LFO can achieve some interesting effects, it is sometimes desirable to create more chaotic sounds, and the cyclic nature of an LFO makes this a little difficult. While it's possible to pick one of the noise LFO presets or draw in a random waveform, this can still sound cyclic. One way to try to overcome this is to use one LFO to control an audible parameter, and then use a second LFO to influence the speed of the first. This can lead to some interesting and unusual effects.

Firstly, load up a sample which is of a reasonable length (10 seconds plus), with distinct sounds in it, such as a spoken phrase or a part of a song. Next, set up stepLFO 1 with a sine wave set to a rate of 3.000Hz.

Now use the modulation matrix to send stepLFO 1 to rate (linear) by 95%. When you play the sample you will get a 'scratched vinyl' effect, with the sound playing backwards and forwards, and moving through the sample. This is an interesting sound, but clearly cyclic as you can hear the movement back and forth.

Next, set stepLFO 2 to one of the noise waveforms, and to 2.000Hz. Use the modulation matrix to send stepLFO 2 to stepLFO 1 rate, and set this to 3.00 octaves.

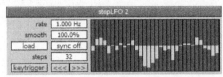

Now when you play the sample you will get a similar effect, but the speed of the changes through the sample will be altering each time, and it will sound far less predictable.

modulation routing			
1	stepLFO1	+95.0%	rate (linear)
2	stepLFO2	3.00oct	stepLFO1 rate

Using Groups

While the editing you have been doing above is creative, it can be tedious when you have multiple sample zones which you want to apply the same settings to; often you will want to make the Amp EG settings the same, or apply the same filter, etc., to a number of similar-sounding samples, and to do this individually is extremely time-consuming; if you have an octave of samples then you have 12 edits to do (one for each semitone). If you have multiple samples per note (as velocity splits) then it will be even more so.

Fortunately, shortcircuit has a way round this, and that is to use Groups. A group is a container for a number of keyzones, and once they are in a keyzone they can be edited as one. Only the settings that you change in the group are applied, all the other settings stay as the individual sample originally was.

Firstly, create a number of keyzones. In the example shown, a number of samples of sung notes have been recorded, and then spread across an octave of keyboard - on the next page we see the 8 keygroups.

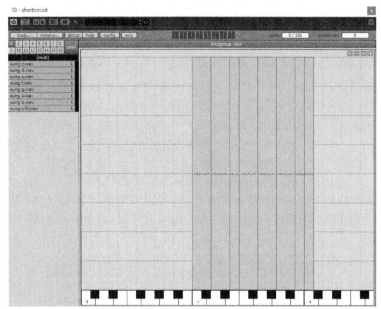

Next, we will create a group. This is done by right-clicking in the area where the samples are listed. A menu appears.

Pick **new group**, and you will see the group appear in the list on the left, above the samples you currently have. You can rename it in the group section at the bottom left of the main part of the shortcircuit window.

Now the samples need to be put into the group. To do them all, click on the first one in the list, and **SHIFT-click** on the last one - this will select all of them - and then right-click and pick **Move To >** and pick the group you have named (Singing in the example) - you should see they are now in the group as they will be indented with the group's coloured bar to the left of the sample names.

Tip: When you have more than one zone selected, shortcircuit will apply any edits you make to multiple zones, so it is possible to do multi-sample editing without using a group, but groups are more convenient as you don't have to select multiple samples to do the edits.

Now it is possible to use the group settings to apply a change to all the samples in the group. To make a first change, go to the amplitude EG section and click override. The controls will now be active and you will be able to apply the envelope to all the samples in the group. In this example, they have been given a long Attack and Release time to create a smooth pad-like sound.

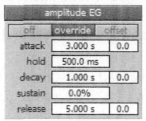

The group offers effects - these can be added in addition to the filters you have applied, and they offer not only the filter effects from the individual groups, but also some new effects, such as Chorus, Delay and flanger. If you have found that having only two filters to apply to a sample is restrictive, adding it to a group will allow you to add more - even if the 'group' only contains the one sample.

Groups are a powerful way of making multiple editing easy, and as seen above they also offer the ability to add extra filtering and/or effects to sounds within them, increasing your sonic palette.

Making your own samples

Of course one of the great reasons for using a sample is to make your own samples - it's not just about replaying sounds and music that others have recorded and created, but being creative yourself; it's amazing how sounds can be re-purposed and put into new contexts in this way, and while sampling has developed hugely from the early efforts of artists such as The Art of Noise who made use of cars starting and other everyday sounds, there are still countless ways in which traditionally non-musical sounds can be used. To do this, record audio (see how to do this on page 439), and then mix it down into a WAV file (see page 636). Often making a mono wav file will be satisfactory (there is no need to produce a stereo file if both channels are the same), and makes for an easier-to-see display in shortcircuit.

Using Loops with the sampler

This mimics the original use of hardware samplers and a MIDI-only sequencer. Each loop is assigned to a specific key, and pressing and holding that key will play the sample, often as a loop which will repeat infinitely. The crucial thing here is making sure that the tempo of the sequencer is correct – often the tempo will be given as a part of the sample name, and it is simply a case of setting the sequencer to this tempo. In this case, the way to tell is to set up a long note (such as 8 or 16 bars long), and then play the sample with the metronome turned on – any small issues with tempo will become apparent towards the end of the section, and the tempo of the sequence can be adjusted to suit. It's important to remember that often a sample's quoted tempo may not be correct and this adjustment can be the difference between a sequence that is spot on and one which loses its feel.

Using samples without a sampler

Several years ago, sequencers could only work with MIDI - Audio wasn't a possibility at all. As a result of this, any time audio or samples were to be used, a hardware sampler would be the only option to do this, and to produce a loop which would repeat seamlessly took some skill to do, as the controls were often difficult to use and often dealt only with numbers.

However, today things have changed dramatically - the integration of Audio capabilities into most sequencers means that audio samples can be dealt with quickly and easily. When wanting to produce a sample which is simply a repeat of a section, it is often far quicker to perform these actions from the sequencer itself instead of using the sampler, as the editing and looping can be carried out visually, and also it's possible to do things quickly that would require a great deal of work to achieve in a sampler (whether hardware or software), such as repeating a section which isn't the beginning or altering the sample's tempo in real time with a tempo change. When using samples for a melodic purpose, the sequencer option is nowhere near as convenient as a sampler and MIDI track.

Using Loops with Cubase

Sometimes you may take a section that you wish to use as a loop to be repeated, such as a four-bar drum loop you have recorded. This is where current sequencer technology is extremely helpful – rather than spending time setting up looped samples in the sampler's edit page (which is possible), you can do everything visually, allowing quick and simple creation of loops, and in addition allowing complex manipulation to be achieved. For the techniques needed to do this (creating a loop, using timestretch and using the Time Warp tool) look at the Audio Editing chapter on page 489.

Exercises

Sample a single note

This is the basis of all sampling. Record a single note on an audio track (see page 439 if you haven't done any recording yet), and then create a .WAV audio mixdown of this (see page 636) - make sure you have good level on this before performing your mixdown. Now import this into shortcircuit (see page 318) and then experiment with changing the key range of the sample, and listening to the effect of playing different notes.

Sample percussion sounds, program basic drumkit

This is an extension of the previous section - creating multiple keyzones, one for each part of the kit. The samples you use could be ones you have recorded (most environments offer the ability to create impromptu percussion instruments), or ones from existing VST Instruments. It is good practice to be able to make mixdowns of each and turn them into samples as there are many occasions where a synthesizer will not offer you the flexibility and programmability that shortcircuit does, so making sure you can create good mixdowns with good level of VST Instruments is an important skill.

Sample singer over 1 octave

Set up a mic and record a singer singing all the notes from C to C in a given octave. Export each one as an audio file with an appropriate name, and then import them into shortcircuit on the appropriate notes. You should then have a playable version of the singer in question.

Extend above and below / detune

Working from the previous example, you can extend the key range of the top sample (make it stretch up an octave) and the bottom one (make it stretch down an octave). How far can a note be stretched before it starts to sound artificial?

Looping

Looping of samples is important to allow them to last longer than the original recording did. With the singer example, experiment with the looping controls (as seen on page 326) to allow the sound to play constantly and smoothly. Experimenting with crossfading can be an important tool in this technique, as sometimes it is not possible to loop smoothly with some samples.

Single-cycle looping

As seen on page 328 it is possible to create some extreme textures using this technique. Practice it on a number of different sections of an audio file - full mixdowns make a good sample to work on as they usually have sections with high level and a wide range of frequencies present.

Modulation

All of the techniques so far have been 'standard' sampling techniques, but shortcircuit's most powerful abilities lie in its modulation - the ability to use one signal to control another. With the modulation section it is possible to control nearly any aspect of the sample via almost any other. Start out with something simple, such as the filter example shown on page 324 and velocity on page 326, and then move to the more advanced topics as shown on page 332. There are a near-infinite number of ways you may want to alter a sample in this way, and when you combine multiple modulation sources to control a single parameter, or use one to control the signal which is then controlling another, then there are many new sounds which can be generated - using one LFO (or another modulation source) to control another, as shown on page 334 is a great way to come up with completely new and dynamically-changing sounds.

Summary

Sampling is an extremely important technique for a Music Technologist to master – it gives quick access to a huge range of textures and timbres, and also allows for the creation of new and interesting sounds, as well as the use of found sounds which otherwise would be impossible. The manipulation of audio for use in samples can be extremely simple or as complex as you wish it to be, and the use of envelopes to control level and filtering can make a mundane sound into an interesting one.

Automation

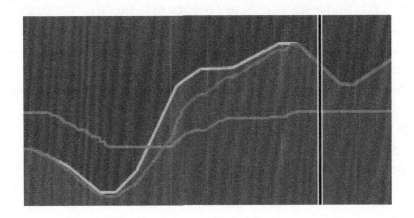

Automation is one of the key ways to get more detail into any Cubase project, whether it is strictly MIDI only, MIDI using VST Instruments, Audio or any combination of those elements. In short, Automation allows you to get Cubase to alter a parameter automatically and repeatably. In addition, this data can be edited just like any other in Cubase, and added to progressively allowing the creation of incredibly complex pieces.

Basic Principles

Firstly, it's important to realise that Cubase can automate a great many parameters (from now on, for the sake of convenience, we will refer to them as controls). This can include settings for channels within Cubase, audio effects, VST Instruments. However, there are some things that cannot be automated – it is down to the programmer of the VST effect or instrument to decide what can be automated so sometimes a control cannot be. In addition, it's important to remember that you can control or create automation data in a variety of ways, as we'll see, and also that automation data looks the same regardless of what the destination is, although the units that it works with will change depending on the destination of that information.

There are a few things to remember with automation which will help you when working with it. Firstly, by default automation data is copied with a part when it is moved or duplicated, so if you want to create complex automation, then it is probably best to make sure the structure of your project is correct before doing this as moving parts will alter the data that's present.

Secondly, Cubase performs interpolation on the data that you create – it doesn't store every movement you record precisely, but instead thins this information out, and then 'fills in the gaps' between those points - we will see how this works later on.

The parameters that can be automated will vary with each channel type and effect or instrument. Although the way that this information is displayed in Cubase will always be the same, it is important to realise that the way this information is interpreted is down to the destination (be that a MIDI synthesizer, VST audio effect or instrument or Cubase itself), and sometimes this might appear to be slightly odd; for instance, although there are only 8 programs available by default with the Double Delay effect, automating this will allow you to enter many different levels (rather than the 8 'steps' you might expect), a range of each will correspond to one program. This behaviour is down to the programmer of the destination in question.

Controls

There are a number of controls for automation – some appear on the track itself, others only when you have an automation lane being displayed. The global controls are visible above the track listing in the project window.

Control		Description
⌄	⌃	**Show/Hide** controls – shows/hides automation tracks for this channel. Only shown when you hover over it as seen below.
		[M S first automation] [⌃ ● ◄× ∅ ∞ R W]
R	R	**Read** – turns automation read on this channel, playing back any data present
W	W	**Write** – enables writing on this channel, recording new data if a control is altered
☒	☒	**Mute** – mutes the current automation track from playback – works per automation track
🔓	🔒	**Lock** – locks the current automation track and prevents writing to that Cubase track
R	R	**Read All** – toggles all channels read on/off, and also shows if any are active
W	W	**Write All** – toggles all channels write on/off and shows if any are active.

A first piece of automation

The very first thing to automate will simply be a channel fader. This can be on a MIDI or Audio track (either can be automated, although the end results will vary – one will output MIDI data while the other will control internal values for Cubase), so once you have created one, arm the automation system by hitting the write button on the appropriate channel, and then hit play. You can now move the channel fader, whether by doing so on screen (either in the inspector volume control, the inspector channel or the mixer itself), or physically with an external mix controller if you have one – in any case the end result will be the same, your movements will be recorded by Cubase.

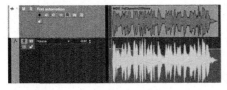

Once you have made some movements, hit stop, disable the write control (click it again to turn it off), and then use the Show control for the channel in the project window to reveal the automation data you have just created.

It should look something like the automation shown above. The movement of the control is represented in the automation line, and if you have the control visible (in the inspector or the mixer) then when you play it back, you will see the control moving, and hear the effect of it.

To disable the automation, click the R – you can either do this on the inspector or on the Volume automation track – both do the same.

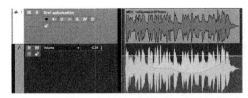

The automation becomes inactive (pale), and you can see the 'current' level is now shown as a straight line.

You may also notice that your original movements of the controls have been reduced by Cubase – it 'thins' the automation data out to what it considers to be the minimum necessary to effectively reproduce your performance – in this case the fader movements have been reduced to a start and stop point for each line, rather than tracing the entire movement precisely. This is an important concept to grasp, as we will be editing the data later on.

Here is the original movement of a control – each dot represents a change in position in time. While this is totally accurate, in many cases it is not needed, so Cubase will 'thin' this data out, and only store the points which it feels are relevant.....

.....which would look something like this – where the 'curve' was nearly straight, none of the movements are kept, only ones which make a discernible change from a straight line. This is not played back like this, however.....

... here is how Cubase 'fills in' (interpolates) the gaps between these points, actually creating a more detailed version of the data (being able to calculate a precise point at any given time).

This stores less information and makes editing easier; rather than having to edit several points, moving just the one will alter the entire line. If you play back this data and look at the relevant control, you will see that Cubase responds as if you had moved the control yourself. Also, whenever you move the play position to a location, the current automation settings for that time are reproduced as well.

Creating Automation Data

Another way to create automation data is to draw it. To do this, make sure you have an automation track visible, and the automation enabled by clicking **R**.

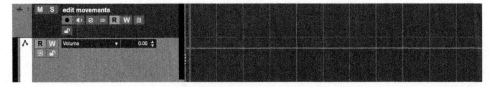

Clicking at a point on the line (here in the second beat of the first bar, on the volume line) will create an automation point.

Clicking elsewhere will create another point - here it has been dragged down after clicking to create a fade-out effect.

We have already seen how to create data with the mouse, but it's possible to use tools other than the Object Selection tool to create data, as seen in the table below.

Icon	Mode and use
	Line – creates a straight line, which will usually consist of just two points, start and end.
	Parabola – creates a parabolic curve, usually abbreviated to 3-4 points. To get the "right" curve may necessitate drawing right-to-left.
	Sinewave – a sinewave. Amplitude is varied with the mouse, frequency by the snap setting
	Triangle – functionally similar to sinewave, but with a triangular output.
	Square – as above, but with a squarewave generated.

Whenever editing or creating automation data with these tools, it's important to realise that Cubase simply interpolates (fills in the gaps) between automation points, so be aware that you may only need to move a few points to achieve a desired effect. In addition the ability to create curves and edit multiple points quickly is something to experiment with as familiarity with the tools available will allow you to create the desired effect in an expedient manner.

Editing Automation Data

Once you have automation data, you will probably want to alter it. There are a number of ways to do this - the simplest is to click and drag a single point using the selection tool. Hovering on the line whenever there is a change in automation level will lead to a circle appearing on the line. Dragging it...

... allows curves to be created quickly and intuitively...

... and dragging above or below creates a useful fade-out/in shape.

The diamond that appears whenever the mouse is between two automation points...

... allows quick and easy editing of that range by clicking and dragging up or down, creating extra points to allow this.

These are both useful ways of working, but there are much more efficient methods to allow you to work with multiple automation points. You can select multiple points by clicking and dragging to select them, but the Range Selection tool (2 on the keyboard) allows a range of automation to be quickly selected, and doesn't suffer from selecting MIDI/Audio events if you are slightly inaccurate with the mouse. Once you have multiple automation events selected, you can use the following techniques to alter the data. When you have multiple events selected, four square 'handles' appear, allowing you to make quick edits as seen below.

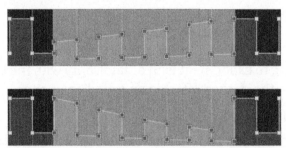

The top corners allow 'fade in' and 'fade out' of the automation data.

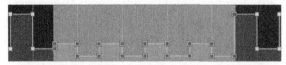

The top middle control allows absolute scaling of the data.

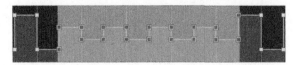

The middle right control allows scaling around the centre.

Range Selection vs Point Selection

In many cases, there is little to choose between selecting the automation points with the Object Selection (arrow) tool and the Range Selection tool. However, the range selection tool acts on the entire range that has been selected, even if there is no automation point present, whereas the arrow tool will only work on points that are present. Being aware of this can help you choose the right tool. Here is some automation.

When the range selection tool is used over a range larger than the points themselves...

... and then dragged down from the top left corner, note the new point created at the beginning of the selection.

Here is the same data that has been selected using the arrow tool...

... and making the same edit to it has slightly different results.

Picking the right tool may take some practice at first, but often choosing the range selection tool will enable you to edit a range of automation without having to create new start and end points - just select the range you want to alter and then those points will be created when you make the edit.

There is an important point to note - it is not possible to drag a single point past another point which originally happened later or earlier than it. If we want to move point the second of 3 points, then we can only do so within the time bounds created by points 1 and 3 – it cannot move past these – here we see the same point moved to its left-most and right-most possible positions.

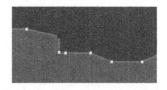

| In its original position | The point moved to the left... | ...and moved to the right |

This can be frustrating when compounded by the next issue – it is possible for there to be multiple automation points which look just like the one when viewed in a zoomed-out view – here is an example; looking at the curve shown to the left, each point looks to be a single one.

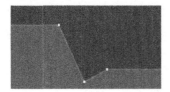

But the lower-most point couldn't be moved to the right, and this was because it was actually two points - the diagram at the right shows this at an extreme zoom level, and the right-most point was stopping the left-most point from being moved further right. Deleting the second point made no difference to the automation output as such, but allowed full movement and editing.

As with notes, automation events can be 'marqueed' around (i.e. click and drag a box), and then moved en masse to their new location. If you want to move an automation pattern to a new location, you can do so by cutting them and then pasting them to a new location (defined by the play position pointer) – if there are any events present in the time range of the pasted material, they will be deleted by the new points.

You may have noticed that there is a control for automation at the top left of the project window, which is usually set to Touch Fader. This is the automation mode, and has several different modes, one of which can be extremely useful for editing.

Mode	Description
Touch Fader	The default – once a control is "touched" (clicked on) the movements are recorded until it is released.
Auto-Latch	This keeps recording even after you have let go of the control, until you disable writing or hit stop – be careful when using this mode!
Cross-over	As Auto-Latch, but with a big difference – when your data crosses over the original data, recording stops.

If you click the **e** to the right of the current automation mode, you will summon the automation panel:

It has a wide range of controls, the most important of which we will cover now.

Trim

Trim mode allows you to make alterations to level-based controls (volume and send levels) by giving you a control which will add relative changes to the existing automation. This is useful for making alterations to existing data which you are mostly happy with but wish to modify.

 Here is the initial data, with a volume curve that we wish to retain, but decrease the overall level of the middle in particular. To do this, we use the automation panel to ensure that ...

 ...Trim mode is selected. As soon as this is done, the channel fader moves to the half-way position, and the automation line reflects this. Now we play the song with write enabled on the track...

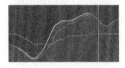 ... and move the fader to give the relative volume change that is required. Note the movements are recorded in the normal way, and you can see the automation output changing to reflect this, with the original shown highlighted.

 Once stop is pressed, the automation now reflects the new values, having been altered suitably. Remember to disable trim mode in the Automation Panel if you want to go back to writing data normally.

Suspending Automation

Sometimes it is desirable to stop automation being read - you may have a passage that you wish to work on without automation happening, or to work out a problem you have in a mix. If you want only specific automation to stop reading back (such as Volume) you can do this using the automation panel - you simply click the appropriate automation type such as Volume, and then all volume automation will stop being read. Clicking it again will re-enable it. It is possible to do the same for writing of automation as well.

Viewing Automation types quickly

The Show column in the Automation panel allows quick display of automation that a project has in it - the various types are present, but Show Used and Hide All are particularly useful when you have a complex project with lots of automation.

Automating more than one parameter at a time

The automation system is not limited to automating one parameter per channel at a time – you can do many at once. To automate a second function, click the small plus at the bottom of your current automation channel - note that these are only visible when you hover over them, much like the show/hide automation controls.

You will see another automation lane which you can then use in the same way as the first one.

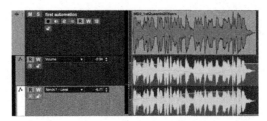

If you want to pick a different destination for your automation, then you can do so by clicking on the name of the current automation parameter, and then picking it from the menu that appears. There are two things to note about this – first, any automation which data which is not currently being displayed is shown at the top of the list with an asterisk next to it, and second, if the parameter you require isn't in the list, then you can use the **More...** option to pick it in a new window which lists every possible parameter to automate, which is quite a list if you have every insert and send in use on an Audio channel, and will include MIDI CCs if you are automating a MIDI or Instrument track.

Bypassing an effect

One of the most common uses of automation is to bypass an effect which is inserted in a channel (such as a delay effect) for part of a piece. As with many automation situations there are a number of ways to do this:

Automate using controls on-screen. Write-enable the track and record the data by bypassing the effect using the bypass button, which can be either on the VST effect window itself , the effect channel (whether in the mixer or in the channel editor) , or in the inspector - all of these will have the same effect.

Draw the data in. This can be done by using the same techniques as shown above for editing data, but first we need to tell Cubase what to Automate. In this case the channel has a MonoDelay as insert 1. The automation track is expanded, and clicking on **Volume** will pop up a menu of possible automation targets, including the one we want – **Inserts:1:MonoDelay – Bypass**. Next the data itself needs to be drawn in. Note that with Bypass is a switch, it has two states, either **ON** or **OFF**, and Cubase will not let you use tools which produce values between this, so you are limited to only using the normal draw tool, and not the line tool or its derivatives.

It is important to bear in mind what we are actually automating – the 'Effect Bypass' control, **not** the effect being ON. This can cause some confusion because of the logical state of the data – it is "Effect Bypass", so when it is ON (up) it means the effect is bypassed, which seems counter-intuitive; most people expect the ON state to mean the effect is ON! This isn't the case – see the example below:

Here is the automation data for our track – this data is shown in the table below, which should make things clearer, showing what happens as the automation data is played back with the rest of the song.

Bar	Automation	Effect Status	Comment
1		Inserts — MonoDelay	The initial state – the bypass is not active, so the effect is **ON**
3		Inserts — MonoDelay	At bar 3, the Bypass is ON, so the effect is bypassed (effect **OFF**)
5		Inserts — MonoDelay	At bar 5, the Bypass is OFF again (inactive) so the effect is **ON** once more.

Automation of MIDI controllers

In many areas, Cubase gives you different ways to do things, and automation means you have that facility with MIDI Continuous Controllers (CCs) – you can create them using the automation controls instead of entering them data 'inside' a part. This approach has a number of benefits – as we have already seen, the automation system 'interpolates' between the data points you create, so to create a long linear increase will only involve creating two points rather than the large number you would have to do editing the data in a part, which makes creation and editing of that information a lot easier. Secondly, although Cubase offers a way of seeing more than one controller at a time (via the **create new controller lane** option in the pop-up menu), this is not as flexible as the automation system, and also is not clearly shown while in the project window – all CCs are viewed in the same way when placed inside a part, while they can be viewed separately while in automation mode.

To automate any CC, firstly view the automation track, as normal. Click on the current parameter (usually **Volume** by default) and you will see the usual pop-up menu. From this menu, select **More...** and you will see a new Add Parameter window, where you can pick the destination you wish to automate. Here we see the usual automation targets, but in addition there is the MIDI Channel group, which expanded shows the All CC group, which when expanded gives us access to all the CCs available – note that Volume (CC# 7) and Pan (CC# 10) are missing from this list as they are already represented in the original list.

You can then pick the CC you wish to automate, and create that automation using the usual controls – bear in mind that some controllers are switches (such as Sustain - CC# 64) so they will only be ON or OFF.

As already mentioned, one of the great advantages of using this method is that you can see the changes of multiple controller data types from the project window, quickly and easily, as seen below.

The following part has three different controllers (**Expression** for volume, **Brightness** to alter the sound's timbre and **Effect 1 Depth** to add reverb), all of which are changing dynamically over these few bars.

Automating Instruments

One of the most commonly-used tasks for automation is to change the parameters of a VST Instrument over time – countless compositions have made use of this sort of facility to add sonic interest to an otherwise repetitive piece of music. To do so is quite simple, but how you do it will depend on whether you are using an Instrument Track, or you are using the VST Instrument Rack. We will demonstrate this for both types with a simple, repetitive 'analogue sequencer' style repeating 32-note figure as a MIDI part, and then play this back using the PG-8X VST Instrument (See page 235 for more on the PG-8X).

Automation of an Instrument Track

Firstly, create an Instrument Track containing a PG-8X synth. Next, create your MIDI data – in this case the Logical Editor has been used to create some random 16th notes (See page 368 for how to do this) – make the part several bars long to give time for the automation to be heard.

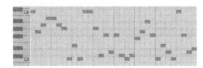

Next, show the automation lane for the PG-8X, and click on **Volume**. A list of parameters will appear - but they may not be the one you are after. If not, scroll down to **More...**, click it and the Add Parameter window will appear. You can expand the PG-8X in the window that appears (by clicking the triangle), and then you will see the entire list of automatable parameters for the instrument in question.

For this example, we want to automate the filter's cutoff parameter, which is called **VCF FREQ** in the list.

Back in the project window the automation track will now be set to **VCF FREQ** and you will see the current value displayed (in this example it was 99.00, but it will vary depending on the sound you have picked). Now enable **Read** and start to add some automation data in. Here is the classic filter sweep, with the filter starting at a low frequency (cutting off most of the sound), and then opening up as the sequence progresses.

However, to make it more interesting, automating another parameter is desirable; repeating the process by adding another automation lane and then picking **VCF RESO** (resonance) from the filter section, and this time making it alter as the sequence progresses:

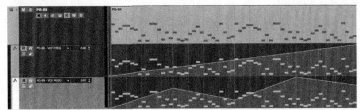

This creates a more interesting sound. This can be repeated for any parameters you want, and of course the ones you want will depend on the synth you are using and your desired effect. Some of the parameters that are available with synthesizers are explained in the Synthesizers section, on page 231.

Automation of a Rack Instrument

The automation of a Rack Instrument is largely the same as for an Instrument Track – you pick the parameters in the same way as you would for an Instrument Track, and automate them in the same way. The fundamental difference is that there are two tracks – the MIDI Track and the VST Instrument Track, which can be some distance apart in the project window. Here is an example.

First, we see the MIDI Track, and the VST Instrument Folder (which is created when the VST Instrument is created in the VST Instruments Rack). Note that the PG-8X has two tracks, one set to **Volume**, one set to **DCO1 WAVE**.

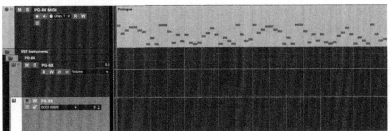

The first track will only give us access to automation of 'standard' mixer functions such as Volume and Pan. It is the second track which we are interested in – click on Portamento to get the pop-up menu for the PG-8X, and then select **More...** to get to the list of parameters and pick **VCF FREQ**.

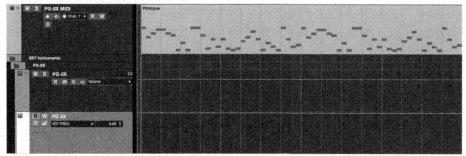

You can now read-enable the track and create the automation data you want for it (the filter sweep shown in the previous section has been created again).

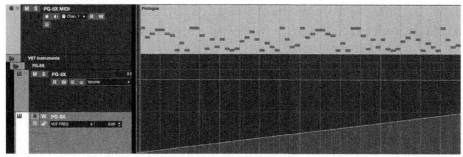

Just as in the previous section, it's possible to add another track (by clicking the show icon at the bottom of the current automation track), and in this case **VCF RESO** has been added and automated.

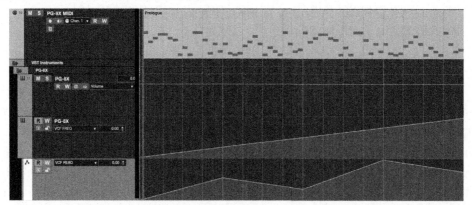

As can be seen from this example, adding the automation is very similar, it is the details that are different. One of the biggest issues with VST Instruments which use separate MIDI tracks is that with a larger project it can become difficult to quickly locate the VST Instrument you are using for automation purposes; if you are aware of the differences between Instrument Tracks and Rack Instruments (see page 34 if you're not sure), then Instrument Tracks can make using automation a lot simpler.

Exercises

Automate Volume

Volume automation is the first step in creating automation, and the one which is most commonly used. Using the instructions on page 343, apply some automation to a part - fade it in, fade it out, and create quick changes as well, learning how automation points cannot move before a previous one or after a following one. Select multiple points and make use of the adjustment handles which appear, allowing the overall level to be altered (top centre) and also tilted (with the corner handles). Delete points, and create them in a number of ways - by clicking the automation line in the lane, and also by using the write control and moving a control on screen.

Automate Panning

Next, create another lane, and use this to automate panning. While the controls and editing are much the same, the pan control's range is different, with the centre being the 'normal' setting.

Automate a Mute

Automating mute controls is important, and a valid alternative to muting parts using the mute tool. Add another automation lane, and mute parts. Note that the automation can only be in two positions - on or off.

Automate Bypass

Automating the bypass of an effect is one of the most common uses for automation, but it can be confusing as when the automation is up (with the bypass on) the effect is off, as outlined on page 350. Practice this a number of times to get the hang of it, noting that as a two-state automation parameter (like mute) it is either On or Off.

Summary

Automation gives the ability to make your music extremely complex in terms of detail and production; the ability to alter just about any parameter means that your project can alter in real time and in a way which would be next to impossible if the changes were being controlled manually. In addition it allows this information to be built up progressively, allowing an extremely complex mix to be created incrementally, and with editing of any information allowed at any time.

The ability to modify the parameters of audio effects and VST Instruments means the possibilities are almost endless, creating far more interest from simple musical parts by altering the tones and timbres as the piece develops, something which has been used to great effect in a wide range of popular music.

Mastery of the automation system in Cubase will lead to you produce far more professional-sounding sequences, recordings and compositions, and is a key skill in which time spent will pay great dividends.

The Logical Editor

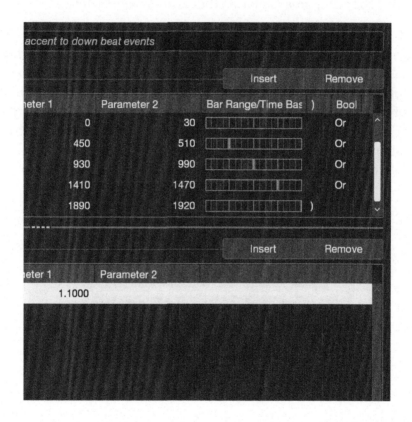

The Logical Editor in Cubase is one of the most powerful tools you can use for MIDI work, but it's also probably one of the least-used. This is a great pity as it can make otherwise tedious editing work quick and simple, and with practice can allow you to produce some varied and interesting effects and also aid your compositional work – it can produce in seconds ideas that could take hours manually.

PRO

The full Logical Editor is only available for Cubase Pro. However, the presets are available to apply to MIDI data in other versions under **MIDI > Logical Editor > Apply Preset....** While this is a limitation, you may find that the presets are still useful, and spending time exploring them can be worthwhile.

Overview

In short, the logical editor is a processor for MIDI data. It is summoned by **MIDI > Logical Editor > Setup....** Note that it can only be opened when suitable MIDI data for it to work on is selected. It has two sections, the filter which decides what kind of information it will work on (from a very general, broad spectrum to a very specific, narrow range) and the action section which decides what to do with the information that has passed through the filter. The logical editor is shown here – the filter section is at the top, and the action section is at the bottom.

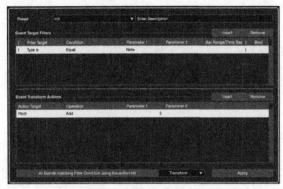

We will now look at each section in detail before moving on to see how the logical editor can help you in a number of common MIDI programming situations.

The Filter Section

The filter section allows you to decide what kind of MIDI information you wish to work on – when working with it, you will need to be familiar with the different kinds of messages that MIDI can transmit (and as a result the different kinds of information that Cubase can record, store and transmit) – see page 55 for details of this. The filter section works with simple lines (allowing selection of certain kinds of data) which can be combined together to make a more complex, selective filter. To do this you can either use an AND (when you want both conditions to be true before the action section will work) or an OR (where you want either one or the other to allow the action section to work). In some situations, you will only need one line in your filter section.

Let's say we have the following information in a part:

Program Change 64

Controller Channel 1, CC 7, Value 80

Note On Channel 1 - C3, Velocity 75

Note On Channel 1 - E3, Velocity 48

Note On Channel 1 - G3, Velocity 65

This sends a program change, sets the volume to 80 and then plays a C major chord.

Selecting Notes

If we wanted to work on the notes only, then our filter line would be straight forward – it would read

Type is Equal Note – i.e. it would just look at the information type, and if it is a note, then it will be altered by the action. If it isn't a note (such as the program change) then it would be rejected and unchanged. Cubase will show the filter settings as an expression, so this is also shown.

If we wanted to select everything but the note then we could change the filter line to read:

Type Is Unequal Note - This is the inverse of the above example, so the Program Change and the CC would be passed onto the action, but the notes would not.

Selecting Notes by Pitch

Often you will want to be more precise. Let's say we wanted to select only the notes that are E in our part (for argument's sake, let's say we have a number of C major chords and we want to turn them all to C minor; we would do this by moving all the E notes down a semitone). To do this we would have to add another line, using **Insert** at the top right of the filter section.

When the new line is added, it will say **Type Equal Note**, so this needs to be changed. Click in the first column and you will see several options. With note data, Pitch is classed as Subtype, so you may need to select **Subtype** from the first column. The Logical Editor will then change the line to read **Pitch**. Next, click on the **Equal** in the same line, and a menu of options will appear – select **Note is Equal to** as this will allow us to select a note regardless of the octave that it is in. Now in the last column click and type **E**.

The first line selects note information only; this combined with the more selective second line which then says only notes of pitch of E are affected by the action.

Note that the two lines are being combined using an **And** – i.e. an event will only pass through if **both** lines are true (in this case, it will need to be a note, **and** the pitch will need to be E). We will see later on that it is possible to use an **Or** statement as well to make for a more flexible filter.

Sometimes you would want to be even more specific, selecting only a note in a certain octave:

| (| Type Is | Equal | Note |) |
| | Pitch | Equal | E3 |) |

The second line now says **Pitch Equal E3**, so only notes with that specific pitch would pass through for processing – any other E (such as E2) would not pass through.

Selecting by Velocity

If you wanted to work on notes which had velocities above 50, you would have the following:

| (| Type Is | Equal | Note |) |
| | Velocity | Bigger | 50 |) |

Here the first line selects notes, while the second line narrows this down further to only notes with a Velocity (Main Value) that is above 50. In our example above this would lead to only the C note and G note being selected – the E would be unaltered.

Filter Section Summary

The Filter Section is where you decide the information which will be passed to the action section. Being aware of the facilities available to you within it is important as it can save you a lot of time selecting data to work on; if you can think of a methodical way that the required information can be selected then you can tell the logical editor how to filter it.

The Action Section

The Action section is where the Logical Editor changes the MIDI data which has passed through the filter. There are a huge range of actions that can be performed, and it is possible to perform more than one action at a time by adding extra lines to the section. We will start out with some simple examples, and then see more powerful ones which are available.

Changing the Pitch

This is a fairly straightforward action:

| Pitch | Subtract | 1 |

It subtracting 1 from Main Value, which is pitch – it will move the note down by a semitone. While this in itself is not particularly powerful (and easily done manually), if it is combined with selecting any E in a part (as shown in the example on page 359) then it would be possible to turn any E into an E♭, changing the example C chords into C minor throughout. Remember that this can be over an entire piece, saving possibly half an hour's work. The action section is actually in two separate parts – firstly there is the drop-down menu which appears at the bottom of the logical editor window.

By default this is on **Transform,** but below we will see all the possible options:

Type	What happens to data which passes the filter
Delete	Passed data is deleted.
Transform	Applies the 'Action' to the data.
Insert	Applies the action to the data, and leaves original notes unaltered.
Insert Exclusive	Applies the action to the data, deletes all data which doesn't pass the filter.
Copy	Applies the action, and stores the result in a new part. Leaves original data as is.
Extract to Track	Applies the action, stores data in a new part on a new track. Removes original data.
Select	Selects passed data.
Extrack to Sublanes	Applies the action, stores the passed data in a new lane on the current track. (See page 13 for more on lanes)
Deselect	Deselects passed data.

This might appear slightly confusing at first, but each has its place. For the most part, if you want to alter data and leave it in the part they it was originally in, then leave the logical editor in 'Transform' mode. If you want to move the data to a new part, then use 'extract'.

In addition to this, there is the action section at the bottom of the editor. This works in a similar manner to the filter section, except that every line you insert is applied in order. There are simple operations such as add and subtract, you can set random values within a range, you can swap values (in the case of notes turning pitch into velocity and vice-versa), fix notes to a scale (a wide range is provided), and also provide a range of values which will be progressively altered between the two locators.

A table showing this working on Controller data should show these operations more clearly – bear in mind that they will only work on existing data, not create data; the only reason to show the "before" data is to give a visual comparison of before and after; note that two settings ignore the original input data's values completely, as shown in the before column for these two settings.

Before	After	Description
		Add (20) – here each value has a fixed amount added to it.
		Subtract (20) – each value has a fixed amount subtracted from it.

		Multiply (1.5) – each value is multiplied by 1.5
		Divide (1.5) – each value is divided by 1.5
		Round (10) – each value is rounded off to the nearest 10, like quantization for values.
ANY INPUT DATA		**Random (0-127)** – input data is irrelevant (apart from position), the output is a random value within the range specified.
		Mirror (50) – this mirrors the values around a point you decide. i.e. if you have a mirror of 50 and input 30, output is 70. If you input 40, output is 30, etc.
ANY INPUT DATA		**Linear Change in loop range (0-127)** – the output is a linear progression between the two locators, in this case 0-127. Original input data is ignored, apart from position.
		Relative Change in loop range (-10 - +30) – similar to the above, but allows adding and/or subtraction from the original values (here subtraction at the left, addition at the right).

In the examples above, controller data has been used for clarity of the diagrams. However, it's important to remember that the Logical Editor can operate on any kind of MIDI data – notes, controller data, program changes, pitch bend and any other data. This flexibility can be daunting at first, but it makes the Logical Editor an extremely powerful tool. Let's look at some typical examples, firstly from some of the presets that are provided in Cubase.

Loading Presets

Cubase 12 introduced a new structure and loading method for Logical Editor presets, as well as a number of new filter types and action targets. This means that finding a preset can be difficult. The quickest way to locate any of the presets mentioned here is to search for it by name. Click the preset area...

... and click in the search area in the popup window that appears...

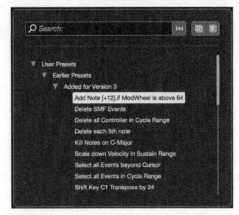

... and type a few letters of the required preset. Any preset whose name matches what you have typed will appear. For instance, typing **random** will summon any preset with **random** in the name:

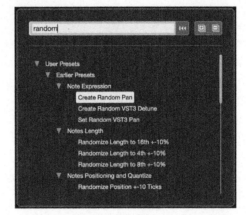

It is possible to scroll this list and find the Random Velocity preset, but probably quicker to type a few more letters to narrow it down to a single choice:

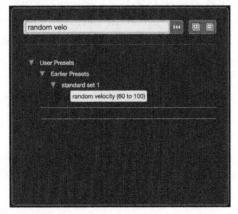

Click the name of a preset to load it.

Random Velocity (60 to 100)

This is a useful one for making a part sound more realistic (with a small range of random values) or to make it sound less so (with a wide range). It consists of the following:

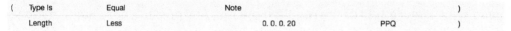

Velocity	Set Random Values Between	60	100

This selects all notes (regardless of pitch) and sets Main Value (velocity) to random values between 60 and 100. Narrowing this range will give a more natural feel, while widening it can have a more drastic effect.

Delete Short Notes

This can be a useful one for tidying up 'sloppy' keyboard playing or MIDI data created by a guitar synth. It deletes any notes which are shorter than 20 ticks long:

(	Type Is	Equal	Note		)
	Length	Less	0. 0. 0. 20	PPQ	)

Note that the action is not set to **Transform**, but **Delete** - all filtered notes will be deleted.

Extract Note (C3 60)

This is a useful one which you can use as a template for extracting other notes. The filter consists of two lines which select only one particular note (by default, C3). Changing this value will allow you to extract other notes, which can be useful particularly when wanting to extract a note from a drum kit to use on a different sound or MIDI instrument.

(	Type Is	Equal	Note		)
	Pitch	Equal	C3		)

Again, here the action is not set to **Transform**, but to **Extract** to move the filtered notes to a new part in the project window.

Tip: Here is our first cautionary note about the logical editor, or more precisely the programming of it. You can see that when you call up this preset, the pitch is not shown as a letter (such as C3), but as a number. While this is correct in terms of the MIDI specification, it is not usual for people to remember that 60 equates to C3, etc., as Cubase normally does this translation. However, when recalling a preset, Cubase doesn't do this, and reverts to 'number' mode. If you want to change the value, you can enter a number, but it is often easier to enter a letter, and this can only be done by re-selecting the **filter target** on our pitch line – click where it says **Pitch** and re-select **Subtype** (which is Pitch). Now the Parameter 1 section will correctly read as a pitch (by default it will be C-2), and will allow you to enter the value as a pitch such as C3. This bug may well be fixed in later versions of Cubase, but it was reported when Cubase 5 was originally released, and has not been attended to at the time of writing.

Downbeat Accent

This introduces a new concept – as well as being able to filter out information by its type, it is also possible to do so via its position in a bar. This gives us the ability to do processing which is based on the timing of an event. To do this, the filter target is set to Position, and then the bar range can be entered, either numerically or by clicking and dragging on the bar range diagram which appears

| Position | Inside Bar Range | | 0. 1. 3. 60 | 0. 2. 0. 60 | | Or |

Here is the setting to catch notes which are around beat 2. Each bar is divided up into 1920 'ticks', so each beat is 480 ticks. The accent downbeat preset actually looks like this:

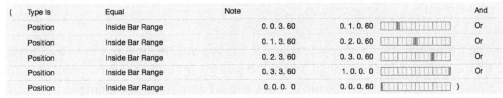

(Type Is	Equal	Note				And
Position	Inside Bar Range		0. 0. 3. 60	0. 1. 0. 60		Or
Position	Inside Bar Range		0. 1. 3. 60	0. 2. 0. 60		Or
Position	Inside Bar Range		0. 2. 3. 60	0. 3. 0. 60		Or
Position	Inside Bar Range		0. 3. 3. 60	1. 0. 0. 0		Or
Position	Inside Bar Range		0. 0. 0. 0	0. 0. 0. 60		)

Here there are 5 "position" filters, because it's not possible to "wrap round" the end of the bar to the beginning and this is set to catch notes which fall slightly ahead of each beat as well as after it; the second line is for 'late' beat one notes, while the last is for 'early' ones.

Note that this filter is more complex than any previous ones. It uses both **And** and **Or** statements - here the data **must** be a note (the statement is part of an And), but can in **any** of the positions (all of which use an Or statement).

The accenting part is simple – it just adds a fixed amount (by default, 30) to the velocity of any filtered notes.

| Velocity | Add | 30.0000 |

Being able to filter events by their position is extremely important, and a tool which you can often use to sequence the way a real musician may accent certain beats.

Delete Black Keys

This preset will remove any 'black key' notes, in any octave. The filter section looks like this:

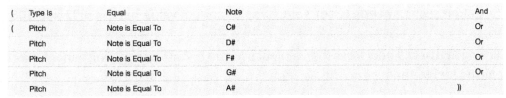

(Type Is	Equal	Note	And
(Pitch	Note is Equal To	C#	Or
Pitch	Note is Equal To	D#	Or
Pitch	Note is Equal To	F#	Or
Pitch	Note is Equal To	G#	Or
Pitch	Note is Equal To	A#	))

As above, it makes use of And and Or statements - the data must be a note, and can be any of the black keys. Also note that the notes are selected using the Note is equal to condition - this allows notes in any octave to be selected, so that the first line will select any C#, whether it is a C#1, a C#8 or anywhere else.

Making a part more realistic

Let's now use the Logical Editor (and some judicious quantizing) to make a badly-programmed drum pattern into a good one. Here is the original part – it just consists of eighth-note closed hi-hats with an open one at the end of the bar, bass drum on 1 & 3 and snare on 2 and 4.

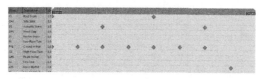

All the notes are at a fixed velocity, and it sounds dull, boring and rigid as a result of this. The first thing to do is to add some swing – in this case just a small amount (7%) has brought some rhythmic life to the part with no other changes.

But the logical editor is going to help us make the velocities far more believable. At present the velocities are all set at 100, which is around the right area, but we will now use the LE to set the velocities of the hi-hats to a random value between 92 and 108. This is done by setting the filter to select notes only (of two different pitches, F#1 and A#1 – here we need to make use of the brackets facility and OR), and then the action to set Main Value (velocity) to random values between 92 and 108.

	Type Is	Equal	Note		And
(	Pitch	Equal	F#1		Or
	Pitch	Equal	A#1	)	

Here, the first line must be true - the type must be a note, but the second bracketed pair allows either one of two conditions to pass – either the pitch is F#1 OR the pitch is A#1 – either will pass the filter. The brackets are important as they enclose the two conditions which are combined by the OR in the right-hand column. While this can appear complicated at first, after a bit of practice you should be able to construct complex filtering arrangements to do the most mundane of tasks automatically.

The action section needs to set Velocity to a random value between 92 and 108.

Velocity	Set Random Values Between	92	108

Clicking **Apply** will now alter the velocities of the hi-hats only, giving a much more realistic feel to them.

But there is a little more we can do – many drummers would accent certain parts of the bar more, and this random approach might accidentally do this, but often won't. If we want to do this, we then need to add an amount to the velocity of each beat – let's add 15 to each one to make this true most of the time. To do this, call up the "downbeat accent" preset, and change the action amount from 30 to 15. This will provide a small accent for each downbeat. Here we see the result of having applied the random velocity operation followed by the "downbeat accent" one – the notes are not all the same velocity, and the beats are accented.

One final action which is possible is to add in a small degree of randomness to the timing of the notes, using this action:

Position	Set Relative Random Values Between	-2	5

This will move the position of the note by a relative random value - taking the original position and them moving it slightly, in this case in a range between a tiny bit earlier and a little bit later; such changes will add a small amount of randomness without making the part sound out of time, and can be done repeatedly. This can either be done to all notes using the simple filter statement below:

(	Type Is	Equal	Note	)

Or it can be combined with a filter which only allows the notes falling outside the downbeats to be processed – this would retain the tightness of the downbeats while adding in a small amount of randomness to the other parts of the bar, again making for a more realistic performance.

(	Type Is	Equal	Note			And
	Position	Outside Bar Range	0. 0. 3. 60	0. 1. 0. 60		And
	Position	Outside Bar Range	0. 1. 3. 60	0. 2. 0. 60		And
	Position	Outside Bar Range	0. 2. 3. 60	0. 3. 0. 60		And
	Position	Outside Bar Range	0. 3. 3. 60	1. 0. 0. 0		And
	Position	Outside Bar Range	0. 0. 0. 0	0. 0. 0. 60		)

Note that the filter uses **And** here instead of Or, as the events would have to be outside **all** of the ranges given, not inside **any** of them as in the previous example. Whenever constructing complex filters, it's important to be clear in your mind what you are trying to achieve. Although it can appear difficult at first, if you are methodical about the way you approach it, you can make a filter which will do what you want it to do.

By applying the above logical editor operation, the pattern is just given a small amount of timing variation that all real performers would display, again adding to the illusion that this has been played by a real drummer. The combination of these small changes in timing and the velocity information will make the drum pattern sound as if it had been accurately and musically played by a good drummer, rather than the original mechanical, rigid performance.

Using the editor for Composition

Firstly, let's make it clear – the logical editor is not a complete replacement for inspiration – you will need that to create a composition, but it does have some use for helping you get more mileage from a phrase or part that you have already created, and this can inspire you in turn to create more interesting and complex pieces.

Generating new pitches

The Logical Editor comes with a preset called **Random notes – C3 to C5**. It should be no mystery what this does – takes your existing note data and alters the pitches (Subtype) to random values between C3 and C5 (note they are shown as numbers here as Cubase does this when recalling a preset, as mentioned before).

Pitch	Set Random Values Between	60	84

This means that the rhythm of the part you have played will be preserved, but the pitches will be totally random. This can be of some use when creating random lines (such as making computer 'bleeping' noises), but because of the totally random nature of the notes generated it can be of less use for diatonic melodies. However, a simple addition will create notes which do fit in a given key.

Pitch	Set Random Values Between		60	84
Pitch	Transpose to Scale	C	Major	

It is important to remember when setting actions that they are applied in order, so the top line is done first, then the second and so on, for each piece of data which is passed through. What happens here is firstly the notes are randomised, and then they are fixed to fit with the chosen key (in this case, C Major, but there are a wide range of scales available). This narrows down the choice of pitches and creates a line which will fit in key, giving a much more musical result. You can alter the range of the notes (in the first line) and the scale to suit your requirements. If you are starting with just this 'melody' you may want to add some chords to create a context for the melody to be heard in; in that way the real sound of the scale you have chosen will become apparent. Listening to just a melody on its own will not give you the real effect, and the choice of chords can really alter your perception of the melody.

Changing note lengths and speed

This is another area which the logical editor can help – although you can use the timestretch tool in the Project Window to alter the duration of a part (and hence the notes inside it), you cannot alter them with the detail that the logical editor can, as the lengths will be altered in the same way as the overall length of the part is. While this is mostly desirable, you may want to alter the note positions and lengths independently of each other, and the logical editor can do this. Let's look at an example.

Here we see the original melody part. If we want to halve the note lengths (for a staccato passage) , we could do this manually, but the logical editor can do it more quickly. The filter section is simply set to event type is notes, so we will not see it here. But the action section is equally simple, as seen below.

Here the length of the notes is divided by two (although a different amount could be set) and the result is seen here:

Each note has halved in length, and even with such a short passage it would be quicker than editing each note manually. With a longer section the savings would be massive, and also adds the possibility of using lengths which would be difficult to do manually, and makes testing different settings out quick and easy to do.

It is also possible to alter the position of the notes without changing their length to speed up their tempo without altering their duration.

Position	Divide by	2.0000

This gives us the example shown below, where the notes have their original lengths (from the first example on the previous page), but their positions have altered to be played at double the tempo.

Again, you can change the tempo using any numerical figure so don't feel that you are constrained using whole numbers – it is possible to create polyrhythmic and indeed even multi-tempo parts and sequences using these techniques (such as overlaying parts of 15 and 16 beats to repeat evenly, which has been heard in a variety of electronic music styles), as seen below.

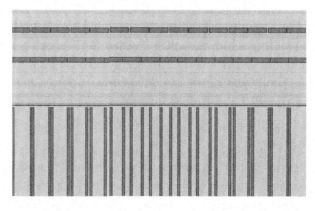

Changing Tonality

Another area where the logical editor can help is the alteration of certain notes. In addition to selecting via MIDI Note numbers, it's also possible to select notes regardless of the octave they are played in – for instance, any C♯ note can be selected using the following line in the filter section – note that the Condition is **Note is equal to**, not **Equal** which selects individual pitches (including the octave that the note is in).

(	Type Is	Equal	Note		And
	Pitch	Note is Equal To	C#	)	

As seen earlier, there is a preset which uses these, called **Delete Black Keys** under the Experimental presets group. You can use this as a basis for a number of different actions, whether you wish to delete notes, or alter their pitch or position. If you want to alter the tonality of a piece, using the logical editor to select the notes which need to change is quick and easy using the Note is equal to condition - then it will just be a case of altering the note as applicable; if you wanted to alter all the F♯s in a piece to F, then it is only a couple of lines away in the Logical Editor:

This line selects all the F♯ notes

(	Type Is	Equal	Note		And
	Pitch	Note is Equal To	F#	)	

Then this line subtracts one from the pitch, changing them into Fs

Pitch	Subtract	1

Exercises

Select a single pitch

The first thing to practice with the logical editor is using the filter section to select the events to work on. The simplest example of this would be to select all the notes of a given pitch within a part. Open up a drum part which has closed hi hat notes in it (F♯1), and use the logical editor to select only those notes, as shown on page 359 and setting the Function to **Select**.

Alter the pitch

This will build on the previous example, by changing the Function to **Transform**, and then using the action section to alter the pitch. The action that you want to apply is up to you, but if you wanted to alter the closed hi hat notes you have selected (F#1) to be open hi hat notes (A#1) then you would use the action section to **Subtype Add 4** to add 4 semitones to the F♯1 pitches to make them into A♯1s. Experiment with different actions to see how they work, as seen on page 360.

Extract all the snares

Another common activity is to extract all of a given note from a drum part; this is useful when you want to change one part of the kit to use a different instrument or patch. This is easily done with the logical editor - set the filter section to select only notes, and add a second line that selects only the pitch D1 (or whatever your snare is in your drum part - it may be E1). Set the function to **Extract** and click **Apply**, and the notes will be moved to a new track with them in; they can now be sent to a different VST Instrument to the rest of the kit.

Select all of a given note

Sometimes it is desirable to alter all of a given note - rather than ones in a specific octave (such as the D1 shown in the previous example), it may be that all of the E notes regardless of octave need to be selected. If we were in the key of C major, we may want to alter all of the Es to E♭s then this would be easily done using the action section to subtract one from each. Find a melodic/chord part where there are notes spread across multiple octaves, and then use this technique to alter the tonality of the music.

Apply velocity changes

As seen in this chapter, the logical editor can make long-winded tasks quick and easy. Take a part you have programmed which has uniform velocities, and use the settings on page 366 to apply small random velocity changes to the notes, making them sound more realistic.

Apply timing changes

As seen on page 366, it is possible to apply a small degree of randomness to the position of the note - i.e. the time that it is played. By doing this to a quantised part, it is possible to make it sound more realistic and human. Do this, experimenting with the numbers for the randomness. Remember that the effect of this is cumulative - each application will move the notes NOT from their original position, but the position they last were, so applying it a number of times will change it more (depending on the numbers you have used, of course).

Summary

The logical editor is a very powerful tool, particularly because it is capable of carrying out tasks which otherwise would be long-winded, repetitive and boring; with a few settings it can alter a huge range of data, such as note velocities over an entire song, or extract a particular note or chord throughout. This can mean a huge reduction in the amount of time it takes you to carry out a task and also an increase in the level of detail you can apply to your sequences.

Whenever you are using the logical editor, it's important to be methodical in the way you approach it, and make a distinction between the filter section (which picks the information to work on) and the action section (which decides what to do with the events which have passed through the filter), and if the editor doesn't do what you were expecting to look in the correct place – often you can use the "select" action to check if the filter section is working correctly without making any alterations to the information, for instance.

With practice, the logical editor will become an often-used tool for you to improve your sequencing, and even to generate musical ideas. As we have seen in the examples above, it's possible to try out editing options that would normally take some time to execute and audition them whereas if they were done manually it would be unlikely that such a range of settings would be tried before patience had expired.

The List Editor

>	Type		Start	End	l
	Program Change		1. 1. 1. 0		
	Controller		1. 1. 1. 29		
	Controller		1. 1. 1. 96		
	Controller		1. 1. 2. 31		
	Controller		1. 1. 2. 72		
	Controller		1. 1. 3. 48		
>	Controller		1. 1. 4. 24		
	Controller		1. 2. 1. 0		
	Controller		1. 2. 1. 96		
	Pitchbend		1. 2. 2. 24		
	Note	♩	1. 2. 2. 72	1. 2. 4. 72	
	Note	♩	1. 2. 2. 72	1. 2. 4. 72	
	Note	♩	1. 2. 2. 72	1. 2. 4. 72	
	Note	♩	1. 2. 4. 24	1. 3. 2. 24	
	Note	♩	1. 2. 4. 24	1. 3. 2. 24	

ARTIST PRO

The List Editor is available in Artist and Pro versions of Cubase, and it allows you to examine MIDI data in detail; a skill which is useful in many situations. You should remember that it is like any other editor, it is just giving you access to the same information but in a different format.

If you open up any MIDI part in the List Editor (**MIDI > Open List Editor**) you will see something like the screen below.

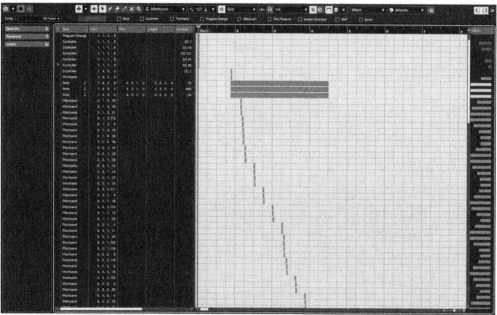

Here the information from the MIDI part can be seen in detail. Each line represents one event – for instance a Note event would take up one line, as would a Controller event, Program Change or Pitch Bend message. Next we see the columns and some information in detail.

Type	Start	End	Length	Subtype	Main Value	Secondary	Channe	Attributes
Program Change	1. 1. 1. 0				90		1	
Controller	1. 1. 1. 0			CC 7	76		1	Main Volume
Controller	1. 1. 1. 0			CC 10	64		1	Pan
Controller	1. 1. 1. 0			CC 121	0		1	Reset Ctrl
Controller	1. 1. 1. 0			CC 91	40		1	ExtEff 1 Depth
Controller	1. 1. 1. 0			CC 93	20		1	ExtEff 3 Depth
Controller	1. 4. 3. 0			CC 1	0		1	Modulation
Pitchbend	1. 4. 3. 0				0		1	
Note	1. 4. 3. 0	4. 3. 1. 0	2. 2. 2. 0	F3	127	64	1	
Note	1. 4. 3. 0	4. 3. 1. 0	2. 2. 2. 0	A#3	127	64	1	
Note	1. 4. 3. 0	4. 3. 1. 0	2. 2. 2. 0	D4	127	64	1	
Pitchbend	2. 1. 3. 30				33		1	

This information is presented like a table, with headings above – they are explained in the table on the next page.

Name	Description
Type	The MIDI event type – Program Change, Note, Controller, Pitch Bend, etc.
Start	When the event occurs, in bars, beats, sixteenths and ticks.
End	In the case of notes only, when the note off for that note happens.
Length	The difference between Start and End (if applicable).
Subtype	In the case of a note, this is the pitch, for controllers it is the controller number, for Program Changes the PC number.
Main Value	A data value - for a note, the velocity, for a controller it is the value.
Secondary Value	The third piece of data – rarely used in MIDI 1.0, but may see more use with MIDI 2.0 devices.
Channel	The MIDI channel that the event originally occurred on.

Underneath this, we see some sample data. We can see that at Bar 1, Beat 1, a Program Change of 90 is sent, and also a number of Controller values are set – volume, pan, modulation, reverb and chorus levels - these are to set the initial parameter values for the part to help make sure the track sounds as the creator intended, rather than possibly inheriting arbitrary values - this is extremely common in MIDI files. Next Pitch Bend is sent - while this is a nominal value of 0, this is actually the 'centre' value of pitch bend; this message is resetting the pitch bend on the track to ensure the pitches are correct. In the fourth beat of the bar, three notes are sent, and the part would continue in a similar manner.

Being able to look up these values and note them is a useful skill - it allows you to see the details of the messages actually being sent. The controller names are given in the Comment column, but the values are "raw" - you should be aware that some values are not as they seem here – in the case of Pan, a value of 0 doesn't mean 'Off' it means 'Left', etc.

Setup Window Layout

By default, the filter may be hidden from view. If so, click the Setup Window Layout button (at the top right of the editor), and turn on sections as needed.

X	Set up Window Layout
☑ Left Zone	☐ Status Line	☑ Value Display
	☑ Filters	

The Filter

The Filter can help you when you are looking for a certain kind of information, and also knowing how it works will make sure you don't miss something out!

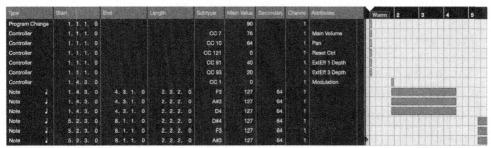

Here we see the filter. If a box is ticked, that kind of information will NOT appear in the list. Clicking **Show All** will clear all the filters that have been set. Taking the part shown in our overview of the list editor, the majority of the information is Pitchbend data. If this is filtered, then the output looks quite different, as seen here.

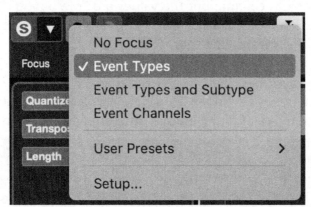

With the pitch bend data filtered out, we only see the remainder, which is a Program change,the controllers being set and 6 note events.

Being able to do this will allow you to home in on the information that you want, without spending a lot of time scrolling through a part, and possibly missing something. However, make sure that you are not filtering something out accidentally. It will still play, but you won't see it.

The Focus Menu

In addition to the filters section, there is also the focus menu, which works in an approximately opposite manner. Click on an event whose type you wish to view, and then click the focus menu to see the available choices.

The most common ones are **Event Types** (which will show any event which is the same type; if you have selected a note then only notes will be visible) and **Event Types and Subtypes** (which will show any event with the same type and Subtype value; if this is a note then it will be of the same pitch, if it is a controller then it will be the same CC type).

Here is an example - a part with a significant amount of mixed data in it. A note has been selected (as this is the type of Event we are interested in).

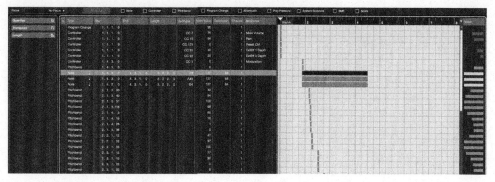

Selecting **Event Types** from the focus menu leads to all other events being hidden from view:

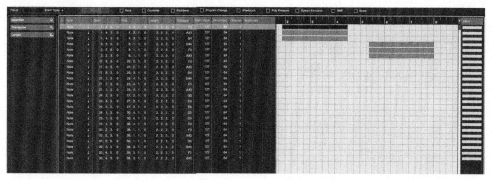

Returning to the original view is achieved by selecting **No Focus** from the focus menu.

Summary

The list editor is most useful when trying to work out what is happening at a low level with MIDI data - this is most commonly needed when working with a MIDI file, as it will allow quick interpretation of data which has been imported, either for analysis or to alter or delete data (such as is commonly needed to remove Program Change information from a MIDI file to allow the selection of different sounds than intended by the creator). While it is not commonly used by many programmers when creating music, it can be extremely important for true understanding of MIDI data.

Scoring

While it may seem outside the remit of many people using Cubase, there are some times when it's important to be able to produce "dots" - music written as standard notation - and it can be extremely useful to be able to produce written parts that are neat and clear, whether you are recording a cover version of a song, are in a band (particularly if you need a 'dep' player to join you), want to get others to play your compositions without hours of group rehearsals and saying "No, no no! It goes like *this!*". This chapter will cover the production of readable and useful scores from a sequence, using Cubase. While there are dedicated score-writing programs available (such as Steinberg's Dorico), for many purposes the scoring that Cubase offers is perfectly adequate and offers some advantages in terms of workflow – if you have been sequencing in Cubase you will be able to go back and change the music without having to re-start your score work.

We will assume that you have already sequenced your piece, and it sounds as you would like it to. It might be assumed that to produce a score, you can simply open up your project, select all the MIDI tracks and then open the Score editor. This will usually produce something that looks like this:

This, clearly isn't a good score – there are many problems with it. It has no title, the instruments may be in the wrong clefs, they look messy and would be difficult to read, amongst other things.

All of these things can be rectified fairly quickly to produce a score which would be easy for a player to read, and which will correctly express your musical ideas in written form.

We will look at the steps you can take to make your scores as clear and readable as possible. Much of the editing will be performed in Page Mode, which shows how the score will look when it is printed out. Edit mode is more useful for editing notes, but in many cases note editing is easier to achieve in the Key editor.

Basics

Before opening the score editor and making changes, it is often best to save your work as a different version (with a new file name) – this is because sometimes to achieve a readable score will mean changes which will make small differences to the sound of the piece (particularly if you have used some detailed MIDI programming techniques), so keeping two versions can avoid any undesirable effects on your original. The score editor can work on one or more parts at a time – it will open whatever you have selected - but it is often best to work on a single part at a time, and once each part is correct, to then work on the complete score. To make working on a complete part at a time easy, glue all the parts on a track together, saving time in highlighting all the parts on a track. Now select a part and hit **CTRL+R**, and you will enter the score editor.

Firstly, a brief note on the difference between Edit and Page mode.

Edit Mode: The score is presented as an unformatted staff which freely changes with the window size, and does not show how the final printed version will look. Changing the width of the window may alter the number of bars on the staff.

Page Mode: The score is presented as it will look on the printed page. The layout and positioning of the staves can be altered to create an appropriate layout for reading. The number of bars on a staff is not controlled by the window width.

You can select Page Mode from **Scores > Page Mode** and vice versa - it will be ticked in the menu when selected, and we will mostly be using Page Mode as we are more interested in the layout than any other factor.

Here is a typical part when opened in the editor in Page Mode:

Here we see that the part isn't easy to read (something we will attend to later), but more importantly we can see some of the basics of the score editor.

In the example above, the first staff is selected – the lines of the staff are blue, and there is a blue rectangle to the left of the staff. Clicking inside any staff will select it, and knowing which staff is selected will be important later on.

You will sometimes find that staves are too close together. If this happens just once, then you can simply select the staff you want to move (the lower of the two), and then drag the staff down using the blue rectangle.

If you want to move all the following staves (i.e. space all of them out more), then you can do the same thing, but hold down the **ALT** key while dragging. This will re-space all the following staves.

You can edit notes by dragging them up and down (to alter their pitch) and left and right (to change their timing). If you want to alter the length of an existing note, you can do so by holding down **CTRL** and clicking on the note-length tool-bar. You can also insert new notes using this toolbar and the note tool.

There is another tool on the main toolbar – the Layout tool. This allows you to re-space bars and notes visually without altering their sound. This can be particularly useful if there is a complex bar that you wish to space out to make it easier to read.

When in Page Mode, you may need to move to another page quickly, which you can do with the Page Selection box, at the bottom right of the window – you can either click the up or down arrows, or you can double-click and enter a page number.

Staff Settings

The Staff Settings Dialog box can be accessed in two ways – either select **Scores > Settings...** or double-click the blue area to the left of a selected staff, as seen to the right. Make sure that Staff is selected in the Score settings box (it is by default).

It contains many options that are useful for deciding the way your part will look. While specific functions will be covered later on, a quick tour now should give you an idea of some of the most useful settings. Here it is possible to set the **Long** (first staff) and **Short** (all other staves) Name.

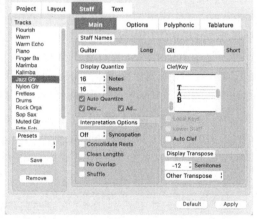

Display Quantize is an important setting – the score editor will not display notes or rests that are smaller than the set values, so if you are using a part with 32nd notes in it, then you will need to re-set these. Cubase has these settings to try to avoid the need for excessive quantization of your original MIDI part; for many situations 16th notes are small enough, and it means that there isn't a large number of odd-length and timing notes because of this setting.

Clef and **Key** can be set here; they are covered in the next section.

One extremely important setting is **Display Transpose**. This allows you to produce music for a transposing instrument, such as the Alto Saxophone. This is a concept that causes confusion for many, but the basic idea is that a written note on a transposing instrument will sound at a different pitch. For instance, if you write a Middle C (C3) on for a saxophonist, it will sound as an E♭, 9 semitones below. Clearly this could be difficult to remember if you didn't do this regularly, so Display Transpose allows you to take your part (and have it still sound at the correct pitch), set the Instrument (a list of the most common is given), and Cubase will alter the notes and the key signature to suit the part so it will still sound the same. It is worth remembering that a Score (with multiple parts, for the conductor) should be in concert pitch (i.e. with none of the parts transposed) while any parts that need to be transposed should be.

Clef and Key

It is imperative to make sure each instrument is in an appropriate clef. This can be straightforward for some instruments, while others will take more thought and work. The clef can be changed using the Staff Settings dialog box, as seen in the previous section.

On the right-hand side is the Clef/Key area, where it's possible to alter the clef of the staff – there are a wide range of clefs provided which should cover most eventualities, including transposing instruments (such as guitars), as well as percussion and TAB (which we will look at later on). You can also select the appropriate key signature for your piece to start in here. Once you click **Apply** you should see the changes made, and if you are happy with them, close the dialog box with the **X** at the top right.

But what if you need to change key or clef during the piece? Key changes in a piece are common, and clef changes are sometimes needed for certain passages. If you need to insert a key or clef change at any point other than the beginning of the piece, click on the appropriate feature in the area to the left of the editing area. Clicking on **Keys** will produce the menu shown to the right. Now click on the key signature you wish to add, and then move over the score. The cursor will turn into a pencil, and clicking at the point you wish to add the signature will create it.

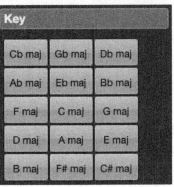

The same idea applies for making a change of clef, and indeed will apply for any of the other features we will add as seen later on.

If you pick the wrong key or clef, you can double-click it and a box will appear allowing you to change it.

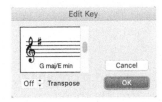

The Properties Inspector

CTRL + ALT + R

Properties of many items in the score editor can be edited directly by showing the Properties Inspector, which changes appearance depending on the selected item. For many editing duties, this will allow quick access to the most-needed settings, once the relevant element is in place in the score.

Here is the Properties Inspector, with nothing selected in the score editor. It shows the relevant settings for the entire part - display quantize, staff mode and staff presets. The appearance of the inspector will alter depending on the selected item - it will show relevant options for the selection.

Here, a note has been selected, and the **Noteheads** section has been expanded by clicking the triangle at the left-hand side. This allows quick editing of the noteheads of the selected notes. In this case, the default is **Auto** which is highlighted. Clicking any of the other noteheads alters the selected notes instantly.

Here, a clef has been selected, and the options available are shown graphically, allowing quick alteration of the clef. If another change is needed and it coincides with an already-displayed clef, then this can be achieved from the Properties Inspector, but insertion at other locations is carried out using the symbols palette on the left-hand side.

Whenever you are making edits in the score editor, check for the relevant property in the inspector as this can greatly speed up workflow.

Drums

If your piece contains a drum kit, then often this will be the next area to require attention. The reason for this is that usually the drums will look something like this:

While this drum part sounds fine, it looks terrible. This is because MIDI drums are played at very low pitches, and in addition these are not the pitches which are used in most drum notation for the kit.

Fortunately, Cubase has a solution for this problem, and that's the Score Drum Map. This provides a translation between the notes that you play on the keyboard and how they should be displayed.

To activate the Score Drum Map, firstly make sure that the MIDI track has the Drum Map turned on (this is in the Inspector in the project window), as seen to the right. Without this set, the next step cannot be completed, something which can lead to confusion.

Once this is on, in the Staff Settings dialog box, go to the `Options` tab, and select **Use Score Drum Map**. Now click Apply and you should see that the score starts to look more like a drum score, and less like a complete disaster.

However, as you can see, it is still not perfect. While most of the notes are now translated by the drum map into an appropriate visual pitch, one of them isn't. To correct this, we will need to listen to the sound which is causing the problem and rectify it, and that will mean editing the Drum Map.

Editing the Drum Map

The Score Drum Map is fairly straightforward - it translates the played (MIDI) pitches to be displayed at a given pitch and with a specific note head. You can access it via `MIDI > Drum Map Setup...` It has 11 columns, but only the first two and last three are of interest for our purposes, as explained on the next page.

Column	Description
Pitch	This is the played (MIDI) pitch of the note – this cannot be edited.
Instrument	The name of the instrument – this is for reference only.
Display	This is the pitch at which it will display – this can be altered to any pitch.
Head Symbol	A pop-up menu gives a choice of 30 different note heads.
Voice	Used in conjunction with Polyphonic mode this allows up and down-stemming of parts

In the previous section, we saw that most of our drum kit was being displayed properly by the default drum map, but the notes in the first bar are not.

Here we can see the drum map itself:

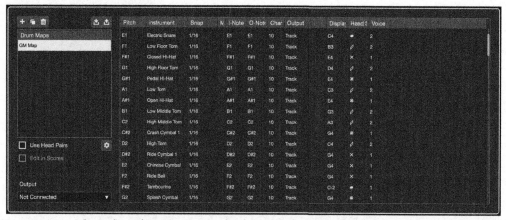

We can see that the Electric Snare (E1) is displayed as C4, with a standard note head symbol. However, when we click on the mis-displayed note in our previous example, the drum map shows us this:

Pitch	Instrument	Snap	M	I-Note	O-Note	Chanr	Output		Display	Head Sy	Voice
F3	High Timbale	1/16		F3	F3	10	Track		C-2	●	2

The sound is correct - it is a High Timbale - but it is being displayed as C-2, five or six octaves below the staff! We need to pick something more suitable (and explain it to our performer if it's an unusual sound), and enter it accordingly.

Pitch	Instrument	Snap	M	I-Note	O-Note	Chanr	Output		Display	Head Sy	Voice
F3	High Timbale	1/16		F3	F3	10	Track		A3	◆	2

Here A3 was chosen, with a diamond head symbol. It was moved to voice 2, for reasons that will become apparent in the following sections. The score first line now looks much better:

This is looking far more readable, but still needs some work to make it easy for a drummer to read. The first element is to stem certain parts of the kit with upstems, some with downstems. This is done using the **Polyphonic** tab of the Staff Settings dialog box. Usually a staff is in **Single** mode – here there are no 'independent' parts on a staff, it's all considered one musical element. However, **Polyphonic** mode allows us to show two musical elements on one line, often indicated by being up- or down-stemmed, regardless of position on the staff. This is done by changing the Staff Mode to Polyphonic. For drums, however, the following changes also need to be made, as shown below.

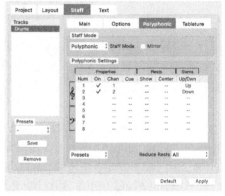

Here we see the Staff Settings Polyphonic tab with the required changes – voices 5 and 6 are turned off, and Voice 1 is set to Up stem. If this is now applied to our drum part, it will show clearly the two parts which are to be played.

However, this looks a little messier in some respects than the previous version.

This is because the note duration is being shown for each part, and this is often unnecessary – when you play a drum, there is no control over the duration of the sound, so displaying it is superfluous. To make the part neater will require some editing of the MIDI data – we will look at the second bar in the example above.

Here is the original bar. It is difficult to read because the tom and bass drum are very short, meaning rests are needed for the remainder of the beat that they are in, and the hi-hat and cymbal are too short at the first beat, meaning another rest is needed.

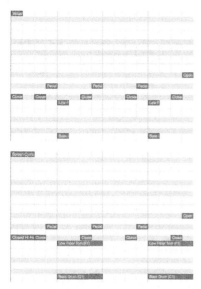

When looking at the part in the key editor, it's clear to see why – all the notes are of different lengths, and none of them use the maximum available length to help make the part look clear. Altering them leads to this.....

..... where the bass drum and tom have been altered to take up an entire beat, while the initial hi-hat and cymbal have been extended to an eighth-note to remove the need for a rest at the beginning. These change mean that the part now looks....

... much cleaner and easier to read. While the rhythm hasn't changed, careful manipulation of note lengths can yield a part which is much more readable.

This may seem long-winded, but in practice it can often be done by selecting large groups of notes and then using **Fixed Lengths** or **Length Quantize** in Cubase. Once you have done a few parts, it becomes quick and simple to do. One thing that you may find helps is to have both editors open at the same time – you can do this quite easily (use **CTRL+TAB** to cycle through the windows until you see both having opened them from the menus), and then you can instantly see the effect your work in the key editor has on your score.

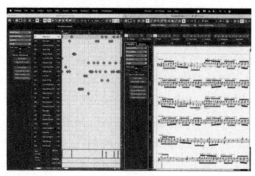

Tidying up note lengths

Another common problem is that note lengths in a part may make it harder to read than it should be – this can be for one of two main reasons:

Firstly, notes can be too short, and make a rhythm more difficult to read as a result. The ideal with a score is to convey musical information while making it as readable as possible. Often parts can be made easier to read by using staccato dots. This is a dot which appears under a note head which halves its duration.

Here is a guitar part, which is a repeated single note, but the rhythm features 16th notes, which some players may have difficulty in reading at all, and which certainly isn't that clear. The cleaned up version is shown below.

This has been achieved by two actions. Firstly, some of the notes have been lengthened to make them display clearly without any rests. Here we see the original:

This is edited to remove any rests. The diagram below shows this, but the notes have been slightly shortened to make their lengths clear - in reality there would be no gap between them:

Next, in the score editor, the notes which have been lengthened are now marked with staccato dots to show the player that they should be shorter than written. This is done by opening the note symbols menu (which is on the left of the score area). The dot is selected, and then can be added to each note by clicking it. Note that you need to have the right staff selected to add a dot. If you have more than one note selected then you will add dots to all of them when clicking on one of the selected notes.

Other note-based symbols are available here, and they will be placed appropriately above or below the note/staff. If you hover your mouse above the symbol, a tool tip will tell you what the symbol means.

Regardless of the player's reading ability, this is much more clear to understand – the rhythmic idea is clear to see, even though they should sound the same.

The second common problem is that notes can be too long. This manifests itself in a messy-looking part, as shown below:

Here the part looks complex – there are several notes which are longer than they should be; this might be desirable for a smooth playback (a legato feel), but it is being misinterpreted by the score editor. Careful attention to the note ends should fix this, and in this case it was simply a case of using Quantize Ends (from the quantize menu on the left of the key editor) to yield the true nature of the part:

This is much clearer! While this was a simplistic example, often a messy-looking part can be fixed with work on the note overlaps.

Multi-Bar rests

When creating parts, there are often times where a performer has several bars of rest together. Printing out parts which show each bar of rest individually can make for a part which is difficult to read, and in addition can be wasteful.

To rectify this, Multi-Bar rests are used instead. To the right we see an original part, which has 6 bars of rest between two phrases; some parts may have much longer breaks.

To turn Multi-Bar rests on, go to the Staff Settings box, and click on the Layout tab near the top. It will look like the screen shown to the left. On the right-hand side the multi-bar rest setting can be altered. The number is the number of bars that are needed to 'trigger' a multi-bar rest; in our case if it was set to 5 or less then they will work, 6 or more they will not (as there are 6 bars of rest). Click **Apply** to see the effect.

Here is the same part with multi-bar rests turned on - the 6 bars of rest is shown as a single bar with the number of bars shown below.

Unpitched Percussion

Often there is a requirement to produce a part for unpitched percussion, and this can be done using the drum map – firstly, turn the drum map on, as seen on page 385 and tick **Single Line Drum Staff**. If you click Apply now, you should see a single line drum staff, and the notes of your part will appear either below, on or above the line. The notes that do this are defined in the two boxes below the tickbox – any notes which fall inside this value will be on the line, those above or below will be displayed above or below the line. However, it is important to remember that these values are taken from the Display part of the drum map – if the notes of your part have not been assigned, they may well be at C-2, and therefore always appear below the line.

However, setting them appropriately will yield something like this:

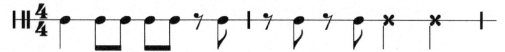

Here is a clear, easy to read part for triangle, with the closed and open triangle being notated with an 'X' note-head.

Guitar Tab

Many guitarists are unwilling or unable to read 'traditional' notation, and in addition there are sometimes occasions on the instrument where specific fingerings or locations on the fretboard are desirable or even necessary.

To do this, once a part has been sequenced accurately, open the part up in the score editor, and then go to the **Score Settings** box, click on the **Staff** Tab, then the **Tablature** tab and select **Tablature Mode**. Clicking Apply will change several settings, making a 6-line staff with the numbers 1-6 as the 'clef', and showing each note as a number on the appropriate string.

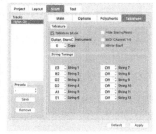

While the Staff Settings box is still open, note a few other settings:

Instrument – This can be Guitar or Bass, with pre-set tunings for 'standard' 6 string Guitar and 4 string Bass. The box below allows setting of tuning for each string, creating possibilities for a open tunings as well as those with extra strings. If you want to create a seven string guitar, it can be added as string 7, often tuned to a B (**B0**) or A (**A0**). If you wish to create a five-string bass, then string 5 can be added, usually as a B (**B-1**).

No Stems/Rests – this is often used for tablature that has no indication of rhythm whatsoever – this can be used to make a clearer-looking TAB, or when the TAB is to appear in tandem with traditional notation (the rhythm can be seen from this).

MIDI Channel 1-6 – this option is given to allow a part which has been recorded using a Guitar-to-MIDI converter that has output each string on a separate MIDI channel, and meaning that each string has its own MIDI channel and will be placed accordingly. Otherwise Cubase will simply make an educated guess as to which string a given note should be on.

Once a part has been set to tablature mode, it will look similar to this:

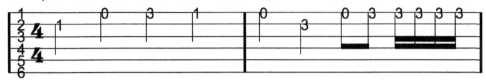

Here the stems are shown, showing the reader the length of notes as well as the fret/string to play them on. However, this is not always seen, and often the stems/rests are omitted and the part is also shown in conventional notation, as seen next.

This is most easily achieved by duplicating the original part, and setting one to conventional notation while one is in TAB mode.

To move a note from one string to another, select it using the arrow, and then right-click, and from the menu, pick **Move to String** and then select the appropriate string for that note.

Chord Boxes

Often a guitar part will include chord boxes, showing a guitarist a particular chord shape. These can be added quickly, and they appear under the **Other** section to the left of the score in the editor. The symbol looks like a guitar chord box, and once you click it, the cursor turns to a pencil, and when you click where you want it to appear, a Guitar Symbol dialog box will appear on screen, as shown below.

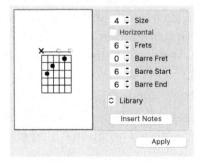

Usually the easiest way to create a given chord is to pick it from the Library - if you click on Library a list will appear of the chords Cubase has already stored. Clicking

Apply will create the chord box, which you can now move.

You can create your own chord shapes by clicking on the strings in the guitar symbol box, and you can add a capo/barre using the three settings to the right of the box. You can also add the notes from the chord to your MIDI part by clicking the **Insert Notes** button. You can edit any chord box you have already created by double-clicking to summon the guitar symbol box, or right-clicking once it is selected to quickly change it to one of the library chords by selecting them from the **Presets** menu.

Making Chord Symbols

Often a part will be read by someone who may wish to use their own inversions of chords, or who isn't good at reading conventional notation – certainly in many instances it's easier to see what's going on when the chords are written in English. Cubase can attempt to work out the chords you are playing in a part – to do this, select the notes you wish to be analysed (often the entire part, so you can use **CTRL + A** to select all), and then go to **Scores > Make Chord Symbols**. Cubase will analyse the notes, and put chord symbols above the staff wherever it thinks a chord change occurs. If any of the symbols that occur are incorrect, you can double-click them to edit them using this dialog box – you can modify any aspect of the chord symbol – key note, bass note, type and tension. Guitar Chord Boxes can be added by right-clicking on a chord symbol and picking **Make Guitar Symbol**.

Strummed Parts

Lots of guitar parts use chord boxes and a style of notation which has the chords printed out and simply shows the rhythm to play, notated as a single note on a staff, making the rhythm much easier to read for many. There are a number of ways to do this in Cubase, but the following will work quickly and easily, although it will result in the part being played on a single note, so this is for score production purposes only. Once a part has been sequenced accurately, we want to produce it on a single-line staff, so we need to make all the notes the same pitch, move them to the right pitch on the single-line staff, and then remove any double notes. Here we see the original part:

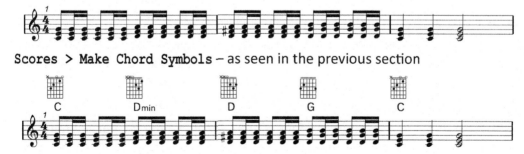

Scores > Make Chord Symbols – as seen in the previous section

MIDI > Logical Presets > Standard Set 2 > Set Notes to Fixed Pitch (C3)
– this changes all the notes to one fixed pitch, C3.

MIDI > Transpose Setup... highlighting the notes only (otherwise your chord symbols will be transposed too) set the value to 11, and click OK, to move all the notes to **B3**, the middle line of the staff, as seen on the next page.

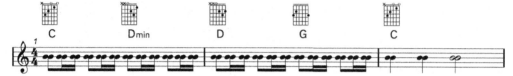

MIDI > Functions > Delete Doubles – this removes any notes which are doubled (in step 1, if you had a 3-note chord, then you would have 3 C3 notes in the same place which leads to messy-looking notes in the score editor as they have multiple heads:

Scores > Settings... – go to the Options tab and set System Lines to 1. This produces the single-note staff, which makes the rhythm reading easy.

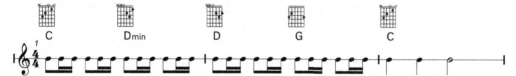

You should now have a part which looks something like this – the rhythm is easy to read, and the chords are shown above the rhythm which should make it easy to read and play.

Staff Modes

We have already seen two modes of the staff – single which suffices for many parts, and polyphonic which has been used for drum parts (and will be explored further later on). There is another mode, and further uses for Polyphonic mode.

Split

Split mode is often useful for creating simple Piano/Keyboard parts where the part is in two staves. This is accessed via **Scores > Settings > Staff > Polyphonic**, and once Split has been activated as the staff mode, it is possible to alter the split point (C3, middle C by default) – any note that is above this will appear in the upper staff, all others below that.

The example above altered this to **B2** to allow the lowest note of the melody to appear in the upper staff. Once this is set, the staff will turn into two staves (by default treble and bass clefs, but these can be altered), and displays the notes as defined by the split point. Here is a simple piano part, but there can be times where there are notes that are above or below the splitpoint that you wish to display on the 'other' staff (for instance when showing that a line should be played with a specific hand, despite the note range). Should you need to do that, it can be achieved by selecting the note/s, right-clicking and picking the appropriate staff from `Display in Staff`. However, this can sometimes create issues with note beaming (where a note's beam links two staves together) which can sometimes be partially overcome by selecting No Overlap in `Scores > Settings > Staff > Main`.

Polyphonic

We have already seen a use of Polyphonic mode, for the drum kit. It can, however, be used for other parts, particularly for vocal music where two different parts (but in the same range) may be notated on the same staff. Again, it is accessed via `Scores > Settings > Staff > Polyphonic`. Once the staff is set to Polyphonic mode, there are a variety of options which can be used. Firstly it is important to turn off the voices you will not be using – for instance, if you are working with a single staff (treble clef), then turn off voices 5 & 6 – if you don't, then you will end up with a bass and treble clef. If you are using Polyphonic mode to create separate parts on one staff, then you should make sure that the upper voice (1 or 5) is up-stemmed, not the automatic setting that is there by default.

Here is a part which is for two voices.

This is a simple part, so it is mostly obvious which voice should sing a given note. However, in bar 3 it is not clear, and bar 4 looks messy as some notes have to be tied as they are crossed by shorter notes. Setting the staff to Polyphonic (with voice 1 set to up stem) provides little change:

This is because by default all the notes are in voice 1, so the lower part needs to be set to voice 2. Selecting the notes and then right-clicking and picking **Move to Voice > Move to Voice 2** will do this. However, selection while in the score editor can be somewhat long-winded, so it's often easier to open the part in the key editor, select the notes there (all of them, using **SHIFT +** click to add to the selection each time), and then open the score editor with them still selected. With the appropriate notes (lower ones in this case) moved to Voice 2, the part now looks like this:

This is an improvement in readability because the individual lines are now more readable, and the different rhythms (in bar 4) are easier to see. However, there are two rests in bar 2, and the rest in bar 3 is oddly-placed. These problems can be overcome using the layout tool – seen on the right – to move the bar 3 rest to a more suitable position, and by selecting one of the rests in bar 2 by right-clicking and picking **Hide/Show**, then re-positioning the other one to a more suitable position.

Adding Dynamics

Another important part of a score is dynamics – the instructions given to the performer to tell them how loud or softly to play a part or phrase. They can be accessed under **Dynamics** on the left-hand-side of the score editor and this is shown to the right. The bulk of the dynamic instructions come from Italian, with *p* standing for piano (quiet) and *f* for forte (loud). More of each letter means going more in that direction, so the progression would be *pppp,ppp,pp,p,mp,mf,f,ff,fff,ffff* from very very quiet to very very loud.

Dynamics			
⌐	*pppp*	*ppp*	*pp*
p	*mp*	*mf*	*f*
ff	*fff*	*ffff*	*fz*
sfz	*sfzp*	*sf*	*sff*
fp	*fpp*	<	>
✕	*p<f*	⌐	⌐
⌐	⌐		

To apply one of these, simply click it to make it active in the palette, and then the cursor will turn into a pencil. You can then apply it; note that a dynamic instruction should appear below a staff, and depending on the contents you may need to reposition it with the arrow tool.

As well as the written dynamic instructions, there are also crescendo and diminuendo (sometimes called decrescendo) lines. These are the lines which show a progression in level, and they are selected in the same way as a written instruction. Clicking and releasing will create one of a preset (short) length, but if you click and drag you will create a longer one. If you have initially placed one, it can be re-sized as shown below.

Here is our original part, which we want to add a crescendo to. This is done by selecting the crescendo from the dynamics menu, then clicking underneath the beginning of the part, dragging to the right and then releasing the mouse to...

...create the bar-long crescendo. Note the two grey handles which control the start and end of the crescendo. If you wish to alter the length or start point, you can do this by clicking and dragging...

...to the new location. Most graphic additions (such as phrase marks) can be altered in this way.

It is also possible to add phrase marks as well in a similar manner — they are named as 'slurs' in Cubase but they are identical in appearance. A phrase mark shows the performer a group of notes to be phrased as one unit, giving more idea of the logical arrangement of the music. By grabbing the middle of the three handles it is possible to increase or decrease the curvature to suit any contour of notes.

Adding Text

Text can be one of the more confusing areas of using the score editor in Cubase — the reason for this is that there are a number of different types of text available, and choosing the right one is important — choosing the wrong one can mean a lot more work becomes necessary on complex or large pieces.

Firstly, it is important to make the definition between Layout text and Project text clear. As the names suggest, Project text will appear on ALL pages. If you want a piece of text to appear on all of the parts that you create for your project (such as the title or composer), then Project text is the way to go. If, however, you want the text only to appear on the current layout (remember that a layout is created for each part or combination of parts that you edit in the score editor) then you will want to use Layout text. But it is important to remember that if you use Layout text when editing a part in the score editor on its own, if you then create a score (with more than one part) then a new layout is used, and that text will not be displayed. If you have text that is to apply to a part but also needs to appear in the score, then use the text from the Other menu.

Text Type	Summary
Project	Appears on all layouts – useful for titles, composer, etc.
Layout	Appears only on the current layout – useful for performer only indications.
Other	Appears on the current layout and any combinations – useful for directions that the player and composer must both be aware of.

If you are creating a score and parts, then you will probably find that Project text is useful for title, composer, copyright, etc, and that Other text is best for directions about the performance.

To create some text, select the text from the appropriate symbol palette (in this example we will create a title for the piece, then credit the composer), and then click on the page, where you want the text to be. The dialog box to the right will appear, and you can enter the text you want in the upper box. There are a number of options, however, that should be noted. Firstly, it is possible to have the text appear on all pages, all but the first, or the first page only.

Typically for a title this will be **Show on First Page**, and in this case it has also been set to the Centre at the top. It is possible to change the font and the font size (you can type a value as well as select one from the drop-down menu) as well as putting the text in a frame or making it bold, italic or underlined. Clicking **OK** will place the text, and if you are not happy, you can double-click it to re-open the dialog box.

Adding a composer would be similar, except it would need to appear on each page, in smaller text, at the top right-hand-side of the page.

If you want to insert lyrics, select **Lyrics** from the **Other** menu, and click under the first note you wish to add a lyric to. Once you have entered the text for that note, you can hit **TAB** to move to the next one. If you want to extend a syllable to cover more than one note, select it and use the arrow tool to drag the grey handle to the right to create a number of ----- to show this.

Bars and Bar Numbers

One extremely common need is to alter the number of bars on a given line – this can either be to make the part appear more readable (either to give enough room for a complex bar or to arrange the lines in a more logical way) or to make better use of the space available. Here is an example – while the rest of the piece is readable, the third bar shown is not – it has more notes in it and is difficult to read at present.

This can be rectified by changing the number of bars on the line. In this case, 3 bars on the line will make it readable. To change the number of bars, use **Scores > Advanced Layout > Number of Bars** and select the number of bars and whether you want it to apply to this staff, or all staves. Often the staff following one you have altered will need to be re-set, but you will then end up with something far more readable.

One other area of spacing that often needs attention is the last bar of a piece – it is not unusual for a score to have one or two bars at the end, and by default Cubase will stretch these across the page, which can look bad, as seen below:

To correct this, use the Object Selection (arrow) or Layout (hand) tool to move the end of the last bar to the left, creating more normal bar lengths and a far more clear indication of the end of the piece:

Hiding and Showing elements

There are times (such as when using Polyphonic mode, above, and when using repeat marks, later on) where elements of the original performance need to be hidden for purposes of clarity. This is easily done – select the element you wish to hide, and then go to **Scores > Hide/Show**. This hides the element from view in the score editor, but it is still there and can still be heard.

Here we see a polyphonic passage which has two rests as a result of both voices having a rest at the same time:

For clarity we want to hide one of them, so we select the lower of the two rests, and go to **Scores > Hide/Show**, and here is the result.

This is fine, but later you may want to un-hide something, and to do that you will need to see it. To do this, you will need to see the filter section to display where elements have been hidden – this is done using Setup Window Layout...

..where **Filters** can be activated, and seen above the main score area.

Once the **Hide** option is active (ticked) then any non-note element that you have hidden will have a **Hide** shown for it at the bar it appears in.

To show the element again, select the **Hide** and delete it with the **Delete** key on the keyboard or the on-screen eraser. The hidden element will re-appear.

Hidden notes are classified separately – they can be viewed with **Hidden Notes** on the display toolbar, and have to be returned to the normal view by selecting them and using **Scores > Hide/Show** to return them to view.

Using Repeat Marks

Another way to make a score or part more readable for the performer is to use repeat marks wherever possible. These are symbols which indicate that the performer should repeat the previous one or two bars, allowing them to perform that section with confidence that they are not re-reading the bars and missing a small difference. Take the following example:

Here bars 3 and 4 are identical. It is easier for the performer if this is indicated as such – we want to hide all the notes in bar 4, and then replace them with a repeat mark. Firstly, click and drag a box round the notes to select them all.

Once this is done, use **Scores > Hide/Show** to hide all the notes.

They are replaced with a rest, which needs to be selected and again use **Scores > Hide/Show** to produce a totally empty bar.

Now, from the **Other** palette on the left of the editor elect the repeat mark and place it in the middle of the bar.

This can be done for two- bar passages (repeating the previous two bars) using ...the two-bar repeat symbol, as shown.

Graphic Elements

Sometimes you will need to replace notes with symbols, for instance if you have accurately sequenced a glissando, it will look messy in the score editor by default. You may wish to use a similar technique to above (hide the notes, then the rests that appear) and use a symbol to replace those notes – this will preserve the playback of the file, while making the score more readable. In addition, you can use the symbols from the "Graphic" palette to add notes and rests which have no effect on the playback; as their name suggests, they are graphic only.

Bracketing Parts together

Sometimes you may wish to place a bracket to show that parts belong together – for instance, adding braces to a piano part, or encompassing a string section or different percussion parts. This can be done under **Scores > Settings > Layout**.

As seen above, a dialog box appears with two columns in it where you can apply braces or brackets – to add them, click on a part to turn the element on, then you can click and drag down the column to encompass more than one part – here braces have been added to the Synthesizer parts (across two staves), while square brackets have been added to the Marimba and Kalimba parts. You can turn off bracketing by clicking again in this column.

Aligning Elements

Often, when producing a score, elements will need to be aligned to make them appear neater – for instance, when chord symbols or guitar chord diagrams have been added, they may need to be aligned. This can be done by selecting the elements you wish to align, and then using the options available under **Scores > Align Elements** to line them up. They can then be moved to their final position as a group (while they are all selected) to retain their relative positioning.

Editing Multiple Parts

Often there is a requirement to produce a Score and Parts for a piece – the score for the conductor, while the parts are for the performers. The Score can be created by selecting all the parts in the project window (CTRL + A) and then opening the Score Editor. Note that a new Layout is created for each combination of parts that you edit, so there may be some formatting lost (for instance, if you have used Layout Text this will not appear in the Score as it is per layout).

A common problem when editing many parts together is that there are too many staves to fit on a page. If this happens, you can reduce the size of each staff (Scores > Staff Settings > Options Tab) by altering the Size setting (often around 70 works well), and then re-spacing the staves to allow them to fit in.

However, bear in mind that some changes (such as the Staff size) affect the Score and Parts, so it is often best to save the song again under a different filename when you are producing a score.

Scoring for sampled parts

Often a part that uses MIDI to control a sampler or samples will not represent the actual pitch of the samples – the sample may be of a different pitch, or may be a longer sample which plays back a number of original pitches. Also the composition may use samples which have been placed and/or edited in the project window, and therefore have no MIDI for it at all.

In either of these cases, to produce a score for the part, you will need to sequence a MIDI track which will not be heard as part of the final piece, but which produces the same pitches as the samples. This can then be edited and scored in the normal way. Note that often for 'spoken' notes it is not possible to produce an accurate pitch, so choose a note that will score well (i.e. at a convenient pitch for display) and then use an 'X' note head to represent this as a note with indeterminite pitch.

Printout

Printing in Cubase is straightforward – once you have made your edits and have the required parts open in the Score editor, simply select File > Print…. and select the pages you wish to print out. Note that CTRL+P does not work, this takes you to the Pool for audio and video files.

Exercises

Produce a part

A common use for the score editor is to produce a part for a musician to play for a recording. Generally this will not need to be a complex score with fully marked dynamics, it is often solely to help the player in conjunction with a recording of what they are required to play. To this end, take a melody you have sequenced in MIDI, and make it clear and readable for printout. This is usually achieved by appropriate quantization, and by ensuring the note lengths are sensible - often when a part has been played in there will be small rests at the end which will make the part look far harder to play than it actually is. Ensure you make correct use of the key signature to minimise the number of accidentals appearing.

Produce a part for a transposing instrument

There are many instruments which are transposing instruments - when they play a C, it will sound at a different pitch to a non-transposing instrument. To get them to sound at the same pitch, their parts need to be transposed. Cubase takes care of this for you, so take your melody from above, and use the Display Transpose feature shown on page 382 to produce a part for a transposing instrument - a task that is far more difficult without this feature.

Produce a strummed guitar part

Guitar parts with strummed rhythms can be extremely useful. Produce one from a set of chords you have already sequenced, using the techniques outlined on page 393.

Produce a drum part

Another common instrument to produce parts for is the drum kit. Using a drum part you have already sequenced, produce a drum score, using the techniques outlined on page 385.

Summary

The Score editor allows the printout of a wide range of notation for performers, but obtaining a readable and meaningful score takes some time – often it is the addition of extra elements such as dynamics, etc., that give the performer a complete picture of the piece. While other programs may offer more facilities, often Cubase can produce everything you need to produce good, readable parts for other musicians.

It is important to remember that a score should be as easy to read as possible, and give enough information to the performer to allow them to accurately reproduce your intentions. Detailed editing of note lengths and addition of relevant symbols will make a score or part far easier for the performer to understand and therefore allow them to pay more attention to creating a musical performance.

Audio

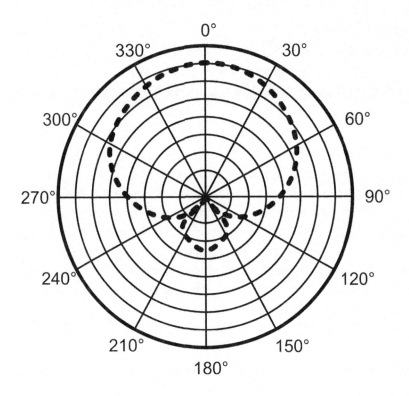

Vibrations of air from the environment around us are perceived by us as sound (often referred to as audio when being recorded). In short, the air vibrates in sympathy with objects, and those vibrations travel through the air towards our ears. Our eardrums vibrate and transfer these vibrations to tiny bones in our ears, and even smaller hairs, and their vibrations are transformed into nerve signals that our brain perceives as sound.

But for us to make a permanent record of a sound, we need to turn it into something that can be recorded – in most cases, electricity. This is the job of a microphone – to turn sound waves into electricity. However, such a simple description ignores the 'real world', and that different items do the same job in very different ways, and each of them has advantages and disadvantages.

The Language of Sound

Before we can describe sound and the process of sound recording accurately, we need to establish some terms which we can use while working, to allow us to understand and express ideas in a clear, concise manner. The first of these is Frequency.

Frequency

Frequency describes how often a cyclic sound repeats. It is measured in Hertz (Hz), which is cycles per second. If a musical instrument is oscillating at 220 times per second, then that note is perceived as an 'A' by us, and it is 220Hz. A doubling in frequency (to 440Hz in this case) means that the note has raised in pitch by one octave – we hear it still as an "A", but an octave above the original sound. Double again (880Hz), and again, another octave interval has been described. This carries on until we reach a point where a sound isn't perceived as a pitch, but more as a high-frequency noise. The same goes when we halve the frequency, giving us two notes below – 110Hz and 55Hz.

However, in both directions we reach limits. In the case of low frequencies, anything below around 40Hz or so isn't perceived as a note, but is 'felt' more than heard. In the case of high frequencies, the upper threshold of human hearing changes with age, illness and exposure to high levels of sound. When newborn, a child can usually hear up to 20-22kHz. However, as time progresses, this upper limit is decreased, until normally in adulthood it is around the 16kHz mark, although this can vary dramatically with exposure to loud noises for long periods, such as going to loud concerts, or a loud working environment, playing the drums or spending your life in nightclubs.

Other animals (such as bats and dogs) can perceive these super-sonic frequencies, but we cannot. There remains some question as to whether or not super-sonic frequencies can affect the way we perceive sound – there is some evidence to support this theory, but that's a debate for another time.

To see the difference between various waveforms, we will be using diagrams which show the sound pressure over time – this is something that is commonly seen in audio editing and sequencing programs. The x-axis (left to right) represents time, while the Y axis (up and down) represents pressure/signal level at any given time.

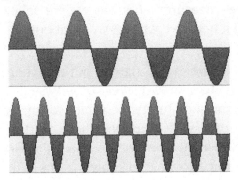

Here we see a diagram showing a Sine Wave, which is at 220 Hz - it repeats 220 times a second, and completes four cycles in the time shown.

Here is another Sine wave, but at twice the frequency - 440Hz. 8 complete cycles happen in the same time as four in the diagram above.

Amplitude

The other unit we need measured is amplitude – this is how loud a sound is, and is independent of frequency – a sound at the same pitch could occur at low level or high level.

The diagram to the right shows a signal that is at the same frequency as the second one above, but at a different amplitude - it is 3dB quieter than the one above.

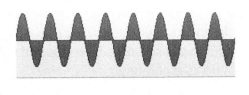

Here is another example - again the same frequency, but the amplitude is 9dB less than the first example (and therefore 6dB less than the one above).

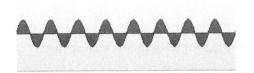

The unit of measurement we will use here is the decibel (dB), which represents a ratio between two different signals. However, what is more immediately important is the way that the decibel works; it is a logarithmic scale, which means it doesn't work in the same was as 'normal' numbers. 0dB in many cases means "no change" - the output is the same level as the input. A change of +10dB means we will perceive the sound as being twice as loud. A change of +20dB means it will be four times as loud, and importantly a change of +30dB will mean the sound seems **eight** times as loud to us; for each 10dB increase, we think the sound has **doubled** in volume. Now consider a negative change: A reduction of 10dB (-10dB) is a halving in volume, -20dB is a quarter and -30dB is an eighth of the volume; again for every 10dB decrease, the sound seems to have **halved** in volume. Silence in many systems is represented as -∞dB - minus infinity. This in theory means it doesn't matter how loud the input signal is, the output will be nothing. The most common error people make is thinking that 0dB means silence; in many systems it doesn't.

It should be noted that the figures above pertain to how we perceive sound; most psycho-acoustic experts agree that +10dB represents what we think of as a doubling in the loudness of a sound. However, +3dB represents a doubling in power; our ears respond differently to actual power measurements. As we are solely concerned with audio and our perception of it here, we will not worry about this fact.

It has been said above that the dB is a ratio between two signals, but to give us an absolute value this needs to be referenced to a known level - otherwise it is merely a relative comparison. There are many such reference values for many different purposes, but when we are concerned with recording there are two references we need to use for our purposes. Firstly when we are talking about digitally recorded signals, dB will make reference to what is known as the "Full Scale", sometimes written as dBFS. These will always be negative, as 0dBFS represents the loudest signal that can be stored in such a file. This is the most common reference point.

Secondly, when referring to sound levels (i.e. in a real environment), the most common references is dB(SPL) which gives a reference point which is the quietest sound a human ear can perceive; this is the reference most often referred to simply as decibels by many. Sometimes db (A) is used, which gives a weighting to different frequencies that approximates the way the ear perceives them; this is useful to approximate how a sound will be heard, where as a db (SPL) level may not do as accurately.

However, often controls' settings will be mentioned, such as the level of a fader or output control, and these will be without a reference, and then they will represent only the relationship between input and output.

Frequency Response Diagrams

Sometimes it is necessary to see the frequencies present in a signal chain, or to see the frequency response of a system (or component). This is done on a 'frequency response diagram', which has frequency as its x-axis, and level as its y-axis. The level is in dB, with most diagrams referencing to a nominal 0dB figure (showing that the system leaves the signal level unchanged). The x-axis (which represents frequency) normally shows the audible range (which we've already seen covers from around 35Hz to 20kHz). To do this in an accurate manner, the x-axis is also graded in a logarithmic scale, which allows the lower frequencies (where a change of 100Hz or so is important) to be displayed accurately while doing the same for the high frequencies (where a change of 100Hz will make little difference); this follows the way we perceive the sound, as an increase of an octave represents a doubling in frequency.

Here are some typical frequency response diagrams, and explanations for their appearance:

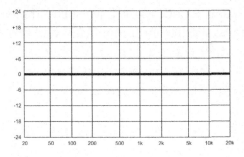

Here is a 'perfect' response – there is no change regardless of the frequency of the input signal.

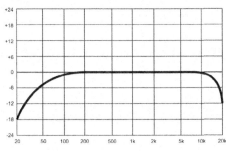

Here is a more typical response curve from something like a microphone – while the majority of frequencies are flat, the extremes of bass and treble are cut

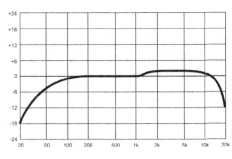

Here is a microphone with a top-end boost – this mic will sound brighter than the one above as it picks up high frequencies more readily.

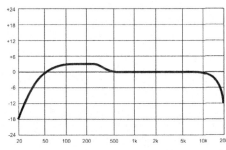

Here is a bass-sensitive microphone – it produces more output from lower frequencies and can pick up lower frequencies than the first microphone.

Although this doesn't tell the whole story of a device's quality or behaviour, it often can give a guide to the performance to be expected, particularly with microphones (most of which come with a plot like this – more expensive models will have an individual test certificate). Often frequency ranges are quoted in terms of ±3dB; they give the range between which the device can stay inside these dB levels, but as we've already seen 3dB is a doubling in energy, so ±3dB is in fact four times difference in energy. Some manufacturers also quote for wider ranges, which tends to flatter their products if that fact is not noted.

Waveforms

The signals we have seen so far have been a sine-wave, which is a mathematical, simple construct. However, real instruments and sounds rarely have such simple waveforms – most sounds are made up of several different frequencies, and this complicates the issue somewhat. Complex mathematical analysis can show some interesting facts about the waveforms that are actually present and the various frequencies, but that is a topic for another time. We will just have a look at some different examples.

Firstly, here are a few waveforms – we've already seen the sine wave, but there are other simple, mathematical ones (in fact there are many, but we'll see the most common ones):

Sine - a smooth repetitive oscillation, derived from motion around a circle.

Triangle - as its name suggests, it is a triangular wave with equal rise and fall times.

Square - in theory this only has two levels, maximum positive and negative, with no transition in between.

Sawtooth - named after the item that it resembles.

White Noise – this is essentially a random waveform, and sounds like a de-tuned radio.

Pink Noise - a random waveform, but with energy decreasing by 3dB every octave, so the higher frequencies are quieter.

Brown Noise - much like Pink, but decreasing by 6dB every octave, sounding less harsh as a result of the lower high frequency content.

Music – note that the low-frequency fundamental tone (of a bass drum) has others superimposed on it.

There is an infinite number of waveforms that could be represented here, but the important thing to remember is that most do not just have a single frequency present, but have many at different frequencies and amplitudes, and that these elements vary with time. A process called Fourier Transformation allows analysis of any waveform into constituent sine waves, but involves very complex mathematics best completed by computers.

Harmonics

While we have seen two fundamental properties of audio signals (frequency and amplitude), there must be more to sound than this; it is possible for a Guitar, Piano and Voice all to play the same note, but each sounds different and can be recognised by the listener as such. One factor is that sounds change over time (see page 412), but another is the presence of harmonics. Harmonics are frequencies present in an audio signal which are higher than the fundamental (lowest) note, and which are a multiple of that fundamental. Many periodic (repeating) waveforms can be broken down into fundamental and harmonic sine waves, and analysis software can show the presence of such harmonics. Use of such analysis software is an important tool in the recording, mixing, programming and synthesizing spheres, and should be considered extremely important.

In the following diagrams we will see the frequency analysis window (using Voxengo SPAN, a free plug-in) - it is much like the frequency response diagrams we have seen above, but it will show the presence of any given frequencies.

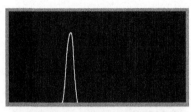

Sine Wave being played at A3 (220Hz). As can be seen from the analyser, there are no harmonics present, just the fundamental. This is why the sine wave sounds quite dull, but also pure - it consists of only one frequency.

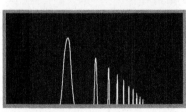

Triangle Wave. In addition to the fundamental there are a number of harmonics present, all quieter than the fundamental, and they get quieter as their frequency increases. This explains the sound of the triangle wave - it has a 'sharper' tone to it than the sine wave, but it is not harsh.

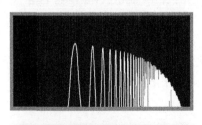

Sawtooth Wave. Note the harmonics - there are more of them, and their amplitude is greater than in the triangle wave. In addition to this, they are present to a higher frequency than we have seen before, giving the sawtooth its characteristic sharp sound.

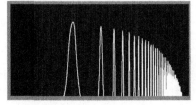

Square Wave. This has a different arrangement of harmonics; they are the odd harmonics, being 3x, 5x, 7x etc. the fundamental frequency, rather than 2x, 3x, 4x, 5x, 6x etc of the Sawtooth. This gives the square wave a more 'hollow' sound.

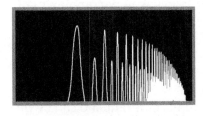

Here is a mixture of two waveforms. You may be able to recognise them from the two previous diagrams, as it is a mixture of Sawtooth and Square waves, with the sawtooth quieter than the square wave, hence its harmonics being lower in level.

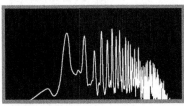
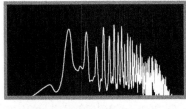

Piano. As we can see from this diagram, it has a much more complex set of harmonics, with their balances being more difficult to describe than the simpler waveforms we saw earlier. Note also the sub-harmonic at around 110Hz, which has a "thud" which is characteristic of the note being played by the hammer mechanism.

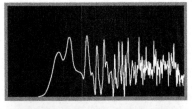

Guitar. Another set of different harmonics, and an extremely complex relationship with the amplitudes of them to the fundamental.

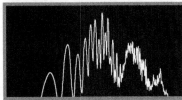

Voice. Finally, the same note being played on an "Aaah" vocal synth sound. Once more, there is another set of harmonics, with different relative volumes to the fundamental.

It should be noted that each of the 'complex' signals shown here will have different harmonics as time progresses; this is one of the features of physical instruments when they are played; while it may be possible to recreate the frequencies present during a snapshot, there are usually changes in harmonics which happen over time to give a sound its character, and programming such changes is a far more complex proposition.

Dynamic Changes

Another important element of an instrument's sound is how it changes in level over time. Some sounds, such as an electronic organ, may not change significantly over time, they will be either on or off. Others will alter as time passes.

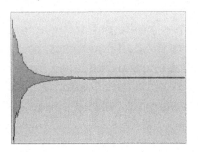

Here is a note (middle C, C3) played on a Piano. It starts out with a near-instant attack to become as loud as it will ever do, and then fades away into silence, despite the note being held down.

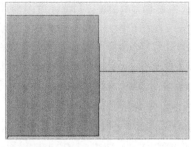

Here is the same note played on a synthesizer. It reaches maximum level straight away, and stays at that level until the key is released. This kind of dynamic behaviour over time is not usual for a 'real' instrument, but commonplace in electronic sounds that can sustain indefinitely.

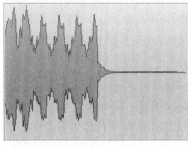

Here an organ is playing the sound, and while it can sustain the note indefinitely, it has a dynamic change over time - the volume alters in a cyclic manner

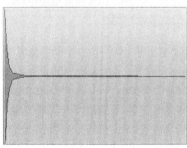

Here the note has been played on a Nylon-string guitar, and the result is similar to the piano, but it decays even more quickly than the piano sound did - only a couple of seconds after the note has been played the majority of its level is gone.

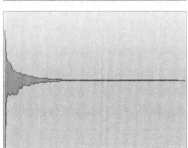

Once more, this time on an electric guitar. This note lasts longer than the nylon guitar sound above, but still decays quickly. This is a characteristic of many strung instruments where they are played by an initial impulse and no more energy is put into the string (plucked or hit, rather than being bowed).

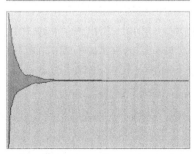

Finally, a bass guitar. While it once more features a similar dynamic change over time, note that there is a difference in the shape of the sound as it decays. It is quite similar to the piano that was in the first example, and here the balance of harmonics would be different to give an audible difference in tone.

Phase

Strictly speaking, phase is the time relationship between two cyclic signals. It is possible to have two waveforms at the same frequency that are not in time with each other, as seen next.

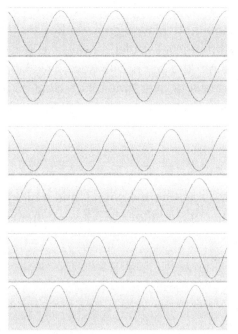

These signals are in phase. They are not only the same frequency and waveform, they also start at exactly the same time. When played back the result would be like the original signal, but with higher amplitude.

These signals are out of phase - the bottom waveform is completely out of phase (180 degrees as it is half way around the 360° cycle). If they were played back together they would cancel each other out completely.

These signals are also out of phase - the bottom waveform is around 45° out of phase with the top one. The sound will not be completely cancelled, but will sound different to the first example.

However, this term is often slightly misused; the term "phase" is often used to define the polarity of a signal - in the second example above are two waveforms which are of the same frequency and start at the same time, but one begins by going positive, the other by going negative. Many recording engineers would refer to these signals as being out-of-phase, which may be true for a simple repetitive waveform such as a sine wave seen in the example, but not for a complex one, as seen next.

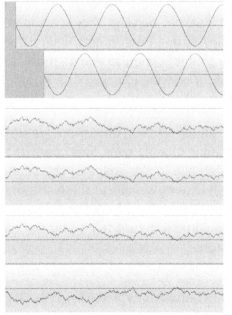

Here the top and bottom signals are the same, but the bottom one starts later, leading to total cancellation (180° out of phase). This can only happen with simple repetitive signals.

Here is a complex signal - it doesn't repeat, so there is no way that a time shift of the lower signal will allow for cancellation.

The only way to achieve complete cancellation is for the signal to be inverted. This can be done in Cubase by right-clicking the audio event in question and picking **Processes > Invert Phase** from the menu.

Whenever we have two microphones recording the same sound source, phasing will occur, and being aware of this and minimising it where possible is one of the most important tasks for an engineer to do; negative phasing (i.e. phasing which makes the sound worse) can completely ruin a recording. The examples shown here use a single frequency, but most sounds consist of many frequencies at once, and the effect will change with frequency, making it something which is extremely important to be aware of - an effect called Comb Filtering can often occur, where the time delay leads to some frequencies being boosted, others being cut, and which looks similar to a comb on a frequency response chart, with negative troughs as well as positive peaks.

As we will see later on, when recording a drum kit or indeed anything where more than one microphone is in use, phasing will happen (due to time delays as the signal passes through the air), and it is possible to make positive use of it (as seen with a mic technique such as MS on page 445), as well as take measures to minimise the problem (as when micing a drum kit on page 466).

Microphone Types

There are several different types of microphone which are in common use today, but the most common types are Dynamic and Condenser (there are also PZM and ribbon mics available which are less commonly used but still have their roles). As we will see, their way of converting vibrations into electricity is quite different, and as a result they have different characteristics.

Dynamic Microphones

Dynamic Microphones rely on the fact that moving a wire through a magnetic field produces a voltage which bears a direct relationship to the movement of the wire thorough that field. The voltage generated by one wire moving through a typical magnetic field is tiny, so the effect can be magnified by wrapping the wire in a coil which moves through the field all at once. This effect is harnessed in the dynamic microphone, which consists of a coil of wire which is attached to a diaphragm which is subject to the sound source – the diaphragm (and hence coil) moves in sympathy with the vibrations in the air, and this means that a voltage is generated that is proportional to that movement; in effect it produces a voltage representation of the vibration of the air. See the diagram below for more on this.

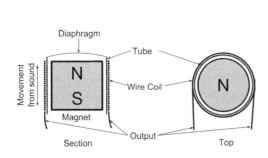

A schematic diagram of the dynamic mic – the wire coil is moved through the magnet's field by vibrations in the air, and this creates a voltage at the output.

A typical dynamic microphone looks like this, although some condenser mics can look similar.

However, like many things in the real world, this is not perfect. Firstly, the coil and diaphragm have mass, so a certain amount of energy is needed to make them move, and this means that the microphone is not as sensitive as it could be. In addition, this has the side-effect that higher frequencies aren't picked up as well as they may not have the energy to move the assembly; it's also possible that they are vibrating too fast for the diaphragm to move in sympathy.

There are upsides. Because of their simple construction, they are cheap, and extremely rugged. In addition, they produce an output which is sufficiently large to not need further amplification before reaching a mixer or recording device – the same cannot be said for the next type of microphone.

Condenser Microphones

A Condenser is an old-fashioned British term for an electronic component, the capacitor. In essence, the job of a capacitor is to store electrical energy, and in this case this is done using two conductive plates which have an air gap between them; electricity can be stored in non-conductive substances and air works perfectly well in this instance. But how does this help us record music? Well, there is a convenient by-product of this electricity being stored – the amount of capacitance changes depending on the distance between the two conductive plates. Now, if we make the conductive plates out of a very thin metal (or metal-covered plastic) then they will be flimsy enough to be moved by vibrations in the air, and that will mean we can measure this amount, and thereby generate a voltage which is a representation of the vibration of the plates, and therefore our original sound. The construction of a condenser microphone is shown below.

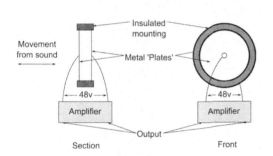

A condenser mic works by using an amplifier to increase the tiny voltage changes brought about by the movement of a capacitor's plate. Without this amplifier the output would be too small to use.

A typical condenser microphone, in its "shock mount", which provides isolation of the sensitive microphone from vibrations of the floor and mic stand.

Note that there is an amplifier included here. This is because the signal from the capsule is very, very small – far too small to be capable of passing down a microphone cable unaffected. So we have a very quiet amplifier inside the mic, which increases the level of the signal to that similar of the output of a dynamic mic. This amplifier needs to be powered – it can be powered either from an internal battery (on some microphone types, such as the AKG C1000), or from the mixer, via 'phantom power'. Phantom power places a DC supply of 48 Volts on the microphone connection, providing enough power to operate the amplifier and (if needed) polarise the plates on the capsule. However, it is important that the phantom power is not turned on until the microphone is connected – plugging it in after turning the power on can permanently polarise the capsule, and damage the microphone in the process. Also bear in mind that a 48v phantom power supply is a high enough voltage to give you an unpleasant tingling feeling or damage some devices if it is plugged into them incorrectly or via incorrectly-wired cables, so ensure that you are working safely when using it.

Ribbon Microphones

As the name suggests, the ribbon microphone uses a single element to pick up sound, and it resembles a ribbon, being a thin strip of metal, which is often corrugated (as seen in the diagram below). This metal strip is placed in a magnetic field, and can vibrate in sympathy with the sound source, and this vibration induces an electric current to flow through the ribbon. This is similar to a dynamic mic (and indeed a ribbon mic is a dynamic mic), but it only has one wire passing through the magnetic field rather than many hundreds, so the output is very low. This means that a ribbon microphone needs an amplifier, like a condenser mic. The physical construction of the ribbon mic means that it will be a figure-8 pattern (see below), and also means that they are generally very good at picking up high frequencies and low-level sounds, comparing well with condenser microphones. However, they are extremely fragile, although improvements in materials technology in recent years has led to them being re-introduced at affordable prices.

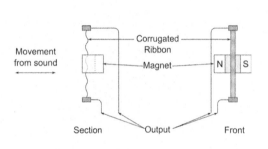

Here we see the ribbon, which vibrates in the magnetic field, producing an electrical output due to electromagnetic induction.

Many ribbon microphones are inspired by the first-generation of ribbon mics which were used by veterans such as Bing Crosby, in an attempt to re-create that sound.

Ribbon microphones are enjoying somewhat of a resurgence, being the current 'retro' item to have. Despite their fragility, they do have something to offer in terms of a unique blend of the characteristics of dynamic and condenser mics, although possibly not the ideal ones. However, they do offer a sound which is generally considered to be worth the downsides of their construction, and many of the 'classic' recordings (particularly of singers from the 1940s) were made using ribbon mics, and as a result they are being used in the quest to replicate the sound of this era.

Boundary Microphones

Boundary microphones (often called PZM, a trademark of Crown International) are an unusual device. They make use of the 'boundary effect' - because the microphone is at the boundary of a space (such as a wall), there are not the usual reflected sounds present (as the wall is the source of these reflections), thereby all the sounds picked up by the microphone capsule are picked up in-phase, providing there are no other nearby reflective surfaces. In addition, because the capsule is so close to the boundary (the metal plate, usually on a wall), there is not vibration but instead a change in pressure at this boundary. They generally use a small condenser element (often an electret one, which is a permanently-charged capacitor used in cheaper microphones), and look unlike most other microphones. They need to be placed on a flat, reflective surface for best results (1m x 1m or more), and produce remarkably good results given their cost and construction.

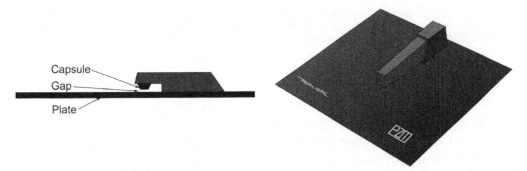

Here we see the layout of the main components of the boundary microphone. The placement of the capsule relative to the plate is the most critical part of the design.

The classic "Radio Shack PZM" microphone. Before the advent of cheap condenser mics, they were a mainstay of many home recording setups.

Boundary microphones have a hemispherical pickup pattern – they pick up well all around the capsule, but clearly cannot pickup sounds from behind the mounted surface (unless the mounting surface vibrates, as is often the case with a large window)

The Boundary microphone was a staple of the home studio scene (and indeed of many smaller professional studios) through the 80s and 90s, and only really fell from popularity as the production of Condenser microphones increased (particularly with Chinese manufacturing), meaning that they dropped in price to a level that most could afford. As a result the Boundary Mic (in particular the classic Radio Shack PZM model, which was ubiquitous beforehand) is now far more rarely seen, although its performance is usually far better than its rarity would suggest.

Summary of Microphone Characteristics

The pros and cons of each type of microphone are summarised in the following table – remember that this is a generalised table, and there can be some crossover in some areas between different specific mics of each type.

Dynamic	Condenser	Ribbon	PZM
Cheap	Expensive	Expensive	Cheap
Rugged, can withstand loud sounds	Fragile, and can be damaged by too loud a sound	Fragile, can be damaged by a loud sound	Reasonably rugged
Inefficient at low levels	Very sensitive, can pick up very quiet sounds	Very sensitive	Sensitive
Needs no power	Needs power	Needs no power	Needs power
Not good at high frequencies	Very good at high frequencies	Good at high frequencies	Good at high frequencies

In this table, it is important to remember that generalisations have been made, and specific devices may exceed or fall below any of the standards shown. It is also important to remember that microphone choice can come down to many factors – for instance Jay Kay of Jamiroquai is reputed to have recorded most of the vocals for his albums using a hand-held Shure dynamic microphone because he feels far more comfortable doing so, and yet the quality of these recordings is very high. Dismissing a microphone as incapable of capturing a specific performance without auditioning it can sometimes be an error – it is quite possible to achieve a good recording of an acoustic guitar with a dynamic microphone, and it is also possible to achieve a good recording of a bass guitar amplifier with a general-purpose condenser mic. Overall, though, the characteristics above should at least provide some idea as to the general performance and abilities of each type of microphone.

Polar Patterns

You will hopefully be aware that your perception of a sound changes dependent on where it is in relation to you – if the sound is behind, it's quieter, and also because of the immense power of your brain you're able to pinpoint the location of most sounds easily. Microphones aren't that advanced, but they can (and do) pick up sounds differently depending on where they are placed. Knowing the pickup patterns of microphones that you are using is important - not only so you can point them in the right direction towards the sound you are trying to record, and away from undesired ones, but also so you can make creative use of the effects that different polar patterns will give you.

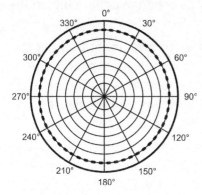

Omnidirectional - the name literally means in every direction. The polar pattern is illustrated to the left. This pattern means that the mic will pick up sounds equally in every direction – it makes no difference where the sound is. Such a pattern is very good for capturing the sound of a room or a performance which is happening all around. However, this can lead to an 'unfocused' sound as the sound of the room's reverberation, etc, is picked up greatly by this.

Cardioid This means 'heart shaped' – if you look at the diagram, it's like an upside-down heart. This shows a microphone which picks up from the front very well, less so at the sides, and which rejects sound that comes from the rear. Cardioid is probably the most commonly-used polar pattern, as it allows the microphone to focus on the intended sound source, without picking up too much of any other sounds (whether that be other instruments, the room, an audience or a foldback speaker on stage). All dynamic microphones are cardioid.

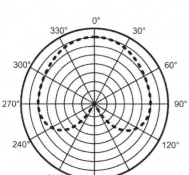

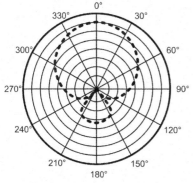

Hypercardioid This pattern is sometimes used as it is more directional that a Cardioid microphone - it rejects sound from the sides better, but at the expense of slightly increased sensitivity at the rear of the pattern.

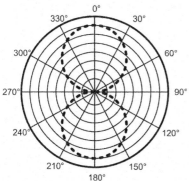

Figure 8 As the name suggests, this is like two small circles, one in front and one behind the microphone. This allows for rejection of sounds from the sides, and means that it's possible to isolate two performing sources easily while rejecting other sounds. It has some other interesting uses such as MS Micing.

While these patterns are idealized versions, it is important to remember that the actual patterns will look similar, and also that they can change depending on the frequency the mic is picking up.

With all these polar patterns, it's extremely important to remember that the patterns shown are 2-dimensional representations of a 3-dimensional phenomenon. The 'omni' pattern isn't a circle, it's a sphere, centred on the microphone itself. The cardioid pattern would look like an apple, upside-down, and the figure 8 one like a couple of balls, one in front and one behind the microphone.

The other thing that's important to remember and know is that some microphones are 'side-firing' and some are 'end-firing'. This means that the pattern can "come out" of either the end or the side of the mic. Dynamic mics tend to be end-firing, while most condenser mics are side-firing. If this is the case, the front of the mic is usually indicated by a marking on the case, the manufacturer's name or a differently coloured grille. We will see how to make use of polar patterns on page 471.

The Proximity Effect

The Proximity Effect is a property of directional microphones (typically cardioid mics) which leads to a boost of low frequencies when a sound source is close to the microphone. It can lead to a considerable boost in these frequencies (up to 16dB), and the exact effect will depend on the microphone in question. It is, however, something to be aware of and experiment with; many singers will make use of the effect when in the studio to create an 'intimate' sound by moving close to the microphone, but when it is used it needs to be done with care and consistency.

Connections

In an audio studio, there are a wide range of connectors used for a variety of different purposes. We will be making use of just a few of them, the majority of which are outlined below.

Name	Appearance	Description	Typical Uses
XLR		A robust, professional shielded connector which has male and female cable-mounted connectors allowing cables to be extended easily.	Microphone connections, balanced line signals.
¼" TRS Jack		A semi-professional connector which offers balanced capability, but difficult to extend and not physically as secure as an XLR TRS stands for Tip, Ring and Sleeve, the three connectors this jack provides.	Signals in patchbays, outputs and inputs of audio equipment including mixers.
¼" Jack		As above, but with only two connections – the Sleeve and Tip.	As above, but unbalanced signals only, often used for instruments.
Phono RCA Jack		A consumer-oriented connection, offering a cheap solution as a shielded connector.	Connecting CD players and other Audio/Visual equipment.
1/8" TRS Jack		Consumer-oriented, easily damaged and not reliable due to small contact area and flimsy construction.	Headphones on consumer items such as MiniDisc players, etc.
TOS Link		Optical connector which latches into matching receptacle.	S/PDIF and ADAT signals (carrying 2 and 8 channels respectively).
Bantam Jack		A smaller TRS-type jack connector, originally used for telephone connections.	Patchbay connections, allowing increased density.

Sometimes a microphone input on a mixer or amplifier will use a ¼" TRS input instead of an XLR and still offer sufficient gain for the low signal from a microphone, but in many cases jack inputs aren't the correct ones to use – whenever possible use an XLR to XLR lead and the correct input on the device you are plugging into and you should avoid problems.

TOSLink connectors are a digital-only connection, usually using a red light to transmit the signals at high speed. They offer the great advantage of providing complete electrical isolation, removing the possibility of any ground loops occurring. The optical fibre for the cables is fragile, though, and must be treated with care.

Bantam jacks are a smaller type of jack connector which were originally used in patchbays for telephone systems (such as when operators were employed to physically connect phone calls), are used in many pro studios for their patchbays due to their high reliability (as they were designed for this) and because they are smaller than a ¼" jack meaning more connections can be fitted in the same space.

Balanced Signal Transmission

Balanced audio signal transmission is far more resistant to interference from electrical and magnetic sources. This is because the signal is transmitted as two versions – one of them is the original, while the other is 'negative' – i.e. the waveform is upside-down, with a positive change in the original being represented as a negative change, etc, as seen below.

When the signals reach the device they are connected to, the inverse signal is inverted again, and then added to the original. This results in a signal which is twice the strength of the original, but that's not the reason for balanced signals being better.

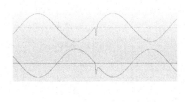

If interference has happened, it will be equal on both the original and negative versions of the signal, as seen to the left. The peak is a negative one on both channels. Once it reaches the connected piece of equipment, however, the bottom signal will be inverted, which means that the interference will then be inverted too, as seen in the next diagram down.

Once these two signals are then recombined in the device, the two interference signals should largely cancel each other out. It's not perfect, as it's rare that identical interference happens on both channels, but usually it is close enough to mostly cancel out their effect and gives a much higher resistance to interference than an unbalanced signal.

If you ever have the choice between using an unbalanced or a balanced output/ input, then the balanced one will usually be the one to use, particularly in an environment with lots of electrical noise.

Gain

The gain control is probably the most important control that you will set – an incorrect setting can totally wreck a recording, and the damage that is done is generally irreparable, and obvious even to the casual listener. We will now examine why this is the case, and how you can avoid these problems and get the best out of your equipment.

The gain control sets how much amplification is applied to the signal coming from the microphone – the original signal from the mic is at a very low level, and needs to be boosted for the circuitry in the mixer to work on it. Even if you have a digital mixer (where most of the processing is done digitally), you need to set the gain correctly so the converters are being used at their optimum. The gain control allows us to minimize the effects of one element which is present in all electronic devices - noise.

All electronic components produce noise when they are in use; some more than others, but the effect is cumulative. Despite the efforts of design engineers and improvements in components, all equipment produces noise, and we need to minimise the effects of this on our recordings. To do this we need to increase the gain of the amplifier to ensure that the signal is as loud as is possible in comparison with the noise, while ensuring it doesn't become too loud and get distorted.

Let's examine what happens as the gain control is altered. We will assume that the input signal is unchanging throughout these three examples. The bar in the middle of each diagram represents the noise level in the circuit – it has been hugely exaggerated for the purposes of illustration, but the principle stands.

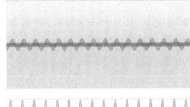

Here the gain is too low – the desired signal level is little greater than the noise level, so if it is amplified after this then the noise will also be amplified, leading to a large amount of hiss.

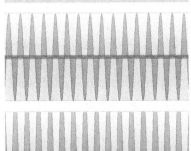

Here the signal level is good – it is high in comparison to the noise level, giving a good signal-to-noise ratio, and minimizing any issues there may be with noise.

Here the gain is too high, and the originally sine-wave input signal is now flattened off at the peaks as the circuit cannot handle the desired levels, leading to undesirable distortion.

Setting Gain

Once you have placed your microphones (something we will look at later on), make sure you are viewing the actual signal level the microphone preamp is seeing – this will vary depending on the equipment you are using, but is often performed by using the "pre-fade listen" (PFL) control for a channel, or by setting the channel's fader to 0dB (remember that 0dB doesn't mean off, it means the control is having no effect, so in this case the fader is letting you see the level the mic preamp is seeing). You will need to see this signal level on a meter (this may be per channel, or many PFL controls convert the master output meter into a meter for the PFL'd channel). Once you can see this signal, get your performer to perform at the loudest level they will do during the piece you are recording – this is extremely important as their overall volume level may be different from any other piece they play. Now alter the gain control until their peak level reaches around -3dB, possibly lower (down to around -6dB). This gives the recording system some 'headroom' so if they are louder there will not be distortion immediately. Many performers get louder when they play 'for real', so bear this in mind when you record – some get a lot louder, and you may need to account for this. As you get to know your performers better you will have more of an idea in advance of what they will do – some get dramatically louder when performing for real, whereas others provide a good level while practicing.

When you start to make a first recording, if the signal level is too high, reduce the gain to the correct level while the player is still performing, and once you are confident this is correct, stop the recording and re-start from the beginning. Any recording that has the gain altered during it cannot be used (particularly as the reason for turning gain down is distortion), but often it will provide good practice for the performer.

If you follow this simple procedure, you will not have a problem with distortion or noise – the signals that you pass into your mixer (and therefore your recording system) will be at (or very near) the optimum, meaning that noise levels will be low, and that also you will have optimised the sampling process if you are using digital equipment.

The Mixer

Audio mixers come in a wide range of shapes and sizes, from small mixers (such as a Spirit Notepad) to large, fully-automated mixing desks (such as those by Neve and SSL), and everything in between. However, they all do similar tasks, and share a number of basic controls – and because of this paradigm, many software-based "mixer channels" such as those in sequencing packages and hard disc recorders follow a similar layout. We'll look at a simple generic mixer channel, and the controls that it features.

Firstly there is the input; this can either be on a three-pin 'XLR' connection (as normally used by microphones), which provides a balanced connection, allowing the elimination of interference, or via a ¼" Jack plug, which can be balanced or unbalanced. Normally inserting a Jack disables the XLR input.

Phantom Power Sometimes this is switched per channel, sometimes per group of channels, and sometimes for every input. Usually it is a push or slide switch, either marked as "Phantom" or "48v"

Gain This is the first stage that the signal entering the mixer reaches. It is an amplifier circuit, whose purpose is to change the incoming signal to the optimum level for the rest of the mixer's circuitry. This is done to minimise noise within the mixer, as each stage adds a fixed (small) amount of noise, so by increasing the level of the desired signal the effects of this noise are minimised.

Equalisation (EQ) The EQ facilities that are provided on mixing desks vary widely; some provide just simple low and high frequency level controls, while others offer four (or more) bands of fully-controllable EQ circuits, and many stages in-between. There are three main controls to an EQ circuit, the latter two may be omitted depending on the mixer:

a) **Level** This control allows the addition or subtraction of the frequencies controlled by the EQ circuit; normally it is graded in decibels (dB), and often offers a wide range of alteration (typically ± 12dB), with 0dB (no change) in the centre of the range, typically at the 12-o'clock position.

b) **Frequency** In the simplest mixers there is no frequency control, and the EQs will work at fixed frequencies. However, for more control some provide the facility to alter the frequency that an EQ circuit will operate on. The range of this frequency will normally be tailored to the specific band in question, allowing each to be set to the desired value. Normally these controls are marked in Hz and kHz.

c) **Q** This is the most advanced control for an EQ, and it controls the 'quality factor' of the EQ circuit; in essence this sets the width of frequencies that the EQ circuit will work on; at low Q values the circuit is not 'picky', and works on a wide range of frequencies centred on the desired value. Setting to a high Q will mean that the EQ will work on only a narrow band of frequencies, leading to a more intense and focused sound.

Auxiliary Sends These controls allow the signal from each channel to be sent to a different destination; this is normally a physical output on the mixer which can be connected to an effects unit or monitoring system. By having a separate control for each channel it is possible to choose which signals and how much of them get sent to the output. These sends take two forms – Pre- and post-fader. In a Pre-fader send, the level sent does not alter when the

volume fader (see later) has its level altered. A post-fader send's level is dependant on the volume fader level – when the fader gets turned down then the signal is no longer sent from the auxiliary output. Generally Pre-fader sends are used to set up monitoring and similar applications (which need to be independent of the final mix), while post-fader sends are used for effects (so they get turned off when the faders are turned down).

Pan   Most mixers are stereo, providing two outputs – left and right – which is the way that most audio systems work; surround sound (which typically uses 6 channels) needs a more complex arrangement that we won't cover here. The Pan (Panorama) control allows the positioning of each channel's signal in this stereo field, from far left through centre to far right.

Volume Fader   This is the final control in the channel; it controls the output level of the channel, and can reduce the output level to its minimum (-∞) through no change (0 dB) and normally giving some additional boost too (often 6 dB)

A basic mixer will now just pass the signal to its master section, which is usually a stereo volume control sometimes with extra features. A more advanced mixer will have alternate destinations to send the audio to (called busses), and these are normally selected using switches, allowing the signals to be routed to whatever equipment is connected to these outputs, in addition to (or instead of) the main stereo outputs.

We have looked at the features of a typical analogue mixer, but most digital mixers feature similar controls; some do this with physical controls that mimic those shown above; others do so by having one set of controls that can be used for whichever channel you decide. Some have most of their controls on-screen, with just a few 'soft' controls to alter them.

This shows how a typical physical mixer channel looks, but often you will be doing your mixing using a channel which exists only in software, where you move on-screen controls to make the same changes. Most audio sequencing software (such as Logic, Cubase, Sonar and ProTools) duplicates the layout above faithfully with the exception of the gain control (as the signal is already digital). With software it's sometimes possible to alter the structure of the channel, and also automate any controls that are present.

Cubase 13 Mixer Channel

Displays the most important settings on the track, with Inserts on the left, Sends on the right, and a large EQ area. Each of these areas can show alternate information, as the channel is packed with features.

Cubase 6 Mixer Channel

This has the channel fader on the right, with the routing section above it. There are eight insert effect slots, followed by the EQ section (with graph above and controls below), and finally the 8 assignable send controls.

Cubase SX 3 Mixer Channel

The same information is present (Inserts, EQ, Sends, fader), but with a different appearance and layout. Note the much smaller area for visualising the EQ curve.

Pro Tools Channel

Here is a channel in another piece of music production software, Pro Tools. The channel on the left is a bare channel, with no effects or EQ present. The one on the right has had these added, and has facilities similar to Cubase.

Logic Channel

Apple's Logic follows the same rationale as Pro Tools, starting with a bare channel, allowing complete configuration. While this offers the ultimate in choice, it can mean more work in initial setup.

These channels come with nothing inserted in them – if you want an EQ, you need to add one manually. While this may seem like a lot of work, it means you can tailor your needs for each channel, using only the processing power you need for each one, and also can use high-quality EQ on each channel if you have one.

Using frequency diagrams, we can see more clearly the way EQ controls (particularly Q) work:

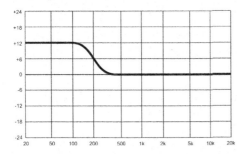

This first plot shows the effects of turning a typical "bass" control up – all frequencies below it are boosted from the original "flat" response – here the control is set to "+12 dB". Such an EQ is referred to as a "shelf" EQ, because of the flat shelf seen to the left of the diagram.

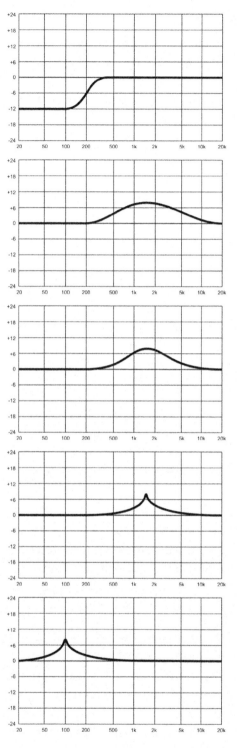

This is the same control turned down to "-12dB" – the shape of the curve is the same, but cutting instead of boosting at these frequencies. While this is a "low shelf" EQ, it is possible to have high shelf EQs as well, which work on all frequencies above their set point.

Here is a mid-boost control (centred around 1500Hz) where the Q is low – it is boosting a wide range of frequencies either side of the set value, and has an unfocused sound.

The Q has been increased to make the filter more selective, and you can see the results here – the peak value is unchanged, but a narrower range of frequencies is being altered.

The Q has now been increased further to make a pronounced peak, and as a result of this the centre frequency can be heard more clearly. This will usually give quite an artificial sound to the EQ, but is very useful for pinpointing frequencies and specific effects.

Here the frequency has been changed to centre on 100Hz.

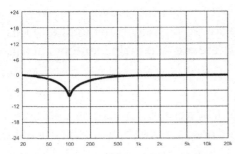

And here the gain control has been altered to cut 10dB rather than boost as in the above diagrams.

The important thing to do with all these settings is to hear their effect as they work on music, not simply alter the controls to see the effect on the graph on screen. Getting a feel for what frequencies each instrument or sound occupies will take some time, but it will be hugely beneficial to your recording and mixing skills once you get it. Spend time experimenting with tracks you have recorded of different sounds, using EQ to cut and boost different frequencies and hearing the effect that this has. Remember that EQ is never a substitute for good recording practice, but it can allow more creative alteration of a recorded sound and to accentuate the character of a track.

Analogue and Digital

Typically the signal in an analogue system is a voltage which represents the sound being listened to at any one time; at some point the signal gets turned into the physical movement of air (such as by headphones or speakers), which our ears then pick up and convert to a signal which our brains interpret as sound. A basic signal path can look like this:

Signal	Microphone	Mixer	Headphones	Ear	Brain
Air Pressure	Electrical signal (tiny)	Electrical signal (larger)	Electrical signal (larger)	Vibrations	Nerve signals

In this example at all points the signal is a representation of the original sound, whether it's as air pressure or an electrical signal. This is how analogue systems all work, with voltages representing signals. Even when recording onto a storage medium (cassette, vinyl, etc) the sound is still represented as a signal whose level is proportional to the original vibration, meaning that storage equipment is simple, and meaning the stored information can be easily deciphered.

However, computers are digital for the most part. This creates advantages and disadvantages; a couple of the advantages are that being digital makes the circuits simple (read cheap) to produce, and that they can work at extremely high speeds (because they only have two states, on and off). The disadvantage is that

431

the computer cannot just take in a voltage like the example above; some way of converting the signal into a form that can be stored digitally is needed, and this is where things get a bit more complicated. There are two main elements of this that we need to examine.

Bit Depth

Firstly, storing a number: When using a digital system, it can clearly only store two numbers, 0 and 1. To store larger numbers needs more than one binary digit (bit for short). Using two bits means we can store four states (00, 01, 10, 11), and so on. Each bit that we add doubles the number of values that can be stored, and as the table shows it's not long before we can store very large numbers indeed.

Bits used	Values available
1	2
2	4
3	8
4	16
5	32
8	256
16	65,536
24	16,777,216

But why do we need to know this? Once we have the ability to store large numbers in the memory of a computer, it's a simple task to design a circuit that looks at a voltage (which can be a representation of an audio signal) that outputs a digital code – this is called an Analogue to Digital Converter (ADC for short). This means we can now represent (and store) the voltage value of an audio signal inside a computer. This process is called sampling. One variable for this process is the "bit depth", the number of bits that are used for this conversion, and the more bits used, the finer 'steps' into which the signal can be sampled. At 8 bits there are only 256 steps available, but at 16 bits there are 65,536, and that leads to a reasonably faithful representation of the signal. At 24 bits the representation is extremely good indeed. CD audio is recorded at 16 bits, while DVD-Audio is recorded at 24 bits. The process of playing back the stored signal is the reverse, and involves a Digital to Analogue converter (DAC). The diagrams on the next page illustrate what happens when a signal is sampled with different bit depths.

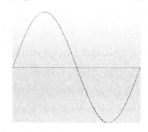

16 bits. This is CD-quality audio, and gives enough levels to represent most signals faithfully. The sine wave input is clearly smooth.

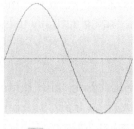

8 bits. Halving the number of bits reduces the number of levels by a factor of 256 – although the waveform is still reasonably smooth, there are some areas of error, and this will translate to a slightly different sound - more noticeable on some material than others.

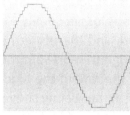

6 bits. There is now some clear "stepping" of the signal, and when re-played it will sound far more harsh than the original, smooth sine wave.

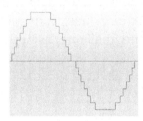

4 bits. This only has 16 possible levels, and as a result the once-smooth sine wave has become more like a stairway. It will sound harsh and somewhat distorted as a result of this.

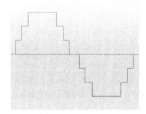

3 bits. Now there are only 8 possible levels, compared with over 65,000 in the 16 bit example. The waveform is drastically altered from the original, and this leads to many unpleasant side effects.

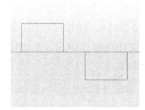

2 bits. The original smooth sine wave is now reduced to something much more like a square wave, and while the frequency may be the same as the original, there is little else that is.

These examples show how different bit depths can alter the sampled sound (and therefore the sound that is played back). The first generation of samplers (and PC soundcards) were 8 bit, but the rise of CD audio meant that 16 bits became the de facto standard for digital audio – after all, most recordings will end up using this format, so it seems to make sense to use it, particularly as it was chosen after a considerable amount of testing.

However, there are a number of recordists who prefer to use 24-bit recording, particularly for music which has a wide dynamic range (such as classical music) as such a system is more capable of handling these differences between the quietest and loudest sounds. While these recordings may still end up on CD, it is possible that they will be re-mixed onto higher-resolution formats in the future (such as

DVD-Audio or SACD), and it is also possible using dither (which involves some clever mathematics) to maximise the number of bits your recording actually uses if you record in 24 bits and then master down to 16 bits.

Sample Rate

There is another element to an audio signal; it changes with time, and quite rapidly at that. The range of human hearing (when we're born at least) is from around 35 vibrations per second (Hertz, or Hz for short), to 20,000Hz (20kHz). This means that if we want to record sounds without an obvious loss in quality we need to be able to record signals up to that upper threshold, and therefore the signal that we wish to record needs to be sampled often enough to represent the audio. Initially common sense would think that sampling at the rate of the highest frequency we want to record would be enough, but the diagram below shows that's not quite the case. You can see that at the four sampling points (shown with the dotted arrows) the two sine wave signals have the same values; from this data alone it wouldn't be possible to tell which signal was the 'real' one, as both would give the same values at these points.

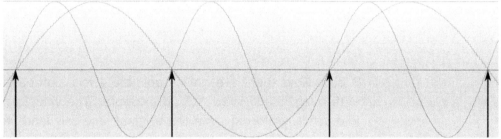

In fact it turns out that the sampling rate needs to be just over twice the frequency of the highest sound that we want to capture; this means that the frequency needed to capture audio for human-range hearing is 44100Hz, which is (not by coincidence) the speed at which CDs are sampled and played back. DVD-Audio is at 192kHz, which means that it can capture far higher frequencies, which some believe have a non-audible but perceived effect on the listener.

The effect of sample rate can be shown with the two diagrams below. Both use a 16-bit ADC, but the first is operating at half the speed of the next and the frequency is then halved again in the last one, and it's clear to see that the lower-rate sample provides a less accurate representation of the original signal, despite both operating at the same bit depth.

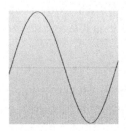

Here is the original signal, sampled at 44.1kHz. The waveform is smooth, and a good representation of the original analogue waveform. Remember that for all of these examples, there is 16 bits of resolution; only the sampling rate (on the horizontal axis) changes.

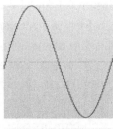

Here is the same signal sampled at 22.05kHz - half the speed above. The waveform is still a fair representation of the original, although it is showing some changes from the decrease in sample rate. Bear in mind that a more complex signal could be affected more as it could contain higher harmonics which would not be sampled at all.

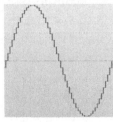

The sampling frequency has once more been halved, and the waveform is now clearly stepped, with audible distortion present in many cases. If a complex sound was sampled like this, it would be noticeably different from the original signal.

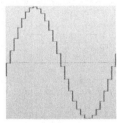

Finally, the speed is halved again - this is now only an eighth of the original frequency, and the steps are marked. Any complex audio sampled at this frequency would be severely altered by this sampling, and many high frequency harmonics would disappear completely.

Taking these two concepts together allows us to record audio and store it inside a PC or Mac; this is what happens whenever a recording is made by a computer, and the reverse process happens when playing back any digital audio, either from a PC/Mac or a DAT player, CD player or any similar device. However, making these recordings generates a large amount of data; at CD speeds each second generates 44,100 16-bit numbers; indeed a minute of stereo audio at CD speed takes up 10 Megabytes of space.

Storing audio in less space

The next area to look at is how to reduce the amount of space that recorded audio takes up; as we just saw a minute of CD-quality (16bit, 44.1kHz) audio takes up 10MB; a minute of DVD-A quality audio (24 bit, 192kHz) takes up 60MB. Clearly this makes storage space an issue, and particularly when wanting to transfer audio over bandwidth-limited links such as the Internet. While the speed of Internet access is constantly increasing, it is still desirable to store audio in less space, making any transfers quicker, and reducing their cost and improving availability.

There are several ways to approach this problem; the first is to use settings when recording the audio to use fewer bits or a lower sample rate. However, this leads to a reduction in quality of the audio which is normally unacceptable - the examples above with low sample rates and bit depths show this clearly.

A second method is to use compression technology to make the data smaller without losing any information; this is commonly seen on Windows and macOS typically as "zip" and "rar" files. These systems all work in similar ways, looking for patterns in the data to reduce their size. However, audio data is often semi-random and unpredictable (depending on its contents), and therefore there may only be a small reduction in the size of the file. The following table shows the differences in results when compressing different audio files, all of which were 5 seconds long, mono 16-bit 44.1kHz WAV files, meaning they were originally 435kB.

As can be seen from the table on the next page, the results of such compression varies greatly on the data contained within, but it's certainly safe to say that the complexity of most musical recordings will mean that the space saved will not be that great – around 5-10% for the examples of full music tracks that were tested.

File type	Description	Size	% of original
Pulse	A square wave at 220Hz	3kB	0.69
Sine Wave	A 5kHz sine wave	4kB	0.91
Sine Wave	A 220Hz sine wave	8kB	1.83
Kick Drum	A kick drum recording (sparse)	183kB	42.1
Kick Drum	A kick drum recording (busy)	215kB	49.4
Bass Guitar	A bass guitar recording	333kB	76.6
Guitar	An electric guitar recording	376kB	86.4
Music	A section of a song (rock)	400kB	91.9
Music	A section of a song (classical)	410kB	94.3
Music	A section of a song (dance)	417kB	95.8
Noise	White (random) noise	431kB	99.0

The third way is more involved (in terms of technology) and takes advantage of the deficiencies in human hearing. Extensive research has shown that human hearing has a wide range of characteristics that are far from a theoretical 'perfect' ear. Amongst other things, the presence of some frequencies masks others, and also louder sounds mean that quieter sounds cannot be heard, even if they are still present – for instance the 'whine' of a computer hard drive can't be heard when someone is singing (loudly) in a room, but as soon as they have stopped it will be heard again, as well as more subtle occurrences of this phenomenon. In addition, the frequency response of our ears is not flat – we are more sensitive to some frequencies (those that human speech is made up of) than others.

All this research was put together to come up with algorithms that could take an audio file and remove the components that couldn't be heard by the human ear. It took years and much testing, but finally this led to pieces of software that can encode audio by compressing it in this manner. There is now a proliferation of compressed audio formats – MP3, Ogg Vorbis, ATRAC (which MiniDiscs use), Real Audio, Windows Media Audio (WMA), Dolby Digital and DTS amongst others - and in general these are referred to as "lossy" compression as data is lost during this process (even if we can't perceive it).

With many of these systems, the degree of reduction can be decided by the user when encoding the file - from very little (which is somewhat pointless) through a large reduction of file size with little change in audio quality perceptible to extreme (where there is a discernible loss of quality, but with greatly reduced file sizes). ATRAC (the Sony format) works on a fixed reduction of 5:1, as it's controlled by hardware (inside the MiniDisc recorder). The measure of the reduction is commonly referred to as the "bit rate" of the audio, which describes how much information is used to describe each second of the music.

Most audio that is downloaded from the Internet (both legally and not) is in a compressed format, and normally at a bit rate which means that most listeners cannot hear a difference between the original audio and the compressed version – 128kbps is commonly used, both for MP3 and WMA formats. Real audio typically works at a lower bit rate as it is generally designed to be 'streamed' – downloaded in a real-time format so that it can be listened to without downloading the full file. Dolby Digital works on a bit rate of 384kbps, but that is used to encode six channels (5 full-range and one subwoofer channel). Ogg Vorbis is similar to all these others (offering better quality than MP3), but with one (important) difference; it is 'open source' and therefore free to use; encoders for all other formats need to pay licence fees to the developers.

The table below shows typical values for stereo audio encoded in different ways

File Type	Extension	Format	Bitrate	Size/min	Quality
Wave	.wav	Uncompressed	1280kbps	10MB	Perfect
Zipped Wave	.zip	Compressed (no loss)	1280kbps	9.5MB	Perfect
MP3	.mp3	Compressed (lossy)	128kpbs	1MB	OK
MP3	.mp3	Compressed (lossy)	64kpbs	0.5MB	Poor
WMA	.wma	Compressed (lossy)	128kbps	1MB	OK
Ogg Vorbis	.ogg	Compressed (lossy)	128kbps	1MB	Good

For the most part when working with Sequencing and recording, uncompressed files will be used, whether Wave (.wav) on PC, or Audio Interchange File Format (.AIFF) on the Mac, but it's important to know how the compressed formats work, as often you will be working with basic tracks in this format (when working with track downloaded from the Internet, for example), or making a final mix which will be posted on a website. Compressed formats are becoming more and more popular, particularly as they offer the ability to add digital rights management (DRM) protection; this is the music industry's attempt to stop illegal downloads and police the use of digital media, a technology which is being integrated into new computer operating systems.

With experimentation, you will find that certain sounds are addressed by the lossy compression codecs more effectively than others. For instance, often sounds which are high in frequency and last for some time (such as cymbals) can be easy to hear processing artefacts in, and reverse cymbals even more so.

Spend some time making mixdowns which use different bit rates and listening to the difference between them to hear what happens as you reduce the amount of information the file can convey, and the quality as a result of this change. If you are making a mixdown to be distributed, it is important that you strike the right balance between quality and size – many artists feel that the 'standard' 128kbps MP3 file is not of a high enough quality to hear the end result of their works, and some will prefer much higher bit rates to achieve better sound quality while still achieving a reasonable degree of compression.

Summary

The basics of audio recording hardware have been outlined here – the most important things to remember are the different microphone types and their characteristics as this will often help you make decisions when doing a recording. In addition, awareness of polar patterns will help you understand where to place the microphones for the best results, and allow you to make the most of a physically compromised recording situation. Knowing what connects to what and with which kind of connector is also valuable as you will know how to interface different pieces of equipment and understand why something may not be working as you expected.

In addition to this, taking care to select the appropriate sample rate and bit depth will mean you can be sure that what you are recording will sound as you intended. You will also understand the reasons that sample rate and bit depth can alter the sound of your recordings. In today's society being able to reduce the size of audio while preserving quality is important as online distribution becomes evermore pervasive. Understanding what you are actually doing to a piece of music when you use an encoder such as MP3 is important if you are to ensure that all your hard work in recording and producing your music is not lost before the listener gets to appreciate it.

First Recordings

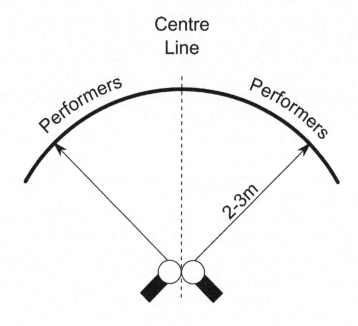

When starting out in recording, it can seem quite daunting to begin with, as there are many things to take into account – the equipment can be unfamiliar, and there are quite a few things to get right before a recording can be made. With that in mind, it is probably best to put some time aside for yourself to become more familiar with all the equipment, and to just make some trial recordings where the act of recording is the important element, not what you are recording.

With that in mind, you will need to set up your recording equipment. This setup will vary depending on the equipment you are using, but typically it will consist of similar elements, and there are some parts which will be common to all recording setups.

Firstly, you will need a sound source to record. This could be yourself (whether talking, singing or playing a musical instrument), or some other source of sound, be it a person or a device. At first, it really doesn't matter other than it makes a sound that you can record – you can become more selective as you get better at recording.

Secondly, you will need a microphone and connecting lead. The microphone type isn't that important at first, and it may well be best to start out using a dynamic mic as you will not have to worry about phantom power, or damage to the microphone.

Thirdly, you will need your recording hardware. While this may be a variety of setups in a more general sense, we will be concentrating on recordings made using Cubase, with an external soundcard to allow high-quality audio into and out of the computer. There are many different options that will fulfil these criteria, so you will need to fine-tune the instructions given here to suit your exact setup.

Fourth, you will need some way of monitoring the recording. This can be headphones, but it is often better to use speakers providing they are of good quality. Once set up, your recording system will look something like one of the diagrams below.

Recording using a Computer

Recording using a computer can vary considerably – it can be very simple (just the computer), or more complex, with a multiple input/output soundcard and mixer. We will look at both examples. Firstly the most simple setup possible (which is attainable with just about any computer), with one or two microphones connected, and a pair of active speakers connected to its output.

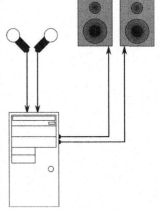

This simple setup is as basic as is possible with a PC – the microphones plug into the PC, as do the speakers. All control of the recording process is done on the PC, and the quality of the recording is largely dependent on the quality of the computer's soundcard. While they have improved greatly in recent years, they are far from professional in terms of quality, but can be a good starting point (and often better than many cassette multi-trackers from years gone by).

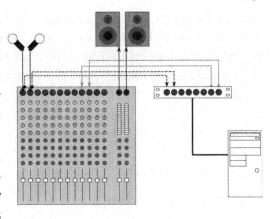

To the right is a complex setup with a mixer and a soundcard with more inputs and outputs. This setup is very similar to the first one - the PC handles all the audio recording - but uses the mixing desk to amplify the signals and send them to the PC, and also to monitor the signals coming back from the PC.

It is not uncommon to have a hybrid of these two setups, often where the computer outputs directly to the monitor speakers while having the inputs via a mixing desk, but sometimes the other way round – there are a near infinite number of possibilities.

Whenever you start working with a new setup, it's important to establish the signal flow in the studio – without knowing what goes where, it can become confusing and difficult to work out why things aren't working properly (or how to fix them if they're not). Never be afraid to ask questions about connections, and if you need to make a diagram to show what goes where, then do so!

Preparation for the recording

You should have the microphone connected to one of the inputs (usually input 1), and the monitoring setup connected to the output of the recorder/PC.

Once you have done this, it is time to set the levels. As mentioned in the First Recordings chapter (on page 439), setting the gain is the single most important setting you will make on a recording as getting it wrong will leave you with either a noisy signal or a distorted one.

Many computer soundcards or converter boxes do not have any meaningful level metering, so the only way to set the gain is to use the input mixer on the software you are using as a meter. In the case of Cubase, it is possible to view each input channel in the mixer and use this as a meter for the level as you adjust the gain. In Cubase Artist and Elements, you will need to open the channel mixer (**F3**), set the fader to 0dB and monitor the signal from there.

Once this appropriate steps have been taken, you can use this meter to set the gain to give a level of around -3dB when the performer is at their loudest in this performance. Leaving 3dB is usually enough for most performers, but some do get louder when performing 'for real', and it is not unusual to have to give some more headroom. For the this first recording, this should be enough, however.

The next step is to Record-enable the track you are going to record on. Once you have created a track (**Project > Add Track > Audio** and select **Mono** from the new window that appears), you will need to make sure that the new track will record from the input you have chosen – in Cubase

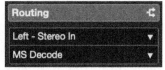

this is done in the inspector, as shown to the right. If you have a multi-channel soundcard, then you may need to use the VST Connections window to route the soundcard's input to the appropriate Cubase input – see the Audio Setup chapter (page 654) for this. You will then need to record-enable the track in Cubase, and you are ready to record.

Making the recording

When making your first recording, it is usually best to just hit record and then make some sound, just to ensure that the setup is working. If it isn't, then you will need to be methodical to find out what isn't working – it could be any element of the signal chain, from the microphone right through to the speakers/ headphones. Some logical deduction should see the problem found quickly, and is part and parcel of recording, especially when you are using a new or unfamiliar setup. Remember that when your are trying to find a fault, never assume that anything is working - you need to prove each component works before you can eliminate it.

Once you have made the sound you want to record, hit **STOP** and go back to the beginning of the recording. Before doing anything else, ensure you put the track back to **PLAY** – many recordings have been ruined by leaving a track in 'record' and then accidentally recording over it! (Remember, Undo - **CTRL-Z**) Once you have done this, play and listen to what you have recorded. While it should be an accurate recording of what was performed, you may well find it sounds different, especially if it is your own voice and the first time you have recorded it.

At this point, it is a good idea to spend some time experimenting with recording a variety of instruments or sounds, and also using the different microphones that you have – the more that you do of this, the better. You will learn far more by experimentation and analysis of what you have done than by any other means – experience really does count when recording.

Once you are happy with operating the recorder, the next thing to try is to record with two microphones at the same time. While the setup will be similar, you will have to record on both tracks at the same time, ensuring that you record-enable both tracks. You can either record the same sound/instrument using two microphones placed differently, or record different instruments at the same time. Whichever you do, make sure that the gain control for each channel is set appropriately.

Once you have done this, you can try the next stage, which is recording tracks at different times – this is how the Multitrack recording you will do later on will be completed (see page 455). To do this, make a recording on the first track, and then turn off monitoring so you can hear the recording. You will need some way of monitoring what is already recorded (often using headphones fed from the mixer/recorder, sometimes using a headphone amplifier too). Next, record something different on the second track – don't worry if it doesn't 'fit' with what you've recorded on the first one, the concept of recording things at different times is what's important. To make a recording on a second track, you usually have two options – you can either use a microphone plugged into the second channel of the desk/recorder/soundcard, or in many cases you can pick a different input – on most multitrack recorders it is possible to select a different input for any track, and in Cubase it is possible to select a different input from the Inspector (see the "Routing Audio in Cubase" section in the Audio Setup chapter on page 654).

Once you have made the recording of the second track, play them both back, and you should be able to control the levels of the tracks independently. Once you are comfortable with this, you can build up a track which works musically, and which each element has been recorded separately. The possibilities for this are nearly endless; a solo performer can play all the instruments of a band (this is how Lenny Kravitz, amongst others, plays everything on his own recordings), or can provide their own harmony vocals, or create rhythmically impossible parts.

At first, the novelty of being able to record at all is probably enough to keep you occupied for some time. But after a while (as with all things) you will be able to discern differences and become more picky about the way you record.

To this end, see if you can answer the following statements - do this by recording the same performance a number of times on different tracks – this will allow a direct comparison between them.

- What difference does moving the microphone nearer to and further away from the sound source make?

- Does the microphone pick sound up in the same way from all directions?

- Does moving the microphone from one side to the centre and then the other side of the instrument or speaker make any difference?

You should find that moving the microphone further away from the sound source will make it quieter (which is fairly obvious), but also that the character of the sound will change with distance, and the sound of the room itself will become more of a factor.

Many microphones are directional, as discussed in the Audio chapter on page 420. You should be able to work out what polar pattern of microphone you have (if you don't already know) by listening to the different ways it picks up sound from different directions.

You should also hear a difference when moving the microphone to different positions on the instrument or speaker. With speakers, the sound is generally thinner and harsher when in the centre, warmer at the outside, while instruments vary greatly depending on their construction.

Ambient Recording

While many recordings which are made today make use of multi-tracking and close-mic techniques (as we will see later on), being able to make a technically simple recording using a pair of microphones to record and entire ensemble is a useful technique to learn, so we will now look at how this is done.

Firstly, the ambient recording, as the name suggests, makes use of microphones which capture the ambient sound in the room in which the performance is happening. The easiest way to think of this is to think of the microphones as the ears of a listener. By choosing the appropriate microphones and placing them in the right location, we will capture the sound of the performance as a listener would hear it. To do this, we need to select a microphone type which will pick up very low levels of sound, much like our ears are capable of doing. This means that generally a dynamic microphone isn't the right choice, and a condenser mic is; although it is possible to make a recording using a good dynamic, generally a condenser will perform better.

Most recordings made these days are in stereo. This means that there are (at least) two different microphones used each of which captures what is happening to one side or the other of a 'listener's' position. We will be doing this for this recording, and to that end it's important to choose a microphone of which you have access to a pair that are the same make and model; otherwise the recording could sound off-balance and quite odd.

Microphone placement

There are a number of different ways of placing two microphones to create an ambient stereo recording. We will look at three of them. Each has its strengths and weaknesses, and its own followers. No method of recording is perfect, and as a result often a combination of these techniques is used, but for the sake of simplicity it is best to pick one of the three.

Spaced or "AB" Pair

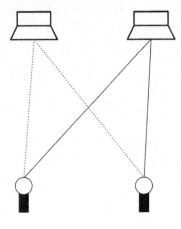

This method uses two microphones which are placed some distance (typically more than 30cm) apart, facing the direction of the performance. This is the most basic method of making a stereo recording, but can suffer from problems relating to the distance between the microphones (especially when listening on headphones), and is also often used near a rear wall of a venue which creates issues with reflections. This creates a feeling of width because the distance between the mics means there is a delay in signals from off-centre sound source reaching the far mic.

Coincident or "XY" pair

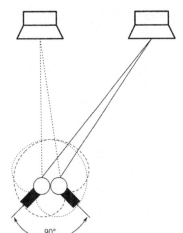

This method uses two identical mics which have a cardioid or other directional pickup pattern. They are placed as close as possible to each other, with the direction of pickup at 90 degrees to each other in one plane (looking from above), and flat in the other plane. This provides a good stereo image and minimises undesirable side-effects, such as phasing, which are inevitable when using two microphones to record a single sound source. It creates a feeling of width because the pickup patterns reduce the level of off-centre sound sources.

MS Mic'ing

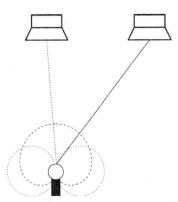

MS stands for Middle and Sides. This is a more advanced technique which uses two microphones, one to pick up the 'middle' signal (either cardioid or omni) and one to pick up the 'sides' signal (always a figure-8). These two signals are recorded onto separate tracks (no mixing must happen between the signals), and when played back, the signals are decoded (by feeding the M signal to the centre of the mix, while feeding the panned S signal in phase in the left channel, out of phase in the right channel), and the original stereo sound field is reproduced.

The advantage of this method is that the 'width' of the stereo image can be controlled by the amount of S signal that is played back, and the M signal is always perfectly mono-compatible and suffers from less phasing than any other method.

At the moment these considerations may mean nothing, but in the future they will do, and MS offers a useful way to record in stereo that gives options after the event which the other methods shown here do not.

MS Recording and decoding

We will look at how to achieve MS decoding in Cubase, with and without a plugin to do it.

Without a plugin

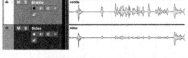

Firstly you will need to record two mono audio tracks; one will be the middle mic, and the other will be from the sides mic.

To achieve the decoding, the sides track needs to be duplicated, by right-clicking on the track in question, and selecting **Duplicate Tracks**

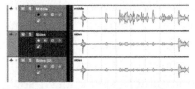

Here is the result of the duplication - the bottom track is the duplicated sides track.

Next, the track which has just been duplicated needs to be phase inverted, this is done by **SHIFT-right-clicking** on the audio event on the track, and picking **Processes > Invert Phase**. See page 579 for more on applying audio processes.

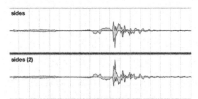

Here the effects of the phase reversal can be seen - the bottom track is now 'upside down' - note the negative peak at the beginning of the original sides track is now a positive one.

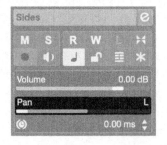

The two sides tracks need to be panned - this is what creates the phase cancellation that allows MS to work. Pan the first sides track to the left, the second to the right (this may need to be reversed, it will depend on the mic setup).

You should now hear a stereo representation of what you recorded. You can alter the balance between the two sides mics and the middle mic to control the stereo width.

With a plugin

An alternative way to decode MS is to use a plugin; in this example we will use the free Voxengo MSED plugin, available from http://www.voxengo.com/.

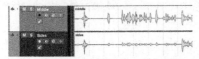

As in the previous example, you will need to record your two mono audio tracks, middle and sides.

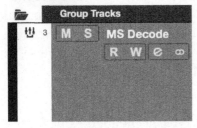

Next, create a stereo group track. **Project > Add Track > Group Channel Track**. Call this group MS Decode. This is an audio track through which we will route both the Middle and Sides tracks, and then place an effect on that group which will turn the Middle and Sides signals into a stereo output.

In the group, Insert the MSED plugin. This is done by clicking in the inspector on the Inserts tab, and then clicking in one of the empty boxes and selecting MSED from your plugin selection. This is covered on page 538. If you don't have MSED see the section in the Audio Setup chapter on downloading and installing plugins on page 662.

Set the MSED plugin as shown here with the mode set to **decode**. This will take the middle signal from the left channel, and the sides from the right, and decode that MS signal to a stereo one. The plugin takes care of the inversion of the sides channel and its panning, making decoding much simpler to achieve once you have it set up.

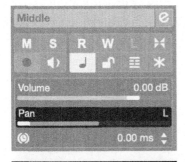

The audio now needs to be routed to the MS decoding group. Firstly, pan the tracks - pan the middle track to the left, and the sides track to the right.

Now set the output of both the Middle and the Sides tracks in the inspector to the MS Decode group.

On playback, you should hear a stereo representation of your recording. You can alter the stereo width and other options using the controls on the MSED plugin.

MS recording works by the mics phasing with each other to cancel signals out, and can only do so because of the polar patterns of the mics used, particularly the figure 8 of the sides mic. It is extensively used in a wide range of recording situations and can allow more creative use of the stereo field as it can be manipulated afterwards. To some listeners it offers a more 'natural' sound, but this depends heavily on the mics, sound sources and recording environment. It is also useful for recording individual instruments as the Middle mic is usually useful on its own anyway (as it would be the way many instruments would be recorded anyway, as seen in the Multitrack recording chapter on page 455).

Setting up

To make an ambient stereo recording, two mics are typically needed – one for the 'left' signal, one for the 'right'. This will mean two identical microphones, and cables to suit. The preferred way to connect these up is with XLR connectors – they provide a fully-shielded balanced connection that also means there is no safety issue with the phantom power connection – this is the power for the amplifier and capsule in a condenser mic. The setup should be with two microphones, plugged into the inputs of the recorder using two XLR leads, with the microphones mounted on stands so they won't fall over – don't over-extend booms, and make sure that one of the legs of the mic stand is below the boom to make it more stable.

Next we need to place the microphones. This is one area where only guidelines can be produced. There is never and absolutely right or wrong way to mic up any sound source, only a starting position. After that, it's best to use your ears and experience to guide you to produce the best result. For this performance, you will want to place the microphones as shown in the diagram below as a starting point – after that, experimentation is the order of the day. Remember when setting up that you need to be aware of the positioning of things like cables – make sure that you've not set up a tripwire for the unwary, as it'll either hurt someone or wreck your recording....

Here we see a typical ambient recording setup:

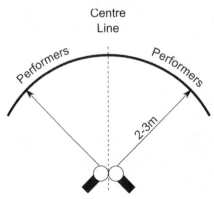

As can be seen, the performers are in an arc around the microphone, at around 2-3 metres away from them. The microphones are set up with an imaginary centre line, with the performers in a balanced arrangement either side of this – these two factors are extremely important in achieving a recording that sounds balanced.

Next, get the performers to play the piece, and listen. If there is something wrong with the sound of the instruments, or there is an imbalance between the performers, then the easiest way to fix it is to make the corrections now – guide the performers to play in balance, and make any other alterations that you might want. And important part of the recording process is just to listen to the sound source and make judgements based on that – it's a common misconception that technology can save a bad performance; it can, but to do so often involves far more work than getting it right in the first place, particularly when you are just starting out recording. Make sure the instruments are in tune, that they sound good, and the performers sound in balance, and your recording will be much, much better as a result.

Now we can deal with the recording hardware itself – firstly, if you are using condenser microphones, they will need to be powered. Some (like the AKG C1000S) have an internal battery, and a switch to turn the mic on and off – make sure this is turned ON. Many condenser microphones do not have a battery, and need to be powered by 'phantom power' which places a 48v DC power supply on the cables of the microphone, meaning the mic cable not only carries the signal from the mic to the recorder, but also delivers power to the microphone. The method of turning phantom power on varies on each recorder, but it is often on a switch either by the channel, or a group switch which may turn several channels on at once. The phantom power is sometimes labelled as +48v.

Important! NEVER turn phantom power on before connecting a microphone – it is possible to permanently damage a microphone by connecting it up after phantom power is turned on, so make all your connections first and then turn the power on.

Once the performers are playing well, it's time to set the microphones to the best level for the recording. On a digital recorder, the highest level that can be recorded is 0dB – everything recorded in practice is quieter than that, and as we've seen previously, that means a negative level; -3dB is quieter than 0dB and so on. The ideal situation is to get a recording that is at 0dB, but this is rarely achieved in practice, as trying to go over this level can lead to distortion which we don't want. Often a performer will play more loudly during the actual performance than the level check, so it's always best to leave them some "headroom" so that the recording will not be distorted if this happens. To do this, get the performers to play the loudest part of the piece, and then set the gain on the input channels to reach a peak level of -3dB at maximum – being below this (down to around -6dB) is OK, but being lower than this may increase the noise in your recording, so this level is quite important.

The gain control's name can vary on different audio interfaces; the controls can sometimes be called 'gain', sometimes 'trim', sometimes 'level'. Monitoring the input signal level can vary depending on the version of Cubase that you have (lower versions have mixers without the input channels), but sometimes you can monitor accurately using meters on the audio interface. A final check is to listen to the signal coming from the microphones; often your ears can be the best judge of whether a signal is distorting or not.

As this is a stereo recording using two microphones, it's important that the gain is set equally between the two channels – this will help ensure a well balanced stereo field. Set one microphone's gain, and then set the other to the amount you have come up with. If that's now too high, reduce both channels equally.

Sometimes it's not possible to get the signal level to the ideal, as the sound source may not be loud enough, the microphones may not be sensitive enough, or the recorder/mixer may not have enough gain to do this. If this happens, move the microphones closer to the sound source (although not closer than 1.5 metres as this is an ambient recording, not a close-miced one), and then try to get the performers to play as loud as they can. As with many things, do the best that you can in the circumstances – very few recordings are actually perfect!

Next, we need to record-enable tracks. Your recording is done on a digital multi-track recorder or sequencer, and again the way to record-enable a track will vary on each machine/setup. On many multi-trackers there will be a dedicated button for record-enabling a track (often it will go red or flash when in 'record' mode, while in many sequencers individual tracks have record-enable buttons on-screen.

Making the recording

This is where the recording proper starts. The first thing to do is to make sure there's as little extraneous noise as is possible - mare sure that everyone in the area has turned their phone off – putting it on silent isn't enough as if someone phones or texts it will still put out interference that the recording setup will capture, and wreck a recording. Ensure that doors and windows are closed, and there are notices so people won't just rush into the recording area. If your recording venue has a noisy air conditioning or heating system, see if you can turn it off, and remember that some light fittings make a fair amount of noise, so if it is possible to turn them off (and not inconvenience your performers) then do so.

Once your performers are ready to record, start the recording and give them a signal to play – it's important to rehearse this so they know when to play, as this will minimise the amount of editing you need to do at the end of the recording to remove large silences. Monitor the performance as it is being done, but don't stop the recorder until around 5 seconds after they have finished – many good ambient recordings have been ruined by people hitting **STOP** before the last notes have died away completely.

Listening back

To listen back to the recording you've made, firstly you need to set the panning of the channels correctly – generally this will involve a 'pan' control on the recorder or software that you are using, but you need to make sure that the left microphone channel is panned left, and right to the right – this will allow you to hear the stereo sound field that you are capturing.

Rewind to the beginning of the piece, and listen through it, with a critical ear – listen out for mistakes, imbalances and any other noises that don't belong. At this stage you may not be able to make detailed critical appraisals of a recording, so it may take several listens before you can decide if the recording should stand or not. If it doesn't, simply go back to the start of the recording and do another one.

If you are unsure of what to listen for, ask yourself if the recording satisfies the following criteria:

- Can you hear any background noise?
- Is there any distortion?
- Is it a good performance?
- Is the stereo placement of the sound sources represented well?
- Can you hear each instrument?
- Is this a good representation of the original performance?
- Are the recording levels high enough?
- Is it enjoyable to listen to?

If you are satisfied on all these points, then it's certainly a good starting point. If you're not, then you should address the issue (be it gain, mic placement or a 747 landing during the performance) and then try again.

If you are satisfied with the recording, you can pack up the recording equipment – your recording session is over, but you still have some work to do with the recording - firstly, there may well be EQ to add.

EQ

Equalisation (or EQ) is the process of adding or taking away certain frequencies within an audio signal. A simple EQ uses two controls, treble and bass, to add or subtract high or low frequencies – most of us have seen or used controls like this in the past. But when we're recording music, there are more complex and subtle EQ controls that we can use to enhance a recording. There are full details of the various EQ options available to you in the Effects chapter, on page 537.

In the ideal world, your ambient recording would be made in an acoustically perfect space, with perfect instruments and players, and using very expensive, totally faithful recording equipment. However, this isn't the case, so often EQ needs to be added to improve the recordings that we've made. On the ambient recording there is little scope for this, other than some general EQ which can help improve the recording.

Firstly, listen to the recording and assess whether it has enough high frequency content – does it sound a little dull? Using your recorder or software's controls (again, identified separately for each piece of equipment), add in some high frequency EQ – typically 3 to 6dB of boost at around 10kHz. This should brighten up the recording.

Secondly, listen to the bass content – depending on the source material, there may or may not be enough bass. Adding or taking away up to 6dB at around 100Hz should improve this.

It is important when making any changes like this to listen to the recording with and without the EQ that you have set up – is really an improvement? If it is, then keep it. If it isn't, then don't!

Trimming the recording

The next area to look at is whether or not you have captured any extra silence (or noise) at the beginning or end of your recording. If you listen to any commercial recording, you won't hear long gaps before or after a piece of music, and the same should go for your recording. Hopefully you had a good arrangement with your performers and they started promptly, but if not, then the beginning and end of the piece will need to be trimmed to remove these silences. How this is done varies between each recording setup, but generally it will involve marking the position that the recording proper starts (making sure not to cut off the beginning or end), and then using a 'slice', 'trim' or 'edit' control on the recorder to remove the unwanted part. For details on how to do this in Cubase, see the Audio Editing chapter on page 489 , and trim the audio and apply suitable fades as well.

Mixdown

Your recordings will usually end up either on CD or as an uncompressed (.WAV or AIFF file) file when you have finished - even if they are to be distributed as a lossy format such as an MP3, that conversion should only happen after everything else has been done without any chance of loss, by keeping with WAV or AIFF until the end of the process. Mixing down onto CD will usually be completed using CD recording software to transfer the WAV or AIFF files to the CD in audio format. To perform an export of the audio in Cubase, see the Mixing chapter on page 636. Once you have the recording on CD, you can listen to it anywhere and have a final, archived copy of it.

Exercises

Record something

The most important first exercise you can do with recording is to actually record something. It doesn't matter what you record at this point, what is important is that you get used to setting up the equipment and whatever else is needed for you to record, and actually going through the process of recording. You can become more fussy about what you are recording and the way you are doing it once you have confidence in setting up and making a recording. Try to record a variety of sounds - music, speech, everyday sounds.

Experiment with mic types

In the audio chapter on page 415 we looked at microphone types. You should have access to at least a dynamic and a condenser mic, so take the opportunity to record something using both types of mic. The experiment is much more valid if you set both up at the same time and as close to each other as possible, and then use them to record the same performance at the same time - then you know the only variable is the microphones you have used. Listen back to the tracks and see if you can hear the differences between the two mic types.

Experiment with stereo mic placement

On page 445 there are three main ways to record in stereo. While at the moment the differences between them may not be apparent, by recording with each setup you will hopefully start to appreciate that the microphone placement alters the way the recording sounds. As above, record something with the three main mic setups (A-B, X-Y and MS) - if you have the equipment to make all these recordings at once, all the better. In addition, you should hopefully find that any kind of stereo recording adds an extra dimension to your recordings, in many cases helping bring it to life and become far more engaging for the listener.

Summary

When making your first audio recordings, there are number of different challenges to overcome - learning how to place your microphones, how to connect everything up, how to use your recording software/hardware, and on top of that artistic and technical assessment of what you've done when you finally have made a recording. It's very easy to find all the challenges overwhelming, so making some simple recordings using ambient mic setups will give you the best chance of making a good recording and overcoming any difficulties you have. It is important to remember that ambient recordings can be extremely useful and in many styles of music will be the preferred method of recording, so they should not be viewed as solely a beginners' technique. You should make a number of recordings and listen and assess them to allow you to feel confident in your abilities before moving onto a multi-track recording which will be a much more complex affair, as seen in the Multi-track recording chapter.

Multi-Track Recording

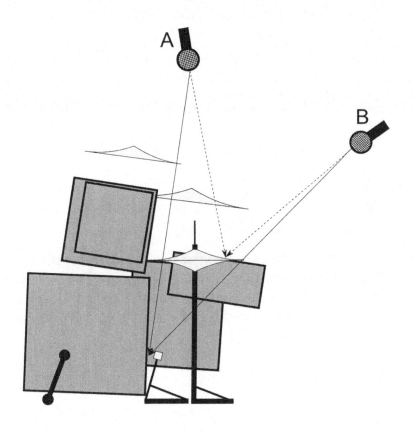

Your first recordings were ambient recordings, usually using 2 microphones to make a 'realistic' recording of a performance, using the placement of the microphones to capture the ambience of the performance and its environment. The next level of recording is a multi-track recording, often referred to (slightly inaccurately) as a close-mic recording as the mics are not always close to the sound sources. This will involve a lot more time as the instruments will mostly be recorded separately, and they will each require setting up separately. There are advantages and disadvantages to multi-track recording:

Advantages

- Far more control over the levels of each instrument – most instruments are recorded in isolation meaning that level can be controlled during mixdown.

- Less compromise in terms of the sound of each instrument – microphone location is not compromised by issues of bleed and physical restriction

- One person's mistake will not ruin the entire recording, just their own 'take'.

- Effects can be applied to individual instruments.

Disadvantages

- Far more time consuming than an ambient recording.

- More equipment and planning is necessary

As you can see, the disadvantages are generally outweighed by the advantages – most recordings that you hear that are released commercially will have been created using the multi-track techniques that you are going to learn, and with careful planning and execution, you will be able to make recordings which are of an increasingly professional level.

Recording Techniques

The first thing that we need to learn is the fundamental principle of all recording. With this simple idea, you will be able to make the most of your recordings, regardless of your equipment, abilities or talent, whether you are making your first recording, or making your 20th album. And that is summed up with two words:

Quality Control

It's a simple concept, but when put into practice, it will make your recordings better. And that is simply to make sure that each and every step of the recording process has been done to the highest level that you can do. But it doesn't start out with microphones, leads, a recorder or expensive monitor speakers. It starts with a simple thing, your ears. You need to listen to what you are going to record, and decide whether it can be improved or not. Forget to do this and you make more work for yourself at best, and compromise your recording at worst. It's a common misconception that you can "fix it in the mix" - this is to a degree true – it's possible to fix a wide range of things, but that takes a lot of practice and skill. It's far simpler, easier and you will always get a better result if you make the thing that you're recording sound good. Here's a quick list of things you can listen for and correct on each type of instrument you might commonly come across. However, it's not exhaustive list – you must use your ears and common sense!

Instrument	Problem	Solution
Drum Kit	Rattles	Find the rattling part – commonly loose components, broken/loose snare, or missing felt washers (cymbals)
	Ringing	Toms and bass drum often need damping – use moongel or gaffa tape and small bits of towel (toms) or a blanket/towel (bass drum)
Guitars	Dull sound	Old strings – particularly on Acoustic Guitars
	Tuning	Make sure the guitar is in tune, but also intonated correctly. Old strings will often not tune properly
Singers	Tuning	Some singers need time to warm up, others are sensitive to the level in their headphones. Singers can also need to feel comfortable to perform well.

Once you've done these things, then your recording work will be much easier.

Planning

One of the largest issues with making a recording, particularly a multi-track one, is a lack of planning. This can show itself up in many ways, and can be a lack of planning on the part of the recordist as well as the performers. Preparation is the key to success for both parties:

Recordist

Anyone recording a piece should have planned for every eventuality before starting to make the recording; failure to do so will at best mean a lot of time is wasted, and at worst will mean the recording needs to be aborted. The first phase of planning a recording is working out in detail the song which is to be recorded. This means a detailed song plan needs to be constructed first, as seen on the next page:

Time	Section	Bars	Instruments	Comment
0:00	Intro	1 – 8	Guitar Drums	Guitar Riff is repeated, distorted sound Drum fill at end
0:17	Verse 1	9 – 40	+ Bass +Vocals	Bass follows intro guitar riff, guitar plays chords
1:25	Chorus	41 – 56	+ B. Vox	Backing Vocals repeated throughout
1:59	Verse 2	57 – 89	- B. Vox - Guitar	Just Vocals, Drums and Bass. Delay on Vocal

A table like this will show a song in detail, and provides a good reference for the recording session – it's possible to refer back to it and know for sure that there are a certain number of bars in a verse, or that there are two choruses at the end, etc. It might sound odd, but it's quite possible (and indeed common) for musicians to make mistakes or forget the structure of a song when in the studio; they may be comfortable when playing along with the original of a song, but having to play the entire thing from scratch can be very different (often they may not even realise they are taking cues from other performers).

Performers

If the performers who are to be recorded are not well prepared, the recording session may end up too long, or even a complete waste of time. The ensemble need not only to be able to play the piece to be recorded, but need to know it well enough that they can play separately when needed without becoming lost. This can often be particularly challenging for some players who rely on the vocalist to let them know where they are in the song, and if this isn't going to happen, they can get lost easily. Practicing beforehand without a singer is a good way for them to overcome this, but sometimes a singer providing a rough track which is fed into the performers' headphones is necessary.

If the performers are well prepared and able to play the piece accurately and repeatably then the recording session will be productive and short, and the end result will be much better. Often performers expect a recording engineer to perform miracles and rectify their errors or omissions – while this is possible, it's always best to make sure everything is right in the first place.

Microphone Placement

When placing a microphone, there are no rules, only guidelines. At the end of the day, it's all about the sound that you get. But there are good guidelines, which will allow you to place the microphones well initially – from that point you can tailor the sound you want by listening and modifying the position. Additionally, if you have very little time in which to work (as is sometimes the case, if you are recording a gig or have limited studio time), they will at least mean you can get a workmanlike, functional sound quickly and simply. When you first start recording, microphone placement could be a complete mystery, so having a good starting point will allow you to start making recordings, and learn and experiment. However, you should be making sure that each sound you record is at the optimum, and spending some time on microphone placement to achieve this. It is always a good idea to become comfortable recording each type of instrument in isolation before trying to do so as part of an important recording - as with most things, practice will improve your abilities to listen, compare and produce a good final recording. Most engineers and producers of your favourite songs will have done the same tasks hundreds if not thousands of times, and their first recordings were probably nothing to shout about. With that in mind, we will now look at a guide to microphone placement for some common instruments and sound sources.

Amplified instruments

When we amplify an instrument, a speaker becomes the sound source, and we need to mic it up to get a good sound. The sound that is heard close-up varies quite widely depending on the position of the microphone, but on the next page is a good starting point for a typical close-mic recording.

Here we see the view from the front of the amplifier. The microphone is placed at the edge of the cone, facing in towards the centre of the speaker. This position usually gives a 'warm' tone, which often sounds similar to that heard in the room (which is affected by the acoustics of the environment). Moving the microphone to the centre will usually given a sharper, thinner tone, while changing the angle of the mic can fine-tune the tone that is heard.

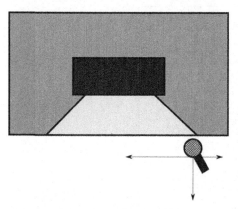

Here is the view from the top (the amp is a cutaway), showing the angle to the centre, and also the distance from the cone – usually around 20mm will be a good starting point – this allows the proximity effect to give a bass boost, making the sound warmer. Experimentation with the position of the mic is important, with the arrows showing movement that should be tested to achieve the desired sound.

In the diagrams above we can see that the microphone is placed at the edge of the speaker, facing in slightly – around a 30° angle. This generally gives a reasonably 'warm' sound, which usually approximates the tone that a listener would experience, and because of the short distance to the speaker compared to any other instruments in the room this gives maximum separation. However, if we want to fine-tune the sound, we can do this. Usually, moving the microphone to the middle of the cone will give a harder, 'colder' sound – this can often be useful when wanting to give a guitar or bass sound more 'attack', and angling the microphone towards the centre or edge will usually fine-tune this sound to a colder or warmer sound respectively. In addition, if you move the microphone back from the speaker, you usually get a sound which is softer in nature, and sometimes more representative of the actual sound the performers are hearing.

Multiple Microphones

It is not uncommon to use two or more mics when recording an amplifier, particularly for guitars; the sound from a close mic will be quite different to the sound in the room, and placing one further back can often give a more 'natural' sound. There is more to the technique than this, though - as seen in the Audio chapter, when multiple microphones pick up the same sound source, then phasing usually occurs, altering the tone when both signals are heard together. There are many different ways that phasing can be used when recording amplifiers, but there are not many options when you only have two microphones - if you have the option to invert the tracks' phases individually, then you have only two options:

Mic 1	Mic 2	Result
+	+	A
+	-	B
-	+	B
-	-	A

The first and last will sound the same (as both have the same phase relative to each other) and the second and third (for the same reason) this gives only two options. However, introducing a third mic to the setup will give four options:

Mic 1	Mic 2	Mic 3	Result
+	+	+	A
+	+	-	B
+	-	+	C
+	-	-	D
-	+	+	D
-	+	-	C
-	-	+	B
-	-	-	A

There is a setup used by several producers which is shown below, using three microphones.

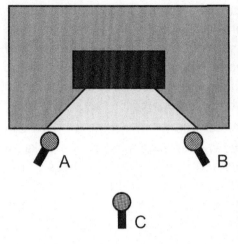

Here is the setup, seen from above. Mics A & B are both dynamic, placed near the edge of the cone. Mic C is a condenser mic, about 30cm back from the centre of the cone. By changing the phase in the combinations shown (when mixing), it is possible to obtaining some extreme EQ effects; due to the nature of the placement and acoustics, it is not entirely predictable what will happen, but experimentation with this technique will lead to some guitar sounds which have individual character and will stand out well in a mix.

This is not the only method by which you can use multiple mics to record an amplifier, but it is a useful one; there are a near-infinite number of possibilities, and remember that you can combine this multi-mic setup with another such as a room mic to give you ambience from your recording environment.

Acoustic Instruments

Acoustic Instruments often give more of a challenge to the recordist, as they generally differ far more than a speaker/amplifier combination - most will produce a different tone from different parts of them, and being able to capture this is a challenge. To get the best sound, the approach should usually be of listening to the performer, and moving around them to find the area in which the 'best' sound is, and then placing the microphone in that location. Often the sound that's required will depend on the recording that you want to make – for example, in a solo classical guitar piece, you may want a very full sound, whereas if the same guitar was being used to fill in some rhythm parts in a piece will full band, you might want a thinner sound. However, we will look at good starting points.

Acoustic Guitar

The acoustic guitar is a complex device which emanates sound from many parts of its body – not only the sound hole, but the entire front of the guitar, back, sides and even the neck. In general, placing the microphone in front of the guitar, between the neck and the sound hole will give a reasonable sound, but there can be much mileage gained by moving the microphone around the guitar, including placing it behind and above the instrument in a similar position to where the player may hear it from, or from moving the microphone up the neck to get a thinner, more percussive sound. Each guitar is different, and each player's technique will lead to a slightly different result. If you have enough tracks spare (or want a full and varied guitar sound) then you can use a coincident pair to record a guitarist's performance in stereo.

Here we see the basic positioning for a single microphone. The tone obtained can be altered dramatically by moving the microphone from the soundhole area to the fretboard, and fine-tuned by changing the angle between the guitar and microphone – start out with it at 90 degrees to the fretboard.

Here is the stereo mic placement. This can work really well as each microphone picks up a slightly different sound and nuances of the playing, leading to a rich, full sound. Again, it can be tuned by moving the position of the mics as with the diagram to the left.

Another technique that can work well is an MS pair , as it allows more creative use of the stereo field after recording, and in many cases gives a "deeper" impression of stereo.

While experimenting it is possible you will find multiple positions that are desirable, and it's perfectly acceptable to use more than one microphone on the guitar at once, although you will need to be aware of the effects of phasing when you do this.

Double Bass

The double bass can be a challenging instrument to record, particularly depending on the player's technique. However, a good starting point is to place a low-frequency capable microphone (such as an AKG D112 or Shure PG52) around 20-30cm in front of the right-hand f-hole as you are facing the player. This normally will pick up the bass adequately as well as most of the fingering sounds, although moving the microphone up to the fingerboard area can pay dividends.

It is also sometimes desirable to add a second mic which will pick up the fingering and fretboard noises, placing this further up the instrument above the fretboard (providing it doesn't hinder the player), although with this it is important to listen to both mic signals together during a practice performance to ensure that phasing is not adversely affecting the sound achieved.

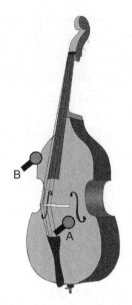

Here we see the double bass, with microphones placed as suggested – microphone A (either a low-frequency capable dynamic or a condenser) will suffice for many situations, while the optional microphone B (usually a condenser) will pick up any fingering and fretboard noises.

Whenever you are multi-micing an instrument, make sure that listening to the two microphones together doesn't mean a less pleasing sound. Phasing between microphones always occurs, but the effect can be negligible, beneficial or negative. Experimentation with positioning will usually eradicate any problems that happen.

Piano

The piano can be a challenging instrument to record for a number of reasons. Firstly, it can produce an enormous range of frequencies, more than nearly every other instrument. Secondly, it is unusual to have access to one for a long enough period to experiment with the considerable number of different mic techniques which are possible with it, and thirdly some pianos can be difficult to record due to extraneous noise from damper and pedal mechanisms being difficult to mask. It would be possible to write an entire chapter solely on piano mic techniques, so only the briefest summary will be given here, from which you can experiment to get the best results.

The Grand Piano

A grand piano should be recorded with the lid open; the sound propagates best by doing this and with the lid closed the sound will be compromised at source. A general principle is that the closer the mics are to the instrument, the more attacking and clear the sound will be, so two different general areas of micing will be covered, as well as specific changes.

The first is to place the microphones above the strings (typically around 30cm), with one mic covering the left-hand of the keyboard, one covering the right. This will generally give a bright, modern sound, with a sharp attack. Movement of the individual mics both along the strings' length and to/from the strings will allow fine-tuning of the sound.

463

Secondly is to use a coincident stereo pair or an MS pair in a similar location. This will alter the sound considerably due to the lack of phasing between the mics which would happen with a spaced pair, and gives more control in the case of the MS setup. The exact position of this pair of mics will be subject to some experimentation, particularly when considering that the sound is generated not only by the strings of the piano but the soundboard too. Movements within the body of the piano will change this considerably, so making a number of test recordings is vital.

For some styles of music a close-mic setup will not be suitable, in which case moving the mics away from the piano to a more ambient setup will be advisable; in general there will be more of the sound of the room captured as a result of this and in addition the attack of the instrument will be decreased, giving a far less upfront sound, more typical of a classical recording or similar. Again, experimentation with positioning and the specific mic setup used is worthwhile if you have time; a spaced pair will give a very different sound to a coincident pair or an MS setup.

Upright Piano

The upright piano is a more common sight where space is limited, and needs different treatment to record it adequately. While the instrument has a lid, it is only a small one, and contributes differently to the way the sound propagates. While the number of techniques that can be used is probably as numerous as there are engineers, a couple of good starting points are outlined next.

Firstly, with the lid open, placing a spaced pair at either end of the instrument - this will allow clear definition between the low and high notes and allow wide panning between the low and high notes (giving the listener the impression of being sat at the piano) should you wish, but there will be some phasing issues which may be a problem.

Replacing this setup with a coincident or MS pair as shown in the next diagram can be worthwhile and will lead to a different sound, typically with a more neutral tone due to the lack of phasing issues.

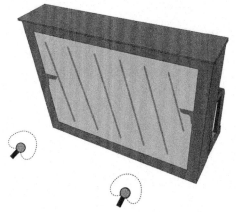

Sometimes it is possible to get good results by miking the piano up from the rear - the soundboard is typically clearly audible from the back of the piano and if it is physically possible to do so then placing the mics here will work well, particularly if a more ambient sound is required.

Vocalist

There is one sound which most people are an expert on – they hear this sound every day, and are used to judging its character for various reasons; that sound is the human voice. This is unlike just about every other sound source, which means that in general it's probably the one which you should spend most time and care on recording. In addition, most of the time the voice provides the story for the song, and that can be important as most people will be paying more attention to it than any other sound. So, how do we mic up the voice?

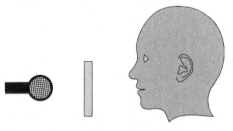

Typically using a condenser mic, placed on a stand around a foot in front of the performer. Sometimes a 'pop shield' is needed – this is a gauze or foam device which is placed between performer and microphone and diffuses the 'ball' of air which is fired at the microphone during certain sounds such as "P" and "B".

Not all singers do this, and some more than others, but if you get this problem (sounding like a low rumble or wind passing by the mic), then it can ruin an otherwise ideal vocal take. Make sure you test your vocalist's performance before recording them, as they may only have one good take in them and it would be a shame to miss it because of a small oversight.

Drum Kit

The drum kit can be a challenging instrument to mic up as it is essentially a number of instruments played by the same person, and as a result of this can take as much time to set up as the rest of the band (there can often be as many microphones on a kit as on the other performers, and in addition these microphones can interact with each other, meaning some fine-tuning is needed before the kit sounds as good as possible). However, the initial placements can be done as follows:

Bass Drum

The positioning of the Bass Drum mic can be extremely critical – a small movement of maybe 20mm can totally transform the sound you get from the microphone. There are a number of different places that the mic can be placed, and experimentation is definitely key to getting a good sound.

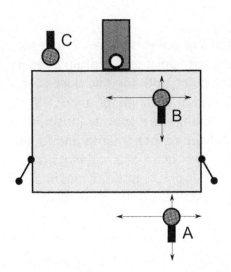

Here is a bass drum seen from above (a section through it so we can see inside). There are two common areas to place the mic - A is usually used when the drum has a front skin on, while B is commonly used inside the drum to mic up the head which is hit by the pedal. Mic position C can sometimes be used to add some attack to the sound directly from the beaten head. However, experimentation is order of the day, by making trial recordings and noting the different sounds obtained from each.

To get a 'tight' sound (as featured on many contemporary recordings), one way is to place the microphone fairly close (within 50mm, sometimes as close as possible without touching) to the skin of the drum that is being hit by the drum pedal beater – the closer, the more 'tight' the sound will be as the sound of the skin will be picked up more than the sound of the drum - in position B on the diagram above. Moving the mic from side to side will change this balance too – moving to right behind the beater can give a really hard, clicky sound, whereas moving to the outer edge of the drum generally gives a smoother, softer sound, but the acoustics of the drum are a complex thing, and there are no hard and fast rules for this; sometimes position A will yield surprisingly attacking and full results. The only way to get the 'right' sound is to experiment, either having someone move the mic for you while you listen, or making test recordings as you move the mic and then listening back to them.

Snare

Snare drums can make or break the sound of a recording – they are usually one of the most prominent things in a mix (listen to most songs very quietly, and you'll usually hear two things – the voice and the snare drum). There are a massive range of sounds, and this change of sound can come either from the snare itself, or from the positioning of microphones.

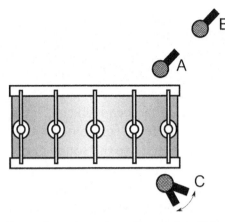

A good starting point is shown in the diagram to the left - position A is often given as the starting point, with the mic close to the top head, and at an angle of about 45° to the skin. Moving the mic away (position B) will often given a more smooth and forgiving sound. The snare drum gets its name from the snares on the bottom, and mic C is picking these and the bottom skin up.

Note that changing the angle of the mics (as shown with mic C, but applicable to all) will often change the sound quite dramatically, and the desirable part of the skin to point the mic at may change with each drum or even drummer. Many drum mic clip setups will give you a position similar to A and C, but you may find (given time) that placing the mic on a conventional stand and being able to move it further away from the drum gives more options in terms of sound. Often the top and bottom snare mics will add different characters to the overall drum sound, and may need quite different processing (such as gating) to allow them to work together; it's often the case that a bottom snare mic will have a lot of rattle when not being played as the snares vibrate sympathetically to other parts of the kit being played.

Toms

Toms are very similar to the snare drum, so the same goes for them. Bear in mind that each one is different, however, and a position which you like on one tom may not be optimum for the others in a kit. You may, however, find that the overheads pick the toms up adequately, and you don't need mics for them. You may also find that you don't have enough tracks free to be able to afford to record them separately.

Overheads

Here is one place where the "close mic" recording name falls down - by definition the overheads will be at some distance from parts of the kit that are being recorded, but they will add an overall feel of the kit and cover any parts which have not been mic'd individually. We will see a number of methods of using overheads, somewhere in front of and above the drum kit, and they will pick up the cymbals, etc. Depending on the number of tracks you have available (see the section on page 477), you may end up using a pair or even a single overhead to record the majority of the kit, possibly all the toms and maybe even the snare. While current trends may be for many mics to be used on the kit, it is possible to get a good sound using just two carefully-placed overheads, as seen in the last method that follows.

The first four setups are more conventional, with the mic setup being based around an imaginary centre line of the drum kit, and changing microphones and/or positions to suit.

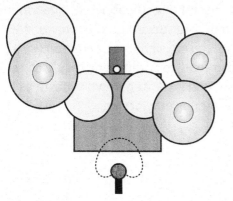

Mono. Here a single mic is centrally placed in front of the kit, and picks up every element. While most recordings will be in stereo, this setup has been used successfully, and depending on the tracks available to you, it may be the only option if other elements are to be close-mic'd. While it may not be the ultimate in refinement, there are fewer phasing problems, and many great recordings have used this to good effect.

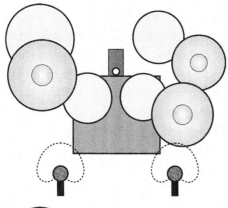

Spaced pair. The two mics are at a distance of around 1.5m apart, and facing towards the kit. The stereo image generated is as a result of their distance apart, but this leads to phasing problems, generating issues with tonal changes and also some 'smearing' of the sounds as the slightly delayed signal in one mic will adversely affect the punch of individual drum hits.

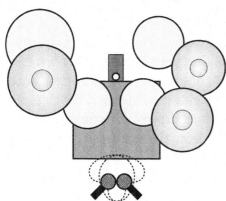

X-Y pair. There are two mics (at around head height) which are covering the whole kit. Note that in this setup, the microphone on the right will pick up the left of the kit and vice versa. The close proximity of the mics eliminates much of the phasing problems of the setup above, and also the timing issues, leading to a more accurate sound.

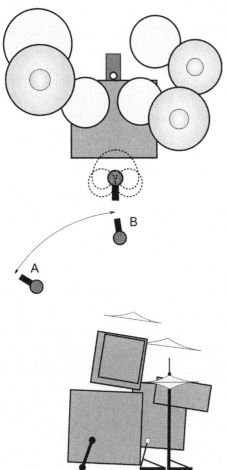

MS setup. The middle mic is a cardioid one, much like the first mono setup. The figure 8 mic is placed directly above it, and when the signals are decoded (see page 446) then the stereo signal is recreated. This setup can lead to a different result to the X-Y setup, and it is often down to taste as to which a listener may prefer.

In the cases above, from the side the microphone setup will look something like this – the mics should be placed at around 2M from the ground, and slightly in front of the kit (depending on space requirements). They can be placed in a number of different positions, from A which is in front of the kit and angled slightly down, to B which is above the kit and straight down; each will produce a different sound as they will pick up the lower parts of the kit differently.

There are other methods for placing drum overhead mics, one of which is credited to recording engineer Glyn Johns, where instead of attempting to capture a "symmetrical" overhead pattern, they are placed with one roughly above the snare drum, and another behind and to the right of the drummer. Their distances from the centre of the snare and the bass drum beater are identical which avoids phasing issues. It is possible to add a snare and bass drum mic to the setup (Glyn Johns usually did this), and then the two signals from the overheads are panned left and right, although not to the extremes.

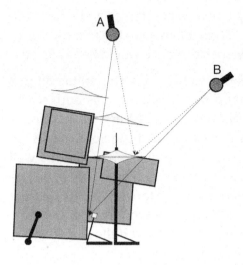

Here is the side view of the setup. Mic A is above the snare drum, pointing directly at its centre, and is usually set around 70cm from the drum (Two drum stick lengths will usually do). Mic B is pointing over the drummer's right shoulder, again at the centre of the snare, and the same distance from it as Mic A is. Next, attach a piece of string to the kick drum beater, and run it up to the front of Mic A, and then down to the centre of the snare. Mark the string where it touches Mic A, and keep the ends fixed to the kick beater and the centre of the snare.

Next, you will need to adjust the position of Mic B (using the string) to ensure it is the same distance from both the kick beater and the centre of the snare - this is done using the string you have just marked, making the process fairly quick. You now have two mics which are placed the same distance from the kick and the snare and as a result they will suffer far less from phasing. Getting these distances right is important, so spend some time ensuring they are as close as you can.

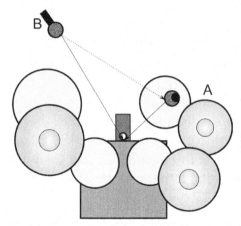

Here is the setup from above. The distances may not look the same in this diagram, but remember that the placement is in three dimensions, so Mic A will typically be higher up than Mic B. Once they are in position, they should be set so they both achieve the same level when the kit is played (unlike X-Y and spaced setups where the gain should be the same rather than the level).

The distance from both the snare drum and kick drum is the same for both mics, so they will be 'phase-coherent' - the sound from both will reach the mics at the same time, and as a result this method avoids lots of problems which other overhead methods (particularly a spaced pair) suffer from, and can give good results even without any close mics to augment them.

Making use of Polar Patterns

On page 420 we saw the different polar patterns that are available to us, but what use are they? When making a multi-track recording one of the main uses is to choose pickup patterns and locate the performers in a manner to minimise pickup of other unwanted sounds (often referred to as bleed). Take the example of recording a singer who plays electric guitar, and wants to play and sing at the same time. If this was just set up without any thought given to the recording process, the setup could closely mimic how a live performance would be achieved:

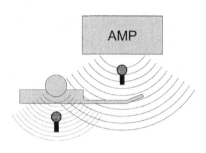

In this case the sound from the guitar amp is being picked up by the vocal mic as both sound sources (voice and amplifier) are 'on pattern' – both mics are cardioid, and the vocal mic is receiving sound from the guitar amplifier as well as the singer. This is undesirable as there will be less separation and therefore less control at the mixing stage. In addition the amplifier needs to be set quite loud as it is behind the singer.

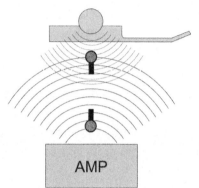

A far better solution is shown to the left - The amplifier is in front of the singer, directed at them. This has two benefits – firstly the amp is 'off pattern' of the cardioid vocal microphone (drastically reducing how much it is picked up), and secondly the amplifier can be quieter as the performer can hear the guitar very well even at a low level.

The end result is much better as the performer is happy (they can hear the guitar and themselves equally well and feel comfortable) and the bleed from the guitar amp is reduced because of good placement and pattern choice and also because the level is much lower. While this placement example is a simple one, such planning can reap rewards in the studio. Sometimes limitations in foldback (headphones) for performers can mean they will want to play as if they are playing live, while other players will never feel comfortable with headphones and then will perform badly as a result, leading to a bad recording. There is little point in making a perfect recording of a bad session!

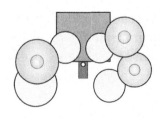

In the next example, the rhythm section for a track is being recorded all in one take. The drummer and bass player like to hear each other as they would do in a live situation (often the case, making the drummer more confident of his location in the song). They may initially set up as seen to the left, much as in a live situation.

However, this is not ideal – the overheads in particular will pick up the sound of the bass amplifier fairly efficiently, leading to a compromise when mixing.

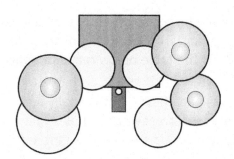

A much better solution is shown to the left. As with the guitarist and amplifier, the bass amplifier is now projecting sound directly at the drummer, meaning he can hear well at a lower amplifier level, and that the overhead microphones will pick the bass up to a far smaller degree. The bass drum mic is a cardioid one, so will also reject much of the bass amplifier's sound.

Often a small amount of thought put into instrument/amplifier placement can drastically improve the amount of bleed that a microphone will pick up, and all without the use of screens between performers. While screens are not a bad idea, they can often leave performers feeling isolated (as can providing all monitoring via headphones), and careful placement can minimise the need for them.

Experimentation

You may have noticed that the above list of microphone positions is not complete. This is because there are a near-infinite combination of instruments, performers and recording spaces in which to place your microphones. Every eventuality cannot be covered, so if you come across a new situation in which to record (such as a trio of nose flute players), there is only one thing to do – experiment! Here is where two factors come into play – firstly your knowledge of the equipment you are using and how it works. Knowing how a microphone picks up is important, both in terms of polar pattern and frequency response. The second factor is to listen – get the performer to play, and move around them to see if there is a "sweet spot" where they sound really good. You can then place your microphone/s to pick this up. Make a trial recording and see if the end result is good. If it isn't, then try again. Even if it is good, you may be able to improve it, so make a note of where you have placed the mic, and then try some alternatives.

How placement alters the sound

Anyone who has studied acoustics in depth will tell you that the way sound propagates through a room is extremely complex – if you look at how complicated ripples on a pool become when they hit the sides, think about this happening in three dimensions instead of two, with different waves superimposed on top of each other – and that as a result of this, it can be difficult to predict exactly what will happen without access to several pHDs and a computer! However, microphone movement relative to a sound source does have some general rules which can be applied.

Firstly, when moving a mic away from a sound source, apart from the obvious drop in sound level, the sound of the room it is in will become more dominant. This is usually heard as an increase in reverb as the reflections from the wall become more significant. However, tonal effects can also become apparent, and in addition the sound can become less harsh as the increased amount of air being moved can attenuate high frequencies.

Secondly, placement relative to the sound source (in terms of left & right, up & down) can drastically alter the tone of the recording. This is usually most apparent with a speaker, and while the observations in the table below may not apply to every amplifier, they are repeated often.

Thirdly, changing the mic's polar pattern can have an effect – both tonally and in terms of capture of room ambience. This depends on several complex factors – the sound source, the room and how the mic picks up frequencies differently when in different patterns.

There are many possibilities when using these three variables, some of them are shown in the table on the next page. This was done in a recording studio, using a CAD M179 multi-pattern condenser mic, a Shure SM58 dynamic mic and the left-hand speaker of a Line6 2x12" combo in a medium-sized room. The comments made on the sound were aggregates from 10 listeners, although the agreement between them was considerable in any case.

No	Mic	Position	Distance	Pattern	Comment
1	Dyn	Centre	5cm	⌓	Thin sound with harsh attack and little low frequency
2	Dyn	Edge	5cm	⌓	Full, powerful sound with good attack
3	Dyn	Centre	1m	⌓	As 1, but quieter, slightly less attack
4	Dyn	Edge	1m	⌓	As 2, but quieter, more natural sounding
5	Con	Edge	5cm	⌓	As 2, but more high frequency pickup
6	Con	Edge	5cm	8	As 5, but with some room sound
7	Con	Edge	5cm	O	As 6, but with more room sound again, fuller tone
8	Con	Centre	1m	⌓	As 1, but with some room sound and less harsh
9	Con	Edge	1m	⌓	As 5, but with more room sound, very natural sound

It's important to remember that these changes will vary in every experiment – sometimes quite surprising results can happen, and that is why you can never be 100% sure that a given mic in a given position will work best; as you become more familiar you will have a better idea of what happens, but there can always be surprises in store. Only with experimentation and making quick test recordings can you be sure that you have achieved the best possible results – it's rare to achieve the optimum sound with your first microphone placement.

The 3 to 1 rule

As mentioned previously, whenever you have multiple microphones recording the same sound source, phasing will occur. The effects of it can be positive or negative, and difficult to predict. There is, however, a technique which will help you minimise its effects, and that is the 3 to 1 rule, which states that the distance between microphones should be three times the distance between the mics and their sound source. In essence this means that the microphones you use will be much closer to their sound sources than they are to each other. This will minimise bleed between microphones, and therefore reduce the chances of any unwanted (and often unexpected) phasing happening between tracks. If you are recording a number of performers together at the same time, your positioning of them should try to take this rule into account as it will greatly reduce any problems you will have when mixing. Note that this does not apply to using multiple mics on a single sound source - if you tried to apply this rule to drum overheads, if they were a metre above the kit they would need to be three metres apart!

DI

When an instrument or amplifier has an electrical output (such as electric guitar, bass, keyboards, etc), it is possible to connect to this directly and avoid using a microphone. Some instruments and amplifiers provide an output which is electrically compatible with a microphone input on a mixer/recorder, but many don't. In this case, a device called a DI box is necessary. This unit will perform level and impedance matching to allow the two pieces of equipment to work together in an ideal way.

Here is a typical DI box. It has jack inputs (for the instrument), and XLR outputs (for connection to the microphone inputs of the desk/recorder). It is an active model, so needs to be powered, either by a battery or by phantom power. It has two channels, so can work for a stereo instrument, and other options such as switches to alter input level to suit the instrument or amplifier it is connected to. One important thing to remember when using a DI box is that it isn't a microphone, so you will get NO bleed from other instruments if present. The sound from a DI can be quite different from the sound of a mic, giving you more creative possibilities and also solving problems while recording.

Budgeting for tracks

In a perfect world, you would be able to use as many tracks as you needed. However, there are nearly always limitations placed on the number of tracks you can record; until the 1960s, two or three tracks was generally the limit for audio recording, but the advent of the first four-track recorder quickly led to 8, 16 and 24-track recorders becoming the norm in professional studios, and this didn't change much for some time (although it's possible to link multiple recorders together, and some have been produced with larger track counts). Digital tape recording systems allowed multiple machines to be linked together and meant that 48 or even 72-track recording was a possibility in high end studios, although few offered this and many studios still only offered 8 or 16 tracks into the 1990s.

However, the advent of computer-based recording software (such as Cubase, Pro Tools and Logic) and modern, powerful computers has meant that it's possible to record many more tracks than this with relatively inexpensive hardware - many computer setups will allow you to record over 100 tracks without too much trouble, and in addition be able to integrate many different effects on each track as well. This can be extremely important for unlimited creativity, but it is also useful sometimes to apply limits and to see how much you can do with limited resources.

A typical recording session

While it is, of course, impossible to list every possible recording situation, below is a table outlining the recording of a song involving a range of instruments and the use of 24 tracks in total.

Trk	Instrument	Microphone/Recording Method	Take	Notes
1	Bass Drum	Shure BG52 Low-frequency sensitive Dynamic Mic	1	
2	Snare Drum	Shure SM57 Dynamic Mic	1	
3	High Tom	AKG D440 Dynamic Mic	1	
4	Mid Tom	AKG D440 Dynamic Mic	1	
5	Floor Tom	AKG D440 Dynamic Mic	1	
6	Overhead L	CAD M179 Condenser Mic, set to Cardioid	1	X-Y Pair
7	Overhead R	CAD M179 Condenser Mic, set to Cardioid		
8	Bass Guitar DI	DI via DI Box	1	Same Take
9	Bass Guitar Mic	AKG D112 Low-frequency sensitive dynamic Mic		
10	Guitar 1	Shure SM58 Dynamic Mic	2	
11	Guitar 2	Shure SM58 Dynamic Mic	3	
12	Acoustic Guitar	AKG C414 Condenser Mic, set to Omni	4	
13	Lead Guitar 1	Shure SM58 Dynamic Mic	7	Same Take
14	Lead Guitar 2	AKG C414 Condenser Mic, set to Cardioid		
15	Tambourine	CAD M179 Condenser Mic, set to Cardioid	12	
16	Congas M	CAD M179 Condenser Mic, set to Cardioid	11	MS Pair
17	Congas S	CAD M179 Condenser Mic, set to Figure 8		
18	Vibes M	CAD M179 Condenser Mic, set to Cardioid	5	MS Pair
19	Vibes S	CAD M179 Condenser Mic, set to Figure 8		
20	Keys 2 L DI	DI via DI Box	6	Stereo
21	Keys 2 R DI	DI via DI Box		
22	Lead Vocal	AKG C414 Condenser Mic, set to Cardioid	8	Pop screen
23	Backing Vocal 1	AKG C414 Condenser Mic, set to Cardioid	9	Pop screen
24	Backing Vocal 2	AKG C414 Condenser Mic, set to Cardioid	10	Pop screen

As can be seen from the table, the drums and bass were recorded at the same time to give the best feel in the rhythm section, and after that the rest of the track was built up using overdubs of single instruments at a time. An MS pair was used for the Congas and also for the Vibraphone, and a total of 12 separate recordings made up the end result.

The recording sessions

Instrument order to record

It is of particular importance that this aspect of the recording process is thought about beforehand. Many recordings have been made difficult or scrapped because of a lack of planning. Why? There are two main reasons.

Getting a good foundation. Like it or not, the rhythm section of a band is the foundation onto which the rest of the song is built. If the drums and bass aren't up to standard, the rest of the song will never be good enough. It is common practice to record the drums and bass together, as this often gives the drummer a structure to work to (as they often key from the bass player's changes), and also leads to a better recording as they tend to 'groove' better in person.

Starting the song. This is really important. Firstly, if everyone starts at the same time, but the drummer and bass player are recording first, then a count-in needs to be recorded so the subsequent performers know when to start – this might sound obvious, but it's forgotten a lot more than you might think! Also, often the first instrument to be heard isn't the first instrument to be recorded – there might be an acoustic guitar intro or an unaccompanied vocal. If that's the case, you need some way of guiding your performers accurately. The most common way to do this is get the drummer to do a count-in, and then click for the correct number of bars. They should click quietly so this can be edited out after the event – really loud clicks can be difficult to get rid of as the kit may still be vibrating from them.

Playing along to a backing

In an ideal world, the performers for your recording would know the song inside out, and be able to play it without any backing to play along to. However, this is sometimes not the case, particularly when working with little notice or a dep player; you may need to use a drummer who is not familiar with the song, and they may want to play along with the original to allow them to hear the song's structure as they play. This can be done, but to allow an effective start, you will need to provide a count-in to the original song; this can usually be done easily in Cubase by finding the tempo of the first bar of the song (see the Tempo Mapping section on page 90), and then creating a simple drum part which will provide the clicks to warn the drummer (or whoever starts the song) that they are about to start; it is only by doing this that the beginning of your recording can be in time.

Click Tracks

It is sometimes necessary to have a drummer play along to a click track, but if you are planning to do this make sure that your drummer can do so efficiently and musically. It may seem unusual, but playing drums in time to a click or metronome is not a simple skill, and many drummers who are otherwise extremely talented find it very difficult to do – check before planning your recording!

Overdubbing

In some situations, it might be possible to record the entire performance and all the performers in one go. That's not always desirable or possible - if you don't have enough physical inputs on your audio interface, you'll have to do an overdub. Overdubbing sounds complex, but it's really just playing back what you've recorded so far to the performer (usually via headphones so that the sound of the other tracks isn't re-recorded, unless you are using a "DI") and then recording their performance on another track. It's a good way to build up a complex recording, and also has the great advantage of allowing each performer to record alone, which means that there will be no 'bleed' from other instruments being picked up on the microphone at the same time – this element gives you complete dynamic control of the mix, as you can control each instrument's level independently. It also means that a mistake during this take won't ruin the other performances – something that wouldn't be true if you recorded everyone together.

To set up overdubbing depends on the individual equipment setup that you have, so we will look at the process rather than the details. If you are using Cubase then once you have recorded your first track, you will need to create more audio tracks, pick the correct input for them if applicable (for more on this see the Audio Setup chapter on page 651), and then record.

An example

We will see a quick example of a simple overdub - in this case, three percussive tracks, all played by the same person. First, the recording of track 1.

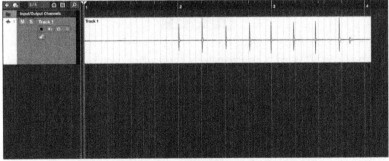

Next, another audio track is added, and while listening back to Track 1, the performer records Track 2.

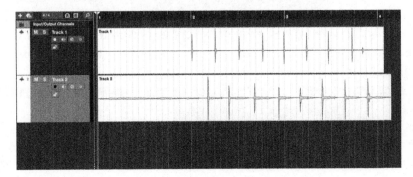

The process is repeated again - now Track 3 is added, and recorded by the performer.

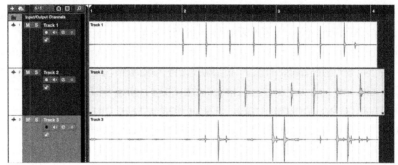

Note that a mistake at any point in the recording process will only affect the track being recorded at the time - all the others will be unchanged, and this is one of the key strengths of the technique. It is possible to add many tracks to such a setup; while in the past the number of tracks that can be recorded would be limited by the recorder, most computer-based recording setups are capable of recording or playing several hundred tracks at once, allowing extremely complex recordings to be created.

Setting the record mode

Like MIDI (as seen in the Sequencing chapter on page 11), there are different record modes for Audio, and we will look at them briefly here. The Audio record mode is set by clicking on the Transport Bar.

Picking the audio recording mode can be important - particularly if you need to record a number of takes of a section to allow a perfect take to be assembled.

Keep History

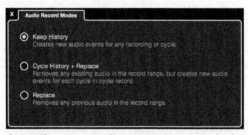

This is the default mode. When an audio event is recorded on top of another one, the other one remains 'underneath'. Here we see a track, with an existing part which starts at bar 3.

Recording over this (to bar 4) produces a part which is 'on top' of the older material - note the hatched area of the overlap.

It is still available quickly, however - trimming the new recording back reveals the original.

Replace

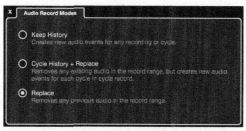

In replace mode, audio is replaced with any audio which is recorded on top of it. Here we see a track, with an existing part which starts at bar 3.

Recording over this (to nearly bar 4) replaces the material of the older part.

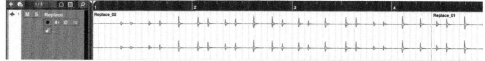

Trimming the new part back doesn't reveal the old audio.

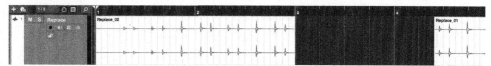

It should be noted, however, that as Cubase is a 'non-destructive' audio editor, the original take is still available - it is simply a case of trimming the part to reveal the hidden audio.

Cycle History + Replace

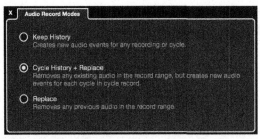

Cycle History + Replace allows the creation of history when in cycle mode, but replaces the audio when not in cycle mode, so if you are not in cycle, it will work in the same way Replace does.

Cycle recording and Lanes

There are some occasions when you will need to record multiple versions of a section (or possibly even an entire song) - sometimes this will be down to the performer needing several attempts to get the recording right, and other times it will be for more creative reasons, when trying different versions to assess later. In both circumstances, using Cycle Record can be useful. The record modes shown above are slightly different when in cycle mode, as seen here.

Keep History and Cycle History + Replace

When in cycle mode, both these modes do the same thing - for each cycle they create an event for each lap of the cycle, and each one is stacked on top of the others. This may appear somewhat cumbersome, until advantage is taken of lanes - the lanes system allows multiple audio events to be visible simultaneously on the same track (although only one can play at any one time). If recording is completed in cycle mode, after the first lap it will look like this:

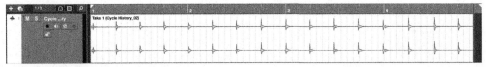

After lap two, there is another take:

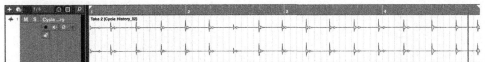

And finally, lap three, with take 3. Note that Stop was pressed before the end of the lap.

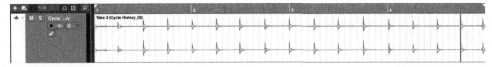

With the mouse in the track in question, each part is hatched, showing that there is at least one part below.

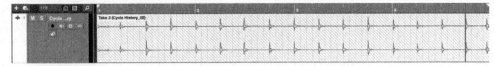

Using the lanes button reveals what is actually happening

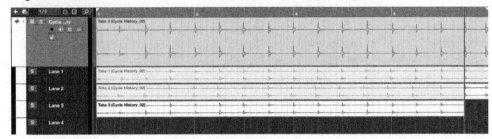

For most of the playback, Take 3 is being used, with a small section from take 2 at the end. To alter this, use the Comp tool, as seen on page 522.

You can cut the events on the lanes just as you would on a normal track, and mute them as you wish - Cubase will only allow one event to be played back at any time. Once you have made your edits, click the hide lanes button on the track, and it will return to the appearance of a normal track.

Replace

Replace works in the same way in cycle mode as normal recording - you will only get the version from the last lap of the cycle.

Dropping In

It is a fact of life that people make mistakes - even the best performers will make them, so it's important to be able to deal with this in an efficient manner. One of the strengths of multi-track recording is that it's possible to re-record only the track of the current performer, and replacing small sections of a take with new material is often needed.

Here we see a recording of a vocal part. Nearly all of the vocal is OK, aside from a problem around 1:36. The entire phrase between 1:34 and 1:40 needs to be re-recorded. The performer is still in the same position, with the mic still setup in the same way, and the gain is unaltered. To perform the drop-in, the song is played from earlier (to allow the performer to know where they are, and to get ready to perform, or even to play/sing along with the track), and at the appropriate time, record is hit (* on the numeric keypad), while still in play.

The track goes into record mode, and will record the new section.

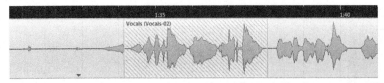

Hitting * again will take Cubase out of record mode, while the track will play on - if needs be you can leave it playing and then drop in to replace other sections. If you have finished doing drop-ins, you can of course hit Stop. It is important that you hit record before the performer starts the phrase in question as you want to capture all of the part. On tape-based systems, it was important to do this at exactly the right place, so that wanted material happening before the drop-in was not lost, but with a non-destructive system such as Cubase this is less important (but not a bad skill to perfect as it can save editing time). If you need to edit the entry and exit points of the drop-in then refer to the Audio Editing chapter on page 490.

Using Punch In / Out

If you are working alone, or are particularly worried about dropping in at an exact point, you can use Cubase's Punch In feature. This allows you to set a position you want the drop in to occur, and then to set Cubase to automatically start recording when it reaches that point. You can also set a Punch Out point - where Cubase will stop recording and revert back to play mode. First, activate Punch In (and optionally Punch Out) using the buttons on the transport bar. Punch In is the middle of the three buttons shown below, and Punch Out is on the right.

Next, set the Punch In and Out points using the red triangles that have appeared on the ruler - much like setting the locators.

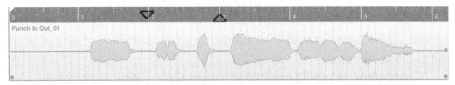

Finally, the project is played from before the Punch In point - long enough for the performer to get in the swing of things - and once the Punch In point is reached, Cubase will go into record mode. When the Punch Out point is reached, it will drop back into play. The new section will now have been recorded.

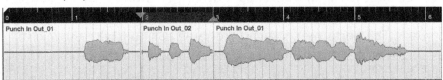

The 'Lock' button to the left of the punch buttons locks the Punch In and Out points to the locators - this can greatly speed the setup of these points, particularly if you have already been using the locators to listen to a section that needs replacing.

Providing Foldback for Overdubs

Foldback is the signal that you send to your performers so they can hear what is already recorded when performing for overdubbing. The way you provide foldback for overdubs will depend on the recording setup that you are using - as with recording setups, it's not possible to cover every eventuality, but we will look at some general ideas and tips.

Performer hears control room mix

With most simple recording setups, this is the setup that you will be using. For most standalone multitrack recorders, there is not the provision to provide a different mix for foldback, and in many simpler computer-based setups this will also be true - if you have a soundcard with only one stereo output, then this will also be the case. Often there will be a headphone output or amplifier which is connected to the same signal that is heard in the control room. In this case, the performer will hear the same mix as you will do in the control room. To this end, you will need to tailor your listening mix to suit the performer. This requirement can vary as much as performers themselves - some will like a lot of themselves in the mix, others far less. What's important is that you try to give them what they want; this can mean you are unable to hear what you want in the control room, but you will be able to do so after the recording has taken place.

Performer hears their own mix

In some setups, it is possible to provide a dedicated mix for the performer to hear. This setup was common in multitrack recording studios before computers became commonplace, and many mixers provided Pre-fader sends for this purpose. With a multi-output soundcard it is possible to have such a setup using Cubase, and in addition Cubase provides the Control Room mixer which if used allows the setup of such mixes. In this case it is possible to give the performer whatever mix they desire, while still listening in context in the control room.

General Tips

Firstly, as said above, the most important thing is to ensure the performer gets what they want to perform to - in general they will know what will help them the most. However, a headphone mix that is too loud or too quiet can cause issues; if it's too quiet then the performer will usually strain to hear the backing and drift off. If it's too loud, they may have problems hearing themselves correctly, have issues with pitch, and also the sound from the headphones may bleed into the mic (common with singers), so be aware of these points as you work.

If your monitoring setup makes it difficult for the performer to hear themselves well, it's sometimes useful to get them to remove one side of the headphones so they can hear themselves via that route.

If you need to provide reverb for a performer, you can do so as an insert or a send on the channel in question.

If you are monitoring via the computer (as you may well be), this is the time that latency is most noticeable. Try to reduce it as much as you can while keeping the recording setup reliable - see the Audio Setup chapter on page 651 for more on this.

Assessing the tracks

Being realistic about performances and the way they have been recorded is an important skill to learn. You will be judged not only on the quality of the recording that you've made in terms of microphone choice and usage, effects and mixing, but also that you've had the skill to differentiate between a good and a bad performance. This part of recording can be difficult, not only because it means you need to be able to assess performances on a wide range of instruments, but also because of the personal nature of it. No-one likes being told what they've done isn't good enough, so it's always important to be diplomatic about anything that you say, and also to encourage your performers – it's much better to be positive about what was good, rather than negative about what was bad. But at the same time, you need to be able to be firm about whether a performance was good enough, and if it wasn't and the performer can't do it any better, then it's either time to take a break for them to do some practice, or to get someone else in who can do the job.

In addition, it's important to be objective about the performers that you have, and what they are adding to your recording. This is the number one reason why you should not play on your own recordings for A level. Very few people of any age (let alone at 17-18) are objective about their own performances, and can therefore either spend a lot of time trying to fix mistakes which aren't there, or be happy with a recording which is sub-standard.

Once you have all the tracks you need recorded, you may need to do some editing – often there will be small errors that you can address or improve parts of the original performance – for these things, see the Audio editing chapter, page 489.

You can then move onto the mix. It is not uncommon to 'mix as you go' when making a recording, particularly if it is a large recording that takes place over a number of sessions, but the most important factor is making sure that each track is as well performed and recorded as is practical. Mixing is covered in full in the mixing chapter on page 619, with procedures and techniques to help you get the most out of the tracks you have recorded, but always remember that you should aim to make recordings of the highest quality – only then will you have a mix which is also as good as it can be.

Exercises

Basic Overdubbing

Overdubbing is the most important technique with multi-track recording. Recording different parts at different times while the new parts play along to the previously recorded ones is a technique which takes some skill to master, particularly as it means a new level of setup as you have to provide a mix for the performer to listen to which will allow them to play along with what you have already recorded. To this end, your first overdubbing should be something extremely simple, so that you can concentrate on the procedure rather than worrying about the quality of the music. The simplest setup would involve just one microphone, a pair of headphones for foldback and then the performer recording something simple such as counting on the first track, and then on the next track carrying on with the count, so that the first track contains 1 2 3 4 and the second one contains a pause (while the first plays) and then 5 6 7 8 and so on. Doing this will allow you to get the process up to speed.

Build up a track with multiple overdubs

Once you are comfortable with the technique above, build up a simple musical piece using the same techniques. Start out with something simple, such as a single drum playing a simple rhythm and record it. Now add more complex parts to the original beat you have created - you can do this with percussion instruments fairly easily, and also consider adding pitched instruments as well. You can experiment with microphone types and placement on each track, and start to concentrate on the quality of recording as the process becomes more familiar.

Record a simple blues

The next stage is to record a piece of music. To keep things simple, it is often a good idea to record something where the music will be easy to play and the structure straightforward, and a Blues often fits this bill easily - it's usually fairly simple to ask a drummer to play a 12-bar blues pattern and they will be able to do this without needing a click or other performers to play along with. Next you can add the bass, guitar, keyboards and vocals. This process will be a significant step towards recording for real.

Compare microphone positions

One of the most important ways to improve the sound of your recordings (and one which many overlook) is to experiment with microphone placement. Positions you are given from books and the Internet are always best guesses - there are far too many variables in play in an acoustic environment to guarantee that any given position is the 'right' one, even before considering differences in desired sound. The only way to get to know what is happening is to experiment, and the best way to do this is methodically, trying different locations, different polar patterns and different mic types. A small positional change in a close mic on a drum or amplifier can reap huge rewards, so spend some time experimenting, and record the results on separate tracks so you can directly compare the results. When you make a recording you should never settle for the first position you have placed the mic, as often it will not be the optimum one.

Drop in and edit replacements

Performers will make mistakes during your recordings, and dealing with them quickly and efficiently can be the difference between a really productive session and a difficult one. Practice recording part way through a part to replace some of it by playing from a few bars before the error, and getting the performer to play along with the track as soon as they can. You can press record as soon as they are comfortable, and Cubase will seamlessly record the new part on top of the original. Once you have recorded the part you want, you can then edit the transition from the old part to the new to make it inaudible - usually you will find a small silence before a note which will allow you to do this. For more details, see using the Trim tool in the Audio Editing chapter, page 490.

Summary

Multi-track recording is an important skill to master, for the reasons described at the beginning of this chapter – it is possible to record the same performer many times, obtain complete isolation between performances and replace minute parts of a performance to obtain a perfect recording. But this comes hand in hand with an overhead in terms of the amount of work needed, and the skills needed to make the recording. If you build the recording on solid foundations then you should be able to make a recording which will be of excellent quality and be worth listening to for a long time. Multi-track recording is also a complicated area to master - it involves many separate considerations, some of which are technical and some are aesthetic, and combining these to create a pleasing recording is a task which takes time and practice. There are few absolutes when working in this discipline, and asking 10 different producers how they perform a given task will usually yield 10 different answers. Experimentation, listening and experience are all key to achieving the best results when recording, and attention to detail is critical throughout the process - only a fastidious approach will allow you to get the most out of a recording at each stage and lead to an end result which can be mixed to produce a great final product. The more you record and the more you listen, the better your recordings will be as you become more familiar with the technical tasks to be completed, allowing you to concentrate on making aesthetic judgements about your recordings and producing a better end result, which you can then mix (see page 619).

Audio Editing

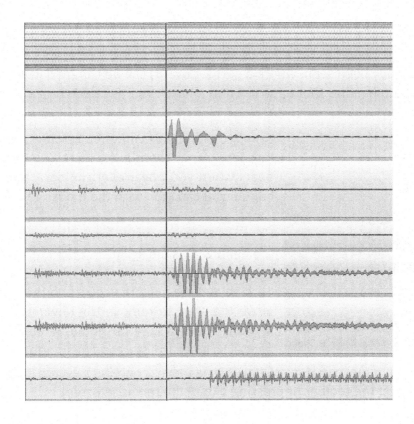

One of the most powerful techniques available in modern music production is the ability to edit audio down to individual sample level. This means it is possible to make extremely accurate edits and make changes that would be next to impossible using traditional techniques, and fix errors of timing and performance that would otherwise have ruined a recording. This is not to say that a bad performance can be made into a good one (although many have tried) – it's always best to make sure you have a good recording in the first place – but it is possible to fix an error which would have rendered an otherwise good performance unusable.

The tools that Cubase gives you allow you to edit the audio in a number of different ways, and can be used in different contexts. Firstly we'll see what each tool can do, and secondly how to use them for differing editing purposes.

The Tools:

Trim

This has already been seen, where a part (or event) can be trimmed in length using the square handles that appear when a part/event is selected or the mouse hovers over it.

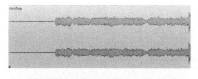

Here is the original event. You can see at the bottom left corner there is a square - this only appears when you hover over the part, and is the handle you can grab with the mouse to move.

Here is the same event, having been selected - the handle is visible again.

Clicking and dragging the square to the right will move the start to remove the unwanted audio. In many cases, a fade in should be applied (see below) to make the start sound smooth.

Contents do not move unless you have sizing moves contents selected (by clicking and holding on the toolbar or pressing 1 until the tool is selected).

Fade

Fade in and out is achieved using the triangular handles that appear when an event is hovered over – use for simple fades in and out and overall level control of an event

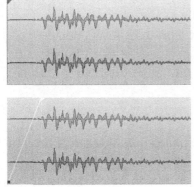

Here is the beginning of the audio above at a high level of zoom. The triangular fade handle is at the top left. Clicking and dragging it to the right will fade the audio part in, avoiding the possibility of any clicks or unwanted sudden starts...

Here we can see that the fade has been applied, with the line showing clearly the fade; the wave-form will alter to reflect what will be heard as well. Removing the fade is done by moving the fade handle back to the start of the event.

Event Envelopes

Envelopes can be applied to events. This is done with the pencil tool (you will see it change appearance when it is over an audio event).

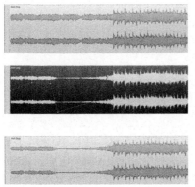

Here is the original audio event, which is played at full volume throughout. Using the pencil tool we can add points which will ...

... alter the level of the part throughout, as can be seen from the waveform. This is attached to the part, so moving it will not alter the effect.

Here is the same event but de-selected - note that the Event Envelope is still visible, but not as clearly as when it is selected (the same applies when using other tools).

Holding down **SHIFT** while using the pencil will allow you to remove envelope points, as will dragging an existing point off of an event.

Cutting audio

Whenever you are working with samples in Cubase it's important to be as efficient and accurate as possible – often you do not need to use the scissors tool as you can just re-size a piece of audio instead of cutting it and then deleting a section.

Another important technique to master is making accurate edits, and one of the best ways of doing this is to make use of your natural timing. Rather than spending a long time trying to decide which part of a sample is the right one, often just hitting **STOP** (**SPACE** by default) is accurate enough, just make sure that you do it in time with the beat and mostly you will be within a fraction of a second of the right place. Practicing this technique can save you many minutes of editing time which can really add up on a complex piece.

To practice these techniques (and particularly creating loops as shown below), start out with really simple drum loop; this can often be done visually with very little difficulty as the bass drum beat is clearly visible as seen below. This is a very easy thing to recognise, and by making your cuts at a point that you decide (such as the first large positive cycle) you will be able to achieve clean and precise edits with little problem. Once you can do it quickly and easily with such samples, move onto more challenging loops.

Creating a loop from a sample

Creating loops from samples is an important skill to have. It can be quite straight-forward, but being accurate is important, not only in terms of making sure the audio loops properly, but also making sure that the beginning of the sample is timed correctly – otherwise you will have relative timing issues with other samples or MIDI that you use.

Firstly, import the track you want to create the sample from – it will look something like this:

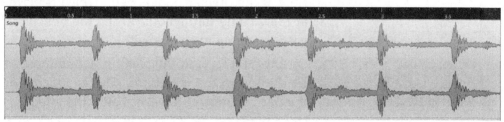

The next step is to trim the beginning of the sample to make it start where the beat starts – in the case of this sample there is a clearly-defined bass drum beat, with a short silence before it. Trimming the silence is very important to get the timing of the sample right. Here it is, seen in more detail.

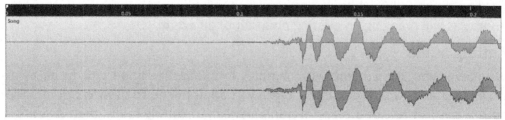

Next, the sample has been trimmed to remove the silence – here it has been trimmed to the start of the first large "positive" cycle, giving a clear and definite point to edit to (this will become important later on). The sample now starts at the same time as the bass drum beat happens.

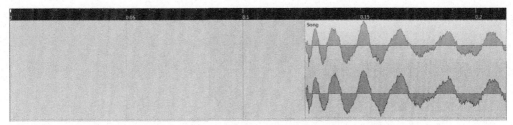

The next stage is to listen to the sample and decide how much of it to use – usually this will be a number of bars, in this case only one bar is needed. Here we see the sample having been stopped using the space bar at the appropriate point:

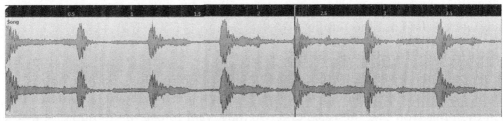

And here is the same point, zoomed in on – as can be seen it's not far off at all.

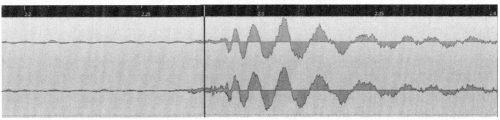

This makes it very clear where to make the cut using the scissors tool – again the first large positive waveform has been selected (as in the first step), meaning we are using the same reference point for each edit; as long as the original playing is in time, it should loop properly. The next diagram shows where the actual cut took place.

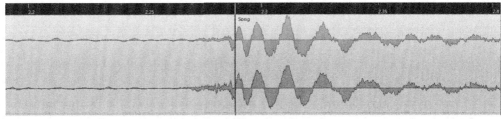

The next step is to check that the sample will loop musically – this is done by selecting the sample, hitting **P** and then playing it with cycle turned on (click on the transport bar or hit / on the numeric keypad).

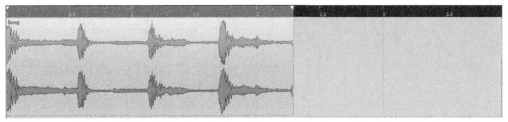

Whenever you do this make sure that you're not being convinced by what you see but by what you hear – sometimes a sample will look right and be wrong, and vice versa. If it sounds wrong, alter the edit until it loops smoothly and without feeling 'pushed' or 'dragged'. Once you have listened to this sample and it loops OK, you may want to find out the tempo.

Finding the tempo of a sample

Often commercial and downloaded samples will have their tempo marked on them (such as 130drumloop.wav), but if you've taken or made a sample your-self then this won't be the case, and you may want to use the tempo of it as the tempo for your song. This used to be a case of trial-and-error (setting the tempo and seeing if it is right), but the Time Warp tool makes it easy to find a sample's tempo.

Once you have created your loop , move the sample to start at Bar 1, Beat 1 (make sure snap is turned on for this). This is important as otherwise the Time Warp tool will not work as desired, so even if the sample appears at another time move it to this point. You will have something similar to that seen on the next page.

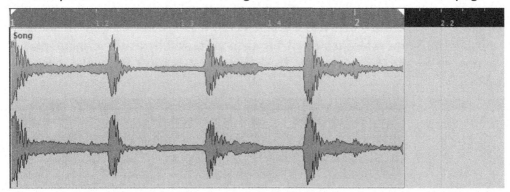

As you can see, Cubase's tempo is not the same as the tempo of the sample – here Cubase is running too quickly, so Bar 2 happens before it should do (it should happen where the sample ends as it's just one bar long). This could be altered with trial and error, but it's much simpler to use the Time Warp tool. Make sure snap is turned on and set to **Events** – this will allow us to snap to the back edge of the sample. Now select the Time Warp tool and move over Bar 2 on the white area of the project window - **not** on the ruler. You can now click and drag Bar 2 to where it should be (i.e. at the end of the sample).

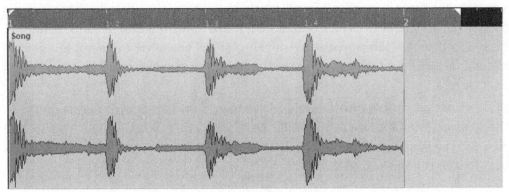

Cubase has calculated the tempo of the sample precisely, and repeats will work without issue, and the sample will now fit with any MIDI data that you add to the project. Note that the locators are based on tempo, so the right one will need to be re-set if you want to keep looping that part.

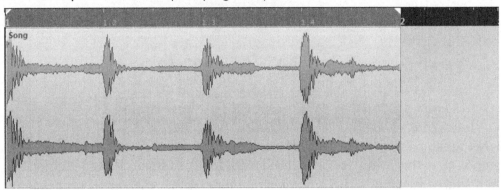

Altering the Tempo of a sample

Sometimes you want to make a sample fit to a specific tempo – either you have MIDI which is already in place, or you want to make two different-tempo samples fit together. This is easily achieved; firstly create your loop as shown in the 'Creating a loop from a sample' section.

Using timestretch

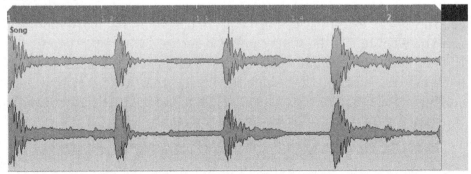

Next make sure that the sample starts at the beginning of a bar, and that you know how many beats or bars it is (when listening to the sample, not to Cubase)

– remember that Cubase isn't intelligent enough to realise how long the sample should be, so you will have to listen and make that judgement, and always be clear about which tempo you are thinking of – Cubase or the sample. Ensure the click is turned off when you are listening to the sample to find out how many beats it is.

Make sure that snap is turned on and set to grid and an appropriate setting, either Bars or Beats for most situations. Next, click and hold on the Arrow tool and pick `Sizing Applies Time Stretch` from the menu – the cursor has a little clock next to it to remind you of this.

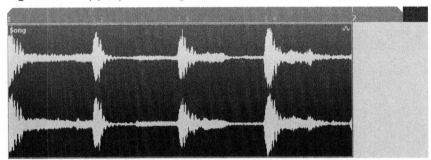

Click on the sample to select it (and make the white 'sizing' handles appear) and then drag it to the appropriate length.

Here the sample has been re-sized and therefore time-stretched to fit the desired tempo. Note the "wave" symbol at the top right - this shows that the sample has been altered in tempo. This is done in real-time; rather than apply processing to the sample and create a new file, Cubase applies this when you play your project back; this is important as it means you can make multiple changes to the time stretching of the sample and the quality will be as good as it can be. However, to aid this there is another setting that you should be aware of - the algorithm as on page 497.

Making a sample follow Cubase's tempo

There is an another way to alter the tempo of a sample, and that is to tell Cubase the original tempo, and let it alter the sample's tempo to match the current tempo. This can be extremely useful if you are unsure of the final tempo of your song, or you want to use the same sample in sections where the tempo differs. Firstly, find the tempo of your sample as seen on page 494. Here, the sample has the tempo of 105.652. Next, open the Pool, with **CTRL+P**. You may need to expand the Audio tree (click the plus to the left of Audio if there is one), and then you should see all the audio files within your project.

Find the sample in question, and then enter the sample's tempo in the Tempo column. Now, click in the **Mus** column which will set the sample to be in the musical mode.

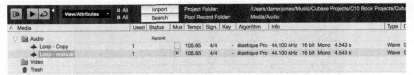

Here we see the sample in question on the top track, and another sample (the same sample, but a different audio file) which is not set to musical mode. Note that the top sample has a musical note at the top right, showing that it is in musical mode.

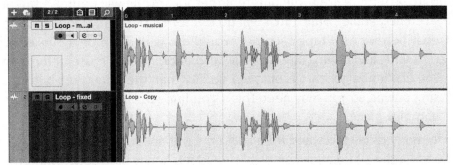

If we change the tempo of the project, the musical mode sample will be stretched to suit, while the other sample will not - it will play back at the original speed.

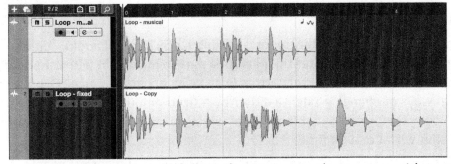

The musical mode sample will follow the tempo track, so even with extreme changes such as a tempo which alters within a bar (a ramp tempo event, see page 94 for details on the tempo track), it will stay perfectly in time, as seen below (note the ruler divisions get smaller as time passes with the increasing tempo).

Changing the Algorithm

In the past, there have been a number of problems with time stretching using Cubase, but Version 6 saw the introduction of the élastique Pro algorithm - this is the mathematical process which is used to time stretch samples, and has vastly improved the sound of time-stretched audio. There are different modes that can be used, and in addition it is possible to select the "Standard" modes which were used in previous versions of Cubase, which is sometimes desirable if you wanted to make use of the odd behaviour that they exhibited at extremes of time stretching.

To pick the algorithm for a given sample, you will need to double-click it to open up the Sample Editor - this is much like the key editor for MIDI, and the setting we want is at the top right of the window; you will see a box with the current Algorithm.

It will probably be set to **élastique Pro - Time**. You can select other modes here, and then hear how it changes the sound when it works.

The élastique Pro algorithm has three basic modes - Pro, Formant and Efficient, and within each there are three different methods; Time will optimise the timing of the stretched audio, while Pitch will do the same for pitch. Tape mode makes the stretch behave as a tape recorder would do, with pitch being linked to the time, so as you slow down, the pitch will also alter, making it useful for many effects. The efficient algorithm is of lower quality than the other two, but uses less processing power, so you may need this if you find you are overloading your CPU with a complex piece.

While in many cases the standard algorithms will not be desirable, the way that they degrade the audio at extremes of time stretch may be creatively interesting; such processing has become a feature of some styles of music, so it's important to be aware of its presence.

Changing Pitch

A common area to need adjustment is the pitch of a piece of audio – either when being used creatively (to alter the pitch of a part to make it fit with other parts or change its quality), or to correct errors in an original performance. Cubase offers several ways of changing pitch – either by a fixed amount that will apply to the entire selection, or using an 'envelope' which can be drawn, showing how the pitch shift will alter with time.

If you want to alter the pitch of an entire audio event, the easiest way to do this is using the information line at the top of the project window.

There are two parameters - **Transpose** and **Fine Tune** that will allow you to alter the pitch of the event - Transpose is set in semitones and Fine Tune in cents (100 of these make up a semitone). Depending on your monitor and project window size, they may not be visible, so you may need to right-click on the information bar and deselect some other parameters from the list that appears to allow you to access them.

Note that when you shift pitch this way, it is done in real time, and applied using the Algorithm that you have selected for that part; as with time stretching this can dramatically alter the sound of the audio, and some selection may be necessary to get the desired effect. Another way to do this is to select an event and then **SHIFT-right-click** and choose `Processes > Pitch Shift` and a new dialog box will appear. See page 579 for more on applying audio processes.

Transpose Mode

Here is the "fixed" pitch shift section, called Transpose – it offers a fixed amount of pitch shift which can be set using the controllers in the left-hand section (the Semitones is the most usual control, but the Cents slider offers the ability to tune to less than a semitone which can be handy for samples which are not at concert pitch).

There is a graphic representation at the top of your selected pitch shift values, and you can click on the keyboard to move the blue (destination) pitch. Bear in mind that this is only showing a relative change in pitch – Cubase does not detect the key of your original audio file. You can alter the Pitch Shift Base in the box on the right to make your calculations easier, but this makes no difference to the end result.

There are different Pitch Shift Modes available here; the right one will depend on the original audio material, so experimentation and experience will be the only way to learn here.

The edits that you make here are applied instantly, as Cubase uses Direct Offline Processing to apply the effect - depending on the processes that have already been applied to the event, you may see a list in the left-hand side of the window. For more information on this, see page 579.

Envelope Mode

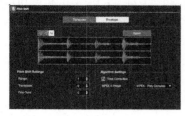

For more complex/creative use of pitch shift, Envelope mode offers the ability to change the amount of pitch shift applied as the sample progresses. To access it, click the **Envelope** button and you will see a screen like the one shown to the left. It has two main areas - settings (at the bottom) and the envelope at the top (your sample will be placed in the background of this to make editing easier).

The first setting to alter is Range in the Pitch Shift Settings section – this controls the range that edits made in the envelope section will have. For our example below it will be set to 2 semitones. The other controls in this section allow editing of points which are created in the envelope section – they can be altered graphically (the only way to alter their timing is graphically), but you can do so using these controls if you want to make precise changes.

Creation of points on the envelope is done graphically, by clicking on the envelope area, or grabbing an existing point and moving it. Points are deleted by dragging them outside of the white area. Here an end point has been created, and dragged up to the maximum. This would mean a progressive alteration in pitch from original at the start of the sample, rising to two semitones higher by the end. The transition would be smooth between the two extremes, as shown by the line.

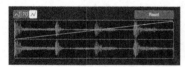

Here more points have been created - the sample will start at the original pitch, and move to nearly 2 semitones sharp before going down to nearly 2 semitones flat. It will then return to the original pitch. However, this movement may sound odd as there is a sudden change in pitch 'direction', because the line is a straight one between each point.

The **Curve Kind** buttons at the left allow for different smoothing modes, which mean the line can become a smooth curve, making for far more natural sounding results – this would sound much more like the sound of a 'real' performance than the example above, although both would have their places

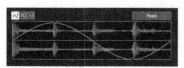

As with the Transpose mode, Cubase processes the audio instantly based on your settings.

Often when making these kind of edits, trial-and-error will be the only way to achieve a good end result – when fixing the pitch of an errant singer, getting the right amount of re-tuning (often just a few cents' worth) can take several attempts, but it is usually worth it in the end.

Timing

As music technology has become more prevalent, our perception of timing has changed greatly. Computers are capable of extremely accurate and mathematically precise timing, and our exposure to this has for the most part made us more demanding – things that were considered to be 'tight' in the past seem far less so now, so the bar has been raised in one area. To achieve this, editing of timing will sometimes be necessary. When working on a part which will be heard once it is important, but when a part will be repeated many times (such as a sample used as the basis for a track) it is imperative that it is correct.

Editing of timing can be as simple as moving an entire phrase 'forwards' or 'back' to change its feel – a small change in such timing of a part can transform how it feels, from being 'pushed' to 'laid back', and can take a mundane-sounding recording and make it fit perfectly.

However, most editing which involves re-timing is not as simple as that – the problem is that there may be continuous notes being played but the timing between them needs to be altered, meaning that if this was just done using the scissors, parts would overlap (if they needed to be moved together) or leave gaps (if they were moved apart). Using a combination of cutting and timestretching can allow a new part to be created that is perfectly in time but also doesn't have gaps or jumps.

After this section we will see how to do this using Cubase's AudioWarp feature, but first we will see how to do this using the tools in the project window; while AudioWarp is useful, it is good to be able to do it using the scissors and time stretch as this then gives the ability to fix errors by replacing sections seamlessly. In addition, you may use software that doesn't have AudioWarp, so being able to do it (and understand how it works) with simpler tools is always a good basis to start from.

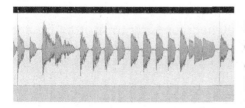

Here is the original guitar part. It loops OK overall, but it has been played a little inaccurately – some of it is in time, some is a little late and some is a little early.

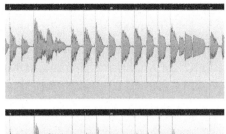

The first thing to do is to cut the part in the places that we know should fall on the beat or off-beat (listening to it will tell us where these are).

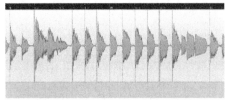

Next, these sections are placed where they should be – note that some leave gaps while others overlap. The part sounds in time now, but there are gaps which need to be bridged.

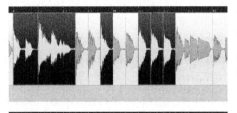

To rectify this, the sections need to be timestretched. For sections where a gap is left, it is easy to grab hold of it and timestretch it to fill the gap (the ones completed are shown highlighted here)

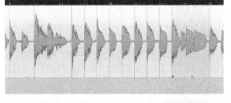

The end section is different - it is too long, and is overlapped by the next bar, so it's not possible to grab the end and timestretch it.

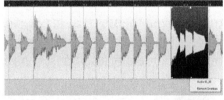

To do that, we need to move it to the front, by clicking on the triangle at the bottom, and selecting it from the menu that appears...

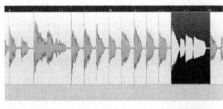

... to move it to the 'top', over the other audio segments. Now it can be timestretched to shorten it and fit into the gap properly.

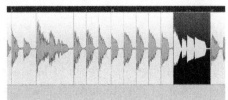

As seen here, the end section has now been timestretched correctly to fit it all in, and the entire section plays correctly.

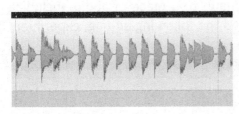 Finally, select all the events that have been edited, right-click and select **Audio > Bounce Selection** and when asked, select Replace to replace these events with a single audio event, making further editing much easier.

Care at each point is needed when making these kinds of edits – regular checking back to the metronome or another part to match to is important. Bear in mind that any timestretching always has an impact on sound quality, and that algorithm chosen (as seen on page 497) will be important, depending on the type of audio you are working on.

Using AudioWarp

The example above involved cutting, positioning and timestretching audio to create a seamless edit of a guitar part. AudioWarp allows this editing to be done within the audio editor or the project window, and without using several different tools. We will see how to do the same edit as shown above but using AudioWarp, in the audio editor. Use in the Project Window is covered on page 506.

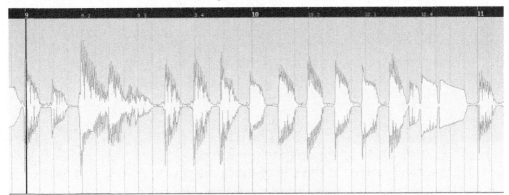

Here is the guitar part seen in the previous example, but opened in the audio editor.

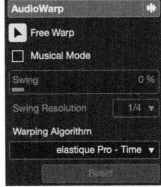

Here is the AudioWarp section, seen on the left of the audio editor window. We will be using free warp, which will allow us to insert tabs (think of them as handles that we can place to stretch the audio with), and also to reset all the warping that has been done.

Musical mode allows quick changes to be made to a piece of audio, including applying swing to it - once you have mastered the following editing, experiment with it to see how powerful it can be.

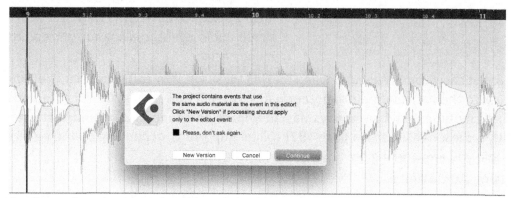

The first tab to be placed will be at the beginning (to fix this in time and stop it from moving). Doing so brings up a dialog box warning of shared audio - click **New Version** as then only this part will be altered.

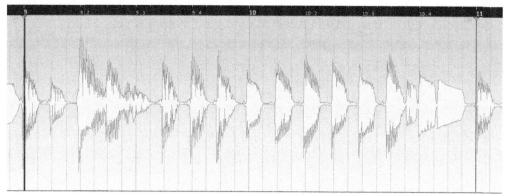

Next, another tab is placed at the end of the audio segment - this is to fix the end in time. Now we have set the points we want to keep static...

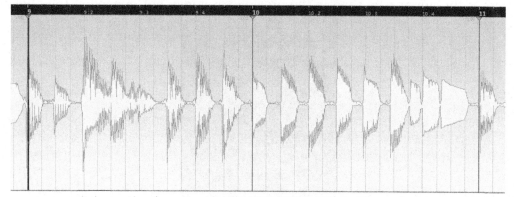

... we can click on the (previously early) audio at bar 10, and move it back in time, so that it happens at exactly the right time. Cubase takes care of all the timestretching needed to achieve this without any other tools.

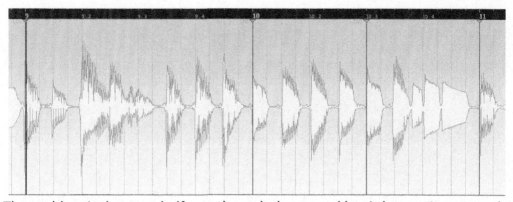

The problem is that now half way through the second bar is happening too early, so it is clicked and dragged later to correct this.

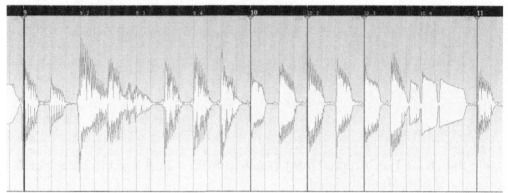

This creates smaller timing issues at the second beat (which is seen corrected here - it had become too late)...

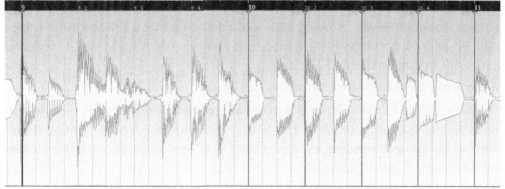

... and also at the fourth beat, which was also too late. Now the entire second bar is perfectly in time.

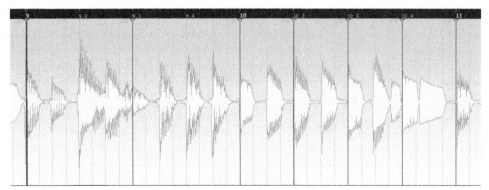

A similar process is now performed on the first bar - beat 3 is moved into time...

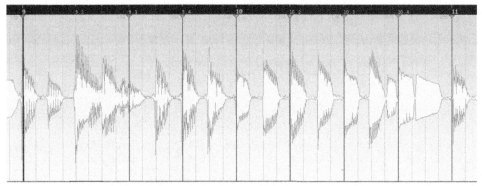

... and then beat 4 is corrected from its new position. Beat 2 in this case sounded correct so it was left unchanged.

As is clear to see, using AudioWarp greatly increases the speed at which this kind of editing can be performed - it removes a great deal of the work needed to correct any timing errors and 'fill the gaps' between such samples. Both techniques are important, however, as being able to do it the first way allows you to understand what is going on, and also to use these techniques to patch audio together that didn't belong in the first place.

AudioWarp in the Project Window

It is also possible to use AudioWarp in the project window. This can be solely for convenience, but can also allow the warping of multiple tracks. To use Audio-Warp in the project window, click and hold the Time Warp Tool on the toolbar, and a pop-up menu will appear:

Select Free Warp, and the toolbar icon will change:

You will need to zoom in to a suitable scale for the tool to work. Click on the audio event that you want to warp, and you should see a warp marker appear, with 1.00 above it, showing that it is not currently altering the speed of the audio:

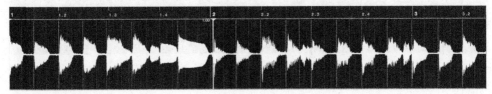

Clicking and dragging the warp marker to a new location will warp the audio, and show the speed change that is in action:

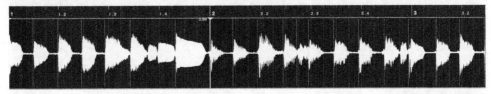

Creating and dragging subsequent markers works in the same way, although you can click and drag them to their new locations in a single action.

AudioWarp on Multiple Tracks

In the Project Window

It is possible to perform the same warping on multiple events at the same time - this is often useful when you have tracks which are in time with each other, but not other elements in a project. To perform the warp, firstly select the events. This can be done using the Free Warp tool by clicking the first event, and then **SHIFT + Clicking** on other events to warp, so they are selected at the same time:

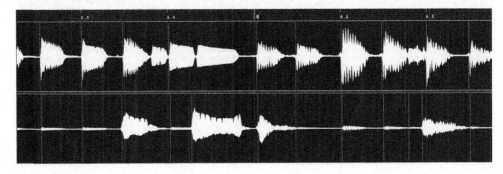

Next, click on one of the events - just as with the previous example in the project window. Warp Markers will appear in the same location on all the selected events:

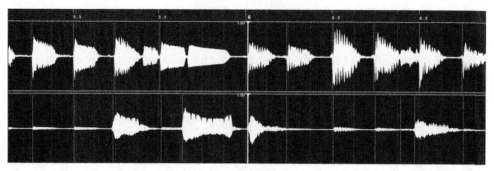

Now, perform the warping as needed. Both events will be warped in the same way.

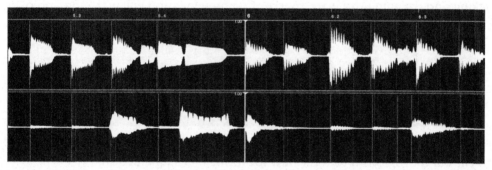

Note that it is possible to perform additional warping on a single event. Deselect all events (by clicking on empty space in the project window), and then warp the desired event as normal. In the example below, another marker has been added to fix the timing of the bottom track. (Both have been selected so the markers can be clearly seen).

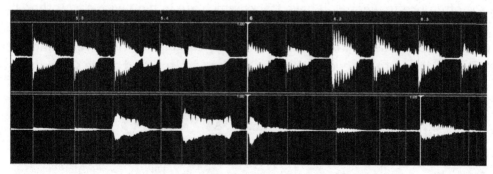

In The Audio Editor

It is also possible to perform AudioWarp editing on multiple tracks while using the sample editor. To do this, select the desired events, and then open them in the sample editor `Audio > Open Sample Editor`, and you will see that multiple events are open in the editor:

The other samples will be seen faintly in the waveform display, 'behind' the first sample data. This may be more or less clear, depending on the audio data in question.

Now, select the Free Warp tool, and perform the edits as seen previously. All the opened events will be warped:

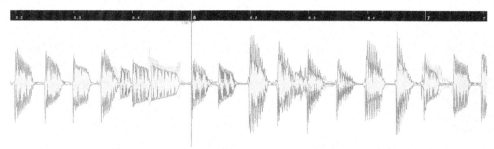

This can be confirmed by selecting the Free Warp tool in the project window and selecting the warped events:

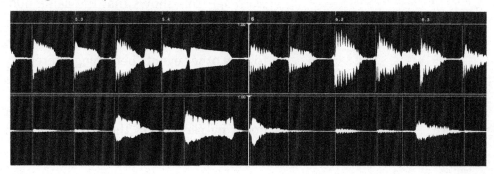

VariAudio **PRO**

One of the most important features of Cubase since version 6 is VariAudio. It provides the ability to analyse a piece of monophonic audio, and then alter the pitch of the notes and even vibrato within each note. While it can be a complex tool to use, the basics will allow you to perform edits which would have been difficult if not impossible manually.

The audio event has been opened in the audio editor, and set to the VariAudio tab on the left-hand side. At the moment nothing has been analysed or altered, but if you click the pitch and warp tool on the left...

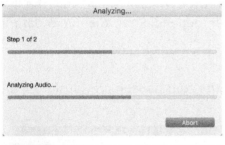

The audio will be analysed by Cubase to work out where each note is, and the pitch of it, along with any inflection within each note (bending of notes, being out of tune and vibrato are all detected by it). Once this has finished...

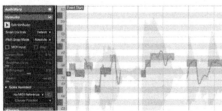

You will see the individual notes in the editor, along with a line representing the momentary pitch. Note that vibrato appears as a wobble in the line (seen in the highest note in the middle of this section).

If you try to move any of the notes (or make any other edits) then you may get this warning - this shows that the same audio material is used elsewhere in the project. You will normally want to click **New Version** to stop other events becoming altered.

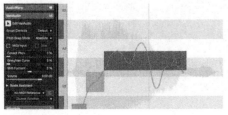

Now VariAudio is active, and you can select notes by clicking on them (note that the highest note has been selected).

Here the pitch of the highest note has been changed, by selecting it and moving it down with the cursor keys - it can also be dragged. Playing this back alters the audio to reflect this change and can be seamless depending on the change and the audio.

Correct Pitch - the slider on the left can correct the pitch; the original was sharp and oving the slider over progressively alters it to reflect the 'correct' pitch.

Straighten Curve - this slider will flatten the black line, reducing the intonation within the note in question. Here it has been set to 50% and the vibrato is noticeably reduced.

Here straighten has been set to 100%. The note is devoid of any intonation or vibrato and sounds quite robotic. Doing this with all the notes (**CTRL + A** beforehand) is a quick way to simulate over-autotuned audio.

Handles View. By default there are four handles on a segment. The top and bottom ones control the pitch curve and quantize settings (as do the sliders seen earlier), but the left one is for...

Warp Start. This control allows quick Audio Warp editing of the segments - note how the waveform of the previous note is now stretched out, and the triangles at the top showing where warp tabs now exist.

Warp End. As with Warp Start, the end handle quickly enters a warp tab. Note that audio that is not assigned a pitch (after the note) is still stretched when using this control.

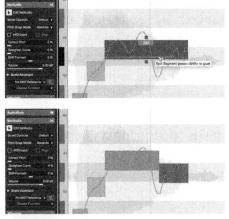

Split Segment. Hovering the mouse over the line at the bottom of the segment will allow splitting of the segment into smaller sections, allowing more detailed control.

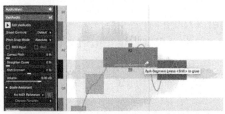

Two Segments. The original segment is now split into two, allowing control of each part individually - note that Cubase now sees the end as a different pitch than when it was part of the main note.

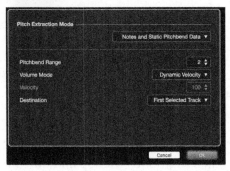

Glue Segment. To glue any segments together (even those that were always separate), hold down **SHIFT** while hovering over the line at the bottom, and then click to glue the following segment.

Extract MIDI. Clicking `Choose Function` at the bottom of the VariAudio section will give options to create a MIDI part from the VariAudio data, which can be useful for providing accompaniment or scoring, depending on the audio in question.

VariAudio is extremely powerful, but it is a complex function with many options to explore. In addition as it relies on such a complex analysis of the audio, it can be quite demanding for a computer to analyse long sections. The detection is not perfect, and depends on a number of factors, so you may well need to rely on a number of methods to achieve your desired result.

Using Snap

You will already be familiar with using 'snap', but it has a number of different modes. They can be selected using the drop-down menu next to the button that turns snap on and off.

Grid Mode

This is the default mode - it allows you to move your events and parts to accurate locations using musical units – placing parts at bar, beat or quantize-setting based grid positions. This is extremely useful when working with sequenced music, allowing you to quickly place events at musically-coherent locations.

Event Mode

Changing snap to 'events' means that any edits that you do will snap to other events; this can be very useful for matching different events together (where they are not easily located using musical units), and also when editing audio to make one event lead directly into another. The front edge of the event/part that you are moving will snap to other events, and this is often the beginning or end of another part.

Cursor Mode

This mode can be extremely useful for making detailed edits – events will snap to the cursor, and placement of the cursor can be done extremely accurately:

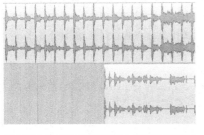

Here are two audio parts, and we want to synchronise the start of the second with a specific point (a bass drum beat) in the first. The first thing to do is play the first part and hit STOP when the sync point occurs...

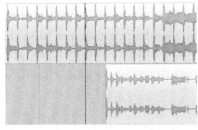

... which will give us a fairly accurate position for the sync point, but next we need to zoom in...

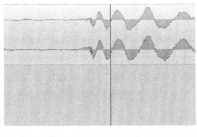

... and it's clear that although it is close, it is not perfectly in time...

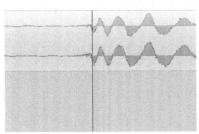

... so we move the play position line to the exact point at which the sync occurs. Once snap is turned on and set to events ...

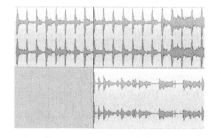

... it's quick and easy to zoom out and move the second part to align perfectly with that point.

Shuffle Mode

Shuffle Mode can be extremely useful in some situations – it only allows events to be placed where there is another event to the left to place it next to – it's as if gravity is pulling sideways and the events need to be supported by another one. This can make it extremely quick when editing events together (such as compiling a number of different takes) which need to be butted against each other.

Audio Editing Examples

Next there follows a number of practical examples on how editing techniques can be used in a variety of situations.

Fixing a timing error

There are often times when a recording can be compromised by a small timing error – often a mis-played drum beat or 'lumpy' fill. As has been said before, re-recording is usually the best way forward, but sometimes this isn't possible, and editing is needed instead. First we will see how to perform a real-world fix using timestretching alone, and then using AudioWarp

Using Time Stretch

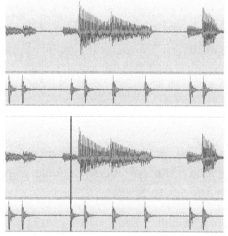

Here is the original part, a bass part where the player has played too early. For comparison below is the bass drum, which is in time, giving us an excellent reference point to use in our edits.

The play position pointer is set to where the bass drum is played - the bass guitar above is clearly too early.

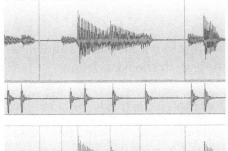

Initial cuts are made after the note that happens before the mistake, and just before the note that follows.

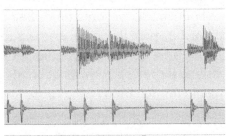

Next, cuts are made at the start of each note in the phrase - there are four, which should match in timing with the bass drum notes below.

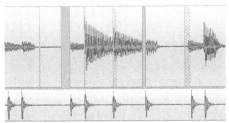

With snap turned off, the notes are moved to the correct time; note that this creates gaps in some areas, and overlaps in others - these will be fixed next, but getting the timing right needs to happen first.

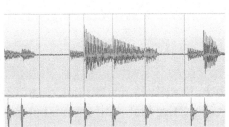

The selection tool is set to `Sizing Applies Timestretch` and snap turned on and set to events. The gaps are filled by timestretching the audio that happens **before** them - the silence before the first note becomes longer, etc. This retains the timing of the notes.

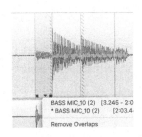

Events which overlap will often be placed 'behind' the following ones, and they will need to be moved 'forward' to allow them to be timestretched. This is done by clicking the triangle at the bottom of the event in question and picking its name from the menu.

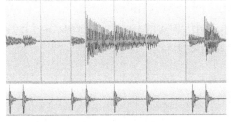

Now it is possible to timestretch the overlapping notes to the correct length, shortening them so they end where the next event starts.

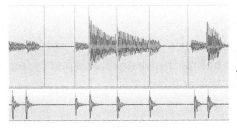

Here is the finished edit, which sounds perfectly in time with the bass drum.

This method of editing is perfectly valid, and has been in use for some time. Being able to do edits this way is an important skill to master, even if you have access to AudioWarp. The reason for this is that you will then be able to edit audio parts which did not belong together to work seamlessly as if they had always been that way. However, if you are making a simple change in timing, then AudioWarp may be the quicker option, as shown next.

Using AudioWarp   # ARTIST PRO

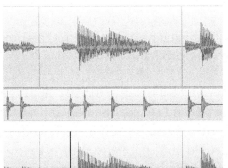

Here is the original part again - above is the bass which has been played too early, below is the bass drum part which is in time and makes an excellent reference point.

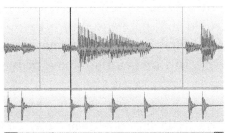

Once more, the play position has been set to show where the first note should happen - it's currently too late...

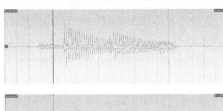

... something which can be seen clearly in the audio editor window. Selecting the Free Warp tool on the left, and clicking and dragging the note...

... will soon fix this. However, this has an impact on the placement of all the following audio which will be timestretched as a result, leading to...

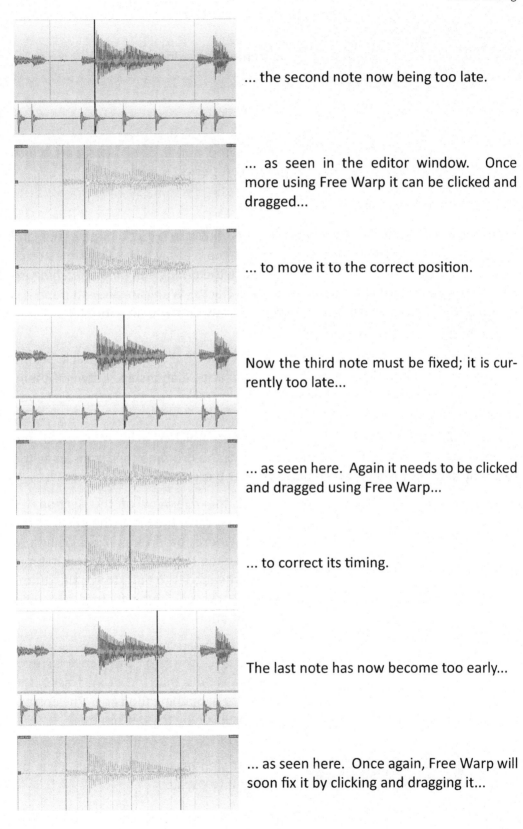

... the second note now being too late.

... as seen in the editor window. Once more using Free Warp it can be clicked and dragged...

... to move it to the correct position.

Now the third note must be fixed; it is currently too late...

... as seen here. Again it needs to be clicked and dragged using Free Warp...

... to correct its timing.

The last note has now become too early...

... as seen here. Once again, Free Warp will soon fix it by clicking and dragging it...

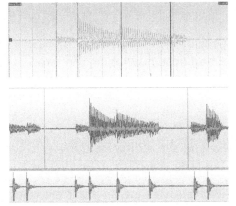

... to the correct location.

Here is the entire, fixed bass part which now plays perfectly in time.

Both methods are valid, but generally using AudioWarp is quicker and easier, and allows correction and alteration to occur much more easily than using Timestretch alone. The next example will show how to use the timing and time-stretching examples seen previously on a number of drum tracks. With care and attention it is possible to fix errors which would have previously wrecked an entire take.

Fixing Multitrack Drum Tracks

The following example uses Cubase's feature which allows all the tracks within a folder to be edited while maintaining the phase relationships between them. This is extremely important when editing multi-tracked parts as otherwise audible problems could occur.

The example below has a number of instruments which have been recorded, and the drum track is out of time at the beginning; the drummer has come in a little too early and has taken a couple of bars to get back into time.

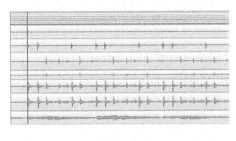

Here is the overview of the section we want to edit. On the left is the entry of the drums, where the drummer is playing too early. On the right, the drummer is in time. What is needed is to timestretch the drums to move the beginning to the right by a small amount

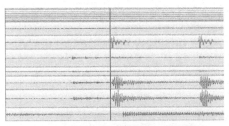

Here is a close-up of the above screen, showing clearly that the drum tracks (the top 6) are happening too early. The correct timing is given by the bottom track.

The first step here will be to turn **Snap** on and set it to **Cursor**.

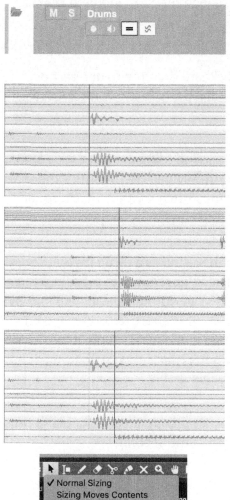

Here is the key - Group Editing must be turned on for the folder track that contains the drums. Without this there could be phase errors when multiple tracks are timestretched.

Here the cursor has been accurately set to the beginning of the drum part, and the tracks have been cut. This is done by cutting on the folder track, rather than the individual tracks.

A cut is now performed at the point where the drums are back in time - this is done to limit the scope of the timestretching; if it wasn't done then the entire track would be altered in timing.

Back at the beginning, we can see the difference in timing between the current drum beginning (the cuts made to the left), and the desired entry timing (with the cursor, to the right).

Next, we will need to timestretch the audio, so click and hold on the arrow on the toolbar, and select **Sizing Applies Time Stretch**

The part on the folder track is timestretched to the cursor point, and all the audio tracks are edited accordingly. This is all done with the correct phase relationship because of the edit group setting being active.

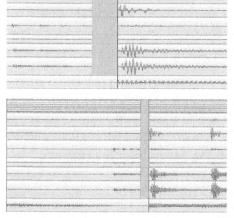

The final issue is the small snare roll which happens before the drums start playing the pattern. This doesn't need to be timestretched, but does need to be moved into the correct place.

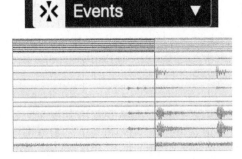

Firstly, change the **Snap** mode to **Events**.

Now, click and drag the folder part over, to move all the parts to the correct location.

With intelligent use, placing tracks inside a folder and using the Edit Group setting can save a great deal of time, but more importantly will try to ensure there are no phase issues resulting from edits such as timestretch - without it, there can be audible artefacts from this sort of processing.

Replacing a section

Most pop songs feature a fair amount of repetition, and as a result it's quite possible that one chorus or section/player in it will have 'good' and 'bad' performances of the same material. Being able to use the best performance can help improve a recording and make it sound more consistent. If the recording has been done using a click track (or the tempi of the sections is identical for any other reason) then it's a straightforward job to remove one and replace it with another. If not, editing and timestretching will be needed to achieve this.

Without timestretch

Here is a straightforward example where the song contained a double chorus. The first version the singer did was far better than the second.

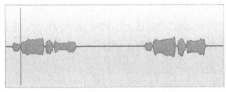

Here is the original vocal track, with the first (wanted) chorus, and then the second, inferior version.

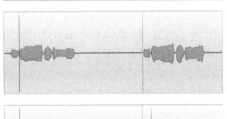

The first step is to cut accurately where the second chorus starts - this provides a timing reference.

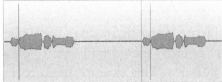

Next, the first section is duplicated, has its beginning trimmed, and with snap set to events is placed to start where it should do. It sounds far better than the original.

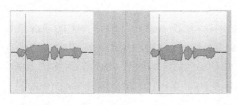

The final step is to trim and fade the parts as normal, removing the possibility of any unwanted noises being heard - particularly as repeating them would be highly unusual.

With timestretch

Sometimes a song will change tempo, and that means that a straight replacement is not possible - it will drift out of time, so will need to be timestretched to get the replaced version to fit with the music.

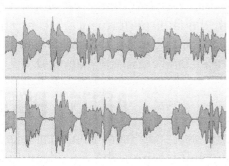

This example shows two tracks throughout - the top one is the original take (for reference), the bottom will be the edited version. This is easily done by duplicating the original track - often useful for this kind of work. Here we can see the bottom track has the chorus copied from earlier in the song, and it starts out in time, but soon drifts off as the song is quicker here.

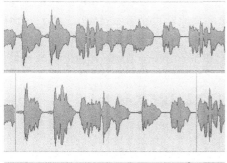

The chorus has been cut accurately (with snap off) to the start of the verse that followed it. This gives us an accurate point of reference for the work performed in the following stages.

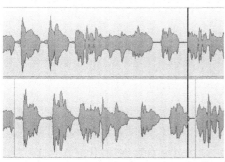

Next, the play position is set accurately to the start of the verse on the original track. This is the length we want the new section to be, and the difference is clearly visible on the bottom track. To set this accurately you may need to zoom in further than the screenshots here.

Snap needs to be turned on for the next stage, and set to Cursor - this will allow us to use the play position as an accurate reference for the edit we are performing.

The selection tool needs to be set to `Sizing Applies Timestretch` from the drop-down menu that appears when you click and hold on it in the tool bar (or repeatedly press 1)

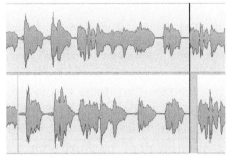

Now the chorus is timestretched by clicking and dragging on the right-hand bottom corner, and it is set to the correct length. Playing it back (without the original track) now sounds correct as the better version is in time with the later performance. To finish the edit, the following verse would need to be reinstated, and crossfading applied.

Comping

ARTIST PRO

Comping is taking a number of recordings of the same part (such as a vocal take) and then creating the best version from these different takes. It's a really useful skill to have and often will allow you to make the best of a recording session; it's rare for singers to perform at their best all the way through a single take, often they will prefer one part from one take and others from different ones. On the next page we see a vocal which has been recorded using cycle mode to create three takes across three lanes.

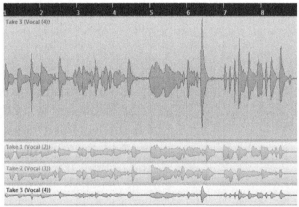

At the moment the version that will be heard is the third take in its entirety, and the waveform shown on the main "Vocal" track reflects this. It is possible to cut the takes up into separate sections and then selectively mute them using the Scissors and Mute tools (and without the comp tool, this is the only way of doing this), but the Comp Tool (seen on the right) makes the job easier. If you are using a version of Cubase without the comp tool, you will still be able to do this, but you will have to switch tools whenever applicable.

In our example, the first thing needed is to replace bars 5-7 - the third take version of this was not good, so the comp tool was selected, and a cut made at bar 5 - this is done by holding down ALT while clicking on one of the takes.

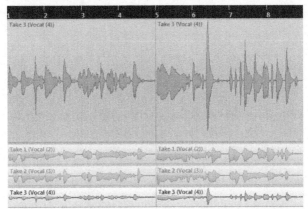

The same was done at bar 7.

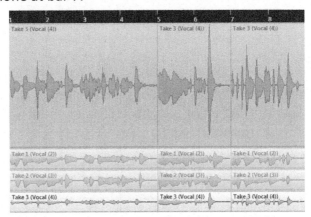

The comp tool will allow us to pick the take we want to hear - rather than having to mute one take and unmute another, it does this for us. Clicking on take 2 between bars 5-7 lets us hear this, and note that this change is reflected in the waveform on the main track.

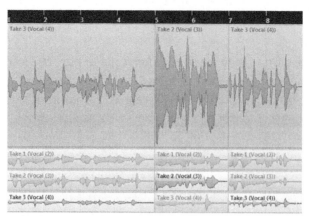

At bar 7, take 1 is the one we want, but the note starts slightly before the beat, so is being cut off.

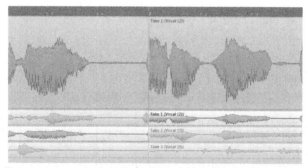

The comp tool allows us to alter the border between sections of a comp quickly and easily. With snap turned off, it's simply a case of clicking and dragging the border between the two to suit the audio.

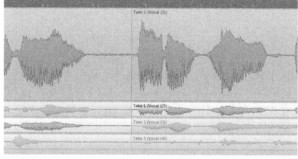

Here is the final comp. It can be left as it is, in multiple lanes, but often it is desirable to turn it into a single audio file. There are a number of ways to do this, but picking **Audio > Bounce Selection** from the right-click menu will produce a single audio file from your comp.

Fixing Pitch Errors on a Vocal

It is not uncommon for singers to mis-pitch notes, particularly during more demanding and longer sections. There are two ways to approach this - all versions of Cubase will allow a basic edit to take place, but the full version also allows a much more flexible solution. First we will look at the 'basic' editing technique.

Using Pitch Shift

This makes use of the techniques outlined in this chapter on page 498.

A Simple Example

Here is the vocal part that needs editing. The last note but one is a bit flat. Fortunately it is isolated with a gap before and after so...

... it is straightforward to cut either side of it to allow it to be altered.

Next it must be selected, and then in the info line at the top of the project window...

... the pitch is altered to correct it; it was a bit flat so a 20 cent sharpening makes it in tune.

A more complex example

The above example was simple as there was a gap before and after the note, and the whole thing was out of tune. When a note is a part of a longer continuous sound (such as part of a word or phrase), then a different technique is usually needed.

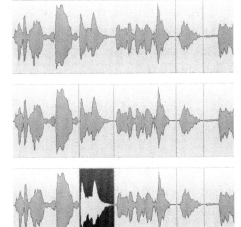

Here is the part - we can see the fix from the previous section, but there is a word that needs to have a syllable or two flattened...

... so it is cut out as before to isolate it...

... selected, and then from the right-click menu, **Processes > Pitch Shift** is selected. The Envelope tab from the new window is selected to...

... bring up the dialogue box as seen previously on page 499. This will give access to smoothly-altering pitch shift rather than applying a single change to the entire section.

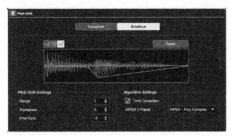

With some experimentation (and auditioning by playing this section), this is the curve that was found to correct the sharpness in the phrase. Exiting the window will leave the changes applied.

Most examples will need a combination of the two approaches to achieve all the desired editing.

Using VariAudio

PRO

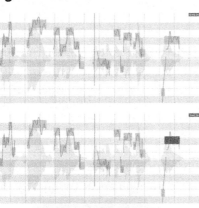

Here is the original vocal part - it is the same one seen in the previous section. It has been analysed to allow VariAudio to work (see page 510), and we can see the notes and the inflection within them.

Here the note we want to work on is selected - it is the last note in the phrase, and a keyboard is shown representing the pitch on the vertical axis. Cubase has analysed it as being slightly sharp:

From the info line, here is the analysis - it is 10% sharp.

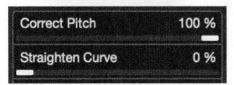

To fix this, **Correct Pitch** can be used (or the note can be clicked on and dragged to the new pitch destination).

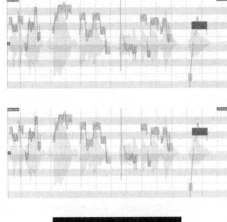

Here Quantize Pitch has been used to move the note to the 'correct' pitch, but listening to it reveals that it doesn't sound right; the analysis may be incorrect or other factors may lead to this.

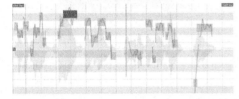

By clicking on the note and using **CTRL** and the up/down cursor keys, it is possible to move the note by a single cent (%) at a time. Listening and altering it led to it being slightly sharp of the original pitch, as seen to the left...

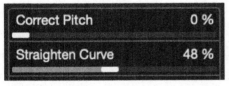

... and confirmed in the info line.

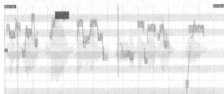

The next note to attend to is the highest note in the section - it is selected here, but needs different treatment as the note goes sharp at the end, so the inflection within it needs to be altered.

Firstly the inflection is decreased using **Straighten Curve**, in this case by around 50%. The effects of this can be seen...

... here as the line is less extreme, and the note sounds more in tune. The next problem is the ending which is still too sharp.

To perform the next change, the VariAudio Smart Controls need to be set to 'All', giving access to more advanced features. This is set in the VariAudio menu in the left zone, as seen here.

The note seen previously has been zoomed in on to see in more detail the inflection of pitch throughout - the ending is too sharp, and needs to be edited seamlessly.

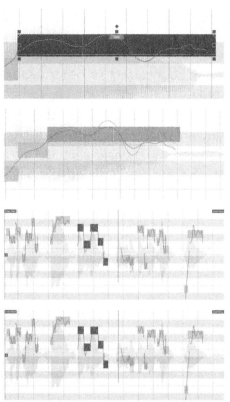

Hovering over the note shows the full range of handles available. The one needed in this case is at the top right - **Tilt**. Clicking and dragging it will alter the inflection within the note.

This is the edit in progress, showing the original inflection, and also the new end result. The line is lower at the end (as it is being tilted down), and it now sounds in tune.

The last change to make here is the next group of notes after the high note - they are all a little sharp, so the first step is to select them (click and drag round them with the mouse)...

... and then to move them down, again in this case using the keyboard with **CTRL +** ↓ until they sound in tune.

Removing Breaths

Some singers breathe in quite audibly before a phrase; depending on your taste and the situation this may not be appropriate. While it is possible to remove such sounds with gating (and is always worth a try), there may be other, desirable parts of the performance which are quieter so gating will not be possible. In this case, cutting and removing these sections is fairly quick, and means each section can be taken on its own merit, making for a far more musical performance.

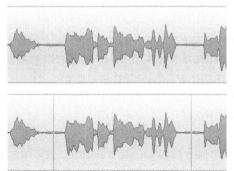

Here is the original vocal part. The quiet sections are not silent - there are breaths taken which are distracting from the nature of the piece.

To start, each one is cut; it is possible to cut more accurately (and cut on each side of the breath) but as trimming will be needed, it is quicker to just cut in the middle and ...

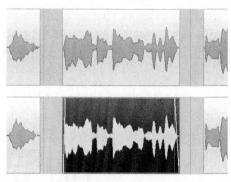

... then trim each part suitably - zooming in may be needed to get these edits done accurately, but more important ...

... is that each part has suitable fades applied - quick fade in and a longer fade out. One part is highlighted for clarity, but all have them applied.

Changing What Someone has Said

Creative use of a pre-existing recording of a speech or commentary is quite a common technique today; it's possible to go from a simple replacement of a word to a complete change in what has been said - a technique which can totally transform the meaning of a speech. The example below will take an interview and change it from mentioning a group of people at the end of a sentence to a specific person, changing the meaning greatly; both components were taken from the same interview so they sound the same.

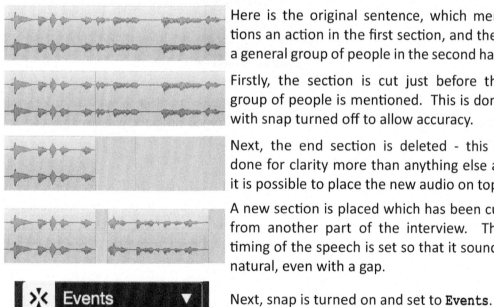

Here is the original sentence, which mentions an action in the first section, and then a general group of people in the second half.

Firstly, the section is cut just before the group of people is mentioned. This is done with snap turned off to allow accuracy.

Next, the end section is deleted - this is done for clarity more than anything else as it is possible to place the new audio on top.

A new section is placed which has been cut from another part of the interview. The timing of the speech is set so that it sounds natural, even with a gap.

Next, snap is turned on and set to **Events**.

Now the gap can be accurately trimmed - it is covered with 'silence' from before the second section, but sounds slightly unnatural as there is a sudden change of level.

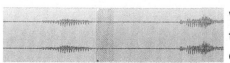

While zoomed in, the second section is trimmed to overlap the first, over a period of about half a second.

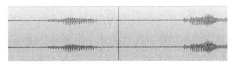

Pressing **X** will create a crossfade between the two samples, smoothing the transition and making it sound as if it had never been edited.

In this example there was silence before the second sample; if there isn't then finding an area where there is 'silence' and splicing that in will do - this will just involve crossfading the end and the beginning of the section you have inserted.

Audio Alignment

There are often situations where it is important to align the timing of different audio takes. As technology has improved, the method of achieving this has changed; originally it would have been to re-record the second take, then editing made it progressively easier to achieve perfect timing. Audio Alignment takes this a step further, and automates the process. Clicking the button opens the Audio Alignment Panel.

Here we see the panel. The **Reference** is the audio clip whose timing we want to follow, and the **Targets** are the file(s) that we want to alter to suit the Reference. Adding them is as simple as selecting an audio recording and clicking the relevant + button.

Audio Alignment Example

Here we see two clips of nominally the same material. The desired result is to make the bottom clip in time with the top one. This could be done manually, using Audio Warp (as seen on page 503), but this can be long-winded, and if there are multiple tracks to align, it can be extremely time-consuming. To achieve this in Audio Alignment, the process is quick and simple.

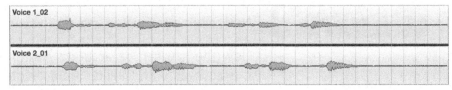

First, the desired Reference clip is selected.

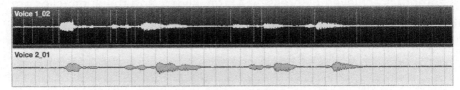

+ is then clicked in the Reference section of the Audio Alignment window. The clip is now shown here, with a waveform representation below.

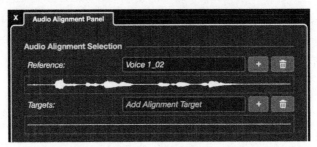

The same process is repeated for the Target clip - selecting it in the project window...

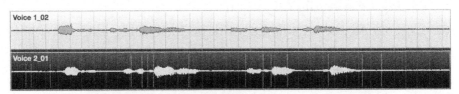

... and then clicking + in the Targets section:

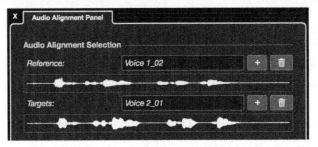

The alignment is achieved by pressing **Align Audio,** and the audio clips are now aligned.

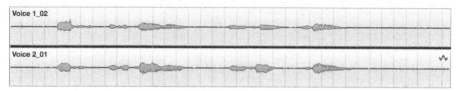

Note that the Target clip now has an icon at the top right to show that Audio Warp is active on it, and opening up the part in the audio editor shows the warp tabs that are in place.

Manual Editing After Audio Alignment

Sometimes Audio Alignment will not work perfectly - the audio may not align well, with some areas which are not timed correctly. An example is shown below - the first half and end are in time, but the third phrase is too early.

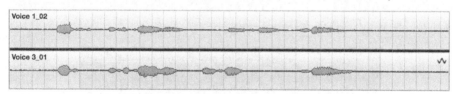

Because Audio Alignment uses warp tabs, it's easy to correct any issues that have occurred. The techniques are the same as those used with Audio Warp on page 503, but we will take a look at this specific example. Below we can see the two clips, and the cursor is currently placed where the third phrase should begin - note that the bottom clip is much too early.

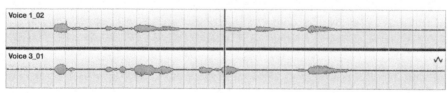

Keeping the cursor in place as a timing reference, the clip is opened in the audio editor:

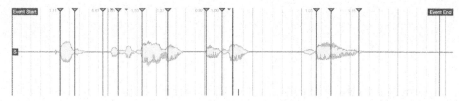

It's clear to see that there are two tabs for the phrase we are interested in, and both are before the cursor. We will move the second one to be much later than it currently is...

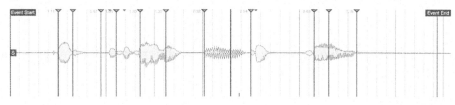

... to make room for the first one to be moved to where it should be.

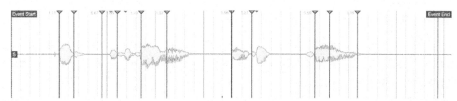

Back in the project window, we can now see that the beginning of the phrase is aligned correctly.

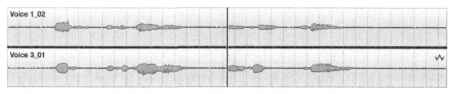

With the cursor now moved to the correct location for the second part of this phrase, it's also easy to see that the second phrase is currently too early.

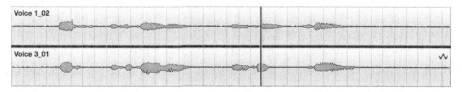

Looking at this in the audio editor shows the warp tab that's before the cursor...

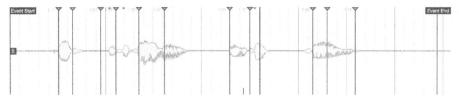

... can be dragged to the right to put it in the correct place:

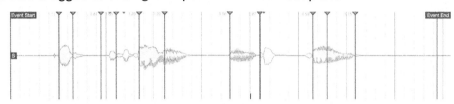

In the project window, we can now see the entire phrase is in time, and sounds accurately aligned.

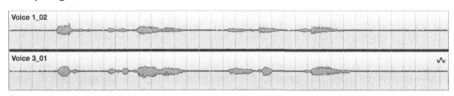

Alignment Precision

It's possible to select the amount of alignment to achieve a 'looser' feel, in a similar manner to Soft Quantize for MIDI (see page 84). Here we see a Reference (top) clip and a Target clip...

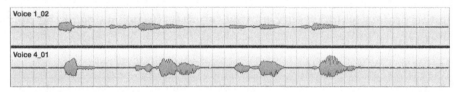

... being aligned with a precision of 50%:

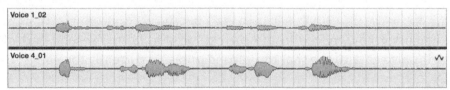

Note that the timing is improved, but it is not completely aligned. As with soft quantize, it's possible to press **Align Audio** multiple times, and each time the target will move closer to the reference by the set amount, as seen on the next page:

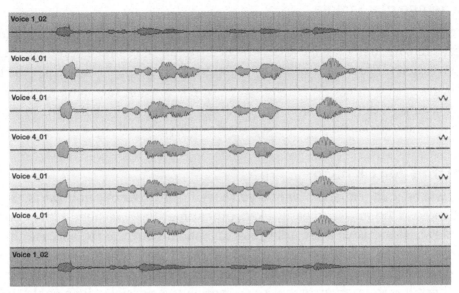

The reference clip is shown as a darker track here, at bottom and top to make visual assessment of the movement easier.

Multiple Clips

It's possible to align multiple clips at once - simply select more than one clip in the project window before clicking the + button to add the Target clips. After doing so, the **Targets** section will have a triangle in it...

... which summons the menu to allow viewing of a given clip. Clicking **Align Audio** will align all the selected clips at once.

Exercises

Create a Loop

One of the most common tasks to perform is to make a loop from an existing recording. Doing this accurately is made easier by Cubase's graphic display as in many cases it is easy to see where the beat begins (often as it is marked by the attack from a bass drum), but it is still a task worth practicing particularly with more challenging material where the waveform may not be as clear (when there are other instruments present the bass drum may be less visible). Import a piece of music which you want to loop, and follow the procedure on page 492. Do this on a number of different pieces of music to give you a variety of audio to practice on.

Find the Tempo of a sample

Sometimes you will need to find the tempo of a loop. To do this, firstly ensure that your loop really does loop correctly, and then use the procedure on page 494 to find the tempo of a sample, using the Time Warp tool.

Alter Tempo of a Sample

There are two main ways to alter the tempo of a sample. The first is using Timestretch, as seen on page 495. Practice this on the sample you have looped above. Note that you may need to experiment with the algorithm to get the best sound, as seen on page 497. The other way is making the sample follow Cubase's tempo, as seen on page 496. Both are valid in their own right, so ensure you know how to use both for maximum flexibility.

Find Errors and Fix Them

There will be many situations where you have errors to fix on audio parts. Sometimes they will be small and easily fixed, other times they will need a lot of editing to achieve. If you have a recording already, find an error to fix, and use the appropriate techniques shown on page 514 onwards to fix them. Remember that there is usually more than one way to fix any given error, and often re-recording is the best way to fix an error, but this is not always possible. Being able to fix a wide range of errors in audio recordings is a hugely useful skill and will only come with practice, so find as many errors as you can and improve your skills.

Summary

Learning to edit audio is an important skill for anyone working with it in Cubase - even if you are solely working with it as a recording tool and not intending to make any changes via editing, there will be situations where a performance can be improved by editing it, even if only to remove noises which should not be present. However, many modern music styles are based on the techniques covered in this chapter, and mastering them will give you access to a great deal more creativity and the ability to fix issues in a performance which would previously have meant it would be unusable. This is not to make it a replacement for a good performance, but many excellent recordings have been compromised by small errors which could be repaired seamlessly to save them, and many 'classic' pieces of music relied on similar techniques, albeit using magnetic tape, a splicing block, a razor blade and sticky tape to achieve edits which can now be done in seconds. As with everything, practice will make perfect, and allow you to see more possibilities when presented with a situation that requires these skills.

Effects

Effects are a huge part of the recording and mixing process. They can take a mundane performance and make it much more interesting, they can create interest and set up a mood or theme, they can make parts fit together than otherwise wouldn't do, and generally give us a lot more scope for making an interesting and creative recording, even if the listener doesn't actively know that's what's happened.

Send and Insert Effects

The way in which audio is passed through an effect is extremely important – not only in terms of the sound of the effect, but in today's computer-based recording systems it can also dramatically affect the number of effects which are available. There are two ways of passing signals through an effect unit – Send and Insert (sometimes called different names by different manufacturers, but these are the 'proper' names for them).

Send Effects

With a send effect, there is only one effect unit, and it is shared by as many channels as is desired. What happens is that a certain amount of each channel's signal can be passed into the effect, with all of the audio signals to be passed through the effect unit being mixed together before passing into it.

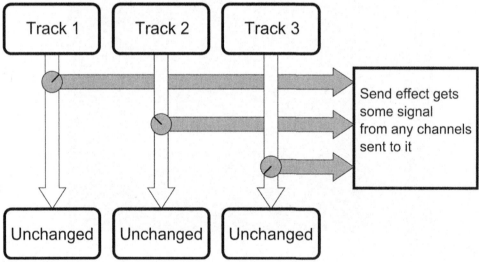

Here is the schematic of a send effect setup - the signals from each track pass from top to bottom (as conventional signal flow in a physical mixer), and there is a Send control which allows some of that signal to be sent to the effect unit in question. Each track has its own send level, and in this case Track 1 has the most signal going to the effect, while Track 3 has the least.

This is most commonly used arrangement for effects like reverb – changing the reverb effect will alter the sound of all the channels, allowing greater control over the whole mix quickly, as well as saving processing power if you are using a computer-based recording system. If you have an effect you wish to apply to more than one channel, a send is usually the best way to approach this.

538

In Cubase, setting up a send needs a number of steps. The first is to create a track for the effect, and this is called an FX track (say it out loud and you'll realise why); this is done in the normal way, although when you choose to create one you will be presented with a new dialog box, where you can pick the effect that you want to use (the effects you have will vary depending on the plugins you have installed), and the configuration of the audio.

In most cases you will pick stereo, and then select the effect from the list - in the example Mono Delay was chosen. You will then see a new track appear in the project window, in a folder marked FX Channels, as seen below.

You have now created the Send effect which is ready to be used, but currently nothing is being sent to it, so it will not be heard. The next steps need to be performed on any track/channel you wish to send to the effect.

In the sends section of the inspector, there are 8 send slots. Here we see slot number 1, ready to be assigned to our Mono Delay effect. To do this, click on the triangle at the right to get a pop-up menu of the available send destinations...

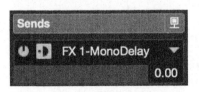

... and pick the effect from the list. This assigns send 1 on this channel to the effect. Note that different channels can have the same effect on different slots, but it makes sense to keep the same effect in the same slot on all of them.

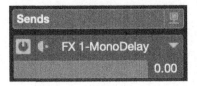

Next, turn the send ON using the power button at the top left. The slot's appearance changes and the controls can now be used. Here the default send level is 0.00dB, sending the track at unaltered level to the effect.

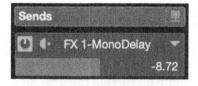

To alter the send level, click on the send at the point where the level is currently set, and drag it to the left to decrease it, or to the right to increase it.

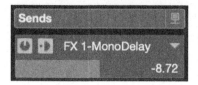

Normally the channel fader controls the signal level sent to the effect, but sometimes it should be independent. Click the button to the right of the power button to toggle the send between Post-fader (as it was originally) and Pre-fader.

Insert Effect

An insert effect works on one channel only. As the name suggests, it is inserted into the signal path of a single channel, and as a result one effect would be needed for each channel it is to work on. This is required by dynamic effects (ones which alter the level of a signal) as they need control of the entire signal in order to change its level. Sometimes it is useful for other effects, such as a delay or similar which will only be applied to the channel in question.

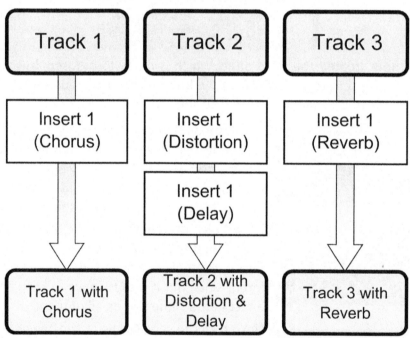

It is a common 'beginner's mistake' to only use insert effects – this can be very wasteful of resources and often means a lot more work to change a sound if it's been applied to several channels. Whenever you can economise on the number of effects you are using without a change in sound, you should do so. However, inserts are the best way to add an effect to a single channel, and easy to set up. You can add up to 16 on a channel in Cubase, as shown below.

Here is the insert slot in the inspector. There are 16, and the effects are applied in order of the slots. To create an insert effect, click in the dark grey area...

... and select an effect from the list. It will instantly be applied to the channel in question. The effect's parameters can be accessed using the small **e** button.

In the inserts view, the inspector shows the used slots plus a first empty one to save space. By default, only slots 15 & 16 are post-EQ and fader. This can be altered by right-clicking on a slot and choosing `Set as last Pre-Fader slot`, or by dragging the dotted line denoting this change up or down. The line may not be visible in all views, so the right-click option is often preferred.

Effect Types

On the following pages there is an outline of some of the effects that you will need to know. While the field of effects is changing due to advances in technology making new processes possible, these are the basic effects which will allow you to listen to and analyse many commercial recordings, as well as produce successful recordings of your own.

Reverb

In short, Reverb is the simulation of the acoustics of a physical space. That space can be small (like a bathroom) or large (like a cathedral). It can be hard and reverberant (like a church), or soft-sounding and dead (like being out in the snow). But most importantly, what it does is to trick the brain into thinking that it's hearing the sound of a particular space. Our hearing is an extremely complex sense, which allows us to gain a great deal of information about our environment – the size, composition and the location of sound sources within it. Reverb tricks the brain into thinking that this is what it's hearing. In addition to this, it can also allow us to make sound sources appear to be in the same environment (by putting the same reverb on all of them), or to make them stand out (by deliberately omitting one or more sound from the reverb). Reverb adds three-dimensional depth to a recording – the same sound will sound 'distant' if some suitable reverb is applied, or 'close' when the reverb is absent.

There are many ways of creating a reverb sound – initially this was done with a speaker and microphone in a hard-walled room, and then using springs vibrated by an electromagnet with a coil picking this vibration up. As technology has increased in complexity, so have reverbs – the latest 'convoluting' reverbs use incredibly complex measurement of real acoustic spaces and fiendishly difficult mathematics to create very realistic simulations of reverberation in this spaces. Generally, they are applied as a send effect – sharing one reverb between several channels. This means that firstly we save on processing power or cost, and secondly if you want to change the reverb for the whole track, you only have to edit one device, not 10.

In the following diagrams we can see a visual representation of the effect of adding a reverb to a short, pulsed sound.

Here we see the initial short, pulsed sound at the left of the diagram, with the rest of the time being complete silence. In the real world this rarely happens (the room we are in will nearly always reflect some sound), but this approximates a close-mic sound in a 'dead' room.

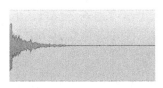

Here reverb has been added. Note that the initial sound is almost unchanged, but then the reverb begins, and it fades out over time, but also see that it is not a smooth fade, but there are fluctuations in the level as the sound decays, mimicking a real room in an effective manner.

Delay

Delay is different to Reverb in that it creates clearly defined 'echoes' of a sound – individual copies that can be heard separately from the original sound. Usually a delay will have three main controls. The first is the delay time, often ranging from a few milliseconds (heard as a very fast echo, much like the effect commonly applied to old Rock 'n' Roll records), to maybe 10 seconds (a really long delay, leading to a slightly odd 'dreaming' feel where things repeat).

The next control is 'feedback' – this controls how much of the delayed signal is fed back into the delay, and it therefore controls how many times the sound repeats – if it's turned right down then it will only repeat once, but if it's up it may repeat many times (getting quieter each time), or even repeat infinitely. This can lead to some interesting (if slightly unnerving) end products.

Again, it can help to see a visual representation of this effect.

Here we see the initial impulse, the same as seen in the reverb example. It has been kept deliberately and artificially brief to make the following diagrams as clear as possible.

Here we see the result of the delay – there is the initial (original) sound, followed by several distinct delayed versions of it, which decrease in volume with time.

Here the delay's feedback control has been turned up, and there are more repeats of the original sound.

Here the feedback control has been turned right down so there is only one repeat of the original sound.

If the original sound had been longer than the delay time then it would have overlapped – it's common to use this to make a phrase sound like a constant loop.

Many delay effects have a tempo-based mode which will allow you to quickly set the delay times to musical divisions of time – with modern audio sequencers, they will also change with tempo if your song has a tempo track.

Tremolo

Tremolo is a rapid change in volume. This was one of the first effects to be created with an electronic circuit as it is quite simple – it's just a cycling of the volume of a amplifier. This sound is commonly used on guitars but can be used on a wide range of other sources. Its effect can be seen below:

Here we see the original waveform, in this case just a constant tone generated by a program. The volume doesn't change at all over the 5 seconds that we see on screen.

Here is the effect of the tremolo – the volume alters many times over the course of the 5 seconds, creating the pulsing sound of a tremolo effect.

The speed, depth and waveform can usually be edited to create a wide range of sounds, from a soft slow sweeping sound to a more aggressive on/off sound - simply changing the waveform can make an enormous difference to the sound of a tremolo.

Distortion

Distortion is an extremely common effect – indeed a lot more common than you may think. There are different kinds of distortion, some desirable, some undesirable, and this can change depending on context – for instance, when recording an orchestra, it is unlikely you would want any distortion of any type, but when recording a rock band you may want lots of it.

Firstly, strictly speaking distortion is the altering of a waveform from its original shape – this could be said to apply to a number of processes described here, but we will limit it to effects that do so in a certain manner – the type seen in the Audio chapter, where the signal peaks and troughs reach the limits of the equipment handling them, and become flattened.

This results in a signal which can sound harsh, depending on the original sound. This can be extremely undesirable for some equipment, or pleasing for some others. This is because each piece of equipment distorts in a different manner, and produces different harmonics as a result of this.

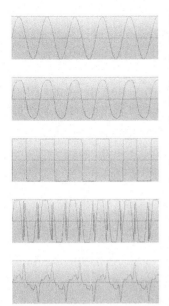

Here is our original signal - a sinewave, which is smooth and regular, with no clipping at the bottom or top, and a waveform that is symmetrical.

A 'valve' distortion has been applied here, resulting in smooth changes to the original waveform and a pleasant sound.

Here is a more extreme distortion with an extremely distorted and 'squared off' waveform, leading to lots of harmonics and a harsh sound.

Here the waveform is even more distorted, with the peaks seeming to fold back on themselves, leading to a very harsh sound.

Another example of distortion - again the waveform is clearly regular, but little like the original signal other than being the same frequency.

As can be seen, distortion can take many forms, from the subtle to the extreme. Many older recordings (from the 50s and 60s) have quite a high level of distortion on them, particularly on the vocals, but it sounds good because the equipment had a pleasing tone when distorted. Some more modern equipment (particularly early and cheap transistor/solid-state based gear) sounds very sharp and unpleasant when it distorts, while valve-based equipment has seen a renaissance as users realized that it distorts in a pleasing way – the harmonics that are generated are generally even which gives them a more musical quality.

There are three words often used when making reference to distortion – Overdrive, Distortion and Fuzz. They have somewhat imprecise definitions; Overdrive and Distortion are often used interchangeably, and Fuzz generally refers to a very specific, extreme and harsh-sounding distortion popularized by Jimi Hendrix and many early 70s rock bands. For many there is a preferred order of use – Overdrive being the most subtle, then Distortion, then Fuzz for extreme sounds. Many guitar sounds are distorted, and simply using this term will be correct.

When talking of distortion, reference is often made to guitars, but the sound of a guitar amp is often more than just the amplifier itself – the speaker plays a great part in altering the sound of the amplifier, smoothing off many of the higher, less pleasant frequencies. Without this (or a speaker emulator) many guitar amps sound quite unpleasant.

Chorus

Chorus is one of the most commonly-applied effects to guitar sounds, but can be used in many other contexts. It consists of a varying in pitch of the original signal, an artificial vibrato mixed in with the original sound. Depending on the depth and speed of the vibrato, the effect can vary from being a subtle 'thickening' of the original tone to sounding very wobbly and out of tune. This effect is achieved by passing the original signal into a very short delay, and the speed at which the signal is retrieved from the delay is altered, producing an output signal which varies up and down in pitch from the original. The two main controls for this effect are speed and depth, although some more advanced chorus effects have others.

Flanger

A flanger is very similar to a chorus effect, but it adds an extra control – feedback. As with a 'straight' delay effect, this feeds the signal coming out of the delay line back into the input. With a flanger this can greatly accentuate the effect, and even make it self-oscillate, which will vary from a 'whooshing' sound to a constant whistle. Again, flangers are most commonly applied to guitars, but have a wide range of other uses too.

Phaser

A phaser is another (short) delay-based effect. In this case, the original signal is delayed by a small amount, and this produces phasing, which accentuates certain frequencies and cancels others, because of the relationship between the delay time and the wavelength of those frequencies. The delay time is usually oscillated, meaning that the affected frequencies will alter with time, making this another cyclic effect, but a fairly distinctive one.

EQ

EQ is short for Equalisation. If you have made an ambient recording, you may have used some general EQ to correct some general issues with the end result, working with bass and treble. However, EQ can be a very precise tool that allows the sound of a recording to be sculptured, and also make similar and different-sounding sources to fit together. It has many creative uses, and we'll take a look at it here.

There are several kinds of EQ, but generally the main difference you will see will be the number of controls. A most basic EQ may only have one control, which will be cut or boost. It will work at a fixed frequency, and the control will just decide how much is added (boost) or taken away (cut) at this frequency. Some hi-fi units have 'bass' and 'treble' controls, and these work in this way.

The next type of EQ is a 'swept' EQ. This adds a "frequency" control – this allows the frequency that the EQ control will work at to be tailored. This gives more control over the effect, and an EQ that has this facility can usually be tuned to give the effect that is desired.

The next level of EQ is a 'parametric' EQ. In addition to the controls offered by a swept EQ, there is also the "Q" (quality) control – this adds a facility to control the width of frequencies that are altered by the EQ, from low Q (very general, affecting a wide range of frequencies) to high Q (affecting a narrow band). This allows the EQ to be tailored for the specific application, be it targeting a specific frequency (such as a vibration or unwanted resonance) or a slightly wider range (contouring EQ as we'll see later).

In addition to these types, there are also "shelving" EQs – these work on anything above or below their set frequency, allowing a wide range of frequencies to be altered, often useful when wanting to cut or boost bass or treble in a broad sense, as well as offering the ability to make very thin or dull-sounding tracks, such as simulating a track being heard on a radio or on the other side of a wall.

A final type is a high-pass or low-pass EQ. This allows everything above/below the set frequency to pass, and blocks everything else. This is a dramatic and extreme EQ to apply, and can be extremely useful in some situations.

On the next page is a representation of the various types of EQ, using a frequency diagram with low frequencies on the left, high on the right, and showing cut and boost in the vertical axis. In Cubase the different EQ settings can be entered at the bottom, and changing the EQ mode is done by clicking on the current EQ mode to show a pop-up menu of those available.

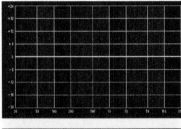

Here is the original, unchanged graph. The response of the channel is flat, meaning that nothing is changed at any frequency.

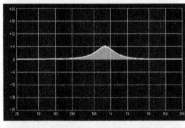

Here +6dB of boost has been applied at 800Hz. We can see the boost not only affects the original frequency, but a wide range of frequencies each side (to a lesser effect). This is because the 'Q' is low, making the filter unselective.

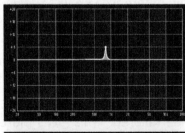

By only changing the Q to make the filter more selective, we see that the other frequencies around the centre are altered far less (in most cases not at all) – this makes the filter more targeted, and can be useful in many situations.

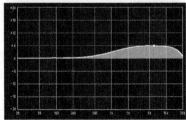

Here we see a +6dB boost applied at 6000Hz, with a low Q value.

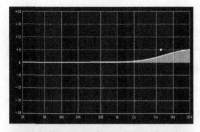

Here the settings are the same, except the filter is now in "High Shelving" mode, meaning any frequencies above the set point are boosted.

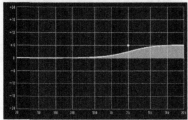

As can be seen here, when moving the centre frequency down, all frequencies above it are boosted, at around the 6dB level.

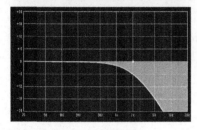

Here the EQ has been set to Low Pass - everything above it is blocked, while that below is allowed to pass.

Using EQ in Cubase

The previous examples have been theoretical explanations of different common types of EQ. The next step is to apply them in Cubase. Each channel in Cubase has a built-in EQ section which offers the three most common types of EQ - Pass (High or Low), Shelving (Low or High) and Parametric. To access the EQ section, open the channel with the Edit Channel button - the **E** in either the Inspector or on the mixer. You will see a screen like the one below.

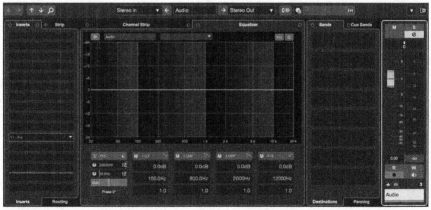

The centre section of the Channel Settings window shows the EQ section. It can also show the Channel Strip, which has built in dynamics processors. If they are showing then click the Equalizer heading in the central section and you will see the EQ section, which has two main areas - the controls at the bottom, and the EQ curve at the top.

Viewing Modes

There are three modes to this section - all function in the same way, but offer different ways of viewing the EQ. You can select the modes from the menu summoned by the gear icon at the top right of the EQ section.

Knob Controls mode. Here the EQ section's controls are represented by knobs, as you would see on a physical mixer. The controls show their settings when you hover the mouse over them, but usually return to a mode where you can't see the value without moving over them.

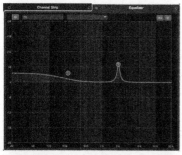

No Controls mode. Here the controls are entirely absent, and the whole space is taken up with the EQ curve graph. This can be useful when combined with the keyboard modifier controls shown later on in this section, and the extra space is useful for viewing exactly what is happening.

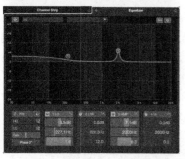

Equalizer Controls mode. In this mode, the EQ section's controls are represented by sliders, and there is always a numerical readout of the current setting of the controls. This gives the most information, and is the mode preferred by the author for using the EQ.

The four main EQ sections are labelled as LO, LMF, HMF and HI, meaning Low frequency, Low-Mid Frequency, High-Mid Frequency and High Frequency respectively, but this is misleading; any of the EQ sections can be set to any frequency. EQs 2 and 3 only operate in parametric mode, while the other two have alternatives; they default to shelving mode, but can be set to parametric or pass mode if you require them to.

To change the mode, click on the graphic representation of the current mode at the top right of each EQ section, and a pop-up menu will appear allowing you to choose the mode you want.

Parametric I
Low Shelf I
High Pass I
High Pass II
Parametric II
✓ Low Shelf II
Low Shelf III
Low Shelf IV

EQ Modes

You may notice that there are multiple options for each EQ type - two parametric, two pass and four shelf modes. Each has a subtly different EQ curve, as seen in this example showing the four different Low Shelf modes for band 1.

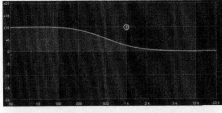

Mode 1. The slope of the EQ is fixed, and the Q control does nothing.

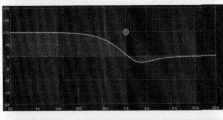

Mode 2. The slope of the EQ can be altered using the Q control, but a high Q leads to a band of cut above the set frequency (when the EQ is boosting).

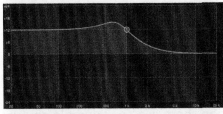

Mode 3. The slope of the EQ can be altered using the Q control, but a high Q leads to an increased boost band below the set frequency.

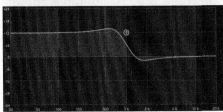

Mode 4. The slope of the EQ can be altered using the Q control, but a high Q leads to a cut above the set frequency and an increased boost band below the set frequency - a combination of mode 2 and mode 3.

Awareness of the different modes' performance can be useful, as it can save using two bands of EQ to achieve the same result as one correctly chosen one can do.

Editing EQ

It's possible to alter the EQ settings using the display - each band appears as a dot with a number, and moving this dot will alter the EQ's settings, something which can allow for increased resolution and quick movement. There are modifier keys on the keyboard which make alterations easier. If you hold down **CTRL**, the EQ frequency will be fixed, allowing gain to be altered without changing the frequency. Holding down **ALT** will fix the gain, allowing the frequency to be altered. Finally, holding down **SHIFT** will allow the Q to be set - without knowing this keyboard modifier, it's not possible to alter the Q from the display area.

Pre Section

The Pre section includes two filters: a low cut and high cut filter. While this is welcome and can free up band 1 and 4 from such duties, there are a couple of issues to keep in mind. Firstly, their names - remember that a low cut filter is the same as a high pass, and vice versa. Secondly, they work before the analyser section that we will see in the following section, so you will not see the before/after comparison that you will see with the other bands. In addition to these, the section includes a phase invert button, and a gain control that can be useful, particularly when the channel fader doesn't have enough gain.

Spectrum Analyser

The EQ section has an important tool when EQ-ing - it has a real time spectrum analyser built in. This means that Cubase analyses the audio passing through the channel in real-time, and shows the levels of each frequency present in the signal. The display makes is much easier to understand what is happening with a signal in terms of the frequencies present in it, and to help you decide what EQ processing you will perform. You can see the effect of any EQ that you apply in real time, with the spectrum display showing the final result.

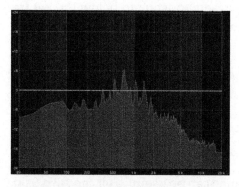

Here we see the frequencies displayed for a track. There is a clearly audible peak in the part, visible in the graph at around 700Hz. In addition there is a considerable amount of energy in the very low frequency range, which appears to continue below the range visible. When listened to on monitor speakers, this made for an uncomfortable "thud" sound in the part, and the speakers moved in a clearly visible manner - not something that is desirable.

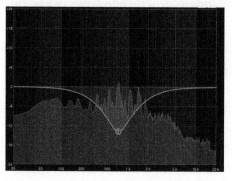

Firstly the dominant 700Hz peak is addressed, with a parametric EQ band centred on 500 Hz. The difference that the EQ makes is visible when comparing the peak with the diagram above. To see this effect in real time, bypass the EQ to see the unprocessed signal.

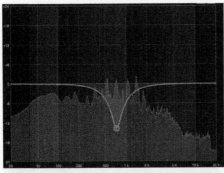

Next, the EQ's range is narrowed by altering the Q control to reduce the width of frequencies cut by the EQ. The effect of this change can be seen as the peaks either side of the original highest one are now being altered far less, and are of a similar magnitude to the central peak.

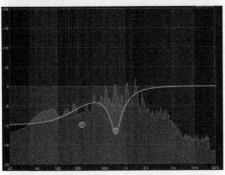

Finally, the lowest frequencies are treateed by applying Band 1 (Low Shelf), and reducing the level by around 12dB. The frequency of band 1 has been set to a little over 200Hz to allow it to give the desired reduction without altering the low-mid frequencies too much.

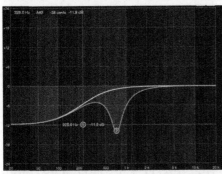

The overall EQ curve is presented in the spectrum analyser window, but it is possible to see the effect of any single band by hovering the mouse over its control point on the spectrum analyser window. Here, band 1 (Low Shelf) has been highlighted, and its effect is shown as the white line on the EQ curve...

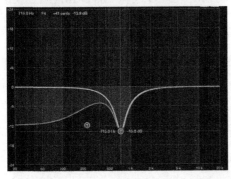

... while here band 2 is shown, illustrating that it still has a symmetrical effect on the frequencies around the set value, and the overall 'slant' is solely due to the effect of band 1.

The ability to see as well as hear effects of EQ is extremely important, and should not be underestimated as an analysis and learning tool. After using these tools for some time, analysing the sound of tracks and applying EQ will become far more natural.

Channel Comparison

An important part of applying EQ is sculpting the frequency balance between different tracks - as illustrated on page 561. To this end, the EQ section allows two channels to be compared quickly without leaving the Channel Settings window. This can make EQ decisions much easier, as it's possible to see the settings (and spectrum) for two channels at the same time. The controls for channel comparison are located at the top of the EQ section:

Comparison mode is enabled with the button at the left of the section, and you will see that the controls are then illuminated:

The left-hand area displays the reference channel - the current channel - and at the moment the EQ section will still work in the normal manner. The power of comparison mode is only available once another channel in the project is selected. This is done using the right-hand area, which allows selection of any suitable track in the project, via a drop-down menu that is triggered by clicking it.

It is now possible to alter the EQ of the reference or comparison channels by clicking on the appropriate button at the top - note that the EQ controls change colour to remind you which channel you are altering. Seen below is the change made by switching between the two selected channels.

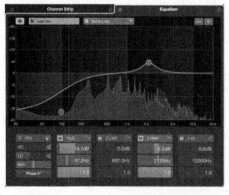
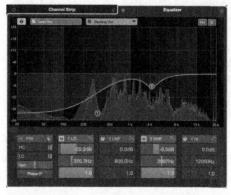

It is also possible to solo each channel or both of them to allow fine-tuning without needing to access the solo buttons elsewhere. This allows for a much faster workflow, and use of this while mixing is illustrated on page 633.

PRO

Frequency 2 EQ Plugin

Cubase's channel equalizer offers four bands of EQ plus a high and low pass filter, but there are often times when more bands of EQ are needed (such as mixing a complex collection of instruments using the EQ techniques shown on page 633), or where more extreme types of EQ will perform a task more efficiently. To this end you can use the included Frequency 2 plugin. It offers 8 bands of EQ, and a number of features that are not available on the standard channel EQ section. Frequency looks like this:

While a number of the controls will be familiar (each band has frequency, gain and Q controls), there are a number of new features, settings and controls to cover.

EQ Display

Frequency offers 8 bands of EQ, and each one is represented on the graph with a coloured dot, plus a line showing the individual EQ's effect in that colour. With simpler EQ settings, the line for a band will coincide with the line showing the overall EQ curve, but when bands interact, the curve for each band will be clearly separate from the overall EQ curve.

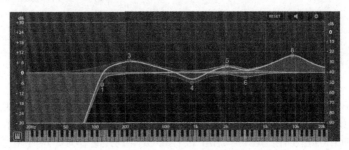

Piano Keyboard

As seen above, there is a piano keyboard covering the entire frequency range at the bottom of the EQ curve. This can be extremely useful for tuning a band of the EQ to a particular note. Each band is shown with the set frequency being represented as a coloured stripe on the note in question. The piano keyboard can be turned off with the button at the bottom left of the frequency response graph.

Single / Multi EQ view

As there are many controls per EQ band, there are two views available. Multiple, which is the default, and Single. The mode is toggled using the switch at the right-hand side of the EQ display:

In multiple mode, an overview of each band's settings is visible, but the display for each can either show the EQ or dynamic EQ settings - not both.

In single mode, all the controls for a given band are shown at the same time, and the band being viewed is chosen along the top of the lower section.

EQ types

The six 'middle' bands (2-7) all offer four EQ types, allowing much more flexibility than the default channel EQ - particularly when combining multiple filters together to achieve a response that is not otherwise possible (such as multiple shelving EQs).

554

Peak

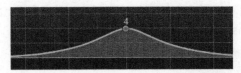

The standard parametric EQ as seen as default in channel EQ bands 2-3. Note that the Q factor can be up to 20, compared to the standard EQ's 12, allowing a more selective EQ.

Low/High Shelf

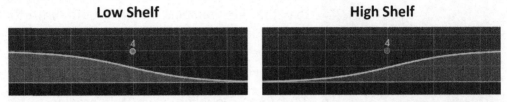

Each band can operate as a shelf EQ, allowing a wide range of frequencies to be altered by each band.

Notch

The Notch setting offers an EQ which has a much narrower bandwidth by default - compare these two graphs, with both set to the same setting. In many cases, notch is selective enough to only alter one note, even in the upper midrange where an eq with a wider bandwidth would be altering those surrounding the set frequency as well.

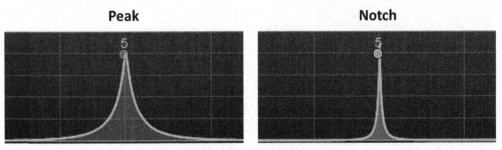

Note that the notch covers a much narrower bandwidth than the peak mode, despite the same Q setting. This can be extremely useful for working solely on a particular frequency, and as the name suggests, it is most often used to create a "notch" at a given frequency, to cut out a specific sound (such as mains hum when there is no other option).

Cut

Bands 1 & 8 offer additional modes - cut - offering different dB/octave curves to suit different situations:

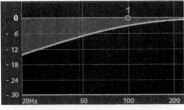

6db/oct - A relatively gentle rate of attenuation, providing a gentle, progressive decrease below the set point.

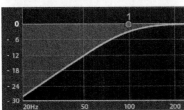

12db/oct - A more severe gradient, and note that the filter remains closer to 0dB above the set frequency than with 6dB. This is a similar filter curve to the High/Low pass which is in the Cubase Equalizer on each channel.

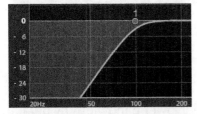

24db/oct - Doubling again, this provides a significant increase in the definition of the filter, but also means that frequency setting will be more critical; the effect of this filter on audio which is around the set frequency will be severe enough to be noticeable.

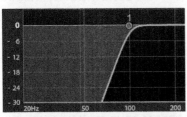

48db/oct - Another doubling, offering a very large difference across a narrow frequency range. Any audio which is around the cutoff frequency will be noticeably altered if its frequency changes. Care must be taken that audio does not move around the set frequency.

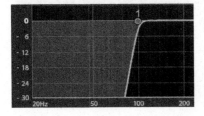

96db/oct - The steepest gradient available. While this can be useful for some purposes (particularly when trying to rectify problems with recordings), it is not without drawbacks and needs to be approached carefully to ensure the resulting audio is not highly variable in level.

While the steepest curves may appear instantly desirable, it is important to remember that with the steeper curves, any audio that crosses the set frequency will be dramatically altered in level, so careful application is important; the lower dB/Octave EQs provide a much greater safety margin, so try to use minimum value that achieves the desired effect.

EQ Modes

In addition to the standard EQ mode where the audio in both channels has the same EQ applied to it, Frequency also offers the ability to apply a different EQ curve to the left and right channels when used on a stereo track. There are three modes, selected by clicking the triangular buttons in the top bar of the EQ. If Frequency is applied to a Mono track, the mode will be set to Mono with no option to alter it.

Stereo Mode

This is the default mode, where both left and right channels have the same EQ curve applied to them. There is only one set of controls, and only one point on the EQ curve.

L/R Mode

Here each channel has its own set of EQ settings, allowing the application of different EQ curves to each channel. Each channel has its own tab at the top of the section, and can be turned off individually. The EQ points are shown on the curve with an L and an R.

M/S Mode

Here the EQ is applied in terms of Middle and Side allowing a different EQ in the extremes of the stereo field (Side settings) in contrast to the centre (Middle). This can offer creative possibilities as well as allowing some compensation to be made for the microphone used when doing MS recording (see page 445). The EQ points are shown on the curve with an M and an S.

Dynamic EQ

Frequency 2 offers the ability for EQ bands to be controlled automatically in response to audio signals. This means it can work in a more subtle way than a static EQ, as judicious setting of it will allow Frequency to alter the EQ setting appropriately at the right time. Needless to say, this isn't a topic that anyone just starting with EQ should trouble themselves with, but once you have more of a handle on the subject, you may find this facility useful. For the sake of clarity, a single band will be used in these examples, and viewed in Single mode so that all controls are visible at all times.

To turn on dynamic EQ for a given band, switch on the dynamics section. Once audio is playing, you should notice that the **Input** section level display is active:

Note that the side-chain section is active. This is normal, and should be left at the default for the time being. This is not currently an 'external' side-chain (as seen on page 565), but reflects that Frequency is intelligently filtering the audio that triggers the dynamic EQ (the **Auto** button is active) to allow you to get the best results. You may want to alter this in future, but for the time being, leave it on **Auto**.

Next, some EQ cut on this band is applied. This sets the maximum cut that will happen in this band. Playing audio will show that the EQ curve is now changing dynamically (depending on the signal being passed through) - as seen below.

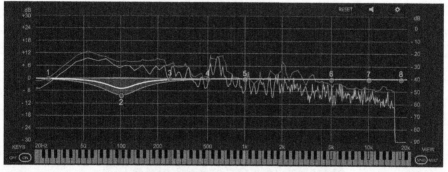

In this part there is a significant amount of energy in the frequency band, and as a result, the EQ curve is approaching the minimum.

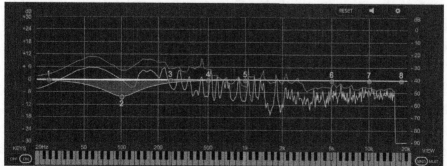

Here, there was less energy present, and as a result, the EQ was not as active - note that the effective EQ curve is almost at the 0dB horizontal line.

558

This shows how the EQ can be used to level out the differences in frequencies present; in this case, it is reducing the overall level in this band when there is lots of energy present in it. When there is less, it passes unaltered.

It is possible to reverse the situation by applying boost when dynamics are turned on - and in that case, the signal will be boosted when there is more energy present. Rather than evening the signal out, this will increase the difference between the low-energy and high-energy states.

Start

The start control provides a baseline for the EQ when dynamics are enabled. It allows contouring of the EQ curve to provide a starting point other than the 0dB line.

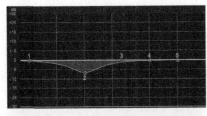

Here is the default of 0dB, where the EQ curve will start when the signal is below the threshold.

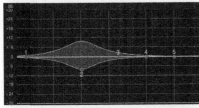

Here, the start control has been set to 10dB, providing boost in this band until the input signal is over the threshold, and then the EQ will be decreased (progressively to -8dB in this case).

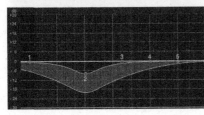

Here, the start is set to -10dB, providing more cut in this area until the dynamic threshold is reached.

With appropriate use of the start and gain controls, most dynamic 'before / after' situations can be catered for.

Threshold and Ratio

The **Threshold** control is useful for altering the amount of dynamic EQ - the signal needs to exceed this amount for the EQ to start working, and the ratio controls how extreme the EQ is above this level. These controls work in the same way that they do for a compressor, so if you need to investigate this further, see the section on Compression on page 562.

Side-chain

Frequency 2's dynamic EQ can be controlled by an external signal by setting the side-chain control to one of its 8 side-chain inputs. This advanced use is covered on page 569.

Other Controls

Inv

Each band has an Inv button. This inverts the gain setting, which makes using the "seek and control" technique outlined on page 627 quicker. Pressing the Inv button again returns the gain to the original polarity.

Lin

Each EQ band in frequency can be placed in Linear Phase mode. This applies some time compensation to allow for the inevitable delay that happens when EQ-ing any audio material. This compensation can restore integrity in the signal which may be lost otherwise, although there is some argument that the sound of an EQ may be dependent on this delay. Pressing the Lin button means that frequency will apply an appropriate delay compensation, but you will hear a small drop-out as you press the button as Cubase re-compensates for the change of the overall delay through frequency - this is nothing to worry about, just an explanation of the inner workings. Note that Linear and Dynamic EQ are mutually exclusive - turning one on will turn the other off.

Output

Adding EQ to any audio will change the overall level, and to help compensate for and control this, Frequency includes a level bargraph meter with peak hold at the top, and an output level slider. This allows control over the output of Frequency, which may be critical depending on the plugins which follow - while Cubase has a significant amount of headroom to avoid internal distortion, it is possible that a high level output may give undesirable results from a plugin. It also means that it's possible to compensate for the changes in level that Frequency is introducing to allow direct comparison when bypassing the effect, in a similar way to the method shown for the Multiband Compressor on page 642.

Auto Listen for Filters

When this button is activated, moving any filter control (whether on the frequency response graph, or the controls below) will set the output to audition only the effect of the filter. This can be extremely useful when trying to 'zero in' on a particular frequency, tone or notes.

Settings

The settings panel allows the control of a number of characteristics of the display of the audio spectrum and EQ curve. The defaults are usable and sensible, but you may wish to fine tune Frequency's appearance.

Applying EQ

EQ (equalization) can be studied in great depth – there is a huge range of options that can be applied, and because of the nature of musical instruments and recording the possibilities are almost endless. But some general pointers can be given here:

Firstly, you shouldn't normally need to use EQ to 'fix' problems with a sound source – your recorded source should already be of a good quality. However, there are occasions where there is no option but to 'fix' a problem – whether this is to remove a certain frequency that is causing problems, to alter the tonal makeup of a recorded track or to boost a frequency range which is deficient.

To pick the frequency to work on (whether you wish to cut or boost), it's usually best to set the EQ for a reasonable amount of boost (around 6dB), and then set the Q to a reasonably high value (around 6 or more). Now altering the frequency control will produce audible results, and allow selection of an appropriate frequency. Once you have found this, you may find that altering the Q value will give some benefits (lower Q for a more general effect, while higher values give a focused effect), and then you can alter the gain to give the required amount of boost or cut.

Complimentary EQ

When working on a larger recording, it is not uncommon for there to be more than one part for a given instrument, and making them fit together can be difficult. However, there is a simple 'trick' which, when applied to tracks that are competing for the same frequency range can allow them to sit together in a mix, and still be heard.

Firstly, listen to one of the tracks, and using the EQ technique above, pick a frequency range that, when boosted, amplifies the 'personality' of the part; this could be a certain range of frequencies that the notes are played in, or it could just pick up on part of the sound of the instrument. Do this with a fairly high Q factor (start at around 8), and add between 3 and 6 dB. Make a note of these values and the frequency you have used. Now go to the other tracks, and make a cut in EQ using the same values – this gives to one track and takes from the others. Now repeat this if necessary with the other tracks in the group – boost one of the tracks that has been 'cut', and cut the other tracks. With some experimentation, it's possible to make tracks fit together that usually would be difficult to do so. This is best done using channel comparison, as seen on page 552.

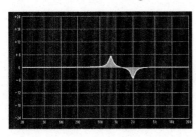

Here is the first instrument. It has had a boost applied at 800Hz (its 'characteristic' frequency) , and a cut at 2kHz (the characteristic frequency of the other instrument).

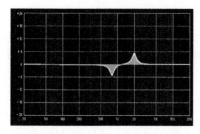

The second instrument's EQ looks like this – essentially the opposite of the first's EQ (boost for cut and cut for boost). The two will now sit together far more easily in a mix, as one instrument has control of one range of frequencies, while the other has control of the other set.

This technique may take some time to get the hang of, but it is well worth experimenting with as it can improve many mixes.

Compression

Compression is a dynamic effect – it works on the level of the signal, so to work effectively, it needs to be used as an 'insert' effect, not a send effect (although it is possible in some situations to use it in conjunction with a send, this is not the normal mode it is used in). The basic concept behind a compressor is that it reduces the dynamic range of a signal – i.e. It makes the difference between the loud parts of a track and the quiet parts less. In effect this is done by the compressor 'listening' to the signal passing through, and when it gets loud, it turns this down. There are two basic controls to a compressor – the threshold and ratio.

Threshold

This control sets the level above which the compressor will start to work. It is usually calibrated in decibels, and referenced to 0dB, so it will usually be a negative number, with a higher number meaning a lower level. Using this control it's possible to pick the signals that will make the compressor work.

Ratio

The ratio controls how much the compressor turns the output signal down once it has gone over the threshold. If the ratio was 2:1, and the input signal was 6dB over the threshold, the output would only be 3dB over the threshold after the compressor. If the ratio was 4:1, then the output would be 1.5dB over, and so on. In short, the ratio controls how strong the effect is once it has been triggered by the signal going over the threshold.

An example is shown below, using a drum loop.

Here is the original drum loop – note that there is a marked difference in level between the bass drum beats (first, third, fifth and eighth hits), and the others.

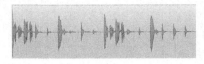

Here some compression has been applied, reducing the level of the louder beats. Make-up gain brings these back to their original level, but also increases the level of the quieter parts, decreasing the difference between the two, and making the average signal level higher. Taking this to extremes....

....leads to there being nearly no difference in level between the originally quiet and loud beats, plus the average signal level is a great deal higher. The sound of this loop is completely different as a result.

This is the most basic use of compression, to even out the levels in a performance. Often there will be too much dynamic range (the difference between the loudest and quietest sounds) in a performance, and reducing this is desirable; a compressor allows this to be achieved quickly and easily once you understand how it works. The amount of compression that you want will vary depending on the sound source in question, the performance and the style of music, and is difficult to quantify as a result; sometimes it is even desirable to compress so heavily that it becomes audible, but this is unusual; most of the time compression is applied in a way that the listener is not aware of. Compression applied to a number of tracks will also make balancing between them simpler, as there will be fewer changes during the course of a piece; carefully applied compression can make mixing a song much easier to do, another reason why it's vital to spend time learning how to use it.

More controls

Compressors come in many shapes and sizes, even when as plug-ins. Nearly all will offer Threshold and Ratio controls, and many offer extra controls, such as Attack (how quickly the compressor starts to work), Release (how quickly it stops working when the signal drops below the threshold) and make-up gain, and possibly others. We will now look at these other controls, all of which allow the compressor to be more flexible and useful.

Make-up Gain

Make-up gain is a really important control for a compressor – remember that the compressor reduces dynamic range by turning the loud parts of the signal down. Therefore, without make up gain, the peaks of the signal would be quieter. It is this control that is turned up to increase the level of the compressed signal (sometimes back to where the peaks were originally) – without it, the level would be lower. It is a fair rule of thumb to set make-up gain to be somewhere near equal to the peak value of gain reduction meter – in this way your signal peak will be where it was before the compressor. Some compressors offer an automatic setting, but the way this is applied can vary greatly and sometimes lead to some unpredictable results, so be prepared to use it manually.

Attack

The explanation of compression above neglects a very important factor, and that is that the audio changes over time, and the way it does so is an extremely important part of its character. Some sounds take a long time to change, others do so near-instantly. If the compressor just worked regardless of the speed of change, then the results can be undesirable; sometimes we want the initial attack of a sound to pass through the compressor unaltered, and have it work only on the remainder of the sound. The way we control this is with the attack control.

The attack control alters how long the compressor takes to start working after the threshold has been reached. By setting a long attack, we can let a desirable beginning of a sound through unaltered, retaining the start of the sound, and then applying compression later on. These timescales can be very short, depending on the sound in question. Here we will see an example:

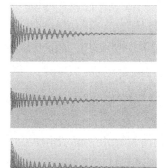 This one of the original kick drum waveforms - they vary in level and we want to use compression to even them out, so we apply some...

... and the result doesn't sound good. The attack is set to 1mS which means the initial 'hit' of the sound is being compressed too, making it sound very weak.

Setting the attack to a more suitable level (about 20mS in this case) allows the initial 'hit' of the drum to pass unaltered, but the rest of it is compressed.

Release

The release time is how long the compressor takes to go from compressing the signal (when the threshold has been reached) back to 'normal'. This is important as effectively a volume control is being altered; if it did so instantly then the effect would be extremely noticeable, so compressors change between the two settings smoothly using release time to do this. On many compressors it can be altered, and this allows release to be set to suit the audio in question. While few offer as short a time as the attack (in the case of the Cubase compressor, the minimum is 10mS compared with 1mS for attack), it can still be critical. Bear in mind that if you have a signal which is repeating often (such as a bass drum) setting the release to be too long can mean the next signal is compressed because the release time for the sound before has not passed, as seen below:

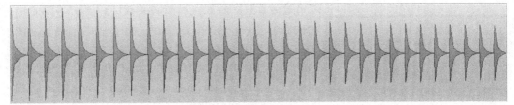

Here the release time is gradually increased, and as a result the later bass drum beats are compressed (including their initial hit) because the release time has not expired before the next bass drum happens. It's crucial to ensure this isn't happening as it can be extremely confusing to work out why the compressor is still active.

One of the most important things to remember with compression is that it usually takes people time to get the hang of it – often it will seem to be confusing how it works, so the best thing to do is to find an example to work on (such as the drum loop shown above) and spend time playing around with the settings on it to understand it. You can also use a vocal sample where there are two levels – quiet and loud – and set the compressor to reduce the difference in level between the two by setting the threshold above the quiet sound (so the compressor doesn't work on it) but below the loud sound (so that it does) – this is a commonly-needed setting with many singers' performances, so being able to do this is a useful tool. Once you understand how it alters level, you can then work on changing the way it works over time with the attack and release controls.

Side-chain

ARTIST PRO

Some compressors (such as the one included with Cubase) allow what is known as side-chain compression. This means that an external signal can be used to control the compression. In a 'normal' compressor the signal that controls the effect is the same signal as is being processed - when that signal gets louder, it triggers the compressor.

With a compressor that allows side-chaining, a different signal can be sent to the compressor to control the amount of compression. This may on the face of it seem an odd thing to do, but it allows some useful possibilities. We will firstly look at how to set side-chaining up, and then at a couple of the creative possibilities that the technique offers.

Setting up

You will need two tracks - one track to be compressed, the other to control the compression.

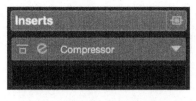

On the track to be compressed, add a VST3 compressor (indicated by the three stripes to the right of the name in the list) as an insert effect, such as the one included with Cubase. It must be a VST3 compressor, as only they have the ability to use side-chaining.

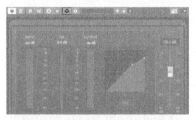

Activate the side-chain, using the control highlighted to the left. This allows the compressor to take the external signal to control the compression. Once this is highlighted, click the triangle to the right of it to summon...

... The Side-Chain Inputs window. Here it is possible to select any track in the project that generates audio (Audio, Instrument, Group and FX Channels) to use as side-chain inputs for the compressor, by clicking **Add Side-Chain Input**.

Here, a track called 'Trigger' was selected. By default, Cubase will turn the send on and set the level to 0dB, which should give you a functioning side-chain setup. You can set the send to be prefader with the button towards the right of the window.

The compression on the first track is now being controlled by the signal on the second track. We will now look at some creative possibilities offered by this technique.

Ducking

'Ducking' is most commonly used by radio DJs to automatically drop the level of the music they are playing when they start talking - the music is turned down by the compressor as soon as they speak, and once they stop, it returns to the original level. However, it can be useful when mixing music as well, as it allows the automatic control of level tracks to take place. A common use for this is in a rock band context, to subtly drop the level of the guitars in a mix when the singer is singing. To be effective this needs to be subtle, but it can be another way of resolving conflicts between tracks which use a similar range of frequencies.

Our mix has three guitar tracks in it. They have been set to use a group track (see page 621 for details on this) so the audio from all of them is passing through this group.

A compressor is inserted into the group, and side-chain is turned on.

On the vocal track, the compressor's side-chain is selected as a send, turned on and turned up to 0dB. Note that this channel has other sends already set up and active - this is to illustrate that the send for the side-chain is just like any other send, and the method shown in the previous section is a faster way of setting up a standard send to control a compressor via its side-chain.

Finally, the compressor is set to gently compress the guitars whenever the singer is singing. Subtlety is extremely important in this situation - the drop in the guitars' level should not be noticeable, so only a few dB should be registered on the gain reduction meter at the maximum compression (i.e. when the singer is at their loudest).

This technique can make mixing an easier task as the potential clash between similar-sounding instruments can be mitigated in part by doing this, but as said above, doing so in a subtle way that is not obvious to the listener is the key.

Kick Drum side-chaining

A common use for side-chaining in a lot of modern dance music is to use a kick drum to produce dramatic changes in another signal, typically a sustained chord pad. While the connections between the tracks are similar as the previous example, the outcome is quite different.

Here is the track we want to compress, a synthesizer playing a pad chord sound. The level is fairly consistent throughout the part.

As in the other examples, a compressor is added as an insert, and side-chain is activated.

Here is the track we want to use to compress the signal - in this case it is a kick drum part which we want to use solely as a control for the compression; we do not want it to be heard in the final mix. Firstly, the send is selected, turned on and turned up to 0dB.

Next, we want to make sure the track will not be heard. To do this, the fader will be turned down to -∞dB, but that would mean the send would stop working, so we need to set it to be in pre-fader mode, as seen on page 540 - shown by the colour.

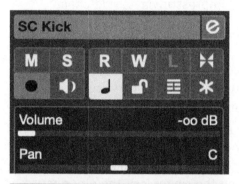

Now we can turn the channel fader down to -∞. The kick drum will no longer be heard, but will still control the compression, as the pre-fader send is no longer dependent on the channel fader level.

Returning to the synth pad track, the compression now needs to be set to a suitable value to produce sizeable changes in level. In this example, the settings were with a high ratio (8.00), and the threshold set reasonably low (-33dB). To get the dynamics of the compression correct, the release time was shortened to 168mS as the default was too slow.

There is one more issue. If the compressed track is soloed, the compression will no longer work as the side-chain send track will be muted. To fix this, long-click on the Solo button, and it will turn to a D - this means Solo Defeat, so it will not be muted when other tracks are soloed.

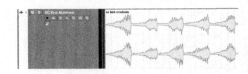

Here is a mixdown of the effect applied to the track in question - the effect of the compression can clearly be heard, and it has now gained a strong rhythmic feel from this treatment.

There are many situations where side-chain control of compression can be beneficial in a mix, but the two examples shown above show the most common ones - the first being a subtle addition to level control in a track to make mixing a simpler affair, while the second makes a dramatic change to an existing sound and creates a new musical effect.

Multiple Side-chain inputs

The ability to have multiple separate side-chain inputs is useful in any effect or instrument where separate signals are needed. In the case of Frequency 2, this can allow a signal to be altered by multiple other signals, offering fine control over the EQ in response to other elements in the mix.

Here is an example - only two EQ bands (2 and 6) will be used for this example, for the sake of clarity. There are three channels present in the project - a kick drum sample, a snare sample, and a loop (which is full frequency, and includes existing kick and snare):

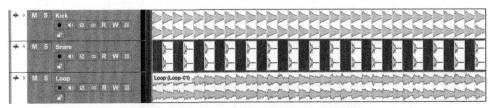

Frequency has been set up with two bands active. Band 2 is reducing the kick of the track (centred on 48Hz)...

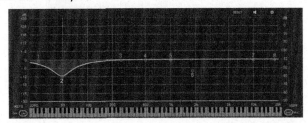

... while band 6 is set to cut high mids, prominent in the snare sample that we want to hear clearly:

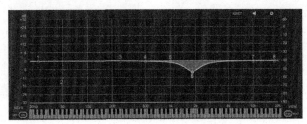

Next, Dynamic EQ is turned on for each band, and the **side-chain** is set appropriately for each - Side-Chain 2 for band 2 and Side-Chain 6 for band 6:

While it would be possible to use any of the side-chains, it makes sense to use the same number as the EQ band in most situations. Next, side-chain is activated at the top of frequency ...

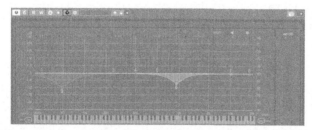

... and the audio tracks are chosen as the side-chain inputs. Note the drop-down menu for selecting the side-chain input, which in this case offers the choice of 8 individual side-chain inputs:

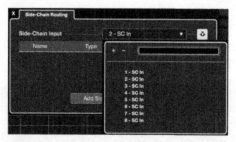

Once the appropriate side-chain input is selected, setting up the source is done in the usual manner as seen on page 566.

SC In 2 (from Kick)   SC In 6 (from Snare)

   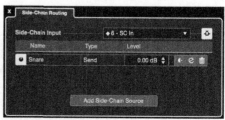

Also note the diamond next to any side-chain input which has a source configured:

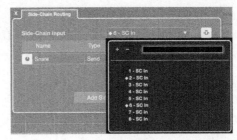

With these both setup, Frequency will now work as intended, with each band of EQ being triggered by its respective side-chain signal. Band 2 becomes effective, decreasing the bass on the loop when the kick sample is playing - as seen below:

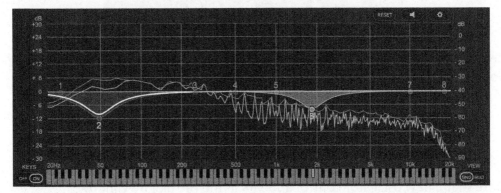

When the snare sample plays, it triggers band 6 to reduce the upper midrange, as seen below (note that band 2 is also active as the kick plays on every beat).

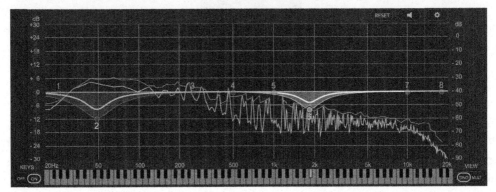

Usage in this manner allows semi-automated mixing, with the ability to apply complimentary EQ as mentioned on page 561 - for instance, cutting the upper midrange on a guitar group whenever the vocal is present - clearing space but allowing the guitar group to be unaltered when the vocal channel is silent.

Side-chain in VST Instruments

It is also possible to send audio to a VST Instrument for processing, if the VST Instrument supports it. Retrologue allows this, treating the audio sent via the side-chain to be processed in the same way the audio created by the oscillators is.

Setup

Here is the initial setup, containing two tracks. One track is the audio which will be fed to the side-chain (in this case a drum loop), and the other is an Instrument track containing Retrologue.

Retrologue needs to have the side-chain input activated in the title bar of its window:

Note that a new oscillator control appears in the retrologue window:

This needs to be turned up to become active. In addition, Oscillator 1's level control is turned down to zero so that only the side-chain audio will be heard. As with the other side-chain examples, the side-chain input is fed from the audio track.

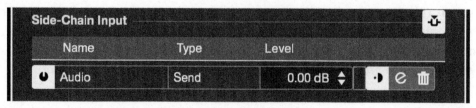

This is set to Pre-Fader to allow audio to be sent even if the channel fader is down. To allow us to hear only the audio passing through Retrologue, the channel level is turned down to zero:

Audio is now being passed to Retrologue's filter section when the track is played, but it will not be audible. This is because Retrologue's amplifier and filter sections need to have MIDI input to trigger their envelopes. This can be live via a MIDI device, or programmed onto the track:

The audio will now be audible, and the tuning of the filter and amplifier settings in Retrologue can be altered to suit the desired effect (the default settings in retrologue will pass the audio almost unaltered, so until changes are made, the effect will be underwhelming).

The initial settings of Retrologue's filter - the cutoff is set to 22kHz and resonance is turned right down; the filter isn't altering the audio.

Setting the cutoff to around 1kHz and the resonance to 5 gives a greatly altered sound, adding some darkness and "grit" to the tone.

Turning up the distortion increases this considerably.

While this will be typical of a common filter effect with a plugin, the ability to control the envelope of the amplifier and filter using more complex MIDI data leads to a much greater range of possibilities.

Changing the MIDI part on the Retrologue track to a note per beat:

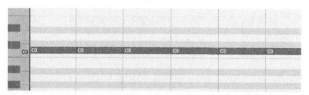

Allows more rhythmic use of the filter and amp envelopes to create new textures from the original audio. The variation and control of the envelopes can be increased by turning up the VEL control in an envelope:

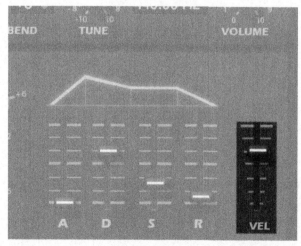

This allows the velocity of a note to alter the magnitude of the envelope signal, allowing a MIDI part like this:

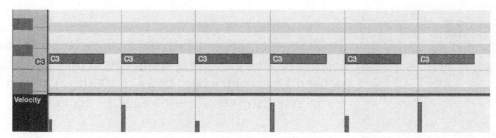

To produce a complex effect, with the filter opening according to the velocity of the note. With some time spent on creating appropriate variations between the Amp and Filter envelopes (and the degree of velocity control for each one), it is possible to create a complex, evolving sound, and when linked with the ability of the Logical Editor (see page 357) to create complex MIDI information, there is an enormous amount of experimentation and discovery possible.

Multi-band compression

PRO

Multi-band compression is an extension of the standard compressor - in essence it divides the incoming audio into a number of frequency bands, and then each one is compressed separately. These signals are then re-combined, leading to a signal which can be of a higher average level in each frequency band than would be the case with a single-band compressor. Imagine a track which has a loud low-frequency sound (such as a bass drum), and less energy in other frequencies. In a single-band compressor, the loud bass drum would be what the compressor is sensing and working on, and the other sounds would be reduced accordingly. When the signal is divided up into separate frequency bands, then the bass drum will not stop the other sounds from being compressed separately, leading to higher average levels in each band.

Here we see Cubase's Multiband compressor (MBC). It has four frequency bands (shown at the top), and each one is compressed separately, with the controls for each band and its transfer graph shown below the frequency area. There is an overall output level meter, and an overall output control on the right hand side.

Here the MBC is in action - each band has signal passing through it, and some are being compressed. The second band has the highest level, and is being compressed more than any of the others.

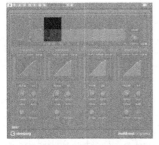

The frequency range of each band can be controlled to tailor it to the audio being compressed. Here the top of band 1 has been moved down to 100Hz, so it is only compressing the very lowest-frequency audio.

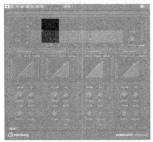

Here the top of band 1 has been moved to around 300Hz, allowing it to compress not only the bass drum, but also most of the fundamental tone of the bass guitar as well. This can sometimes lead to better results, but experimentation is always the key - it's just not possible to prescribe exactly what will work best.

Individual bands can be increased in level, by up to 15dB. This allows a general change to be applied to the sound of the signal being processed. It is important to remember that this is not compression being applied, just a level change.

Here the other bands have been reduced in level, making for a great difference between band 2 and all the others. This is an extreme effect, and due to the nature of the filtering that occurs can lead to some interesting sounds; not recommended for an entire mix, but useful for special effects.

With the levels in the frequency area set to normal (0dB), adjustment of the compression for each band can be performed. Here is the threshold control for band 2, which is set in the normal way, although the nature of multi-band compression can generally mean more conservative settings are needed.

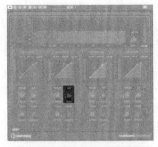

Next, the ratio is being set. Again, it is easy to over-do MBC, so careful and conservative setting of the ratio is usually order of the day.

If you want to hear what the band in question sounds like without being compressed, the bypass control is shown here, and selecting it allows the selected band's audio to pass without being compressed, allowing for A/B comparisons to take place.

There is also a Solo button, which mutes all the other bands. This can be particularly useful when trying to set frequency ranges as it is very difficult to hear what's happening without making use of this.

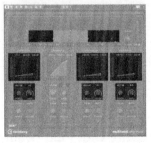

Here the compressor has been set to an extreme setting, with bands 1, 3 and 4 reduced in level as much as possible, and compressed as much as possible, leading to an extreme effect with only the audio of band 2 really audible.

Multi-band compression can be applied to entire mixes, group channels or even individual instruments. Such techniques have become extremely common in the last 20 years or so, and have led to recordings which sound 'bigger' than many in the past, but this change has not been without cost. Use of multi-band compression in a real context is covered in the Mixing chapter on page 642 and should be applied very sparingly if you are to avoid a tiring final mix, or one that sounds over-compressed.

Limiting

A limiter is essentially a compressor with a very high ratio (usually above 10:1) and a fast attack time. It is designed to ensure that a signal does not go over a certain level, and to do so while avoiding high levels of distortion. This can be beneficial in a live recording situation where gain may have been set too high to catch an occasional loud sound, but can also be extremely useful in many modern music production styles where sounds need to be as 'loud' as possible. With a limiter it is often possible to increase the average signal level of a track, as seen below.

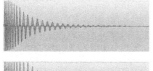

Here is the original bass drum. While the peak is at maximum level, it soon decays to a much lower level, and the average level is not high.

With suitable limiting applied, the average level is higher as there are a number of peaks at the maximum level, leading to a much 'louder' bass drum.

Such use of limiting is not what limiters were originally designed to do (to 'catch' the occasional peak or sudden transient), but is increasingly common in styles of music where loudness is desirable.

Gating

In the perfect environment, there might never be a need for a gate. But in the imperfect world where unwanted noises are present, gates can be very useful. In short, a gate cuts off a signal once it goes beneath a certain level. This can be very handy when recording in an environment which has high background noise (such as a school), as it means it is possible to remove this noise during portions of the performance when there is silence (or rather, where there should be). In addition, it can be useful when using a sample of a piece of music either for the dramatic effect of suddenly cutting off the sound, or to use a vocal line and cut out the music in between phrases. A simple gate would have just one control, threshold. Below this level, the output is silent. Once the input signal goes above the threshold, it is passed to the output unaffected. This allows the removal of low-level noise, and sometimes the salvaging of otherwise unusable material. An example is shown below.

Here is the original audio waveform, with loud (wanted) and quiet (unwanted) sections

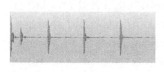

Here we see the effect of putting a gate on with a relatively high level – only the louder sections can pass, the quieter parts are cut out completely. This gate has a very quick 'release' time, leading to a choppy sound. However, it's possible to alter the release time....

... to get a smoother closing action to the gate – this sounds far more musical than the example above, although both have their uses.

Like compressors, gates are usually more complex, featuring extra controls:

Attack

This is how quickly the gate opens once it has been triggered. It can be useful for controlling the transient (initial attack) at the beginning of a sound, particularly with drums where they have been recorded with multiple microphones, or where the mic positioning leads to too much attack.

Release

This controls how long the gate takes to close after the signal has gone below the threshold. Tuning this will alter the sound's decay, and can change it from a natural sound (with a longer decay) to a very short, artificial sound (when the release time is very short). Setting too long a release time can mean the gate will never close, so it is important to experiment with the release time to ensure this does not happen.

Side-chain filtering

Some gates will allow the signal that triggers the gate to be filtered - this can help tune the gate to open only to the wanted signal, by making it sensitive only to that sound. It is, however, important to remember that once a gate is open, all frequencies will be passed; there is no way for it to selectively open and allow only a specific sound through. If an unwanted sound happens at the same time as a wanted sound, both will be heard.

Direct Offline Processing

In version 9.5, Cubase introduced Direct Offline Processing (DOP) offering a way to apply multiple effects and processes to a selected piece of audio, also becoming the default method of applying any audio processes (**Audio > Processes**). In the past, audio processes were applied directly to the audio, with limited scope for making changes later in the workflow. DOP provides a quick way to apply processes in a way that facilitates quick working, but also allows changes to be made later on in the workflow. An couple of examples of this in action should illustrate the possible applications.

Applying a single process

Often your workflow will involve applying 'utility' processes, such as Normalise, Reverse, Invert Phase, Stereo Flip, etc. Previously these would have been applied to the audio file directly, and it was not always possible to go back to the version of the file before the process was applied. With the advent of DOP this has changed - selecting most of the options under **Audio > Processes** now summons the Direct Offline Processing dialogue box, with the selected process listed on the left, and any options for the process in the right-hand side of the window.

Here, **Normalize** has been selected, with a single control to select the appropriate peak audio level.

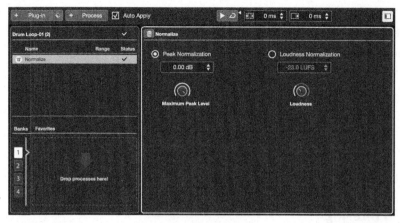

Altering the control produces instant results in the audio file, as seen below.

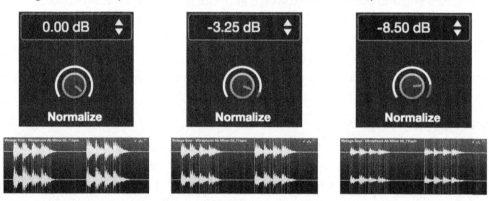

Closing the dialogue box leaves the current state of the process applied to the file - it doesn't need to be confirmed - and note the appearance of the icon at the top right of the audio event, showing that a process (or processes) has been applied.

If you have auditioned the process and decided that you don't want to apply it, you need to remove it from the list on the left. This is done by selecting the process and hitting **DELETE** (or right-clicking and selecting **Delete** from the pop-up menu). Bear in mind that the list may have other entries in it, depending on the history of the processing applied as your project progresses; the last entry will be the process that you have just been auditioning.

Making a process permanent

You can apply a process permanently to an audio file by right-clicking on the process list, and selecting 'Make All Permanent' - bear in mind that this will alter the file in the audio pool, and in many cases leaving Direct Offline Processing in place can allow you to go back to the original audio should you desire.

Applying Multiple Processes

The real power of Direct Offline Processing becomes apparent when applying multiple processes, as the following example will illustrate.

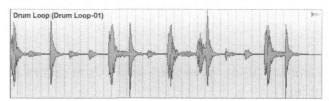

Here is a 2 bar drum loop. The desired end result is to apply a small amount of 'reverse reverb' to give the loop an other-worldly feel, but to keep the original audio playing forwards. This would normally mean processing to reverse the audio, applying reverb, and then reversing the audio again (returning the original audio to playing forwards, but reversing the reverb sound). To apply this would normally mean at least one mixdown, and most importantly if the reverb setting was wrong, it would mean another mixdown from the source drum loop and attempting it again; something which can get tiring quickly!

However, applying these processes can be done in Direct Offline Processing simply, and the nature of the processing means it's possible to alter an effect in the middle of the chain of processes without having to re-do the following processes manually - they are done automatically.

To apply the processes using DOP, the audio part is selected, and then the window opened with **Audio > Direct Offline Processing**.

The blank window looks like this:

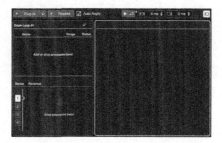

To apply an effect or process, click on the relevant menu and select the one you want - here, **Reverse** was chosen:

The audio is processed straight away:

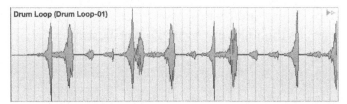

Next, reverb was applied, using **Roomworks**, with a short reverb and fairly dry setting for a subtle effect.

Again, the audio is processed straight away:

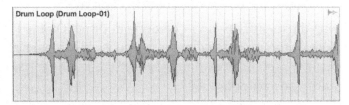

Finally, **Reverse** was added again, putting the original audio back to its original state, and leaving the reverb reversed.

The 'pre-reverb' can be seen before each of the original drum hits:

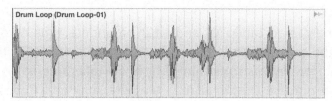

It's possible to edit the settings of any part of the chain and hear the effect straight away - changing the reverb mix is quick and easy, and the post-reverb reverse is also done automatically, speeding the workflow immensely:

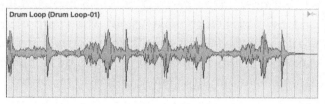

Exercises

Insert effect to several channels, note difference

If you haven't heard any of the effects in the chapter, the first thing you will want to do is familiarise yourself with their sound. The easiest way to do that is to insert an effect into an audio track with audio on it, and listen to the results. Being able to recognise effects is important as they will vastly increase your creative abilities when making any kind of music, whether a MIDI sequence or an audio recording. Experiment with the controls on the effects; some will be immediately obvious, others may take some experimentation and research to work out. What is important is that you spend time working with effects, and getting used to their sound.

Set up FX channel, setup sends

As seen on page 538 the other way of using effects is as sends, via an FX Channel Track. Create one now, and put an effect in that track which will be clearly heard, such as a delay or reverb. Now, as the section starting on page 538, assign a send for a channel that you want to send to the effect, making sure that you turn it on and turn it up so that it can be heard. Note that if you have soloed a track and then assign an effect, you will need to re-solo the track to hear the effect, as Cubase will not solo the effect track you have added until you do so.

Use tempo matching to create musical delay-based effects

A number of effects (mostly delay-based) feature the ability to sync their cyclic element to Cubase's tempo. It is often desirable to have musically-based delay times, so spend some time experimenting with these settings, noting that a number of different divisions are available - not only straight note values, but also dotted and triplet values as well.

Use of EQ

EQ is an extremely important tool, and often an underestimated one. Being familiar with all the controls available to you and having an affinity for the kind of frequencies you can hear is something which will take time but is important to master. To help practice this, import a complete song into Cubase, and spend some time working with the EQ controls to hear the effect of different EQ settings. You should experiment not only with the frequency and gain settings, but also the effect of the Q setting, and the different types of EQ available to you - remember there is not only a bandpass EQ, but also high and low shelving EQs as well as high- and low-pass EQs to make use of. The appropriate situations for each will vary, but knowing the facilities available to you will greatly increase your effectiveness. Make use of the complimentary EQ as described on page 561 as it will become extremely important when you start to mix more complex pieces of music.

Use of compression

Compression can take some time to understand, and even longer to master. Spending some time working with it on single tracks will allow you to understand not only how it works, but also how it sounds. Find (or record) an audio track with excessive dynamics, such as a softly sung phrase followed by an extremely loud one. Set up a loop around them, and spend some time using the compressor's controls to reduce the difference between the loud and quiet sections - remember that the threshold sets the point at which the compressor starts to work, so in this example you will probably want to set it just above the level of the quiet signal. Varying the ratio will control the difference between the two sections, although it's important not to use too high a ratio as this can sound artificial, particularly on voices. As with many skills, compression will take time and practice to master, but making use of it to help control dynamic range and increase the average signal level of a recording is extremely important, particularly for helping you deal with difficult mixes.

Use of gating

As seen in the main text, a gate can help reduce the effects of bleed on multiple close-mic'd drum kits amongst other tough recording areas. When you have recorded a drum kit, listen to the bass drum mic alone, and hear how the rest of the kit is often picked up. By setting the gate to an appropriate setting, it is possible to remove a great deal of this (although remember that when a gate is open, everything comes through including the unwanted signal, it has no way to differentiate between the two). Run through the procedure shown on page 630 of the Mixing chapter and listen to the effect that removing the bleed has on the overall sound of your kit. You should also practice using the gate to get rid of unwanted background noises, as often found in many recording spaces; a gate can save you a great deal of editing time removing such sounds.

Summary

Effects are the cornerstone of much modern music production, and being aware of their sounds and possibilities is one of the pre-requisites of anyone interested in recording or production. Careful listening will allow the identification of effects even when used in combination and heard in context rather than isolation, and with this skill it becomes possible to deconstruct many recordings and learn from those who created them. Modern computer-based Digital Audio Workstations (DAWs) give access to effects that studios of the previous generation could only dream of, in terms of facilities, number and cost, and being able to know how to use these effects and their controls will benefit the recordist greatly.

The Mix Console

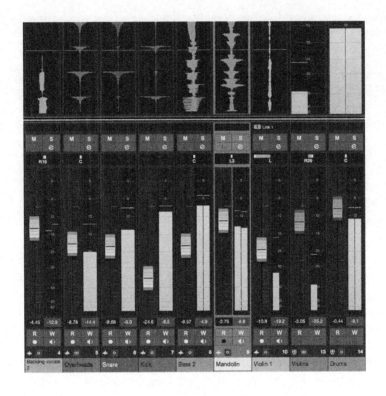

Cubase 7 introduced a completely new mixer - known officially as the mix console - and with it the largest change in the program since the introduction of Cubase SX 1 in 2002. Now the mix console is more powerful than ever before, and as a result of this has more features to learn. Time spent learning these features will be repaid with much faster workflow and improvements in the sound of your project. This chapter will look at each section of the mixer and give practical examples of the features inside in use.

Opening the Mix Console

The mix console is opened by selecting **Studio > MixConsole**, or pressing **F3** on the keyboard. You will see a window similar to the one shown below.

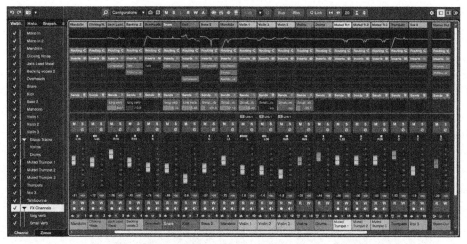

The Mix Console window behaves like Cubase's other windows - it can be resized, moved and maximised, and on a multi-monitor setup it will maximise to take up an entire monitor (rather than the entire desktop). From Cubase 8 onwards, the window handling has been much improved on previous versions, and this contributes greatly to improved workflow (and reduced user frustration!)

It's possible to have up to four different Mix Consoles open at the same time, with different settings, so bear this in mind when you are working on a large project - suitable customisation can allow you to work much more efficiently (such as having one Mix Console viewing inputs only, available quickly).

Mix Console Sections

The Mix Console's default view has four main areas:

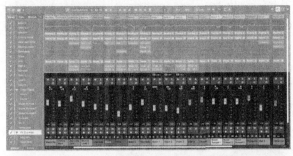

Channel Faders - the area most used, giving access to the most commonly used components, the channel faders and pan controls.

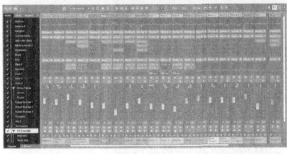

Left Zone - this area allows channels to be hidden, moved to the left or right of the mixer, and for the history of edits to be viewed. If the left zone is not visible, use the buttons at the right side of the toolbar, or **CTRL + ALT + L** to view it.

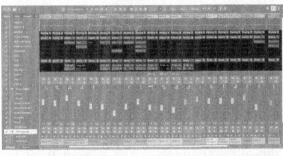

Racks - this section allows access to the detailed parameters for the channels, with EQ, insert and send effects and the channel strip accessible

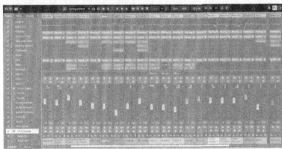

Toolbar - provides viewing option and access to automation and channel linking controls.

Each of these areas will be examined in detail on the following pages.

Zooming and View

The main areas of the mix console can be altered in size - by clicking and dragging the dividing line between them, it's possible to increase the height of the fader section (and correspondingly decrease that of the racks section), and the fader area will change size to fill the new space it has.

Here is the fader section reduced in height as much as possible:

Here is the fader section increased in height as much as possible:

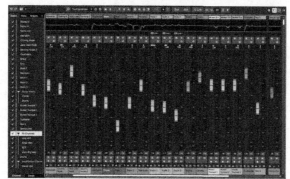

In addition to this, the horizontal width of the channels can be altered, using the standard zoom in/out keyboard shortcuts, **G & H**. Channels can be set from very wide...

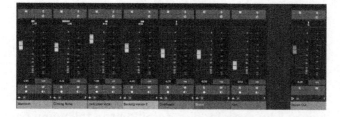

...to narrow.

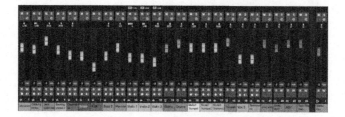

The zoom of the rack section height can also be altered, and this is easiest done using the toolbar buttons (if this isn't visible, right-click to Customize the Toolbar):

Channel Faders

This section is the one that is most associated with the mix console, and probably the area that will get the most use. It's at the bottom right of the mix console, and offers a channel fader and a number of other controls for each channel present in your project.

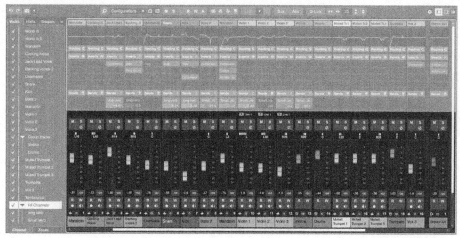

Mute, Solo, Listen and Edit

This section indicates and controls when those settings have been made - Mute and Solo are the same as have been discussed in the Sequencing chapter on page 9. Listen is used when the control room is active (which is not covered in this book), while Edit brings up the channel edit dialogue box where it's possible to set EQ, Inserts and Sends.

Pan Control

This sets the channel's position in the stereo field - if you are working with an audio track then it can go from Left to Centre to Right, with 100 steps on either side of centre. The default position is centre (C). For a MIDI track, the effect is similar but there are 63 steps either side, and the default position is "Off" where no data is sent. Not all synths respond to MIDI Pan controls, but many do. Note that the pan control can be disabled with the power button.

Channel Fader and Meter

This shows the current setting for the channel fader (volume), and a meter showing the current audio level. For a MIDI track, the fader will show the current setting of MIDI Volume (CC 7), which will be set to Off as default. This doesn't mean the channel is off, it means that no value has been set, so the MIDI synth will play at the default volume. The channel meter shows the current note's MIDI Velocity, not audio level.

Automation, Monitor and Record

This section indicates and controls the current automation status - Read and Write - as covered in the Automation chapter on page 342. The monitor control is available here, which will switch the channel over to output the input signal. The final control is Record enable, to set the track to be recorded on when record is pressed on the transport bar.

Name

The track name is visible here with the track number above. The name can be edited by double-clicking it. Once the track is selected, a pop-up menu is available at the right, allowing the track's colour to be picked:

The Channel Right-Click Menu

Right-clicking in the mix console window once a channel has been selected brings up a menu which has a number of useful features.

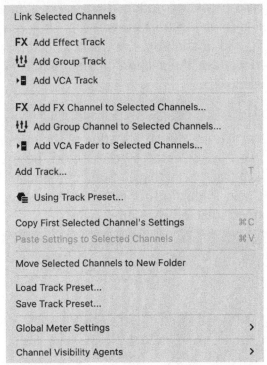

Link Selected Channels

FX Add Effect Track

Add Group Track

Add VCA Track

FX Add FX Channel to Selected Channels...

Add Group Channel to Selected Channels...

Add VCA Fader to Selected Channels...

Add Track...   T

Using Track Preset...

Copy First Selected Channel's Settings   ⌘C
Paste Settings to Selected Channels   ⌘V

Move Selected Channels to New Folder

Load Track Preset...
Save Track Preset...

Global Meter Settings   >

Channel Visibility Agents   >

Firstly, it's possible to add Effect, Group and VCA Tracks here, as well as adding any other type of track using the **Add Track...** entry. Other useful functions such as **Copy** (and Paste) are available, but the most useful entries are specific to this menu - the ability to add Group, FX and VCA Faders to selected tracks, speeding your workflow by removing extra steps from the process.

Adding Group Channels to selected channels

As seen on page 621, group channels can be extremely useful, providing a common fader, dynamics and effects processing for a number of tracks together, simplifying mixing and also providing options that tracks alone cannot have (such as compression applied to all the tracks together). They can be created directly from the mix console, and in addition, the tracks selected will automatically be added to them. Here we see the section of the menu that is presented when multiple tracks are selected:

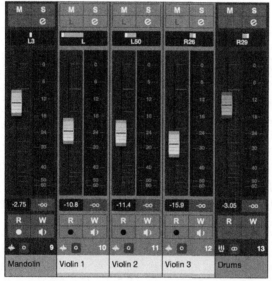

We will now see this in action. Here is a section of the mixer, showing our three guitar tracks, which we have selected by clicking on the first track's name and **SHIFT-Clicking** on the last track, selecting all three of them. If we wanted to select tracks that were not next to each other in the mix console, we could do so by holding down **CTRL** as we selected each one.

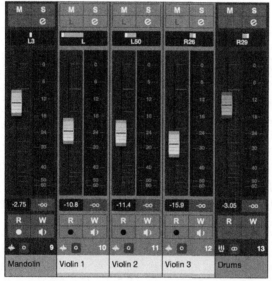

Right-clicking in the racks area summons the menu, and **Add Group Channel to Selected Channels...** is picked.

The **Add Group Channel Track** dialogue box appears, and the group channel name is entered - here **Violins** was chosen.

The Group Channel is created, and the routing of the selected channels is now altered to be through the new group.

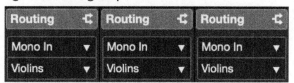

Adding FX Channels to selected channels

This works in a similar way to the previous section, but creates an FX channel instead of a group channel, and we will see an example of this in action. Here is a section of the mixer, with three channels selected. Note the current settings in the sends section - the first and third tracks have an FX send, but the middle one doesn't.

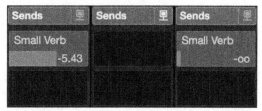

Right-clicking on the fader area summons the menu, and **Add FX Channel to Selected Channels...** is picked.

The **Add FX Channel Track** dialogue box appears, and the FX for the track is picked - here RoomWorks was chosen.

The FX Channel is created, and a send for that FX channel is created in each of the original selected tracks.

There are two points of note here - firstly, the send used is the first available one on each channel - note that for the first and third channels (which already had send 1 in use) this is send 2, while for the middle channel it is send 1. Secondly, note that the levels will be whatever was previously set in the project - in the case of the first and third channels, this is at -∞, but for the middle channel (whose send had previously been used and then discarded), it is at the level the send was when it was last used.

Using this feature can be a real time saver - it is extremely common to have to add an FX channel to the majority of tracks in a project, and adding a reverb to all of the tracks is now a much quicker process as the FX channel can be created and assigned in one action.

The Left Zone

The left zone is located on the left-hand size of the mix console, and has four functions - Visibility, Zones, History & Snapshots.

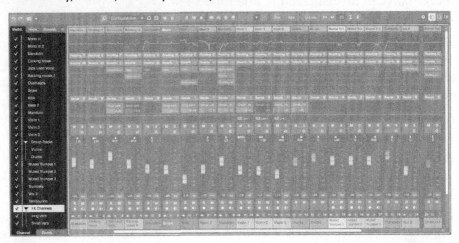

Visibility

Channel

This allows tracks to be visible or hidden in the mix console. By de-selecting the track (clicking on a tick) the track will no longer be visible in the mix console. Clicking the same area again will return the track to visible status.

This can be useful when there are a large number of tracks present or when you want to concentrate on a few without any other distractions.

Zones

By default all of the channels present in a pro-ject will be visible in the mix console, and if there are more than can be displayed at one time then a scrollbar will appear below the channels to al-low all of them to be viewed. Sometimes there are channels that you want present at all times, regardless of the viewing position of the other channels, and the Zones panel achieves this.

There is a white dot for each track - initially this is in the centre, as all the tracks default to being in the centre section of the mixer. However, clicking to the left or right of this position will make the track 'stick' to the left-hand or right-hand side of the mix console, and it will always be viewable in this area.

This is often useful for output channels (as keep-ing an eye on the output as you are working is often useful), or for inputs (so they can be seen quickly if you want to record straight away).

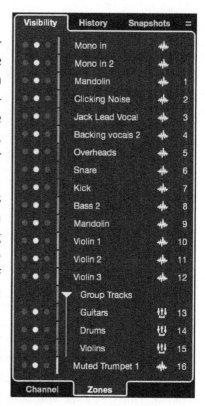

Note that when a channel has been fixed to either edge of the mixer, the area where the track number is becomes grey to give you an indication of what has happened.

History

In this mode, the history of changes made in the mix console (including FX set-tings) are available to undo and redo. This can be stepped through using the key-board (**ALT + Z** to undo, **ALT + SHIFT + Z** to redo), or by clicking in the list.

Snapshot

Snapshots allow you to capture all the settings of the mixer in one easy step - this allows different mixes to be created within a single project, without having to save a project as multiple different files.

A snapshot is captured by pressing the snapshot button that looks like a camera at the top left of the mixer.

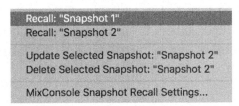

All of the current mixer settings will be stored with this snapshot. You can now experiment with wildly different mixer settings and not have to worry about getting back to a specific point in the mixer's undo history - you can just recall a snapshot using the menu at the top (by clicking the triangle to the right of the camera):

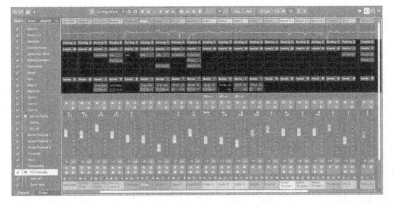

...or by clicking the button to the right of the snapshot in the list. Note, however, that this is not currently capable of storing automation for insert effects, so if you have created a mix with an insert effect in one snapshot and it is not present in another, you will lose the automation that you have created for it. Cubase will warn you about this possibility.

Channel Racks

The racks section is located at the upper right section of the mix console window.

The racks section shows the majority of the channel's settings - Routing, Pre, Inserts, EQ, Strip, Sends, Cues, Quick Controls and Panel. The majority of this information is available elsewhere, but this is a convenient location for all information about a track, and most importantly allows instant comparison between the settings of different channels.

Here is the channel rack section for one track, showing the Routing, Pre, Inserts, EQ and Strip sections, all of which are collapsed. To expand a section, click its heading (here, **Pre** was clicked).

The controls for the section are now visible - the control we are interested in is the Low Cut control which is currently set to **53Hz**, but is turned off. Clicking the power button which appears when hovering over the control...

...activates the control (note the change in its appearance). In addition the indicator next to the rack section is now 'on', indicating that a process inside that section is active.

Clicking the indicator bypasses the section - note the change in colour of the indicator, and also that the controls of the Low Cut also become grey, indicating that it is no longer working.

While editing of individual controls is possible in the channel rack, it is also extremely useful for comparing settings across a number of tracks, and editing them quickly. Here the sends section has been expanded, showing the send effects that have been used on different tracks for a quick comparison:

Editing of those sends is achieved quickly - levels can be dragged to alter them, and sends can be set up by clicking on the drop-down menu in the same way they are in the inspector - see page 538 for details on this.

The Strip

The strip section behaves slightly differently to the other racks, in that it contains up to 5 effects (plus the EQ) inside the section. If expanded then it will look as below:

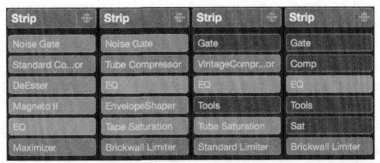

Active effects are indicated by illumination, and they can be edited by clicking the e that appears when hovering over each section.

The effects inside the strip section are covered in detail on page 602.

The Sends Right-Click Menu

While right-clicking anywhere on the mix console will bring up a menu of options relevant to that section, one point of note is the menu that appears when right-clicking on a send in the sends section of the channel rack. It is seen below.

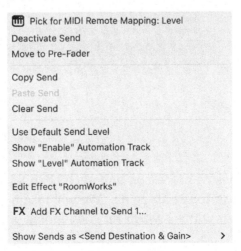

Use Default Send Level

This sets the send to 0dB, which can make the task of setting the send to a high level much quicker than clicking and dragging.

Show "Enable" and "Level" Automation Track

This option will display the (most commonly used) selected automation tracks in the project window - this can be much quicker than using the automation selection menu when in the project window, particularly when there are a great many parameters available from multiple sends.

EQ

The EQ section is covered in depth in the Effects chapter, on page 547.

Channel Strip Effects

The Channel Strip contains a variety of useful processors, providing dynamic effects and channel processing. They can be accessed either in the MixConsole's strip section (where each can be edited individually one at a time as a pop-up), or in the Channel Strip section in the Channel Settings Window, where they are all accessible at the same time:

Note that some of the effects (all three compressors and the Maximizer) offer expanded editors with more controls, accessed via their own e button at the top of their section.

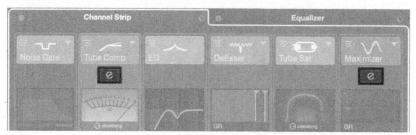

There are five categories of processor, and each channel can have one of each type active if you choose to use them all. We will take a brief look at each category and the processors within , which vary depending on the version of Cubase you are running.

Gate

As discussed in the Effects chapter on page 578, a gate can cut out audio below a set threshold. The channel strip gate offers similar facilities to the one in the Effects chapter, but without using an effects insert slot.

Comp

The compression section offers three different compressors, each with their own distinctive sounds and methods of operation. The standard compressor offers similar facilities to the one discussed in the Effects chapter on page 562, while the tube compressor adds a drive and mix control to emulate valve compressors with a level of distortion in them. The vintage compressor works in the manner of a classic compressor where the input control controls the amount of compression - there isn't a threshold control as such.

Tools

The envelope shaper provides a different form of dynamic control, where the attack and release rates of the audio are controlled - this controls the rate of change of the audio, allowing the envelope shaper to smooth out fast transients, and working well on tracks with a wide dynamic range. The De-Esser is a compressor with a side-chain sensitive to unwanted frequencies in speech, helping reduce unwanted sibilants.

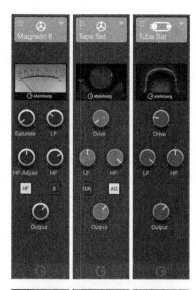

Sat

The saturation section emulates the subtle distortion and compression that is generated by vintage technologies - magnetic tape and tube (valve) amplification. They have subtle differences, and all three impart a smoothly, subtly distorted tone to the audio.

Limit

The limiting section of the channel strip provides three different kinds of limiters. In essence, a limiter is a compressor with infinite ratio - it stops the audio output going over a set level, regardless of the input level. Each of these processors does so in a different way, and experimentation with them is the only way to ensure you are using one which works well with your audio material.

Changing the order of the Strip section

The order of the effects in the strip section has been chosen carefully and makes sense for most applications, but sometimes it's necessary to apply them in a different order. Fortunately, the effects in the strip section (and the channel EQ's placement within them) can be re-ordered. This can be done in the channel settings window or the channel strip section in the MixConsole. The left-hand-side section (which usually shows insert effects) can be set to Strip by clicking in the top section, as seen overleaf.

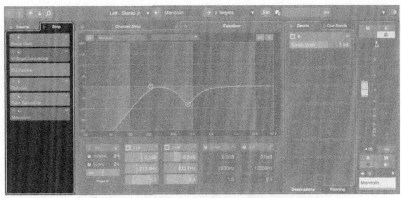

To re-order the strip effects, simply click and drag the section you want to move to its new location. Here the EQ Position has been moved from the third slot to the fifth:

Re-ordering can also be achieved by dragging the section headers in the channel strip area of the audio channel.

The Toolbar

The toolbar collects a number of useful facilities and tools, and is located along the top of the mix console window.

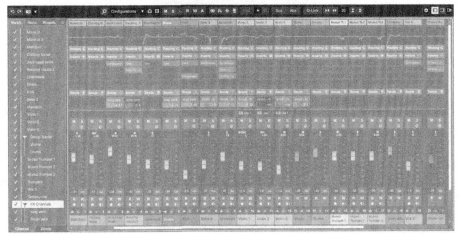

We will look at the useful options available here, from left to right.

Setup Window Layout

The Window Layout button is the box with small cog at the top right and clicking it provides a pop-up menu, enabling/hiding areas of the mix console , including which sections are included in the racks. Once you have selected the areas you wish to use, click outside the menu, or hit **ESC**. The areas which are not present by default are covered in on page 613.

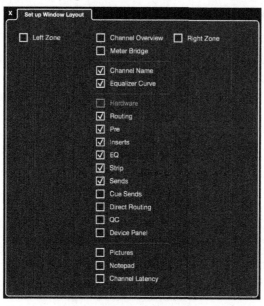

Channel Filter

The Channel Types menu alters the types of channel which are visible in the mix console and in the channel selector. By default it is set to all channels, but here it is possible to quickly hide any given type of channel.

Configuration

It's possible to save configurations of visible channels here - once you have the channel types you want visible, click on **Configurations** and pick **Add Configuration** from the menu that appears. You will then be prompted for a name.

The name and number will now appear in the button, and if channel types are hidden then the button will reflect this by becoming orange.

The menu will expand to reflect the different configurations you have saved, and you can use the menu to Add, Update, Rename and Delete configurations, as well as alter their positions.

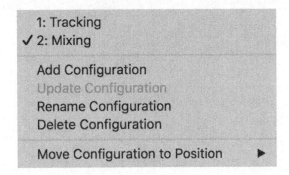

Channel Name and Equalizer Curve

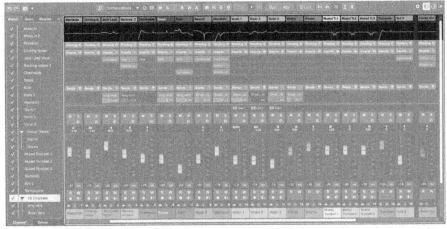

By default, the top section shows the channel name and Equaliser Curve. The channel name can be useful when navigating the mixer on a larger project or screen. The Equalizer Curve gives an overview of the currently-applied EQ for the channels in view, providing quick visual comparison between channels.

Hovering the mouse over the EQ for a given channel will show the EQs applied as individual dots which appear on the diagram:

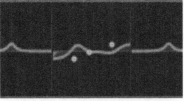

Moving over the dots will show which EQ band is active for that particular EQ:

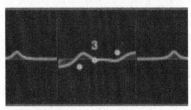

Clicking on the dot will allow that EQ to be edited in a larger-scale popup window:

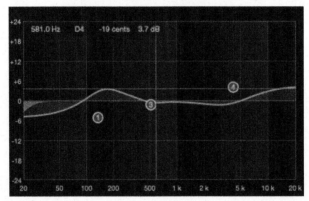

Note that the same keyboard modifiers apply as to the channel settings EQ curve - **CTRL** fixes frequency, adjusting gain only. **ALT** fixes gain, adjusting frequency only. **SHIFT** allows Q to be adjusted.

Agents

The agents menu offers a quick way of showing only tracks which are relevant at a given time - it alters the setting of the visibility section of the channel selector, depending on the option chosen from it, saving a lot of time in picking channels to examine, and in the case of large, complex projects it can allow the pinpointing of a track which is difficult to locate (such as one playing an extraneous noise which is proving hard to find).

Show All Channels
Show Only Selected Channels
Hide Selected Channels

Show Channels for Tracks with Data
Show Channels for Tracks with Data at the Cursor Position
Show Channels for Tracks with Data between the Locators

Show Channels that are Connected to the First Selected Channel

Undo Visibility Change
Redo Visibility Change

Mute, Automation and Bypass

This next section holds a number of buttons which allow control and override of muting, soloing, automation and sections of the rack.

Mute, Solo and Listen

This section shows whether any Mute, Solo or Listen controls are active, and if they are they can be deactivated globally by clicking the appropriate button. These work in the same way as the buttons on page 9.

Read, Write, Suspend All Automation

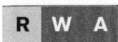

This section shows whether any Read or Write for automation is currently active, and can disable and enable them for all tracks. These controls work in the same way as those in the section on page 343.

The **A** control suspends the reading and writing of automation while it is active, which can be useful when working on a track which has a parameter automated which is making editing difficult (such as an automated mute) - again, this is the same functionality as described on page 349, but the button works for all parameters.

Bypass Rack Sections

This section allows the bypassing of Inserts, EQs, Channel Strip and Sends - to do this click on the appropriate button and you will see the bypass becomes active in the rack section.

Note that there is no indication that these buttons have been used - the only indication given is in the rack itself, with the racks showing bypass in the same way as indicated in the section on page 599.

Linking channels

While group channels can be extremely useful, the ability to link channels in the mixer offers a different way to approach the problem of treating multiple channels in the same way, and also offers the ability to make changes which would not be possible using Group channels.

Here are three channels that are to be linked, to allow their volumes to be controlled as one:

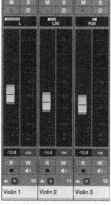

Once the three channels are selected, the Link button is pressed in the toolbar:

This will summon the menu where the parameters to be linked are selected:

Making a change to the volume fader of one of the channels will alter the others by the same amount:

Note that a new area has appeared above the pan control, showing the link group that the channels belong to. It's possible to edit the link from here, and also link an unlinked channel to an existing group. Remember that changes made to any linked parameter of a channel in the group will be reflected in all the other channels.

Linking limits:

In the example above, a decrease on one channel led to the others being decreased by the same amount. It's important to note that the behaviour of the controls will alter once their limits have been reached.

Faders

For the channel faders, the behaviour is different at the top and the bottom.

Here we see the three channels that have been linked:

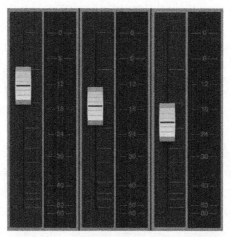

When the right-hand fader is moved up, it will not move any further once one of the other grouped faders has been moved to the top (+6dB).

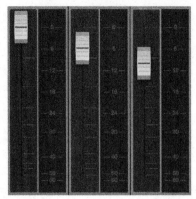

However, when moving down, the other faders will 'catch up', enabling the faders to all fade out to -∞ dB.

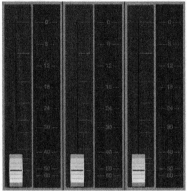

An important point to note here is that the faders will retain their relative balances once they are turned back up.

Pan

The pan control behaves slightly differently - it locks the parameters of the linked channels together, and once one of them reaches a limit, the others will move no further. Here we see the three pan controls that have been linked:

Moving the right-hand control to the right stops at 75 because the middle pan control has reached the limit.

Moving the left-hand control to the left moves all the way to the limit as the other controls do not reach the limit first.

Suspend

Sometimes it is useful to momentarily un-link a parameter to allow the relative settings to be adjusted. This is easily done by clicking the **Sus** button. When this is active, the linking is temporarily suspended, and any control that is altered is done in isolation. Turning **Sus** off will resume the linking. Note that the **ALT** key can be used to turn suspend on momentarily, saving moving up to the toolbar to activate it.

Absolute

Activating the Absolute button will lead any of the linked channels to take on the exact value of any control that is moved in that linked group. This can be useful when a number of parameters need to be set to the same value, such as an effect send or when resetting a section of the mixer.

Q-Link

Q-link is a temporary linking of selected channels - any parameter on a selected channel which is altered will be reflected in all the other channels.

If you get in the habit of using linking and Q-Link whenever you have channels which need the same action applied to them in the mixer, it will greatly speed up your workflow in Cubase.

Sections not shown by default

Some sections of the mix console are not shown by default, so we will now take a look at them and their functions.

Overview

The overview section is shown below.

It adds a meter bridge which allows quick viewing of levels across all channels within the project. This can be really useful for checking that channels are not peaking, particularly as it contains a peak meter which shows the highest level recorded on that channel. To reset the meters, click in one of the meters on the mixer's main channel section - the channel peak mixers will be reset, as will the overview ones.

Meter Bridge

The Meter Bridge section is shown below.

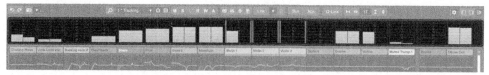

It shows meters for each channel, in a wider format that is complete with calibration markings in decibels. Each channel meter is the same width as the channels, so it may not show all the channels at once. The peak meters are reset either by clicking in the meter bridge area, or by clicking in a channel meter in the main mix section (as for the Overview peak meters). In addition to the standard PPM mode, the meters can also be set to Wave mode, showing the waveform as it plays back, giving a different view useful for noting transients. This can be activated by right-clicking on the meter area and setting the Meter Type to Wave.

Pictures

The pictures section is shown below.

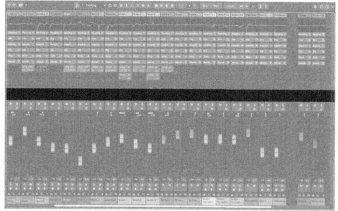

The pictures section allows each track to have a picture for ease of reference. To add a track picture, double-click in the picture area on the track you want to add a picture to, and the Track Pictures Browser window will appear.

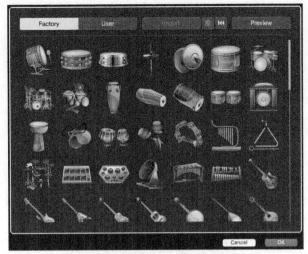

Pick a track picture and it will be added to the track. Here the mix console has a picture added for each track, speeding the recognition of the contents of that track, particularly on a large monitor and from a distance.

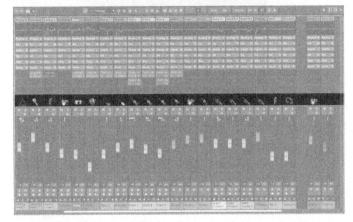

Notepad

The Notepad section is shown below.

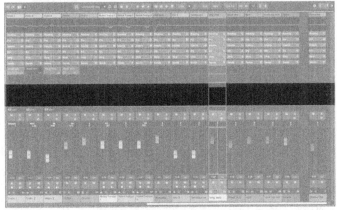

The notepad allows you to add text to each channel - useful for notes on future edits, or comments on the content of the track.

To enter a note, click in the notepad area, and you will be able to enter some text.

Once you have finished, click outside the box and your note will appear. Hitting **ESC** will cancel the editing without saving changes.

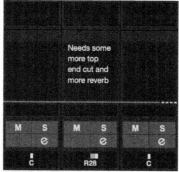

Note that there is no scrollbar on this section, and no indication of extra text present which is not being viewed. The notepad area can be resized, providing you have enough space on screen.

The Control Room / Meter section is shown below.

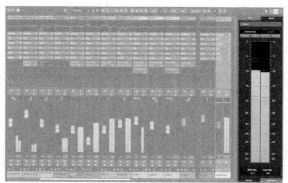

The Control Room / Meter section provides two modes of functionality - Control Room works in conjunction with Cubase's Control Room mode which provides more complex output and monitoring functions than the standard configuration, but as it is a complex area and not normally in use in workstation setups, it is not covered in this book. As a result we will look solely at the Meter mode, which provides some useful features.

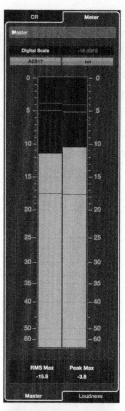

Master Mode

In master mode, the meter provides with a clear indication of the output level in a much larger format than the stereo out channel on the mix console. In addition to the maximum peak level (the same figure as given on the stereo output channel), there is also an RMS (Root Mean Square) Max, which is a clearer indication of the average signal level.

Loudness Mode

In loudness mode, the meter is metering the loudness rather than the peak level. Loudness and its measurement is a complex subject that is outside the scope of this book, but suffice to say that two pieces of audio with similar instrumentation in them and the same peak level can sound very different in terms of loudness. The loudness meter is a tool to combat this and ensure that tracks are of similar loudness, something which is particularly important in broadcasting where programmes can be vastly different in terms of loudness. It gives a number of different readouts which allow the engineer to measure the loudness of the audio with far more precision than the master mode can do. If you wish to investigate further, the EBU produces freely-available documents outlining the measurement processes here and the reasoning behind them.

Summary

The Mix Console provides more than just the ability to mix channels together. It has a variety of facilities which make working in Cubase faster - group and FX channel creation and allocation directly from the mixer, linking of channels for editing - and tools to allow you to process the audio within your project with much more accuracy than without. Learning the tools and facilities it has is important for working quickly and efficiently in Cubase, and that ideal is paramount - the less time you spend worrying about technicalities, the more time you can spend being creative.

Mixing

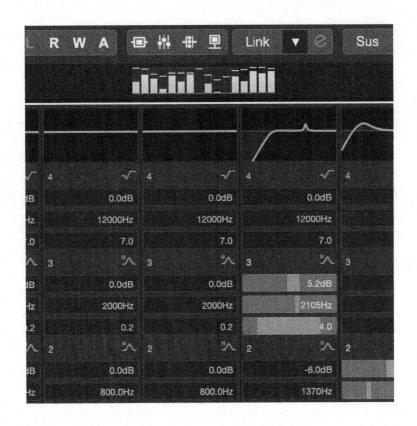

Mixing a track should be viewed in many ways as being one of the most creative parts of the recording process – it is dependent on the recording of tracks that are well captured, but after this there is the possibility of improving the sound of the tracks to make them sit well together, and create a coherent recording from these building blocks. While it is possible to simply set levels and make a mixdown (see page 636), you can often greatly improve the sound of a recording without making huge changes to the character of the recording if that is your objective, but it is also possible to make the mixing process far more creative and drastically alter the sound of the original performance. While this chapter cannot cover every eventuality (there are an infinite combination, after all), it will describe the general process which applies to many recordings.

Importing Tracks

If you have made your recording in Cubase, you can skip this step, but if you have made your recording elsewhere and have wave files to import, or have downloaded stems, then you will need to import them into Cubase to mix. t

Create a new, empty project, and use **File > Import > Audio File** and locate the audio files. If you click and drag a box around them in the file selector, you can import all of them at one time – make sure that **Copy files to Working Directory** is ticked, and when Cubase asks, click **Different Tracks** so they get imported to different tracks.

If you have imported your tracks, you may need to sort them into a more logical order – certainly it is a good idea to move all the tracks of a similar nature or instrument together – drums, bass, guitars, vocals, synths, etc. The actual order you use is obviously up to you, but remember to solo each track and name it so you can refer to it quickly in future.

Trimming the tracks

Your tracks may well look something like the screen in the section above. We can see that each track is the full duration of the piece, and this isn't needed in this case – there are periods where each instrument is silent.

To create a 'clean' sounding recording, it is often a good idea to trim out any sections of silence – this will result in the wanted information being easier to hear, and often an easier mix to control. You can trim the parts from start and end, and also make cuts into them to then trim to the correct lengths.

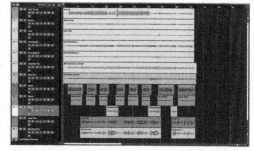

Add Group Channels

Group Channels Tracks are one of Cubase's tools that make mixing a much easier and quicker process. If you have a number of microphones on one instrument (such as on a drum kit), or a number of similar instruments (such as guitars or vocals), then using a group track will make you able to control the levels of all of those instruments together.

You can still control the relative balance of them individually, but then the overall level is easy to control as it will be controlled with just one fader. To do this, firstly add a Group Channel track directly here, or as shown on page 594. Name the Group – here two have been created, called **Drum Grp** and **Vox Grp**.

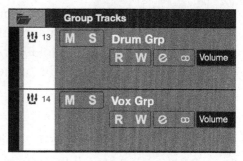

If not already done (when creating the groups), route the channels to the appropriate group – this can be done in the Inspector or in the Mixer.

Here we can see the pop-up menu appearing in the mixer for the output and groups. Once selected, the mixer/Inspector will reflect this change.

To set the relative volumes of the tracks in a group, use the channel faders to set this. If you want to set the overall volume of the tracks, instead of having to move all the faders, you can now do so with the Group fader instead. In addition, if you solo the Group, you can hear the entire group soloed which allows far quicker comparison of sounds and levels in context.

Add Folder Tracks

While Cubase offering many tracks allows great power, it can sometimes mean that the monitor is full of tracks and it is difficult to see what is really going on in the project window. Folder tracks offer a solution to this, and one which is particularly relevant when mixing drums or several guitars or vocals. Folder tracks allow other tracks to be placed inside them and can be "collapsed" meaning they will then only occupy one track on screen, while still working in the same way. This means when you are not working on the tracks in question they can take up little space without having to mess around with zoom settings. There are two main ways to create a folder track - either create the folder track and add the tracks manually, or to select multiple tracks and to move these tracks to a new folder. We will look at both methods.

Firstly, create a folder track, and name it – here it has been named drums. This is a 'container' into which other tracks (audio and MIDI) can be placed.

Next, click on the track (in the track column, not in the main section of the window) and move the track into the folder track – you should see a green arrow in the middle of the folder track.

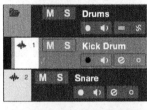

Here the track can be seen as being 'inside' the folder as it is slightly inset to the right.

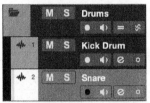

Once you have done this, move the rest of the tracks you want inside the folder into it. Here we see the second track (Snare) has been added, but the principle is the same for all the tracks.

Now you can press the folder icon on the track, and it will collapse, so it will only take up one track's worth of space on screen, while still working in the same way. To expand the folder, click on the icon again.

The second method is to select multiple tracks (Click on the first track, **SHIFT-Click** on the last to select them), and then right-click on one of them. From the menu that appears, select **Move Selected Tracks to New Folder**:

Once the folder track has been created, you can name it.

Note that folder tracks aren't only for convenience in display – anything you do to the folder track will be reflected in the tracks inside the folder track.

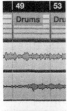

Here we see the folder track has been cut at bars 49 and 53.

Next we see the folder track has been trimmed back to bar 51, using the 'selection' tool and the editing handles that appear on any selected part.

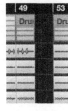

On 'opening' the folder, we can see the same edit has been applied to all the tracks inside the folder track.

Whenever you have tracks which might need the same editing applied to them, or tracks that logically group together, Folder Tracks offer a quick way to handle them and tidy up the project window.

Panning

While there isn't time to get into an in-depth explanation of the reasoning behind it, you should be aware that stereo (or any system which uses more than one speaker) alters the sound of a recording, and that alteration depends on the location of the sound within the sound field – a sound which is panned to one side will sound subtly different to one which is central (and being played by two speakers simultaneously to give the effect of being in between them). To minimise this effect, it is a good idea to pan your tracks before you do anything else in a mix. Granted there are situations where the panning will alter during the mix, but it is a good starting point. Panning can be done in the inspector or in the mixer, and it's often a good idea to use the view from the mixer to be able to view these alterations at one time.

Remember that you should be creative with your panning – it's a good idea to think about an imaginary band layout, and move the pan controls to reflect this – generally it's not good to be too extreme with most of your panning, but often with drum overheads placing them hard left and right will work well, and give some depth to the mix.

Set Levels

Next, listen to the track, and set levels. You may wish to do this by listening to one section or group of instruments, or you may want to listen to the entire mix together and adjust everything at once – many people find that they need to start out mixing a smaller number of tracks at first – make sure you listen to the effect the changes you make are having to the overall mix. Remember that at this point you are not setting final levels, just roughly setting the levels so you can make more detailed changes and judgements about the sounds – there should be no automation or similar data created yet. Remember when you are mixing to listen at a variety of levels, and never listen at a level which will make your ears tired for an extended period – it might sound good to you when it's loud, but you are not capable of making an objective judgement for long at a high level.

Effects

The use of effects is widespread in modern production, and almost unlimited – as a result it's not possible to cover every eventuality. There may be specific effects you wish to add (such as delay or chorus), and typically some form of reverb will be needed too.

When using a computer for mixing, it is important to be aware of the amount of processing power that you have – no matter how powerful a computer is, it only has a finite amount of power available, and if you exceed this, you will need to take steps to allow your mix to continue. But there are ways to minimise the amount of processor power that is needed, and one of them is to share effects between channels. This can't be done with dynamic effects (which need to work solely on one track), and when an effect is only needed on one channel – both of these effects should be used as an insert effect.

Where you wish to use the same effect on a number of channels (such as a reverb or a delay effect), it is best to use Effects (FX)Tracks – there will be one instance of your effect, and you will send a certain amount from each channel to that effect. To do this, create a new FX Track, as seen on page 538. Set the Track to stereo, and insert the desired effect (in this case, reverb). The project window will now show the new track (in an FX Tracks folder), but you will not hear any difference at the moment – some audio from each track needs to be sent to the FX Track now. For convenience, rename the track to something short, such as "Reverb"

This can be done in the mixer or inspector – we will show the mixer, but the procedure for the inspector is the same. Ensure that **Sends** are visible - if not, enable them as seen on page 606.

Click an empty send slot, and a pop-up menu will appear, listing the FX Tracks you have created and any groups as well. Select the FX Track you want.

The send is now routed to the FX Track, but there are two more steps to take before it will be set correctly.

Click the Power button to activate that send (shown as you will see when you hover over it) – the send will turn blue as seen in the next picture.

Now set the level you want to send by clicking on the indicator and dragging to the left or right. The level will be shown as seen here.

625

Note that if you have a group channel and want to have the effect across the entire group at the same level, there is no need to set up sends on individual channels, you can just use a single send for the group. If you want to have differing levels within the group then you will need to have a send for each Track, rather than the Group Track - remember this is easy to do with Q link - see page 613.

Above we see a number of different tracks, each of which has had Reverb added to it, but different amounts for each.

The choice of effects to add to a mix will be down to your discretion, but one of the most common effects to use is reverb. Because it simulates a physical space (something which isn't always captured when making a close-mic recording), it can make the recording sound more natural than without, and also tricks the brain into thinking the performers are all in the same physical location, which helps to tie everything together. Careful use of reverb can create a "3-D" image to the listener – a sound which has less reverb applied will sound closer to the listener. Often adding a lot of reverb to a low-frequency sound (such as a bass or kick drum) will 'muddy' the mix, but not always. A common beginner's mistake is to use a reverb which is too big and too loud – it doesn't have to be a huge-sounding reverb which simulates a cathedral to be effective – rather than picking something which reflects a real acoustic space and subtly adds to the ambience of the recording.

Individual Sounds

Whenever you mix a piece of music, it is important to keep the original goal in mind – to make the entire piece sound good. Whatever style you are working on, this is the objective that shouldn't be forgotten, and it is often easy to spend a very long time working on one sound, only to find that it doesn't work well with anything else. To this end, make sure that you constantly refer back to how that sound works in context. It is not uncommon to find a sound which sounds wonderful in isolation (such as a bass guitar) which doesn't work as well in context as a much more rough and ready track. It is important that each component of your recording is done so with an eye on quality, but this end should be tempered with the end result in mind.

With that point made, it's now time to listen to the recording in more detail. It's usually a good idea to make some notes as you go – just brief pointers such as "0:35 – guitars muddled" and so on, which will remind you which areas you need to fix. Some things may be immediately apparent, while other issues may take some time and experimentation to solve – certainly experience will make the most difference, so experimentation is key in gaining this experience. Always change one thing at a time, and make sure that it is an improvement before moving to the next area. If something isn't improving, go back to the original and work from there, trying something different.

While there are no 'one size fits all' suggestions, the following areas should be examined with most tracks to ensure that you get the most out of each track in a recording – sometimes simply doing a small amount to each track will transform a mix.

Compression

Compression is one of the most important tools in the mixer's arsenal. It can transform the sound of a recorded track from being dull and lifeless to having much more presence, and also help a track stand out by greatly increasing the average level of a track. It is rare to hear a modern recording without any compression at all, and indeed most will have compression on many tracks, as well as overall compression (which should be applied as a part of the 'mastering' process, after the mix itself is complete), so taking some time to experiment with compression and its effects on each track will pay dividends in terms of making your mix louder while preserving the dynamics of the original performance.

EQ

Correct use of EQ can take some time to master, but with practice it becomes easier to do. While you should never need to EQ a track to 'fix' a problem with it (this should have been taken care of during the recording phase), there are sometimes occasions where you have to do this - whether this is to remove a certain frequency that is causing problems, to alter the tonal makeup of a recorded track or to boost a frequency range which is deficient.

It is also possible to use EQ as an effect to dramatically alter the quality of a track – this has become popular in recent years, using EQ to alter the sound of backing vocals, for instance, to create contrast while retaining the same performer. Usually this is done using drastic bass cuts, creating a very mid-range biased sound (sounding like a telephone, popularised by many female artists), or using a low-pass filter which has its frequency reduced or increased over a period of time (such as used on many house remixes of older tracks).

EQ Settings

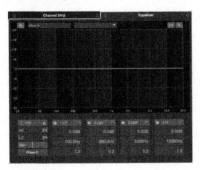

Firstly, open the channel settings, using the 'e' button on the channel in question. The screenshots will show just the EQ section of the channel in question - this part of the window can contain the Channel Strip, so if the EQ is not shown, click the `Equalizer` heading at the top of the window.

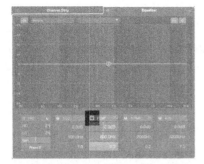

Here, band 2 has been turned on, using the "power" button at the top left of that EQ section. Note that the controls in that band are now active – gain (top control), frequency (middle control), and Q (bottom control) – this is how wide a band of frequencies the EQ will work on, as we will see later.

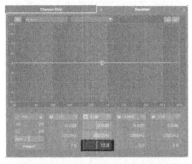

Here the Q has been set to 12 using the bottom control. The reason for this is simple – when the EQ is very focused it's much easier to hear its effect. Once you have centred it correctly, you can decrease the Q (and increase the width of frequencies it works on) to make it a more general effect.

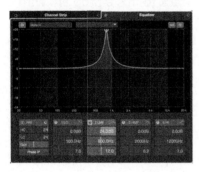

Next, turn down your monitoring level! The reason for this is that the extreme boost you are about to add will usually create distortion and if you're listening on headphones, could damage your hearing. So be careful, and then increase the gain by either altering the gain control to the right, or dragging the point on the graph upwards. You should now hear a very boosted, harsh, midrange sound.

Now, sweep the frequency from low to high, slowly, either by using the frequency control, or by dragging the point from left to right. You should hear the various frequencies being accented within the sound that you are listening to – the number of noticeable tones will differ depending on the sound you are processing. On a simple sound (such as a bass drum) there may only be one or two. One a complex one (an entire mix, a group of instruments, etc.) there may be many points at which a noticeable change is made.

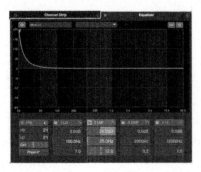

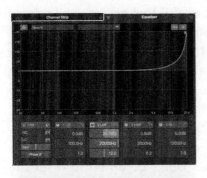

Here the frequency has been moved all the way to the right at the end of the sweep – it may take several sweeps to find the frequencies that you are after. Remember that you will want to boost to find a frequency, even if it is a tone that you want to decrease in level, such as a ringing or resonance. It's much easier to listen to a boosted sound than a cut one, so use boost to find the frequency that you're after.

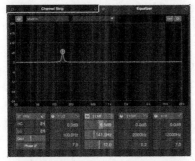

Here we see the frequency has been selected (141Hz which is the 'thud' of a drum in this case), but the amount was too much. The next step is to set the gain correctly – with the amount used above this will nearly always sound artificial and have too much of an effect. Here around 6dB of boost has been added, which is emphasising the desired part of the drum in question.

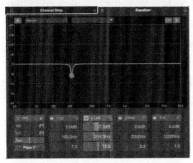

Here a cut has been applied instead – this is reducing the unwanted frequency in a drum, minimising the effect of any problems at that frequency. This is often used on drums that are 'ringing', and to remove harsh, unwanted frequencies in other instruments – often it is possible to make a sound sit far better in a mix using this technique.

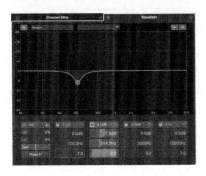

Here the same settings have been used, but the Q has been decreased, meaning the EQ works on a wider range of frequencies (as seen in the diagram above). This makes an EQ sound less 'focused', but can be useful for creating a more "general" effect – rather than boosting just a specific frequency, a more general effect can be what's needed, boosting or cutting the whole bass range rather than just a specific area of it.

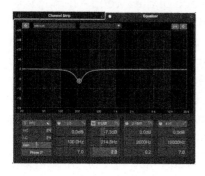

One of the most useful techniques while doing all of this? Turning the EQ off for comparison – it's easy to think that you're making a difference when in fact you aren't, so use the bypass button (top centre, seen activated here) to turn all the EQs off and hear the original unprocessed signal. You can then quickly hear if the EQ you have applied is having the effect you want, and if it is a positive change. Don't be afraid to reset the EQs (load the !Reset EQ preset) and start again – your ears should tell you if what you're doing is working or not.

As seen in the Effects chapter, it is easier to pick out a specific frequency by increasing the gain and the Q to pinpoint a frequency, regardless of whether the end result is a desired cut or boost. You can use this to accentuate any characteristics of a specific track, or to give a more general effect, such as adding a high shelving filter to make drum overheads or acoustic guitar sound 'brighter'.

Use of "contouring" EQ on similar-sounding parts (or those which seem to clash) is an extremely important technique which can often make parts fit together that seem incompatible beforehand. Many producers and mix engineers talk of giving each instrument its own range of frequencies, and this is done using this technique. Of course there will be frequencies present in each track that fall outside its own range, but the idea is to give prominence to one instrument (or group of them) in a specific frequency band. This will be covered in a later section.

Making drums sound better

One of the most common problems when comparing a self-recorded track to a commercial recording is that a lot of the sounds seem a bit "weak" in comparison, and the drum kit is possibly the most noticeable area for this to happen. While such production values aren't needed for all styles, many recordings will benefit from a bass drum which has real power, a snare which has punch and clarity and overheads which are clear and clean. Achieving this can be quite difficult for the beginner, but the following may help for many mixes.

Firstly remember that you need to have recorded a good sound in the first place. It is possible to improve just about any recorded track, but the better it sounds when untreated, the better the end result will be when you have processed it. If you have a bass drum sound which is weak and has very little low frequency energy, no amount of gating, compression or EQ will make it sound as good as a well recorded one which has been treated in a similar manner.

Secondly, it's important to remember that what sounds good in isolation will not necessarily work well in context, so listen to at least the whole kit sound often as well as a single track on its own.

To start out, solo just the bass drum. You will usually find that there is some bleed from other parts of the drum kit, and this is part of the problem – if you try to just turn up the kick drum, you're also adding the sound of other parts of the kit. To the right we see a well-recorded kick drum, but you can clearly see bleed from the snare (the small lump half way through) - this isn't wanted. To rectify this, insert the Gate plugin from the dynamics menu.

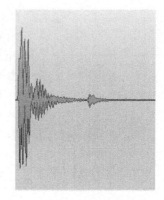

Here we see the gate plug-in, with its default settings. The function of the gate is covered on page 578, but we will be doing something specific here, tuning the gate to be most sensitive to the bass drum. Turn down the release to 10mS (so the threshold can be clearly set), and then ...

... expand the Side-chain section (click the **SC** at the bottom left), and turn 'monitor' on - this allows us to hear the filtered sound that is triggering the gate. It's important to realise this isn't the end result, we are just able to hear the signal that the gate is being triggered by when we do this.

Next, we want to make the gate more specific, and this is done by setting the Q to a higher level, in this case 3. The Q setting will depend on what you are trying to gate - on many drums you can be quite specific, but on some instruments you will need a lower Q value to allow a wider range of frequencies to trigger the gate

While listening to the track, the frequency now needs to be set. This was done by playing the track and sweeping the control until the characteristic frequency of the sound is heard. The more you do this kind of thing, the better your initial idea will be of the frequency needed.

Now monitor is turned off (as we have finished tuning the listening filter), and the threshold needs to be adjusted. Before we tuned the filter, the gate was opening at the default of -20, but we need to reduce this value now as the filtering has removed some of the signal. A value of -30dB worked OK, with the state LED going green on bass drum peaks.

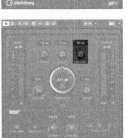

Finally, the release is tuned to suit the instrument in question. When set at the default value of 150mS, the snare drum bleed still got through as it was less than that time between bass drum and snare bleed. This setting (50mS) led to a much tighter-sounding bass drum, with no evidence of the snare sound previously between.

Careful adjustment of the controls is vital for a good result, so listen to the track while making a visual check of the track's signal to make sure that no important notes are being missed - it is not unusual to find that parts of a track are being completely gated out if careful attention to levels has not been paid - it's easy to miss out the beginning of building fills, etc. on the drums if you don't do so.

You may find that the sound is a little artificial when you have gated it. Careful tuning of the threshold and release times in particular can help with this, but remember that you will be mixing the drums in with the overhead sound which will often cover up these problems, and they are less of an issue than the areas fixed by this.

EQ

Next, some creative EQ can work wonders – targeted EQ is a really powerful tool to improve the sound of many instruments and make a mix work well. In this instance, we want to accentuate the drum's characteristic frequencies – this can vary depending on the drum, context and the end result that you are after, but with most drums you will find that there are multiple frequencies which can be boosted, each of them leading to a different character for the same drum.

In the case of the bass drum, there are usually two or three ranges which can increase the power of the drum's sound. The basic procedure is shown in the EQ section above – with most bass drums you will find that there are various frequencies that can be highlighted which will enhance either the low-frequency 'thud' of the drum or accent the attack of the drum at higher frequencies; doing this can completely alter the character of what you have recorded or be used just to accentuate what is already there.

Finally, you may want to add compression to the drum – this can often be the case where original playing inaccuracies (in volume) are not desired, and a 'flatter' effect is more desirable, with even-volume hits. Insert a compressor on the track, and depending on the level of the signal on the track, you may need to alter the threshold control to get any compression (the amount is given on the gain reduction meter), and often you will find that just a few dB of compression will make a great difference to the sound. Remember that a good general rule is to set the `Make-Up Gain` control to the same as the reading that you see on the Gain Reduction meter – this will mean that the signal's peaks are at roughly the same level as they were before the compression, and means that the average signal level will be more than it was before (as the quieter sounds will have been turned up).

When performing this same routine on snare drums, there are often more frequencies to consider – on many occasions the snare drum will have some undesirable frequencies which need to be removed (home in on them using boost, and then cut them by moving the point below the 0dB line on the EQ graph), and in addition you may find that two or three bands of EQ are needed to get a good sound – as well as the sound of the body and the skin, there are also higher-frequency elements to consider with the snare itself.

You should now find that the kit sounds much better as the bass and snare drums have more power and bite – often this means they can be turned down compared to the initial settings on the mixer. The overheads often benefit from a high-frequency boost (using band 4 which is pre-set to be a "High Shelving" filter, meaning that it boosts everything from the set frequency and above), a few dB at 5-10kHz will often achieve this, adding brightness and 'shine' to them.

Finally, overall compression. As we have seen elsewhere, compressors increase the average signal level when used properly – they are a two-stage process where firstly the higher-level peaks are turned down (with correct setting of the Threshold and Ratio controls), but then this entire processed signal is boosted with the make-up gain control, meaning that typically the peak signal level is the same as before, but the lower signal levels are boosted far in excess of their original level, making for a much higher average energy level, and a much 'louder' sound. Applying a small amount (only 2-4dB) of compression to the drum group (i.e. to the whole kit) can really help make the entire kit sound bigger and more powerful.

Conflicts

Often there are elements within a mix that conflict with each other – this can be similar parts played on the same instrument (such as multiple guitar or vocal parts), or sometimes different instruments that conflict (where they are vying for the same range of frequencies). If required (this isn't always an undesirable situation), this can be fixed in a number of ways, the first of which is using EQ to give each instrument 'control' of a certain range of frequencies. The idea behind this is to allow an instrument a range of frequencies where it will be dominant over other sounds – this makes it easier to hear without having to boost the level excessively. It is covered in the Effects chapter, on page 561, but we will look at it in a specific application here.

The first stage is to find out where the 'characteristic' frequencies of the instruments in question are – if they are both guitars, you might think that they would need the same frequency range (and indeed identical guitars playing identical parts may well do) but often you will find that different parts are centred around different frequencies. Once you have found this frequency, the idea is to apply some boost to that frequency on one instrument while cutting that frequency on others that conflict with it.

Below is an example, which makes use of the channel comparison mode, as seen on page 552. Note that low cut has been applied to both channels in addition to the complimentary EQ - it is often the case that other EQ will be needed.

Here we see one of the channels – in this case the characteristic frequency is around the 1.4kHz area, and a boost has been applied to this channel. The other channel's characteristic frequency is around 3.4kHz, so here a cut has been applied. The other channel...

... mirrors this with a boost at its characteristic frequency, and a cut at the frequency of channel 1. This allows the two tracks (in this case, backing and lead vocals) to be heard more clearly without either needing to be turned up in the mix.

Secondly, panning. Humans hear things in stereo, and we are very good at differentiating between sounds that are similar provided they are in different positions. This is referred to as the "cocktail party effect" – when you are in a large group of people, all of them are producing similar sounds all in a similar range of frequencies. We can still differentiate between them (and listen to the person we want to), and this is aided greatly by hearing in stereo. By placing similar-sounding parts in different parts of the stereo field, the listener will find it easier to hear two separate parts rather than one conflicting one.

Thirdly, effects. Aside from side-to-side differentiation (using panning), it is also possible to separate parts from each other by adding effects (and particularly reverb) to them – this allows the brain to separate them. In the case of reverb a great deal of our depth perception comes from the amount of 'room sound' that accompanies a sound; with more reverb we perceive the sound to be further away.

Building the Mix

Once you have EQ-ed your tracks, you may find that you need to re-set the levels between tracks. At this point, don't include any automation data – if there are sections which need more or less level, then just make a note of them, and instead try to get the majority of the track in balance. Once again, you may find that you need to do this section by section – don't be afraid to 'start again' from the rhythm section if you find that you're not getting the results you want. With practice you will be able to mix more tracks more quickly, but at first make sure you get things right, and this takes time. Be ready to have to listen to the track many times over to get the balance right.

There are several ways you can approach the control of needing to change levels as the mix plays back:

Automation

As covered in the automation chapter, you can automate the channel faders, controlling the levels up and down. This can be very useful, but you need to be sure that the levels you are setting are right – if you want to change them afterwards (let's say you decide an instrument is too loud throughout) then you'll have to change all the automation for that channel to achieve this.

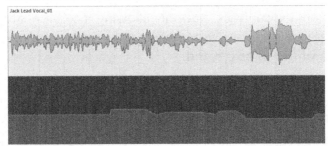

Using the volume setting

Whenever you click on an audio event, it has a square 'handle' at the top, and dragging this up and down alters the playback volume of that event. By carefully cutting the events to suit, you can create an automation of sorts, but bear in mind that the relative changes you have made (i.e. the difference between this event and the next one on this track) will not be lost if you change the channel fader level – this means you can change the overall level of this track in the mix while preserving the changes you've just made.

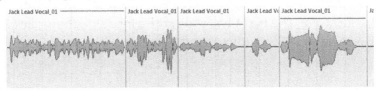

Using Event Envelopes on events

This is a more complex version of the default volume settings (fade in, fade out and level) that are applied to each event by default – use the pencil tool to add and edit them – once you change tools the curve will be seen as a line on top of the audio event, and you will still be able to use the volume setting and fade in/out as shown above. Holding the shift key will turn the pencil in to a rubber to remove points from the curves.

You should be listening for balance throughout the piece, and remember that it's often worth looking away from the computer screen as you mix – it's not uncommon to want to change something just because it "looks wrong", so make sure it's your ears that are guiding you, not your eyes.

Remember it is possible to automate effects as well (and indeed just about any parameter within Cubase and most effects/synthesizers as well), so you can alter the level of them and their parameters as you go. A common use for this is to have a delay on a vocal track, but only allowing it to be heard at the end of phrases, but there are many situations where automation of an effect will allow a cleaner and clearer mix to be created.

Using compression

You may already be using compression on some of your tracks, but be aware that it's possible to use it to help you mix, using the Ducking technique which is shown on page 566 - you can use this on some tracks to make some of the mix automatic, such as the example shown which uses the vocal to slightly reduce the level of the guitars, helping reduce conflicts between the two.

Mixdown

One of the most common tasks you will need to do is to create a mixdown of your work - this is making an audio file of your current project. While it should be a fairly straightforward process, there are a number of things that need to be checked to achieve a good mixdown. Firstly, however, we will cover the process of creating the mixdown. Cubase will create a mixdown of whatever is audible between your locators. The first task is to set the locators, then, click **File > Export > Audio Mixdown**. The audio export window will appear.

Artist   Pro

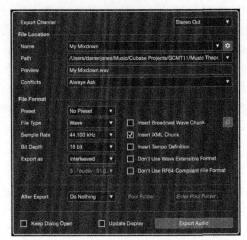   

The Cubase Pro export window offers a multitude of options that will not be covered here, but regardless of the version you're using, the most important settings for you to export your track are covered below.

File Location

Name - It's always a good idea to make it descriptive, and add version numbers or dates if you will be making a number of files to compare.

Path - this is the location where the file will be saved. Make sure you know what it is so you don't spend ages looking for it after mixing the file down. Cubase has the option to use a project mixdown folder (which is automatically created when you make a new project, and is located as a sub-folder inside your project folder), which you can access by clicking the triangle at the right of the path section, and selecting **Project Mixdown Folder**. Any recently-used folders will appear here as well. You may prefer to use a single mixdowns folder for all your mixdowns, in which case, select it by picking **Choose...** and locating it.

File Format

The File Format section is where choices are made about the audio file that will be exported. The main choice is the File Type, but there are typically three options to select which will make a difference to the exported audio file. If you are making a file to burn to CD, for commercial release or for archive purposes, then you should use Wave File. If you are making a file for release over the internet or listening on an audio player, then choose MPEG 1 Layer 3 file - this is an MP3.

File Type - Wave File

This is an uncompressed audio format, with every detail preserved. The sample rate and bit depth should be chosen to suit the destination, and for many uses a 44.100 kHz 16 bit audio file will be fine, but if you are concerned about quality and dynamic range then 24 bit will give you considerably more (at the expense of a 50% larger file).

File Type - MP3

This is a compressed audio format, and it does this by discarding elements which we are judged not to notice. Generally, setting the sample rate to 44.100 kHz will suit most situations; setting the bit rate to suit the situation (by altering the quality and therefore the size of the file) is the main option to be concerned with. For general use, 192kbps will be OK, but if you are concerned about quality then using a higher bit rate (and making a larger file) is a good idea - certainly there will be very little difference between a 320kbps MP3 and a wave file to nearly all listeners.

Export As

Here it is possible to select the number of channels in the output file. For most purposes **Interleaved** will be the desired choice (stereo output in a single file), but there will be occasions (such as producing samples for use elsewhere or checking compatibility) that **Mono Downmix** will be wanted, outputting a single mono channel.

After Export

The options here will change, depending on the other software you have installed.

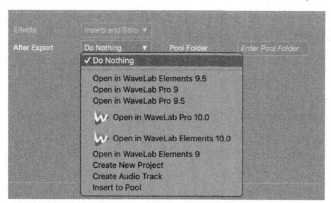

Here the option to open the resulting file in Wavelab is present, but the bottom three options are often useful:

Create New Project - this will import the mixdown into a new project, which is often useful for assessing the final mixdown (if you don't have a dedicated audio editor such as Wavelab), or to use the output of a project as a sample for manipulation in a new project.

Create Audio Track - allows re-importation of the mixdown into the current project, often useful when effects such as a reversed section of a project are needed.

Insert to Pool - this imports the audio file into the Pool, but doesn't place it in the project. This is useful when the location or length of the mixdown needs to be chosen.

In most situations, you will select **Do Nothing**. The next part of the process will be listening to your mixdown outside of Cubase, as assessing a mixdown without visual feedback is a useful technique.

Accurate Mixdowns

While the above covers the process - typically your visit to the window will be short - but there are a few things to look out for to ensure you create a good mixdown.

Setting locators

As mentioned above, the mixdown is only of the area between the locators, so setting them accurately is important. A quick way to set it round everything is to hit **CTRL + A** (select all) followed by **P** (set locators around current selection). For many mixdowns this will be adequate, but you will need to check if any effects you have used will extend beyond this time and would be cut off by it - if so, move the right locator to a suitably later position. A mixdown should not have a long silence after it, so you may need to audition the end a few times to get this right.

The correct tracks

Ensuring that the tracks you want to export are being played, and the tracks that should be silent are too is important; many a mixdown has been ruined by an unwanted visitor or most of it being silent due to an important track being muted.

Levels

Your mixdown level should be high, without distortion. To ensure this you will need to pay attention to the master fader level.

Here is the master fader, usually labelled as Stereo Out in Cubase. This is the channel through which your mixdown will be made, so getting the level of the mixdown right will depend on getting this level right. If the level is too high, then the signal will be distorted at some point in the mixdown. This will be indicated by the CLIP indicator in the channel (which can be reset by moving the fader or clicking in the clip), as well as the peak level readout showing a positive number (digital signal levels are measured as a negative value in dB, all of which are below the theoretical maximum of 0dB). If the signal level is too low, then detail can be lost; this is because the number of bits used to encode the digital signal is effectively decreased, and as seen on page 432 this means there is a reduction in the number of levels available, so the signal is less accurate. Unless the mixdown is severely below the maximum level this effect will not be too noticeable, but it is good practice to avoid this.

Here the level is too high - the peak meter shows a level of 2.1, and the CLIP indicator highlights this. The master level needs to be reduced, in this case by around 3.2dB (to -3.74dB), leading to a peak of -1.1dB

Here the level is too low - the peak is -22.1dB, which is far too low and will reduce the quality of the mixdown, as well as be quiet. The mix level needs to be increased, in this case by 21dB. The levels within the mix may need to be altered, as the master fader does not have enough gain available to increase the levels this much.

Here the level is good - the highest peak is -1.1dB, within the desirable window of between -2.0 and -1.0dB. While the theoretical maximum is 0.0dB, it is safer to aim for a maximum level of -1.0dB as this avoids some complex technical issues which can occur.

If Cubase's clip indicator has come on for the master output, then your mixdown will have distortion in it. If the levels are too low playback will be quiet and the quality will be compromised if this happens to an extreme degree. To get the output level right (making sure this is the playback level, NOT the fader level), you may need to play the track a number of times and make appropriate adjustments. AES / EBU recommends a peak value maximum of -1.0dB, so aim for a window of within 1.0dB below this. To check the levels, reset the peak indicator and play the song in its entirety. The peak level will now be displayed, and correcting it will be a case of altering the master fader position although you may need to make alterations to automation if you have used it on the master fader.

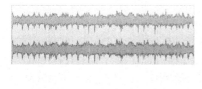

Here is a section of a song which has been mixed down with the correct level - there is no distortion as none of the peaks are reaching (or above) the maximum level.

Here is the same section, but mixed down with levels that are clipping. Note that the peaks are distorted as they have 'flattened out' where they would need to exceed the maximum level. This mixdown would be totally unacceptable.

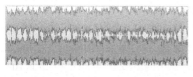

Here is a closeup of the mixdown above - the flattened peaks can be clearly seen, and clearly heard as distortion.

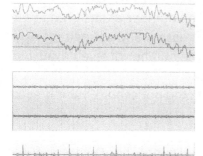

Here is the same mixdown with the level far too low. There will be subtle distortion occurring due to a lack of resolution of the mixdown.

Here is a signal showing the difference between the mixdown made with too low a level, and the correct level.

While this example has been amplified to show the effect and it would not be particularly audible in many examples, it illustrates the problem, and shows that setting the correct level is important to make the most of your project.

It should only take a few attempts to get the mixdown level correct, and it's a good idea to pay attention to it as you work so only minor alterations are necessary when you come to perform a mixdown. With these three areas taken care of, the mixdown should be free of problems.

Compare your work

Throughout the mixing process, it is easy to lose objectivity. Indeed, as anyone who has seen an optical illusion or a magician will tell you, it's possible for your senses to be fooled. One way to counteract this problem is to make reference to commercial material in a similar genre (or the original recording, should you be recording a cover version). In this way you will have an absolute source of reference, and remove many of the variables from the listening equation. While most professional recordings will have been worked on by engineers, producers and mastering engineers with years of experience and as a consequence will often sound 'better' than your recordings, it is a good idea to listen and compare to these – not only do they give something to compare to, they can also offer inspiration and a level of work to aim at. If your mix doesn't sound as "loud" as a commercial track, that may well be because it has not had multi-band compression applied; this will come at the final stage.

Rough mix & notes

An often underused part of the mixing process is to make an initial mix and spend some time listening to it. There are a couple of reasons for this.

Firstly, when you are working on a mix, your ears get tired. If you have heeded the warning earlier in this chapter, you shouldn't have been listening at high level for any length of time, but even so your ears (and brain) get tired after listening to and concentrating on a mix for a while. An initial mix will give you the chance to listen to exactly what you were doing but to make decisions after the event.

Secondly, it is not uncommon to make decisions which seem odd upon reflection. This is particularly true when first mixing recordings. An initial mix will allow you to review your decisions and act accordingly.

It is often best to leave the listening process for a couple of days – this gives you a chance to forget about many of the little issues you may think are there, and once you do listen to the mix, you are listening 'fresh'. In addition, ensure that you are in the right frame of mind and physical condition to listen in detail – it's no good doing so if you're tired or you've had a loud night out before and your ears aren't at their best.

Listen to the track once without making any notes, and then listen through again and make notes on anything in the mix that you don't like, and also things that you do – if there is something specific, make sure that it is retained.

Another useful tip is to listen to a mix on a number of systems, in a few different locations. For complex reasons, stereo systems which may look similar on paper can sound quite different to each other. In addition, the environment in which we listen to music alters the sound as well. It isn't possible to make a mix which will sound identical in different locations, but it is not a good idea to rely on listening on only one setup as it may have a characteristic which distorts your assessment of your own mix. Many professional studios simulate listening on 'consumer' grade speakers by having different monitor speakers (and in some cases a 'boom box' too) to make comparisons of their mixes.

Re-mix and A/B mixes

Once you have made notes on the original mix, open your project and re-save as a new file. This will give you the option of re-visiting your original mix should you want (or need!) to do so. It is a really useful technique to create a separate project in Cubase which contains only your final mixed-down versions of the song, and in this way you can compare each mix as it is created, and check that you really are moving forwards, not backwards. Once you have listened to the new mix and you are sure that you've improved the original deficiencies, make notes on the new one and return to the Cubase mix project to make those alterations. You may need to repeat this process several times, but at each stage ensure that you are actually improving the piece, not just going round in circles or being insecure about the end product.

Final editing and mastering

Once you have a final mix you are happy with, you may think that this is the end of the process, but there are some steps to take before that happens. If you have a dedicated audio editing program (such as Wavelab, Sound Forge or Audacity) then it's possible to use that to trim any silence from the beginning and end of the file, and also to apply any fade in or out that is needed. These processes can be performed in Cubase as well – once you have your original mix file, you can create a new project in Cubase that you re-import the stereo audio file into, and then perform the following operations.

Multi-band compression

This is a technique which is applied to recordings in many genres – pop, dance, rock all now have recordings which make use of this technique. As you have already seen, it is possible to compress a signal to increase its average signal level (see the Effects chapter for details of this if you need a reminder). What Multi-Band Compression does is to split the audio signal up into a number of different frequency bands, and then allow each of them to be compressed separately (see page 642 for full details on this). This means that it's possible to get as much energy as possible in each frequency band, rather than just overall. It can lead to mixes that sound 'louder', but also to allow them to be brighter and bassier at the same time, depending on the settings of the compressor that is used. MBC is quite different to using EQ – it's important to remember that. It is possible to compress one band more than another to alter the tonal balance of the mix, but this doesn't sound the same as using EQ, as dynamic changes are happening to each frequency band.

Many multiband compressors use 3 or more bands - the one included with Cubase uses 4. Correctly selecting the frequencies at which the bands start and stop is an important part of using a multiband compressor, so we will take a look at an example.

Here is the MBC, having been applied as an insert effect to the Stereo Out of the mix in question. It is compressing the entire mix, and we want to improve the perceived loudness of the mix a little bit - at present it sounds a bit weak.

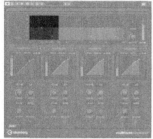

First, band 1 is soloed, and then the right-hand frequency limit is adjusted. In this case, it was adjusted to include the bass drum and the fundamental tone of the bass. It will take some practice and judgement to decide where to set the boundaries between frequency bands, but the more you do the easier you will find it.

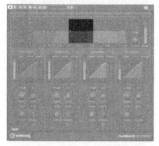

Next, band 2's upper frequency is adjusted. In this case it was adjusted to include the tones of the guitar, but to leave the brighter sounds predominantly in the next band, as much of the music's energy was already in this area, which was sounding a bit over-crowded.

Finally, the point between bands 3 and 4 was set, with band 3 soloed. Increasing it above 10kHz didn't seem to add much, but when band 4 was soloed in this position it was clear that there was audio present there, and this was left in band 4 to be compressed individually.

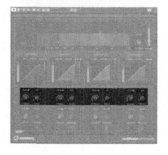

Next, each band was soloed in turn, and the compressor settings adjusted to achieve some compression, without each band being audibly compressed; it is very easy to get an over-compressed sound when adjusting these controls, particularly when they are not soloed. Regular bypassing is important to help avoid this.

Here we can see the results of the compression - as well as the momentary signals, each band has a peak compression meter (the numbers above), and this shows the highest amount of compression applied. Each band is being compressed a reasonable amount, but importantly...

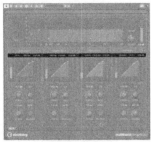

... it is more than on the default settings as seen here. The peak meters are useful tools for seeing what's happening over the course of a piece, and can easily be reset by clicking on the number.

Next, the output needs to be set correctly. It is possible to do this by altering the main out fader, but this means it is then not possible to directly compare the compressed and uncompressed signals using the bypass button as the levels will be dramatically different (usually making the compressed signal sound quieter). To set this correctly, reset the peak meter on the master output (click the smaller number) and play back the entire track from start to end. The peak meter will read the highest value seen in the track, which in this case was +5.0dB. We want to achieve a peak level of around -1.1dB, so to do this we will now set the master fader to -6.1dB. Naturally your numbers will vary from this, but the idea is the same.

Now reset the peak meter and play the track back again, and you should see a peak value of -1.1dB; sometimes you will need to re-adjust due to rounding up or down. The next step is to turn the compressor on, reset the peak meter, and play the entire track back again. Bear in mind that because the compressor is changing the mix dynamically, the peak level may happen at a different time to the uncompressed mix.

Here is the result of the mix playback with the compressor turned on. The peak level is now -8.3dB, which is 7.2dB lower than our desired output level of -1.1 dB. While we could alter the master output level to accomodate this change...

... it's a much better solution to use the output control on the Multiband Compressor to do this. Here it has been set to 7.2dB, which means that we get the same peak level if the compressor is working or if it is by-passed. This allows a direct A/B comparison between the signals, and gives a much better idea of what the MBC is really doing.

The use of Multi-Band Compression is a complex subject, and it's important not to over-do it - err on the side of caution if you are at all unsure, and be sure to A/B your compressed and uncompressed mixes to be certain you are improving it. Many mixes sound 'loud' at the expense of sound quality. They are distorted (although in a specific way which may not be immediately obvious to the casual listener), but unfortunately there is what is sometimes referred to as a "loudness war" happening with commercial recordings, with each new release trying to sound louder than the last, but being extremely tiring to listen to in the long run:

INMUCHTHESAMEWAYASIFEVERYTHINGWASINCAPITALSWITHOUTANYSPACESALLTHETIMEYOUGETTHEFEELINGTHATTHEPERSONWHOWROTEITISSHOUTINGANDTHERE'SNOTHINGINTHETEXTTOALLOWYOURBRAINTODECIPHERWHAT'SGOINGONSOITJUSTGIVESUP

There is no way to compete with this while retaining the quality of the original recording, so when you use Multiband Compression, make sure you do so sparingly, just to add a boost to your final mix, not to make up for deficiencies in it (make sure you only add this afterwards, not during the mix process), and don't try to compete with a mix that has a huge average level and sounds massive in comparison to your first mixes - remember that many of the people producing these mixes have been doing so for many years and have a great deal of experience.

It is often a good idea to keep mixdowns of your work as you go, and then to listen to them in comparison to each other. In the case of final mix compression it can also be interesting to view the effect on the overall dynamics of the piece, as well as sometimes being a useful analytical tool to see what is happening if something isn't going to plan.

Here we see two mixes of the same song (the one mixed above, in fact). One has been mixed down without any final processing, while the other has MBC applied.

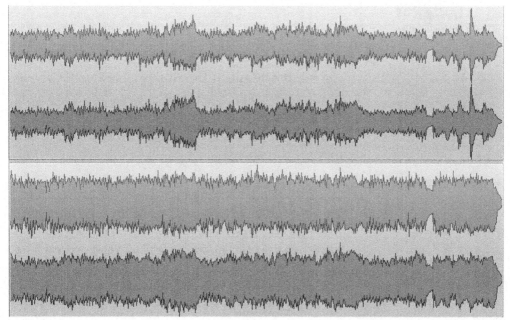

The top mix is uncompressed, while the bottom has been Multiband compressed. It's clear to see why such treatment has an effect on the overall sound - the average level is much greater in the bottom track (5dB louder, in fact), and while there are still dynamics present in the second mix, they are not as extreme as the first. This could have been achieved to a degree using full-band (standard) compression, but the MBC has worked to increase the overall level in a more efficient manner; for instance the large transient peak towards the end of the original mix (which reaches maximum level) is far less prominent in the bottom mix, and this is partly due to the way that MBC works; a standard compressor would have reduced the level of all frequencies in the mix, while an MBC will not do.

Normalising

Normalising is a simple process. It doesn't alter the sound quality at all - all it does it takes the maximum level in a recording (whatever it may be) to the real maximum (0dB). Effectively, it just turns the volume up to the maximum it can be in a recording. This is important as often a mix may be several dB under the maximum and then sound quiet as a result of this when played on CD.

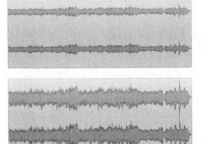

Here is the original audio file. The loudest part of it is right near the end (a peak), and that loudest part is around -8dB, so the entire file is quieter, and overall not loud enough for a final mixdown.

Here the file has been normalised. The loudest peak is now at 0dB, and everything else has been made 8dB louder. It's important to remember that this has just made the entire file louder.

Some multi-band compressors produce an output that is at or very close to 0dB, so you may find that this has little or no effect. To normalise a file in Cubase, right-click on your chosen mixdown track and select **Processes > Normalize** from the pop-up menu. Ensure **Peak Normalization** is set to 0.00 (100%) and close the window. However, if you have set your output fader correctly throughout the mix process (as seen in the steps on Multiband compression on page 642) then you should be around 0.1dB under maximum anyway, and normalising will not make a significant difference. It is also possible that in context on an album a track's desired maximum level may be less than 0dB anyway; it is not always the case that every track has to reach the maximum, but this can be edited when compiling an album.

Topping and Tailing

Sometimes you may need to "top and tail" your chosen normalised mix – this is editing the file to the correct length, and adding a small fade-in and fade-out at the beginning and end to ensure smooth, click-free playback.

Appropriate fades need to be applied to the end of audio files as well, and they generally fall into two types. If you have a "musical" fade to apply to the track, you should do that after the processes above – it should be the last thing you do to your file. Some tracks need a lengthy fade out, and whatever you have decided to do, make sure that it works well when the track is listened to – sometimes it is best to start the fade at a musical point (such as the beginning of a repeated section or bar/bars) as this makes most sense compositionally.

The first kind of fade is for a track which will not 'fade to repeat', but merely needs the end to be trimmed suitably.

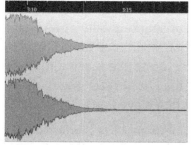

Here is the end of a song where the cymbals fade away over 10 seconds or so. While this is OK, towards the end (as the wanted sounds die out) there is some noise present which we want to remove as much as possible - while this should have been done during the mix, it is not always possible, so...

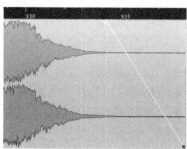

.. a 5-second or so fade is applied to the end of the piece, creating a more natural fade-out of the wanted and unwanted sounds. Generally if such a fade is applied over a suitably long period, the listener will not notice the change, even if there is a reasonably high level of unwanted noise present in the original recording.

The second type is a 'repeat to fade', or a fade-out as it is often known. Here the music will keep repeating, and the level will be reduced gradually over a period of time (often 20-30 seconds).

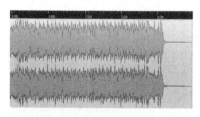

Here is the original end of the mixdown. It is too long, and contains a section where the musicians played an improvised and unwanted finish, so the first task is to trim out the unwanted section (about 20 seconds) using the trim handle to leave...

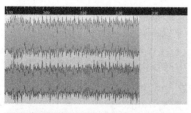

... the mix the correct length. The next stage is to use the triangular 'fade' handle (blue triangle at the top right) and drag it to the left to ...

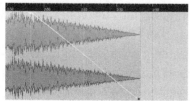

... create a fade out, here around 30 seconds long. Note that the displayed waveform reflects the actual output, and can be seen to fade out at the end.

Exercises

Mixing

The main exercise for this chapter is to perform mixes in the manner shown in the chapter. While it is not possible to cover every eventuality, and mixing itself is an enormous subject which has been covered in a great many large and detailed books, getting familiar with the tools you will use and actually making mixes will teach you a great deal. Follow the instructions from page 620, and mix your recording. Do not worry about applying Multi-Band compression when you are first mixing - it's far more important to concentrate on the basics of getting your tracks sounding good, and getting their levels in balance. Remember that use of compression can help you to avoid excessive dynamic changes and can ease the mixing process in doing so.

Make your mixdown into a format that you can listen to in a variety of places, and listen to it a number of times. You will almost certainly notice things that you want to change, so make a note of those issues and improve them, and make another mix. By repeatedly doing this you will improve your mix and also your ability to listen, concentrate and analyse what you are doing.

Multi-Band Compression

Only when you are producing a mix that you are happy with should you start applying multi-band compression, as seen on page 642. This should be thought of as a final addition to your mix, not something which is used constantly to cover up deficiencies in a mix. Remember that the recordings you have heard will nearly all be by professionals, many of them having decades of experience, using equipment which will be high quality and high budget. Set yourself realistic targets for your recordings and they will improve as you progress.

Summary

Mixing is a creative tool and when well executed it can be the difference between an average and a very good recording. There are many aspects to creating a good mix, and attention to detail at each step of the process will pay dividends. However, it is a complex task, and as such requires dedication and practice to achieve a high level of success. Using the outlines above, it should be possible to create mixes which will enhance your recordings, and each time you make a mix you should feel you have improved your skills and abilities. Listening is an extremely important part of the mixing process, as well as a full understanding of the technical details of the processes, techniques and equipment used. Given practice and time, you should be capable of making good mixes of your recordings that sound well balanced on a variety of playback systems.

Audio Setup in Cubase

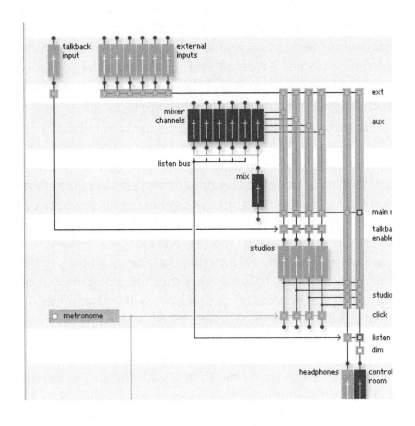

As sequencer setups become more complex, there are more settings to be aware of, and also more things to go wrong! This chapter covers a number of issues which may help when you have a problem with a Cubase setup. You may never need the information in here, but it is likely that at some point you will do, and understanding what's happening inside your DAW will help you when working with it as well.

Latency

In a computer recording setup, latency is the delay between an event occurring and that event being recognised or producing a result. For instance, when you press a key on a MIDI keyboard, there is a short delay while the electronics inside the keyboard recognise which key has been pressed and how hard, another delay while the message for that is sent out of the MIDI output, another one when the audio/MIDI interface gets the message and so on. Each of these delays is tiny, but they do add up. When a system is working well, it is not usually noticeable, and indeed in the case of MIDI there is rarely a problem – the amount of information handled is small, and is dealt with quickly and efficiently.

However, with Audio there can be a problem. Some background may help here. When PCs were first made, audio wasn't a part of their specification. Over several years, various different ways of playing sounds were added, and as a result of this audio became a more standard component and was integrated into Windows. But there was a big issue – the audio was generally for playback only, and certainly not for real-time processing. To ensure that it all worked smoothly, a technique called "buffering" was used. The reasons for this are sound – despite being very fast, computers can only do one thing at a time, so they divide their attention between many tasks by changing what they are doing many thousands of times a second, giving the impression of doing many things at once. To allow them to do this with audio, a 'buffer' is used. When a signal is received by an audio interface, it is converted to digital numbers, and these numbers are stored in a buffer, which may contain many hundreds (or thousands) of these numbers. At some point the processor will have time to deal with the audio, and may deal with several hundreds of these numbers in one go, and then go back to doing something else. By maintaining this buffer, the interface never has to 'wait' for the processor, and the processor always has enough work to get on with once it turns its attention to the sound. The same happens when a sound is played – the processor stores its output in a buffer intermittently, while the interface deals with these numbers and turns them into sound on a regular basis.

The big problem with this is when the buffers are large. By default the Windows buffers add up to nearly a second, meaning that if the computer wants to produce a sound, you will not hear it until nearly a second after it has been produced! Clearly this is no use for playing a keyboard "live", and as a result of this the ASIO standard was developed. An ASIO driver gives far more direct access to the interface from an audio application, meaning that the buffers can be far smaller, reducing latency greatly. Not all interfaces have an ASIO driver, but if yours does, you should use it.

As a good source of comparison, it takes sound around 1mS (1 thousandth of a second) to travel 1 foot. When you have an interface with a latency of 2mS, the delay is around the same as if you were 2 feet away from a speaker – minimal. It is only around the 10mS area that it becomes noticeable for most people. If you don't have access to an ASIO driver, then you can record your MIDI using a non-software synth (such as an external hardware unit or one with a built-in interface), and then use the software synth afterwards. Remember that often a lower latency makes greater demands on the computer, so if you are mixing you may wish to increase the latency to lower the load on the system and allow more processing.

Altering the driver and latency

The driver can be altered by going to **Studio > Studio Setup** and clicking on **Audio System**. You will then see a screen similar to the one shown here – you can pick the ASIO driver here (Windows has **Generic Low Latency ASIO Driver**, and macOS defaults to **Built-In Audio**). If you have another entry, then using that will usually work best – a dedicated ASIO driver should be installed with any suitable interface.

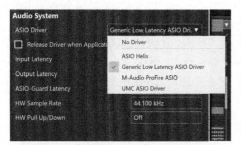

Clicking on the current driver will produce a list of all the drivers on the system. Here we see a choice of 4, currently selected is the Generic Low Latency ASIO Driver - this is the driver that will work with the most interfaces, but at the expense of highest latency.

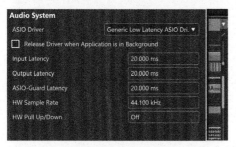

The key pieces of information are outlined here - the Input and Output latency being the most important ones. Here the Generic Low Latency ASIO Driver is selected, offering 20mS of Input and Output latency. This is low enough for on-screen events to seem in time with audio playback, but not for instruments to be played in real time.

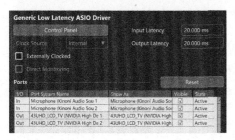

Clicking on the driver in the left-hand pane leads to this screen, showing the latencies, plus the input and output ports that the driver has. In this case there are two of each, often forming a stereo input and a stereo output.

Under **Visible** column it is possible to hide or show any of the ports that the interface has, although most of the time it will be best to leave them all visible (if they have been hidden they cannot be selected in the Audio Connections window which is explained later on).

Routing Audio in Cubase

One of the things that can create a great deal of confusion is that of audio routing in Cubase. The problem arises because Cubase needs to be able to deal with a wide range of interfaces, some of which only have a stereo input, some of which might have 32 or even more.

To make Cubase able to address the wide range of interfaces available, the Audio Connections window was introduced. What this does is allows Cubase to use a software input (which can be named anything you like), and then connect this Cubase input to a 'real' input in the Audio Connections window. The upside of this is that you can create your own input routings and access as large or as small an interface as you wish – it is very flexible. The downside is that sometimes an input you select for a track in Cubase may not be 'connected' to the actual interface input you were expecting, and you might record the wrong thing (or even just silence) as a result.

To overcome this, let's look at a few different situations, and how you edit these connections. To access the Audio Connections window, select **Studio** > **Audio Connections**. The Audio Connections window will appear, as shown to the left.

Here it is showing **Outputs**, although most of the time the **Inputs** tab is where we will be working, so click that.

If you click the Inputs tab, you will see the inputs that Cubase currently has set up - in this case called (**Stereo In - Left** and **Right**), and then the **Device Port** column, which shows the physical inputs that are connected to this – in this case the Microphone inputs of an interface

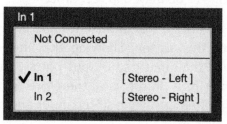

Clicking on one of the Device Port column entries will show a pop-up menu, and this menu lists all the inputs that the interface has. In this case it is a simple laptop setup, so there are only 2 inputs, as seen to the left.

This is a simple setup, and there is very little to create confusion here – Cubase only has two inputs (arranged as a single stereo input), and the computer's interface only has two inputs (arranged as a single stereo input) – everything will connect, largely, as we would expect.

This setup is the most common default, as many computers have two inputs, either arranged as a stereo one using a stereo mini jack, or using two separate inputs which are labelled left and right. If you want to make a stereo recording then this input can be selected on a stereo track, and all will work as expected.

The first issue comes when recording on a Mono track. To make life somewhat easier, Cubase allows you to pick individual inputs from within a stereo input when you are recording on a mono track.

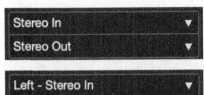

Here is a stereo track, with the stereo input selected on it.

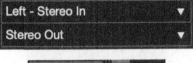

Here is a mono track, and note that it will record from the left input only - audio on the right input will **not** be recorded.

Here is the menu as the input is being selected - note that Left and Right appear as choices within the Stereo In. Either can be chosen and then recorded from.

For many simple recording setups this will be as complex as matters get. The problem comes when you have a more complex recording setup. If Cubase only had a stereo input, it would be impossible to record more than two channels at a time, which is no good for a multi-track recording where you might want to record 8 or more channels at once.

To allow for setups like these, Cubase allows the creation of more input buses – this is a way of connecting signals. In the case of a recording setup where it's possible to record 8 tracks at once, then usually you would want to have 8 input buses, normally arranged as 8 mono inputs.

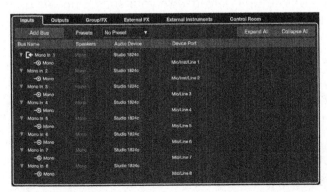

Here we have 8 inputs on the interface, and they are routed to 8 busses in Cubase. If you want to record a microphone you have plugged into channel 5, you should be able to select Mono 5 – this would give you access to anything coming in on the interface's fifth channel.

To create such a setup, click the **Add Bus** button, and then select **Mono**, and set the number of inputs you want to create. Now you will need to route them appropriately in the right-hand column of the window – usually you would want to route Mono In 1 to input 1 on the interface and so on to avoid confusion.

There is a problem, however. If you wish to record on a stereo track then you will not have a stereo input to record from. To achieve this, you would need to create a stereo buss in Cubase, and then route the appropriate inputs from the interface to that. This can mean that the same input can be available on more than one buss – in the example shown below, there are 8 Mono inputs, and a Stereo input. Both the Stereo inputs and Mono channels 1 & 2 are using the same input on the interface, they just arrange them differently.

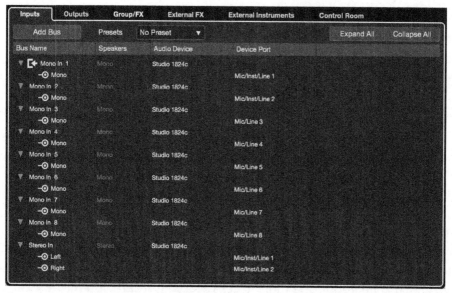

Here we see the setup described above. There are 8 Mono inputs, but in addition at the bottom there is a single Stereo Input (used in this case to record overheads for a drum kit). The Stereo Input and Mono Ins 1 & 2 both address ports 1 and 2 on the interface, but this is not a problem.

Practice with Audio Connections will allow you to be able to record any channel you want in any way you want. This setup is saved with your song, and will only be altered if you change interface (usually if you play the song back on another PC).

Tip: Probably the most useful tip for the Audio Connections window is to name the inputs and outputs clearly – by default Cubase uses some very long-winded names (such as ASIO DirectX Full Duplex Driver Stereo Out), which are far more clear when changed to something more concise such as "Stereo Out". In the same way, it's a good idea to use names such as the examples shown above – "Stereo In" and "Mono In 1", etc. This will make you far less likely to have a routing issue, and end up recording the wrong thing.

Plugins

A significant change occurred with the release of Cubase 9 - it has changed to being 64-bit only. On the face of it, this will make little difference to the casual user - Cubase will look, sound and function in the same manner as before. It does, however, lead to an issue which may make for difficulty for some users, and that is using plugins.

32-bit or 64-bit?

Originally the majority of VST plugins were 32-bit; this was the only option available when the VST format first arose, and many software creators made 32-bit plugins because the tools they had available worked that way, and there was little demand for 64-bit plugins. In the last few years, however, the limitations of running a 32-bit version of any piece of software became apparent, and that was the amount of memory that the software could use - 4GB. A few years ago, this would have been adequate, but as software became more complex and plugins relied on larger sound libraries, the limit became a problem as the 4GB includes Cubase as well as every plug-in that was running. A change to 64-bit was inevitable, and arrived with Cubase 9 in 2016. By default Cubase cannot use 32-bit plugins, so a solution has to be found, and the three possibilities are outlined below.

Obtain 64-bit versions

This is the best, simplest option. All of the plugins that come with Cubase are now 64-bit, and work out of the box with no issues. Nearly all new plugins (with few notable, free exceptions) will be 64-bit, and you will probably have installed a 64-bit version without realising it. If a 64-bit version of the plugin is available and installed, it will solely be a case of pointing Cubase at the appropriate folder, as seen on page 663.

Abandon 32-bit plugins and find alternatives

This option can be difficult for many users, as there are many plugins they have come to rely on over the years that are not available as 64-bit plugins. Often this applies to freeware plugins (in some cases built with tools or libraries which aren't available in 64-bit), products which are now considered as unsupported by the manufacturer, or products whose creators no longer exist. While there may be an alternative, the particular sound or features of any given plugin may not be replicated exactly. This is the least attractive option of the three.

Bridge 32-bit plugins to 64-bit.

The final option allows the use of most 32-bit plugins in a 64-bit host such as Cubase. It involves the use of a third party piece of software that allows Cubase to talk to the 32-bit plugin, and work as it did in previous versions. There is some setting up to do, but once it is done, there is little difference between the 'bridged' plugin and using the original - the main one being that keyboard shortcuts no longer work for Cubase if you have the plugin window in focus (because the plugin is now a separate program running on the computer).

Bridging plugins using JBridge

This next sections will show you how to bridge your 32-bit plugins to 64-bit using JBridge. Jbridge is a third party piece of software available here:

https://jstuff.wordpress.com/jbridge/ - Windows

https://jstuff.wordpress.com/jbridgem/ - Mac

(Author's note: I have no connection with the creator of JBridge, it is merely a tool which has worked very well in my own studio to allow continued use of plugins such as shortcircuit which I find invaluable.)

Jbridge is paid software (at the time of writing, it costs €14.99), so you may need to judge whether or not it is worth it for you. You can install it as a trial for free, which is a good way to test if it will work with a given plugin before paying for it.

Bridging plugins on Windows

You will need to know two folder locations - the location of your 32-bit plugins, and another folder where you will store the 64-bit versions. One suggestion is to have a folder structure like this, with a folder for the 32-bit versions of the plugins (VST Plugins Free) and another one for the 64-bit versions of the plugins and bridging files. It's often a good idea to keep paid and free VST plugins in separate folders as this can make management, updating and moving to a new computer simpler.

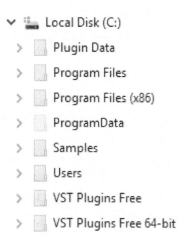

Once you have installed JBridge, you will have a program called Jbridger to run, which looks like this:

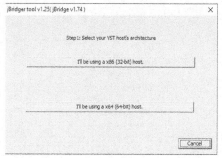

Click the second option (I'll be using a x64 (64-bit) host, and the step 2 window will appear:

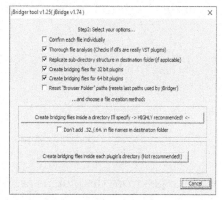

For most purposes, the default options as shown are adequate, so click the first of the two buttons (the one with **HIGHLY recommended** on it). The next window is used to select the folder with the original 32-bit plugins in. In this case, **C:\VST Plugins Free**\ was selected:

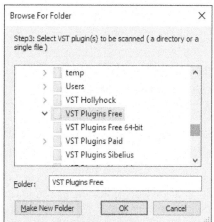

Jbridger now scans the plugins in the folder - this may take some time depending on the number of plugins you have. Jbridger will now ask you select a folder for your new bridged (64-bit) plugins to be stored in.

In this case, `C:\VST Plugins Free 64-bit\` was chosen:

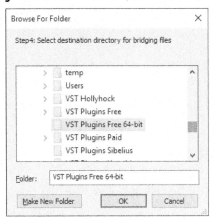

Jbridger will now run each of the plugins in the original 32-bit folder, which may take some time.

You may see a number of messages from the plugins as each one runs; some will not run via Jbridge, so be prepared to click OK; you will not be able to use that plugin in the future, so it may be worth considering removing it permanently from the original 32-bit plugin folder.

Once Jbridge has completed the scan, the last step is to point Cubase at the 64-bit plugin folder you have created, as seen on page 663.

Bridging Plugins on Mac

You will need to find a location to store your 32-bit plugins and place them there. One suggestion is to create a folder called VST-32 in \Library\Audio\Plugins\VST for 32-bit.

This will keep the 32-bit plugins separate, making any fault-finding or deletion easy. It's often a good idea to keep paid and free VST plugins in separate folders as this can make management, updating and moving to a new computer simpler.

VST Plugins on Mac have a .vst extension, as seen above.

Once you have installed JBridge, you will have a program called **jBridgerM** to run (from the Applications folder), which looks like this:

If you've used the suggested folder above, all the default settings are correct to bridge the plugins into 64-bit, so click **I'll be using a 64bit VST Host**

JbridgerM now scans the plugins in the folder - this may take some time depending on the number of plugins you have. Here it can be seen in progress. Don't worry if it looks like it's not doing anything, providing that the currently Processing plugin changes regularly:

> 2 - Choose your VST host's architecture to start the operation:
>
> Processing /Library/Audio/Plug-Ins/VST/Soundtoys/EchoBoyJr.vst...

You may see a number of messages from the plugins as each one runs; some will not run via Jbridge, so be prepared to click **OK**; you will not be able to use that plugin in the future, so it may be worth considering removing it permanently from the original 32-bit plugin folder. Once Jbridge completes the scan, it will show you the total of plugins it has processed and bridged:

> 2 - Choose your VST host's architecture to start the operation:
>
> Done! 22 files analyzed, 1 32bit plugin(s) bridged, 0 64bit plugin(s) bridged.
> You can now exit this application and start your VST host.
> Bridging files were placed in /Users/darrenjones/Library/Audio/Plug-Ins/VST/PluginsBridgedFor64BitVSTHosts/

Next, run Cubase. You will probably see a 'Blacklist' message, showing that the 32-bit plugins have been added to the blacklist. This is normal, as Cubase cannot run them, so just click **OK**.

You should now find that you can access the plugins via the usual route - here **Project > Add Track > Instrument** now shows the bridged plugin in the menu:

The default for Cubase is to scan the /Users/{your username}/Library/Audio/ Plug-Ins/VST folder, in which jBridgerM stored the bridged plugins. If yours don't appear (or you want to add another folder), follow the instructions in the next section.

Apple Silicon

In 2020, Apple began transitioning their computer line-up to their in-house silicon. While this offers the potential of increased performance, it means there is the possibility of increased complexity when running Cubase. By default, Cubase will run in native Apple Silicon mode, which should give access to the full performance of the system. This does, however, mean that only plugins which are compiled to run on Apple Silicon will work by default, and these will only be VST3 Plugins.

If you want to use any plugins which are created for Intel-based systems, or VST2 plugins, this is made possible by enabling Rosetta 2 mode, which allows the software to be translated to run on Apple silicon.

To do this, make sure Cubase is closed, and then use Finder to navigate to the Applications folder, and open up the properties for Cubase (⌘ + I). In the window, tick the option to **Open using Rosetta** and close the window. Cubase will now be in Rosetta 2 mode, and VST2 plugins and Intel-only VST3 plugins will be available. VST2 plugin paths in the Plug-In Manager will be visible as seen on page 663.

There is an impact on performance when running in Rosetta 2 mode, so in general this option should only be enabled when it is needed. If it is disabled and you attempt to load a project with a VST2 or Intel-based VST3 plugin, you will get a warning that the plugin is not available, but the project will load normally in other respects.

Installing Plugins

Cubase comes with a number of VST Plugins already installed. Some of them are Audio Effects, the others are Instruments. One of the greatest strengths of VST is that anyone with the skills can release a plugin, and many have done this creating a wealth of free plugins which you can use. There is an ever-changing selection of them which you can download for free, and while some may not be particularly useful or high quality, there are hundreds that are, and many rival the quality of commercially-available ones. Installing them is something that you will need to do, and the two main ways of doing it are covered here.

Using an installer

Most commercial plugins and some free ones come with an installer which will detect your VST Plugins folder and install the plugin to that location. If that is the case, you will have no problems as it's just a case of clicking OK a few times. A problem can arise when the installer doesn't detect your plugin location correctly (which can sometimes happen with older installers) - then you will need to tell it where the plugin folder is.

Locating the VST Plugins Folder

The Plugin Manager (since Cubase 8) enables management of VST plugins. While there should be a standard location for plugins, the actual location will depend on which version/s of Cubase you have installed, the order, and other settings that may have been applied. To find the currently-used location(s) of your plugins, go to **Studio > VST Plug-in Manager**, and you will see the manager.

At the bottom of the manager there is a cog, and clicking it will reveal the VST2 Plug-in Path Settings, showing the folders that Cubase is currently using for VST plugins. The folder locations will usually start with a C:\ on Windows systems, whereas on Mac OS they will start with / - typical settings are shown below.

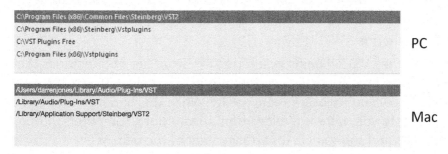

PC

Mac

Adding a location for VST2 Plugins

You can add a new location by clicking on the + in the plugin manager's Path Settings area:

In the PC example above, one has been added for Free VST Plugins to keep them separate from the default plugins. You could do this or use an existing folder now that you know the location of it. Keeping different categories of plugins separate (free plugins, paid-for plugins, for instance) is a good idea - particularly because it can make sharing your collection of free plugins (or moving them to another computer) a much simpler process as they are all in the same location.

Copying the file manually

Most free plugins do not come with an installer, they will consist of one or more files (usually .dll files on Windows, .vst files on Mac) which are the plugins themselves. If that's the case, you will need to copy them to the VST Plugins folder manually. To find the location, follow the directions in the previous section, and then copy them to the location you need.

In both cases, you will need to restart Cubase or click the Rescan All button in the Plug-in Manager window to start using them.

Arranging your plugins

There are two common types of VST Plugins - VST2 and VST3. VST3 plugins allow side-chain inputs (amongst other advantages), but VST2 is still a popular standard, and many plugins are VST2. While it is possible to search for a plugin quickly by entering a few characters of its name, arranging plugins into categories is still useful - a plugin's function may not be apparent from its name, and if you install a set of plugins from a manufacturer, they will often be grouped together by name instead of use. If you have a lot of plugins, it's easy to forget about some of them, and if you're looking for that perfect reverb, you may forget that one is called OrilRiver - or another non-descriptive name - and miss out if your plugins aren't arranged in categories.

Arranging VST2 Plugins

It's possible to arrange VST2 Plugins by altering the structure of directories they are stored in on the computer - moving them to new folders with structures as shown here will allow you to locate them easily. While the actual structure you use is of course up to you, here is a folder from the author's computer, showing some of the folders and sub-folders for arrangement of the plugins.

With the plugin files (.dll on PC, .vst on Mac) arranged appropriately, this makes for much quicker navigation of categories of effects and instruments. VST2 Plugins can be arranged either using the method in this section, or in the method in the following section - both will achieve a similar result. The advantage of moving the files of VST2 plugins is that moving to another computer requires only the movement of the plugins; Cubase will scan the folders and represent this structure in its menu. If you use the method in the next section and have to re-install, you will have to re-create the structure within Cubase. When installing many free plug-ins you have to move the file from your downloads folder to a VST plugin folder, so the extra time to put it in the right place makes this a simple way to keep on top of this.

Arranging VST2 and VST3 Plugins with Plugin Collections

Cubase creates a 'default' plugin collection which contains all of the plugins it finds - both VST2 and VST3, Instrument and Effect. This is often adequate for many users (particularly if combined with arrangement of VST2 plugins in the previous section), but if you want to change the structure of VST3 plugins' arrangement in the menu, then you can do it in the Plug-in Manager (**Studio > Plug-in Manager**).

On the right of the window, there is the current plugin Collection - Default - and this can't be edited. Clicking the + at the top right of the window will allow creation of a new collection. Pick Add All Plug-ins...

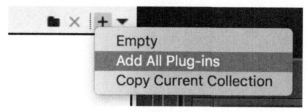

...and then name it in the window that follows

The new collection can be edited by creating folders...

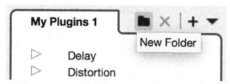

... and clicking and dragging plugins to their desired new location.

Note that the Plug-in Manager works in two modes - Effects and Instrument. Click on the headings in the window on the left-hand side to change between them. A new collection needs to be added for each if you wish to manage them, but the procedure is the same for both. When creating a new Plug-in in a project, note that the menu that appears has the name of the collection you are using at the top of it.

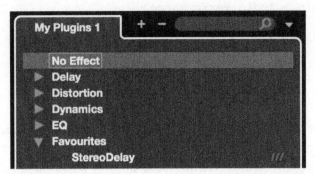

If you want to switch between collections, click on the triangle at the top right of the Plug-in Manager window, and use the menu to select or delete as appropriate (note that you can't delete the Default collection, so Delete doesn't appear in the menu when you have it selected).

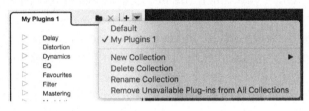

Shortcircuit (Windows Only)

As mentioned in page 318 of the Sampling chapter, Shortcircuit is an extremely powerful and versatile sampler, and is available for free as a Windows-based VST Instrument. It has, however, one drawback for use in some environments, and that is that one of the effects available in the filter section is named in a profane manner. If this is a problem, then it is possible to alter the plugin .dll file to change the name to a more pleasant one. If you load the .dll file into the freeware XVI32 editor, you can search for the string `bitf` (using **CTRL+F**), or you can go to offset **B26D3**. In the right-hand pane you will see the offending text, and you can click on it to edit it. Below are the relevant lines, with the altered text highlighted.

Once you have made these changes, you can save the .dll file, re-open Cubase and the effect will have been renamed.

Troubleshooting

A common issue with any computer-based recording setup is when the system is suffering from glitches, crackles and output breaking up. While this book cannot replace the skills and knowledge of a competent technician, there are a few common issues which can be easily and quickly addressed.

Firstly, it's a good idea to use the Audio Performance window to allow you to view how the system is handling the stresses you are placing on it. You can summon it with **F12** or `Studio > Audio Performance`.

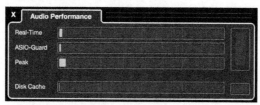

It shows Cubase's assessment of the Processor load (`Real-Time`, `ASIO-Guard` and `Peak`) and Disk load (`Disk Cache`), with a bar graph for each, and an overload 'light'. Monitoring this window while your project plays back can usually give a clue as to where the problem lies.

CPU Overload

It's important to realize that there is only a finite amount of processing power in any computer. Once you reach the limits, you will suffer from glitches. There are ways round this (discussed later on), but if you are simply suffering from having used too many effects or VST Instruments (and the amount you can use will vary depending on your computer's specification), then there is little that can be done. However you should have an idea of how many you can expect to run by comparing it with your system's previous performance and those of other similar systems.

If your system is suffering from glitches without excessive VST load, then it can come from a number of areas. Firstly, you should check that you have no other processes on the system that are running and taking up CPU time.

Checking CPU Load on Windows

Do this by pressing **CTRL + SHIFT + ESC** and going to the **Processes** tab.

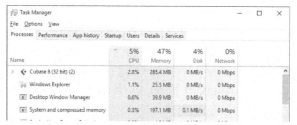

Click the CPU column twice – this will sort the processes by the amount of processing time they are using, with the highest at the top. Cubase should be the largest user of CPU use, but if you have something else presenting a major load on the CPU you may find it here – you will need to do some detective work to find out what a given process does, but usually putting the process name into a search engine will give you a good idea.

Checking CPU Load on Mac

To check the CPU load on Mac, navigate to `Applications > Utilities > Activity Monitor` in Finder. Once launched, you will see a window similar to the one below. If the CPU Column isn't arranged in reverse order, click on the heading until it is (highest CPU load first).

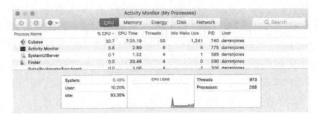

If another process is using significant CPU load, you can investigate what it is, and if needs be quit it from within Activity Monitor by selecting ⌥⌘Q

Disk Access

Excessive load can come from another area, when a disc is being accessed. Most systems don't suffer from this, but some still do. If you do find this, go to **Studio > Studio Setup**, click the **Audio system** tab, the bottom section of the right-hand pane shows options which may help.

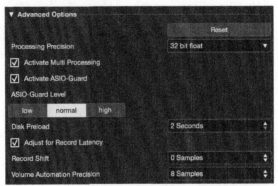

Altering the **Audio Priority** and **Disk Preload** amount can yield results here, although it may take experimentation to find out what works best on your system.

Disk Overload

Disk overload is when Cubase cannot get all the file information it needs at the right time. This can happen for a number of reasons.

Firstly, the disk may just be too slow. This isn't too common as today's systems offer high transfer rates, but it is possible with older disks or large projects. There are other, more likely causes, however.

Fragmentation can be a problem – this is where a file gets stored in a number of locations around the disk, rather than in one continuous space, effectively multiplying the amount of work the disk has to do to retrieve a given file. If you have any disk issue, defragment the drive first to ensure this isn't the problem. Bear in mind that the default Windows defragmentation software is neither efficient nor quick, and freeware alternatives such as Defraggler offer a much better solution.

External drives can be a source of problems too – sometimes they offer inferior performance, despite the drive itself being quick the electronics that transfer the data to the computer and the link itself (older standards of USB in particular) may not be fast enough to provide all the data in time - again this is a problem which is becoming less common as hardware improves, but it's always worth checking.

Trying to run a project from a CD-ROM is always a recipe for disappointment - it will not be able to supply the data quick enough, so copy it all onto your hard drive and open the project from there. Flash drives are often quick enough when playing back smaller projects, but many struggle to work well when being used to record to as they can have much slower write speeds than when reading. If you have problems with a project stored on an external hard drive, try using **File > Backup Project** to save the project onto the computer's internal hard drive, and then open it from there – then the files will all be stored on a local hard drive, and should solve such issues.

Getting more from a system

As already mentioned, there is a limit to the amount of processing any DAW can do, and sometimes that will be reached during a session. If you can't substitute some of the elements you have (such as processor-intensive effects or Virtual Instruments) then you will need to cut down the processor load in different ways.

Freeze

Freeze is a built-in feature of Cubase, and in essence this makes a mixdown of the track/instrument in question and then unloads the effects and/or VST Instrument, freeing up the load it was placing on the system.

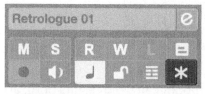

Here is the freeze control in the Inspector.

Here is the freeze control in the VST Instrument rack.

When freezing an audio track, the only option is the "Tail Size" – this is the length of time after the final audio on the track that the mix will take in – the default of 5 Seconds is usually long enough, but if you have an extremely long delay or reverb, this may need to be extended.

When freezing a VST Instrument, the option is given to freeze just the VST Instrument (allowing the channel that it uses to still be kept 'live' for edits to EQ and effects) or Instrument and Channel (useful when CPU-intensive effects are also employed and you are happy with them).

The major disadvantage of Freeze is that it is not possible to do further editing on the track while it is frozen – to do this you will need to Unfreeze it (click the freeze button again), make your edits and then re-freeze it. While this may seem a little long-winded, it does at least allow a processor-intensive track or session to run on even a low-powered system.

Economising

One extremely common problem that many suffer from is inefficient use of effects plugins – this stems from not making enough use of effects which can be configured as send effects (placed in an FX Channel), meaning that each track can have its own instance of an effect, despite the settings being the same across several channels. In the most common case, this happens with Reverb plugins, which also tend to be CPU-hungry. Whenever you run out of processing power, look at your mixer and see if there is any way you can economise on the number of effects you are using – if you have several similar or identical plugins on different channels (and they do not need to be run as inserts, such as dynamic effects), then make a new FX channel with that effect in, and remove the inserted effects you were using. While it is not usual to be able to economise in this way on dynamic effects, it can sometimes be possible by using group channels with those effects in.

Some plugins are also extremely CPU-intensive, and it can be worthwhile seeing if a substitution will work just as well; several free VST plugins sound good, but use a lot of CPU power.

Exercises

Set up Inputs

If you have an interface which has more than 2 inputs, then you will need to create inputs in the Audio Connections window to access them. This procedure is outlined on page 654, so run through it and make mono inputs to allow you to address each input individually. You should also practice creating stereo inputs, and altering the input ports for them to allow you to use stereo tracks efficiently in your recordings

Route audio inputs

The second step when using multiple inputs is to use the inspector to choose the appropriate Audio Connection for the audio track you want to record on. Familiarise yourself with this as whenever you are making a multi-track recording you will need to do this for each track.

Install a plugin

Installing freeware VST plugins is a great way to expand your sonic palette, and with the huge variety of high-quality free plugins available, it would be bizarre not to make use of them. Download a VST plugin from a reliable source, and install it, as shown on page 662.

Summary

While it is possible to work using a computer without knowing all of the information in this chapter, most of it will be needed at some point during your work within Cubase. Being able to route audio is vital if you are to record anything more than the simplest setups, and being able to manage a computer-based sequencing setup is something that most users need to do in order to work efficiently. Being au fait with all the aspects covered here will allow you to work well, even when your system is being taken to its limits by the ever-growing range of complex and power-hungry plugins.

Binary,
Hexadecimal
and MIDI
Communication

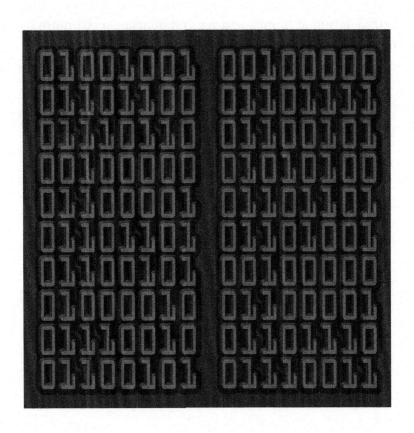

While this information isn't necessary to understand or use MIDI, it is useful to allow you to understand MIDI fully and in depth. While the information present here refers to MIDI 1.0, the same communication is present (with increasing amounts of data) in MIDI 2.0.

Binary

Computers at their lowest level are only capable of understanding two states – ON and OFF, represented as 1 and 0. All the information that modern computers process is stored as zeroes and ones, (called Bits, from Binary DigIT and all other information is stored as groups of these digits, often referred to as Bytes (a group of 8 bits is a Byte).

When counting in decimal (the system we have all grown up with), we fill a column up with all the available digits, starting at 0, then 1,2,3 up to 9. As we don't have a larger number to fit in that column we then expand into a new column with a 1, and re-start our original column from 0. Once we reach 9 again, we add another one to the second column (10s) and re-start our original count again. This repeats until the 10s column is filled, and then we carry into the next column (100s) and so on.

With Binary these same rules apply, but because we only have two values, the columns are worth different amounts, and we end up using a LOT more columns very quickly. This is difficult for us, but easy for computers.

Binary	Decimal
0	1
10	2
11	3
100	4
101	5
110	6
111	7
1000	8
1001	9
....	....
1111	15

We start out with 0, and then move to the next value, 1.

This is as high as this column can count, so we then put a 1 in the next column (which in this case is worth 2), and reset the original. We then increase the units to 1.... but to move to the next number...

.... we have to add another column, which in this case represents 4. The previous process repeats again, increasing in value until we've reached the maximum we can do with three bits – that's 7 in total. To represent a larger number (in this case 8) we need to...

... add a column which represents 8s. Once more the same process repeats adding numbers as we count up until our new maximum (15).

And once more the process is repeated, adding a new column, 16s. With these 5 columns it's possible to represent numbers up to 31. To represent 32 or larger we need to add another column, which represents 32. The pattern repeats with columns doubling in value each time – 64, 128, 256, 512, 1024, 2048, 4096, 8192, 16384, 32768 and so on. These values explain the commonly-seen values for computer-related numbers such as memory sizes, etc.

10000	16
10001	17
10011	18
.....	.....
11111	31

When MIDI was created, 4 bits were allocated within the datastream for the channel, and this explains why there are 16 MIDI channels – 4 bits allows us to count from 0 to 15, which is 16 channels in total. Much of the data which is transmitted starts with an actual value of 0 – when you send something on MIDI channel 1, it is represented at binary level by a 0, channel 2 by a 1, and so on. You don't need to worry about this for the most part, but there are some times when it becomes important – for instance some software packages show program changes in the value 0-127 (which is the 'real' transmitted value), but most use the range 1-128 (as using program change 0 was thought confusing to musicians) – it's important to be aware of which you are using or you may be one value out!

Hexadecimal

While computers can deal with 0s and 1s quickly and easily, humans can't. To make communication between programmers easier, a system called hexadecimal was adopted. As the name suggests, it uses 16 different values per column (as opposed to binary's 2 and decimal's 10), which may seem an odd choice, but as we will see it makes computer-related communication easier.

Hex	Decimal
0	0
1	1
...	...
9	9
A	10
B	11
C	12
D	13
E	14
F	15

As with decimal, we start out with 0, and can count up to 9, BUT we don't move into a new column yet – the letters A to F are used to represent values from 10 up to 15.

Now we have filled our first column and need to move into the next one, in this case worth 16. The counting of the units works as before, running from 0 through to 9 and then A through to F. We now have to add...

... one more to our 16s column and carry on as before going from 0 up to F in this column...

... and so on...

...until we reach the maximum we can hold in two digits, meaning we will now have to move into another column. In this case it is worth 16 times 16....

...which is 256, and the process begins again...

10	16
11	17
...	...
1D	29
1E	30
1F	31
20	32
21	33
...	...
2D	45
2E	46
2F	47
30	48
....	...
3F	63
40	64
....	...
...	...
FC	253
FD	254
FF	255
100	256
101	257
etc.	etc.

Now this may seem to be overly complex, but the reason that hexadecimal is used is because each hexadecimal digit can hold the same values as four binary digits (the range 0-15). As computers have developed, sets of 8 bits have become commonplace, and these can be represented as two hexadecimal digits rather than 8 bits (which is unmanageable for most humans) – rather than having to read 11001001 just C9 can be used. Decimal doesn't divide up well into binary 'column' values, so that's why Hexadecimal makes representing such values more clear.

MIDI 1.0 Transmission

As mentioned in the How MIDI Works chapter on page 55, MIDI 1.0 is a serial protocol, transmitted at 31.25kHz. MIDI 1.0 devices transmit messages as groups of 8 bits, giving a total of 256 different possible values for each message. However, the MIDI 1.0 spec differentiated between status bytes (which are instructions) and data bytes (which are values for the preceding instruction) – they always look different, and this is transmitted using the first bit – if that bit is 1 then it is a status byte, otherwise it is a data byte. This means we have 128 total values for data (0 – 127) and 128 possible status bytes (instructions). Those instructions are divided amongst the 16 channels giving us 8 possible message types, as we will see in the table below.

MIDI Message	Name	Description	Value 1	Value 2
80 8F	Note Off	Sent when a note is released	Pitch	Velocity
90 9F	Note On	Sent when a note is pressed	Pitch	Velocity
A0 AF	Aftertouch	Sends pressure for individual keys after they have been pressed	Pitch	Aftertouch Value
B0 BF	Control Change	Controls various parameters of the synthesizer	CC Number	Controller Value
C0 CF	Program Change	Alters the basic sound a synthesizer is producing	Program Number	N/A
D0 DF	Channel Pressure	Overall pressure for this channel (rather than Aftertouch which is each key)	Channel Pressure	N/A
E0 EF	Pitch Bend	Movement of the pitch wheel which allows bending of notes, typically ±2 semitones	Pitch Bend LSB	Pitch Bend MSB
F0 FF	System Messages	Various messages settings modes and allowing data transfer	Varies depending on the message type	

All the messages apart from System ones have their channel 'embedded' in them – the second hexadecimal digit represents the channel (with a 0 being channel 1, 1 being channel 2, up to F being channel 16). The system messages do not use this system – as their name implies, they are system-based and have 'global' consequences. System Exclusive messages (starting with an F0) were extremely common in the early days of MIDI as a means of transmitting data between devices; many synthesizers and samplers did not have a means of storing programs and data externally, and this allowed the data to be transmitted to a sequencer and saved or sent to a third party. With the advent of software synthesizers and more affordable storage, the use of System Exclusive data has declined greatly, but it is still useful, as are the other system messages - they can provide access to parameters which may not be editable by any other means.

Data bytes take the value 0-127 which are represented as 00 to 7F in hexadecimal – they look different to a status byte, and it is this that allows 'running status' to work (see the Communication section on page 56 for this).

In-depth knowledge of how MIDI transmits data isn't necessary to allow you to successfully use a sequencer, but if you have a good idea of what's going on at the lowest level, you should find understanding new concepts and the transmission of MIDI information a lot easier. Most MIDI 1.0 devices' manuals include a MIDI specification, which should show what the device is capable of sending and receiving and in the case of many synthesizers there is a detailed explanation of specific MIDI messages that the device can understand and interpret; often reading this can reveal features that aren't otherwise obvious (such as being able to program the sounds of the synth, or control filtering in real time).

Sending larger values

While 128 separate values may be adequate for many settings (such as volume), sometimes a wider range of values is needed to send a message. One of the messages that needs more than 128 values is pitch bend – if the pitch bend range of a synthesizer was set to +- 12 semitones, then each semitone would only be covered by around 5 values, which would clearly be audible as step instead of a smooth change in pitch. There is a way round this, and it is to increase the range of values (by 128), and then use two bytes to send that value. The Most Significant Byte (MSB) is multiplied by 128, and then the value of the Least Significant Byte (LSB) is added to it. In this way, instead of 128 values, a total of 16384 values are possible. Possibly the easiest way to envision this is to think of each change in the LSB being a tiny fraction (1/128) of the larger MSB value, as seen in the diagram to the right – for each value of the MSB there are 127 values of LSB that provide "fine tuning", as it were.

In fact, the General MIDI specification provides these LSB values for many of the controllers you will already be using – Modulation, Volume, Pan, Expression (indeed all the controllers up to number 31), but in practice they are not used as the resolution is unnecessary – there is no perceptible difference between these smaller values (and indeed even a single-unit change in the MSB may not be audible in many cases).

There is a caveat to add to this - when viewing pitch bend it is common to see 0 as being in the middle, with negative and positive values from there, but in fact the messages are sent from 0 to 16384, with the mid-

678

dle value (8192) being the default, usual value for 'no pitch bend'. However, this is another case of making things easier to understand – the actual value that is transmitted will still be from 0-16384.

Summary

While much of the information in this chapter may seem to be dry and academic, it forms an important part of understanding why MIDI 1.0 works in the way that it does; particularly in terms of the number of channels and data values available to a programmer, but also the actual messages that are sent; this allows you to understand the limitations that may be presented by the MIDI 1.0 specification, and in turn how to think of ways around these limitations. MIDI 1.0 is a well-thought-out specification which has lasted a considerable length of time; it is not perfect but was clearly extremely forward-thinking and given the huge penetration it has achieved in the music technology market, it will be with us for some time to come, so being aware of its technicalities is time well spent for anyone interested in learning how to program music competently. While MIDI 2.0 looks to build on the capabilities of MIDI 1.0 and fix many of its shortcomings, at the time of writing it is not widespread, and most people referring to MIDI will actually be referring to MIDI 1.0 capabilities, not MIDI 2.0.

Glossary

A

A-B Pair - see spaced pair.

ADSR - see Envelope.

ADC - Analogue to Digital Converter. An electronic device which takes an analogue input signal (such as that from a microphone) and converts it into a digital signal. It is the ADC which marks the boundary between the analogue world and that inside a computer or other digital audio device, and its quality is critical for achieving a good recording.

Ambient placement - Microphone placement which is distant to the sound source - typically 1m or more. Ambient placement allows the recording environment to alter the sound of the recording, and is often used where the atmosphere or acoustics of an environment are desirable.

Amplifier - A device for increasing the power of a signal, using external energy such as a power supply to achieve this. An amplifier's most important quality is Gain.

Amplitude - A term for the loudness of a signal, a measure of the difference between the peaks and troughs of an oscillating waveform.

Analogue - A system where a continuous input signal (such as a sound wave) is represented by another continuous signal (such as an electrical signal) - the new signal is an analogy of the original, hence the name.

Attack - The initial phase of a sound. In the context of an Envelope, it is the time taken for the envelope to reach maximum level after a key is pressed.

Attenuate - to reduce in amplitude; making a signal quieter.

B

Band Pass Filter - A device which passes frequencies in a given range, and rejects those outside that range.

Bit Depth - The number of bits of information recorded for each sample in a digital audio system. The number of bits will control the dynamic range of the system, as the difference between the loudest and quietest sound the system will depend on the difference between one bit being used and all of them. CD Audio is 16 Bit, giving 65,536 different levels of audio. DVD Audio is 24 Bit, giving 16,777,216 levels, allowing for vastly increased detail and less noise generated due to the differences between successive samples.

C

Cardioid - A Polar Pattern where the most sensitive area is at the front of the microphone, while the rear should reject sound completely. The sides will pick up sound at a level between these two. See Polar Patterns on page 420.

Compressor - A device which reduces dynamic range of an input signal (the difference between the loudest part and the quietest) automatically, by setting a threshold level above which a signal will be turned down. See page 562.

Condenser Microphone - A microphone which uses the capacitance of a capsule to turn sound into a voltage. See page 417.

Close Mic - Microphone placement where the microphone is close (under 30cm, often much less) to the sound source, reducing the influence of the environment on the recorded signal.

Coincident Pair - A stereo mic technique where the two microphones are placed as close as possible to each other to minimise phasing.

Cutoff Frequency - The frequency at which a filter begins to reduce a signal - going above or below this frequency (depending on the type of filter in question) will increase the amount of attenuation.

D

DAC - Digital to Analogue Converter. An electronic device which takes a digital input signal (from a computer or similar system) and turns it into an analogue signal, which can then be amplified and listened to in the physical world.

DCA - Digitally Controlled Amplifier. A term used in some synthesizers where an amplifier was controlled by a digital signal. See Amplifier.

DCF - Digitally Controller Filter. A term used in some synthesizers where a filter was controlled by a digital signal. See Filter.

DCO - Digitally Controller Oscillator. A term used in some synthesizers where an oscillator was controlled by a digital signal. See Oscillator.

Decay - The time taken for a signal to go from one level to another lower level. In the context of an Envelope, the time taken for the signal to go from the maximum (reached at the end of the attack phase) to the sustain level (which could be zero).

Decibel (dB) - A logarithmic unit representing the ratio of a physical quality, most commonly used to represent amplitude of an audio signal or physical sound.

Delay - A delay is an effect which stores a sound, and then replays it after a period of time. The delayed signal may be played back once or a number of times, depending on the feedback control (which sends the output signal back into the delay).

Digital - A system which uses numbers to represent an input signal. In a digital signal the incoming signal is converted using an ADC to a stream of numbers which represent the original signal. When this signal is to be replayed, the reverse process is used with a DAC converting the signal back to the analogue domain. The sample rate and bit depth control how close the digitised signal is to the original.

DI Box - Direct Injection Box, a device which allows a high impedance signal (such as that from an electric guitar) to be connected to a low impedance input (typically a microphone input on a recording device). Without such a device, the impedance mismatch would lead to high frequency signal loss, amongst other

683

problems. See Impedance.

Dumb controller - A MIDI controller keyboard which has no sound generating capacity of its own; all it generates is MIDI data which is used by another device (often a computer, but possibly a synthesizer) to create sound from the performance information.

Dynamic Microphone - A type of microphone that uses a magnet and a moving coil to convert sound into an electrical signal.

Dynamics - The volume of a sound or note or performance.

E

Effect - A device or plugin which alters an input signal sound to change the way it sounds. There are a wide range of effects available (see page 537).

Envelope - A unit which generates a signal which alters over time, typically in response to a key being pressed on a synthesizer. The output signal from it can be used to alter the Amplifier, Filter or Oscillator in the synthesizer, creating a sound which changes over time as opposed to being static.

EQ - Short for Equalisation, the altering of frequency response using filters. Many audio devices incorporate filters such as band-pass and shelving filters which can be adjusted from their nominally flat response to alter the tonal character of audio passing through them.

F

Fade - A gradual changing in volume, often a fade in or fade out at the beginning or end of a piece of music.

Feedback - When talking in an effects context, feedback is the amount of the output signal from an effect which is fed back to the input. In a delay, this will control the number of repeats of any given input material.

Figure 8 - A polar response pattern which resembles a figure 8, having two strong areas of response which are 180 degrees apart, with two weak areas perpendicular to that axis.

Filter - A filter selectively attenuates or boosts audio dependent on frequency. The frequency range that a filter operates on allows categorisation into types such as shelving, band pass and high/low pass.

FM Synthesis - A type of synthesis where audio is generated by modulating one oscillator's frequency by at least one other, with both being in the audio frequency range. Developed mostly by Yamaha in the 1980s, they were popular for a time, but extremely difficult to program.

Frequency - A measurement of how fast an oscillating signal is repeating in a given amount of time, usually cycles per second which is Hertz (Hz).

Frequency Response - A description of the range of frequencies at which a given piece of equipment will respond adequately. Humans are typically given the hearing range of 20Hz to 20,000Hz (20kHz), and this would be a fair approximation of the ear's frequency response.

Fundamental Frequency - The lowest frequency present in a waveform or sound.

G

Gain - A measurement of how much an amplifier increases a signal (or in some cases, decreases it). Usually measured in dB.

Gate - An audio processor which only allows audio to pass through once it has gone above a certain level (the Threshold level).

General MIDI - An extension to the original MIDI specification which standardised a number of functions and facilities, allowing MIDI data created on one manufacturer's systems to play back adequately on another manufacturer's. General MIDI became the standard for many MIDI devices, including computer soundcards and mobile phone MIDI playback.

Graphic Equaliser - A type of filter which features a number of band pass filters whose controls are arranged as a series of vertical sliders, giving a graphical representation of the frequency response generated by the settings.

H

Harmonics - A component frequency within a sound which is above the fundamental frequency. Harmonics contribute greatly to the tonal quality of any sound, defining its character.

Harmonic Distortion - Added harmonics which were not present in the original signal, such as overtones added by a distortion effect.

Hertz (Hz) - The SI unit of frequency, cycles per second.

High Pass Filter - A filter which passes high-frequency signals, but attenuates those at and below its cutoff point.

Hypercardioid - A polar pattern which is similar to a cardioid pattern, but has a small area of low response at the rear of the pickup pattern, akin to a cross between a cardioid and figure 8 pattern.

I

Impedance - Electronic circuits present an opposition to a current passing through them. This is sometimes known as resistance but strictly speaking that is only for Direct Current signals; when talking of alternating current (such as an audio signal) then this is called impedance, the measure of how much a circuit will impede a signal passing through it. Impedance should be matched between input and output devices or undesirable consequences will occur. See DI Box.

Insert - Where the entire audio signal passes through the effect, and the output is entirely dependent on it. Most often used for dynamic effects such as compression or gating which would otherwise be unable to perform their desired roles (as they need to have control over the channel's volume to work effectively). Compare Send.

J

Jack Plug - A type of audio connector commonly used on guitars, basses, keyboards and many other common audio devices.

L

LFO - Low Frequency Oscillator, an oscillator which generates an output which is below the audio range, and is typically used to control parameters on devices which are processing or creating audio to create a cyclic effect which can be heard. A typical example would be routing an LFO to an audio oscillator's pitch, altering the pitch to produce vibrato.

Limiter - A type of compressor with a very high ratio, which will stop audio from exceeding the threshold level, regardless of how much above it the input signal becomes.

Line Level - A standard for signal level when passing between pieces of equipment, albeit with several 'standards'; -10dbV which is a signal of 0.316V RMS (for consumer equipment) or +4dBu - 1.228V RMS (for professional equipment).

Linear - A system where the output is a multiple of the input, and therefore bears a direct relationship to it, such as an amplifier. Many circuits are non-linear as they alter the circuit considerably.

Low Pass Filter - A filter which passes low-frequency signals, but attenuates those at and above its cutoff point.

M

Microphone - A device which converts acoustic energy to electrical energy, essential for modern recording devices all of which record electrical signals.

MIDI - Musical Instrument Digital Interface. A standard to allow communication between digital music devices such as keyboards, synthesizers, samplers and sequencers.

Mixdown - The act of taking a recording with more than one track and producing a final output, often in the form of an audio file or CD.

Modulation - Using one signal to alter another one (or its generation).

Monophonic - An instrument which can only produce one note at a time.

Monotimbral - A synthesizer which can only produce one timbre at a time.

Multitimbral - A synthesizer which can produce several (more than 2) timbres at a time.

N

Noise - An unwanted random addition to a wanted signal.

Normalising - Processing a recorded audio file so that the peak level is made to be the absolute maximum possible (0dB in a digital system). This makes ALL the file louder, so the relationship between loud and quiet within the file is maintained.

Nyquist Frequency - In digital audio systems, only audio which is below half the sampling frequency can be correctly reproduced, and this is called the Nyquist frequency, as it was discovered by a mathematician called Harry Nyquist.

O

Octave - A relationship in musical notes, representing a doubling in frequency.

Omnidirectional - A Polar pattern where a microphone is equally sensitive in all directions.

Oscillator - A component which generates a repeating waveform, usually used in synthesizers to create the initial waveform (often Sawtooth, Sine, Square, Triangle) for further modification.

Overdubbing - Adding supplementary tracks to a recording while playing along with previously recorded tracks.

P

Pan - Placement of audio in a stereo audio field.

Patch - Used to describe a group of settings on a synthesizer, typically representing a given sound or effect.

Phantom Power - A way of powering microphones using the microphone cable (usually 48V DC) to avoid the need for extra cabling.

Phasing - Descriptive of the relationship between two signal sources; they can be described to be phasing when playing both together produces an audible effect in terms of frequency response, although in fact nearly all signals mixed together will have phasing effects that may or may not be audible.

Pink Noise - A noise with a frequency spectrum where the volume decreases with frequency, at 3dB per octave. It sounds like the more well known white noise, but with less high frequency content.

Pitch - A musical term to describe the frequency of a given note.

Pitch Bend - A MIDI message which allows the continuous control of the pitch of notes within a set range, allowing notes to seamlessly change pitch.

Polar Pattern - Describes the way in which microphones pick up sound with respect to direction. See Cardioid, Figure 8, Hypercardioid, Omnidirectional.

Polyphonic - An instrument which can produce more than one note at a time.

Preamplifier - An amplifier which prepares a small signal for further amplification or processing. Often used with microphones to take the small mic signal to line level where it can be further processed by a mixer or recorded.

Proximity Effect - An increase in bass response which occurs when a sound source is close to a microphone. Does not occur with omnidirectional mics, as it is due to phasing within the microphone from direct and reflected sounds used internally to create polar patterns.

Punch In/Out - The act of automatically dropping into and out of record to allow sections of a recorded track to be replaced.

Q

Quantisation - The movement of events (usually MIDI notes) from their original positions to the nearest point on a grid. With a carefully chosen grid, this will mean the events happen at the 'perfect' time.

R

Release - In a synthesizer's envelope generator, the release phase is triggered when the note is released, and is the time taken to go from the current level (usually the sustain level) to zero. Usually heard as how long a note takes to fade away.

Resample - To alter the sample rate of a piece of digital audio, without changing the pitch. The maths behind this can be complex and can alter the audio as a result of any issues with processing.

Resonance - The tendency of a system to oscillate at a particular frequency - such as a bell or other percussion instrument having a specific pitch when played. When resonance is present in a filter this will lead to the amplification of that frequency, and with enough resonance making that frequency clearly audible.

Reverb - A simulation of the acoustic effects of a physical environment.

Ribbon Microphone - A type of microphone which uses a thin metal ribbon placed in a magnetic field to generate an electrical signal.

S

Sample - In a digital audio system, a single 'snapshot' of the audio level at a given point in time. Also the act of sampling a piece of audio.

Sampler - An electronic musical instrument which uses recorded sound as the basis for sound generation.

Sample Rate - The speed at which a digital audio system samples incoming or outgoing audio, often 44100 samples per second.

Sawtooth - A type of waveform common in subtractive synthesizers, with an upwards ramp and an instantaneous drop to zero to start the next cycle.

Send - In mixers, a method of directing a portion of a signal to an alternative destination, usually an audio effect.

Sequencer - A software or hardware device which can record, edit and play back music, typically using MIDI as well as audio files.

Side-chain - Controlling the level of an effect (typically a compressor or gate) by using a different signal than the one being processed.

Sine Wave - A waveform with a smooth repetitive oscillation, based on plotting of a point's rotation around a circle.

Spaced Pair - A stereo mic technique where a pair of microphones has a relatively large distance between them.

Spectrum Analyser - A device or software which breaks input audio down into a number of frequency bands, and displays the level at each of these bands, showing the relative distribution of frequencies in the audio signal.

Square Wave - A waveform which alternates regularly between two extremes, with instantaneous transition between the two states.

Subtractive Synthesizer - A method of synthesis which starts with a harmonic-rich waveform and then uses an amplifier and filter to subtract from the original waveform for the desired output.

Sustain - The portion of an envelope generator's output which is reached after the Attack and Decay phases have been completed, and is a set level which is maintained indefinitely while a key is pressed.

Synthesizer - An electronic instrument capable of producing a wide range of electronic sounds. Synthesizers can take many forms, including Subtractive, Additive, FM and Sample-based.

T

Tempo - The speed (usually in beats per minute) of a piece of music.

Timbre - The tone colour or quality of a musical note.

Transient - A high-level, short duration sound at the beginning of a waveform.

Transpose - The act of changing the pitch of a note or piece of music.

Triangle Wave - A repetitive waveform which has an upwards ramp phase followed by a downwards ramp phase, both at the same rate of change.

Tube - see valve

U

Unidirectional - A term for a microphone which responds only in one direction, typically a cardioid pattern.

V

Valve - A device which controls electric current through a vacuum, typically in a sealed glass container.

VCA - A Voltage Controlled Amplifier - typically the amplifier in a synthesizer, often controlled by an Envelope Generator. See Amplifier.

VCF - A Voltage Controlled Filter - typically the filter in a synthesizer, often con-

689

trolled by an Envelope Generator. See Filter.

VCO - A Voltage Controlled Oscillator - typically the oscillator in a synthesizer, often controlled by a keyboard. See Oscillator.

Velocity - In a MIDI system, velocity is a measure of the speed that a note has been pressed on a keyboard, closely related to how hard the key has been pressed.

Vocoder - A system of filters which is controlled by one signal, allowing another one to pass. Usually the control signal is a human voice, while the signal that is filtered is a synthesizer. The control by the voice leads to the output sounding voice-like.

VST - Virtual Studio Technology. A standard created by Steinberg for audio plug-ins, enabling third-parties to create virtual instruments and audio effects which other applications (such as Cubase) can then make use of.

W

Wave - In audio, a waveform such as Sine, Square, Triangle and Sawtooth (see waveform). In computers, a file format for uncompressed audio (see WAV).

WAV - Waveform Audio, a file format created by Microsoft and IBM for uncompressed audio.

Waveform - The shape and form of a signal such as a wave.

White Noise - A random signal with all frequencies represented equally. Often heard as a pitchless sound, as every frequency is present.

X

XLR - eXtended Locking Round, a type of connector with (typically) 3 pins, and a sturdy locking construction. Typically used on microphones in the studio, but can be used for line-level signals as well as a wide range of other signal uses.

Keyboard
Shortcuts

One of the fastest ways to improve your speed in Cubase is to make use of keyboard shortcuts. With one hand on the mouse and the other on the keyboard, you will be able to work much more quickly and efficiently. While Cubase has user-definable shortcuts and there are a great many set by default, it is useful to know some of the most productive shortcuts, so they are outlined below. Where the shortcuts are different between platforms, Windows is shown in the first column, and Mac in the second. Note that the transport keys are missing on a Macbook because of the lack of a numeric keypad. For clarity of the main text, the keyboard shortcuts shown are for Windows, but nearly always translate so that ⌘ is pressed instead of **CTRL** and ⌥ pressed instead of **ALT**, which should allow a macOS user to make use of them in the main text with little effort.

Editing - based

CTRL + S	**⌘ + S**	Save
CTRL + A	**⌘ + A**	Select All
P	**P**	Sets the locators round the current selection
CTRL + D	**⌘ + D**	Duplicate the currently selected part
CTRL + K	**⌘ + K**	Opens the repeat dialog box
J	**J**	Toggle Snap on and off
M	**M**	Mute current track/s
S	**S**	Solo current track/s
Q	**Q**	Quantize
↑↓	↑↓	Move selected notes up/down a semitone
SHIFT+ ↑↓	**SHIFT+ ↑↓**	Move selected notes up/down an octave
CTRL + C	**⌘ + C**	Copy selection to clipboard
CTRL + X	**⌘ + X**	Cut selection to clipboard
CTRL + V	**⌘ + V**	Paste selection (at current play position)

Transport - based

1 (num)		Go to the left locator
2 (num)		Go to the right locator
- (num)		Rewind
+ (num)		Fast Forward
/ (num)		Toggle Cycle on and off
* (num)		Record
SPACE	**SPACE**	Toggle Play on and off
,	**,**	Go to start of project
.	**.**	Swap main and secondary timebase
C	**C**	Toggle Click on and off

Window - based

F2	Toggle Floating Transport Bar
F3	Toggle Mixer
F4	Toggle Audio Connections Window
F5	Toggle Media Bay
F11	Toggle VST Instrument Rack
F12	Toggle VST Performance Window

Tool - based

1	Select the Selection (arrow) tool, cycle mode if already selected
2	Select the range selection tool
3	Select the scissors tool
4	Select the glue tool
5	Select the eraser tool
6	Select the zoom tool
7	Select the mute tool
F9	Cycle through tools to the left
F10	Cycle through tools to the right

View - based

G	G	Zoom out horizontally
H	H	Zoom in horizontally
F	F	Toggle Autoscroll (follow) on and off
CTRL+ALT+L	⌘+⌥+L	Toggle Left Zone visibility
CTRL+ALT+E	⌘+⌥+E	Toggle Lower Zone visibility
CTRL+ALT+R	⌘+⌥+R	Toggle Right Zone visibility

Index

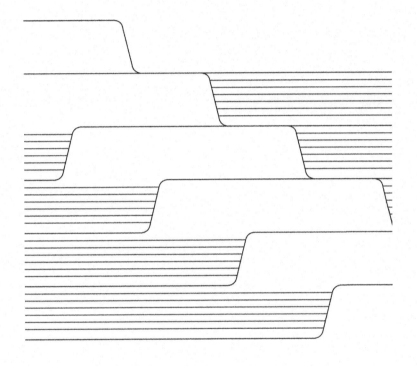

Index

A

B

C